The United Nations
Volume I

The International Library of Politics and Comparative Government

General Editor: David Arter
Associate Editor: Gordon Smith

Titles in the Series

The United Nations Volume I: Systems and Structures

Edited by

Sam Daws

and

Paul Taylor

with Sara Lodge

Ashgate

DARTMOUTH

Aldershot • Burlington USA • Singapore • Sydney

Published by
Dartmouth Publishing Company Limited
Ashgate Publishing Limited
Gower House
Croft Road
Aldershot
Hants GU11 3HR
England

Ashgate Publishing Company
131 Main Street
Burlington
Vermont 05401
USA

British Library Cataloguing in Publication Data
The United Nations. – (The international library of
    politics and comparative government)
    1. United Nations
    I. Daws, Sam II. Taylor, Paul
    341.2'3

Library of Congress Cataloging-in-Publication Data
The United Nations / edited by Sam Daws and Paul Taylor.
        p.   cm. — (International library of politics and comparative
    government)
        ISBN 1-85521-738-4 (hardback)
        1. United Nations. I. Daws, Sam. II. Taylor, Paul Graham.
    III. Series.
    JZ4984.5.U549   1999
    341.23—dc21   98-55701
                                                                                CIP

    ISBN 1 85521 738 4

This book is printed on acid-free paper.

Printed and bound by WBC Book Manufacturers, Bridgend, Mid Glam.

Contents

PART III   THE UN, STATES, AND NON-GOVERNMENTAL ACTORS

PART IV   THE UN SECRETARIAT AND SECRETARY-GENERAL

Acknowledgements

The editors and publishers wish to thank the following for permission to use copyright material.

Cambridge University Press for the essay: Sally Morphet (1995), 'The Influence of States and Groups of States on and in the Security Council and General Assembly, 1980–94', *Review of International Studies*, **21**, pp. 435–62. Copyright © British International Studies Association, published by Cambridge University Press.

Carfax Publishing Limited for the essay: Leon Gordenker and Thomas G. Weiss (1995), 'Pluralising Global Governance: Analytical Approaches and Dimensions', *Third World Quarterly*, **16**, pp. 357–87. Copyright © 1995 Third World Quarterly.

Columbia University for the essay: Richard Falk (1995), 'Appraising the U.N. at 50: The Looming Challenge', *Journal of International Affairs*, **48**, pp. 625–46. Copyright © 1995 The Trustees of Columbia University in the City of New York. Published by permission of the *Journal of International Affairs* and the Trustees of Columbia University in the City of New York.

David Davies Memorial Institute of International Studies for the essays: Simon Duke (1992), 'The UN Finance Crisis: A History and Analysis', *International Relations*, **XI** (2), pp. 127–50. Copyright © 1992 International Relations; Antonio Donini (1988), 'Resilience and Reform: Some Thoughts on the Processes of Change in the United Nations', *International Relations*, **IX** (4), pp. 289–315. Copyright © 1988 International Relations.

Elsevier Science Ltd for the essay: Erskine Childers (1995), 'Financing the United Nations: Some Possible Solutions', *Futures*, **27**, pp. 161–70. Copyright © 1995 Elsevier Science Ltd.

Foreign Affairs for the essays: Paul Kennedy and Bruce Russett (1995), 'Reforming the United Nations', *Foreign Affairs*, **74**, pp. 56–71. Reprinted with permission of Foreign Affairs. Copyright © 1995 by the Council on Foreign Relations, Inc.; Jesse Helms (1996), 'Saving the U.N.: A Challenge to the Next Secretary-General', *Foreign Affairs*, **75**, pp. 2–7. Reprinted with permission of Foreign Affairs. Copyright © 1996 by the Council on Foreign Relations, Inc.; Brian Urquhart (1995), 'Selecting the World's CEO: Remembering the Secretaries-General', *Foreign Affairs*, **74**, pp. 21–6. Reprinted by permission of Foreign Affairs. Copyright © 1996 by the Council on Foreign Relations, Inc.

Indian Society of International Law for the essay: Muchkund Dubey (1995), 'Financing the United Nations', *Indian Journal of International Law*, **35**, pp. 157–67.

The Johns Hopkins University Press for the essay: Dianne Otto (1996), 'Nongovernmental Organizations in the United Nations System: The Emerging Role of International Civil Society', *Human Rights Quarterly*, **18**, pp. 107–41. Copyright © 1996 by The Johns Hopkins University Press.

Lynne Rienner Publishers, Inc. for the essay: W. Andy Knight (1995), 'Beyond the UN System? Critical Perspectives on Global Governance and Multilateral Evolution', *Global Governance*, **1**, pp. 229–53. Reprinted from *Global Governance: A Review of Multilateralism and International Organizations*, **1** (2). Copyright © 1995 by Lynne Rienner Publishers, Inc. Used with permission of the publisher.

MIT Press Journals for the essays: Giulio M. Gallarotti (1991), 'The Limits of International Organization: Systematic Failure in the Management of International Relations', *International Organization*, **45**, pp. 183–220. Copyright © 1991 by the World Peace Foundation and the Massachusetts Institute of Technology.

New Republic for the essay: Michael Lind (1995), 'Twilight of the UN', *New Republic*, **213**, pp. 25, 28, 30–3.

Norwegian Institute of International Affairs for the essay: Raino Malnes (1996), 'Democracy in the United Nations. For and Against', *Forum for Development Studies*, (1), pp. 5–34.

B.G. Ramcharan (1990), 'The History, Role and Organization of the "Cabinet" of the United Nations Secretary-General', *Nordic Journal of International Law*, **59**, pp. 103–16. Copyright © B.G. Ramcharan.

Sage Publications Ltd for the essays: Daniele Archibugi (1993), 'The Reform of the UN and Cosmopolitan Democracy: A Critical Review', *Journal of Peace Research*, **30**, pp. 301–15. Copyright © The Journal of Peace Research. By permission of Sage Publications Ltd; Erskine B. Childers (1995), 'Breaking the Realists' Cabal: Citizens' Rights in the UN', *Development*, **4**, pp. 15–21. Copyright © 1995 The Society for International Development. By permission of Sage Publications Ltd.

John Wiley & Sons, Ltd for the essay: Michael Gurstein and Josef Klee (1996), 'Towards a Management Renewal of the United Nations – Parts I and II', *Public Administration and Development*, **16**, pp. 43–56 and pp. 111–22. Copyright © 1996 John Wiley and Sons Limited. Reproduced with permission.

World Peace Foundation for the essay: Leland M. Goodrich (1947), 'From League of Nations to United Nations', *International Organization*, **1**, pp. 3–21. Copyright © 1947 World Peace Foundation.

The Editors are very grateful to Virpi Timonen and Rebecca Sutton for their valuable research assistance in the preparation of these two volumes.

Series Preface

The International Library of Politics and Comparative Government brings together in one series the most significant journal articles to appear in the field of comparative politics in the last twenty-five years or so. The aim is to render readily accessible to teachers, researchers and students an extensive range of essays which, together, provide an indispensable basis for understanding both the established conceptual terrain and the new ground being broken in the fast changing field of comparative political analysis.

The series is divided into three major sections: *Institutional Studies, Thematic Studies* and *Country Studies*. The *Institutional* volumes focus on the comparative investigation of the basic processes and components of the modern pluralist polity, including electoral behaviour, parties and party systems, interest groups, constitutions, legislatures and executives. There are also collections dealing with such major international actors as the European Union and United Nations.

The *Thematic* volumes address those contemporary problems, processes and issues which have assumed a particular salience for politics and policy-making in the late twentieth century. Such themes include: democratization, revolution and political change, 'New Politics', nationalism, terrorism, the military, the media, human rights, consociationalism and the challenges to mainstream party political ideologies.

The *Country* volumes are particularly innovative in applying a comparative perspective to a consideration of the political science tradition in individual states, both large and small. The distinctive features of the national literature are highlighted and the wider significance of developments is evaluated.

A number of acknowledged experts have been invited to act as editors for the series; they preface each volume with an introductory essay in which they review the basis for the selection of articles, and suggest future directions of research and investigation in the subject area.

The series is an invaluable resource for all those working in the field of comparative government and politics.

DAVID ARTER
Professor of Nordic Politics
University of Aberdeen

GORDON SMITH
Emeritus Professor of Government
London School of Economics and Political Science

Introduction

The United Nations provides a wall upon which historic handwriting may be inscribed . . . to which realism must pay attention, whether or not idealism inspires respect.[1]

Definitions

The phrase 'the United Nations' appears every day in newspapers and on the television news. It is used interchangeably to refer to the member states of the Organization; the bodies, such as the Security Council, upon which they sit; and the civil servants who constitute the UN Secretariat. The United Nations is all these things. To its most faithful supporters it is also the cornerstone of international law and legitimacy: an essential and practical embodiment of the ideals of multilateralism, international cooperation, and the application of morality to the international sphere. To its severest critics it is an irrelevancy in a world defined by power politics – at most an expensive talking shop with a bloated bureaucracy. Both addressing and moving beyond a simplistic characterization of 'realist' and 'idealist' approaches, the chapters in this two-volume compendium reflect the wide breadth of views that exist in both academia and policy-making circles on the utility, functioning and future of the UN system.

The scope of this compendium

The 50th anniversary of the founding of the UN in 1995 concentrated attention upon reviewing past performance, and evaluating future direction and potential reform. Whilst supplemented by essays from the UN's early years, this compendium rests primarily upon significant contributions from this crucial and reflective point in the UN's history. Literature on the UN is extensive and growing, and reference is made in the Introductions to important sources published elsewhere. The forty-eight essays assembled in these two volumes span the political and ideological spectrum from right to left, from interventionism to isolationism, and from unilateralism to multilateralism. This first volume, in four parts, presents the structural and systemic aspects of the UN. We begin by addressing the UN's institutional development, from its Charter origins to recent debates on UN reform. Part II tackles the perennial and fundamental issue of the financing of the work of the Organization. Part III examines the multiplicity of actors in the UN system, with a particular focus on states and non-governmental organizations. Finally, we examine the evolution, recruitment, and potential reform of the UN Secretariat; including the appointment and changing role of the UN Secretary-General.

Part I: UN Institutional Development and Reform

The early years

The United Nations did not emerge from a political and historical vacuum. In the first chapter in this volume, Leland Goodrich highlights significant continuities between the League of Nations and its successor. Goodrich asserts that 'anyone desiring to understand the machinery [of the UN], how it operates, the conditions of its success, must look to the experience of the past . . .' (p.21) This essay is typical of studies from the early years of the UN (Russell and Muther (1958); Lee (1947)), which place the new organization in its historical context. More recent studies have revisited the origins of the UN Charter (Friedlander, 1984).

Paucity of theory on reform

Literature on UN institutional development flourished again in the 1990s, reflecting and influencing efforts at reforming the Organization. The remaining chapters in this section address this more recent debate. The first is a review essay by W. Andy Knight on the theme of global governance and multilateral evolution (Chapter 2). Knight notes with alarm the paucity of theory underlying much of the recent work on UN reform. He concludes that the UN must develop a long-term adaptation strategy whilst engaging in the inevitably pressing agenda of immediate political events, even if this task can be likened to 'trying to change the wing of an aeroplane whilst it is still in flight' (p.252).

Democracy in the UN context

Many advocates of UN reform make claims that their proposals would make the Organization more 'democratic'. Democracy is not an easy concept, however, to apply to an international organization (Claude, 1956). The voting procedure of the General Assembly was established by applying the democratic principle of 'one person, one vote' to sovereign states (Archibugi, Chapter 3). This results in a country such as Palau, with a population of 19,000, having the same *de jure* voting power as China, with a population of over a billion. Malnes (Chapter 5) assesses whether this system can be designated as democratic. He finds that there is support for a 'one state, one vote' system if one applies the defences of democracy conceived by John Stuart Mill or John Rawls (1971 and 1985) to the UN (see also Held, 1992 and 1995). Malnes acknowledges, however, that the General Assembly can be deemed democratically flawed if one accepts Righter's (1995) call for account to be taken of population or financial contribution (see also Franck, 1995). Righter goes further to argue that the current UN voting structure is also *pragmatically* deficient since it does not yield a workable international organization. This position validates those who argue for the introduction of weighted voting in the General Assembly (Manno, 1969).

    The Security Council was established as a body of limited membership, with a composition designed primarily to be effective rather than democratic. As such it gave particular privileges to the five permanent members, in part as a reward for operating within the constraints of UN multilateralism, and in part as payment for their expected military and financial contributions (Daws, 1997). The ten (originally six) non-permanent members were, similarly, elected on the basis of specific criteria, including their contribution to international peace and security, as well as the principle of equitable geographic distribution. However, much has changed since the Charter was framed in 1945. There has been an increase in the size of UN membership from 51 in 1945 to 188 in 1999. There has also been growing concern at the apparent lack of transparency in Council decision-making. This increase in membership, along with pressure from states seeking permanent membership, such as Japan and Germany, led to the establishment in 1993 of a General Assembly Working Group to examine possible changes to the size, composition, voting procedures, and working methods of the Security Council (Ciechanski, 1994; Schwartzberg, 1994). To date, member states have been unable to agree on substantive issues relating to the expansion of the Council or changes to its voting procedures (Choudhury, 1988; Fassbender, 1998; The South Centre, 1997; and Winkelmann, 1998). Despite the logjam in the Working Group, a number of proposals have been adopted in recent years with the aim of increasing Council transparency (Bailey and Daws, 1998).[2]

The UN's future: an enhanced role or terminal decline?

The 50th anniversary of the founding of the United Nations served to stimulate a wealth of literature assessing its past performance and promoting alternative visions of its future role (Eban, 1995; Kirgis, 1995; Kothari, 1995; Neuhaus, 1995; Seara-Vazquez, 1995; and Singh, 1995). In Chapter 4 Kennedy and Russett provide a wide-ranging analysis of the challenges facing the UN in the realms of peace and security, and economic, social, and institutional reform. In their view, the half-century anniversary presented the international community with two choices: to reduce demands on the organization, allowing it to perform reduced functions adequately within existing resources; or to value an enhanced role with a commensurate increase in resources and functions. The authors favour the latter course.

In contrast, Lind (Chapter 6) and Helms (Chapter 7) advocate a significantly diminished role for the United Nations, and a radical overhaul of its bureaucracy and finances. Lind regards the overrunning of the 'safe areas' of Srebrenica and Zepa by Bosnian Serbs as irrevocably discrediting the United Nations. Advocating national-interest realism as an alternative to both liberal internationalism and xenophobic isolationism, he concludes that 'the UN should be allowed to wither away into irrelevance, as it was doing before George Bush unwisely, if temporarily, revived its importance' (p.33). Senator Jesse Helms argues that the UN must be 'saved from itself' through dramatic downsizing. Like Lind, he objects to what he sees as the supplanting of national sovereignty by the organization, and as a remedy he advocates a 50 per cent cut in UN staffing, the replacement of assessed regular budget contributions with principally voluntary funding, and the creation of an option for the US to refuse funding for particular UN peacekeeping operations. As well as contributing to the academic literature, Helm's views have had direct political influence, through his chairmanship of the US Senate Committee on Foreign Relations.

Gallaroti (Chapter 8) echoes the sentiments of Lind and Helms, but approaches the subject from a theoretical perspective. He argues that the limitations and drawbacks of international organizations, including the United Nations, have traditionally been understated, and that international organizations can be a source of, rather than a remedy for, disorder. He points to the tendency of governments to see the passage of a UN resolution as absolving them from further responsibility to act. In this vein, Adam Roberts and Benedict Kingsbury (1993) argue that the UN has potentially worked against international security through its function as a perceived, but in practice unfruitful, substitute for arms control. As well as blaming international organizations for acting as a substitute for responsible domestic policies, Gallaroti rejects the idea that the UN is a useful safety valve, promoting 'jaw-jaw instead of war-war'. As a solution he recommends more limited managerial functions for international organizations.

Other scholars, whilst recognizing the merits of some of Gallaroti's arguments, ultimately counter such criticisms by pointing to the many concrete achievements of international bodies in the fields of peace, human rights and human development (Taylor and Groom, 1988).

Part II: UN Financing

The entire budget of the UN and its specialized and technical agencies for the world of 5.7 billion people, including funds for development, peacekeeping and humanitarian relief, is about $11 billion a year. That is about what Americans spend in a year at beauty parlors and health clubs. It represents just under $2.00 per human being alive on Planet Earth, while governments are still spending about $150.00 per capita of humankind on military establishments. The U.S. *makes* over a billion dollars a year out of hosting the UN and out of UN procurement awards to U.S. companies.[3]

For much of its history, the United Nations has been faced with reluctance on behalf of many of its members to fund its work. In particular the US, the largest assessed contributor to the Organization, is currently its largest debtor, owing over $1 billion. The withholding of dues from the UN by a state rarely reflects inability to pay, but rather a dissatisfaction with specific UN programmes, or a belief that withholding is the best lever by which to secure national advantage within the Organization.

The chapters in this section provide an historical review of past financing precedents and difficulties, and examine future reform options. Duke (Chapter 10) portrays the current financial crisis as originating with the Congo crisis of the early 1960s, and intensified by US republican dissatisfaction with 'the tyranny of the Third World majority' and the resultant Kassebaum-Solomon amendment in the US Senate in the mid 1980s.[4] He explores a number of future options: that other industrial countries pay more of the UN's finances to reduce the assessment of the United States; that penalties for late payment, or incentives for timely payment, be introduced for the UN regular budget; and that taxes be levied on international goods and services. While considering the merits of the *ad hoc* approach taken in financing the Persian Gulf War, scaling down the activities of the UN, and the introduction of weighted voting for financial decision-making, Duke views the full and unconditional payment of outstanding financial arrears as the most desirable outcome.

Erskine Childers (Chapter 9) argues forcefully for the full and prompt payment of UN financial assessments. He regards this as a mandatory legal obligation upon each member state, which therefore should not be made contingent upon changes in UN management or policies. He supports the 1985 proposal of Swedish Prime Minster Olaf Palme that a ceiling of 10 per cent should be placed on the assessed contribution of any member state, and follows Duke in examining various forms of international taxation (for example, on arms sales, air and sea travel, or international currency transactions) that could be introduced as a means of providing a more secure income for the UN system. Other key authorities in this area are McDermott (1994) on the financing of UN peacekeeping and peace enforcement; Mendez (1995) on paying for peace and international development; Taylor (1991) on changing US attitudes towards UN financing; and D'Orville and Najmann (1994) on new income sources for the Organization.

In Chapter 11, Muchkund Dubey echoes Officer (1994) in providing a developing-country perspective on UN financing. Dubey charts the declining share of the UN regular budget paid by the United States, from 50 per cent in 1946 to 33 per cent in 1952, 30 per cent in 1955, and then 25 per cent from 1972 to the present day. He laments the steady growth in voluntary contributions to UN bodies. Voluntary contributions were originally introduced solely to finance technical assistance programmes, but by the 1960s were being used for many other purposes. Dubey argues that 'Today, by and large, the UN Organizations do what the governments of the countries making major voluntary contributions want them to do'.[5]

Part III: The UN, States, and Non-governmental Actors

The UN was founded on the principle of state sovereignty, and the Charter framed largely to prevent or resolve disputes between states. The designation of *apartheid* in the 1960s as a threat to international peace and security was an early challenge to such an inter-state focus for the UN. In the 1990s these challenges multiplied. Global and transnational phenomena such as terrorism, drugs, human-rights abuses and humanitarian disasters were increasingly regarded as potential threats to international peace. Emphasis shifted to addressing often complex intra-state conflicts and the need for democratization within states.

States, groups and blocs in the UN system

In the first reading in this section, Falk (Chapter 12) reviews the effect on the UN of an increasingly globalized world economy and the changing role of states. Morphet (Chapter 13) contributes to a growing literature on the formation of groups and blocs of states within the UN system (Ball, 1951; Holcombe and Sobel, 1996; Holloway and Tomlinson, 1995). She shows how, in the post-Cold War period, changes have also occurred in the influence and political groupings of states in the UN Security Council and General Assembly. She concludes that the old West, East and non-aligned pattern of groups was principally replaced, from 1985 onwards, by a permanent member/non-aligned split.

Non-governmental organizations

Chapters 14 to 15 analyse the relationship between non-governmental organizations (NGOs) and the UN. Much recent literature in this area has focused on the impact of NGOs on specific UN conferences or sectors: food (Van Rooy, 1997); human rights (Weissbrodt, 1977); the environment (Willetts, 1996) and women (Chen, 1995; Laugen, 1996). Gordenker and Weiss (Chapter 14), in a wide-ranging introductory essay, go beyond individual sectors to address definitions, historical, legal, and political dimensions, and an analytical framework for understanding the role of different actors.[6] The works of Donini (1995) and Uvin (1995) similarly reflect the wider political complexities of UN–NGO relations. Otto (Chapter 15) reports on the attempts of some developing countries to review and reduce NGO access to UN meetings. She also applies theoretical perspectives to understanding NGOs and inter-national civil society – exploring liberal-realist, liberal-republican, and post-liberal positions. In the final chapter in this section, Childers (Chapter 16) challenges the realist assumptions that he sees informing much contemporary debate on the United Nations. He argues that the assumed power of certain states, in particular the Western permanent members, is illusory, but that such assumptions have disempowered the majority of the world's states. He sees the mobilization of citizens, both as individuals and collectively in NGOs, as the path to a more democratic UN.

Part IV: The UN Secretariat and Secretary-General

The UN Charter establishes a Secretariat headed by a UN Secretary-General (Article 97), consisting of independent civil servants accountable to the Organization, rather than to governments (Article 100), who are recruited on as wide a geographical basis as possible (Article 101). In practice, both the independence of Secretariat members and the geographical basis of their appointment have come under strain. Two perennial difficulties still face the Secretariat: poor management practice resulting in inefficient use of human and financial resources, and interference by member states in the daily running of the Secretariat. Such state interference includes micro-management, protection of nationals from dismissal, and lobbying for the placement of nationals in particular Secretariat positions (see Bulkeley, 1990).

Antonio Donini (Chapter 17) analyses recent initiatives for reform of the UN Secretariat in the context of developing a theory for understanding change in the UN system. He points to a divergence between a Northern approach of streamlining and restructuring UN institutions and a Southern agenda where political challenge to the existing world order is more important than managerial reform. Donini recognizes and assesses the significant contribution made by Maurice Bertrand and others at the time of the UN's 40th anniversary, the work of the 'Group of 18' member states, and the lever of financial conditionality applied by the United States in the 1980s.

In contrast to Donini's international-relations based approach, Michael Gurstein and Josef Klee (Chapter 18) apply management theory to contemporary initiatives to restructure the UN Secretariat. They give prominence to developments in the UN Department of Administration and Management including the Integrated Management Information System (IMIS), the establishment of the Office of Internal Oversight Services, overhauls of personnel and financial management, and the application of new technologies. They conclude that adequate resources and board-level direction from states is a more effective route to UN reform than a focus on 'waste, fraud and abuse' (p.120). The changing role of the UN Secretariat has been explored by other authors (Van Boven, 1991).

The question of the role of the UN Secretary-General came to the fore in 1996 with the decision of the United States to veto the reappointment of Boutros Boutros-Ghali. The Secretary-General has long been required to perform a balancing act, working as a servant of member states, yet also as a guardian of the ideals embodied in the UN Charter. The difficulties inherent in this position are explored by James (1959) and Newman (1998). In Chapter 19 B.G. Ramcharan reviews the evolution and functions of the Executive Office of the Secretary-General. Elaraby (Chapter 20) further explores the political dimensions surrounding the Secretary-General's role. Brian Urquhart (Chapter 21) who has worked at or around the UN since its foundation, reviews the lack of any adequate selection process for the post of Secretary-General. He points out that the absence of a search procedure or even an interview with the candidate would be rejected as a bad joke by any serious institution in the private sector.

Conclusions

Do we really think that politics among nations are the politics of working out common interests, or are they the politics of working out an adjustment between standing differences? The answer which the Charter gives is: 'A little of both, please'. It is this double quality of the perfect and the practical, the dream and the deed, the hope and the fear, that makes the Charter so hard to apply.[7]

In this volume we have examined structural and systemic aspects of the United Nations. This will provide a foundation for a detailed consideration of the Organization's functions and performance in Volume II. Through presenting diverse, and at points diametrically-opposed, perspectives, we have aimed to reflect the wide-ranging literature that exists on the Organization. Differences extend not just to means – the balance to be struck between the 'dream' and the 'deed' – but also to ends – whether the fundamental objectives of the UN are reasonable, tenable and practicable.

Notes

1 Claude, Jr. Inis L. (1984), *Swords into Plowshares: The Problems and Progress of International Organisation* (4th edn), New York: McGraw-Hill, p.239.
2 Reisman (1993) regards the problem as one of a 'constitutional crisis' in the relationship between the General Assembly and the Security Council.
3 Erskine Childers, Foreword to Phyllis Bennis (1996), *Calling the Shots: How Washington Dominates Today's UN*, New York: Olive Branch Press, p.x.
4 Duke (1992), p.136.
5 Dubey (1995), p.161.
6 See also Gordenker and Weiss (1995b).
7 The Hon. Paul Hasluck M.P. Address to the University of Sydney, Australia, 22 October 1954. Source: Australian Archives, Canberra, Series no. A5954/1 Item no. 1834/2. File: 'The Revision of the UN Charter'.

Bibliography

Archibugi, Daniele (1993), 'The Reform of the UN and Cosmopolitan Democracy: A Critical Review', *Journal of Peace Research*, **30** (3), pp. 301–15.

Bailey, Sydney D. and Daws, Sam (1998), *The Procedure of the UN Security Council*, Oxford: Oxford University Press.

Ball, M. Margaret (1951), 'Bloc Voting in the General Assembly', *International Organization*, **5** (1), pp. 3–31.

Bulkeley, J. Russell (1990), 'Depoliticizing United Nations Recruitment: Establishing a Genuinely International Civil Service', in Paul Taylor, Sam Daws and Ute Adamczick-Gerteis, *Documents on Reform of the United Nations*, Aldershot: Dartmouth.

Chen, Martha (1995), 'Alter Engendering World Conferences: the International Women's Movement and the United Nations', *Third World Quarterly*, **16** (3), pp. 477–93.

Childers, Erskine B. (1995a), 'Breaking the Realists' Cabal: Citizens' Rights in the UN', *Development*, **4**, pp. 15–21.

Childers, Erskine B. (1995b), 'Financing the United Nations: Some Possible Solutions', *Futures*, **27** (2), pp. 161–70.

Choudhury, Humayun Rasheed (1988), 'United Nations Reforms: Some Reflections', *Ethics and International Affairs*, **2**, pp. 155–71.

Ciechanski, Jerzy (1994), 'Restructuring of the UN Security Council', *International Peacekeeping*, **1** (4), pp. 413–39.

Claude, Jr. Inis L. (1956), *Swords into Plowshares: The Problems and Progress of International Organisation*, New York: McGraw-Hill.

Daws, Sam (1997), 'Seeking Seats, Votes and Vetoes', *The World Today*, October, pp. 256–9.

Donini, Antonio (1988), 'Resilience and Reform: Some Thoughts on the Processes of Change in the United Nations', *International Relations*, **9** (4), pp. 289–315.

Donini, Antonio (1995), 'The Bureaucracy and the Free Spirits: Stagnation and Innovation in the Relationship between the UN and NGOs', *Third World Quarterly*, **16** (3), pp. 421–39.

D'Orville, Hans and Najman, Dragoljub (1994), 'A New System to Finance the United Nations', *Security Dialogue*, **25** (2), pp. 135–44.

Dubey, Muchkund (1995), 'Financing the United Nations', *Indian Journal of International Law*, **35**, pp. 157–67.

Duke, Simon (1992), 'The UN Finance Crisis: A History and Analysis', *International Relations*, **XI** (2), pp. 127–50.

Eban, Abba (1995), 'The UN Idea Revisited', *Foreign Affairs*, **74** (5), pp. 39–55.

Elaraby, Nabil (1986), 'The Office of the Secretary-General and the Maintenance of International Peace and Security', *Revue Egyptienne du Droit International*, **42**, pp. 1–42.

Falk, Richard (1995), 'Appraising the U.N. at 50: The Looming Challenge', *Journal of International Affairs*, **48** (2), pp. 625–46.

Fassbender, Bardo (1998), *UN Security Council Reform and the Right of Veto: A Constitutional Perspective*, The Hague: Kluwer Law.

Franck, Thomas M. (1995), *Fairness in International Law and Institutions*, Oxford: Oxford University Press.

Friedlander, Robert A. (1984), 'Power Politics and International Order: Pre-Charter Origins and Post-Charter Views', *Year Book of World Affairs*, **38**, pp. 43–58.

Gallarotti, Giulio M. (1991), 'The Limits of International Organization: Systematic Failure in the Management of International Relations', *International Organization*, **45** (2), pp. 183–220.

Goodrich, L.M. (1947), 'From League of Nations to United Nations', *International Organization*, **1**, pp. 3–21.

Gordenker, Leon and Weiss, Thomas G. (1995a), 'Pluralising Global Governance: Analytical Approaches and Dimensions', *Third World Quarterly*, **16** (3), pp. 357–87.

Gordenker, Leon and Weiss, Thomas G. (1995b), 'NGO Participation in the International Policy Process', *Third World Quarterly*, **16** (3), pp. 543–55.

Gurstein, M. and Klee, J. (1996), 'Towards a Management Renewal of the UN: Parts I and II', *Public Administration and Development*, **16** (1), pp. 43–56; and **16** (2), pp. 111–22.

Held, David (1992), 'Democracy: From City States to a Cosmopolitan Order', *Political Studies*, **40**, Special Issue, pp. 10–39.

Held, David (1995), *Democracy and the Global Order*, Cambridge: Polity Press.

Helms, Jesse (1996), 'Saving the UN – A Challenge for the Next Secretary-General', *Foreign Affairs*, **15**, September/October, pp. 2–7.

Holcombe, Randall G. and Sobel, Russell S. (1996), 'The Stability of International Coalitions in United Nations Voting from 1946 to 1973', *Public Choice*, **86**, pp. 17–34.

Holloway, Steven K. and Tomlinson, Rodney (1995), 'The New World Order and the General Assembly: Bloc Realignment at the UN in the Post-Cold War World', *Canadian Journal of Political Science*, **18** (2), pp. 227–53.

James, A.M. (1959), 'The Role of the Secretary-General of the United Nations in International Relations', *International Relations*, October, pp. 620–38.

Kennedy, Paul and Russett, Bruce (1995), 'Reforming the United Nations', *Foreign Affairs*, **74** (5), pp. 56–71.

Kirgis, Frederic L. Jr. (1995), 'The Security Council's First Fifty Years', *American Journal of International Law*, **89** (3), pp. 506–39.

Kirkpatrick, J.J. (1984), 'The United Nations as a Political System', *World Affairs*, **146** (4), pp. 358–68.

Knight, W. Andy (1995), 'Review Essay: Beyond the UN System? Critical Perspectives on Global Governance and Multilateral Evolution', *Global Governance*, **1** (2), pp. 229–53.

Kothari, Rajni (1995), 'Globalisation and "New World Order": What Future for the United Nations?', *Economic and Political Weekly*, **30** (40), pp. 2513–17.

Laugen, Torunn (1996), 'Balancing Effectiveness and Legitimacy: UNICEF's Follow-Up of the World Summit for Children', *Forum for Development Studies*, No. 1, pp. 63–86.

Lee, Dwight E. (1947), 'The Genesis of the Veto', *International Organization*, **1**, pp. 33–42.

Lind, Michael (1995), 'Twilight of the U.N.', *New Republic*, **213**, 30 October, pp. 25, 28, 30–33.

Malnes, Raino (1996), 'Democracy in the United Nations. For and Against', *Forum for Development Studies*, (1), pp. 5–34.

Manno, Catherine Senf (1969), 'Selective Weighted Voting in the UN General Assembly: Rationale and Methods', *International Organization*, **20**, pp. 37–62.

McDermott, Anthony (1994), 'United Nations Financing Problems and the New Generation of Peacekeeping and Peace Enforcement', Thomas J. Watson Institute for International Studies Occasional Paper no. 16.

McIntyre, Elizabeth (1954), 'Weighted Voting in International Organizations', *International Organization*, **8** (4), pp. 484–97.

Mendez, Ruben P. (1995), 'Paying for Peace and Development', *Foreign Policy*, **100**, pp. 19–31.

Morphet, Sally (1995), 'The Influence of States and Groups of States on and in the Security Council and General Assembly, 1980–94', *Review of International Studies*, **21**, pp. 435–62.

Neuhaus, M.E.K. (1995), 'The United Nations' Security Role at Fifty – The Need for Realism', *Australian Journal of International Affairs*, **49** (2), pp. 267–82.

Newman, Edward (1998), *The UN Secretary-General From the Cold War to the New Era: A Global Peace and Security Mandate?*, Basingstoke: Macmillan.

Officer, Laurence H. (1994), 'An Assessment of the United Nations Scale of Assessments from a Developing-country Standpoint', *Journal of International Money and Finance*, **13**, pp. 415–28.

O'Neill, Barry (1996), 'Power and Satisfaction in the United Nations Security Council', *Journal of Conflict Resolution*, **40** (2), pp. 219–37.

Otto, Dianne (1996), 'Nongovernmental Organizations in the United Nations System: The Emerging Role of International Civil Society', *Human Rights Quarterly*, **18**, pp. 107–41.

Ramcharan, B.G. (1990), 'The History, Role and Organization of the "Cabinet" of the United Nations Secretary General', *Nordic Journal of International Law*, **59** (2/3), pp. 103–16.

Rawls, John (1971), *A Theory of Justice*, Oxford: Oxford University Press.

Rawls, John (1985), 'Justice as Fairness: Political not Metaphysical', *Philosophy and Public Affairs*, **14** (3), pp. 223–51.

Reisman, W. Michael (1993), 'The Constitutional Crisis in the United Nations', *American Journal of International Law*, **87**, pp. 83–100.

Righter, Rosemary (1995), *Utopia Lost: The United Nations and World Order*, New York: Twentieth Century Fund Press.

Roberts, Adam and Kingsbury, Benedict (1993), 'The UN's Roles in a Divided World', in Adam Roberts and Benedict Kingsbury, *United Nations, Divided World*, Oxford: Oxford University Press.

Russell, Ruth B. and Muther, Jeannette E. (1958), *A History of the United Nations Charter: The Role of the United States 1940–1945*, Washington: Brookings Institution.

Russett, Bruce and Sutterlin, James S. (1991), 'The UN in a New World Order', *Foreign Affairs*, **70**, pp. 69–83.

Schwartzberg, Joseph E. (1994), 'Towards a more Representative and Effective Security Council, *Political Geography*, **13** (6), pp. 483–91.

Seara-Vazquez, Modesto (1995), 'The UN Security Council at Fifty: Mid-life Crisis or Terminal Illness?', *Global Governance*, (3), Sept–Dec, pp. 285–96.

Singh, Rai (1995), 'A Historical Perspective For Change in the United Nations', *India Quarterly*, **51** (2–3), pp. 1–20.

South Centre, The (1997), *For a Strong and Democratic United Nations: A South Perspective on UN Reform*, London: Zed Books Ltd.

Taylor, Paul (1991), 'The United Nations System Under Stress: Financial Pressures and Consequences', *Review of International Studies*, **17**, pp. 365–82.

Taylor, Paul and Groom, A.J.R. (1988), *International Institutions at Work*, London: Pinter.

Urquhart, Brian (1995), 'Selecting the World's CEO: Remembering the Secretaries-General', *Foreign Affairs*, **74** (3), pp. 21–6.

Uvin, Peter (1995), 'Scaling up the Grass Roots and Scaling Down the Summit: the Relations between Third World Nongovernmental Organizations and the United Nations', *Third World Quarterly*, **16** (3), pp. 495–512.

Van Boven, Theo (1991), 'The Role of the United Nations Secretariat in the Area of Human Rights', *New York University Journal of International Law and Politics*, **24**, Fall, pp. 69–108.

Van Rooy, Alison (1997), 'The Frontiers of Influence: NGO Lobbying at the 1974 World Food Conference, The 1992 Earth Summit and Beyond', *World Development*, **25** (1), pp. 93–114.

Weissbrodt, David (1977), 'The Role of International Nongovernmental Organizations in the Implementation of Human Rights', *Texas International Law Journal*, **12**, pp. 293–321.

Willetts, Peter (1996), 'From Stockholm to Rio and beyond: the Impact of the Environmental Movement on the United Nations Consultative Arrangements for NGOs', *Review of International Studies*, **22**, pp. 57–80.

Winkelmann, Ingo (1998), 'Bringing the Security Council into a New Era: Recent Developments in the Discussion on the Reform of the Security Council', in Jochen A. Frowein and Rüdiger Wolfrum, *Max Planck Yearbook of United Nations Law: Volume One*, The Hague: Kluwer Law.

Part I
UN Institutional Development and Reform

[1]

FROM LEAGUE OF NATIONS TO UNITED NATIONS

by LELAND M. GOODRICH*

I.

On April 18, 1946, the League Assembly adjourned after taking the necessary steps to terminate the existence of the League of Nations and transfer its properties and assets to the United Nations. On August 1, this transfer took place at a simple ceremony in Geneva. Thus, an important and, at one time, promising experiment in international cooperation came formally to an end. Outside of Geneva, no important notice was taken of this fact. Within the counsels of the United Nations, there was an apparent readiness to write the old League off as a failure, and to regard the new organization as something unique, representing a fresh approach to the world problems of peace and security. Quite clearly there was a hesitancy in many quarters to call attention to the essential continuity of the old League and the new United Nations for fear of arousing latent hostilities or creating doubts which might seriously jeopardize the birth and early success of the new organization.

This silence regarding the League could well be understood at a time when the establishment of a general world organization to take the place of the discredited League was in doubt, when it was uncertain whether the United States Senate would agree to American participation, and when the future course of the Soviet Union was in the balance. Though careful consideration had been given within the Department of State to League experience in the formulation of American proposals, it was quite understandable that officers of the Department, in the addresses which they delivered and reports which they made on the Dumbarton Oaks Proposals, should have for the most part omitted all references to the League except where it seemed possible to point to the great improvements that had been incorporated in the new Proposals. Nor was it surprising, in view of the past relation of the United States to the League and the known antipathy of the Soviet Union to that organization, that Secretary of State Stettinius in his address to the United Nations Conference in San Francisco on April 26, 1945, failed once to refer to the League of Nations,

* LELAND M. GOODRICH, Professor of Political Science at Brown University and Professor of International Organization at the Fletcher School of Law and Diplomacy, was Secretary of the Committee on the Pacific Settlement of Disputes of Commission III at the United Nations Conference at San Francisco. He is co-editor of the *Documents on American Foreign Relations* series, co-author, with Edvard Hambro, of *Charter of the United Nations: Commentary and Documents*, and a former Director of the World Peace Foundation.

or the part of an American President in the establishment of it.[1] In fact, from the addresses and debates at the San Francisco Conference, the personnel assembled for the Conference Secretariat, and the organization and procedure of the Conference, it would have been quite possible for an outside observer to draw the conclusion that this was a pioneer effort in world organization.[2] Since the United Nations came into being as a functioning organization there has been a similar disinclination on the part of those participating in its work to call attention to its true relation to the League of Nations.

While the circumstances which make it necessary for those officially connected with the United Nations to be so circumspect in their references to the League of Nations can be appreciated, the student of international organization is free, in fact is duty bound, to take a more independent and objective view of the relations of the two organizations. If his studies lead him to the conclusion that the United Nations is in large measure the result of a continuous evolutionary development extending well into the past, instead of being the product of new ideas conceived under pressure of the recent war, that should not be the occasion for despair, as we know from the past that those social institutions which have been most successful in achieving their purposes are those which are the product of gradual evolutionary development, those which in general conform to established habits of thought but which nevertheless have the inner capacity for adaptation to new conditions and new needs.

While progress largely depends upon the discovery and application of new ideas and techniques, it has always been considered the test of practical statesmanship to be able to build on the past, adapting what has been proven to be useful in past experience to the needs and requirements of the changing world. Thus the framers of the American Constitution, while they created much that was new, did not hesitate to draw heavily upon the institutions and principles which were a part of their common background of experience in America and in England. At the time of the establishment of the League of Nations, the view was commonly held, certainly with more justification than today in relation to the United Nations, that something really unique was being created. However, we have come to recognize that even the League system was primarily a systematization of pre-war ideas and practices, with some innovations added in the light of war experience. Sir Alfred Zimmern has expressed this fact very well in these words:

> . . . The League of Nations was never intended to be, nor is it, a revolutionary organization. On the contrary, it accepts the world

[1] United Nations Conference on International Organization, Document 15, P/3, April 27, 1945.

[2] For an authoritative description of the Conference, see Grayson Kirk and Lawrence H. Chamberlain, "The Organization of the San Francisco Conference," in *Political Science Quarterly*, LX (1945), p. 321.

FROM LEAGUE OF NATIONS TO UNITED NATIONS 5

of states as it finds it and merely seeks to provide a more satisfactory
means for carrying on some of the business which these states trans-
act between one another. It is not even revolutionary in the more
limited sense of revolutionizing the methods for carrying on interstate business. It does not supersede the older methods. It merely
supplements them.[3]

We have come to recognize the various strands of experience—the European Concert of Powers, the practice of arbitration in the settlement of
disputes, international administrative cooperation, to mention only a
few—which entered into the fabric of the League. Should we be surprised
to find that what was true of the League of Nations is even more true
of the United Nations?

Those who have thus far attempted a comparison of the United Nations
with the League of Nations have, generally speaking, been concerned
with pointing out the differences.[4] Furthermore, comparison has been
made of the textual provisions of the Covenant and the provisions of the
Charter, not taking into account actual practice under the Covenant.
Such a basis of comparison naturally leads to an exaggerated idea of the
extent of the gap which separates the two systems. If in similar fashion
the Constitution of the United States as it existed on paper at the time
it became effective in 1789 were compared with the Constitution as it is
applied today, the conclusion undoubtedly would be that a revolution
had occurred in the intervening period. Obviously, any useful comparison
of the League and the United Nations must be based on the League system
as it developed under the Covenant. If that is done, it becomes clear that
the gap separating the League of Nations and the United Nations is not
large, that many provisions of the United Nations system have been
taken directly from the Covenant, though usually with changes of names
and rearrangements of words, that other provisions are little more than
codifications, so to speak, of League practice as it developed under the
Covenant, and that still other provisions represent the logical development
of ideas which were in process of evolution when the League was actively
functioning. Of course there are many exceptions, some of them important. But the point upon which attention needs to be focused for the
serious student of international affairs is that the United Nations does
not represent a break with the past, but rather the continued application
of old ideas and methods with some changes deemed necessary in the
light of past experience. If people would only recognize this simple truth,
they might be more intelligent in their evaluation of past efforts and more
tolerant in their appraisal of present efforts.

[3] Alfred Zimmern, *The League of Nations and the Rule of Law*, London, 1936, p. 4.
[4] See, for example, Clyde Eagleton, "Covenant of the League of Nations and Charter of the United Nations: Points of Difference," in Department of State, *Bulletin*, XIII, p. 263.

6   INTERNATIONAL ORGANIZATION

II.

Space does not permit a detailed analysis with a view to establishing the exact extent to which the United Nations is a continuation of the League system. All that is attempted here is to consider the more important features of the United Nations system, particularly those with respect to which claims to uniqueness have been made, with a view to determining to what extent in general this continuity can be said to exist.

Relation to the Peace Settlement

One point that has been made in favor of the United Nations as a special claim to uniqueness is that its Charter is an independent instrument, unconnected with the treaties which are in process of being made for settling the political and economic issues of World War II.[5] In contrast, it is argued that the League, by virtue of the fact that its Covenant was made at the Paris Peace Conference, and incorporated in each of the peace treaties, was from the beginning so involved in the issues of the peace settlement that it was never able to overcome the initial handicap of being a League to enforce the peace treaties. It is true, of course, that under the Covenant and under other provisions of the peace treaties, the League had placed upon it certain responsibilities in connection with the carrying out of the peace settlement.[6] This connection was not, in the early years of the League, regarded as an unmixed evil. One distinguished observer, while recognizing that a principal function of the League was "to execute the peace treaties," concluded on the basis of the first years of experience that this connection on balance served a useful world purpose.[7] It might be suggested that the criticism that later came to be made of the League on the ground of its relation to the peace treaties was primarily an attack upon the treaties themselves and would have been directed against any international organization which proved incapable of revising them. Without further arguing this point, however, the question can be raised as to how different will be the relation of the United Nations to the peace settlement following World War II?

While the Charter is a separate instrument and was made at a conference called specially for the purpose, the United Nations will inevitably become intimately and directly associated with the peace treaties once they are made. For one thing the original Members of the United Nations were those states that were at war with one or more of the Axis powers at the time of the San Francisco Conference. Furthermore, the interpre-

---

[5] See, for example, Clyde Eagleton, "Covenant of the League of Nations and Charter of the United Nations: Points of Difference," in Department of State, *Bulletin*, XIII, p. 264.

[6] See, for example, the provision of the Treaty of Versailles relating to the administration of the Saar Basin and the protection of Danzig. *Treaty of Peace with Germany*, Part III, section IV, Annex, chapter II, and section XI.

[7] W. E. Rappard, *International Relations Viewed from Geneva*, New Haven, 1925, p. 14–16.

FROM LEAGUE OF NATIONS TO UNITED NATIONS 7

tation to date of the provisions of Article 4 of the Charter makes it clear that the conduct of a non-member state during the war is an important factor in determining whether that state shall be admitted to membership. While Article 107 dissociates the United Nations as a peace organization from action taken in relation to enemy states, once the peace treaties have been made they will become part of the existing economic and political order on the basis of which the United Nations will seek to maintain peace and security. It is difficult to see how an international organization for maintaining peace and security, such as the United Nations is, can do so on any other basis. Furthermore, in connection with the making of the peace treaties, we already see the United Nations being called upon to exercise important functions of administration or guarantee similar to those which the League was asked to perform. Thus the United Nations guarantee of the special regime for Trieste parallels very closely the League guarantee of Danzig in its basic conception, and the proposed role of the United Nations in connection with "territories detached from enemy states in connection with the Second World War"[8] is almost identical to that of the League in relation to "colonies and territories which as a consequence of the late war [World War I] have ceased to be under the sovereignty of the States which formerly governed them."[9]

In this same connection we should consider the respective powers and responsibilities of the two organizations in regard to the revision of the two peace settlements. One serious criticism made of the League of Nations was its ineffectiveness as an instrumentality for the revision of those provisions of the peace treaties which had come to be recognized as unfair and unjust. Under the Covenant of the League the Assembly was empowered to advise the revision of treaties which had become "inapplicable" and the consideration of international conditions whose continuation might affect the peace of the world.[10] This provision remained a dead letter from the beginning, due to the Assembly's lack of power of decision and means of enforcement.[11] How much more effective is the United Nations likely to be in this respect? According to Article 14 of the Charter the General Assembly may recommend measures for the peaceful adjustment of any situation, regardless of origin, which is likely to impair friendly relations among nations. While there is no specific mention made of the revision of treaties, the General Assembly is clearly authorized under this Article to discuss any situation having its origin in unsatisfactory treaty provisions and to make recommendations thereon.[12] There is, however,

[8] *Charter of the United Nations*, Article 77.
[9] *Covenant of the League of Nations*, Article 12, paragraph 1.
[10] *Ibid.*, Article 19.
[11] Frederick S. Dunn, *Peaceful Change*, New York, 1937, p. 106–11.
[12] See discussion in Leland M. Goodrich and Edvard Hambro, *Charter of the United Nations: Commentary and Documents*, Boston, 1946, p. 104–06.

8   INTERNATIONAL ORGANIZATION

no obligation on the part of Members to accept any recommendation
that may be made. Thus the power conferred under this Article does not
go substantially beyond that of the Assembly under Article 19 of the
Covenant and there is the same chance, if not likelihood, that the United
Nations will be ineffective as an instrument for treaty revision. Furthermore, while the Security Council is given broad powers to take necessary
action to maintain peace and security, the powers which the Council
has to bind Members are limited to those falling within the general
category of enforcement action and do not extend to the power to impose
upon parties to a dispute or states interested in a particular situation any
particular terms of settlement or adjustment. That was made clear in the
discussions at San Francisco.[13]

Basic Character of Two Organizations

The statement has been made that the United Nations is "potentially
and actually much stronger" than the League of Nations.[14] That statement might lend itself to some misunderstanding, particularly in view of
the fact that it is only one of many statements that have been made
suggesting that the United Nations inherently is a more powerful organization and therefore more likely to achieve its purpose by virtue of
the specific provisions of its Charter than was the League of Nations.

We can start, I think, with the fundamental proposition that the United
Nations, as was the League of Nations, is primarily a cooperative enterprise and falls generally within the category of leagues and confederations
instead of within that of federal unions. Except in one situation, neither
the United Nations nor its principal political organs have the authority
to take decisions binding on Members without their express consent.
Without this power, it is impossible to regard the organs of the United
Nations as constituting a government in the sense of the federal government of the United States. The essential character of the United Nations
is specifically affirmed in the first of the principles laid down in Article
2 of the Charter where it is stated that "the organization is based on the
principle of the sovereign equality of all its members." This principle was
not expressly stated in the Covenant of the League of Nations, but was,
nevertheless, implicit in its provisions.

Since both the United Nations and the League of Nations are based
primarily upon the principle of voluntary cooperation, the point that
needs special consideration is whether, more or less as an exception to the
general principle, the Charter contains provisions which give to the organs of the United Nations greater authority than was vested in the corre-

[13] See Goodrich and Hambro, *op. cit.*, p.   *Handbook on the New World Organization*,
152–53, 155–59.   New York, 1946, p. 16.
[14] Louis Dolivet, *The United Nations: A*

FROM LEAGUE OF NATIONS TO UNITED NATIONS　　9

sponding organs of the League. In this connection a great deal of emphasis has been placed upon the provisions of the Charter regulating voting in the General Assembly and the Security Council. It is, of course, true that under Article 18 of the Charter decisions of the General Assembly can be taken by a two-thirds majority of the members present and voting, instead of by unanimous vote of those present, as was the requirement for the League Assembly. It must be borne in mind, however, that on questions of policy the General Assembly can only recommend, and that consequently any decision taken is a decision to make a recommendation. Also, it is quite unfair to compare these provisions without taking into account the practice of the League Assembly under the Covenant. In several important respects the rule of the Covenant was interpreted so as to bring actual League practice fairly close to the provisions of the Charter.[15] For one thing, it was provided in the rules of the Assembly that a state which abstained from voting was not to be counted as present, with the result that abstention was a means by which certain of the consequences of the unanimity rule could be avoided. More important, however, was the rule which was established in the first session of the League Assembly, that a resolution expressing a wish, technically known as a "voeu," might be adopted by a majority vote. This had the effect of making possible a whole range of Assembly decisions by majority vote which did not differ in any important respect from decisions which may be taken by the General Assembly by majority or two-thirds votes.[16] Furthermore, it should be noted that the League Assembly early came to the conclusion that the decision to recommend an amendment to the Covenant under Article 26 might be taken by a majority vote,[17] with the result that the power of the Assembly to initiate amendments actually could be exercised more easily than under the Charter of the United Nations. Thus it would seem erroneous to view the provisions of the Charter with respect to the power of the General Assembly to make decisions as representing any fundamentally different approach from or any great advance over the comparable provisions of the Covenant of the League of Nations as interpreted in practice.

When we turn our attention to the Security Council we find admittedly that an important change has been made. Under the League Covenant the Council was governed by the unanimity rule except in procedural matters, and this proved a serious handicap, particularly when the Council was acting under Article 11 of the Covenant. It was possible for a member of the Council, accused of threatening or disturbing the peace, to prevent any effective action under this Article by the interposition

[15] See Margaret E. Burton, *The Assembly of the League of Nations*, Chicago, 1941, p. 175–205.

[16] See C. A. Riches, *Majority Rule in International Organization*, Baltimore, 1940, p. 24.

[17] League of Nations, *Records of the Second Assembly*, Plenary Meetings, p. 733–35. See also, Burton, *op. cit.*, p. 187.

of its veto, as happened in the case of Japanese aggression in Manchuria in 1931 and the threat of Italian aggression in Ethiopia in 1935. Under the Charter it is possible for a decision to be taken binding Members of the United Nations without their express consent. Furthermore, this decision may require specific acts upon the part of the Members of the United Nations and is not to be regarded as a simple recommendation as was the case with decisions taken by the League Council under Articles 10 and 16.

Nevertheless, there are important points to be kept in mind before we conclude that a revolutionary step has been taken. In the first place, a decision by the Security Council can only have the effect of a recommendation when the Security Council is engaged in the performance of its functions under Chapter VI, *i.e.* when it is seeking to achieve the pacific settlement or adjustment of a dispute or situation. Furthermore, while the decision of the Security Council with respect to enforcement action under Chapter VII is binding upon Members of the United Nations, including those not represented on the Security Council, such decisions cannot be taken without the concurrence of all the permanent members of the Security Council. Consequently, in a situation comparable to that of Japanese aggression against China in Manchuria in 1931 and the threat of Italian aggression against Ethiopia in 1935, where the League Council admittedly failed on account of the unanimity principle, the Security Council would be prevented from taking any decision. Under the Charter the Security Council has power, which the League Council did not have, to take action against the small powers, but the experience of the past would seem to show that it is not the smaller powers, acting alone, who are most likely to disturb the peace. When dealing with threats by smaller powers acting alone the League Council was reasonably effective; it failed only when small powers had the backing of great powers. In spite of important changes in the technical provisions of the Charter, one is forced to the conclusion that so far as the actual possession of power is concerned, the United Nations has not advanced much beyond the League of Nations and that in comparable situations much the same result is to be anticipated. In the last analysis under either system success or failure is dependent upon the ability of the more powerful members to cooperate effectively for common ends.

Finally, the provisions of the Charter with regard to amendments and withdrawal follow in all essential respects the provisions of the Covenant and the practices developed thereunder. Under both Charter and Covenant no amendment recommended by the Assembly can become effective until ratified by the great powers. The Covenant was a little more restrictive than the Charter in one respect, requiring ratification by all members of the League whose representatives composed the Council,

FROM LEAGUE OF NATIONS TO UNITED NATIONS   11

plus a majority of all other members, thereby giving any Council member a "veto." On the other hand, the Charter, while limiting the "veto" to permanent members, requires approval by two-thirds of the Members of the United Nations. In practice, the charter provisions are not likely to have substantially different results.

Likewise, with respect to withdrawal, the League and the United Nations systems do not differ in any important respect. The Covenant of the League expressly permitted withdrawal under certain conditions which were not, however, enforced in practice.[18] The Charter says nothing about withdrawal but it is understood on the basis of a declaration adopted at San Francisco that the right of withdrawal can be exercised.[19] No doubt influenced by the League practice and conforming to it, it was decided that no legal conditions should be attached to the exercise of this right and that no attempt should be made to force a state to remain a Member, although it was made clear that a moral obligation to continue as a Member exists and that the right of withdrawal should only be exercised for very good reasons.

Basic Obligations of Members

Enumerated in Article 2 of the Charter are certain basic obligations of Members of the United Nations. These include the obligation to settle disputes by peaceful means in such a manner that international peace and security are not endangered, the obligation to refrain from the threat or the use of force against the territorial integrity or political independence of any state, and the obligation to give assistance to the United Nations in any action taken under the terms of the Charter. Similar commitments phrased in somewhat different language and with somewhat different meanings were to be found in various Articles of the Covenant.[20] From the point of view of form the Charter does represent a somewhat different approach in that these basic commitments are grouped together as Principles binding upon all Members. The phraseology of the Charter in certain respects undoubtedly represents improvement. For instance, the provision of Article 2, paragraph 4, by which Members are to refrain "from the threat or use of force against the territorial integrity or political independence of any state" represents an advance over the corresponding provisions of the Covenant which made it possible for members to take refuge in the technicality that an undeclared war in the material sense was no war and that therefore such use of armed force did not constitute a "resort to war." On the other hand, in one important respect, the basic

---

[18] Article 1, paragraph 2.

[19] For text, see UNCIO, *Verbatim Minutes of the Ninth Plenary Session*, June 25, 1945, Document 1210, P/20, p. 5–6; for text and comment, see Goodrich and Hambro, *op. cit.,*

p. 86–89.

[20] Articles 10; 12, paragraph 1; 13, paragraphs 1 and 4; 15, paragraphs 1 and 6; 16, paragraphs 1 and 3; and 17.

obligations of the Members of the United Nations may prove to be less satisfactory since, in the matter of enforcement action, the obligation of the Members of the United Nations is to accept and carry out decisions of the Security Council and to give assistance to the United Nations in any action taken under the Charter, while under Article 16 of the Covenant, the obligation of members extended to the taking of specific measures against any state resorting to war in violation of its obligations under the Covenant. While this obligation was weakened by resolutions adopted by the Assembly in 1921, it nevertheless proved capable of providing the legal basis for important action against Italy in 1935.

III.

The element of continuity in the progression from League of Nations to United Nations is perhaps most obvious when we examine the structure of the two organizations. The General Assembly is the League Assembly, from the point of view of the basic principles of its composition, powers and procedures. We have already seen from an examination of voting procedures that the practical difference between the League provisions and their actual application and the Charter provisions has been greatly exaggerated. The powers of the General Assembly, as compared with those of the League Assembly, have been somewhat restricted, it is true. The General Assembly's powers of discussion under Article 10 of the Charter and succeeding articles are fully as broad and comprehensive as the League Assembly's powers under Article 3, paragraph 3 of the Covenant. Only in respect to the making of recommendations has the power of the General Assembly been limited, and this, it can be argued, is in line with the practice which developed under the Covenant according to which the Council, and not the Assembly, ordinarily dealt with disputes and situations which endangered peace and good understanding.[21] The significant difference is that under the Charter a party to a dispute cannot by its act alone transfer the dispute from the Council to the Assembly, as was possible under Article 15, paragraph 9, of the Covenant.

The Security Council, from the point of view of composition, is the old League Council. One important change, however, has been introduced into the Charter. The League Council had general responsibilities and functions, whereas the Security Council is a highly specialized organ. Instead of having one council with broad powers as did the League, the United Nations has three, among which the various functions and powers of the League Council are divided. To a certain extent this new set-up was anticipated in League practice. At the time when the League's prestige as a peace and security organization was low, the Assembly created a special committee known as the Bruce Committee to inquire

[21] See Burton, *op. cit.*, p. 284–374.

FROM LEAGUE OF NATIONS TO UNITED NATIONS 13

and report on the possibilities of giving the economic and social work of the League greater autonomy. This Committee recommended the establishment of a new organ to be known as the Central Committee for Economic and Social Questions to which would be entrusted the direction and supervision of the work of the League committees in this field.[22] This proposed Committee, while it never was set up, was in effect the forerunner of the present Economic and Social Council.

So far as the Trusteeship Council is concerned, there is a somewhat similar background of development. While the Council was responsible under the Covenant for the supervision of the administration of mandates, in actual practice the Council came to rely very heavily on the Mandates Commission which, under the Charter, has come to be elevated to the rank of a principal organ, responsible not to the Council but to the General Assembly. This very responsibility of the Trusteeship Council to the General Assembly was to some extent anticipated in the practice of the League. Over the protest of some members, the League Assembly early asserted and exercised the right to discuss and express its opinion on mandates questions. While the Council was technically responsible for the enforcement of the provisions of the Covenant, there can be little doubt but what the Assembly exercised a real influence both on Council action and upon the mandatory powers.[23]

The Secretariat of the United Nations is clearly a continuation of the League Secretariat, not only in name, but also largely in substance. While the Charter provisions would permit its organization on somewhat different lines, with separate staffs for the principal organs of the United Nations, it seems clear that the conception of a unified Secretariat has prevailed.[24] "The role of the Secretary-General as the administrator of the United Nations derives from that of his counterpart in the League of Nations," [25] but has clearly assumed greater importance and scope under the provisions of the Charter. Due to political circumstances and the personality of the first holder of the office, the Secretary-General of the League never came to exercise a strong guiding hand in the direction of the League's work. The Charter of the United Nations, however, both expressly and by implication, gives the Secretary-General greater power and seems to expect more constructive leadership from him. More particularly, the role which the Secretary-General will be called upon to play in connection with the coordination of the work of the specialized agencies will require the exercise of initiative and strong leadership.[26]

---

[22] *League of Nations, Monthly Summary,* August 1939, Special Supplement.

[23] See Quincy Wright, *Mandates under the League of Nations,* Chicago, 1930, p. 133–35.

[24] See Report of the Preparatory Commission of the United Nations, PC/20, 23 De-

cember 1945, p. 84–94; Walter H. C. Laves and Donald Stone, "The United Nations Secretariat," *Foreign Policy Reports,* October 15, 1946.

[25] Laves and Stone, *op. cit.,* p. 183.

[26] *Ibid.,* p. 186 et seq.

14　　　　　　　　INTERNATIONAL ORGANIZATION

With respect to the Court, it is clearly recognized that, while it was decided to set up a new Court under a new name, it will be essentially the same as the Permanent Court of International Justice.[27] The fact that this Court is regarded as one of the principal organs of the United Nations does not in substance distinguish it from the Permanent Court. For purposes of expediency it seemed advisable to maintain the fiction that the Permanent Court of International Justice was independent of the League system, but a careful examination of the actual organization and work of the Court will leave no doubt that the Court functioned as fully within the framework of the League as will the International Court of Justice within the framework of the United Nations.

IV.

Like the League of Nations, the United Nations is a "general international organization" in the sense that its functions and actions cover the whole range of matters of international concern. Both the Preamble and the statement of Purposes contained in Article I of the Charter make this clear. In fact this generality of purpose and function is more explicitly stated in the Charter than it was in the Covenant, though in the practice of the League it came to be fully recognized. The Charter of the United Nations, in its general arrangement and substantive provisions, divides the major activities of the Organization into three categories: (1) the maintenance of international peace and security, by the pacific settlement of disputes and the taking of enforcement measures; (2) the promotion of international economic and social cooperation; and (3) the protection of the interests of the peoples of non-self-governing territories.

The Pacific Settlement of Disputes

The Charter system for the pacific settlement of disputes,[28] while differing from that of the League in many details of substance and phraseology, follows it in accepting two basic principles: (1) that parties to a dispute are in the first instance to seek a peaceful settlement by means of their own choice; and (2) that the political organs of the international organization are to intervene only when the dispute has become a threat to the peace, and then only in a mediatory or conciliatory capacity.

The obligation which Members of the United Nations accept under Article 2, paragraph 3 is to "settle their international disputes by peaceful means in such a manner that international peace and security, and justice, are not endangered." Under Article 34, paragraph 1, the parties to any

[27] UNCIO, Report of the Rapporteur of Committee IV/1, Document 913, IV/1/74 (1). See also Manley O. Hudson, "The Twenty-Fourth Year of the World Court," in *American Journal of International Law,* LX (1946), p. 1–52.

[28] For detailed analysis, see Leland M. Goodrich, "Pacific Settlement of Disputes," in *American Political Science Review,* XXXIX (1945), p. 956–970.

FROM LEAGUE OF NATIONS TO UNITED NATIONS 15

dispute "the continuance of which is likely to endanger the maintenance of international peace and security, shall, first of all seek a solution" by peaceful means of their own choice. Furthermore, by the terms of Article 36 of the Statute of the Court, Members may by declaration accept under certain conditions the compulsory jurisdiction of the Court. Declarations made by Members of the United Nations accepting the compulsory jurisdiction of the Permanent Court of International Justice and still in force are declared to be acceptances under this Article.

The legal obligations which Members of the United Nations have thus assumed are substantially the same as the obligations of League members under the Covenant and supplementary agreements. The Covenant itself did not place upon members of the League the obligation to settle all their disputes by peaceful means. However, forty-six states accepted the compulsory jurisdiction of the Permanent Court by making declarations under Article 36 of the Statute.[29] By Article 2 of the General Pact for the Renunciation of War of 1928 (Kellogg-Briand Pact), the signatories agreed that "the settlement or solution of all disputes or conflicts of whatever nature or of whatever origin they may be . . . shall never be sought except by pacific means."

The powers of the United Nations organs for the pacific settlement of disputes are substantially the same as those of the principal organs of the League. Under the Charter, as under the Covenant, the functions of political organs in this connection are limited to discussion, inquiry, mediation and conciliation. It is clear from the words of the Charter and from the discussions at San Francisco, that the Security Council has no power of final decision in connection with its functions of pacific settlement.[30] The Charter does, however, seek to differentiate between the functions and powers of the General Assembly and the Security Council in a way that the Covenant did not do. More specifically it makes the Security Council primarily responsible for the maintenance of peace and security, does not permit a party to a dispute to have the matter transferred at its request to the General Assembly, and limits the power of the General Assembly in principle to that of discussion. This constitutes an important departure from the textual provisions of the League Covenant which gave the Council and Assembly the same general competence and expressly allowed a party, acting under Article 15, paragraph 9, to have a dispute transferred at its request to the Assembly. It is significant, however, that out of some 66 disputes that came before the League, only three were actually brought before the Assembly under this provision. It would thus appear, and this is the conclusion of a careful student of the Assem-

[29] See Manley O. Hudson, "The Twenty-Fourth Year of the World Court," *op. cit.*, p. 33.

[30] See UNCIO, Report of the Rapporteur of Committee III/2, Document 1027 III/2/31(1), p. 4.

16   INTERNATIONAL ORGANIZATION

bly,[31] that actual practice under the Covenant resulted in a differentiation of function. This the Charter seeks to make obligatory.

In certain other respects the Charter system departs from the League pattern, but the importance of these differences can be greatly exaggerated. The elimination of the requirement of unanimity in voting theoretically increases the power of the Security Council, as compared with the League Council, in dealing with disputes and situations, but considering that the Security Council can only recommend, and that in League practice, agreement of the great powers was likely to result in the necessary agreement among all members of the Council, the practical importance of this difference is not likely to be great. Furthermore, under the Charter provision is made for the consideration by the Security Council and General Assembly of situations as well as disputes, but this does not mean any increase in the powers of the United Nations organs, particularly the Security Council, as compared with those of the corresponding organs of the League. In fact, it can be argued that the provisions of the Charter suffer somewhat in flexibility and capacity for growth, as compared with the corresponding provisions of the Covenant, because of the greater detail and consequent rigidity of certain of its terms. A comparison of experience under the Charter to date in the peaceful settlement or adjustment of disputes and situations with that of the League gives little basis for a confident conclusion that the Charter system is inherently better than, or for that matter, significantly different from, that which operated under the terms of the Covenant.[32]

Enforcement Action

It is in respect to enforcement action that the provisions of the Charter seem to offer the most marked contrast to the provisions of the Covenant,[33] but here again when we compare the Charter provisions with the way in which the Covenant provisions were actually applied the differences do not appear so great. The League system, as originally conceived, was based on the principle that once a member had resorted to war in violation of its obligations under the Covenant, other members were immediately obligated to apply economic and financial sanctions of wide scope against the offending state. The Council was empowered to recommend

---

[31] See Margaret E. Burton, *The Assembly of the League of Nations*, p. 284 et seq.

[32] On the operation of the League system, see William E. Rappard, *The Quest for Peace*, Cambridge, 1940, p. 134–207; Burton, *op. cit.*, p. 284–374; and T. P. Conwell-Evans, *The League Council in Action*, London, 1929. On the work of the Security Council to date, see Clyde Eagleton, "The Jurisdiction of the Security Council over Disputes," in *American*

Journal of International Law, XI (July, 1946), p. 513–33; and United Nations, *Report of the Security Council to the General Assembly*, A/93, October 3, 1946.

[33] For analysis of the United Nations system for the enforcement of peace and security, see Grayson Kirk, "The Enforcement of Security," in *Yale Law Journal*, LV (August 1946), p. 1081–1196.

FROM LEAGUE OF NATIONS TO UNITED NATIONS   17

military measures which members of the League were technically not required to carry out. As a matter of fact, in the one case where the provisions of Article 16 were given anything like a real test, the application of sanctions against Italy in 1936, acting under the influence of the resolutions adopted by the Assembly in 1921,[34] the members of the League established a mechanism for the coordination of their individual acts, and proceeded to apply selected economic and financial measures. No recommendation was made by the Council for the application of military measures.[35]

The Charter makes the Security Council responsible for deciding what enforcement measures are to be used to maintain the peace. Obligations arise for Members of the United Nations only when such decisions have been taken. This is a further development of the principle recognized in the 1921 Assembly resolutions and in the application of sanctions against Italy, that a central coordinating agency is needed to insure the taking of necessary measures with the maximum of effectiveness and the minimum of inconvenience and danger to the participating members. However, the provisions of the Charter go much further than did the Covenant in providing for obligatory military measures and advance commitments to place specific forces at the disposal of the Security Council. Even though certain members of the League, notably France, were insistent upon the need of specific military commitments, little was done in League practice to meet this need. The Geneva Protocol of 1924 was one notable attempt to meet this demand, by methods which in certain respects anticipated the Charter, but it never came into force. The framers of the Charter, no doubt recognizing this as a defect in the League system, sought to remedy the deficiency by providing in some detail for military agreements between members of the United Nations and the Security Council, and for a military staff committee to assist the Security Council in drawing up advanced plans and in applying military measures.

It can, however, be queried whether the Charter system will be more effective than the League system, in view of the requirement of unanimity of the permanent members of the Security Council. If we imagine its application in situations such as the Italian-Ethiopian and Sino-Japanese affairs, it is difficult to see how the United Nations would achieve any better results than did the League. Like the League, but for somewhat different technical reasons, the United Nations, in so far as its enforcement activities are concerned, is an organization for the enforcement of peace among the smaller states. If the permanent members of the Security Council are in agreement, it will be possible to take effective action under

[34] League of Nations, *Records of the Second Assembly*, Plenary Meetings, p. 803.
[35] For summary of this experience, see *International Sanctions* (A Report by a Group of Members of the Royal Institute of International Affairs), London, 1938, p. 204–213.

the Charter. It is not likely that such agreement will be reached to take measures against one of these great powers or against a protégé of such a great power. Consequently the sphere of effective enforcement action by the United Nations is restricted in advance, even more perhaps than was that of the League. Within the area of possible operation, the actual effectiveness of the United Nations system will depend upon political conditions which, if they had existed, would have also assured the success of the League of Nations.[36]

Administration of Non-Self-Governing Territories

Here we encounter new names and phraseology in the United Nations Charter, but the substance is very much the substance of the League mandates system. There are, of course, important differences. For one thing, Chapter XI, "Declaration Regarding Non-Self-Governing Territories," is definitely an addition. The idea, however, is not new, as it has been accepted by various colonial administrations in recent years, and has found expression both in official statements and in authoritative writings on the subject.[37] However, it is new to have embodied in an international instrument a definite statement of principles binding upon all states engaged in the administration of non-self-governing territories and to place upon such states the additional obligation to make reports to an international authority.

So far as the trusteeship system, strictly speaking, is concerned, it follows in general the lines of the mandates system.[38] The three categories of A, B, and C mandates do not appear, but due to the freedom allowed in the drafting of trusteeship agreements, there can be the same, if not greater, variety of provisions. Like the League mandates system, the institution of the trusteeship system is not made obligatory for any particular territories; it is simply declared applicable to certain territories to the extent that they are placed under it by agreement. Following the practice under the mandates system, the trusteeship agreements, according to the Charter, are to be made by the states "directly concerned." They must in addition have the approval of the General Assembly or the Security Council, depending upon whether or not they apply to strategic areas, but neither organ has any authority to draft and put into effect a trusteeship agreement for any territory without the specific approval at least of the state in actual possession of it.

The machinery for supervision and the lines of responsibility have been changed in that for trusteeship areas other than strategic areas the ad-

---

[36] See Kirk, *op. cit.*, p. 1082.

[37] See, for example, Baron Lugard, *The Dual Mandate in British Tropical Africa*, 2nd ed., London, 1923.

[38] For detailed analysis of the United Nations trusteeship system, see Ralph J. Bunche, "Trusteeship and Non-Self-Governing Territories in the Charter of the United Nations," in *Organizing the United Nations*, Department of State Publication 2573.

FROM LEAGUE OF NATIONS TO UNITED NATIONS   19

ministrative authorities are responsible to the General Assembly and its agent, the Trusteeship Council. As has been pointed out above, however, this change as compared with the League mandates system, was to some extent anticipated in League practice by the right which the Assembly asserted and exercised to discuss and make recommendations with respect to the administration of mandated territories. There is, however, in the Charter one important power vested in the United Nations organs, though in somewhat qualified form, which the Council and Mandates Commission of the League did not have and the lack of which was regarded as a serious weakness of the League system. I refer to the provision for periodical visits to the trusteeship territories which should make it possible for the Organization to get information on the spot and thereby check upon and supplement the reports of the administrative authorities.

International Economic and Social Cooperation

Perhaps the most important advance of the Charter over the Covenant of the League is to be found in its provisions defining the objectives, policies, machinery and procedure of international economic and social cooperation. In this respect, the Charter offers a wide contrast to the Covenant, which had only three articles dealing specifically with the subject. In fact, the Preamble of the Covenant, containing the statement of purposes of the League, made no specific mention of cooperation in economic and social matters, though the very general phrase "in order to promote international order and cooperation" was relied upon to justify numerous activities for which no express authority was to be found.

It is, nevertheless, true that the League in practice was a quite different matter.[39] It has been generally observed that the most permanently worthwhile activities of the League of Nations were in the field of international economic and social cooperation. There was in the course of the League's existence a tremendous proliferation of organization and an impressive record of substantial achievement in making available necessary information, in promoting administrative and legislative action by member states, and in dealing directly with international economic and social evils by administrative action. We have seen how in 1939 the recognition of the scope and importance of this work led to the proposal that a Central Committee for Economic and Social Questions should be set up to coordinate League activities in this field.

Apart from the provision for a separate economic and social council there is one important organizational difference between the League and United Nations systems, a difference which may prove to be of great

---

[39] See, for example, Denys P. Myers, *Handbook of the League of Nations*, Boston, 1935, for evidence of the relative importance on a quantitative basis, at least, of the League's economic and social activities during the first fifteen years of the League's existence.

importance, depending upon how the provisions of the Charter are applied in practice. Whereas the League technical organizations dealing with health, economic and financial cooperation were developed within the framework of the League and operated under the general direction and control of the principal League organs, the approach of the United Nations has been a different one. This time we have proceeded on the assumption that special needs as they arise should be met by the creation of appropriate autonomous organizations and that subsequently, these organizations should be brought into relationship with each other and with the United Nations by agreements negotiated by the organs empowered to act in such matters. The result is that instead of having a number of technical organizations functioning within the general international organization and subject to the general direction and supervision of its principal organs, as under the League system, we now have a number of specialized inter-governmental agencies, each operating within a defined area and more or less independently of the others.

Such a system clearly has possibilities as to the range and type of action that may be taken which were denied to the League system operating more completely under the influence of political considerations. On the other hand, there are obviously certain advantages in having some effective coordination of the operation of these various agencies as there will be many points at which their interests and activities will overlap.[40] Under the Charter the proposal is to take care of these common concerns by the special agreements referred to above. It is too early to be certain as to what the practical consequences of this approach will prove to be.

V.

To the student of international organization, it should be a cause neither of surprise nor of concern to find that the United Nations is for all practical purposes a continuation of the League of Nations. Rather it would be disturbing if the architects of world organization had completely or largely thrown aside the designs and materials of the past. One cannot build soundly on the basis of pure theory. Man being what he is, and the dominant forces and attitudes of international relations being what they are, it is idle to expect, and foolhardy to construct the perfect system of world government in our day. Profiting from the lessons of past experience, we can at most hope to make some progress toward the attainment of a goal which may for a long time remain beyond our reach. The United Nations is not world government and it was not intended to be such. Rather it represents a much more conservative and cautious approach

[40] See Herman Finer, *The United Nations Economic and Social Council*, Boston, 1945, 121 p.; also *Report of the Preparatory Com-* mission *of the United Nations*, PC/20, December 23, 1945, p. 40–48.

FROM LEAGUE OF NATIONS TO UNITED NATIONS   21

to the problem of world order. As such, it inevitably falls into the stream of institutional development represented by the League of Nations and its predecessors. Different names may be used for similar things, and different combinations of words may be devised to express similar ideas. There may be changes of emphasis, and in fact important substantive changes, deemed desirable in the light of past experience or thought necessary in order to meet changed conditions. But there is no real break in the stream of organizational development.

The student of international organization must recognize the United Nations for what it quite properly is, a revised League, no doubt improved in some respects, possibly weaker in others, but nonetheless a League, a voluntary association of nations, carrying on largely in the League tradition and by the League methods. Important changes have occurred in the world distribution of power, in the world's economic and political structure, in the world's ideological atmosphere. These changes create new problems and modify the chances of success or failure in meeting them, but the mechanics remain much the same. Anyone desiring to understand the machinery, how it operates, the conditions of its success, must look to the experience of the past, and particularly to the rich and varied experience of that first attempt at a general international organization, the League of Nations.

[2]

Global Governance 1 (1995), 229-253

REVIEW ESSAY

Beyond the UN System? Critical Perspectives on Global Governance and Multilateral Evolution

—————— ⊕ ——————

W. Andy Knight

Erskine Childers (with Brian Urquhart), *Renewing the United Nations System*, Development Dialogue 1994:1 (Uppsala, Sweden: Dag Hammarskjöld Foundation, 1994), 213 pp.

Shridath S. Ramphal and Ingvar Carlsson, *Our Global Neighbourhood: The Report of the Commission on Global Governance* (New York: Oxford University Press, 1995), 316 pp.

Rosemary Righter, *Utopia Lost: The United Nations and World Order* (New York: Twentieth Century Fund Press, 1995), 420 pp.

Mihaly Simai, *The Future of Global Governance: Managing Risk and Change in the International System* (Washington, D.C.: United States Institute of Peace Press, 1994), 402 pp.

James S. Sutterlin, *The United Nations and the Maintenance of International Security: A Challenge to Be Met* (London: Praeger, 1995), 143 pp.

Oran Young, *International Governance: Protecting the Environment in a Stateless Society* (Ithaca, N.Y.: Cornell University Press, 1994), 221 pp.

The year 1995 marks the fiftieth anniversary of the United Nations. No one should be surprised if an atmosphere of festivity and jubilation should accompany such an occasion. After all, this second-generation multilateral organization has reached a milestone never realized by its immediate predecessor, the League of Nations. The six books listed

230   *Beyond the UN System?*

above should inject a needed sobering element into the commemoration activities, particularly because they reveal serious problems (stemming from both exogenous and endogenous sources) that confront the world body today and imply that, unless major adjustments are made, we may have to look beyond the UN system to meet the myriad of demands of the twenty-first century. Yet these studies also offer a glimmer of hope that the UN can be reformed, even though the prescription for change varies from author to author.

While "prospects for UN reform" may be the main theme that runs through four of these studies, there is a broader, and much more interesting, leitmotif that unites them—the theme of "global governance and multilateral evolution," an aspiration and process that can be observed by analyzing that nexus between the expansion of international society and the striving of that society toward the creation of a regulatory framework within which conditions for peaceful interaction between people across the globe can blossom. Therefore, I have divided this review into two distinct parts. The first part summarizes the books and contrasts the different critical perspectives they bring to bear on the larger issue. The second part critically analyzes the books' differing answers to specific questions about the evolution of multilateralism and the direction of current reform efforts.

Part 1: Six Critical Perspectives

One of the troubling features of the international organization field is the paucity of theory. From among the six books covered in this review, only the Young book is explicitly devoted to theory building, and the empirical and historical material presented in this collection should provide a useful basis for those interested in developing their own theories of multilateralism or global governance. The Righter, Sutterlin, and Childers and Urquhart books, as well as the Commission on Global Governance report, lean toward the problem-solving epistemological approach, whereas the Simai and Young studies have elements of both problem-solving and critical epistemologies.

Utopia Lost

Righter is a British journalist who specializes in international affairs and has written two books on the subject. *Utopia Lost: The United Nations and World Order,* her third major book, is a damning indictment of most of the UN system. Only her "pet" organizations, the Bretton Woods institutions, escape relatively unscathed. According to the author, *Utopia Lost* is a Popperite title that implies a distaste for comprehensive blueprints—something she considers part of the "UN disease." She sets out, in a deconstructionist manner, to explore the institutional, political, and ideological dimensions of the malaise afflicting UN organizations and attempts to uncover how and where the problems arose in the first place, and why some global organizations, such as the International Monetary Fund (IMF) and the World Bank, have adapted better than others. Her primary goal in dissecting UN failures is to see where restructuring is needed, where it is hopeless, and what kind of alternatives must be found.

The book is divided into four main sections. Part 1 presents an interpretative history of the creation of the UN system. In it she exposes conceptual and structural contradictions of the UN Charter, inherent tensions between human rights and nonintervention principles, and institutional design faults. Part 2 chronicles the paralyzing impact of the Cold War environment on UN operations. It shows how East-West political and ideological tensions within the organization were exacerbated by decolonization and the North-South ideological rift. Here, Righter argues that the failure of the Western industrialized UN members to respond to this challenge in other than a defensive and patronizing manner is largely to blame for the state of the organization today and its inability to reform itself.

Part 3 attempts to show that the reason the World Bank and the IMF have been more successful than all the other UN agencies at modernizing and adapting to changed world conditions lies in their more pragmatic and demand-led orientation. This particular section of the book reveals the author's skewed reasoning. Righter seems to relish the Reagan administration's decision to withhold a percentage of its UN assessed contribution because it "forced governments and secretariats alike to recognize the need for radical rethinking of the UN's roles" rather than continue along the path of "tinkering with utopia" (a reference to the long and largely unproductive series of attempts at administrative, financial, and structural reform in the organization).

Part 4 is addressed primarily to Western governments. It lays out a number of policy options with respect to UN reform. The first is the typical antiorganizational recommendation of opting out of the organization. The second is the attempt at implementing structural and process reform from within. The third is a status quo tactic that would continue "facade management" of UN organizations. And the fourth is the author's preferred strategy of "positive discrimination"—i.e., letting the worst-managed UN agencies wither away instead of trying to reform them, and using the power of the West's purse, its organizational abilities, and political influence to build up those parts of the UN most capable of good work.

International organization specialists will find this book to be a selective historical account of the UN's institutional evolution, written from a very narrow functionalist perspective in a sensationalist, atheoretical, journalistic style. On the surface, this book appears to be relatively broad in scope, in that it touches on a wide range of subjects. However, a careful reading will

232   *Beyond the UN System!*

reveal a quite limited and thin analysis. The most in-depth analysis in her investigation is of the UN's bureaucratic inefficiency and ineffectiveness. Limiting one's inquiry in this way is not necessarily a bad strategy. However, the preoccupation with "navel gazing" seems to have left very little room for what could have been a more substantive contribution to the debate about the future direction of the world body.

Whatever strengths this book has tend to be outweighed by its weaknesses. There is a plethora of major deficiencies and important omissions. Here are a few examples. For a book that purports to deal with the failed efforts at reforming the UN system, the failure to analyze one of the most important efforts at restructuring the organization (the Group of Eighteen reforms) is surprising. Relatedly, several recent and important studies dealing with the subject of UN reform are never referred to or consulted.[1] In addition, Righter accepts too uncritically the position of World Bank and IMF officials, and this apparently blinds her to the problems those organizations have wrought on the world's poorest countries through their patronizing, heavy-handed strategies of political conditionalities, structural adjustment, and lending. No mention is made in the Righter study about the fact that in 1990 there was a global surplus of $180 billion, while developing countries' indebtedness soared to eight times that figure, and in the meantime the IMF had siphoned off $1.7 billion in interest and principal payments from those poor countries. Righter also fails to mention the World Bank's own internal assessment, which showed that out of eighteen hundred current bank projects in 131 states, 37.5 percent of the projects completed by 1991 were considered failures.

Righter's positivist problem-solving epistemology lends itself well to the functionalism of the Mitrany school. The functionalist orientation can be used to explain her apolitical stance and her decision to eschew analysis of UN security operations. The weakness of this approach is that it fails to take into consideration the kind of political analysis found in the Childers and Urquhart and Sutterlin works or the broader structural analysis of the impact of changes in the global political economy on the UN, which Simai addresses at length in Chapters 12 and 13 of his book and which is also dealt with in substantial detail in Chapter 4 of the commission report. Along with the absence of any major contribution to theoretical development in the international organization field, this book also suffers from unsubstantiated charges, sweeping and unqualified generalizations, imperfect analogies, half-truths passed off as evidence, inadequately supported conclusions, faulty reasoning, unclear arguments, questionable assumptions and premises, and biases and prejudices wrapped up in sanctimonious objective rhetoric. These, and not the fact that Righter is an "outsider," contribute to the weaknesses that will damage the credibility of the book.

W. Andy Knight   233

The United Nations and the
Maintenance of International Security

Sutterlin's book, *The United Nations and the Maintenance of International Security: A Challenge to Be Met,* provides an interesting counterpoint to Righter's analysis. While it also doesn't make any significant contribution to theory in the field, it fills a major void in Righter's research: the author focuses on the UN's peace and security mechanisms, and he does so as an informed "former insider." Bruce Russett, in his foreword to the study, shows why Sutterlin's interpretation of the evolution of the UN's role in peace maintenance has some credibility. Not only did the author serve in key positions under UN Secretaries-General Javier Pérez de Cuéllar and Kurt Waldheim, but he also contributed substantially as adviser to the current secretary-general, Boutros Boutros-Ghali, in the drafting of the widely read *Agenda for Peace.* Sutterlin now works at Yale University's program on the United Nations, the site of the research staff of a high-level independent commission on UN reform that was created at the suggestion of the UN secretary-general.

This rather succinct book is structured around four basic questions: To what extent are the UN's security mechanisms competent and relevant? Where did the concepts underlying the organization's functions originate? How can the UN be strengthened and changed? Are the purposes on which the organization is based still relevant and adequate for the realities of our new era? He concludes that while at the moment the capacity and potential of the UN to maintain international security and build peace are in question, the present constellation of international relations provides a propitious moment for enhancing the effectiveness of the world body's security apparatus. A recurrent theme in the book is the need for state leaders to seize the "opportunity to adapt the sound principles" on which the UN was founded "to the vastly altered circumstances of a changed world." Chapter 1 sets the backdrop by examining the old principles on which the UN was founded and the new realities it faces today. This is followed by successive chapters on conflict prevention, peacekeeping and intrastate conflict, peace enforcement, peace building, nuclear security in a multipolar world, the potential use of regional organizations in maintaining the peace, and the challenging role of the UN secretary-general. In the end, he issues a challenge for governments and peoples to work toward enhancing the UN's security apparatus.

Sutterlin demonstrates a much more sophisticated understanding than Righter of the limitations placed on the UN system's ability to function in the post–Cold War era. While Righter places the blame primarily on the imperfections of the Secretariat and specialized agencies, Sutterlin argues that the UN's failed performance lies in a number of factors—e.g., the changed nature of conflict, the anachronism of diplomatic tools, and the degree of authority available to the organization in given circumstances. He is careful to point out that the UN's individual failures in places like Bosnia, Angola, and Rwanda "should not be seen as negating the value of achievements or the validity of UN endeavours to protect human security." This more positive evaluation, however, downplays Righter's legitimate concerns with the fatal errors that certain key UN personnel have made in carrying out specific mandates.

This book provides a good balance of historical reflection and case study analysis. Its language is accessible to all students of international relations, even those who have little or no prior in-depth knowledge of the UN system. If there is a problem with Sutterlin's work, it is that it does not go far enough in its recommendations. The author limits himself to adaptive, piecemeal reforms rather than entertaining any drastic or transformative changes to the organization, and in doing so he reveals a conservatism that might prove out-of-step with the requirements of the changing times.

Sutterlin's work can be categorized as one of "utopian realism." His normative idealist position is tempered by a tendency to embrace a classical realist position. On the one hand, he recognizes the importance and power of the dominant states within the UN and the international system at large; on the other hand, he is not prepared to accept the pessimistic view that international organizations can accomplish little without the major powers.

Our Global Neighbourhood

Our Global Neighbourhood: The Report of the Commission on Global Governance goes beyond an examination of the problems of the UN system to look at the broader problematic of global governance. In doing so, it casts the net much wider than the books by Righter and Sutterlin. This report, put together by a group of prestigious international figures (headed by Sir Shridath Ramphal, former secretary-general of the Commonwealth, and former Swedish prime minister Ingvar Carlsson), adopted as its task to review existing arrangements of global governance against a backdrop of "profound, rapid and pervasive change in the international system—a time of uncertainty, challenge and opportunity." The authors set out for themselves the goal of making a contribution to improving the way the globe is governed. The prepublication publicity for this report seemed overstated (on its cover are the words "the most important book of the decade"), but its seven chapters constitute a rather comprehensive analysis of the concept, values, problems, and potential of global governance.

The report tries to reconcile existing global institutions with the emerging requirements for a more inclusive and democratic global governance arrangement that would address the demands of nonstate actors, and to goad state leaders into recognizing the need for a world institutional system that is much more responsive to the interests of all nations and people.

In Chapter 1, "A New World," the concept of global governance is first defined in a way that exposes the normative state-society leanings of the commission. What follows is a relatively detailed examination of the substantive changes in military, economic, social, and environmental fields that have occurred in the international system since 1945. Chapter 2 delineates the core values of "the global neighbourhood"—a reformulation of the "global village" concept. This neighborhood is depicted as one that is interconnected due to the communications revolution and the broader complex interdependence phenomenon. However, its diversity and pluralism make it difficult to reach agreement on common action and a common set of core values, such as respect for life, liberty, reciprocity, caring, integrity, respect for human rights, respect for democratic principles, and the rule of law. Yet this is precisely what the world needs at this critical juncture, according to the commission. This chapter also tackles the thorny issue of adapting established norms of sovereignty and self-determination to a world pervaded by seemingly paradoxical trends of globalization and fragmentation—perhaps the greatest challenge to global governance in the global neighborhood. Next, the report addresses ways of promoting common security in light of the expanding concept of security. Here the commission advocates the development of a new set of norms for security policies. Their wish list is by no means original, but it is packaged in a way to appeal to the state-society complex's need for safeguards against threats to security—a departure from the traditional statist approach to security.

Chapter 4 deals with the challenge of managing economic interdependence and the environment. A strong case is made for the adoption of a multilateralist "subsidiarity" framework in which economic responsibility can be allocated to institutions of global, regional, national, and local governance in a manner that would lend itself to efficiency and competence. The commission makes an argument similar to Righter's that global governance cannot be limited to public sector activity. Multinational financial and banking companies "account for a substantial and growing slice of economic activity," and their business is generally global in scope. Similarly, other nonstate actors, such as the Red Cross and Green Crescent, are playing a growing role in governance at the global level. While these bodies may not be able to substitute for an effective intergovernmental structure, in the authors' opinion, they cannot be excluded from playing a role in global governance. This chapter ends with a consideration of the controversial idea of a global taxation system that would help finance the activities of global governance.

236 _Beyond the UN System?_

The report then addresses the issue of reforming the UN system and introducing a global civil societal element in the decisionmaking of the world body, while Chapter 6 proposes ways of strengthening international law by moving toward compulsory jurisdiction for the International Court of Justice, creating an international criminal court, and developing better monitoring, compliance, and enforcement regimes. The final chapter is a call to action; in it, the commission's prescriptive proposals are summarized and an implementation strategy outlined.

There is very little in the way of original thought in this book. It reads more like an accumulation of ideas and proposals presented before by organizations such as the Club of Rome. Decidedly liberal institutionalist, the study also contains the hint of a state-society model of global governance.[2]

Renewing the United Nations System

According to Childers and Urquhart, the objective of _Renewing the United Nations System_ is to provide an analysis of the UN's present condition and to suggest changes that might allow the organization to function in a more systematic and effective manner. Like the Righter and Sutterlin books, this study has a problem-solving and structural-functionalist orientation. It is the fourth in a series produced with the support and funding of the Dag Hammarskjöld and Ford Foundations that have dealt with specific UN reform issues, such as improving leadership, reorganizing the Secretariat, and oiling the UN humanitarian emergency machinery. The subject matter of this book is broader in that it is devoted to reform of the overall UN system.

The authors identify a graduated and feasible sequence of steps for bringing about reform and restructuring the UN system that are likely to improve the situation for the organization. Their recommendations are circumscribed by the practical realization that what is ultimately needed for the UN to be efficient and effective—i.e., "major constitutional transformation" of its disparate elements into an integrated whole—is "not attainable now." The study therefore produces a number of "less radical" organizational change proposals. Childers and Urquhart's diagnosis of, and solutions for, the problems that exist in the UN system are sometimes at odds with Righter's. Part of the reason may lie in the fact that both Childers and Urquhart have developed a much more nuanced understanding of the political and bureaucratic complexities of the universal transorganization than Righter because they have been "insiders."

The framework of analysis for _Renewing the United Nations System_ consists of an introduction that sets out the post–Cold War challenge for the UN system; a description of the UN system as it is today, warts and all; a brief history of the origins of the organization—how it developed and why, and of the actual intentions of its founders in order to understand "why the system has not operated as well as it could"; a carefully argued case for revamped UN machinery to bring about global equity and sustainable development; a critical examination of the lack of a central brain for the UN's operational development activities—i.e., all development cooperation with, or assistance to, developing states; a diagnosis of the problems that need to be solved in the UN's human rights and humanitarian relief machinery and operations; a set of recommendations for practical reform to the intergovernmental decisionmaking structure and machinery of the UN; an analysis of the financial management and leadership problems in the organization and how they might be solved; and a revelation of the factors responsible for the denigration of the international civil service, including undue governmental pressures to place nationals in key positions, cronyism, uncompetitive salaries, deadwood and mediocrity, gender imbalance, and absence of an ombuds function for addressing cases of malfeasance and injustice.

The final two chapters deal with (1) developing a more democratic UN in which "we the people" can be brought back into the picture and (2) alerting governments to the urgent need to heed the warning signs of pending disaster to the global community. As Childers and Urquhart put it: "The instruments for such action do not need to be invented. The UN system is in place, however much updating and strengthening it may need. The UN system needs the urgent and sustained attention of all governments. They are directly responsible for it, and it is their responsibility to ensure that at long last the warnings are heeded." The reader will benefit from the excellent summary of conclusions and recommendations from the analyses of each chapter.

The Future of Global Governanace

In *The Future of Global Governance: Managing Risk and Change in the International System,* Simai seeks answers to two overarching questions: (1) What are the major political, economic, technological, environmental, and societal changes that confront international society at this juncture, and (2) given what is known of these changes, what new institutional adjustments will have to be made to guarantee a peaceful and stable world? In this work, he draws on three decades of accumulated research, mostly as a UN insider, reflected in three major publications: *Toward the Third Millennium* (1976), *Interdependence and Conflicts in the World Economy* (mid-1970s), and *Power, Technology and the World Economy* (1990). Some of his research findings over this period have also appeared in four volumes published by the UN Development Programme (UNDP) and the North-South Round Table.

238   *Beyond the UN System?*

This book is divided into five parts: the historical development of global order concepts and the need for formulating new ones; an analysis of the new realities and formations in the global political system; a review of the search for collective security in an era of intense global economic competition; considerations of global multilateral cooperation; and conclusions that assess the challenges and opportunities facing governments and individuals as we head into the twenty-first century. A reading of Simai's work reveals the eclectic nature of his thinking. He is able to combine analysis from comparative politics, political economy, history, and sociology into an institutionalist framework. This allows him to part company with several of the authors discussed in this review. For instance, he comes to the conclusion that despite the rhetoric that suggests an international consensus on the need to revitalize multilateral institutions, most national policymakers have not indicated much willingness "to support a higher level of international multilateral cooperation."

The final part of this book, "Holding the World Together," explores ways of making multilateralism work during a period of transition in which the parameters and regulating forces cannot be fully determined. Simai concludes that it may be too early "to draw a comprehensive and credible picture" of the end state of the current global changes. Yet he draws some tentative conclusions about what the impact of these changes will likely be on the emerging world order and how to reconcile the disparate worldviews of the major actors in the international system.

Instead of focusing on the institutional details of multilateral governance, as most of the other authors have done, Simai suggests that decisionmakers and analysts would be better off trying to gain an understanding of the nature and structure of cooperation and the complex international processes where it needs to be applied. He adopts what he terms "an unconventional systems theory framework," which is little different from a global systems perspective except in its embrace of a structural/historicist element. He conceives of the global system as encompassing the entirety of relationships among the actors that influence processes and changes beyond nation-state frontiers. That system, we are told, operates within a structure that has traditionally been dominated by states but has now made room for other important actors—nongovernmental organizations (NGOs), transnational corporations, and others—who have demonstrated an interest in managing destabilizing forces and risks. Further, the global system for Simai is conceptualized as embedded within social, ideological, and cultural structures as well—structures through which power may be concentrated, diffused, and transformed. At the base of the system is a political subsystem consisting of the totality of the relations between states. At the next level are those relations that are formed between states and nonstate actors and conditioned by a number of forces such as domestic political motivations. The next rung is a subsystem dominated by what the author calls the "price makers"—a handful of leading economic powers—whose decisions result in a permanent condition of adjustment for the smaller states or the "price takers."

International Governance

The final author, Oran Young, like Simai, does not limit his analysis to any particular international organization. His work is more broadly theoretical than any of the others reviewed here. *International Governance: Protecting the Environment in a Stateless Society* evolved from one of Young's previous works, *International Cooperation: Building Regimes for Natural Resources and the Environment.* It demonstrates the evolution of the author's thinking concerning international institutions in recent years. There are four major starting points for this study: 1) that the study of international regimes must be set more broadly in the context of the concept of "new institutionalism" within the social sciences, 2) that the concept of international bargaining has emerged as a way of thinking about the creation of international regimes, 3) that "effectiveness" is an essential element in the study of international governance systems, and 4) that there is a need to integrate the works of those who study international regimes with the contributions of students of international law and organization.

Those familiar with Young's pretheoretical studies on the linkage between international regimes and global governance will recognize the author's penchant for clarifying terms. This book is no exception in that regard. Young defines *governance systems* as social institutions—i.e., sets of rules that guide the behavior of participants engaged in identifiable social practices. This distinguishes governance from government—government being the material entity established to administer the provisions of governance systems. Here he draws heavily on the Rosenau and Czempiel text, *Governance Without Government: Order and Change in World Politics,* to which he made a seminal contribution. For him, governance encompasses both formal governmental and informal nongovernmental activities. His emphasis on intersubjective meanings as a base from which governance springs is a major contribution to the debate on global governance and multilateral evolution. Clearly, Young's regime focus helps him to see beyond the UN system and other formal multilateral bodies. In fact, the author demonstrates in this book that there are certain conditions in which the operations of formal governmental structures "are not only insufficient to ensure that growing demands for governance are met but also may be unnecessary for the provision of governance." Another useful conceptual

240   *Beyond the UN System!*

contribution is his differentiation between the "new institutionalism" and neoliberalism. What accounts for the preoccupation with new institutionalism? According to Young, there are four main factors: 1) the remarkable surge in demand for institutions to cope with broadening and deepening interdependencies, 2) the loss of confidence in the standard institutional tools such as private property rights and command- and control-type public regulations, 3) increased interest in the broad spectrum of institutional arrangements available to solve coordination and cooperation problems, and 4) research achievements in this area—in other words, success breeds success. The development of the "new institutionalism" can have negative consequences for formal international organizations, such as the UN system, particularly if they are viewed as "decisions frozen in time."

Chapter 1 of *International Governance* provides an excellent literature review on international regimes and governance systems linked to the broader dialogue of "new institutionalism" from other fields of study. In this chapter, Young provides a solid analytical vantage point from which the reader can track and assess the rapid growth and interest in the concept of international governance. For those interested in the environmental area of study, this chapter briefly introduces the reader to a treatment of the environment as a central issue in international relations. The material in Chapters 2 through 8 is further divided into three parts. The first is devoted to illustrative cases (on the global climate regime), which offers a good background for thinking about international governance systems in a generic way; the second focuses on theoretical issues arising from the notion of governance without government; and the third discusses the relationship between the "new institutionalism" and international relations, international organization, and international law. In his conclusions, the author defends a view, not generally held by regimists, that students of international law and organization have much to contribute to the building of knowledge about international governance systems. While the focus of this work is on environmental issues, the underlying argument pertaining to governance systems is generic enough to be easily applied to other issue areas, such as security, human rights, economics, and so forth.

This book, more than any of the others under review, makes a significant contribution to the development of a theory of international organization. The reason for this may lie in the fact that the author is able to separate his thinking from the traditional and worn functionalist and systems perspectives and utilitarian, power politics, and cognitivist perspectives to introduce a model of institutional bargaining that can explain regime formation. That model's defining characteristics include the significance of multiple actors, consensus rules, integrative bargaining, the veil of uncertainty, problem-solving activity, transnational alliances, and shifting involvements. In developing this model, Young makes a number of substantive contributions to the understanding of multilateral evolution and global governance. We learn from him one of the important characteristics of global governance systems—i.e., that they reflect the underlying configuration of power in international society. This means that such arrangements must of necessity be transitory—they come and go with the shifts in fortunes of the most powerful actors. The author also hypothesizes that international governance systems will tend to evolve in ways that their founders can neither predict nor control; that governance systems work best when they reflect and build on larger sets of ideas; that success is difficult to achieve when governance arrangements run counter to prevailing ideas; that robust governance systems require a balance between inclusiveness and workability as well as some degree of flexibility—i.e., the capacity of a governance system to adapt to changing circumstances without losing its identity; and, finally, that shifts in the intellectual underpinnings of a governance system can erode its viability. The challenge for the student of multilateralism will be to put these hypotheses through rigorous testing against the mounting empirical evidence that is now available.

Part 2: Three Key Questions About Reform

1. How do current concepts of "global governance" relate to what we know about the earlier evolution of multilateralism?

While multilateralism is by far the most promising conceptual approach for understanding and explaining the place of international organization within the broader context of world politics and for theorizing about adaptation and transformation processes in international organs, it has in the past "been relatively neglected in international relations theory."[3] Today we are witnessing a virtual growth industry in the field of multilateral studies. Why is this the case?

There seems to be a greater recognition these days of the importance of having a historical view of the multilateral process. Ruggie alerted us to the fact that multilateralism is more than "the practice of coordinating national policies in groups of three or more states."[4] It also embraces the principles and norms that order the relationship of states[5] and can be conceived as "an architectural form" or deep organizing principle of global society. In this sense, multilateralism existed before the advent of modern international organizations and has always been linked to an evolving governance process.

Simai reminds us that most ideas about multilateral organization and world order, presented as original to the twentieth century, actually appeared long before. Clearly, modern multilateral practices have benefited from concepts and routines tried in previous attempts at organizing and governing societies of states. An understanding of the evolution of this historical and structural process is therefore essential to explaining and predicting the nature of change in the concrete entities that embody the traits of multilateralism and in the social institutions that frame the context of their development and contribute to shifts in the design of world order.

The authors reviewed here demonstrate only a superficial grasp of the significance of the longer historical/structural process that resulted in the emergence of international organizations. But many of them realize that the historical structure (which can be conceived as a triad linking ideas, material capabilities, and institutions) has been evolving and will continue to change—not in any predetermined direction but according to the demands and challenges of international society at any given time. The demands of international society in 1945 were quite different in many respects than those today. Thus, it is useful to question whether the institutions and organizations established at that time are still relevant. It is on this point that Righter's contribution is valuable. She correctly points out that multilateralism is "an established, ineluctable, part of our lives" (a position on which the other five authors agree); that the rapid evolution of new forms of multilateral cooperation, increasingly more sophisticated and flexible than previous forms, has outflanked the activities of the traditional global intergovernmental institutions because those institutions are either defective, inefficient, ineffective and largely irrelevant, or a combination of all of the above; that while the UN system has no doubt contributed to the rapid evolution of multilateral cooperation since 1945, its future impact on this process is in doubt and could depend on the extent to which the organization is able to demonstrate "relevance" in dealing with the new demands of the international community; that excessive fidelity to particular institutional molds (such as the UN system as designed in 1945) will inhibit further development of international collaboration; and that the UN is not synonymous with multilateralism or international governance—it is merely one vehicle for accomplishing these things.

In light of the preceding discussion, it is imperative that we begin a process of rethinking the concepts of global governance and multilateralism. Each of the books reviewed has contributed to this process in one way or another. The Commission on Global Governance makes the case that *governance* ought to be defined as "the sum of the many ways in which individuals and institutions, both public and private, manage their common affairs." Based on this definition, the concept of global governance should therefore be broad enough to embrace "the whole exciting patchwork of institutions, processes, and people which together make society." In other words, the commission agrees with Righter and Young that global governance cannot be limited to the activities of the formal (but embryonic) governing structures and processes of the UN system or regional organizations, or the more informal, issue/function-specific international regimes. Those who would advocate a single model of global governance—whether it be in the form of an intergovernmental and pluralistic set of decision-making and security apparatus or a more amalgamated, less accommodating construct such as a world government—are open to the charge that their vision is either too exclusionary or suffers from the fatal flaw of practical unattainability.

Clearly, at this juncture in our history, we cannot speak as though we have arrived at any coherent, or viably aggregated, form of global governance. What we have can best be described as partial governance with very few linking-pin connections that could give it a truly holistic and global shape. It would seem, however, that there has been a kind of evolution in the multilateral activity of human society whose trajectory bears evidence of a progressive, albeit not consistently unilinear, development in the direction of what might be called global governance.

The commission report also makes a worthy effort at defining what should be considered the work of global governance today. For this group, such tasks include maintaining peace and order in the global neighborhood, expanding economic activity, dealing with the problems of pollution and greenhouse warming, combating diseases, curbing the horizontal and vertical proliferation of weapons, preserving genetic diversity, deterring terrorism, warding off famine, saving endangered species, solving economic problems, developing fair ways of sharing the earth's resources, halting drug trafficking, and tackling the problems of AIDS and other fatal diseases—and the list goes on. As does Sutterlin, the group calls for the global adoption of a set of core ideas and values that can unite people of all cultural, political, religious, and philosophical backgrounds. The values would have to be appropriate to an increasingly crowded and diverse planet. One such core value could be "the democratic principle," which can serve to shift the responsibility for global governance from intergovernmental institutions to "we the people." Simai agrees, in part, with the commission's normative stance in arguing that governance during this transition period requires a system of international cooperation that is more democratic, complex, and flexible than the current one. It will therefore require a system that is broader than the UN system.

2. How does the UN's own history affect the prospects for UN reform?

As the Childers and Urquhart study reminds us, the second generation of the modern multilateral organization, the United Nations, was founded on more than utopianism. Its founders injected a degree of "realism," "reason,"

244   *Beyond the UN System?*

and "intellectual analysis" to the discussions leading up to the San Francisco conference of 1945. One of the major problems for the UN is the way it is judged by those who interpret the intent of the founders as that of trying to create a supranational body, or a global government. Sutterlin, Childers and Urquhart, and, to some extent, Righter remind us that the intent of the founders was much more circumscribed. The UN was intended to be an association of independent sovereign states.

The founders had no way of knowing the extent to which many of the principles on which the world body was built would be challenged as the modern era comes to an end and a postmodern one begins. UN Secretary-General Boutros Boutros-Ghali, while respecting states' fundamental right to sovereignty, has recognized that the "time of absolute and exclusive sovereignty" has passed.[6] Issues that were once considered under the category of "domestic jurisdiction" are now being placed on the international agenda. Complex interdependence and globalization forces are turning the world into a truly "global village." In addition, the end of the Cold War has resulted in unprecedented demands on the UN system. The only hope of dealing with these problems is to develop progressively a global-governance structure that can be responsive to the variety of needs and demands of the next millennium. Can the UN system become that structure? Based on the analysis of the above authors, the answer is "probably not." Can it become a linking pin for that governance structure or the central mechanism for the facilitation of global governance? Again, based on the analysis provided by the authors, the answer is mixed—both "probably yes" and "probably no." The unanimous verdict is that the UN system will have to make some vital changes if it is to remain relevant to the new multilateralism and to global governance.

Just about eight years ago, several commentators predicted the demise of the United Nations. Most of them were advocates of unilateralist state foreign policy, like the Heritage Foundation in the United States and the Adam Smith Institute in the United Kingdom, who either secretly or openly cheered at the prospect of eliminating an organization that, in their view, was overly politicized, excessively bureaucratic, anti-Western, antidemocratic, lethargic, wasteful, expensive, ungovernable, inefficient, ineffective, irrelevant, even dangerous, and possibly a nuisance. Some of them were openly critical of the UN for allowing itself to be hijacked by tyrannous Third World majorities in the General Assembly, who used their voting advantage to pass useless resolutions and to side with communist countries against the United States and the rest of the Western industrialized world. Essentially, underlying those criticisms was a general view that the world body in its first forty or so years of existence had not been able to do what was intended by the UN Charter and instead had created more problems than it was able to solve in the process. A few of these critics even went so far as to recommend that their national government bail out of the organization rather than continually plough resources into it.[7]

This kind of analysis tended to be placed within the context of a so-called decline of multilateralism during the mid-1980s. Some, particularly U.S. political scientists and some journalists, had even ventured so far as to claim that multilateralism was indeed dead and that the UN system, the institution that most embodied that concept, should perhaps be taken off its life-support system and given, if need be, a kind of Kevorkian send-off or even a more ignominious burial—not unlike that given to the League of Nations in the late 1930s. This position gave the false impression that the UN was somehow inextricably linked to all activities of multilateralism. The largely U.S.-fostered financial crisis in the organization put the UN on the brink of insolvency in the late 1980s and threatened to be the final nail in the institution's coffin.

The predicted demise, however, proved somewhat premature. In fact, public criticism of the UN subsided, at least temporarily, as defrosting of Cold War conditions produced a propitious climate in which the UN Security Council appeared to have thrived. As Sutterlin points out, the council was relatively successful in resolving a number of outstanding conflicts across the globe—its crowning achievement being the decisive action taken against Iraq during the 1990–1991 Gulf War. That action momentarily silenced those critics who had claimed, for valid reasons, that the Security Council's security apparatus was incapable of functioning in the way the charter had envisaged. The UN emerged from the Gulf experience operating much closer to its founders' vision and was perceived as "a stronger and more effective institution."[8]

Righter, however, does not agree with that perception. While she admits that the end of the Cold War and the Gulf War experience effectively ended the marginalization of the UN and gave the impression that the organization had revived itself, she contends that the world body did not undergo any renaissance as such. In fact, according to the author, by being jettisoned into the global spotlight, a number of the organization's deep-seated inadequacies were revealed. What are some of these inadequacies?

For one, the Righter and Childers and Urquhart books agree on the position that decades of efforts at institutional reform in the organization have produced too few improvements. Righter's criticisms of the UN bureaucratic machinery as cumbersome, complicated, slow-footed, and unaccountable continue to be largely valid. Her evidence of drift, bureaucratic infighting, and transorganizational malpractice has been well documented elsewhere. It is also fair to say, as I do, that there is still too much verbal obfuscation in the main plenary bodies of UN organizations, too much

empire building among the specialized agencies, and too much disorganization and incoordination throughout the entire system. All of these blemishes
certainly detract from the original idea of the universal organization.

But some of the criticisms of the UN by Righter as well as by others
are not valid, in that they do not address the real problems of the UN system. For example, Righter's concern with the extravagance of the UN budget becomes moot when one realizes, as the Childers and Urquhart study
reminds us, that the overall global expenditures of the organization (including those from its regularly assessed, voluntary, and peacekeeping
budgets) total about $10.5 billion a year. This is less than the amount the
United Kingdom spends on public administration and police. The expenditures of the UN proper, including the amount from the vastly expanded
peacekeeping budget, is $4.1 billion—an amount comparable with what is
spent by New York City's fire and police departments. Childers and
Urquhart put criticism of the amount the UN spends on all of its activities
(less peacekeeping and other emergency costs) into proper perspective
when they reveal that U.S. citizens spend approximately the same amount
on cut flowers and potted plants each year. Another one of her charges,
that the UN is unproductive except for its paper factory, falls into the category of sensational-journalistic hype.

To assert, as Righter does, that UN machinery is kept in place over-
whelmingly "for the benefit of its international staff, armies of consultants,
and conference goers" belittles the extraordinary commitment that many
Secretariat staff members have demonstrated over the years in trying to
ameliorate the suffering of people and improve conditions for a large portion of the globe. Several other of her charges, such as that "idealistic
vagueness" prevents the UN from functioning, are so vacuous that they
erode the scholarly credibility of her study.

Many of the Righter-type criticisms of the world body have been
made before, especially by those who would prefer to see a world without
the UN. But will this fetishism with improving the organization's efficiency and effectiveness prove to be the correct strategy for dealing with
the underlying problems of the UN? Based on the past record, probably
not. Underlying most of the analysis on the reasons why the UN system
has consistently failed in its efforts at reform is the notion that very little
learning has taken place within the organization.

3. What reforms should be made?

The Urquhart and Childers book lays out specifically how the UN reform
process can benefit from "learning." In light of the cumulative experience
of the organization's reform attempts, the authors note that many of the
weaknesses of the system stem from the poor quality of the people appointed

by governments to important leadership positions; that the mechanistic shuffling of units is usually confused with installing the ability to generate teamwork and transorganizational coordination; that some decisions regarding reform are made because of dissatisfaction by some member states with the administrative leadership within particular organizations—as was the case with Amadou Mahtar M'Bow in UNESCO and Edouard Saouma in the Food and Agriculture Organization (FAO); that insufficient care is taken to ensure that reorganization efforts are accompanied by proper retraining of staff or necessary rewriting of senior job descriptions; that avoidance of needed restructuring by introducing palliative reforms will not solve problems that are structural in nature; that governments should be more specific in their reform and restructuring proposals to make sure that the proper lines of responsibility are drawn that will strengthen coordination between organizations and units; that sufficient responsibilities and resources should be directed to those organs that will best serve the interests of the global community; that "reform impact reports" should precede any implementation of organizational changes; and that follow-up reports on each reform effort (along with its implementation) should become standard policy and be recorded in a computerized data bank for further reference.

The authors then go on to list a number of detailed constructive efforts that might improve the UN's efficiency and effectiveness. Some of the most prominent of these include reverting to the original idea of a common seat of the UN system that would house all global-level elements of the UN Secretariat, including UN development and humanitarian organs and funds, the five major specialized agencies (ILO, FAO, UNESCO, UNIDO, and WHO), a UN parliamentary assembly with increased status for NGOs, and a unified UN Public Information Department with state-of-the-art communications technology; creating a UN consultative board; fully implementing the original Special Agreements between the world body and its specialized agencies; consolidating UN budgets; making the Administrative Committee on Coordination (ACC) a true executive committee of the entire system; ensuring UN leadership in international economic cooperation by establishing a post of deputy secretary-general for international economic cooperation and sustainable development; streamlining the UN's operational development activities in the field under single offices; transforming the Trusteeship Council into the UN Council on Diversity, Representation and Governance—a body responsible for addressing the unresolved legacies of former empires, the aspirations of cultural and ethnic groups within existing states, and the growing phenomenon of the spread of democratization; establishing the rank of the high commissioner for human rights at the level of deputy secretary-general; appointing an independent ombuds panel to judge the human rights performance of the UN system; reorganizing of the Department of Humanitarian Affairs into two divisions (one for early warning analysis and the other for purely operational assignments); creating a UN humanitarian security force to protect UN and NGO emergency personnel, transport vehicles, and supplies; completely overhauling the UN's deliberative machinery; improving the financial management of the organization and its system of accountability and oversight; reviving an old proposal to create a common UN system staff college network in order to improve the quality of the international civil service; and creating a more democratic UN system by establishing a people's assembly to operate alongside the UN intergovernmental machinery.

Sutterlin proposes a number of ways to improve the UN's ability to manage conflicts that are also based on organizational learning. But he also has a word of caution for those who recommend predetermined formulas for dealing with the broad variety of threats to human security. For instance, the author warns that the new preoccupation with trying to create criteria for UN intervention may be counterproductive. On the one hand, such criteria might help expedite council decisions and improve the UN's rapid-response capability. But these could also prove to be debilitating in certain circumstances. Each crisis is seen by the author as sui generis, involving to a different degree the interests and concerns of individual council members. Thus, any guidelines that seek to predetermine the reaction of council members to a particular conflict "are likely to be untenable," according to Sutterlin, and could place the world body on the sidelines as nothing more than a witness to indiscriminate slaughter and genocidal acts.

He also notes that not all conflicts can be prevented. Therefore, there will continue to be a need for reactive responses to unexpected violent outbreaks across the globe. The answer to this problem is suggested in the commission's report—i.e., the development of an independent UN rapid-reaction capability. In this regard, the Canadian government has committed itself to devise such a capability to help avert catastrophe in world trouble spots.[9] Such commitments to a more independent role for UN troops will mean that UN member governments will have to be willing to accept some risks of casualties in theaters of conflict where their national interest may not necessarily be at stake. To justify such actions may require a redefinition of the national interest in a way that allows state leaders to protect their citizens' interests and at the same time deal responsibly with those global interests that intersect with the more narrowly defined ones at home; this will demand the acceptance of a new ethic. As Sutterlin puts it, "It is in the national interest of every country that the coming century be a century in which ethical considerations figure in the shaping of government policies and of global public opinion. All countries and peoples will be safer as a result" (pp. 138–139). But there is also a more pragmatic reason for encouraging this new conceptualization of the national interest. The outflow of refugees from conflictual regions in places such as Africa or the Balkans may spill over the borders of neighboring states in numbers that are too large to be absorbed practically. This could result in conflict over scarce or limited resources in the receiving countries. Terrorist groups formed out of the dissatisfaction with unjust regimes can disrupt the social tranquility of countries that are foreign to those groups.

To the charge that the UN is overextended, Sutterlin retorts that "it is within the power of the world community—if the UN, regional organizations, NGOS, and governments work together—to limit the intensity of such critical situations through preventive measures and peace-building" as well as through the maturation of early warning devices. But this requires a change in mind-set by the major industrialized countries about the requirements of national security and the allocation and distribution of foreign aid. It helps if UN member governments would realize that prophylactic treatment can be more costly than emergency treatment. As Sutterlin correctly points out, savings from reductions in national military spending could be put toward the development of proactive strategies designed to prevent the outbreak of conflict. But this is a decision for governments, and, as Simai notes, they have so far shown little inclination in this regard.

The commission proposals for changing global governance are perhaps even more comprehensive and sweeping than those of the Childers and Urquhart study. These prescriptive recommendations can be broken down into the following categories: improving security, strengthening the socioeconomic bodies, democratizing the intergovernmental and political institutions, and empowering the legal element.

In the security field, the commission recommends revising the UN Charter so that the Security Council can authorize action in intrastate conflicts (but only when the security of people is so extensively violated as to require humanitarian intervention); strengthening the preventive mechanisms of the UN (i.e., early-warning mechanisms, a comprehensive system of information collection); enhancing the UN's rapid-response capability by creating a UN volunteer force; improving the secretary-general's fact-finding capacity; reactivating the Military Staff Committee; increasing funds for peacekeeping operations in order to keep up with the increasing demands in this area; renewing the NPT for an indefinite period; creating new nuclear weapons-free zones as a means of confining the spread of nuclear weapons; establishing a demilitarization fund to help countries reduce their military commitments; and negotiating a worldwide ban on the manufacture and export of land mines.

In the socioeconomic area, the report calls for establishing an apex body, the Economic Security Council (ESC), which would be as important as the current Security Council; quickly implementing the proposed plan for a World Trade Organization; reforming the decisionmaking structure

2.50   *Beyond the UN System?*

of the Bretton Woods institutions to make them more democratic; enhancing the role of the IMF by enabling it to enlarge its capacity to provide balance-of-payment support and to play a more active role in promoting policy convergence in major economies, releasing a new issue of Special Drawing Rights, and improving its capacity to support nominal exchange rates; strengthening the World Bank's role in development financing through an enhanced International Development Association and by extending its financial intermediation role through greater use of guarantees and the cofinancing of big projects; instituting a more radical debt-reduction strategy for heavily indebted low-income countries; fortifying the capacity of insurance markets to meet the economic costs of disasters in poor and small countries; charging levies on the use of common global resources—such as flight lanes, sea lanes, ocean fishing areas, and the electromagnetic spectrum—essentially to provide money for global purposes; exploring the possibility of an international tax on foreign currency transactions; and creating an international corporate tax base for multinational companies.

To democratize the intergovernmental and global political institutions, the report suggests enlarging the Security Council to make it more representative of the entire UN membership by creating a new class of five "standing" (rather than permanent) members, whose status would be reviewed around the year 2005; raising the number of nonpermanent (rotating) members from ten to thirteen; phasing out the veto in the Security Council after the year 2005; creating a Forum of Civil Society, reminiscent of the Kantian cosmopolitan model of international organization, which would convene each August before the annual session of the General Assembly; transforming the now outmoded Trusteeship Council into a body responsible for overseeing and maintaining the global commons; creating a Council for Petition that would hear the complaints of members of international civil society concerning threats to their security; eliminating ECOSOC, UNCTAD, and UNIDO and merging the Second and Third Committees of the General Assembly; enhancing the UN's capacity to advance the rights of women, beginning with the promotion of more women to senior Secretariat positions; radically improving the procedure for appointing a secretary-general and restricting the appointment to a single term of seven years; and applying consistently Article 19 of the UN Charter, which calls for the disenfranchisement of member states that are grossly in arrears; and revising the formula for assessed contributions so that the UN is not dependent on too large a contribution from any single member state.

In the legal area, the commission proposes limiting World Court judges to a single ten-year term and developing a system to screen potential members for jurisprudential skills and objectivity; encouraging states to include in future agreements and treaties provisions for the settlement of interstate disputes; giving the UN secretary-general the right to refer at an advanced stage legal aspects of any dispute to a full bench of the World Court; appointing a distinguished legal adviser to provide independent advice to the Security Council on international legal propositions that might develop within that body; encouraging the council to make greater use of the World Court as a source of advisory opinion on matters that might have some relevance for international law; and establishing an international criminal court with an independent prosecutor or panel of prosecutors of high moral character, level of competence, and experience.

Many of these suggestions are not original; but, taken as a package, they highlight the amount of adjustment that is required if the UN is to become not only an efficient and effective world body but also one of the relevant global-governance institutions of the next century. Failure to implement these changes might mean that the organization could either be bypassed or suffer the fate of its predecessor, the League of Nations.

Conclusion

The breadth of analysis contained in the works reviewed here, as well as the package of prescriptive reforms offered, makes these books essential reading at a time when observers of international organizations and regimes are unclear about the future of multilateral bodies. On the whole, these six books constitute a set of timely and important contributions to the debate over UN reform and to the broader question of which direction global governance and multilateral evolution will take in the next millennium. Whether the UN system will be a central player in the new multilateralism is still an open question. Its relevance to the twentieth century will depend very heavily on its flexibility and adaptability and on the extent of the competition it receives from other multilateral players in the global-governance arena.

If we are to believe the combined analysis of all the authors reviewed here, the fifty-year-old UN system is now left with two basic choices: dissolution or succession. Given the persistence of the idea that the fate of humankind depends on state-society collaboration and cooperation around common security issues, dissolving the UN can be considered nothing more than "throwing out the baby with the bathwater." As several commentators have noted in the past, the elimination of the UN today may only result in the reinvention of the wheel tomorrow. This being considered, it makes much sense to utilize the current propitious environment to bring about the changes that would make the world body relevant to the twenty-first century and beyond. To be successful, this sort of change will require much more than tinkering with organizational charts, shifting financial envelopes, reordering bureaucratic priorities, downsizing headquarters

252   *Beyond the UN System?*

and field operations, streamlining managerial and administrative procedures, or oiling the intergovernmental machine. While these issues might be considered important, they have generally resulted in a concentration of focus on reformist prescriptions that are limited and narrow in scope and superficial and short-term in vision and effect.

It seems much more important at this critical juncture that we begin to develop a long-term adaptation agenda (and strategy) that focuses on the requirements of international society and, then, on how the UN system can be adjusted to help. Such an approach should not treat the UN as a given and must recognize that the immediate political agenda, which generally engages the responsibilities of states, will have to share the stage with longer-term structural issues that have tended recently to depend to a proportionately greater extent on a broader range of social forces. It is this mix of state/societal, immediate/long-term action that will be necessary if we are to adapt existing global-governance arrangements to the emerging conditions of a postmodern era. The problem, however, for the above scholars (as well as those scholars interested in the subject of global governance and multilateral evolution) is that, given the turbulence of the present transitional period, the required task will not be unlike "trying to change the wing of an airplane while it is still in flight."[10] It is an assignment that demands every ounce of our imagination and that will have to involve both reflexive adaptation and learning strategies if we are to prevent a disastrous crash. ⊕

Notes

The author is assistant professor of political studies at Bishop's University, Lennoxville, Quebec. He was formerly research fellow and lecturer in international organization at the Centre for International and Strategic Studies at York University.
1. None of the following important and recent works on UN reform is mentioned in the author's study: J. Martin Rochester, *Waiting for the Millennium: The United Nations and the Future of World Order* (Columbia: University of South Carolina Press, 1993); K. P. Saksena, *Reforming the United Nations: The Challenge of Relevance* (New Delhi: Sage Publications, 1993); Joachim Müller, *The Reform of the United Nations*, vol. 1 (New York: Oceana Publication, 1992); Joseph Baratta, *Strengthening the United Nations: A Bibliography on UN Reform and World Federalism* (New York: Greenwood, 1987); Yves Beigbeder, *Management Problems in the United Nations Organizations: Reform or Decline?* (New York: St. Martin's Press, 1987); David Steele, *Reform of the United Nations* (London: Croom Helm, 1987); Daniel Bardonnet, ed., *The Adaptation of Structures and Methods at the United Nations* (The Hague: Hague Academy of International Law; Martinus Nijhoff, 1986).
2. On that latter point see Keith Krause and W. Andy Knight, *State, Society, and the UN System: Changing Perspectives on Multilateralism* (Tokyo: United Nations University Press, 1995).

3. These points have been made by John Gerard Ruggie, "Multilateralism: The Anatomy of an Institution," *International Organization* 46, no. 3 (Summer 1992): 567, and by James Caporaso, "International Relations Theory and Multilateralism: The Search for Foundations," *International Organization* 46, no. 3 (Summer 1992): 630.

4. The nominal definition provided by Robert Keohane, "Multilateralism: An Agenda for Research," *International Journal* 45 (Autumn 1990): 731.

5. See Ruggie, "Multilateralism," p. 567.

6. Boutros Boutros-Ghali, *An Agenda for Peace* (New York: United Nations, 1992), par. 17.

7. Examples of such critics include Charles Krauthammer, "Let It Sink: Why the US Should Bail Out of the UN," *New Republic* 197, no. 3 (24 August 1987): 18–23, and Burton Pines, ed., *A World Without the United Nations: What Would Happen if the United Nations Shut Down* (Washington, D.C.: Heritage Foundation, 1984).

8. See Lucia Mouat, "Prestige High, UN Looks Stronger," *Christian Science Monitor,* 11 March 1991, p. 4.

9. A core working group has already been assembled by the Canadian Departments of Foreign Affairs and National Defense to put together a feasibility study and comprehensive action plan for the creation of this rapid-reaction capability. Canada has already committed one hundred thousand dollars to the study. The final report will be completed in June 1995 and will be submitted to the UN secretary-general for the fall General Assembly.

10. A comment made to me by J. Martin Rochester in recent correspondence.

[3]

© Journal of Peace Research, vol. 30, no. 3, 1993, pp. 301–315

The Reform of the UN and Cosmopolitan Democracy: A Critical Review*

DANIELE ARCHIBUGI
National Research Council, Rome and Global Security Programme, Faculty of Social and Political Sciences, Cambridge

With the end of the Cold War has come a new generation of proposals aiming to reform the existing international organizations and even to create some new ones. This article critically assesses these proposals, subdividing them into: (i) projects to institute a UN Second Assembly with members elected by 'world citizens' rather than nominated by national governments; (ii) prospective reforms of the International Court of Justice to extend its functions beyond the role of arbitration between states; and (iii) proposals to restrict the use of the veto power of the permanent members of the Security Council. These proposals are an attempt to upgrade international democracy and are here considered in the light of the systems of states theory. On the one hand, these proposals intend to go beyond the current confederal structure of the UN in aiming at direct participation of the peoples in world affairs. On the other hand, they reject the idea of developing a federal state on a world scale. They suggest a third and largely unexplored model of international organization which – to borrow a term employed by Immanuel Kant – is here named cosmopolitan democracy.

1. Introduction

Reform of the United Nations has been under discussion for decades. Although many reforms in the workings of the UN have been undertaken during the postwar period, really radical proposals, involving a substantial change in its functioning, have remained a dead letter.[1] The principal obstacle was the rivalry between the two superpowers, which paralysed any attempt to endow international organizations with enhanced powers. It is not therefore surprising that one effect of the end of the Cold War should be a relaunching of the debate on the reform of the international organizations, including the UN.

Revitalizing international organizations means placing a bet on the role of law as a constituent part of any future world order. Even if the norms of international law have until now been held in contempt by member states and overturned for political considerations, it is still to be hoped that such norms can constitute a more stable point of reference in post-Cold War international relations.

The fervour with which reform proposals had been advanced was quickly 'cooled' by the Gulf War. It became palpably clear that law could lend itself to ambiguous interpretations, and that international organizations, the UN included, could initiate actions clearly at odds with those intended by the proposed reforms. However, even if in the wake of the Gulf War the international climate has become less idyllic, the proposed reforms have not lost their value. Their declared aim is in fact that of eliminating, or at least reducing, those periodic oscillations in international relations which existing institutions have proven unable to contain. A commitment to these reforms is therefore necessary if at times of heightened international tension they are not to be ignored as unrealizable nor to be written off as useless in moments of comparative calm.

This paper undertakes a critical review of some of the reforms that have been proposed concerning the UN. While widely debated, they have as yet been granted little space on the agenda of international diplomacy. The reforms may be subdivided thus:

(i) projects for creating an Assembly of the Peoples of the United Nations, which would directly represent citizens rather than their governments;

* I thank Luigi Ferrajoli, Jeffrey Segall, Franco Voltaggio, the Editor and two referees of *JPR* for their comments to previous drafts.

302   *Daniele Archibugi*

(ii)   proposals for the reform of the International Court of Justice;
(iii) proposals to modify the Security Council, and, especially, the veto power of its permanent members.

These ambitious proposals have been widely supported by pragmatic argumentation, while less attention has been given to the underlying theoretical rationale. This article, therefore, will concern itself more with the latter. The proposals to be considered belong to a specific current of peace thinking: that which proposes to enhance global security by creating appropriate international legal institutions. First, however, we need to specify both the potential and the limits of what I shall call, following others, *legal pacifism*.

2. *Legal Pacifism: Underlying Rationale*
A commitment to the value of peace unites individuals with various motivations, instruments and objectives. Full and precise taxonomies of peace thinking have been developed (Bobbio, 1984; Ceadel, 1987; Harle, 1989; Scheler, 1931). Legal pacifism, as one possible means for confronting the problem of war and peace, shares the merits and limitations of every judicial approach to social problems, being essentially normative. It differs from other forms of peace thinking in that it concerns itself not so much with the causes of conflicts as with ways of preventing and resolving them.

The judicial approach encounters special problems in the international sphere, which is a system characterized by the absence of a central authority capable of imposing a sentence on those – mainly states – who are found guilty by the court. Consequently, an essential part of the work of legal pacifism involves attempts to create supra-national institutions with legislative, judicial and executive powers.[2] Not all advocates of legal pacifism, however, deem it necessary to create an international executive power. William Ladd (1840), for example, held the creation of a legislative power and an autonomous international judicial power essential, but considered that the executive power should be exercised solely by public

opinion, which he optimistically baptized 'the queen of the world'.

From one point of view, the importance of legal pacifism is enhanced by the absence of an international executive power: while the internal disputes within individual states may be resolved without recourse to force, since there exists an executive power with many instruments at its disposal to impose its will on the parties, in the international sphere there exist only two alternatives: either to submit to the decision of an arbitration which lacks the means for coercion or instead to accept that conflicts will be regulated according to considerations of political opportunism – not least the relative force at the disposal of the contenders.

From this perspective of wilful worldly wisdom the merit of the judicial approach lies not so much in its intrinsic ability to overcome problems that result from interstate rivalry, as in the absence of more efficacious solutions. It is not surprising therefore that the battles waged by legal pacifists have been at the same time both huge successes and total failures.

The success of legal pacifism cannot be denied when we recall that today's international institutions themselves and the norms of international law are indeed its fruits. Institutions such as the UN and the EC are much more highly developed than would have been imagined possible by those thinkers and philosophers who as early as the 17th and 18th centuries had envisaged international institutions with the responsibility for guaranteeing peace and cooperation between peoples (Archibugi, 1992). The same goes for today's international law, which is certainly much more highly developed than could have been imagined from any 17th or 18th treatise on the law of nations (Bull et al., 1990).

On the other hand, the role of legal pacifism appears of scant import if we consider whether it has succeeded in holding in check and regulating international conflicts. For nearly half a century UN actions have been repeatedly ignored or circumvented by member states. In all the conflicts both great and small, both explicit and latent, the rules dictated by the raison d'état have taken precedence over legal principles. Indeed, the actions of the international institutions have proven efficacious only in those cases where an accord, implicit or explicit, already existed between the more powerful states. Where such agreement was lacking, the effects have been insignificant. In other words, the role of international organizations has been most significant when least needed, and irrelevant when most needed.

Legal pacifism has thus achieved an excellent logical construction, but one with little impact in reality. The discrepancy between precept and reality is barely counterbalanced by the fact that the former has become an integral part of international politics. The invasions of Afghanistan, of Granada, of Panama, etc., have been condemned by the international community and public opinion on the grounds of principles of law: without these principles, any condemnation would have remained exclusively moral.

Legal principles, in other words, are in part constrained to be the precursors of reality by being declarations of good intent rather than of actual positive legal rights. These principles must therefore be assessed not on the grounds of their probable effective application in the world today, but on the grounds of their utility in an indeterminate future. The Universal Declaration of Human Rights was a declaration of good intentions 45 years ago and still is to a great extent today, but by following its outlines it has been possible on a daily basis to defend some fundamental and quite concrete principles.

3. *Proposed Reforms*

The reform proposals to be considered here are intentionally ahead of our time, at present not supported by any of the principal powers on the international stage. Yet they represent an attempt to create a world order based on consensus and the rule of law.

The following body of literature on the reform of the United Nations will be reviewed here:

(i) The Conferences on a More Demo-

cratic United Nations (CAMDUN Conferences). To date, three have taken place, at the New York UN Headquarters (13–15 October 1990), at UNO-City, Vienna (17–19 September 1991), and the third in Accra (26–29 November 1992) (Barnaby, 1991; Segall & Lerner, 1992).

(ii) The conference organized by the Lelio Basso International Foundation for the Rights and the Liberation of the Peoples (Rome, 15–16 April 1991) on the theme of 'The UN between War and Peace' (Falk, 1992, Ferrajoli & Senese, 1992).

(iii) A study promoted by the Ford Foundation and the Dag Hammarskjold Foundation on the institutional reforms needed in the ambit of the UN (Childers, 1990; Urquhart & Childers, 1990).

(iv) The new UN Charter proposed by Harold Stassen (1990), one of the original authors of the 1945 Charter.

The following sections present a critical analysis of reform proposals in the light of the most complex political theory of legal pacifism. They will be treated in three groups: those relating to the creation, in the ambit of the UN, of a peoples' Assembly; those concerned with the International Court of Justice; and finally those concerned with the Security Council.

4. *A UN Peoples' Assembly and its Political Theory Implications*

The most radical proposal from the CAM-DUN Conferences concerned the institution of a UN Second Assembly, which, in accordance with the preamble of the UN Charter ('We, the Peoples of the United Nations'), would represent the peoples rather than their governments. This is certainly not the first time that such an ambitious proposal has been put forward: a World Parliament is an idea that has been dear to philosophers for centuries. In recent years, however, a number of new proposals have been made to the extent that a review of these proposals has been found necessary (Newcombe, 1991).

304   *Daniele Archibugi*

Most present-day proposals have reached an impasse more on the possible procedures for 'electing' this second assembly than on the duties with which it is to be entrusted. Indeed, paradoxically, even the subdivisions of electoral colleges are being discussed before any specification of the powers of the assembly has been made. This is a considerable stumbling block, since there are robust theoretical arguments to justify and give credibility to such an ambitious institution which need to be emphasized. It must be explained why the governments, who represent the states in the General Assembly, should not be the sole institutions authorized to represent the citizens of the world.

An analysis of this sort requires us in the first instance to recognize the state as the central figure in international relations today. The very notion of thinking and acting politically presupposes the individual's citizenship in a state; there can be no politics without a *polis*. Notwithstanding that states may be imperfect institutions of the human communities, since linguistic, religious, ethnic and cultural homogeneity may be lacking, they will always constitute the first and chief institutional point of reference for the individual.

The function of states is not only that of allowing individuals the right to participate in the running of the *polis*, but also, importantly, that of representing their own citizens at an international level. Individuals have no role in the international community, except as citizens of a state. As Martin Wight (1966) has wittily noted, even the Pope, the individual who might be considered most inclined to set aside secular power, did not feel at ease in the sphere of international relations until he had become the first citizen of a state.

The recent collapse of some nation-states – most notably Yugoslavia and the Soviet Union – makes it clear how problematic it is for individuals devoid of a state to have voice in today's international arena. These cases lead to a search for other and more progressive models of organization of international society.

The deep identity crisis currently faced by several nation-states (far beyond the dissolution of the Soviet Union and Yugoslavia: I am here also thinking of the emergence of regional conflicts in countries as diverse as the United Kingdom, Italy and Spain) should not necessarily lead us to believe that we are experiencing the end of a form of political organization which has lasted, in one way or another, for several centuries. We must differentiate between the crisis of the nation-states to be credited to internal contradictions (such as the rise of ethnic conflicts) and those which are related to the difficulty of coping with international integration.

Once it has been accepted that states play the role of an oligarchy in the realm of international politics, limits must be set. If the state, as an institution based on the inhabitants of a particular territory, acts in its own specific interests, then it obviously cannot satisfy the needs of its own citizens if it is operating in an international community devoid of other institutions.

The first justification for the existence of the state is that of security: the *Leviathan* liberates the individual from the terrors of the natural state, and thus provides conditions sufficient for his/her acceptance of the role of subject. Following on this observation from Thomas Hobbes, an organic theory of the power of the state has been constructed, positing the impossibility of extending the social contract beyond the state's frontiers and leaving international relations in a condition of anarchy (Bull, 1977).

The weak point in the Hobbesian line of argument lies in the fact that individuals cannot be considered free from a condition of fear as long as they are still exposed to the threat of war. Until the state can make the threat of war disappear, its promise to liberate its subjects from the dangers of war cannot be considered fully realized, and consequently the subject has not the obligation to obedience.

In the nuclear age, the ability of *Leviathan* to 'wound' prospective aggressors can no longer be considered a method of fulfilling the above promise; as strategic studies have shown, the states least exposed to a nuclear threat are those who neither possess them nor belong to alliances armed with nuclear weapons (Prins, 1983). This is the crucial contradiction for the state: on the one hand the full realization of *Leviathan* requires it to seal a pact of peace with other states, yet the state cannot undertake this without significantly changing its sovereign power.

Still more problematical is the situation for those states which are obliged by reason of their constitutions to fulfil the wishes of their own citizens, i.e. the democratic states. The absence of truly international institutions often presents them with dilemmas. Are they to defend their citizens' interests at the expense of other states, or are they to follow the rules of international democracy at the expense of their own citizens? They thus find themselves in a contradictory situation which can be solved only by entering into a contractual relationship with other states (this is a point emphasized by Held, 1991, 1992).

To find a way out of this contradiction, political theory indicates essentially two ways for arriving at an institutionalized system of states: the first is to set up a confederation of sovereign states, in which each member would renounce its sovereignty insofar as its relations with other states were concerned, while the second would be to enlarge the experiment already undertaken inside the individual states, and thus substitute the multitude of sovereign states with a worldwide *Leviathan*.[3] Neither solution appears to resolve the unsettled problems of the international community.

The confederal model, which took a global form first with the League of Nations and later with the United Nations, is based on the principles of equal sovereignty of states and non-interference. Countries are represented by their governments, which are recognized on the basis of their de facto existence rather than on any grounds of legitimacy. Without these preconditions it would not have been possible to secure the membership of governments and countries with such widely differing political systems and values. The defects of this model are closely connected with its advantages: on the one hand the principle of non-inter-

ference must be safeguarded to avoid 'the big fish eating the smaller' with interventions often dictated by pretexts; on the other hand, this principle sanctions the absolute autonomy of governments in their relations with their own subjects, and the total inseparability of the latter from the actions of their governments. Until a state breaks the rules of the international community, there exists no channel for censuring its activities.

It is not by chance that in the UN, itself blessed with a more advanced legal system, the traditional view of international law has prevailed, as was evident in the Gulf War: on the one hand, no sanctions for the internal abuse of power; on the other hand, sanctions inflicted on all the Iraqi population for a violation of international law committed by their government. In the confederal model, in fact, individuals are represented at the international level by their particular governments only.

The failings of the confederal model are linked to more than the fact that some members have not been democratic. In fact if they had been, the objective of the political struggle would not have been in the sphere of international relations, but rather would have been the achievement of democracy *inside* individual states. The fundamental reason why the confederal model does not of itself secure international democracy is because each institutional state, however democratic, is forced to act on, and represent, the interests of its citizens on the basis of its own raison d'état.

Democratic regimes do not necessarily follow the same principles at an international level: the USA and Israel have constitutions among the most democratic in the world, yet this has not impeded their violation of the most elementary norms of international law. Nor do dictatorial regimes necessarily behave in a like manner in their international relations: the former Soviet Union, for example, carried out not only interventions in open violation of international law – as in Hungary, Czechoslovakia and Afghanistan – but also interventions in support of national liberation movements, for example the Palestinian cause and the anti-apartheid movement.

These appear to be the ambiguities in the concept of international democracy: it may be understood as a *democratic* union of States, regardless of whether some or even all of them are *autocratic*, or as an *autocratic* union of democratic states.[4]

The confederal model has traditionally been opposed to the federal state model. The extension of the federal model to a world scale is based on radical hypotheses, since it implicitly assumes that the existence of a constellation of states is merely a particular inheritance of history (see Hutchins, 1970). The elements which unify individuals across states are seen as just as important as those which link citizens as subjects of a specific state. For a system of states to be founded on democratic principles, its supporters affirm, it is necessary that there be the direct participation of individuals, for example through the vote. The objections to this idea are twofold: the first concerns its feasibility, the second its desirability.

Federal states formed on the basis of a consensual accord of the parties – as with Switzerland, the Netherlands, Germany and, above all, the United States – have come about from the necessity of concentrating their forces for defence against an external foe. However diverse their motivations may have been, these states figure as experiments similar to that of the Hobbesian *Leviathan*. Could therefore the same system function in a dimension devoid of external agents, such as the entire world? There are obvious reasons for doubting that the parties, i.e. the states, would be consensually disposed to transfer their forces to a central power – at least as long as states possess the attributes which characterize them in the modern age. It is of course possible for a federal state to be formed by the imperial imposition of one party on others. However, if this state fails to conform to the rules of democracy at its inception, there is no reason to believe that it will do so once instituted.

As to the desirability of a world federal state, it is necessary to check how much it would be compatible with the effective operation of democracy. The concept of a state presupposes the existence of a unity of purposes in the norms applied by the several parties. For much of the world's population, these norms would seem alien to their particular historical and cultural traditions, and would be considered as authoritarian impositions. The creation of a world state, even in the remote future, can only imperfectly take into account the historical, cultural and, in the widest sense, anthropological peculiarities of the inhabitants of our planet (Thompson, 1992). The current crisis in multi-racial states probably constitutes the best indication of the difficulties inherent in administering large communities. Rousseau's empirical observation that democracy requires small communities in order to function should be constantly borne in mind.

Finally, the making of a world state with a monopoly on force, even if conceived and realized with the most perfect democratic constitutional engineering, would risk being transformed, as does any institution, into something at variance from the original intentions. There could be the qualification, however, that this world state would have such a concentration of force as to render any successful rebellion impossible – but then a world federal state becomes an aspiration which jeopardizes democracy (Berns, 1970).

Could there be a third model, uniting the positive elements of both the confederal and federal models? Is it possible to limit the state's monopoly of decision-making at the international level without ending with a world state? The attainment of democracy at the international level requires us to steer between the Scylla of a mass of independent autonomous states and the Charybdis of a planetary *Leviathan*. To achieve this goal, a new concept of world citizenship must be formulated.[5]

First, it is necessary to clarify that a theory of world citizenship is something completely different from a doctrine of natural rights. Any theory of natural rights is necessarily founded on a notion of the human being as outside an historical context and free of the baggage of social relationships to which the individual is constantly attached. Following the path traced by Rousseau and Kant, it is necessary to found a theory of the Rights of the Citizen, where the citizen is seen as at the same time both a citizen of a state, with which he or she shares some historical and cultural values, and as an inhabitant of the whole planet.

The specific route which leads to world citizenship suggests that the *cosmopolis* could be an end of history and not an attainable phenomenon – a political aspiration which must come to terms with the everyday actual citizenship, exercised by individuals within the narrower bounds of their own *polis*.

To strengthen international democracy, and to overcome its ambiguities, cosmopolitan democracy aims to give voice to citizens in the international community. The development of institutional linkages between national civil societies would help to strengthen democratic procedures both in international society and within the single national components. But this does not imply that current states should be considered as a transitional form of political organization to be dissolved in a federal union which would have the same characteristics of national states but on a larger scale. On the contrary, several of the functions carried out by sovereign states should be integrated into the cosmopolitan model.

The theoretical credentials of every reform project of existing international organizations, and especially those for the formation of an Assembly of the Peoples, are based on recognition of the shortcomings of the confederal and federal models. These projects must be seen as attempts to give an institutional form to a cosmopolitan ideal.

The pragmatic reasons which prompt this institutional innovation may be summarized as follows:

(i) In the principal institution of the international community, the General Assembly of the UN, the electoral criterion of 'one state, one vote', is scarcely 'democratic': the vote of Luxemburg has the same weight as that of China, India or the USA. This means that governments which represent fewer than 10% of the world's population, or less than 5% of the world's gross product, may potentially cast the majority of votes in the General Assembly. As long as the General Assembly has little effective power (as has been the case up to now), one may easily put aside this problem by taking the point of view that the important decisions are taken by the Security Council – or, more realistically, by the superpowers. However, if we are to increase the real power of the United Nations, the problem of the differing sizes of states must be confronted one way or another.

If it is assumed that governments should be the only institution to represent their own citizens, the problem could be easily solved without creating a new institution, simply by giving weighted votes, according to population and/or other criteria, to the governments of each country in the General Assembly. For example, to strengthen the political role of the General Assembly, Stassen (1991) has proposed the weighting of states' votes according to a composite index which includes population, national income and productivity growth.

However, the problem of the differing sizes of states needs to be tackled more radically, leaving aside a confederal logic; in other words by creating a parallel body to serve as the expression of individuals and not of their governments. This means accepting of the principle of non-interference of one state in the affairs of others, as laid down in international law. This principle, however, can be maintained only if supported by an autonomous institution authorized to 'interfere' in the internal affairs of each state. On a limited scale, an experiment of this type has already been realized within the European Community. This is based on, first, a body endowed with effective power, the Council of Ministers, with the 'one country, one vote' criterion; and, second, on a body with limited powers, the European Parliament, elected by universal suffrage and with the number of members roughly in proportion to the populations of the member countries.

(ii) Countries are represented in the UN General Assembly on the criterion of their de facto control rather than that of their legitimacy; in other words, to gain a seat in the Palace of Glass a political force must hold de facto control over a given territory, without necessarily representing all the citizens of that country. Within the confederal model framework, the problem may be solved by establishing that only those governments which democratically represent their citizens may be accredited to the UN. There have been judicial developments along these lines: the failure to recognize the government formed by the coup d'état in Haiti, the proposal to withdraw recognition of the de facto government of Burma and to accredit the duly elected one, etc.

However, to abolish entirely the principle of effective control in bodies such as the General Assembly and the Security Council risks being counter-productive because it could all too easily lead to a marked divergence between legal norms and reality. The consequences could be unpredictable: how many of the current members have the credentials to be members of the UN on the basis of a rigorous application of its own Charter and of the Universal Declaration of Human Rights? How should one treat governments which are de facto but not de jure? Should they be ignored by the 'democratic' international community, or be considered as enemies to be fought? In this last case, how else but by means afforded by other states? This certainly does not mean that the principle of effective control should always prevail over the principle of legality, but the former might be given greater weight in the international community in transient situations or in cases of extreme illegality.

A body representing citizens would have much greater flexibility: those countries which declined to nominate their own deputies according to democratic norms could be excluded, and in controversial cases the Assembly of the Peoples would have the authority to accredit the political forces deemed to be the proper representatives of the population. By means of its very existence the Assembly of the Peoples would constitute an instrument of censure towards autocratic governments, who would see their own citizens voicing opposing views to those that they were putting forward in the General Assembly.

(iii) However, the efficacy of an Assembly of Peoples would be limited to countries with autocratic governments. Even in democratic states there may be significant differences between the opinions expressed by governments and those expressed by the representatives of individuals. In the first place, the Assembly of Peoples would allow direct representation of national minorities and of the opposition. In the second place, it is likely that within the same political force differing tendencies will develop, with the national representatives in the General Assembly more inclined to sustain 'state-centred' policies, and the representatives of the Assembly of the Peoples having a greater propensity towards 'global' policies. Take the case of the European Community: the European Parliament shows a greater propensity towards 'European' or 'global' solutions than does the Council of Ministers.

The most elaborate and realistic proposal for instituting an Assembly of Peoples, and one which has gained the widest support was put forward back in 1982 by Jeffrey Segall and the International Network for a UN Second Assembly (INFUSA). No less than 94 nongovernmental organizations have already supported it, and INFUSA has actively promoted it with a view to getting the UN Secretariat to institute a Commission to study the conditions under which this proposal might be made to work (Segall, 1990, 1991).

Segall's proposal suggests that the 'Second Assembly' should be an exclusively consultative body of the General Assembly. In this case it could be set up without having to modify the existing UN Charter: Article 22 states in fact: 'The General Assembly may establish such subsidary organs as it deems necessary for the performance of its functions'. This means it could be instituted by the General Assembly alone, without requiring the approval of the Security Council (where it might be blocked by the veto of a permanent member).

The electoral system would not differ substantially from that pertaining for the European Parliament: a number of deputies for every country roughly proportionate to its population, even if 'corrected' to safeguard the populations of the smallest countries. In one illustrative scheme of the proposal, out of a total assembly of 560 members, the most populous country (China) would have 31 seats, while countries with up to one million inhabitants would have one seat each.

The electoral criterion proposed by the INFUSA initiative is certainly not the only one. Many other electoral systems could be adopted which would safeguard minorities and allow the assembly to reflect, within certain limits, the real power of the various world regions. Some have hypothesized a weighting criterion which would take account of the income of the various countries, reasoning that this may be a suitable indicator of their relative international power and influence. However, an hypothesis of this type would violate a cardinal principle of democracy: decades ago, income ceased to be an electoral criterion within nations.

Other projects foresee a transitional device. In one of these it is suggested that the nongovernmental organizations recognized by the UN might constitute a Consultative Assembly. Another method proposed for permitting the direct participation of citizens is that of making elective at least one of the five members who make up a national delegation at the General Assembly. It has further been proposed that a national delegation should include members nominated by the opposition as well as by the government.

5. The International Court of Justice
The potential role of the Court was underlined in the course of the Fondazione Basso Conference, while it received less attention at the CAMDUN Conferences. This difference in perception, and also of the evaluation of the priorities to be pursued, demonstrates the urgent need for reaching a systematic and integrated view on projects for reforming international organizations.

As far as the proposed modifications to the Court go, one can only remark that there appears to be nothing new under the sun, in that they do not diverge significantly from those already suggested by Hans Kel-

sen (1944). Kelsen allocated a central role to international jurisdiction in achieving the non-violent resolution of conflicts. He was convinced that an international judiciary would be the first step towards a political world order: 'Until it is possible to remove from the interested states the prerogative of resolving questions of law and transfer this permanently and universally to an impartial authority, all further steps along the road to world peace are to be excluded'. At the same time Kelsen held that the formation of an international judiciary would be the line of least resistance, and would not encounter the same objections that states might pose to an executive power or a worldwide legislature.

Kelsen recalled that 'long before Parliaments became legislative bodies, Courts were instituted to apply the law to specific cases', and that 'we have good reason to hold that international law . . . will develop in the same way as the primitive law of communities from before the development of the state' (p. 58): in other words, that judicial power antedates legislative power. However, Kelsen may have undervalued the crucial difference between the national and the international situation, which, to repeat, consists of the want of executive power in the latter. In pre-state societies, in fact, the executive power was antecedent to the judicial power. This difference can only drastically reduce the role of international judicial power.

The UN Charter, adopted not long after Kelsen's work, largely disavowed not only his predictions but also his hopes. It sanctioned the existence of a core of world governance in a much more marked manner than could have been hoped. On the other hand, the Court became crystallized in an antiquated role and was ill-adapted to incorporate the more innovative elements of that same UN Charter. The Court's Statute poses precise limits on its jurisdiction: in the first place, its jurisdiction is limited solely to cases in which the interested parties decide to apply to the Court in terms of 'a model which is much more arbitrational than judicial' (Ferrajoli & Senese, 1992). In the second place, the Court's competence is

310   *Daniele Archibugi*

limited to relations between states, and it has no jurisdiction over cases which concern relations between individuals and their respective states.

The Court thus reflects a state-centred view of international law, owing more to the League of Nations than to the United Nations. The modifications interpolated into international law have rendered the Court completely baroque, and unable to carry out to the slightest degree the ambitious role that jurists had in prospect for it. Because the Court is an integral part of the present international order, three profound transformations are required, which may be summarized as follows:

(i) Returning to Kelsen's suggestion, the Court's jurisdiction should be made mandatory – as was recently restated in the Fondazione Basso Conference (Ferrajoli & Senese, 1992). It is evident that passing a verdict on matters between states is of little practical use unless this is not accompanied by measures against it (e.g. sanctions); these would have a judicial (and thus a political) merit, above all in cases where the Security Council is unable to approve a resolution owing to the veto of one of its permanent members.

(ii) The Court must furthermore extend its jurisdiction to cover cases which concern the relationship between individuals and their governments. It is absurd that, within the existing order of the UN, individuals must be safeguarded in their relations with their own governments by non-judicial bodies, such as for example the Commission for Human Rights. This means abandoning the human rights sanctioned by the Universal Declaration, and ratified by numerous conventions, to the exclusive sphere of interstate relations, and thus to the inflexible laws of raison d'état.

Rendering the Court a competent judicial body obviously has broad theoretical significance. It would indicate that relations between a state and its citizens also concern the world community, up to the point that this possesses a judicial body independent of both states and interstate organizations. The Court would thus be a body genuinely exercising cosmopolitan law.[6]

It may be objected that widening the competence of the Court to embrace individuals would lead to its becoming so overwhelmed with cases that it would be unable to function. However, once it has been accepted that individuals have the right to turn to international judicial bodies to safeguard themselves in respect of their governments, many expedients may be found to enable the Court to function. Ferrajoli & Senese (1992) have suggested that access might be granted to the Court to a selected number of designated nongovernmental organizations such as Amnesty International. Another criterion might allow individuals to have recourse to the Court after national legal channels had been exhausted, following the procedures already in use at the European Court. A third criterion might be to consider cases collectively rather than individually, and to give hearings to groups of persons against their governments (for example, the Argentinian 'desaparecidos'; banned political organizations; racial, political and religious minorities, etc.). In short, these proposals are not intended to make this body some sort of Planetary Court of Appeal. Its function would be much more effective if it concentrated on flagrant and recurrent cases of the violation of human rights.

(iii) Finally, it is necessary again to take up Kelsen's idea of governmental individual responsibility for war criminals and for the crime of war. Ferrajoli & Senese have proposed a significant extension of Kelsen's idea of enlarging individual responsibility in governments to all breaches of human rights. There are already significant cases where 'crusading judges' in some countries have, on the basis of radical interpretations of existing law, condemned those responsible for crimes against human rights in other countries (discussed in Cassese, 1988, 1990). These cases are significant because the criminals have been both condemned and sentenced in a country not their own. On the other hand, even though these cases may be important, since they appear to be a prelude to a new legal system, they are based on profoundly restrictive criteria and are unlikely to be substantially extended.

It is not by chance that the greater part of these 'crusading judges of international law' come from the more powerful countries, and especially the United States; the sentences they hand down place a great deal of faith in the existing balance of power between states. The judge of a stronger state may condemn the torturer of the weaker, but we can be sure that the reverse does not apply. Noriega is a case in point: there is certainly no shortage of good reasons for the Panamanian dictator to be tried by an international tribunal or even a US one, but there are at least equally good reasons for President Bush being tried before a Panamanian court.

Again, the Court would not have a possibility of directly applying a sentence: in other words, the Court would not have at its disposal the executive powers to imprison a guilty or aggressor dictator and his cohorts, but only the power to condemn him. However, even that condemnation would mark an important first step as a deterrent against committing crimes against human rights: following the condemnation, any legitimate authority could be authorized to implement it. Once the independence of the judicial authority had been established, then the function of the 'secular arm' could be delegated to the states in the absence of a world executive power.

Introducing the principle of individual responsibility would mean establishing correspondence at the international level between the rights of the individual citizen and the duties of other citizens, at least as far as these represent the non-violation of the rights laid down in the Universal Declaration. In practice this would apply to that restricted group of citizens who are able to escape national justice because they themselves hold executive power: that is to say those citizens who perform the function of governors.

6. *Proposals for the Reform of the Security Council of the UN*

The UN Security Council is, according to the existing Charter, the body with responsibility for taking executive decisions.

Decisions on non-procedural questions are taken on a vote of 9 out of 15, but must include a favourable vote by all the 5 permanent members. Aside from any judicial euphemisms, the permanent members hold the right to veto all the decisions of the Security Council. As a result of the existing procedures permanent members avoid the embarrassment of declaring the decision of the majority invalid since only one contrary vote will fulfil this function.

The victors of World War II have arrogated to themselves crucial power over this body of their own creation (Köchler, 1991). Here we are confronted with something with no democratic justification: in no other constitution or organization founded on democratic principles is it accepted that some few members alone may invalidate the decisions of the majority. To understand the legal absurdity of this it is sufficient to imagine what would happen if the power of veto existed within a national political system: it would not be easy to imagine a national government where the ministers of some regions could exercise veto power.

Not only this, but the way in which the superpowers have exercised the veto within the Security Council has far exceeded the intentions of the 1945 Charter. This laid down that: (1) decisions on procedural matters should be taken on a majority vote of 9 out of 15, without requiring an affirmative vote by permanent members (Art. 27, par. 2); (2) parties to a dispute must abstain from voting (Art. 27, par. 3), as every legal logic dictates. In practice, the permanent members arrogated to themselves the right of deciding both which matters were procedural and which were substantive, and whether or not to vote in cases where they were directly involved, thus blocking all resolutions against themselves.

The existence of the veto power also contravenes one of the supposed principles of the UN Charter, which stipulates the equal sovereignty of states (Art. 2, par. 1). It is not therefore surprising that ever since 1945 both smaller states and jurists have been opposed to it. The prominent name is once again Hans Kelsen (1946), who, furthermore, has exercised a crucial role as an ideologue of the United Nations. Of course, it may be argued that a legalistic critique of the veto power is not relevant since it concerns relations which are political rather than strictly legalistic.

At the end of World War II the power of veto could be interpreted as a legal codification of the agreed status quo, with the victorious powers not wishing to oppose each others' freedom of action. If this legal abuse of power has succeeded in halting conflicts, it may have some justification. It would certainly not have been better to have had a Security Council founded securely on democratic principles, but which had also helped to bring about a war between the superpowers: the motto *Fiat iustitia, pereat mundus* constantly reminds us to temper the desirable with the practicable.

However, even if we should judge the power of veto on grounds of its practicality rather than its rationality, it can only be considered today as a sterile inheritance of the past rather than an element of international stability. The world picture has changed profoundly since the end of World War II, and the decline of some powers has seen the rise of others. The most emblematic case has been the relative decline of the UK and France and the rise, above all economically, of Japan and Germany.

Outside the Western World the role of Third World countries has increased enormously in terms of population, wealth and military power. But the most significant and recent change has been the dissolution of one of the superpowers: the Soviet Union. Apart from the entry of the People's Republic of China into the Security Council, no other single change on the world scene has so affected the composition of the Security Council since it was established.

In this new international political situation, the present structure of the Security Council represents the principle obstacle to the smooth functioning of the UN. We need to ask how long it will remain acceptable to preserve the political balance of power resulting from the end of World War II, and whether it is not now time to make the abolition of the veto a principal political objective of the peace movement.

Various proposals for modifying the Security Council have accumulated over the years. Not surprisingly they have remained a dead letter, given that every modification to the UN Charter requires a vote in favour by all the Permanent Members of the Security Council (Arts. 108 and 109, par. 2). This being so, under the terms of the Charter, the General Assembly itself has no sovereign powers over the UN constitution. In this situation, every proposal must take account of the power at the disposal of the permanent members. Obviously, proposals for modifying the Security Council voting procedures are those which stand the least chance of being approved. Nevertheless, the dissolution of one of the permanent members, the former Soviet Union, may constitute an occasion for modifying the Charter – and not only formally. This might be achievable if certain states as well as world public opinion could exercise pressure in this direction.

Let us now consider the proposals advanced during the CAMDUN Conferences, ranging from the 'maximalist' to the 'minimalist'. The latter may be legally less satisfying, but they at least have a greater chance of being accepted.

(i) The most radical is, obviously, that of abolishing the veto *sic et simpliciter*, leaving Security Council decisions subject to a qualified majority vote. Proposals to make the Council completely elective, thus denying the 'Five' not only of their veto power but also the right to serve as permanent members, have received scant attention. Such a model would not only stop the Council from reflecting the existing international balance of power, but would also fail to enhance it democratically: we could imagine a Security Council dominated by the smallest states who had been notably advantaged by the 'one state, one vote' system in the General Assembly. Unavoidably, in a body such as the Security Council, which is entrusted with 'primary responsibility for the maintenance of international peace and security' (Art. 24), there must be countries represented with the necessary force at their disposal.

(ii) A subordinate proposal foresees a

situation where the veto of a permanent member might be invalidated by the unanimous vote of the other members. Thus, one contrary vote would no longer be enough to invalidate a Council decision.

(iii) In other proposals it is suggested that the Security Council should be opened up to the existing regional organizations. A prime candidate for permanent membership would obviously be the European Community. There is no valid reason why France and the UK should be permanent members while other EC countries, Germany to begin with, should have a much subordinate role in the UN. In principle, the Security Council could become a point of contact between existing regional organizations such as the Organization of American States, the European Community, the Organization of African States or the Arab League (Köchler, 1991).

(iv) Stassen (1990) has proposed broadening the Security Council to 18 members, including two new permanent members drawn from among the most populous countries of the 'South' (probably India and Brazil).

(v) Another minimalist proposal, which would not require the approval of the Security Council but only that of the General Assembly, foresees the formation of a Committee of the Assembly composed of 15 members elected in rotation, who would be geographically representative and at the same time not members of the Council. This Committee would assume responsibility for reporting to the Assembly on the initiatives undertaken by the Council for resolving disputes and armed conflicts by peaceful means. This would mean, in other words, creating an entirely elected 'shadow' Security Council, tasked with evaluating the work of the actual Council.

There are many reasons for doubting whether most of these proposals will ever be accepted on a consensual basis – not least because their usefulness, in the end, lies in restricting those members who have most power and who can use fully legal means to block any modifications to the Security Council. However, this does not diminish their merit. It is scandalous that the only state continually to protest against the veto

power of the permanent members should be Libya. Instead it should be principally the Western democracies and the states of smaller size who should be the spokesmen for a progressive transformation in international judicial relations.

7. *Final Considerations*

This paper has considered three concrete proposals concerning the United Nations: those relative to the formation in the heart of the UN of an Assembly of the Peoples; the proposals for the reform of the International Court of Justice; and those on the modifications to be undertaken to the Security Council. The aim was to undertake an analysis of what legal pacifism, and in its ambit what I have defined as the cosmopolitan model, offer to the theory and praxis of international relations.

These proposals inevitably lead in a wider sense to the efforts of those aiming to establish democracy in international society. Democracy does not seem attainable by simply adding together individual democratic states, nor achieving democratic communities of states without questioning their internal constitution. This justifies the proposal of an alternative model of international organization: the cosmopolitan one, which differs considerably from both the confederal and the federal models (Held, 1992, provides additional arguments for cosmopolitan democracy). Proceeding towards the realization of the cosmopolitan model necessarily implies that states will have to allow, on a consensual basis, the world community to interfere in their internal affairs. In the long term, this process cannot but undermine the nature of the modern state, founded as it is on dominion over a given territory and population.

The perspective offered belongs to the tradition that, in an historical dimension, queries how to overcome the state as an institution. It also includes, however, a decisive qualification, in assuming that the persistence of the role of the modern state, as well as its difficulty in fully realizing its promise of democracy, depends largely on its failure to integrate itself internationally with other states (Kaldor, 1990). It suggests that a democratic state is an imperfect political entity as long as there exist no institutions able to link democratically its citizens to the citizens of other states. This is because a large share of the political problems in government agenda, including security and environment, are only partially addressable by intergovernmental organizations, since the interests of one part will often contradict those of the global community.

The debate on the proposals here considered is pervaded by two questions: can they be realized? And, if so, in what measure could they lead to a real transformation in international relations?

With respect to the first question, there is a good possibility that at least some of the proposals will, in the long term, come about. On the one hand, problems typical of our age – such as those concerning the environment and sources of energy or those connected with growing economic integration – indicate that intergovernmental action needs to be strengthened by other organizations, less formal and more dynamic. On the other hand, there is a perceptible tendency towards widening the international community, which implies an irreversible shift towards a progressive reduction de facto of the sovereignty of individual states.

History teaches that the emergence of new institutions is possible only if there are specific interests working in that direction. The transformations occurring in international relations – the end of East/West bipolarism, the emergence of Third World countries as the subjects of international politics, the difficulties experienced by Western democracies in fully realizing themselves within the confines of their own state systems – lend weight to those political and social forces which have an interest in extending the influence and functions of supranational institutions. It is increasingly evident that decision-making is no longer the exclusive province of the *polis*. Any attempt to realize a model of political democracy within a single country must take account of the emergence of a global community: what the cosmopolitan model proposes is, in the end, simply the creation of the appropriate institutions where citizens of the planet may discuss the problems and take the decisions that shape their destiny.

This does not necessarily mean that there must be a substantial transfer of power from the states to the new institutions. Not only would it be unrealistic to expect this, it would not be desirable either. The challenge of the cosmopolitan model is not that of substituting one power with another, but in reducing the role of power in the political process while increasing the influence of procedures. If we view the proposed reforms not as a panacea to cure the ills of the world, but only as an additional way of confronting them, we may better understand their usefulness.

NOTES

1. For a review of the 'realistic' proposals, see Müller (1992). More radical proposals were made as early as in the 1960s by Clark & Sohn (1966) and by Falk & Black (1969). See also Falk (1981).
2. The separation of the executive, judicial, and legislative powers in the international sphere dates back to such now-forgotten peace thinkers as Justus Sincerus Veridicus (1796) and William Ladd (1840).
3. On the classical opposition between a confederation and a federal state, see Friedrich (1968). Middle stations, such as common security communities, not involving the direct participation of citizens in international affairs, can be treated as confederations.
4. International democracy has been the subject of a significant debate among Italian scholars; see the essays by Norberto Bobbio, Luigi Bonanate and Luigi Cortesi in Cortesi (1988).
5. I have indicated the Kantian roots of this attempt in Archibugi (1993).
6. To separate the functions of the Court as an interstate tribunal from its functions as a tribunal for individuals in relation to their own states, it could be divided into two separate sections, the first dealing with international law and the second with cosmopolitan law. A similar model has already successfully been adopted by the European Court.

REFERENCES

Archibugi, Daniele, 1992. 'Models of International Organization in Perpetual Peace Projects', *Review of International Studies*, vol. 18, no. 5, October, pp. 295–317.

Archibugi, Daniele, 1993. 'Immanuel Kant e il diritto cosmopolitico', *Teoria Politica*, forthcoming.

Barnaby, Frank, ed., 1991. *Building a More Democratic United Nations*. London: Cass.

Berns, Walter, 1970. 'The Case Against World Government', pp. 531–544 in Robert A. Goldwin, ed., *Readings in World Politics*. New York: Oxford University Press.

Bobbio, Norberto, 1984. *Il problema della guerra e le vie della pace*. Bologna: Il Mulino.

Bull, Hedley, 1977. *The Anarchical Society*. London: Macmillan.

Bull, Hedley, Benedict Kingsbury & Adam Roberts, eds, 1990. *Hugo Grotius and International Relations*. Oxford: Clarendon.

Cassese, Antonio, 1988. *Violence and Law in the Modern Age*. Cambridge: Polity.

Cassese, Antonio, 1990. *Human Rights in a Changing World*. Cambridge: Polity.

Ceadel, Martin, 1987. *Thinking about War and Peace*. London: Oxford University Press.

Childers, Erskine, 1990. 'The Future of the United Nations: The Challenges of the 1990s', *Bulletin of Peace Proposals*, vol. 21, no. 2, June, pp. 153–163.

Clark, Grenville & Louis Sohn, 1966. *World Peace through World Law*. Cambridge, MA: Harvard University Press.

Cortesi, Luigi, ed., 1988. *Democrazia, rischio nucleare, movimenti per la pace*. Napoli: Liguori.

Falk, Richard, 1981. *The Promise of World Order. Essays in Normative International Relations*. Brighton: Wheatsheaf.

Falk, Richard, 1992. 'The United Nations and the Gulf War', *Democrazia e diritto*, vol. 32, no. 1, pp. 311–331.

Falk, Richard & C. E. Black, eds, 1969. *The Future of the International Legal Order*. Princeton, CA: Princeton University Press.

Ferrajoli, Luigi & Salvatore Senese, 1992. 'Prospettiva di riforma dell'ONU'. *Democrazia e diritto*, vol. 32, no. 1, pp. 243–257.

Friedrich, C. J., 1968. *Trends of Federalism in Theory and Practice*. London: Pall Mall.

Harle, Vilho, 1989. 'Towards a Comparative Study of Peace Ideas: Goals, Approaches and Problems', *Journal of Peace Research*, vol. 26, no. 4, November, pp. 317–351.

Held, David, 1991. 'Democracy, the Nation-State and the Global System', *Economy and Society*, vol. 20, no. 2, May, pp. 138–172.

Held, David, 1992. 'Democracy: From City States to a Cosmopolitan Order', *Political Studies*, vol. 40, Special Issue, pp. 10–39.

Hutchins, Robert, 1970. 'World Government Now', pp. 517–530 in Robert A. Goldwin, ed., *Readings in World Politics*. New York: Oxford University Press.

Justus Sincerus Veridicus, 1796. *Von der europäischen Republik. Plan zu einem ewigen Frieden*. Altona.

Kaldor, Mary, 1990. *The Imaginary War*. Oxford: Blackwell.

Kant, Immanuel, 1795. *Towards Perpetual Peace. A Philosophical Project*, in Hans Reiss, ed., *Kant's Political Writings*. Cambridge: Cambridge University Press, 2nd enlarged ed., 1991.

Kelsen, Hans, 1944. *Peace through Law*. Chapel Hill, NC: University of North Carolina Press.

Kelsen, Hans, 1946. 'Organization and Procedure of the Security Council of the United Nations', *Harvard Law Review*, vol. 59, no. 6, pp. 1087–1121.

Köchler, Hans, 1991. *The Voting Procedure in the United Nations Security Council*. Vienna: International Progress Organization.

Ladd, William, 1840. *An Essay on a Congress of Nations for the Adjustment of International Disputes without Resort to Arms*. London: Ward.

Müller, Joachim W., ed., 1992. *The Reform of the United Nations*. New York: Oceania Publications, 2 vols.

Newcombe, Hanna, 1991. 'Proposals for a Peoples' Assembly at the United Nations', pp. 83–92 in Barnaby, 1991.

Prins, Gwyn, ed., 1983. *Defended to Death: A Study of the Nuclear Arms Race*. Harmondsworth: Penguin.

Scheler, Max, 1931. *Die Idee des Friedens und des Pazifismus*. English translation 'The Idea of Peace and Pacifism', *Journal of the British Society for Phenomenology*, vol. 7, no. 4, pp. 154–166, 1976 and vol. 8, no. 1, pp. 36–50, 1977.

Segall, Jeffrey, 1990. 'Building World Democracy Through the UN', *Medicine and War*, vol. 6, pp. 274–284.

Segall, Jeffrey, 1991. 'A UN Second Assembly', pp. 93–109 in Barnaby, 1991.

Segall, Jeffrey & Harry Lerner, eds, 1992. *Camdun-2: The United Nations and a New World Order for Peace and Justice*. London: Conferences for a More Democratic United Nations.

Stassen, Harold, 1990. *The 1990 Draft Charter Suggested for a Better United Nations Organization*. New York: Glenview Foundation.

Stassen, Harold, 1991. 'We the Peoples of the World', pp. 36–45 in Barnaby, 1991.

Thompson, Janna, 1992. *Justice and World Order*. London: Routledge.

Urquhart, Brian & Erskine Childers, 1990. *A World in Need of Leadership: Tomorrow's United Nations*. Uppsala: Dag Hammarskjöld Foundation.

Wight, Martin, 1966. 'Why Is There No International Theory?', pp. 66–107 in Herbert Butterfield & Martin Wight, eds, *Diplomatic Investigations*. London: Allen & Unwin.

DANIELE ARCHIBUGI, b. 1958, PhD at the University of Sussex (1989), has been a consultant for the EC and the OECD; Researcher at the Italian National Research Council, and Fellow of the Global Security Programme, Faculty of Social and Political Sciences, Cambridge, UK. Member of the editorial board of *Peace Review, Giano. Ricerche per la pace* and *Lettre internationale*.

[4]

Reforming
the United Nations

Paul Kennedy and Bruce Russett

A BETTER INSURANCE POLICY FOR THE WORLD

FIFTY YEARS AGO the free nations of the world met in general
assembly to begin the task of establishing a postwar order that
would secure the peace, advance global prosperity, alleviate poverty
and unemployment, and promote human rights worldwide. These
were lofty goals, but the founders of the United Nations system
were utter realists. Having lived through the economic crisis of the
1930s, the rise of fascist aggressor states, and the horrors of World
War II, these statesmen, from Winston Churchill to the formidable Republican senator Arthur Vandenberg, were committed to creating new international structures to deal with problems that were
international by nature. Part of their realism was the conviction that
they had a responsibility to try to make things work better in the
future through such structures.

A half-century later it is proper that the governments and peoples
of the world should want an assessment of the United Nations' performance. The record is mixed at best, and in recent years the world
organization has been much criticized. It has suffered great humilia-

PAUL KENNEDY is a Professor of History and BRUCE RUSSETT a
Professor of Political Science at Yale University. Since 1993 they have
served as Co-Directors of the Secretariat to the Independent Working
Group on the Future of the United Nations, supported by the Ford Foundation. The views expressed here are their own and should not be attributed to the Working Group or any of its members.

Reforming the United Nations

tions in Bosnia that have eclipsed its peacekeeping successes else-where. It is only just beginning to implement effective global social and economic policies, and its development strategies are under attack from many quarters. It is widely regarded as bureaucratically unwieldy, unnecessarily expensive, and weakened by poor personnel recruitment. These sentiments are particularly strong in the United States, reflecting that country's current politics of frustration, but they are echoed in many other parts of the world.

Yet even if the United Nations' administrative and personnel weaknesses were corrected, the world body would still require reshaping so that it could better respond to the stresses of the early 21st century. In every one of its activities, from peacekeeping to development, from monitoring human rights to overseeing environmental accords, it has been pressed by member states and their publics to play a larger role and to assume fresh responsibilities. During the early 1990s the number of U.N. peacekeeping personnel in the field increased ten-fold, as did the cost of peacekeeping operations. Strains on the social fabric of many nations bring calls for concerted U.N. policies of assistance. In the economic realm, too, the world organization is being asked to produce greater security, equity, and prosperity for all human beings, not just a privileged minority.

These operations, hopes, and expectations far exceed the capabilities of the system as it is now constituted, and they threaten to overwhelm the United Nations and discredit it, perhaps forever, even in the eyes of its warmest supporters. Fifty years old, the United Nations finds itself at a critical juncture, which should be honestly confronted by the member states who are its proprietors and who endowed it with its present features. Two paths lie before the world community. Countries should decide either to reduce their demands on the United Nations, thus giving it a decent chance of carrying out reduced policies with its existing resources, or they should recognize the necessity of improving its capacities and grant it greater resources, functions, and coordinating powers. Avoiding a decision risks condemning not just the organization but the world to a deeply troubled future. This is a much more fundamental issue than improvements to specific parts of the system, welcome though the latter would be.

In light of global circumstances, it would be wiser to take the sec-

Paul Kennedy and Bruce Russett

ond of these two paths and improve the United Nations for the benefit of future generations. A half-century ago member states recognized that a set of international instruments to achieve aims they
could not secure by themselves was very much in their national interest. The world of 1995 is clearly a vastly different place than that of
1945, and the gathering pace of technological change, global demographic growth, and environmental pressures will make the world of
2045 (or even 2020) radically different from that of today. As the
demands on states and governments increase, the need for the world
organization is growing, not shrinking.

The chief reason effective international instruments are required is
an eminently practical one, as the founders realized. Simply put,
states, people, and businesses need an international system to provide
physical, economic, and legal security. They need some form of international police force to deter terrorists and other breakers of the
peace; bodies like the World Trade Organization to head off trade
wars; institutions like those developed at Bretton Woods to assist
emerging economies; international human rights organizations to
guarantee individuals' basic freedoms across the globe; and a myriad
of agencies and offices to ensure such basics as telecommunications
and safe air traffic. If the United Nations system did not exist, much
of it would have to be invented.

POLITICS ON A GLOBAL SCALE

REFORMERS will have to reckon with the fact that there are many
different United Nations—or, at least, that different interest groups
and governments look at the world body differently. The media in
Europe and North America sees the United Nations as mainly taken
up with peacekeeping and security issues in places like Bosnia. To
finance ministers in Latin America or Southeast Asia, the United
Nations is a complex, multiheaded creature whose World Bank and
International Monetary Fund offer (often contradictory) advice on
economic development along with carrot-and-stick incentives. To
women's groups and associated nongovernmental organizations
preparing for the Fourth World Conference on Women in Beijing this
September, it is a set of agencies dealing with education, reproductive

Reforming the United Nations

rights, health care, and the like. To international lawyers and human rights advocates, it is an array of legal instruments and offices that advance the Universal Declaration of Human Rights and subsequent protocols and agreements. To isolationist critics, it is a bloated bureaucracy that is wasting taxpayers' money. For true believers, it is the embryo of Tennyson's "parliament of man, the Federation of the world."

Moves toward reform must take into account that the very different political and ideological stances of member governments, interest groups, and voters will critically influence whether specific proposals succeed or fail. Indeed, unless governments can agree on basic principles regarding the roles of the United Nations and are ready to compromise on changes in the system, years of international gridlock could lie ahead.

> To isolationists, it is a waste of money; to true believers, the "parliament of man."

Finally, there is the touchy issue of states' sovereignty. Although the original members agreed in 1945 (and countries that joined later concurred by subscribing to the charter) to bind themselves in various ways for the common good, they emphasized national sovereignty and prohibited intervention in matters "essentially within the domestic jurisdiction of any state." What they constructed was not an embryonic world government but an international corporation, so to speak, with the nation-states as shareholders. The concern with sovereignty is no less strong today, whether among conservative Americans or governments in Beijing or New Delhi, and any schemes to enhance the United Nations will have to reckon with that sentiment. The organization can only be as effective as member governments, in agreement, desire it to be.

Yet global forces for change are weakening the traditional authority of the sovereign nation-state in ways unforeseen in 1945. For example, if your American dollar or French franc is freely traded in East Asian markets in the middle of the night, to what extent is it still your currency? How can single governments deal with threats to the national interest that may come in the form of global environmental degradation or international terrorism or drug trafficking? How can citizens expect today's beleaguered governments to handle these matters, when authority and influence in many spheres is being relocated

Paul Kennedy and Bruce Russett

away from the national centers, either downward to the regions or upward to transnational actors?

This steady loss of sovereignty will probably make countries more jealous of their autonomy at first. But the only chance U.N. members have in dealing with the cluster of transnational problems is to work out a cluster of transnational responses. This requires creating and empowering more effective international structures and operating procedures, not as ends in themselves but as means to satisfy national needs. But until states arrive at that conceptual breakthrough, efforts to enhance the U.N. system will be checked.

> Threats today come in international forms. So how can national governments cope?

Those who favor improving the world organization should stress that proposals for a U.N. rapid-reaction force to handle the Rwandas of the future and the many other schemes for reform are intended not to reduce the freedom of member states but to buttress the real sovereignty of societies everywhere. By "real sovereignty" is meant the ability to influence outcomes, nationally and internationally, and it has declined in recent decades in countries like France, India, Argentina, and even the United States. Nations will not recover it until they are willing to sink their differences and work together toward common ends.

This notion, however, is immediately tested once one turns to some of the specific areas in which reform of the United Nations is suggested. For purposes of brevity, only five fields for reform are discussed here, and many other important dimensions (human rights, reform of the Secretariat, and on and on) are not considered. But these five illustrate both the problems and the possibilities of reform.

MAKING ROOM IN THE SECURITY COUNCIL

EXPANDING the Security Council seems like one of the more reasonable ways to improve the representative character—and thus the legitimacy—of the world organization in the eyes of its 186 members and their people. Increasing the council's overall size from the present 15 members would allow more nations to participate on a rotating basis in decision-making by this critically important organ. And adding to the permanent membership would permit the Security

Reforming the United Nations

Council to reflect the changes in the global balance since the five victorious powers of 1945 insisted that the charter include special provisions upholding their status and interests.

Yet proposals to promote certain countries to permanent membership are quickly enmeshed in political objections. For example, Japan and Germany have strong claims, as the second- and third-largest contributors to the U.N. budget, but would their neighbors be happy with the change? And given the special responsibility of the permanent members to maintain peace and security, should permanent membership be granted to Japan, whose constitution restricts it in sending forces abroad?

Then, since admitting a Germany or Japan to permanent membership would unduly increase the influence of the "North," it would be necessary to compensate by including a number of states from the "South," especially larger regional powers like India, Brazil, Nigeria, and South Africa. Yet this suggestion provokes criticism from those countries' neighbors. Why not consider instead permanent regional membership on the Security Council, whereby different countries take turns representing their part of the world?[1] Yet how likely is it that Britain and France would cede their historical status as permanent members and trust their interests to a European representative?

> Nations will not recover their sovereignty until they sink their differences and work toward common ends.

The veto right of each permanent member further complicates prospects for Security Council reform. The drafters of the U.N. Charter assumed that the Big Five were to be chiefly responsible for maintaining the peace and defeating aggressors, and therefore should control the use of United Nations forces. Moreover, it was vital that the great powers not opt out of the organization—the shadow of the U.S. absence from the League of Nations loomed large here—so their governments had to be reassured that at least in matters of war and peace their interests would not be overruled. Over the subsequent half-century, however, the veto has been invoked in many other cir-

---

[1] See the interesting discussion in *Prospects for Reform of the United Nations System* (Italian Society for International Organization, Cedam-Padova, 1993), pp. 445-449.

Paul Kennedy and Bruce Russett

cumstances, such as blocking resolutions and opposing nominations. If the number of permanent members on the Security Council was increased, would that not increase the risk of many more vetoes in the future? One solution might be to deny the newer permanent members the veto, but that would confuse things by introducing a third membership category. Some have proposed that the veto be abolished—a splendidly egalitarian idea, but highly unlikely to win approval by the Permanent Five.

The best that can be hoped for is a compromise after negotiation in the General Assembly. An increase in the number of both permanent and rotating members of the Security Council, and a restriction of the veto to questions of war and peace as the founders intended, would not crimp the Security Council's effectiveness but would make it less like the old boys club of 1945.

GIVING PEACE A CHANCE

THE WORLD organization must have better access to well-trained forces to implement the peacekeeping missions agreed on by the Security Council, and such missions must be differentiated from peace enforcement operations so that the confusions that occurred in Somalia and Bosnia will not be repeated. These are the two most important issues in what is one of the United Nations' most important functions: securing the peace.

The first immediately brings up the problem of sovereignty again. Member states always reserve the right to decide whether they will respond to the secretary-general's request to donate troops or other forces to any peacekeeping operation. In this as in everything else the United Nations depends on the whim of governments, and there is definite evidence of donor fatigue, partly because of the embarrassment of the triple crisis of Somalia/Bosnia/Rwanda but more generally because of the unprecedented number of missions undertaken and peacekeepers deployed since 1989. The Security Council is going to have to be more selective in the field operations it authorizes, although deciding what criteria to apply in evaluating a request for intervention could be excruciatingly difficult. Clearly, to approve no additional missions would undermine the purposes

Reforming the United Nations

of the United Nations and set the scene for future horrors.

Had the world body been able to summon battle-ready troops as the tragedy in Rwanda unfolded, the swift interposition of peace-keeping units might have saved tens of thousands of lives. Calls for remedying the situation have led to two alternative proposals: endowing the United Nations with its own rapid-reaction forces, or, through negotiation with member governments, creating within national armed services units ready for immediate deployment for U.N. purposes.

In terms of operational speed and coherence, the first option is superior. U.N. standing forces, sent to a crisis zone on the resolution of the Security Council alone, could quickly carry out an array of peacekeeping and humanitarian actions. The secretary-general would not have to beg governments for peacekeeping contingents on an ad hoc basis, and governments would not be periodically confronted with the delicate choice of whether or not to commit national units. Critics raise objections about costs (a standing force of 10,000 could cost $500 million a year) and logistics (where would it be stationed?, for instance). But the greatest obstacles are political. Are governments willing to let the world organization have its own army of peacekeepers, making it appear to have acquired one of the attributes of statehood?

> What should the United Nations do when bad guys are committing atrocities?

If not, the best alternative would be the creation of specially ear-marked national units ready to be dispatched once the government in question had agreed to the secretary-general's request for a troop contribution. That, of course, is the rub, for delays as governments ponder that request may see a potential tragedy turn into a full-blown disaster. And as the separate national units grapple with language and coordination problems during the operation, they will still be subject to constant scrutiny by their home governments, which naturally will want a say in operational decisions. A U.N. standing force would be far preferable; standby national units are a halfway measure.

The question of distinguishing peacekeeping work from peace-enforcement missions cannot be separated from the above objections. Indeed, the reluctance of many governments to contribute

Paul Kennedy and Bruce Russett

forces to the U.N. stems from their concern that they might become embroiled in an operation whose purposes are changed from time to time. The lessons of Bosnia and Somalia must be heeded, as well as those from more successful missions like the U.N. Transitional Authority in Cambodia (UNTAC). The original elements of a peace-keeping operation, evolved by the United Nations through hard experience, were clear enough; Brian Urquhart describes them in

his 1987 book *A Life in Peace and War*, after four decades of traveling the world for the secretary-general. Both sides (usually governments or putative governments) requested international assistance in maintaining peace, lightly armed blue helmets were interposed impartially, and the good offices of the secretary-general or his representative were used to negotiate a political settlement. However, things are much less clear when the world organization is offering humanitarian aid in circumstances where authority has collapsed or is collapsing, factional struggles are under way, and some of the warring parties refuse to cooperate. What should the United Nations do when bad guys are interfering with humanitarian and peacekeeping operations and carrying out atrocities?

Are governments willing to let the U.N. have its own army, just like them?

The kaleidoscopic and unpredictable nature of such conflicts ensures that no set formula will assist the Security Council when it considers future requests to intervene. But a few prerequisites must be insisted on should a local crisis in which U.N. peacekeeping forces are involved deteriorate and a request be made for *enforcement* of the peace. The entire issue should be carefully examined by the Security Council and concerned member states before the mandate is changed, the peacekeeping troops must be pulled out of harm's way or given adequate protection, sufficient funding (if need be, an open-ended commitment to get the job done) must be assured, and Security Council members and other participating governments must be resolved to enforce the peace. If the above conditions are not present, the proposal for peace enforcement should be resisted. These may seem commonsense requirements, but their absence explains the debacles in Bosnia and Somalia.

Reforming the United Nations

ADVANCING ECONOMIC AND SOCIAL PROGRESS

THIS RUBRIC comprehends a vast panoply of U.N. activities, including those of the World Bank, the International Monetary Fund (IMF), and the World Trade Organization, and accounts for by far the largest portion of the world organization's expenditures. The United Nations' portfolio of duties in this domain rests on the lofty language of 50 years ago, whereby the founding governments pledged "to employ international machinery for the promotion of the economic and social advancement of all peoples." They established the Economic and Social Council (ECOSOC) to coordinate the work of the specialized agencies in international economic, social, health, and related matters and to promote human rights and fundamental freedoms and the advancement of international cultural and educational cooperation.

It is not surprising that the United Nations' role here has been controversial. Some laissez-faire ideologues suggest canceling the entire U.N. economic and social agenda, seeing no sense in reducing government at home while paying for international agencies and programs abroad. The United Nations, which like all public organizations today operates under intense pressures to reduce costs and trim programs, must constantly justify itself to the richer countries that contribute a large portion of its funds. At the same time, the organization is under attack from governments and nongovernmental organizations in developing countries, and their sympathizers in developed nations, for what seem to them its failures in pursuing the noble economic and social goals set out in the charter. Funds for development, these critics say, are completely inadequate, and the world economic order is still stacked in favor of a few countries and companies possessing a disproportionate amount of capital. The constant preaching about the free market from affluent countries, they say, ignores the fact that dire social conditions and lack of infrastructure in developing regions make it difficult to attract investment. The austerity measures mandated by the World Bank and the IMF sometimes lead to cuts in already ill-funded education and social programs.

> No agenda for peace is complete without an agenda for development.

The whole time the gap between richest and poorest around the globe

Paul Kennedy and Bruce Russett

is widening. More radical voices demand a redistribution of wealth, and U.N. controls on Bretton Woods institutions. Moderate reformers recall the 1960s, when global economic growth and a far stronger commitment by the North to reducing the divide gave developing countries hope.

Assuming that neither free market enthusiasts nor supporters of the "new international economic order" succeed in imposing their views of what the United Nations should do or cease doing in this sphere, how might a few substantive reforms help?

Most reform studies have recommended abolishing the unwieldy ECOSOC and erecting new, more effective organs in its place.[2] New permanent intergovernmental organs should be empowered by the member states to develop policies to handle the complex and interrelated socioeconomic matters that confront the world. This implies that the World Bank, the IMF, and other specialized agencies whose autonomy had undercut ECOSOC would be brought into a closer relationship with the rest of the U.N. system. This would occur not through any direct takeover—the major treasuries and finance ministries would oppose that—but simply because the governments that are their chief shareholders finally see that if common tasks are to be carried out effectively greater coordination and consultation is required among all the entities dealing with economic and social affairs.

Such consolidation depends on member states adopting a more holistic view of how to use international machinery to improve the condition of the planet. Like that of the U.N. founders, this view would recognize that real security cannot be achieved without the eradication of poverty. Like Secretary-General Boutros Boutros-Ghali's reports in 1992 and 1994, it would assert that no "agenda for peace" is complete without an "agenda for development." But the latter agenda would concern itself as much with turbulence in global currency markets as with rising unemployment among youth, and be as committed to reducing protectionism as to lowering female illiteracy, for it would see that humankind's prospects are hurt by all these threats to well-being.

---

[2] See, for example, the Commission on Global Governance, *Our Global Neighborhood: The Report of the Commission on Global Governance*, New York: Oxford University Press, 1995; and the Independent Working Group on the Future of the United Nations, *The United Nations in Its Second Half-Century: The Report of the Independent Working Group on the Future of the United Nations*, New York: Ford Foundation, 1995.

Reforming the United Nations

RESCUING COLLAPSED STATES

WHEN THE U.N. founders drafted the charter, they were emerging from a war in which many nations had lost their independence because of the aggression of foreign states and during which the United States (though not Britain or France) had been anticipating the independence of colonial territories. The focus was on state-building and the need to ensure that no member states, especially smaller ones, would suffer outside interference. Yet 50 years later, after Cambodia, Afghanistan, Haiti, and Rwanda, it is evident that a key challenge to international stability is the phenomenon of internal conflicts in which authority implodes, ethnic and religious conflicts erupt, many lives are lost, and millions flee across international borders. Without subscribing fully to prophecies of widespread chaos by writers like Robert Kaplan and Martin Van Creveld, it is not hard to see that a combination of demographic pressures, resource depletion, internal migration, and social stress could lead to the disintegration of other states.

Rescuing failed nations will be expensive, further straining U.N. budgets. Moreover, going in will always be an extremely sensitive proposition politically, both inside the collapsing society and in the developing world, where such collapses are more likely to occur. Many governments in developing nations regard with suspicion the prospect of rescue actions by a United Nations still in their eyes dominated by the richer countries; talk in the Western media of trusteeship and mandates fuels their fears that this could be a form of neocolonialism. They even frown on the use of the term "failed state," suggesting as it does that a country's sovereignty can disappear.

> The original concern was state-building; now, it's states collapsing.

Any motion for intervention, therefore, will have to be phrased extremely delicately. It might be pleaded on ethical grounds that the international community has a duty to assist disintegrating societies and to forestall the widespread breaches of human rights that attend such chaos. In some cases the argument that large-scale cross-border migrations constitute a threat to international stability could be made, as in the U.S. request for action in Haiti last year.

Paul Kennedy and Bruce Russett

If anything more is to be done in this field, the United Nations
must establish procedures open to public view concerning the decision to intervene (it must come at the request of some or all of the
contending parties and be approved by the Security Council, adequately funded, subject to review by the General Assembly, etc.)

and the rescue process itself. Specified U.N.
agencies with clear lines of responsibility
must be accountable for the temporary
guardianship and recovery mechanisms, and
the United Nations must work with the
domestic parties and nongovernmental organizations toward restoring full sovereignty
and returning the country to membership in
the community of nations.

> Should the world body
> be granted a separate
> income? Some want to
> keep the right to cut off
> funds to make a point.

Before all this happens, however, governments will need to
understand another political paradox, which is that the only purpose
of the intrusion by the world organization is to help the peoples
concerned recover their real sovereignty—that is, their capacity to
influence their own fate and to conduct their own affairs peacefully.

BALANCING THE CHECKBOOK

CHARGES that the United Nations misspends the contributions of its
members are widespread, and critics insist that eliminating superfluous
agencies, trimming perquisites, and improving management throughout the organization would yield great savings. Defenders point out
that the United Nations spends relatively little considering all that it is
expected to do—its regular budget in 1994 was $1.3 billion, with peace-
keeping consuming another $3.3 billion—but most everyone would
concede that there is room for further efficiency measures. Some,
such as eliminating various staff positions, have already been carried
out, following recommendations in the 1993 Thornburgh Report,
and Boutros-Ghali appears committed to more. But proposals by the
secretary-general's office to cut agencies and personnel have frequently been blocked by member states. Most important, no amount
of savings will permit the world organization to be solvent if members, especially those in the Security Council, keep adding to the

Reforming the United Nations

United Nations' tasks and operations. Responsibility, in other words, must also be shouldered by the governments.

This applies even more directly to the late payment or even non-payment of countries' annual contributions. The two worst sinners here, to their discredit, are both permanent members of the Security Council and founders of the United Nations: the United States, and Russia, as the successor to the Soviet Union. But other countries add to the arrears so that these typically total up to about half of both the regular and the peacekeeping budget. This keeps the United Nations in fiscal crisis—what would be regarded as an impossible operating situation for any private company and for most member governments. The very least that members might do would be to recommit themselves to pay their assessments fully and on time, as they are legally obliged to do. But this should be accompanied by agreement to revise the formulas for assessing contributions (especially the formula for peacekeeping costs), which are out of date and disadvantage certain powers, notably the United States.

More ambitious reformers suggest, considering the vagaries of the present system and the prospect of increased demands on the organization, that the United Nations be assured an income flow that is larger but also independent of member governments' willingness or capacity to pay on time. Two camps are against this: conservatives who fear that it would free the world body from the displeasure of governments and the threat to withhold assessed contributions, and what might be termed U.N. fiscal constitutionalists, who declare that since the organization is the possession of member states, the latter should be fully responsible for financing it (except for agencies like UNICEF that collect voluntary contributions).

> The historic moment should not be missed. The heads of state should seize it in New York in October.

Yet the case for funding an innovative and reliable revenue flow for the United Nations is strong. The organization ought not to have its work delayed and diminished by fiscal uncertainties. Moreover, governments might welcome not having to cajole reluctant legislatures each year to vote their national assessment, and states in economic distress would be relieved that funding came from a source other than their exchequers. There is no lack of ideas on potential

Paul Kennedy and Bruce Russett

new sources. Most involve taxes on the use of the global commons (a small levy on currency transactions or tickets for international airline flights, for example). Since international business, tourism, and communications rely on international governance structures, the argument goes, a modest contribution to the latter's operating costs seems appropriate. That said, however, all the proposed global taxes raise technical and legal issues that would require detailed study and negotiation through the General Assembly. The question remains: would member states at last permit the United Nations a revenue source other than their own contributions?

ACT NOW OR BE PUSHED LATER

THESE ARE breathtakingly large problems, and in the present political climate readers may doubt that what has been proposed above could ever be achieved, even if they themselves subscribe to such ideas. Yet they might also recall that, despite setbacks, the United Nations has altered and evolved in ways that were striking at the time but are now taken for granted. Meanwhile, decade by decade we move closer to worrying demographic, ecological, fiscal, and socioeconomic thresholds. The world faces a blunt choice between initiating prudent and substantive improvements in the next few years or being forced into emergency measures if and when the situation deteriorates. Since no one can know our global future, is it not worthwhile to invest a small amount of humankind's capital in a worldwide insurance policy—which is what the United Nations is intended to be?

There are really only two paths to follow. Critics can deride the United Nations, its secretary-general, its "bloated bureaucracy," its failures in Bosnia, and so on. After all, there is a subtle argument that the world community needs a scapegoat for its setbacks and embarrassments, and since democratic governments have to deflect criticism from themselves, one of the United Nations' functions is to take the heat. As societies collapse, peacekeeping missions founder, and social stresses mount, there will always be someone to blame—the United Nations.

The alternative is to take advantage of the world organization's fiftieth birthday and the meeting of the heads of state and government in New York in late October during anniversary celebrations, to develop a

Reforming the United Nations

process for considering substantive improvements in the system. While the United Nations is not the inefficient, incompetent body unfair critics depict it to be, it clearly requires a serious overhaul to prepare it for the years ahead. The process has already begun with the formation of study groups in the General Assembly and with the publication of reports on the United Nations' past, present, and future timed to coincide with the organization's half-century. Member states, acting through their permanent missions in the General Assembly, must now push ahead with a sustained examination of the various reform proposals, understanding that no single one will be perfect but that a distillation and then an advancement of the better ideas is urgently required. The historic moment should not be missed. The world owes it to the generations yet to come.

FORUM FOR DEVELOPMENT STUDIES
NO. 1 – 1996

Democracy in the United Nations. For and Against

Raino Malnes

1. Purpose and Plan

The fiftieth anniversary of the United Nations (UN) saw many calls for reform of the organisation, but is reform really called for? This question brings up an array of technical issues pertaining to coordination, budgeting, recruitment, etc. They are currently being debated extensively and incisively by people having intimate familiarity with the UN. But one would also like to sort out the normative problems that lie behind technical issues, and among these is the question whether or not the UN should remain a democratic institution.[1]

Democracy is no marginal subject as far as the UN is concerned. The discussion about the need for reform often boils down to a controversy over the retention or revision of the democratic structure of the organisation. One fairly frequent way of approaching this issue is first to point out problems associated with the current structure of the UN and then to probe the prospect of political alignment around proposals for change. The central question then becomes: what chance do reformists stand of recasting democratic procedures? This article takes another tack, asking only: what speaks for democracy in the UN and what speaks against? An exploration of pro- and counter-democratic considerations is needed because both protagonists and antagonists of reform tend to rest their case on blurred or incomplete arguments. I shall, however, stop short of answering the question raised in the opening sentence: is reform of the UN really called for? This is, of course, what we ultimately want to know, but the answer will not come easily, and it is best to start with an overview of normative considerations that bear on the matter.

Two kinds of normative considerations come into the picture. First, one may ask whether an institution like the UN is legitimate in the sense that those who are affected by it have no justification for complaining about the way it affects them. Assessments of legitimacy are

Raino Malnes

normally premised on principles of justice or arguments about right and wrong with respect to the consequences of policies and practices for people's well-being. It is, in brief, a question of moral evaluation.

Note that an institution that is legitimate in the sense intended here need not be subject of approval by all (or anyone) who care to pass a judgement on it. To be sure, the notion of legitimacy is very often associated with what people actually think about institutions rather than what they are justified in thinking. One hears, for example, that an institution is legitimate insofar as it is widely endorsed. And some even deny the warranty of distinguishing between justified and unjustified ideas on this score. Yet, *pace* moral relativists, we may draw a line between normative assessment of legitimacy and empirical analysis of political opinions. The first turns on moral qualities that institutions, objectively speaking, have or lack; the second has to do with people's perceptions of such qualities. In either case, we take an interest in arguments that are actually advanced in public debate, but when our task is normative assessment, we look for good arguments, while empirical analysis aims at finding out which arguments are invoked most often and by whom.

As this article addresses itself to a normative question – should the UN be democratic or not? – it is an exercise in normative assessment of legitimacy. Yet, the conceptual machinery that I shall avail myself of can serve equally well as a framework for empirical analysis of the on-going debate about the UN. In general, normative theories of legitimacy provide tools also for investigations of legitimacy-cum-popular approval. But on this occasion, we adopt the normative point of view.

The other kind of considerations that normative questions bring up are pragmatic. These have to do with the prospect of implementing legitimate policies and practices. One asks, to paraphrase William Shaw (1980: 133), if a particular institution is apt to win the support of those whose contributions it needs to work properly. Will people comply with its rules? Will it fulfil the purpose of setting up an institution in the first place? Could an alternative arrangement do better? Such concerns are not reducible to questions of legitimacy, as the successful operation of an institution hinges on more than its moral qualities. People's readiness to support it and comply with its rules does not only or primarily depend on whether or not they are justified in withholding support and compliance. Thus, it may well happen that legitimate arrangements appear utterly impracticable, and normative assessment should take both moral and pragmatic considerations into account.

Democracy in the United Nations. For and Against

The remainder of the article divides into ten sections. Section 2 looks closer at the defining features of democratic institutions, while Section 3 dwells on three compelling reasons why democracy is an attractive system of collective choice. Section 4 shows that the three general rationales of democracy reverberate in things that are actually said in support of the current distribution of political rights within the UN. Then attention turns to the criticism that is being raised against democracy in the UN. It branches off in different directions, and Section 5 distinguishes between three categories of argument whose concrete expressions are explored in sections 6 through 10. Section 11 rounds off the discussion by hinting at a framework for more stringent thinking about the need for reform of the UN.

2. What is Democracy?

What is democracy? The question is mostly answered by reference to how political decisions are made within a state; so also here:

> By a democratic procedure I mean a method of determining the content of laws (and other legally binding decisions) such that the preferences of the citizens have some formal connection with the outcome on which each counts equally (Barry, 1979: 156).

I shall pause to spell out the central assumptions of Brian Barry's definition. First, democracy is an attribute of procedures of decision-making, not decisions as such. It is the way people go about the problem of collective choice, not the choices they eventually make, that qualify as democratic or non-democratic. Thus, a democratic decision may well be a decision that for good reasons is highly regrettable. Second, democracy is an attribute of a procedure that translates individual preferences into collective choices. A democratic choice is a function of the configuration of preferences among citizens – and not, say, the configuration of stars at the moment the choice is made. Third, the method for translating preferences into decisions is formalised. There exist fixed rules that define the steps people should take to arrive at a collective choice. Finally, these rules qualify as democratic only if they accord each individual's preference an equal weight when it comes to determining the choice. The exact implications of this criterion are notoriously difficult to delineate, but some are clear. Counting votes one by one is, for example, more democratic than counting male votes twice and female votes only once.

7

Raino Malnes

I take it that Barry's is an adequate definition of democracy. It refers, as I said, to decision-making within a state, but carries over easily to intergovernmental organisations like the UN: a democratic procedure is a method of determining the policies of an organisation such that the preferences of the member-states have some formal connection to the outcome in which each counts equally. This is a straightforward – although, as we shall later see, not an unproblematic – definition of democracy in international organisations.

One question is left open by Barry's definition: who is a citizen? If each person who lives within a state is called a 'member' of the state, which members will have to be reckoned as citizens for the state to be called democratic? (granted that its legally binding decisions are taken by a procedure that otherwise answers to the definition). Was, for example, ancient Athens democratic? Its procedures for collective choice met all the requisite criteria, but the citizens – adult men of Athenian ancestry – were a small sub-set of the members of the state.

The question is best answered by distinguishing between two aspects of democracy (Hyland, 1995: 55-6). The qualitative dimension has to do with the distribution of political rights among citizens. If all citizens have equal rights of participation – if, more specifically, each citizen's preferences count equally – decision-making is, qualitatively speaking, democratic. The quantitative dimension turns on the ratio between citizens who have equal political rights and all those who live within a state. The greater this ratio, the more democratic the state is.

The qualitative dimension seems to allow a definite answer to the question whether a state is democratic or not. Either citizens have equal rights or they have not. But things are, alas, not that simple. As indicated above, the exact implications of the idea that rules of decision-making are democratic only if they accord each individual's preferences an equal weight are notoriously difficult to delineate. Moreover, deviations from this norm can be greater or smaller, and it therefore makes good sense to speak of states as more or less democratic (in qualitative terms) depending on how closely they come to distributing political rights equally among citizens.

As far as the quantitative dimension of democracy is concerned, there is no way of avoiding gradualist assessment. To be sure, if all members of a state are citizens, democracy is perfect on this dimension, but there can be no question of deeming all states that do not display such perfection non-democratic. It is all a matter of degree, but it seems at the same time sensible to say that, below a certain level, the ratio of citizens to members of a state is so low that any talk

Democracy in the United Nations. For and Against

about democracy will be a travesty. I shall not, however, try to pinpoint the critical level.

In view of what has just been said, is the UN a democratic organisation? Three observations suggest that it is. First, the various assemblies and agencies that together make up the UN allow of broad – often universal – participation by member-states in decision-making processes. Second, rights of participation are equal among those who have such rights in any assembly or agency with the exception of the Security Council. Third, decisions are largely taken on the basis the majority principle. These characteristics alluded to – widely distributed and equal rights of participation together with majority rule – are earmarks of democracy as defined earlier. Moreover, the distinction between the qualitative and the quantitative dimension of democracy is a fine basis for clarifying the formula 'one state, one vote', commonly invoked as the core constitutional principle of the UN. It says that each state should have the right to cast one and only one vote, and this implies, first, that the UN is a perfect democracy on the quantitative score, its 'citizens' being coextensive with its members, and, second, that a necessary condition of the UN's perfection on the qualitative score is also fulfilled, as any organisation that accords unequal numbers of votes to citizens will for that reason be less than entirely democratic.[2]

One might ask why it is only a necessary condition of the UN being a perfect democracy in the qualitative sense that each state has the right to cast one and only one vote. Why not a necessary and sufficient condition? Because more has to be known about the method of aggregating votes before we can tell whether each state's preferences count equally. 'One state, one vote' says nothing about how one arrives at a collective choice on the basis of the votes cast. In the UN, this is largely done by means of the majority rule, and it is arguable that this method of aggregation safeguards political equality better than any other method. The commitment to majoritarianism may therefore be said to certify the democratic character of the UN. Yet, we shall later hear of a tendency towards decision-making by consensus, which means that any state opposing a proposal has a veto as regards its adoption. This is naturally seen as a step away from political egalitarianism, and to the extent that this tendency prevails, the democratic credentials on the UN will be weakened. So far, however, we are justified in deeming the organisation democratic.

But more than one kind of democracy is conceivable in international organisations. The institutional structure that was sketched above is a democracy of states – or, to be quite precise, a democracy of

9

Raino Malnes

governments – and if the UN had instead been designed as a democracy of individuals, it might have had a different structure. I shall
return to this issue in Section 6.

3. Three Reasons to Prefer Democracy

A somewhat paradoxical characteristic of debates about the legitimacy of various methods of collective choice is this. On the one hand,
the virtues of democracy seem in little need of defence. Democratic
procedures have a naturalness about them that renders justification of
democracy almost redundant. Isn't it preposterous to ask why decisions ought to be taken democratically? Counter-democratic arguments,
on the other hand, are so suspect that they have to be stated with care
if they are to be taken at all seriously. The upshot is that the contents
and force of the latter come out quite clearly while supposedly stronger pro-democratic arguments remain mute and elliptic. In practice,
then, the virtues of democracy easily appear too lightweight to over-
ride countervailing considerations. An inadequate understanding of
why the burden of proof should be placed on those who dispute the
legitimacy of democracy may well make this burden too easy to discharge. Hence, I shall take the time to elaborate three reasons to prefer democracy to other procedures of collective choice. Some may
lament this long detour into political theory, but it is needed to find
out whether or not, all things considered, the reasons to retain democracy in the UN are stronger than the reasons to abolish it.

What, then, does democracy have to say for it? Basically two lines
of argument are conceivable. First, one may claim that democracy is a
procedure of collective choice that brings good results in the sense
that decisions that are taken democratically are likely to serve the
interests of those who take them better than decisions that are taken
otherwise. This will be called the consequentialist justification of
democracy. It recommends the democratic procedure on grounds of
the consequences it is likely to have with respect to the quality of
laws and policies. Second, democratic procedures may be thought to
guarantee justice in the distribution of political rights, which no other
procedure does to the same extent. This will be called procedural
justification, as it recommends the democratic procedure on account
of its inherent characteristics, without regard to wider consequences
of taking decisions one way or the other.

Consequentialism and proceduralism are two perspectives on legitimacy. They offer divergent definitions of the qualities whose presence or absence render institutions legitimate or illegitimate. Or, to be

Democracy in the United Nations. For and Against

more accurate, they bring up different, but not necessarily conflicting, considerations for determining whether an institution is legitimate or not.

The simplicity of the distinction between consequentialism and proceduralism may be deceptive, as many versions of either mode of justification, as well as mixed arguments, are conceivable. It is, however, hard to think of arguments for democracy that are cast in an altogether different mould. Anyway, a thorough investigation of everything in favour of democracy is not required here. I shall confine myself to presenting three suggestive justifications – two consequentialist arguments and one hovering between consequentialism and proceduralism.

3.1 Mill's arguments

John Stuart Mill (1861/1992) offers two justifications of democracy, both of consequentialist character. One takes its cue from what we may call the welfarist principle. It says that collective choice should be made in the manner that maximises social welfare, the level of which depends roughly on how far people's preferences are being met. This, Mill argues, speaks in favour of procedures that permit broad participation in decision-making processes by those whose welfare is at stake. Under appropriate circumstances, the extent to which laws and policies accord with people's preferences increases with the extent of popular participation in legislation and policy-making.

Mill's elaboration of the welfarist rationale of broad participation rests crucially on a comparison of the presumed effectiveness of various constitutions in (i) making popular preferences known to legislators, and (ii) making sure that these preferences actually guide legislation. For both purposes, there is no better guarantee than extensive popular participation, provided only people are capable of conveying what they want.

> [T]he rights and interests of every and any person are only secure from being disregarded, when the person interested is himself able, and habitually disposed, to stand up for them (ibid.: 58).

It is not that autocratic or socially exclusive governments necessarily conspire to exploit those who lack political rights. The inadequacy of such systems can have far more innocent explanations.

> We need not suppose that when power resides in an exclusive class, that class will knowingly sacrifice the other classes to

11

Raino Malnes

themselves; it suffices that, in the absence of its natural defenders, the interest of the excluded is always in danger of being
overlooked; and, when looked at, is seen with very different eyes
from those of the persons it directly concerns (ibid.: 59-60).

Note that Mill does not say that a procedure that permits broad participation always yields laws and policies that reflect popular preferences. He suggests that this is so only under appropriate circumstances.
Thus, there are things that may offset the benign effect of popular
participation on laws and policies, and one such thing has already
been touched on. Mill says that the opportunity of participation is a
guarantee of good laws only if people are 'habitually disposed' to
stand up for their interests. This is to say that the democratic system
is not a universally superior form of government; its superiority is
contingent on 'the necessary conditions ... for giving effect to its
beneficial tendencies' (ibid.: 46). Mill conjoins his ideal of an optimal
procedure of collective choice to 'a theorem of the circumstances in
which that form of government may wisely be introduced' (idem.).
Generally speaking, the prerequisites of maximising social welfare
through democratic arrangements reside in the 'mental conditions' of
citizens. People must, in particular, be capable of impartial judgment.
They must not stand up for their own interests so ardently that they
have no regard for the interests of others. Mill is particularly alarmed
by the 'dangers of class legislation' which looms where the majority
principle gives free reign to a coalescent and numerically dominant
group (ibid.: 136).

> Looking at democracy ... as the rule of the numerical majority, it
> is surely possible that the ruling power may be under the domi-
> nion of sectional or class interests, pointing to conduct different
> from that which would be dictated by impartial regard for the
> interest of all (ibid.: 128).

This is to say that extensive participation does not guarantee legislation that is sensitive to what citizens generally want. If the members
of society are highly partial and do not divide into groups that neutral-
ise one another, then democratic decisions may reflect 'selfish incli-
nations' and 'sinister interests' (ibid.). This, of course, is the problem
of majority tyranny.
    There is no need to go deeper into Mill's welfarist argument. What
has been said above already amounts to a suggestive, albeit conditional, defence of democracy. If the risk of majority tyranny can be

Democracy in the United Nations. For and Against

deflected, the aim of maximising social welfare is best served by a democratic procedure of collective choice because the interests of all those who are affected by what is done are only secure from being disregarded when they are all able to stand up for them. Like any consequentialist argument, it rests ultimately on a standard of value, but Mill's standard – the welfarist principle – is not liable to create a stir.

Mill advances another defence of democracy as well. He does not see political institutions only as instruments for providing people with what they want, but also as mechanisms that contribute to making people what they are – that shape human character. Thus, 'the merit which any set of political institutions can possess' consists in 'its tendency to improve or deteriorate the people themselves' (ibid.: 35-6). Mill puts forth what we may call a perfectionist ideal with several components, two of which are relevant for our purpose. First, intellectual excellence involves knowledge of theoretical matters as well as 'speculative talent' (ibid.: 64). In its absence, people may deteriorate into 'mere masses of ignorance, stupidity, and baleful prejudice' (ibid.: 31). Second, practical excellence consists in both broad instrumental knowledge and a striving, energetic character. Such qualities characterise a person who is 'self-helping' and 'actively engaged in the attempt to improve [his] own or some other lot'; who 'continually measur[es] his energy against difficulties'; and 'whose thoughts and activities are all needed for, and habitually employed in, practicable and useful enterprises' (ibid.: 67 and 68).

Mill holds that the absence or presence of such excellence is largely determined by what political institutions we find in a society. The 'nature and degree of authority exercised over individuals, the distribution of power, and the conditions of command and obedience, are most powerful of influences, except their religious belief, which make them what they are, and enable them to become what they can be' (ibid.: 39). This is not the place to look in detail at Mill's elaboration of this bold claim, but here is one consideration to support it. Mill maintains that political participation is indispensable to the development of an active character. '[T]here can be no kind of doubt that the passive type of character is favoured by the government of one or a few, and the active self-helping type by that of the Many' (ibid.: 69). He alludes to 'the practical discipline which the character obtains, from the occasional demand made upon the citizens to exercise, for a time and in their turn, some social function' (ibid.: 71). Political office involves responsibilities which elicit foresight, perseverance and other practical virtues to a greater extent than the lighter tasks of private life do. Another reason why democracy fosters

13

Raino Malnes

practical excellence is, in Mill's view, 'the invigorating effect of freedom upon the character' (ibid.: 71).

> [I]t is a great ... stimulus to any one's self-help and self-reliance
> when he starts from an even ground, and has not to feel that his
> success depends on the impression he can make upon the senti-
> ments and dispositions of a body of whom he is not one. It is a
> great discouragement to an individual, and a still greater one to a
> class, to be left out of the constitution; to be reduced to plea from
> outside the door to the arbiters of their destiny, not taken into
> consultation within (ibid.: 70-1).

Psychological hypotheses at this high level of generality are hard to
assess, but Mill's perfectionist defence of democracy has enough
initial plausibility to be counted among the considerations that speak
in favour of democratic procedures of collective choice.

3.2 Rawls' argument

Mill's defence of democracy looms large in political thought of the
nineteenth century, and the same goes for John Rawls' argument in
contemporary political thought. Rawls grounds his assessment of
political institutions in a theory of justice. It defines the lower limits
of how people may tolerably be treated, constituting an 'uncompro-
mising' demand on the political system.

> [J]ustice is the first virtue of social institutions. ... laws and insti-
> tutions no matter how efficient and well-arranged must be
> reformed and abolished if they are unjust. Each person possesses
> an inviolability founded on justice that even the welfare of soci-
> ety as a whole cannot override. ... [T]he rights secured by justice
> are not subject to political bargaining or to the calculus of social
> interests (Rawls, 1971: 3-4).

The interests Rawls takes to be beyond compromise are first and foremost certain personal freedoms.

> [J]ustice denies that the loss of freedom for some is made right
> by a greater good shared by others. It does not allow that the
> sacrifice imposed on a few are outweighed by the larger sum of
> advantages enjoyed by many (ibid.: 4).

Democracy in the United Nations. For and Against

Rawls identifies a category of 'basic liberties' to which he accords the privileged status of absolute rights. Among these are political freedoms of the kind conventionally associated with democracy. Rawls holds that justice requires constitutional guarantees of the freedom to vote, to stand for political office, to set up political parties, and so on.

This argument seems not to share the consequentialist structure of Mill's arguments. It does not, on the face of it, defend democratic institutions by virtue of their benign social effects, i.e. the superior quality of laws and policies enacted by such institutions. Rawls rather asserts that democracy is the best procedure of collective choice – or, indeed, the only tolerable one – because it is the only procedure that respects political freedoms whose violation is inherently wrong.

A detailed presentation of the premises of Rawls' defence of democracy is beyond the scope of this paper. Suffice it to adduce some central elements. Rawls starts from a 'conception of the person'. He assumes two capacities, which are called 'moral powers', to be characteristic of fully developed human beings:

> A sense of justice is the capacity to understand, to apply, and to act from the public conception of justice which characterizes the fair terms of social cooperation. The capacity for a conception of the good is the capacity to form, to revise, and rationally pursue a conception of one's rational advantage, or good (Rawls, 1985: 233).

Consider the moral power to form and pursue a conception of the good. Rawls assumes that an individual can develop and exercise the moral power of freedom only to the extent that he enjoys certain *primary goods*. These are 'things that every rational man is presumed to want' (Rawls, 1971: 62). They are not, however, goals in themselves. Their primacy lies in the fact that any goal a person may set himself depends on these goods for its realisation. 'Primary goods are', Rawls (1987: 21) says, 'singled out by asking which things are generally necessary as social conditions and all-purpose means to enable persons to pursue their determinate conceptions of the good and to develop and exercise their two moral powers.'

Among the primary goods is *self-respect*, or, more accurately, the 'social bases of self-respect', which are 'those aspects of basic institutions normally essential if citizens are to have a lively sense of their own worth as persons' (ibid.: 23). A person has such a sense only if he is aware that he commands the capacity to form and pursue worth-

15

Raino Malnes

while objectives. Self-respect is the conscious possession of this prime moral power.

> The importance of self-respect is that it provides a secure sense of our own value, a firm conviction that our determinate concep- tion of the good is worth carrying out. Without self-respect noth- ing may seem worth doing, and if some things have value for us, we lack the will to pursue them (ibid.: 33).

Rawls says that a person is unlikely to pursue personal objectives if he doubts the worth of pursuing them. This psychological premise borders on an analytic truth. But it points to the more important assumption that self-respect is necessary to lead a free and rational life. Granted the moral value of freedom and rationality, those who are subject to conditions that undermine self-respect suffer intolerable treatment.

In Rawls' view, the presence or absence of self-respect is largely determined by social institutions. He holds, more specifically, that 'self-respect depends upon and is encouraged by certain public fea- tures of basic social institutions, how they work together and how people who accept these arrangements are expected to (and normally do) regard and treat one another' (ibid.: 33). If so, justice becomes a question of eliminating institutional features that subvert self-respect. Principles of justice are guidelines for the design of social institutions that sustain people's sense of their own worth. This goes for standards of political justice in particular. Rawls (1988: 270) says that 'the basic rights and liberties of a constitutional regime are to assure that every- one can adequately develop these [moral] powers and exercise them fully over the course of a complete life as they so decide'.

One thing emerges from this brief overview of Rawls' argument: while it has the appearance of a prodecuralist justification of demo- cracy, it may turn out on closer scrutiny to rest on consequentialist considerations. The central thesis seems to be that democracy is the correct procedure of collective choice because it is the only procedure that sustains people's self-respect. But there is no need here to ascer- tain whether the argument is really preceduralist or consequentialist at root. We may content ourselves with observing that it borrows ele- ments from both modes of justification and – what matters most – that it is a suggestive defence of democracy.

4. Domestic and International Democracy

The arguments of Mill and Rawls focus on decision-making within states, and one may question their relevance to assessments of legitimacy of international organisations. Do the three general reasons to prefer democracy to other procedures of collective choice apply to the UN? I believe they do.

As far as Mill is concerned, there is no great problem. Consider, first, his welfarist defence of democracy. In international no less than intra-national relations, it is arguable that all those affected by a choice are only secure that their interests will be regarded when they are able to stand up for them. It may, of course, seem preposterous to speak of maximising social welfare in the world as a whole, but if decisions are to be taken that affect many countries, it makes perfectly good sense to say with Mill that 'in the absence of its natural defenders, the interest of the excluded is always in danger of being overlooked'.

Second, consider Mill's perfectionist justification of democracy. If it is valid in domestic contexts, it may be assumed to have some validity in the international context, too. It is arguable that political impotence always instills an attitude of general defeatism in people, and that the opportunity of participating and making one's influence felt fosters confidence and a go-ahead spirit whether it is a question of individuals participating in decision-making at the national level or governments taking part in the work of international organisations.

The international analogy of Rawls' argument is, by contrast, not clear-cut. Statements about individuals having a 'lively sense of their own worth as persons' are not easily translated into statements about states. But it takes no great effort to come up with a meaningful translation. Consider a recurring phrase of international law: 'the sovereign equality of states'. It refers to the doctrine that states should be on an equal footing as far as rights of domestic authority are concerned, however much they diverge in terms of size, wealth, power, prominence, and so on. Ian Brownlie (1973: 280) explains that the 'principal corollaries of the sovereignty and equality of states are: (1) a jurisdiction, *prima facie* exclusive, over a territory and the permanent population living there; (2) a duty of non-intervention in the area of exclusive jurisdiction of other states'. But there are other corollaries as well, such as equal rights of participation in international organisations that are empowered to take decisions that may affect all states of the world. A state that is denied such rights is to some extent under the suzerainty of states that have them.

17

Raino Malnes

This observation points towards an international analogy of Rawls' argument about self-respect. The extent to which the government and citizens of a state have a secure sense of their national sovereignty depends, among other things, on institutional features of intergovernmental organisations. Equal rights of participation in such organisations serve to foster people's sense of belonging to a sovereign political entity. This may not be indispensable for a sense of one's own worth as a person, but if we assume, with Rawls, that the latter hinges on a firm conviction that one's determinate conception of the good is worth carrying out, the sense of worth can be jeopardised among people whose political sovereignty is restricted. After all, want of full sovereignty implies that people cannot be sure of their freedom to implement domestically decided policies, which in turn means that they cannot be sure of being free to exercise their moral powers over the course of a complete life as they so decide. This argument comes nowhere near to establishing that an equal distribution of political rights in intergovernmental organisations is a *necessary* condition of self-respect anywhere, but it suggests that deviations from democracy can put self-respect at risk.

One may wonder whether these reasons to put international organisations on a democratic basis are among the reasons cited by advocates of democracy in such organisations. To what extent, in particular, do philosophical justifications of democracy resound in the political debate about reform of the UN? How do the arguments put forth above compare to what is actually said in defence of the democratic structure of the organisation?

Philosophical ideas are certainly not incongruous with views that are voiced in the political debate. Thus, we hear distinct echoes of Mill's two lines of argument. Here, for example, is an intimation of the welfarist defence of democracy:

> Multilateralism as evolved in the UN system does not imply that no decision can be taken in multilateral forums unless all the countries participate in the decision-making. What it implies is that decisions taken should be in the interest of all and that no interest-group should be left out of the decision-making process. It implies that there should be no attempt to impose preferred development strategy or set of measures applicable to all countries. Thus the policies adopted should not seek to promote sectarian interests and multilateralism should be able to take care of the interests of the countries pursuing different social economic

Democracy in the United Nations. For and Against

systems and which are at different stages of development (Saksena, 1993: 142).

If we seize on the suggestion that 'no interest-group should be left out of the decision-making process' so as to avoid that policies 'promote sectarian interests', the principle of multilateralism accords fully with the welfarist justification of universal rights of participation. But what about the disclaimer that multilateralism 'does not imply that no decisions can be taken in multilateral forums unless all the countries participate in the decision-making process'? It is reasonably seen as a concession to the need for indirect, representative democracy in some assemblies where collective choice is made. The point is that no interest-group will be left out although some countries do not participate as long as all are represented. In the same vein, Mill holds that 'all cannot, in a community exceeding a small town, participate personally in any but some very minor portions of the public business'. (Yet, it remains the case that the 'ideally best form of government' is direct democracy – the 'completely popular government' (Mill, 1861/ 1962: 74 and 57-8)).

Consider, next, a replica of Mill's perfectionist defence of democracy. It turns on the democratic structure of multilateral development agencies in particular.

> United Nations involvement in development cooperation is based on a larger concept of partnership between countries, not one of donor and client. No meaningful development can take place in the developing countries without their full involvement and control of their destinies. It is their own mobilization of sources that forms a basis for long-term development. The United Nations and its specialized agencies are organizations where the developing countries themselves play a major part. The role of these organizations in capacity-building through institutional and human resources development is increasingly important both at the global and country level (Nordic UN Project, 1991: 58-9).

There is no denying the congeniality of these considerations and Mill's preoccupation with intellectual and practical excellence. To talk about people being in control of their destinies and mobilising their own resources for development, is to conceive them as self-helping and actively engaged in the attempt to improve their lot, to recall a central element of Mill's perfectionist ideal. And the suggestion that the UN and its specialised agencies foster involvement and control by

19

Raino Malnes

allowing developing countries themselves to play a major part in development efforts, concurs well with Mill's assumption about the invigorating effect of political freedom on people's character. To conclude, both versions of Mill's suggestive defence of democracy reverberate in the ongoing controversy over the distribution of political rights in the UN.

Not surprisingly, it is hard to come by equally elaborate emulations of Rawls' argument about the benign effects of democracy on self-respect and the inherent justice of political equality. This argument has a conspicuous philosophical ring to it that presumably lends it little clout in heated public debates. Still, if it is the case, as sometimes suggested, that multilateralism 'has come to embody a procedural norm *in its own right* ... in some instances carrying with it an international legitimacy not enjoyed by other means' (Ruggie, 1993: 23), the reason may lie in the perceived justice of treating states as equals, regardless of the consequences for welfare or development of practising this procedural norm. Moreover, Rawls' allusion to the relationship between justice and the encouragement of self-respect lurks behind assertions to the effect that 'United Nations development activities are supposed to be processes of genuine cooperation between states respected as equals, for commonly accepted Charter goals' (Childers and Urquhart, 1994: 100). The relevant passage in the UN Charter invokes 'respect for the principle of equal rights and self-determination of peoples' (Article 55). Admittedly, however, this correspondence between Rawls' theory of justice and the ideology of multilateralism can only be established if we permit ourselves some poetic license in the interpretation of trite political statements.

5. Reasons to Recast the United Nations

What can be said against intergovernmental democracy of the kind practised by the UN? Several things, if we are to believe the following tirade.

> It was impossible to take issue with a principle so evidently democratic [as the one state, on vote principle]. But it produced gross distortions: microstates with a combined population of fewer than 90 million could out vote states representing the other 4,900-plus million. And it created the absurd situation in which Western governments providing three-quarters of the UN's regular budgets could be out voted by a two-thirds majority of states that together paid less than 1 percent. However, what mattered

Democracy in the United Nations. For and Against

more than either size ... or wealth was the erosion of the sense of common purpose, which relied on some degree of comparable capacity to participate. Voting democracy took precedence over working democracy, and resolutions became the principal measure of the UN's 'output' (Righter, 1995: 75).

Three lines of argument are contained in this passage. The first says that the UN is undemocratic because it distributes political rights between states without regard to the size of their populations. Many states have too much voting power and some too little. This, of course, is no all-out rejection of democracy as an architectonic principle of international organisations, but an objection to intergovernmental democracy of the kind practised by the UN. The argument suggests, in effect, that the seemingly democratic principle 'one state, one vote' is at odds with the truly democratic principle 'one person, one vote'.

The second argument to be found in the passage above objects to an equal distribution of political rights on the ground that it puts rich countries, who contribute the lion's share of what it costs to run the UN, at the mercy of many poor countries who contribute little. This situation is deemed 'absurd', and the underlying idea seems to be that relative voting power should reflect the relative size of various states' financial provisions to the budget of UN.

When it comes to the question of how political rights ought to be distributed in the UN, the preceding arguments have divergent implications. Yet, they are at one in focusing on legitimacy, suggesting that something is wrong *in principle* with the current distribution. Both are *moral* arguments in that they appeal to our notions of how much influence various states are entitled to exercise; the difference between them lies in their views of whence such entitlements derive. The first argument says that there is too little democracy in the UN, the second that there is too much.

The third argument contained in the passage quoted above is of a different species. It suggests that intergovernmental democracy as practised in the UN is a perverted form of democracy. What offends is not the egalitarian principles that underlie it, but the way it works in practice. A 'sense of common purpose' does not exist and may be unattainable among states whose capabilities are so wide apart. This is not a moral argument for abandoning the current distribution of rights, but a *pragmatic* argument for distributing rights otherwise because the current distribution, however justified in principle, does not yield a workable international organisation.

21

Raino Malnes

It will be evident from the previous paragraphs that criticism of the UN can have many faces. It is raised on different grounds and issues in different proposals for reform. We have, more specifically, become aware of three categories of reasons to recast the UN: (1) moral reasons to recast it because it is either (a) not democratic enough or (b) too democratic, and (2) pragmatic reasons to recast it because it is too democratic. I shall now look closer at all categories by elaborating the arguments invoked above and two more – the latter belonging to category (2).

6. The First Problem of Disproportionality

In a direct democracy, where every citizen is empowered to stand up and speak for himself/herself, political equality is guaranteed only if all citizens cast the same number of votes. In an indirect democracy, where people elect representatives to speak on their behalf, political equality exists only if the number of votes that representatives cast are proportional to the number of people they represent. Or, to be more precise, the voting power of each representative must be set to reflect the size of the constituency that elects him or her.

In view of this, the democratic character of the United Nations can be questioned. Think of governments as representatives of those who live within their respective jurisdictions and imagine the UN as an assortment of representative assemblies. The inhabitants of the world are not guaranteed political equality in fora like the General Assembly, as each government commands one and only one vote, but states differ widely in size. The distribution of voting power among representatives is therefore out of proportion to the size of the constituencies that stand behind them.

There are two ways of solving this problem, which may be called the *first problem of disproportionality*. (Another awaits in the next section.) Daniele Archibugi (1995: 139) writes: 'If it is assumed that governments should be the only institutions to represent their own citizens, the problem could be easily solved ... by giving weighted votes, according to population ... to the governments of each country in the General Assembly.' But Archibugi, for one, favours another, more radical solution: 'creating a parallel body to serve as the expression of individuals and not of their governments' (idem.). The model for this body is 'the European Parliament, elected by universal suffrage, and with the number of members roughly in proportion to the populations of the members countries' (idem.).

Democracy in the United Nations. For and Against

Yet, it is not obvious that the first problem of disproportionality is in need of solution. Two arguments to the contrary are conceivable. First, the problem may be set aside on the ground that it misconstrues the nature of the United Nations. The General Assembly, in particular, is not intended to be a representative body of the citizens of the world, but to be precisely what it is: an assembly of states. It is, indeed, a rarity – a direct democracy realizing political equality to perfection, in that each and every member of the relevant constituency – the international system of sovereign states – has a seat in the assembly and commands one and only one vote.

But this is no good reason to set aside the first problem of disproportionality if one assumes, as I have done above, that the justification of democracy in the UN turns ultimately on its benign consequences for individuals. Such a justification, whether couched in welfarist or perfectionist terms or rooted in concerns about self-respect, sets no store by the rights of states as such. It accords these rights importance only to the extent that they play a role akin to that of political rights which people personally enjoy. When I argued earlier that arguments in favour of domestic democracy also lend support to democratic procedures in the UN, the shift in focus from intra-national to international relations involved no corresponding shift in the primary subjects of moral concern. They remain individuals, and the fate of governments when it comes to the distribution of rights matters only insofar as it affects the fate of individuals in the three respects singled out by the general justifications of democracy.

The second reason to set aside the first problem of disproportionality is stronger. The problem may be set aside because the fate of individuals will not be affected very much by a reform of the UN aimed at achieving proportionality between the voting power of governments and the size of their constituencies. It is arguable that no appreciable addition to the benign consequences of democracy awaits such a reform, and it is therefore superfluous.

This argument seems most convincing if the reform in question consists in replacing 'one state, one vote' with weighted voting, i.e., the least radical solution to the problem of disproportionality. As far as the welfare, character or self-respect of individuals are concerned, it may be assumed to matter little whether the state to which they belong casts one vote in the General Assembly or has its vote weighted by the number of people belonging to this state.

But what about the more radical alternative: direct election of the members of the General Assembly? Does it matter with respect to welfare, character or self-respect whether people are represented by

23

their government or by people directly elected to 'serve as the expressions of individuals'? The answer depends on two things: the import that decisions taken in the UN have on people's daily lives and the extent to which governments are subject to democratic control. The more import decisions have and the less citizens of a state are allowed to influence the composition and policies of their government, the more they may gain from direct control of their representatives in the UN. Thus, democratic concerns go some way to support the idea of recasting the UN along the lines of the European Parliament. There is sometimes something to gain and never anything to lose from doing so. This implies that the rationales of democracy in the UN will be best attended to by converting its various assemblies and agencies into bodies elected by universal suffrage where the number of representatives from each state is proportional to the size of its population. Needless to say, however, this objective has a pronounced utopian ring to it.

7. The Second Problem of Disproportionality

As indicated in Section 5, it may seem objectionable that states who provide the lion's share of the UN's regular budgets can be outvoted by states who provide less than 1 per cent. Those who object to this situation think that a state's voting power should somehow reflect the size of its financial contribution to the organization. The principle 'one state, one vote' is, of course, a bar to any kind of proportionality between political influence and economic strength, and this may be called the *second problem of disproportionality*.

There is no denying the political salience of this problem. It is a central issue in the North-South conflict.

> The one-state-one-vote principle ... has given developing countries a large majority whenever they act as a bloc ... At the same time the industrialized countries have contributed most of the funding of the UN. The crisis at the UN during the 1980s have [sic] to a large extent centered on the problem of striking a balance between influence deriving from financial contributions and influence deriving from voting power (Nordic Project, 1991: 31-2).

Some steps have, indeed, been taken to prevent that the minority of rich countries who submit the bulk of financial contributions are at the mercy of the majority of poor states. First, the egalitarian system

Democracy in the United Nations. For and Against

'was somewhat modified in the 1980s with regard to budgetary issues, where committee consensus is now required to approve the budget, thereby giving an effective power of veto to any country represented in committee' (Simai, 1994: 320). Second, the 'introduction in the 1980s of "consensus voting" (where decisions are taken on the basis of formally required or informally achieved unanimity) represented a compromise between those who wished to maintain the simple majority system based on the one-country, one-vote principle and those who wanted a qualified voting system based on each country's budgetary contribution or another form of weighing' (ibid.: 321).

If one were to take further steps towards weighing votes according to financial contributions, the following reform suggests itself:

> A variety of groups have recommended that the voting on certain issues should be restructured along the lines of the system used in the Bretton Woods institutions. In those institutions, decisions are made by boards of executive directors. Each of these boards has more than 20 members, each representing a constituency – a constituency is usually a group of countries but can also be a single country, such as the United States, which by virtue of its financial contribution enjoys a veto power over many issues. Voting power is weighted according to predetermined quotas based on financial contributions; changes in quotas thus brings changes in voting power (Simai, 1994: 320).

No proposal for weighing votes in this way sits well with concerns of the kind that underlie the general rationales of democracy presented in Section 3. Consider, for example, Rawls' defence of democracy as a safeguard of self-respect. Anyone who finds this argument congenial is bound to have qualms about the Bretton Woods institutions and proposals for recasting the UN in their mould.

> They [the Bretton Woods institutions] operate in accordance with a weighted voting system which reflects the prevailing balance of powers but, above all, the structural adjustment plans of the International Monetary Fund and the World Bank are so tightly knitted into the internal workings of states that they often amount to an out-and-out form of international control. The donors determine the collective objectives, the structures of authority, decisions about prices and investments and the nature of the social compromises to be envisaged (Smouts, 1995: 232-3).

25

Raino Malnes

The second problem of disproportionality can be solved only at the cost of diluting the democratic character of the UN. To insist that the problem should be solved is tantamount to rejecting political equality as the guiding principle – or at least the sole guiding principle – of right and wrong in the distribution of political rights. The alternative conception of right and wrong finds its classic statement in Aristotle's theory of distributive justice. In Aristotle's view, justice consists in proportionality between what a person contributes to an undertaking and the benefits he receives from it. The crux of the theory comes out clearly in the following example:

> ... if X contributes one mina to a business venture while Y contributes ninety-nine, X has a just claim to only one-hundredth of the net earnings ... If X contributes less than Y to the venture but receives the same share, the Y will justifiably complain. Or if X contributes the same but receives a smaller share, X will justifiably complain (Miller, 1995: 71).

Is there room for compromise between a democrat and an adherent to the Aristotelian principle of justice? The answer is yes and no. On the one hand, a democrat who takes her cue from Mill's arguments, stressing the welfarist or perfectionist rationale of democracy, can argue that the benign effects of democracy will to some extent survive concessions to calls for proportionality. The social and psychological mechanisms posited by Mill can remain in force despite inequalities in the distribution of political rights; yet, the more a system deviates from equality, the higher the risk that it fails when it comes to maximising social welfare or breeding an active type of character among people in general. On the other hand, a democrat who starts from Rawls' argument about self-respect will categorically reject the Aristotelian principle.

8. The Problem of Viability

Irrespective of whether or not moral considerations imply that voting power in the UN should be proportional to the relative size of financial contributions, rich countries may channel their resources away from the organisation if they can buy greater influence elsewhere. Thus, however much 'one state, one vote' corresponds to the spirit of the UN, it might be an untenable principle in practice because it creates unfortunate incentives. Democracy can undermine the financial viability of the organisation.

26

Democracy in the United Nations. For and Against

The funding of the UN organizations is unlikely to be increased without a revision of the procedures relating to governance and greater accountability as regards management and agency expenditures. Already many major donors have withheld or are decreasing their contributions to several UN agencies in which they perceive to have little effective say as to how their taxpayer funded assessments are deployed (Nordic Project, 1991: 89).

Among things that tend to substantiate this assumption are '... threats against WHO and FAO, the demonition of UNCTAD, the immobilisation of ECOSOC and the inertia of the General Assembly of the United Nations' (Smouts, 1995: 239). The altered role of ECOSOC is, in particular, adduced as a major example of the marginalisation of the UN.

ECOSOC's original composition provided for in the Charter – only eighteen members ... – reflected its design as a vehicle whereby the great powers could manipulate the agenda and maintain a degree of steerage over economic-social issues ... As ECOSOC expanded in size and grew beyond the control of the U.S. and the major industrialized economies, ... the major powers lost interest in it (Rochester, 1993: 139).

Let us assume the democratic structure of the UN gives rise to this *problem of viability*. There are two things that might be done to avert it, only one of which calls for recasting the distribution of political rights in the UN. In the first place, the distribution of rights may be altered to reflect the relative size of budgetary contributions. Rochester (1993: 147) foresees growing acceptance of this strategy even on the part of those countries whose rights will shrink: 'a continued drift of the UN in the development field might make a growing number of LDCs open to a grand bargain that would replace the illusion of control over the decision-making process with greater concrete payoffs.' This is to say that developing countries may acquiesce in forsaking democracy in the UN.

In the second place, one might try to do away with the problem of viability by reducing the economic dependence of the UN on a small number of rich countries.

... if the United Nations and its affiliated bodies are to emerge as effective and vital mechanisms of international cooperation, the vulnerability of these organizations to domestic political forces in

27

Raino Malnes

one or two states must be substantially reduced. In large measures, this means reducing the financial obligations of any one
member-state to a level that is not life-threatening, should that
member-State decide to use its financial leverage against the
organization (Saksena, 1993: 206).

The latter solution seems all but unfeasible, given the uneven distribution of economic resources among states. But it does not follow
that the former solution should necessarily be implemented. It is
invoked as a response to an alleged *risk* of exodus of affluent states
from the UN, and more must be found out about this risk. How real is
it? Does political equality really breed marginalisation of the organisation? There are reasons for some scepticism on this score. Some of
the things that are taken as premonitions of exodus do not, on the face
of it, bespeak a readiness of rich countries to evacuate institutions
they cannot control. Thus, Rochester (ibid.: 138) notes that 'permanent members of the Security Council did not use their veto power to
block the 1965 Charter amendment enlarging ECOSOC to twenty-
seven seats'. To be sure, he attributes their reluctance on this score 'to
either their willingness to tolerate what appeared at the time to be a
relatively minor incremental change or, alternatively, to their disengagement from ECOSOC already by the 1960s as they had become
disillusioned over their capacity to ride herd over economic-social
problem-solving through the UN' (idem.). Yet, the latter explanation
suffers from the lack of independent evidence to support it, and the
former falls squarely on the fact that the 'doubling of ECOSOC membership to fifty-four in 1973 transpired with little debate' (idem.).

The previous remarks come nowhere near to ascertaining whether
or not a true problem of viability exists, but they clarify what kind of
problem this might be. It is pragmatic, having to do with the risk that
democracy in the UN, however legitimate, can be retained only on
pain of rendering the organisation irrelevant to international affairs.
There is, moreover, nothing wrong about moral concession spurred by
pragmatic considerations. When the best – that is, the most equitable
institution – is the enemy of the good – an economically sustainable
organisation – the best is simply unattainable. If, therefore, the risk of
marginalisation is real, egalitarians – whether right or wrong on matters of principle – will only win a Pyrrhic victory by blocking reforms
aimed at weighing voting power by the size of financial contribution.
But the reality of the risk is no foregone conclusion.

9. The Problem of Unworkable Democracy

We come to another version of the idea that the democratic structure of the UN can be retained only if one abandons every hope of having an organization whose decisions really matter to the course of developments within and among countries. The argument is that 'voting democracy' has taken precedence over 'working democracy', so that the UN's 'output' is best measured in empty resolutions.

> The problem ... was the devaluation of the UN and its agencies as places for 'harmonizing the actions of nations,' as UN conferences were transformed by the new majority into worlds of make-believe. The ringing language of an International Development Strategy, or a resolution calling for general and complete disarmament, or pledges to bring food or health or jobs to all by the year 2000 threw comforting veils over the unworkability of 'debate' between so many participants and the paucity of agreed, achievable, specific decisions (Richter, 1995: 75).

A proposed solution to what we may call the *problem of unworkable democracy* is to distribute political rights so as to reflect 'power realities'.

> In those IGOs which deal with highly technical matters placing a premium on expertise possessed by relatively few states, or which have weighted voting formulas or other arrangements that allow power realities to be reflected more accurately, there is a closer fit between the capacity to control agendas and the capacity to engage members in serious policy formulation likely to lead to the adoption of decisions having policy impacts (Rochester, 1993: 144).

How, then, are votes to be weighted to allow a more accurate reflection of power realities? One might apply the decision procedure of the Security Council wholesale to the UN, vesting great powers with a veto. Or one might, alternatively, revert to the principle of proportionality that came up in the previous two sections on the ground that political power increasingly mirrors financial strength. But before one does anything to either effect, it should be noted that the problem of unworkable democracy, like that of viability, is a pragmatic one. It is not that democracy in the UN involves illegitimacy as regards the distribution of political rights. Once again, the crux of the matter is the risk that the organisation will become marginalised if it does not

29

Raino Malnes

undergo reform, only this time marginalisation relates to its alleged incapacity of taking achievable, specific decisions that have policy impact. And once again, the risk should be taken seriously if – and only if – it is real.

10. The Problem of Inefficiency

The UN is often charged with being an inefficient organisation in the loose and colloquial sense that it is incapable of suiting actions to words. The structure of the organisation allegedly stands in the way of an efficient allocation of the resources at its disposal – an alloca-tion that makes the most out of these resources when it comes to realising goals that the UN sets itself.

It is unclear how this charge relates to the question whether or not the UN ought to retain its democratic structure. In the first place, the tendency towards decision-making by consensus is mentioned as one reason why the UN does not allocate resources efficiently. It often fails to define clear-cut goals and determine priorities. J. Martin Rochester (1993: 146) argues that the '[r]esort to consensus means that some decisions may never be taken, while those that are taken – by calculating the lowest common denominator among over 150 states – may be so amorphous as not to be worth the effort expended'. But the resort to consensus is not bound up with democracy. As indi-cated in Section 2, another mode of decision-making – majority vot-ing – is the proper embodiment of political equality as far as the translation of individual preferences into collective choice is con-cerned. Hence, inefficiency that stems from the tendency towards decision-making through consensus is not an upshot of democracy, but rather results from deviation from standard democratic proce-dures.

In the second place, inefficiency is often attributed to difficulties inherent in coordinating the activities of the large network of special-ised institutions that make up the UN. The need for coordination arises due to the disjointedness of the system of multilateral instituti-ons. It consists of a large number of special-purpose organisations that hang together in a highly decentralised framework. Critics of the system speak of fragmentation, overlapping responsibilities and redundancy. They lament the absence of a 'common controlling brain' which may initiate and oversee the implementation of what Childers and Urquhart (1994: 90-1 and 141) calls 'a holistic develop-ment process' and 'global macro-policies'. The decentralised and fragmented character of the UN system reflects its history. As the

30

Democracy in the United Nations. For and Against

Nordic Project (1991: 27-8) points out, it owes its existence to a functionalist rather than a federalist approach, the relationship between its various branches being contractual rather than hierarchical – the result of a long and highly politicised negotiation process.

Now, should decentralisation and fragmentation really be seen as structural deficiencies of the UN? Or is the large measure of agency autonomy rather valuable? And if fragmentation is a deficiency, is there a realistic prospect of integrating and streamlining the UN so as to put a more centralised system in the place of the current one? These are central questions, but for our purpose, another comes more immediately to mind: are decentralisation and fragmentation bound up with the democratic structure of the UN? The answer is not straightforward. On the one hand, the genesis of many special-purpose agencies can be traced to continuous initiatives of institution-building taken for largely symbolic purposes by developing countries whose numerical strength guarantees their success. On the other hand, the elimination of many such agencies or their incorporation into a hierarchical chain of command will not follow automatically upon reforms of decision-making procedures. The UN will have to be designed *de novo* along holistic lines, and such efforts can, but need not, go hand in hand with reforms of democratic procedures.

All in all, then, there is no straightforward relationship between the problem of inefficiency and the question whether or not the UN should retain its democratic structure. While the two issues may be interwoven in some respects, they are better dealt with one at a time. One thing, at least, is clear: improved efficiency does not follow right away upon reforms of decision-making procedures.

11. Conclusion

This article concludes with four observations. First, there are divergent and weighty reasons to prefer democratic procedures to other modes of decision-making in the UN. I dwelled long on three arguments to this effect in order to bring out virtues of democracy that often remain unstated and may therefore be taken too lightly in political debate.

Second, several objections – moral and pragmatic – have been raised against the existing constitutional structure of the UN. I argued that four such objections merit further consideration. Two are moral arguments: one the effect that the voting power of states should be proportional to the size of their populations, and another to the effect that voting power should be proportional to financial contributions.

31

Raino Malnes

Then there are two pragmatic arguments, one saying that voting power should be proportional to financial contributions in order to avoid the exodus of rich countries, the other saying that voting power should reflect power realities in order to ensure that the UN has political impact.

The two moral arguments have widely divergent implications for reform of the UN; the first deems the organisation insufficiently democratic, the other deems it too democratic. The second moral argument and the first pragmatic one have similar implications; both recommend that 'one state, one vote' be replaced with weighted voting based on budgetary contribution. It is not quite clear what the second pragmatic argument implies as far as institutional reform is concerned.

Third, it is not true, as U Thant is reported to have said in 1964, that 'it is hard to imagine another system by which the voting in the United Nations could be more equitably arranged' (Childers and Urquhart, 1994: 125). If this assertion means that any departure from 'one state, one vote' involves a departure from justice in the distribution of political rights, it begs the question raised by the two moral objections referred above. And if U Thant rather meant that it is hard to *imagine* an arrangement which might replace 'one state, one vote', his view is likewise unjustified, as proportionality between voting power and either population or contribution constitute straightforward alternatives of both simplicity and intuitive appeal.

Fourth, however, it is far from clear that any *prima facie* cogent call for reform of the UN succeeds in establishing that reform is called for, all things considered. The strongest case is presumably provided by the moral argument for proportionality between voting power and population, but this is also the argument that has the most utopian ring about it. Those who appreciate the force of the Aristotelian theory of justice will recognise a moral reason to adjust voting power to the size of budgetary contributions, but it is an open question whether this reason overrides the case for political equality. Finally, counter-democratic arguments of a pragmatic nature pose a serious challenge to political egalitarianism regardless of what appeal equality in the distribution of political rights has on purely moral grounds. But before we conclude that eqality is impracticable, we need to know more about the risk of retaining democracy in the UN.

Democracy in the United Nations. For and Against

Notes

1. One may query the characterisation of the UN as a democratic institution, and I shall later touch on two reasons for doing so, but the general drift of the argument will be that a recognisable form of inter-governmental democracy currently reigns in the UN.
2. The principle 'one state, one vote', as interpreted here, is not fully embodied in the design of every part of the UN. While it governs the work of the General Assembly, to mention only its most prominent embodiment, many specialised agencies and assemblies deviate from the principle in that they do not offer seats to all member-states. Yet, it remains true that the formal methods of decision-making in the UN are democratic to a very high degree.

References

Archibugi, Daniele, 1995, 'From the United nations to cosmopolitan democracy', in Daniele Archibugi and David Held (eds.), *Cosmopolitan Democracy*, Cambridge: Polity Press.

Barry, Brian, 1979, 'Is democracy special?', in Peter Laslett and James Fishkin (eds.), *Philosophy, Politics and Society. Fifth series*, New Haven: Yale University Press.

Brownlie, Ian, 1973, *Principles of Public International Law*, Oxford: Clarendon Press.

Childers, Erskine and Brian Urquhart, 1994, *Renewing the United Nations System*, Uppsala: Dag Hammarskjöld Foundation.

Hyland, James L., 1995, *Democratic Theory. The philosophical foundations*, Manchester: Manchester University Press.

Mill, John Stuart, 1861/1962, *Considerations on Representative Government*, South Bend, Ind: Gateway Editions.

Miller Jr., Fred D., 1995, *Nature, Justice and Rights in Aristotle's Politics*, Oxford: Clarendon Press.

Nordic UN Project., 1991, *The United Nations in Development*, Stockholm: Almqvist & Wiksell International.

Rawls, John. 1971, *A Theory of Justice*, London: Oxford University Press.

Rawls, John 1985, 'Justice as fairness: political not metaphysical', *Philosophy & Public Affairs*, Vol.14, No.3.

Rawls, John, 1987, 'The basic liberties and their priority', in S. M. McMurrin (ed.), *Liberty, Equality, and Law*, Salt Lake City: University of Utah Press.

Richter, Rosemary, 1995, *Utopia Lost. The United Nations and world order*, New York: The Twentieth Century Fund Press.

Rochester, J. Martin, 1993, *Waiting for the Millennium. The United Nations and the future of the world order*, Columbia, South Carolina: University of South Carolina Press.

Ruggie, John Gerard, 1993, 'Multilateralism: the Anatomy of an Institution', in John Gerard Ruggie (ed.), *Multilateralism Matters*, New York: Columbia University Press.

Saksena, K.P., 1993, *Reforming the United Nations*, New Delhi: Sage Publications.

Shaw, W.H., 1980, 'Intuition and moral philsophy', *American Philosophical Quarterly*, Vol. 17.

Simai, Mihaly, 1994, *The Future of Global Governance*, Washington, D.C.: United States Institute of Peace.

Smouts, Marie-Claude, 1995, 'International organizations and inequality among states', *International Social Science Journal*, Vol.144, No. 2.

Raino Malnes

Summary

Raino Malnes, 'Democracy in the United Nations. For and Against', *Forum for Development Studies*, 1996: 1, pp. 5-34.

This article concludes with four observations:

- there are divergent and weighty reasons for preferring democratic procedures to other modes of decision-making in the UN.
- there are significant moral and pragmatic objections against the existing constitutional structure of the UN.
- U Thant's statement that 'it is hard to imagine another system by which the voting in the United Nations could be more equitably arranged' (Childers and Urquhart, 1994, 125) is problematic.
- it is far from clear that any *prima facie* cogent call for reform of the UN succeeds in establishing that reform is called for, all things considered.

34

[6]

TWILIGHT OF THE U.N.

By Michael Lind

In the summer of this year, the U.N. suffered the greatest humiliation of its half-century history. Bosnian Serbs lashed U.N. peacekeepers to flag-poles, as human shields to ward off NATO air strikes, while desperate Bosnian Muslims looted the arsenals of other U.N. blue helmets for weapons to defend themselves. Then, in July, Bosnian Serbs overran the towns of Srebrenica and Zepa, "safe areas" that were not safe, protected by U.N. peacekeepers incapable of keeping the peace. The contrast between these scenes of U.N. impotence and the recent NATO air strikes against Bosnian Serb artillery positions has the clarity of allegory. In the eyes of perceptive observers the United Nations and the philosophy of collective security that it embodies have been finally and completely discredited.

This conclusion will be resisted, of course, by Wilsonian globalists in the United States. During the half century since the end of World War II, globalists have used their predominance in the U.S. foreign policy elite and the prestige media to propagate the notion that there are only two schools of thought about foreign policy in the United States—"internationalism," the philosophy of moral, educated people, and "isolationism," the philosophy of xenophobic, ignorant know-nothings. "Internationalism," moreover, is usually thought to be intimately bound up with the project of subordinating sovereign states to international organizations, of which the United Nations is the archetype. Thus the syllogism of American globalism: he who is against xenophobic isolationism must be for liberal internationalism; he who is for liberal internationalism must support the United Nations; ergo, he who opposes the United Nations must be a xenophobic isolationist. On one side, the party of enlightened Cro-Magnons standing in the U.N. plaza; on the other, the slope-headed Neanderthals with clubs raised, ready to isolate America from the world.

The choice, though, is not that simple. There are not two enduring schools of thought in American foreign policy, but three. The vague category of "international-
continued on page 28

ism" includes two different—indeed, irreconcilable—philosophies of international relations: Wilsonian globalism and national-interest realism. In the conflicts of the twentieth century, American globalists and realists have often allied against American isolationists. Even when they have cooperated, however, globalists and realists have promoted different goals for the United States.

Extreme globalists see the United States and other states as potential provinces of some supra-national confederation of the distant future. Most contemporary globalists, however, hope the human race will one day be bound together not by global bureaucracy but by global trade or global communications. Both types believe that military and economic conflict between sovereign states, like slavery, will fade away as humanity progresses to a higher level of social organization and even morality.

Realists, by contrast, view organized violence as the foundation for both world order and domestic political order. They do not necessarily believe in a balance of power among sovereign states; a realist could endorse a world empire. But that hypothetical world empire would be akin to the regional empires of the past, possessing the means, if necessary, to crush independence movements by force. In the twentieth century, American realists have included thinkers such as George Kennan and Walter Lippmann, who wanted the U.S. to prevent other great powers from exercising world dominion, and others who wanted the U.S. to exercise such dominion itself or in concert with other great powers. A great-power concert or condominium, that is, a world empire shared by several powers, is no more to be confused with a genuine collective-security system than an oligopoly with a free market.

Franklin Delano Roosevelt preferred the idea of a global great-power concert orchestrated by the United States to the equally realist but less ambitious conception of a global balance of power. FDR is often criticized for having had vague ideas about how the world should be organized after World War II. In fact his ideas were not so much vague as unpalatable to Wilsonian globalists, then and now. In 1941, he told an envoy to the Vatican that he did not wish "to reconstitute a League of Nations which, because of its size, makes for disagreement and inaction. There should be a meeting place of nations for the purpose of full discussion, but for management there seems no reason why the principle of trusteeship in private affairs should not be extended to the international field." Increasingly FDR favored a post-war great-power concert of the Big Four: the U.S., the British empire, the Soviet Union and Nationalist China (which in practice would have been an American client). The defeated Axis nations were to be disarmed, and the victors would monopolize military power. In December 1942, FDR told *The Saturday Evening Post* that small states "may as well disarm" because international security "rests with the powers who have the military force to uphold it."

FDR had in mind regional spheres of influence, not a global great-power directorate with universal interests. Each of the four great powers would "police" the lesser countries in its geographic region while contributing to joint four-power bomber squadrons, situated on international bases, which would punish countries that the great powers defined as "aggressors." According to historian Robert C. Hildebrand, "Roosevelt thought that American land forces could be sent to trouble spots in the Western hemisphere, but that only naval and air forces which were manned by voluntary enlistment, should be employed in other areas of the world" (a politically shrewd approach that would have prevented the domestic outrage over the deaths of conscripts in Vietnam). In order to minimize the resemblance of his new concert to the discredited League of Nations, FDR wanted the four-power "management" of the postwar U.N. to be located apart from the universal-membership assembly—preferably on an island base in the Azores or Hawaii.

FDR's postwar vision of regional great-power blocs, imposing peace in their own neighborhoods most of the time and collaborating only in emergencies, was shared by that other great realist, Winston Churchill. Like FDR, Churchill was more interested in winning the war than in drawing up plans for the postwar world (he brushed off a request from the Foreign Office to pay more attention to postwar planning by recommending that it "not overlook Mrs. Glass's *Cookery Book* recipe for Jugged Hare—'First catch your hare.' ") On March 21, 1943, Churchill revealed his bias toward a regional rather than global arrangement of international authority by proposing the creation of "a Council of Europe and a Council of Asia."

The alternative to the Roosevelt-Churchill view of a concert of regional great-power blocs was universalism. The war would have been fought in vain, the globalists believed, if a world legislature, universal collective security and global free trade did not replace spheres of influence and preferential trading blocs (which often were, and are, blamed inaccurately for the Depression and World War II). In the United States, the most important advocate of this view was the elderly Secretary of State Cordell Hull, a former Tennessee senator and fervent Wilsonian.

FDR, who distrusted Hull on this issue, assigned responsibility for postwar planning to Undersecretary of State Sumner Welles, who promoted FDR's idea of "the four policemen." In 1943 Hull connived to force Welles's resignation after Welles was exposed as a homosexual. With Welles gone, and FDR concentrating on winning the war, Hull pushed through his Wilsonian plan for postwar security based on a revival of the League of Nations under a different name. By the time American, British, Soviet and Chinese diplomats gathered at Dumbarton Oaks in Georgetown in the summer of 1944 to discuss postwar planning, the U.S. proposal for the United Nations envisioned an organization little different from the League, with a General Assembly, an executive council (the Security Council) and a Secretariat.

The chief difference between the old League of Nations and its new incarnation involved the veto. The League had been paralyzed by the fact that any member could veto any action; Japan, for example, had vetoed League action against its invasion of Manchuria. The Dumbarton Oaks conferees limited the veto to the permanent members. At Soviet insistence, the veto was made absolute. The debate over this provision took place against the backdrop of the Soviet Union's consolidation of control over Eastern Europe and the growing split between the USSR and the Anglo-American alliance; the U.S. conceded the absolute veto to placate the increasingly hostile Soviets.

George Kennan, the second-highest U.S. official in Moscow, predicted that the East-West division would render the U.N. still-born. He argued that the U.S. should use Soviet intransigence over the veto question as an excuse to "bury" the whole idea and instead draw a line defending Western Europe from Soviet expansion. Kennan recognized that the rivalry between the Soviet Union and the West would prevent the institutionalization of the World War II alliance and, therefore, not only doom the emerging Wilsonian U.N. but prevent any recourse to FDR's realist model as well. In fact, the most successful international security organization of the postwar period was one that was not envisioned by the diplomats at Dumbarton Oaks. It was NATO: an old-fashioned alliance that balanced the Soviet Union by restricting its geographic sphere of influence until Soviet communism was overthrown by Russian nationalists.

During the cold war, the U.N., while irrelevant to the real superpower conflict, served as an arena for rhetorical conflict instead. For much of its fifty-year history the organization was the world's leading forum for anti-American and anti-Western agitation by the Soviets and their allies. Soviet influence at the U.N. grew gradually over time. Postwar plans for continued Western-Soviet collaboration in international peacekeeping broke down immediately. The Soviets began aggressively using the

KURT WALDHEIM, BOUTROS BOUTROS-GHALI AND
JAVIER PEREZ DE CUELLAR BY VINT LAWRENCE FOR THE NEW REPUBLIC

veto in support of their client states (they failed to veto the Security Council resolution against their client North Korea only because they were boycotting the Security Council on behalf of another client, the People's Republic of China, which demanded the seat then held by Taiwan). Soviet influence in the General Assembly—initially stacked with pro-U.S. countries in Latin America—grew rapidly in the 1960s as a result of decolonization.

Self-determination, it soon became clear, was a right limited to those rebelling against European colonial masters, not against successor elites in the Third World. The U.N.'s Congo mission of 1960-1964—the most disastrous U.N. intervention until the Balkan debacle—led to the use of U.N. troops as auxiliaries for the Soviet-backed central government of the Congo, which crushed the breakaway province of Katanga. The U.N.'s bloody assistance to the central government helped usher in one of Africa's most vicious kleptocrats, Mobutu Sese Seko.

By the 1970s, the U.N. General Assembly had become the leading forum for ritualized denunciation of the West and its allies by the Soviet and Third World blocs. The majority in the General Assembly that denounced Zionism as a form of racism took no action to denounce the human rights violations routinely committed by Arab governments. As head of the Organization for African Unity, Idi Amin was rapturously applauded by the General Assembly, and the genocide in Rwanda and Burundi was ignored by the same bloc in the assembly that singled out South African apartheid. U.S. ambassadors to the United Nations Daniel Patrick Moynihan and Jeanne Kirkpatrick became political heroes for many in the U.S. simply by countering the constant stream of vilification directed at this country.

When they were not denouncing the U.S. and its allies, the U.N.'s majority bloc devised schemes for the one-way transfer of wealth from the industrial democracies to their own regimes ("the new international economic order") and for muzzling the free Western press ("the new international information order"). The Law of the Sea Treaty, which the Reagan administration wisely torpedoed, is a baroque monument of the *tiers-mondiste* era at the United Nations. The treaty would have shared the profits of Western mining of the unclaimed sea-floor with Third World countries like Chad, under the theory that the riches of the ocean were the common property of all mankind (by this theory, American fishermen should share a portion of their catch with the landlocked Swiss). International bureaucracy achieved a rococo efflorescence in the agencies enumerated in the Law of the Sea: a multinational government-owned corporation called The Enterprise, an International Tribunal for the Law of the Sea (complete with a Sea-Bed Disputes Chamber), and—not least—an International Sea-Bed Authority, with an assembly and council of thirty-six members elected by the assembly. While this elaborate machinery, by discouraging entrepreneurial companies, would have defeated its explicit purpose of developing ocean resources, it would have accomplished its unstated purpose: providing still more opportunities for employing the cronies and clients of Third World authoritarian rulers.

The corruption of the idea of international organization at the United Nations was inevitably accompanied by the corruption of its bureaucracy. Under Director-General Amadou-Mahtar M'Bow of Senegal, who served from 1974 to 1987, UNESCO became so riddled with inefficiency and so addicted to anti-Western propaganda that the U.S., the major donor, and Britain withdrew in disgust. What M'Bow did to the credibility of UNESCO, Kurt Waldheim had done earlier to that of the United Nations.

A respected European statesman with a secret Nazi past becomes Secretary-General of the United Nations and consistently shows favoritism toward the Soviet Union, which possesses the means to incriminate him—it sounds like the plot of a second-rate thriller, but it actually happened. "It is not in the interest of the United Nations to get involved in this political aspect," Secretary-General Kurt Waldheim told *The New York Times* in 1975, dismissing suggestions that the U.N. protest the mistreatment of refugees by the communist government of North Vietnam. "The criticism comes from the West exclusively.... The rest of the world seems satisfied." As Shirley Hazzard pointed out in *The Countenance of Truth: The United Nations and the Waldheim Case*, the League of Nations had similarly refused to protest the treatment of Jews in Nazi Germany after 1933. Waldheim was thwarted in his search for a third term in 1982. Although the full extent of his participation in Nazi atrocities was not revealed until 1986, Stephen Solarz and TNR had brought his Nazi past to public attention as early as 1980.

After Waldheim's tenure, the debased United Nations had nowhere to go but up. Under Javier Perez de Cuellar (1982-1992) the U.N. recovered some of its lost prestige while preserving its irrelevance to world politics.

The U.N.'s relevance seemed to grow, however, with the end of the cold war. The new policy of cooperation between the United States and Gorbachev's Soviet Union, and then Yeltsin's Russia, ended the paralysis of the Security Council. The Third World bloc in the General Assembly—which had formed in order to exploit the U.S.-Soviet rivalry—began to crumble, its superfluousness apparent after the disappearance of the communist "Second World." Most important of all, the decision by President Bush to present the war against Iraq as a U.N. police action gave a new legitimacy to the United Nations. Talk of a "new world order" stoked the hopes of old Wilsonian globalists and their young epigones.

As fate would have it, just as the U.N. was gaining new credibility the office of Secretary-General passed to a veteran Egyptian diplomat, Boutros Boutros-Ghali, with an expansive vision of the U.N.'s future. Boutros-Ghali wanted to revitalize plans, dormant since the 1940s, for a military arm of the United Nations. He and others also suggested adding "peacemaking" to the organization's "peacekeeping" duties. Franklin Delano Roosevelt and the other Allies had envisioned collective war-making against "aggressor" nations—but by the great powers. Boutros-Ghali wanted the Secretary-General itself to be a great power.

As a rule, U.N. peacekeeping operations had been limited to places where there was already peace to be kept. The new peacemaking, however, involved the injection of U.N. forces into ongoing wars in Somalia and the Balkans. In Somalia, where the modest original mission of U.N. forces to deliver humanitarian aid was expanded into impossible nation-building, the U.N. forces sought to act as kingmakers, taking military action against uncooperative factions like that of General Mohammed Farah Aidid.

In the Balkans, U.N. peacemaking also led to disaster, but by a different route. The misnamed United Nations Protection Force (UNPROFOR), instead of taking sides as U.N. forces had in Somalia, was confined to delivering supplies and defending "safe havens" for refugees. UNPROFOR soldiers were permitted to defend themselves from attack, but not to defend the civilian populations being shelled, driven from their homes, massacred and raped all around them. The representatives of "the global community" acted as passive voyeurs of atrocity, month after month, year after year. Soon the warring sides, particularly the Bosnian Serbs, learned that they need not fear the U.N.—and used the blue-helmeted observers as hostages against threatened NATO air strikes.

The fact that most of the approximately 40,000 U.N. troops in the Balkans belonged to France and Britain—states which are at once permanent members of the U.N. Security Council and major members of NATO—has provided a fascinating test of two international mechanisms for imposing order: collective security and alliance. As Security Council members, France and Britain have participated in an unwieldy and unworkable scheme whereby the five permanent members, working at cross purposes and sharing authority with the Secretary-General, supervise a "dual key" military operation in which NATO in turn shares authority with an international bureaucrat from Japan. As members of the much simpler and more efficient NATO alliance, France and Britain, after earlier misgivings, have participated in the recent bombing campaign that has succeeded in forcing Bosnian Serbs to withdraw heavy weapons from the vicinity of Sarajevo.

Whatever the outcome of the present NATO initiative, there is a general lesson in the debility of the U.N. and the relative efficacy of NATO in the Balkans. An alliance in which decisions can be swiftly made by a few military powers is far more effective than a collective-security organization burdened by too many participants and elaborate decision-making procedures—as FDR foresaw. NATO and the European Community, the two most effective international organizations of the past fifty years, are based on the principles of balance-of-power alliance and regional rather than universal organization—the very principles favored by Roosevelt and Churchill and rejected by Cordell Hull and his fellow globalists in designing the United Nations.

The virtues of the Rooseveltian approach to world order should not be exaggerated. FDR, like Churchill, was thinking only a few years ahead, not planning for half a century. Even if the U.N. had been shaped along Rooseveltian lines as a great-power concert, it would probably have been anachronistic in 1995, thanks to changes in the distribution of power and wealth in the world. The great powers of 1995 are not those of fifty years ago. If the Security Council were designed today, its membership would almost certainly include the United States, Japan, Germany, China and Russia—but not Britain or France, which have not been great powers for generations. It is absurd to have a great-power directorate that excludes half of the world's great powers.

Britain and France will not step down from the Security Council in favor of Japan and Germany. That means that any effort to bring the Security Council in line with contemporary power realities will require adding the second- and third-largest industrial democracies without expelling Britain or France (this is the Clinton administration's proposal). Most observers agree, however, that the General Assembly will never approve the accession of Japan and Germany unless permanent membership is also offered to developing countries like Brazil, India or Egypt.

The United States should oppose such reforms on the grounds that they dilute the authority of the great powers in general and of the U.S. in particular. Why should the U.S. acquiesce in the dilution of its influence in the Security Council by the excessive multiplication of members? A Security Council with seven or ten permanent members would be so unwieldy as to be useless.

Since the Security Council, flawed as it is, is the most workable branch of the U.N., a highly uncomfortable conclusion hovers precariously in the air. It is this: the U.N., bad as it is, can only be made worse by reforms like the radical enlargement of the Security Council. The U.N., then, should not be reformed. It should be abandoned.

The idea that the U.N. has outlived its usefulness is neither new nor limited to political extremists. In 1985, the U.N.'s own Joint Inspection Unit concluded a seventeen-year analysis of the organization with the prescription that the deteriorating world body be replaced by something new. The report suggests that "the time has come to begin to reflect in a serious and ambitious way on the definition of a third-generation World Organization."

Some analysts suggest a great-power concert of the sort that FDR initially envisioned. Even this might be too hopeful. While FDR's notion of the "four policemen" was more realistic than the Wilsonian dream of a world parliament, it was based on the assumption that cooperation among the wartime opponents of the Axis powers could be maintained indefinitely. In reality, of course, the wartime alliance began falling apart as soon as the defeat of Germany and Japan was certain—and the defeated Axis powers were rehabilitated and invited into the new anti-Soviet alliance. The Concert of Europe, established after the Napoleonic wars, suffered a similar fate, succumbing to internal conflicts after a few decades.

The brief life of great-power concerts is not surprising; in the absence of common enemies, great powers become rivals. Respect for agreed-upon spheres of influence can mitigate mutual suspicion but cannot eliminate it. FDR's projected great-power concert, then, was doomed to decay into two or more hostile blocs. The shrewd FDR may even have foreseen this; surely it was no accident that two of the other three great powers in his concert were clients of the U.S. (one of them, China, was not a genuine great power at all). Had FDR's four policemen fallen out among themselves, the most likely outcome would have been a U.S.-led alliance of Britain and China against the Soviet Union, similar to the American-led cold war alliance of Western Europe and a rehabilitated Japan.

A concert, it might be suggested, is a euphemism for an alliance that has outlived its purpose. Besides the difficulty of maintaining unity in the absence of a common threat, the varying rates of growth in wealth and power among countries present a challenge to the would-be framers of international concerts. In addition, even the most modest plans to institutionalize great-power concerts do not—indeed, cannot—take into account economic or political changes that cause a state to drop from the ranks of the great powers (like bankrupt Britain after 1945) or that change its regime, introducing entirely new dynamics in great-power politics (like the communist victory in China in 1949).

But, if you reject not only ambitious collective-security organizations but also institutionalized great-power concerts, you're left with the devices of traditional diplomacy that Wilsonians have vilified for almost a century:

great-power alliances against particular countries and the traditional forum for international discussion known as the embassy. Would twentieth-century history have been much different if there had been neither a League of Nations nor a United Nations—if the tools of nineteenth-century statecraft had been the only tools of twentieth-century statecraft? While counter-factual historical speculation is of limited value, one can plausibly dismiss the post-1945 myth of Wilsonian propagandists that World War II might have been avoided if the U.S. had joined the League of Nations instead of staying out. World War II was caused by the imperialism of Germany, Japan and the Soviet Union (Nazi Germany's partner in the division of Poland and the Baltics). The only thing that might have deterred the aggression of these revisionist great powers was a show of force by the two democratic great powers, the United States and Britain, neither of which was willing to risk a major war to prevent what were then speculative threats. No one familiar with the history of the period can believe that mere U.S. membership in the toothless League of Nations would have convinced the isolationist American public to support sending American troops to defend Czechoslovakia, or Manchuria in the early 1930s, to say nothing of the 1920s. If isolationists were strong enough to defeat FDR's effort to lead the U.S. into the World Court in 1935, they would hardly have allowed him to send U.S. troops to the Rhineland in 1936.

As the League of Nations, with or without the U.S., could not have prevented World War II, so the U.N. did not, and could not, prevent the cold war. Even before the Axis powers surrendered, realists like George Kennan and Walter Lippmann were predicting the likely result of division among the wartime allies—the partition of Europe between the Soviets and an Anglo-American alliance, and East-West competition elsewhere in the world. The fact that the rival powers held seats on the Security Council had no discernible effect on the origin, conduct or conclusion of the cold war. Suppose the Soviets had been present to veto the U.N. Security Council resolution authorizing the "police action" in Korea. Would the Truman administration have meekly abandoned South Korea to conquest by Stalin's client Kim Il Sung? Of course not. The U.S. would almost certainly have come to South Korea's defense under some other legalistic pretext.

I f the League and the U.N. had such little effect on the course of events in the last two worldwide conflicts, what reason is there to believe that either the U.N. or a successor organization would serve as anything more than an additional arena of conflict in a future great-power rivalry? The U.N. would not be able to prevent a cold war between China and the United States or Japan—and might well inflame tensions by permitting opportunistic states in the General Assembly to amplify the propaganda of one side or the other.

Defenders of the U.N. might concede the irrelevance of the organization when the stakes are high and the great powers are involved. But can't the U.N. play an important role in resolving disputes between lesser powers? In theory it might. In practice it seldom has. Former Israeli diplomat Abba Ebban, in a recent issue of *Foreign Affairs*, listed the negotiations to which the U.N. has been irrelevant: "The Austrian State Treaty, which prohibits Austria from possessing nuclear weapons; the termination of the Berlin blockades; the Treaty of Rome establishing the European Union; the end of Algeria's war for independence from France; the American opening to China; the conclusion of the Salt I arms limitation agreement; the Panama Canal settlement; the *Ostpolitik* agreements orchestrated by German Chancellor Willy Brandt, leading to the recognition of the European frontiers; the Rhodesia-Zimbabwe settlement; the establishment of the Conference on Security and Cooperation in Europe at Helsinki; the Egyptian-Israeli peace treaty; the Israeli-Jordanian peace treaty; the Declaration of Principles signed by Israel and the Palestine Liberation Organization; the British-Irish dialogue; the Israeli-Vatican reconciliation; the new agreements between the republics of the former Soviet Union and the Western states...." The list could be extended. To be sure, the U.N. has sometimes usefully provided its good offices for conflict resolution. But countries like Switzerland and organizations like the Conference on Security and Cooperation in Europe can do that. And peacekeeping is best undertaken by countries from the regions involved, which, though probably less neutral, do at least have an ongoing stake in the peaceful settlement of a conflict.

T he final argument for the U.N. is the one that realists find most compelling—namely, that since the cold war, and particularly during the Gulf war, the U.N. has proved a pliant instrument of American policy. Why not continue to use the blue flag to disguise the Stars and Stripes? This clever strategy, alas, founders on the built-in conflict between world opinion and the beliefs of the American public. A U.N. policy that is identified closely enough with American strategy to win lasting public support in the U.S. would be too closely identified with American strategy to win support outside of the United States. No administration can persuade elites abroad that the U.N. is not a mere tool of the U.S. while at the same time persuading Congress and the public that, well, it is. By pretending that the United States must get the permission of the Security Council before it can act, alone or with its allies, President Clinton, like President Bush, has lent the U.N. a prestige it does not deserve, without gaining a legitimacy the U.S. needs. In the future the U.S. should refrain from seeking "authorization" from this misbegotten and discredited organization.

After a half-century of doing little harm and less good, the U.N. should be allowed to wither away into irrelevance, as it was doing before President Bush unwisely, if temporarily, revived its importance. George Kennan was right when he declared that the U.N. should have been buried stillborn at the Dumbarton Oaks conference. If the United Nations did not exist, it would be necessary *not* to invent it. •

[7]
Saving the U.N.

A Challenge to the Next Secretary-General

Jesse Helms

Not long ago, while accompanying U.N. Ambassador Madeleine Albright to an appearance in North Carolina, I was asked by a reporter whether the United States should withdraw from the United Nations. It was a valid question, to which I responded, "Not yet."

As it currently operates, the United Nations does not deserve continued American support. Its bureaucracy is proliferating, its costs are spiraling, and its mission is constantly expanding beyond its mandate—and beyond its capabilities. Worse, with the steady growth in the size and scope of its activities, the United Nations is being transformed from an institution of sovereign nations into a quasi-sovereign entity in itself. That transformation represents an obvious threat to U.S. national interests. Worst of all, it is a transformation that is being funded principally by American taxpayers. The United States contributes more than $3.5 billion every year to the U.N. system as a whole, making it the most generous benefactor of this power-hungry and dysfunctional organization.[1]

This situation is untenable. The United Nations needs to be radically overhauled. Yet Secretary-General Boutros Boutros-Ghali has ignored multiple warnings and stubbornly resisted reform that gets down to fundamentals. On the contrary, Boutros-Ghali has pursued a well-publicized campaign of what he calls U.N. "empowerment." He has protected the bloated bureaucracy, and the number and nature of peacekeeping operations has vastly expanded under his tenure. He has pressed for the establishment of a standing U.N. army and the power to collect direct U.N. taxes.

Now, with U.N. "empowerment" as his platform, Boutros-Ghali has reversed his pledge to serve a single term and is seeking a second one. The Clinton administration has belatedly announced its opposition but has failed to nominate or even search for a replacement, just as it has been complacent in the face of his presumptions to power.

Rather than Boutros-Ghali's "empowerment," the United Nations needs a stark reassessment of its mission and its man-

---

SENATOR JESSE HELMS (R-N.C.) is Chairman of the U.S. Senate Committee on Foreign Relations.

Saving the U.N.

date. The next secretary-general must help develop a bold plan to cut back the overgrown bureaucracy and limit its activities, then muster the political will and leadership to implement it. The reformist zeal of the next secretary-general will in all likelihood determine whether or not the United Nations survives into the next century. For if such a plan is not put forward and implemented, the next U.N. secretary-general could—and should—be the last.

BACK TO BASICS

The United Nations was originally created to help nation-states facilitate the peaceful resolution of international disputes. However, the United Nations has moved from facilitating diplomacy among nation-states to supplanting them altogether. The international elites running the United Nations look at the idea of the nation-state with disdain; they consider it a discredited notion of the past that has been superseded by the idea of the United Nations. In their view, the interests of nation-states are parochial and should give way to global interests. Nation-states, they believe, should recognize the primacy of these global interests and accede to the United Nations' sovereignty to pursue them.

Boutros-Ghali has said as much. In his 1992 *Agenda for Peace*, he declared his view that the sovereignty of nations is an outdated concept: "The time of absolute and exclusive sovereignty . . . has passed. Its theory was never matched by reality. It is the task of leaders of states to understand this." In other words, U.N. member nations, including the United States, should be willing to abandon claims of "absolute and exclusive sovereignty" and empower the United Nations by ceding it a measure of their sovereignty. They should give the secretary-general a standing army and the power to collect taxes—functions that legitimately rest only with sovereign states.

Such thinking is in step with the nearly global movement toward greater centralization of political power in the hands of elites at the expense of individuals and their local representatives. In the United States, Europe, and elsewhere, political leaders are belatedly recognizing the destructive effects of central bureaucracies and state-controlled economic activities and are fighting uphill battles to bring these into check. They are finding, however, that once established, bureaucracies (along with the goodies they dispense) are nearly impossible to dismantle. As the millennium approaches, this virus of centralization is spreading to the global level, and the United Nations is its carrier. Just as massive bureaucracies have taken hold in Europe and the United States, the U.N. bureaucracy has established a foothold on the international stage.

This process must be stopped. In the United States, Congress has begun a

---

[1]There is no single entry in the U.S. budget for contributions to the United Nations. Ambassador Charles Lichenstein, a former U.S. representative to the United Nations, has calculated the $3.5 billion figure thus: the U.S. share of the U.N. administrative budget, $298 million; the U.S. share of the U.N. peacekeeping budget, $1.2 billion; U.S. contributions to all U.N. specialized agencies, $368 million, excluding capital contributions to the World Bank and the International Monetary Fund; the value of goods and services the United States voluntarily contributes toward U.N. peacekeeping and the U.N. system as a whole, $1.7 billion to $2.0 billion. In recent years Congress has withheld a fraction of this amount as pressure for U.N. reform.

Jesse Helms

process of devolution, taking power away from the federal government and returning it to the states. This must be replicated at the international level. Reining in the U.N. bureaucracy goes hand in hand with Congress' domestic agenda of devolution. U.N. reform is about much more than saving money. It is about preventing unelected bureaucrats from acquiring ever-greater powers at the expense of elected national leaders. It is about restoring the legitimacy of the nation-state.

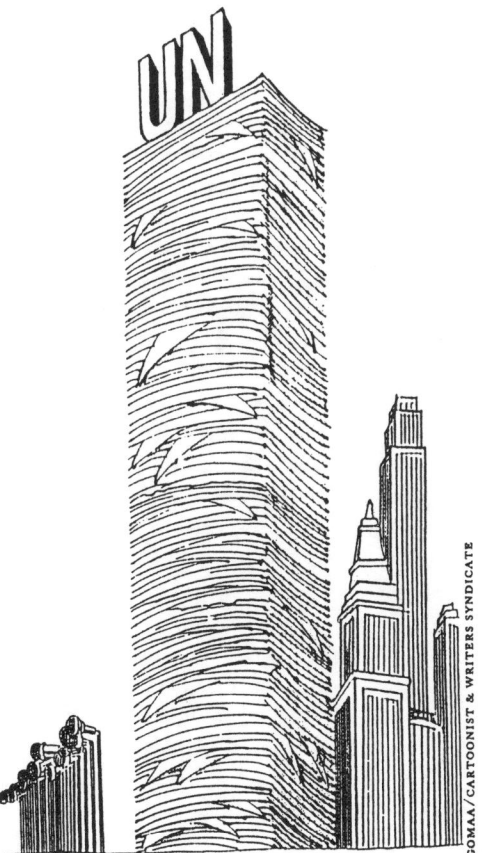

THE BIG PICTURE

How big is the problem? According to the latest official U.N. statistics, the organization is home to 53,744 bureaucrats, comprising the Secretariat bureaucracy and those of the diverse specialized agencies. Hard as it is to believe, some advocates of the United Nations argue that it is not big enough. In his book *Divided It Stands: Can the United Nations Work?* James Holtje writes that "when one considers that . . . [the United Nations is] expected to meet the needs of 5.5 billion people worldwide, the number begins to look small." It is not the job of the United Nations to "meet the needs" of 5.5 billion people—that is the job of nation-states.

But the U.N. bureaucracy mistakenly believes that caring for the needs of all the world's people is exactly its job. From the bureaucracy's vantage point, there are no international, national, or even local problems—all problems are U.N. problems. Thus we have the recent Habitat II conference in Istanbul, where the United Nations spent millions of dollars to address the concerns of cities—an issue that legitimately should be handled by local or national governments.

So what is wrong with the United Nations lending a helping hand on these matters? The issue is not just sticking the U.N.'s nose where it does not belong. By making every problem its problem, the United Nations often makes the situation worse. Instead of helping nation-states solve problems, the United Nations does the exact opposite—it creates a disincentive for states to handle problems that are their responsibility to resolve. When every local or regional problem becomes a global one, the buck stops nowhere. Solving it becomes

Saving the U.N.

everyone's responsibility, and thus no one's responsibility.

The war in Bosnia is a perfect example. Dealing with Serbia's illegal aggression and genocide in Bosnia was the responsibility of the European powers, in whose region the crisis lay, and of the United States, which considers itself a European power. But instead of addressing the issue themselves, the Clinton administration and our European allies pushed responsibility for handling this problem onto the United Nations, which accepted a mission it was incapable of fulfilling. The U.N. peacekeeping operation became an excuse for inaction by the Europeans and Americans, who used the United Nations to pretend they were addressing the problem. As a result, thousands upon thousands of innocent civilians died, while the United Nations, through a combination of impotence and negligence, did nothing to stop the genocide.

The United Nations also complicates matters by giving states with no interest in a particular problem an excuse to meddle without putting anything concrete on the table. Countries that have no natural interest in an issue suddenly want to get involved, and the United Nations gives them the legitimacy to do so without cash or constructive contributions. What, for example, are countries like Togo, Zaire, Panama, or Ireland, or China for that matter, prepared to contribute to bringing about Middle East peace? They have no legitimate role in the peace process, save that which their U.N. membership (and in some cases seats on the Security Council) gives them. What the United Nations ends up doing is giving lots of countries a seat at the table who bring nothing to the table.

By making every issue a global issue, the United Nations is attempting to create a world that does not exist. A United Nations that can recognize its limitations—helping sovereign states work together where appropriate and staying out of issues where it has no legitimate role—is worth keeping; a United Nations that insists on imposing its utopian vision on states begs for dismantlement.

GOALS OF REFORM

Successful reform would achieve the twin goals of arresting U.N. encroachment on the sovereignty of nation-states while harnessing a dramatically downsized United Nations to help sovereign nations cope with some cross-border problems. Such reform must begin by replacing Boutros Boutros-Ghali with a new secretary-general who will go in on day one with a daring agenda to reduce bureaucracy, limit missions, and refine objectives.

Second, there must be at least a 50 percent cut in the entire U.N. bureaucracy. The Clinton administration has made the standard of reform a "zero-growth" budget. This is inadequate. So long as this bureaucracy remains in place, it will continue to find new missions to justify its existence.

Third, there must be a termination of unnecessary committees and conferences. Since its founding as an organization of five organs in 1945, literally hundreds of U.N. agencies, commissions, committees, and subcommittees have proliferated. Today, for example, the United Nations includes a Committee on Peaceful Uses of Outer Space, which counts among its crowning achievements the passage of a resolution calling upon sovereign nations to report all contacts with extraterrestrial beings directly to the secretary-general.

Jesse Helms

In addition to massive, wasteful conferences like the Beijing women's summit and Habitat II, the United Nations continually sponsors workshops, expert consultations, technical consultations, and panel discussions, last year some 7,000 in Geneva alone. Most of these can be terminated at a savings of millions of dollars.

Fourth, the U.N. budgeting process must be radically overhauled. Budgets for U.N. voluntary organizations are currently amassed through a bidding process, where nation-states must make capital investments prior to involvement in specific issues or projects under U.N. auspices. This should be the model for the entire U.N. budgeting system. The secretary-general currently has a budget of roughly $1 billion to pay for the activities of the Security Council, General Assembly, Economic and Social Council, Secretariat, and International Court of Justice, plus the administrative costs of numerous relief, development, and humanitarian agencies. This budget is voted on by the General Assembly, where the United States has no veto, and where every nation—whether democratic or dictatorial, no matter how much or how little it contributes to the United Nations—has an equal vote.

This system should be abolished. Instead, the secretary-general should be limited to a bare-bones budget of some $250 million, and U.N. activities should be funded on a voluntary basis. This would essentially subject all U.N. programs to a market test. Each country would decide the value of programs by how much they were willing to pay. Those programs that are really vital will continue to receive support, while those championed only by the bureaucracy will die of malnutrition.

Some bargaining will naturally result (country X would say to country Y, you help with my project, and I'll help with yours). But this system would dramatically cut down on waste, eliminate freeloaders, empower member states vis-à-vis the bureaucracy in budget determinations, give states a voice in the U.N. commensurate with their willingness to pay while forcing wealthier countries to pay more, and give the United States and others the option not to fund or participate in programs they are currently compelled to support, but which they feel directly violate their interests.

Lastly, peacekeeping must be overhauled. Peacekeeping is the United Nations' fastest-growing industry. In 1988, the total cost of U.N. peacekeeping operations around the world was just $230 million; in 1994, it was $3.6 billion. Of that, the United States was directly assessed nearly $1.2 billion, plus additional in-kind contributions of personnel, equipment, and other support totaling roughly $1.7 billion (all of which was skimmed off the U.S. defense budget).

Not only have costs proliferated—so has the scope of peacekeeping missions. Prior to 1990, most peacekeeping missions were just that: monitoring truces, policing cease-fires, and serving as a buffer between parties. Today, however, peacekeeping has evolved into a term without meaning. It is used to justify all sorts of U.N. activities—everything from holding elections to feeding hungry people to nation-building. As the system now works, the United States has two choices: go along with a proposed peacekeeping operation and pay 31.7 percent of the cost, or veto the mission, which we do not like to do. The system should permit a third

Saving the U.N.

option: allow the United States to let missions go forward without U.S. funding or participation. If others in the world want to undertake nation-building operations, there is no reason the United States should discourage them—so long as American taxpayers do not have to pay for a third of it. This would allow the United Nations to serve the purpose it was designed for: helping sovereign states coordinate collective action where the will for such action exists. And, of course, Security Council members would retain the authority to veto missions they deem wholly inappropriate.

FORCING CHANGE

The time has come for the United States to deliver an ultimatum: Either the United Nations reforms, quickly and dramatically, or the United States will end its participation. For too long, the Clinton administration has paid lip service to the idea of U.N. reform, without imposing any real costs for U.N. failure to do so. I am convinced that without the threat of American withdrawal, nothing will change. Withholding U.S. contributions has not worked. In 1986, Congress passed the Kassebaum-Solomon bill, which said to the United Nations in clear and unmistakable terms, reform or die. That did not work. A decade later, the United Nations has neither reformed nor died. The time has come for it to do one or the other.

Legislation has been introduced in the House of Representatives by Rep. Joe Scarborough (R-Fla.) for the United States to withdraw from the United Nations and replace it with a league of democracies. This idea has merit. If the United Nations is not clearly on the path of real reform well before the year 2000,

then I believe the United States should withdraw. We must not enter the new millennium with the current U.N. structure in place. The United States has a responsibility to lay out what is wrong with the United Nations, what the benchmarks for adequate reform are, and what steps we are willing to take if those benchmarks are not met by a date certain.

The United Nations will certainly resist any and all reform—particularly many of the smaller and less developed members, which benefit from the current system and gain influence by selling their sovereignty to the organization. That is why the next secretary-general has an enormous job to do: his or her mandate will be nothing less than to save the United Nations from itself, prove that it is not impervious to reform, and show that it can be downsized, brought under control, and harnessed to contribute to the security needs of the 21st century. This is a gargantuan, and perhaps impossible, task. But if it cannot be done, then the United Nations is not worth saving. And if it is not done, I, for one, will be leading the charge for U.S. withdrawal. ❷

[8]

The limits of international organization: systematic failure in the management of international relations
Giulio M. Gallarotti

"Nothing in excess" is the warning inscribed on the Temple of Apollo at Delphi and echoed in the literature and mythology of ancient Greece. According to the logic of excesses, too much of anything—even a "good" thing—can be detrimental. This lesson appears to be as relevant for international organization (IO) as it is for other social contexts.[1] Just as poorly managed or "bad" IO can be harmful, "good" IO in excess can have adverse effects.

On the one hand, IO can be counterproductive when management is of the wrong kind or is executed poorly. Critics of the Food and Agriculture Organization, for example, argue that the institution's administration supports a model of agricultural development that is antithetical to private sector growth and therefore inhibits general economic development in Third World countries.[2] On the other hand, excessive IO can be bad even when the management is apparently good. Some have argued, for example, that the provision of abundant liquidity to debt-ridden nations creates a moral hazard in that it gives debtors fewer incentives to promote the economic changes

An earlier version of this article was presented at a seminar sponsored by the Program on International Politics, Economics, and Security (PIPES) at the University of Chicago in May 1989. I gratefully acknowledge the comments of the seminar participants as well as the suggestions of Riccardo Fiorito, Jeff Frieden, Robert Jervis, Stephen Krasner, Duncan Snidal, and the anonymous referees of *International Organization*.

1. Throughout this article, I refer to international organization (IO) and international organizations (IOs) in keeping with the following distinction made in the mainstream IO literature: the term "IO" refers to both the formal (institutionalized) and informal (noninstitutionalized) processes of management, while the term "IOs" refers to the institutions engaged in the formal processes of management. IOs are thus a subset of IO. See J. Martin Rochester, "The Rise and Fall of International Organization as a Field of Study," *International Organization* 40 (Autumn 1986), pp. 753–75; Friedrich Kratochwil and John Gerard Ruggie, "International Organization: A State of the Art on an Art of the State," *International Organization* 40 (Autumn 1986), pp. 777–813; and Inis Claude, *Swords into Plowshares*, 4th ed. (Random House: New York, 1984).

2. See Roger Brooks, "Africa Is Starving and the United Nations Shares the Blame," *Backgrounder* 480, Heritage Foundation, January 1986.

International Organization 45, 2, Spring 1991

that would make them less dependent on foreign lending.[3] In this case, as with the recent case of savings and loans bailouts in the United States, it appears that safety has it price. Similarly, food aid, as traditionally practiced with respect to less developed countries (LDCs), has often served to compound problems of hunger and food dependence because of its "disincentive effects" on domestic food production.[4] And, finally, too much IO may be undesirable if it is costly and has no appreciable effect on international relations.

While IO can be said to "fail" in any of these ways, it is most antithetical to orderly international relations when its failures make international problems worse or generate new problems—that is, when IO itself is a destabilizing force in world politics. In his first annual report on the work of the United Nations (UN), Secretary-General Javier Pérez de Cuéllar sensitized the international community to such destabilizing failings in the multilateral management of interdependence by citing the adverse effects that UN resolutions can have on international security and by admitting that the misuse of the UN has contributed to the global problems facing the organization.[5] In light of the failures of IO, bureaucrats and scholars alike need to reassess the role of multilateral management and its effects on international relations within and across issue-areas. Or, more formally, they need to take into account the limitations of IO when considering the optimal scope and level of multilateral management.[6]

As Friedrich Kratochwil, John Ruggie, and J. Martin Rochester have argued, recent scholarship has increasingly strayed from the study of IO as distinct from world politics and has relinquished much in terms of the normative foundations of the traditional literature on IO. A result is that the processes of IO and international relations have been conflated in a way that makes the specific assessment of managerial processes and institutions more difficult. Furthermore, the analytic modes and conclusions generated by recent work have insufficiently addressed issues that contribute to social engineering at the level of multilateral management; that is, they have provided little food for consumption on the part of international bureaucrats

3. General arguments on moral hazard in the international monetary system have most recently been made by Charles Kindleberger in *The International Economic Order* (Cambridge, Mass.: MIT Press, 1988).

4. See Raymond Hopkins, "Reform in the International Food Aid Regime: The Role of Consensual Knowledge," *International Organization* (forthcoming).

5. Javier Pérez de Cuéllar, *Report of the Secretary-General on the Work of the Organization*, no. A/37/1 (New York: United Nations, 1982).

6. The scope of IO is defined by neofunctionalists as the range of issue-specific tasks involved in a managerial scheme, while the level is defined as the "central institutional capacity to handle a particular [issue-specific] task." See Joseph Nye, "Comparing Common Markets: A Revised Neo-Functionalist Model," in Leon Lindberg and Stuart Scheingold, eds., *Regional Integration* (Cambridge, Mass.: Harvard University Press, 1971), p. 201; and Philippe Schmitter, "Three Neo-Functional Hypotheses About Integration," *International Organization* 13 (Winter 1969), p. 162.

and national policymakers.[7] Historically, the study of IO has to a large extent been coterminous with the study of the structures, roles, and goals of international institutions. The traditional literature has placed much emphasis on institutional origins and developments in the frameworks and objectives of specific organizations and has paid considerably less attention to the effects of these organizations on international relations. Moreover, when scholars have assessed the effects, they have tended to offer a rather benign vision in which the process of multilateral management is characterized as invariably contributing to the stabilization of relations among nations and in which the limitations of management are ignored or downplayed. Thus, traditional contributions to the IO literature have been heavy on the positive side (the stabilizing outcomes of management) and light on the negative side (the failures of management), whereas the recent contributions have been instrumental in addressing the negative side but have taken a somewhat restricted approach to organizational failure. To use Kratochwil and Ruggie's analogy, while the doctor has more recently stopped visiting the patient altogether, the doctor has traditionally visited the patient without systematically diagnosing illness.[8]

In addressing these limitations in the IO literature, this article presents a typology of the systematic (inherent rather than mistake-related) failures of IO. In doing so, it brings the processes and institutions of multilateral management back into focus as phenomena that are sui generis and therefore distinct from the underlying relations they oversee. While its conclusions about the nature of overmanaged relations and the partial solutions that it offers are intended to serve as potential normative guidelines, its focus on the effects of IO is intended to complement the traditional focus on the roles, goals, and structures of international institutions. Thus, by emphasizing the destabilizing effects of IO and presenting a less benign view of the management of international relations, the article makes a contribution toward filling in the negative side of the managerial ledger. In Kratochwil and Ruggie's terms, the present enterprise once more attends to the patient, but with an emphasis on diagnosing illness.

The article begins with a discussion of the managerial approach to IO and the recent revisionist scholarship. It then confronts the managerial vision of IO by offering a more general theoretical approach to understanding the destabilizing effects of multilateral management than has commonly been taken in the critical IO literature. In presenting a typology of systematic failures, it seeks to bridge the gaps in our understanding of why many different institutions and managerial schemes fail. That IO has virtues and can

7. See Kratochwil and Ruggie, "International Organization"; and Rochester, "The Rise and Fall of International Organization as a Field of Study." Regarding the normative rationale for the study of IO, see also John Gerard Ruggie, "The United States and the United Nations: Toward a New Realism." *International Organization* 39 (Spring 1985), p. 345.

8. Kratochwil and Ruggie, "International Organization."

have a positive impact on international relations is not denied. Nevertheless, the article concludes that it is often in the best interest of stable international relations in and across issue-areas to be regulated by IOs that are limited in their scope or level of management. In addressing the general issue of IO failure, rather than addressing why a particular institution or managerial scheme fails, the analysis is thus intended to serve both as a focal point for understanding critical approaches to the study of IO and as an alternative rationale for eliminating the excesses of multilateral management.[9]

The managerial approach to international organization

Traditional IO scholars have tended to take a rather benign view of the process of multilateral management.[10] For these scholars, IO at best provides the necessary management dictated by the growing complexity of interdependence within and between issue-areas. At worst, this management appears as a benign redundancy in functions insofar as it is targeted to bring about order that is already existent in some set of relations. The tone of the literature has for the most part been uncritical both on a systematic and a general level,[11] and any explicit or implicit critiques that have been offered have tended to be issue- or case-specific.[12]

9. Regime analysts and neoliberal institutionalists have argued that big government can be redundant and is unnecessary when limited forms of management are sufficient. But the viability of smaller government is all the more compelling when big government is subject to organizational failure.

10. As Conybeare notes, "Federalists, functionalists, neofunctionalists, and pluralists all agree as to the inherent desirability of world government. . . . It would not be a caricature to infer from the modern IO literature that the world needs more supranational authority to manage interdependence, public goods, and externalities in general." See John Conybeare, "International Organization and the Theory of Property Rights," *International Organization* 34 (Summer 1980), pp. 307–8. The critical focus of my article, however, is not the modern IO literature per se but, rather, those strands in the IO and international relations literature that uncritically profess the need for the extensive multilateral management of international relations and support the benign view of IO from which this prescription stems. Some strands are not overtly managerial in orientation. And in many cases, as pointed out in my article, the logics of their arguments are not antithetical to the usefulness and importance of limited forms of IO.

11. Critiques of domestic government have been far more prevalent and systematic than have general critiques of IO. For a typical example of the former, see Richard Rose, "What If Anything Is Wrong with Big Government?" *Journal of Public Policy* 1 (February 1981), pp. 5–36. An inquiry into the reasons for this neglect would be speculative. Perhaps it is simply a matter of specialization, with IO failing to attract the attention of erstwhile critics of big domestic government who are specialized in domestic political issues. Or perhaps the unpleasant effects of IO are not felt on an individual level to the same extent as the unpleasant effects of domestic government are. IOs do not conscript or tax individuals, for example. Their dues come from nations rather than individuals; their laws do not affect individuals directly; and there is no authoritarian appropriation of human capital and resources. Quite simply, there are fewer reasons for individuals to be angry with IO.

12. There are, of course, exceptions to this trend, notably in the classic literature on integration and interdependence. But even these show limitations. Early neofunctionalists argued that IO can have adverse effects on specific interest groups and elites within nations but have said

According to the functionalists, the growth of technology, the awareness of its possible adverse and positive effects, and the spread and intensification of demands for higher material welfare place increasing pressure on nations to seek what Ernst Haas calls "managerial leadership" at the multilateral level.[13] The growth of "common activities and interests across nations," argues David Mitrany, requires a concomitant growth in the "common administrative agencies" that manage interdependence. International government must grow so that it remains "co-extensive with international activities." Hence, like the activities it must oversee, international management must itself become "all-embracing and all-pervasive."[14] In this sense, the growth of IO is consistent with the ongoing evolution and greater centralization of functions in human society. For a working peace system, notes Mitrany, nations must collectively "take over and coordinate activities hitherto controlled by the nation state, just as the state increasingly has to take over activities which until now have been carried on by local bodies."[15] Thus, the goal of global security is reached through a process involving "a sufficient addition" of managerial functions, which together "would create increasingly deep and wide strata of peace."[16]

For neofunctionalists, the causal link between technological and welfare problems on the one hand and international management on the other is mediated by interest groups and elites, but the vision of IO is quite similar. For them, the process of spillover is the forcing variable.[17] As the pressures for integration spread laterally and vertically, the level and scope of international management must be expanded. According to Haas, the problems of international security, economic development, and technological and scientific interdependence require an "upgrading of common interests" among nations, which is only realizable within "the framework of supranational institutions." The intensification of this "upgrading" in turn requires "continuing supranational activity."[18] For Ruggie, the impact of scientific and technological interdependence on international relations necessitates a "col-

---

much less about the adverse impact on international order and relations between nations. Haas noted that organizations can sometimes fail to achieve their goals, but he did not go on to explore the possible negative consequences of this failure. Morse noted that IO can adversely affect nations by limiting their autonomy, but he did not pursue the manifold consequences of this constraint. See Ernst Haas, *The Uniting of Europe* (Stanford, Calif.: Stanford University Press, 1958), pp. 288–89; Ernst Haas, *Beyond the Nation-State* (Stanford, Calif.: Stanford University Press, 1964), p. 126; and Edward Morse, *Modernization and the Transformation of International Relations* (New York: Free Press, 1966), p. 100.

13. Haas, *Beyond the Nation-State*, p. 31.
14. David Mitrany, *A Working Peace System* (Chicago: Quadrangle, 1966), pp. 52, 63, and 97.
15. Ibid., p. 37.
16. Ibid., p. 98.
17. Of course, even for neofunctionalists, spillover is not a given. Integration has been conceptualized as positive, stagnant, and negative.
18. See Haas, *Beyond the Nation-State*, p. 459; and Haas, *The Uniting of Europe*, p. 287.

lective response'' based on ''mutual accountability.''[19] The collective response will be manifest in ''greater amounts of joint services and joint production, and a greater degree of joint regulation of national activities.''[20] For Eugene Skolnikoff, this interdependence requires that nation-states ''accept a degree of international regulation and control over their nominally domestic activities that goes well beyond the situation today.''[21]

Traditional scholarship in the field of modernization and interdependence has similarly argued that the greater interpenetration of the social and economic spheres that occurs with industrialization necessitates a collective approach to the specific needs of nations. Edward Morse, for example, indicates that ''modernization is accompanied by increased levels and types of interdependences among societies, which require . . . a high level of cooperation.''[22] This interdependence, adds Morse, makes ''international coordination of policies highly desirable'' because the ''attainment of basic domestic policy goals'' can no longer be realized through independent actions.[23]

These managerialist strands in the traditional literature on IO and interdependence have numerous counterparts in the general literature on international relations. For example, Seyom Brown and Larry Fabian would address the problem of the global commons with a comprehensive oceans authority, an international scientific commission on global resources and ecologies, a global weather and climate organization, and an outer space project agency.[24] Stanley Hoffmann, in mainstream fashion, argues that the future of the world order will depend on the growth of IO as a means of integrating inherently conflictual interests and realizing joint gains both in a political and an economic context.[25] In explicating the assumptions underlying Hoffmann's vision, Richard Cooper states that ''where trust is not complete, some form of international organization may be helpful to police the rules and supervise the imposition of penalties for violations of the rules.''[26] Regarding the international political economy, the exhortations of Fred Block and Robert Solomon are characteristic. According to Block, ''If

19. John Gerard Ruggie, ''International Responses to Technology: Concepts and Trends,'' *International Organization* 29 (Summer 1975), pp. 557–83.

20. John Gerard Ruggie, ''Collective Goods and Future International Collaboration,'' *American Political Science Review* 66 (September 1972), p. 875.

21. Eugene Skolnikoff, *The International Imperatives of Technology* (Berkeley, Calif.: Institute of International Studies, 1972), p. 153.

22. Morse, *Modernization and the Transformation of International Relations*, p. 80.

23. Ibid., pp. 85 and 93.

24. Seyom Brown and Larry L. Fabian, ''Toward Mutual Accountability in Nonterrestrial Realms,'' *International Organization* 29 (Summer 1975), pp. 887–92.

25. Stanley Hoffmann, ''International Organization and the International System,'' in Leland Goodrich and David Kay, eds., *International Organization: Politics and Process* (Madison: University of Wisconsin Press, 1973).

26. Richard Cooper, ''Prolegomena to the Choice of an International Monetary System,'' in C. Fred Bergsten and Lawrence Krause, eds., *World Politics and International Economics* (Washington, D.C.: Brookings Institution, 1975), p. 83.

our goal is the improvement of human welfare, this requires subordinating market forces to conscious human will.''[27] Similarly, Solomon argues, ''Co-operation and joint management are still necessary. . . . The international system has tended to follow the evolution that has occurred within individual countries. One of the major lessons learned in the thirties . . . is that the pursuit of self-interest by individual entities in an economy does not nec-essarily bring about optimal results for the economy as a whole.''[28] The high point of this managerialism in international economic relations is embodied in Irving Friedman's call for a ''new Bretton Woods.''[29]

More recently, scholars have taken a much more systematically critical approach to IO and have qualified the traditional arguments about the need for extensive supranational government. IO has been attacked both from the right and the left and both in theoretical and nontheoretical treatises. On the right, the ongoing studies of the Heritage Foundation have expounded a vision of IO, especially as manifest in the UN, as a destabilizing force in international politics because of the inflammatory way it mediates disputes (for example, supporting the positions of guerrilla groups) and the way it generates other managerial failures.[30] A frequent critique of the UN is that it perpetuates underdevelopment because its approach is biased against mar-ket solutions. In exploring the ways in which UN management in and across issue-areas makes the world a more ''dangerous place,'' Abraham Yeselson and Anthony Gaglione have adopted the same destabilizing view of the UN.[31] Others have underscored that deficiencies in the managerial structures of the UN are the sources of its failure and inefficiencies.[32]

27. Fred Block, *The Origins of International Economic Disorder* (Berkeley: University of California Press, 1977), p. 225.

28. Robert Solomon, *The International Monetary System, 1945–1981* (New York: Harper & Row, 1982), p. 379.

29. See Irving Friedman, *Toward World Prosperity: Reshaping the World Money System* (Lexington, Mass.: Lexington Books, 1987), p. 273. More specifically, Friedman calls for a resuscitation of the managerial instruments of the Bretton Woods system, which he and many others believed were strong. Actually, the system reflected rather weak management in con-figuring monetary relations. Relations carried on in a rather haphazard way with occasional multilateral (G-10) and unilateral (U.S.) management.

30. In its journal, *Backgrounder*, the Heritage Foundation has published numerous studies that take a critical view of UN operations. See especially Juliana Geran Pilon, ''The Center on Transnational Corporations: How the UN Injures Poor Nations,'' *Backgrounder* 608, Oc-tober 1987; Thomas Gulick, ''How the U.N. Aids Marxist Guerrilla Groups,'' *Backgrounder* 177, April 1982; and Brooks, ''Africa Is Starving and the United Nations Shares the Blame.'' See also Charles Lichenstein et al., *The United Nations: Its Problems and What to Do About Them* (Washington, D.C.: Heritage Foundation, 1986); and Burton Yale Pines, ed., *A World Without a U.N.* (Washington, D.C.: Heritage Foundation, 1984).

31. See the following works by Abraham Yeselson and Anthony Gaglione: ''The Use of the United Nations in World Politics,'' in Steven Spiegel, ed., *At Issue: Politics in the World Arena* (New York: St. Martin's Press, 1981), pp. 392–99; and *A Dangerous Place* (New York: Viking Press, 1974).

32. Robert Jackson argued, for example, that the UN could be likened to ''some prehistoric monster, incapable of intelligently controlling itself. This is not because it lacks intelligent and capable officials, but because it is so organized that managerial direction is impossible.'' Jackson is quoted in ''The United Nations Agencies: A Case for Emergency Treatment,'' *Economist*,

The leftist literature on IO has tended to take the same pejorative view of supranational structures of governance that leftists normally take of domestic structures of governance: both types institutionalize class hegemony. In the case of supranational government, leftists speak of economic (capitalist) classes of nations as well as social classes. Most of their studies are targeted at specific organizations, while some contributions exhibit a general orientation.[33]

On a more theoretical level, proponents of rational choice and public choice approaches to IO have argued that supranational management is either redundant or the source of inefficiencies in the relations between nations. John Conybeare argues that the market can sufficiently allocate goods and address international problems in relations that do not exhibit high levels of publicness and that supranational management in these relations is unnecessary and would only replicate the outcomes generated by less centralized schemes.[34] John Ruggie and Per Magnus Wijkman marshal similar, albeit more restrictive, arguments.[35] Roland Vaubel sees the collusive and redistributive nature of international collaboration as inherently imposing welfare losses on the international system in general as well as on specific subnational groups.[36]

At the same time that scholars have taken a more critical approach to IO, they have also taken a more decentralized approach to the possibilities for order and cooperation in international politics. This trend is particularly evident in the regime and neoliberal institutionalist contributions to the international relations literature. According to proponents of the decentralized approach, institutions serve as facilitators of cooperation. This suggests positive, rather than critical, sentiments about the role of IO. Where they

---

2 December 1989, p. 23. See also David Pitt, "Power in the UN Superbureaucracy: A Modern Byzantium," and Johan Galtung, "A Typology of United Nations Organizations," in David Pitt and Thomas Weiss, eds., *The Nature of United Nations Bureaucracies* (Boulder, Colo.: Westview Press, 1986), pp. 23–38 and 59–83, respectively.

33. See, for example, Ismail Abdalla, "The Inadequacy and Loss of Legitimacy of the International Monetary Fund," *Development*, vol. 22, Society for International Development, Rome, 1980, pp. 46–65; Cheryl Payer, *The Debt Trap: The International Monetary Fund and the Third World* (New York: Monthly Review Press, 1974); Cheryl Payer, *The World Bank: A Critical Analysis* (New York: Monthly Review Press, 1982); Teresa Hayter, *Aid as Imperialism* (New York: Penguin, 1974); Robert Cox, "The Crisis in World Order and the Problem of International Organization in the 1980s," *International Journal* 35 (Spring 1980), pp. 370–95; Robert Cox, "Labor and Hegemony," *International Organization* 31 (Summer 1977), pp. 385–424; and Peter Cocks, "Toward a Marxist Theory of European Integration," *International Organization* 34 (Winter 1980), pp. 1–40.

34. Conybeare, "International Organization and the Theory of Property Rights."

35. Ruggie and Wijkman, however, are generally positive about the functions of IO with respect to confronting issues of publicness. See Ruggie, "Collective Goods and Future International Collaboration"; and Per Magnus Wijkman, "Managing the Global Commons," *International Organization* 36 (Summer 1982), pp. 511–36.

36. Roland Vaubel, "A Public Choice Approach to International Organization," *Public Choice*, vol. 51, 1986, pp. 39–57.

depart from traditional managerial approaches, however, is in their sensitivity to the conditionality of management. Since relations in and across issue-areas are seen as heterogeneous, rather than homogeneous, the requirements for regulation will vary in scope and level. Some constellations of relations (particularly those with preexisting norms about appropriate policies) will require institutions only to reduce the organization or transaction costs of cooperation, while others will require more careful and extensive regulation.[37]

Although the revisionist literature on IO offers a valuable counterbalance to the traditional managerial view, it nevertheless exhibits limitations in its identification and analysis of organizational failure. The existing critical literature, for example, tends to be disproportionately specific in its targets and orientation. While the work of Yeselson and Gaglione, the studies from the Heritage Foundation, and the literature on bureaucratic failure are specifically targeted toward the UN, the leftist literature has commonly focused on the World Bank, International Monetary Fund, and the UN. Even the work that appears to be of a more general orientation is still quite restricted and sometimes insufficiently systematic in its identification of IO failure. General leftist critiques, such as those of Robert Cox and Teresa Hayter,[38] are fundamentally restricted to the adverse distributional effects of the institutionalization of First World hegemony and are much less concerned with instabilities within classes of nations. Conybeare, Wijkman, and Ruggie are more concerned with why IO might be unnecessary than with how and why IO fails. Although Vaubel is both general and systematic in the identification of IO failure, he is more concerned with the inefficiencies than with the destabilizing effects of IO, and his analysis of inefficiencies is restricted to those generated by the collusive and redistributional nature of IO.

In contrast to the revisionist literature, which offers a restricted critique

37. See the contributions to *International Organization*, vol. 36, Spring 1982, a special issue on regimes. See also Robert Keohane, *After Hegemony* (Princeton, N.J.: Princeton University Press, 1984); and Robert Keohane and Joseph Nye, *Power and Interdependence*, 2d ed. (Glenview, Ill.: Scott, Foresman, 1985). For surveys of the literature on regimes and neoliberal institutionalism, see Stephan Haggard and Beth Simmons, "Theories of International Regimes," *International Organization* 41 (Summer 1987), pp. 491–517; and Joseph Grieco, "Anarchy and the Limits of Cooperation: A Realist Critique of the Newest Liberal Institutionalism," *International Organization* 42 (Summer 1988), pp. 485–507. For other works that are concerned with less managed relations, see Conybeare, "International Organization and the Theory of Property Rights"; Wijkman, "Managing the Global Commons"; W. Max Corden, "The Logic of the International Monetary Non-System," in Fritz Machlup, Gerhard Fels, and Hubertus Muller-Groeling, eds., *Reflections on a Troubled World Economy: Essays in Honor of Herbert Giersch* (New York: St. Martin's Press, 1983), pp. 59–74; W. Max Corden, "Fiscal Policies, Current Accounts and Real Exchange Rates: In Search of a Logic of International Policy Coordination," *Weltwirtschaftliches*, vol. 122, 1986, pp. 423–38; Roland Vaubel, "Coordination or Competition Among National Macro-Economic Policies?" in Machlup, Fels, and Muller-Groeling, *Reflections on a Troubled World Economy*, pp. 3–28; and Martin Feldstein, "Let the Market Decide," *Economist*, 3 December 1988, pp. 21–24.

38. See Cox, "The Crisis in World Order and the Problem of International Organization in the 1980s"; Cox, "Labor and Hegemony"; and Hayter, *Aid as Imperialism*.

of how IO can fail *within* specific issues and institutions, the following general critique of managerialism offers a typology of systematic organizational failure and suggests how IO can fail *across* issues and institutions.

Critique of managerialism: the systematic failure of international organization

The failures of IO, defined here as the negative or destabilizing effects of IO on international relations, can generally be classified as either unsystematic or systematic. While unsystematic failures are related to mistakes or malfunctions in the management of international problems, systematic failures are considered inherent in or endemic to IO.[39] There is no systematic reason, for example, why one supranational organization would make the mistake of overmanaging relations while another would not; why one would be too extreme in demanding adherence to its rules while another would not; or, more generally, why one institution or managerial scheme would be characterized by or result in poor management. While unsystematic failures are stochastic and have a chaotic distribution, systematic failures are determined by bias (by the roles, functions, and goals of IO, which naturally encourage failure) and have an identifiable pattern in their distribution. IO can fail systematically in four general ways that will be summarized briefly here and discussed in detail below.

First, IO can be destabilizing when it attempts to manage complex, tightly coupled systems. Because management of complex relations and issues is one of the goals of IO and because these complex systems are difficult to understand and therefore manage successfully, there are inherent possibilities for destabilizing management.[40]

Second, IO can be destabilizing when its solutions discourage nations from pursuing more substantive or long-term resolutions to international problems, including disputes, or when it serves as a substitute for responsible

---

39. This dual categorization of managerial failure is somewhat problematic because what some consider to be random mistakes of bureaucrats may be seen by others as problems endemic to the bureaucratic structure of IO. Similarly, depending on the manner in which malfunction is defined, IO can be said to malfunction systematically or unsystematically. Further research may improve upon the present typology by suggesting a better differentiation both between and within categories. Nevertheless, the dual categorization is useful as a first-cut approach to the general failures in the process of international management. The alternative presentation of undifferentiated failure does little service to the normative and theoretical importance of distinguishing endemic failures from failures that are more stochastic.

A point that deserves emphasis here is that while IO is by nature prone to several types of failure, it does not follow that IO will invariably fail. A simple analogy is that the inherent or genetic predisposition to diabetes does not always manifest itself as disease.

40. The mainstream IO literature has tended to offer a "complexity" rationale for supranational government: as interdependence becomes more complex and issue-spaces increase in density, the need for IO to orchestrate relations also increases.

domestic or foreign policy. It is in the nature of supranational management to generate solutions and resolutions (output) that address international problems, and to the extent that it does so, it reduces the incentives of nations to come up with better alternatives.

Third, IO can actually intensify international disputes under several circumstances: when it is used as a weapon of confrontational statecraft, when it encourages confrontational solutions to problems, when it creates roadblocks to the resolution of disputes, when it is a source of destabilizing linkages, when it is a source of predatory or confrontational collusion, and when it takes sides in international disputes. In the case of international disputes, IO is by nature prone to confer greater legitimacy to one of the competing factions and thereby shift the moral balance of power. Like other instruments of international competition, then, IO support can be an important instrument of statecraft. This was evident, for example, in President Kennedy's desire to have the approval of the Organization of American States before confronting the Soviets on the issue of Cuban missiles.

Fourth, IO can have destabilizing effects when it is a source of moral hazard. Supranational management is fundamentally based on the desire to prevent crises or provide insurance against the untoward effects of potential crises that emanate from a state's irresponsible behavior. In mitigating the adverse consequences of this behavior, IO reduces the incentives for the state to eliminate the underlying problem, which is the behavior itself.

The principal element of failure in the first category—the management of complex, tightly coupled systems—is essentially a technical one: cooperation yields inferior outcomes because of the technical difficulty of managing systems of relations and issues. The principal element of failure in the other three categories—which we can label adverse substitution, dispute intensification, and moral hazard—is not technical: a technical basis for cooperation does exist, but the political systems act in ways that can make cooperation destabilizing.

Managing complex, tightly coupled systems

Organizations often attempt to manage systems whose problems emanate from what Charles Perrow would refer to as the "complex, tightly coupled" nature of international relations.[41] As with any cybernetic system, the feedback effects of the systems of relations and issues are complicated and frequently unpredictable. And as with any complex chaotic system, these systems commonly exhibit what the chaos literature refers to as a sensitivity

41. The subject of complex, tightly coupled systems is formally explored by Perrow in the context of accidents which involve nuclear power, chemicals, and other high-risk technology and which have adverse effects on the various ecosystems. See Charles Perrow, *Normal Accidents: Living with High-Risk Technologies* (New York: Basic Books, 1984).

to initial conditions, or a macrosensitivity to developments in microconditions. Their complexity and unpredictability are thus a function of the numerous and highly conditional connections between the many variables that contribute to systemic outcomes. As Perrow argues, the complexity of tightly coupled systems makes it impossible to manage them in a way that avoids periodic crises; in other words, catastrophes and accidents are "normal" and are the rule rather than the exception.[42] Not only is IO incapable of avoiding crises, but IO often causes or exacerbates problems by offering solutions that have unpredictable and destabilizing effects.[43]

Contributors to the literature on interdependence, most notably Robert Keohane, Joseph Nye, Richard Cooper, and James Rosenau, have essentially viewed the international political economy as a system with the characteristics noted above and have emphasized the complexity of interdependence emanating from process and issue density (the tight linkage of different economic processes and international issues).[44] The literature has also highlighted the similarities between international political economic relations and the processes of systems theory and chaotic systems: feedback processes are numerous and not fully understood; knowledge about principal relationships is often indirect and inferred; there are strong systemic sensitivities to small changes in underlying conditions; policies and actions are connected in complicated constellations of relations; and simple policy initiatives often generate unintended systemic outcomes.[45]

The period from the mid-1940s to the present, for example, has been one in which international monetary schemes have been aimed at instituting and managing equilibrium exchange rates while economists have continually argued that we do not know what equilibrium rates are *ex ante* and can only know what they are *ex post*. Gottfried Haberler's statement on the equilibrium value of the dollar is representative: "With all due respect, it must be said that we, economists as well as ministers and other officials, simply do

---

42. Ibid.
43. Economists of the Austrian school have underscored this point with respect to attempts at managing complex systems such as markets and prices. Centrally planned economies, contrived price systems, and other forms of control, they argue, produce outcomes that are Pareto-inferior and significantly worse than those effected by a market approach. See, for example, the following works of Friedrich Hayek: *Individualism and Economic Order* (Chicago: University of Chicago Press, 1948), p. 187; *Law, Legislation and Liberty*, vol. 1 (Chicago: University of Chicago Press, 1973), pp. 48–50; and *The Fatal Conceit: The Errors of Socialism* (Chicago: University of Chicago Press, 1988), pp. 85–88.
44. See Keohane and Nye, *Power and Interdependence*; Richard Cooper, *The Economics of Interdependence* (New York: Council on Foreign Relations, 1968); and James Rosenau, *Turbulence in World Politics* (Princeton, N.J.: Princeton University Press, 1990).
45. For a discussion of systems in international politics, see Robert Jervis, "Systems Theories and International Politics," in Paul Gordon Lauren, ed., *Diplomacy* (New York: Free Press, 1979), pp. 212–43. On the subject of chaos, see James Gleick, *Chaos: Making a New Science* (New York: Penguin, 1988).

not know enough to say what the equilibrium exchange rate is."[46] More generally, William Branson argues that the management of exchange rates is well beyond our state-of-the-art methods of rational organization: "With this range of disagreement on [the] economic analysis [of exchange rate equilibration], how are negotiators to reach agreement? The topic is one for the National Science Foundation, not a new Bretton Woods."[47]

There is significant disagreement on a plethora of issues, not the least of which is what economic indicators are a valid reflection of equilibrium. It has been commonly thought that equilibrium is determined on the real side: the exchange rate at which trade balance is encouraged. But even this long-honored wisdom has been called to task both on the empirical and the theoretical side. The U.S. deficit with Japan budged only hesitantly from 1985 to 1987, while the dollar lost 50 percent of its value vis-à-vis the yen during this period. Japanese retail pricing trends showed that the yen-denominated prices of American goods in Japan had remained almost unchanged. Evidently, Japanese importers enjoyed the greater purchasing power of the yen but did not pass the savings on to the Japanese consumer. Hence, the decline of the dollar vis-à-vis the yen effected a redistribution from American exporters and Japanese consumers to Japanese middlemen, rather than eradicating the bilateral trade imbalance. Outcomes such as this have led some economists, Jagdish Bhagwati and Robert Mundell included, to question whether any continued change in the dollar will significantly dent the trade deficit. They argue that because competition in industrial markets is imperfect and because nations can counteract an appreciating currency with more protectionism so as to maintain a trade balance, exchange rates are rendered less effective in adjusting trade flows.[48]

Attempts at managing the complex, tightly coupled system of political economic relations have created a trail of international events that leads to the graveyard of misguided social engineering. The Louvre Accord of February 1987, for example, was negotiated and adopted by the G-7 for the purpose of strengthening the dollar following its sharp two-year decline. It ended up having just the opposite effect in the short run because it was perceived by the market as a signal of the dollar's weakness rather than its strength, and the resulting run against the dollar brought it well below the Louvre target. The G-7 did not anticipate this negative feedback. As it turned out, the intervention scheme initiated a destabilizing self-fulfilling prophecy: investors, thinking that the fall of the dollar was not yet over, took actions that brought such an outcome about. If the accord had not been concluded,

46. Gottfried Haberler, "The International Monetary System: Recent Developments in Perspective," *Aussenwirtschaft,* vol. 42, 1987, p. 379.

47. William Branson, "The Coordination of Exchange Rate Policy," *Brookings Papers on Economic Activity,* no. 1, 1986, p. 176.

48. See "Passing the Buck," *Economist,* 11 February 1989.

the market might have been prepared to accept the Louvre target. In other words, less management might have brought about a better outcome.[49]

Unfortunately, the Louvre story does not end there. U.S. authorities tried to counteract the destabilizing speculation by raising interest rates and demanding specific macroeconomic policies from other G-7 nations. These actions destabilized financial markets during the period in which the Dow speculative balloon was most inflated. The October crash followed. Haberler bluntly called the Louvre Accord "a striking example of how *not* to fix exchange rates."[50] Pointing out the dangers involved when less than well conceived and organized schemes are used in an attempt to manage complex systems, he argued that "the foreign exchange market, like the stock market, is a very delicate and sensitive mechanism that does not lend itself to continued manipulation by a loosely organized group of nations."[51] In this case, the solution made the problem worse because the approach in counteracting the adverse effects of the initial managerial miscalculation was essentially a linear solution to a tightly coupled problem. Decision makers proceeded as if moods in domestic financial markets were isolated from international policy initiatives. They erroneously assumed that policies geared toward the defense of the dollar in international forums would not feed back adversely onto perceptions of prevailing trends in domestic financial markets.[52]

The Louvre Accord was presented to the public in a way that reduced rather than increased confidence. "The accord," noted one journalist, "focused attention on the weakest elements of cooperation. Every time [James] Baker spoke he offered a new version of what the accord was expected to

---

49. For discussions of the Louvre Accord and its results, see "The Show Can't Go On," *Economist*, 21 November 1987, pp. 13–14; Haberler, "The International Monetary System"; and Yoichi Funabashi, *Managing the Dollar: From the Plaza to the Louvre* (Washington, D.C.: Institute for International Economics, 1988), pp. 187–92. It is not clear that defenders of the Louvre Accord are correct in attributing positive externalities to it. The argument that even misaligned rates stabilize trade flows assumes that volatility following the imposition of the exchange rate was less than it would have been if the rate had been allowed to converge by market forces. There is more evidence to suggest that, on the contrary, the imposition and market reaction to it created more volatility than would have otherwise occurred.

50. Haberler, "The International Monetary System," p. 383.

51. Ibid., p. 381.

52. The direction of swings in response to changes or developments in financial markets, currency markets, and other complex systems is difficult to predict, as are the perceptions of investors and other actors. This brings up the question of whether these systems would be more manageable if actors knew more about the manifold effects of different policies. In some situations, even supposedly prudent policies may have adverse effects if actors in systems are adapting to rather than passively accepting policy. (Such adaptive microbehavior typifies complex, tightly coupled systems.) But this could also be the case when actors are cognitively rigid. For example, given a particular nervous state in currency markets, investors may interpret any kind of interest rate policy (even the most prudent one based on knowledge of how currency markets work) as signaling trouble for a currency. An interest rate hike to prop up the dollar, for instance, may be perceived as a signal that the dollar is weak. A rate decrease may be perceived as a signal that U.S. policymakers will let the dollar slip. And finally, no change in the interest rate may be taken as indecision on the part of U.S. policymakers and perceived as a sign of trouble.

achieve, and of the roles of the various partner countries' policies. . . . Each
new disagreement with West Germany . . . made the Louvre agreement seem
hollower than it really was."[53] The April 1987 communiqué of the G-7 on
the state of monetary relations was an especially glaring failure. Baker called
the April meeting of the G-7 "quite successful," but the communiqué failed
to make mention of any specific intentions to support the dollar. A strong-
dollar statement was necessary to get the dollar out of its bearish state, given
that trade figures for February were announced in mid-April and were dismal,
causing dismay among dollar holders. James Vick of Manufactures Hanover
Trust reflected how the market in general perceived this omission and what
it indicated about G-7 intentions when he commented that the G-7 "seemed
to be accepting the current level of the dollar and the downward direction."[54]
This perception was reinforced by the G-7's approval of the new rate around
"the most current levels."[55] These outcomes were further manifestations of
the strong sensitivity of macroproperties to apparently small developments
in international markets.

The managerial pattern continued under James Brady. In November 1988,
following the election of Bush, the dollar declined sharply. This was met
with intervention both by the Federal Reserve Bank and by several European
central banks to keep the dollar from declining to a new low against the yen.
On the second day of this intervention, Brady made the following statement:
"Markets go up and down. I really don't worry about it very much."[56] The
statement was perceived as signaling that the commitment of the G-7 was
not strong and that the dollar might fall even more. This led to foreign
exchange trading that ran counter to the intervention of the central banks
(and, of course, imposed losses on the banks that had purchased depreciating
dollars). One New York banker said, "We've had Brady make several statements early on that have not given the indication that he recognizes or has
the judgment to understand that he has a profound impact on the marketplace."[57]

In the cases of both the Louvre Accord and the Plaza Accord that preceded
it, policymakers failed to accept a fundamental lesson: exchange rates are
not imposed upon markets; they are determined by markets.[58] In 1987, after
Louvre ranges were established and defended, Baker and the G-7 kept talking
(telling the market what equilibrium rates were), but the market failed to

53. See "Almighty Fallen," *Economist,* 14 November 1987, p. 11.
54. James Vick, quoted by Funabashi in *Managing the Dollar,* pp. 189–90.
55. Funabashi, *Managing the Dollar.*
56. See "Brady Avoiding Critics as Group of 7 Gathers," *The New York Times,* 2 February
1989, p. D-1.
57. Ibid.
58. Rates were imposed much more frequently under the Bretton Woods regime in the 1950s
and 1960s than they have been recently. But the size and the sensitivity of exchange markets
were considerably smaller than they are now. And, in fact, the destabilizing money flows of
the 1960s attest to the difficulty of sustaining rates misaligned with respect to the market rate.

listen.[59] In both cases, agreements were ill-conceived because they were attempting to coordinate unstable policy preferences.[60] The outcome was that the nations violated both the letter and the spirit of the agreements, thereby producing bad relations among the participants.[61] These events served to further destabilize financial markets. Investors perceived that the G-7 was unable to impose order on the international monetary system, and this in turn fed back domestically and internationally to create pessimistic investment moods.[62] Decision makers continued to remain out of touch with the complete range of reactions to the nature and effectiveness of their multilateral policy initiatives. And these reactions continued to be principal sources of instability in financial and exchange markets.[63] In sum, for reasons relating to the limitations of regulating complex economic systems, the Louvre and Plaza schemes produced some cures that ended up being worse than the diseases.

The outcomes of policy coordination in recent years are quite consistent with recent theoretical findings regarding the pursuit of collective macroeconomic management in the face of disagreements on the fundamental workings of national and international economies and in the face of limited information. Jeffrey Frankel and Katherine Rockett, for example, have shown that in cases in which nations disagree on the macroeconomic models (an expected situation, since macroeconomies themselves constitute complex, tightly coupled systems) and in which the effects of economic policy are not perfectly predictable because of the complexity and tightly coupled nature of causal relations in economic markets, macroeconomic policy coordination

59. See Funabashi, *Managing the Dollar*, p. 190.

60. See ibid., pp. 28, 29, 34, 205–7, 214, and 228.

61. Especially distasteful were the U.S. threats: the U.S. insistence on a high yen rate; the constant changes in negotiating forums, including at various times the G-2, G-3, G-5, and G-7; and the attempts at unilateral management of the dollar rate, characterized by "talking the dollar down" when others refused to accommodate the downward trend of the dollar. See ibid., pp. 53, 182, 217, and 235–37.

62. An alternative interpretation of the Louvre and Plaza episodes might be that large and responsive capital markets, in combination with high mobility in the flow of goods and capital, have made it necessary for advanced industrial nations to coordinate their economic policies and that failures are a small price to pay for the necessary long-term management. No one would argue that coordination is not valuable or that the market can resolve all economic problems. But the Louvre and Plaza agreements generated significant instabilities that most likely would not have occurred in the absence of intervention. Even the necessity of long-term coordination is no excuse for generating market instability that has short-run effects and might in turn generate lasting effects. Given the adverse outcomes of linear managerial approaches taken in the past, it seems all the more inexcusable to turn to them again and again in the present.

63. For reasons relating to the unpredictability of international reactions to the construction of international managerial schemes in the area of the debt problem, Kindleberger appears cautious about the desirability of even attempting to develop collaborative multilateral solutions. If such attempts were made and fail, he argues, and if this generated pessimistic forecasts about developments in the issue-area, the problem is likely to be exacerbated. See Kindleberger, *The International Economic Order*, p. 12.

can almost as likely be bad for nations in terms of welfare as it can be good. In some instances, constellations of uncoordinated unilateral actions would be preferable to cooperation, especially the type of cooperation founded on linear approaches to market interventions.[64]

These findings point to a common failure for any organization solving problems in complex, tightly coupled systems. There are side effects, many of which are unforeseeable. With respect to the problem of economic development, Paul Streeten notes that "scientists may have a solution to every problem, but development has a problem for every solution."[65] Such conditions put a premium on nonlinear solutions to the problem of poverty. "Single actions which look technically correct," he emphasizes, "can be worse than useless if they are not accompanied by supplementary actions."[66] This is especially true about managing nations toward higher levels of economic development. According to Streeten, "Development is . . . like a jigsaw puzzle. To be effective, several actions must be taken together, in the right order; rural education has to be combined with the improvement of rural amenities or the educated will leave the countryside. The new seeds have to be applied with fertilizers and water at the right time; there must be extension services and roads to get the food to the markets."[67]

Adverse substitution

Nations are continually faced with difficult domestic and international problems whose resolution entails political, economic, or social costs. Although IO can alleviate short-run pressures and provide nations with an "out" from more costly solutions, doing so can be counterproductive in that it discourages nations from seeking more substantive and longer-term resolutions to their problems. To the extent that time horizons are short (which is certainly the case in domestic political systems where political survival is predicated on short-run imperatives) and national leaders are sensitive to differing domestic costs of competing solutions to domestic and international problems (which also appears to be the case), nations will be encouraged to substitute less costly and less viable multilateral schemes for more costly and substantive solutions.[68] The problem of substitution is systematic be-

64. See Jeffrey Frankel and Katherine Rockett, "International Macroeconomic Policy Coordination when Policymakers Do Not Agree on the Model," *American Economic Review* 78 (June 1988), pp. 318–40.

65. Paul Streeten, "The United Nations: Unhappy Family," in Pitt and Weiss, *The Nature of United Nations Bureaucracies*, p. 187.

66. Ibid.

67. Ibid.

68. It has, in fact, been a long-standing characteristic of international economic summitry for leaders to use international agreements to reduce some of their domestic economic and political costs. See Robert Putnam and Nicholas Bayne, *Hanging Together: Cooperation and Conflict in the Seven-Power Summits* (Cambridge, Mass.: Harvard University Press, 1987); and Vaubel, "A Public Choice Approach to International Organization."

cause it is in the nature of IO to solve international and domestic problems. But because of jurisdictional limitations and the bargaining process, the solutions offered by IO are often not substantive.

Secretary-General Pérez de Cuéllar pointed to one of the largest and most prevalent drawbacks of IO substitution in his first annual report on the work of the UN: "There is a tendency in the United Nations for governments to act as though the passage of a resolution absolved them from further responsibility for the subject in question."[69] Particularly in the case of dispute resolution, the tendency has been to offer flimsy "patch job" solutions that reduce the incentives for disputants to find a better way of resolving their differences. This point was emphasized by James Stegenga in his 1968 assessment of the effects of UN efforts in Cyprus: "UNFICYP [the UN Peacekeeping Force in Cyprus] is vulnerable to the charge that it may very well be inhibiting settlement. By helping to protect and thus consolidate the abnormal status quo and by reducing the sense of urgency felt by both sides, the Force may actually be making a negative contribution to what in the long run is the most important requirement, a viable political order."[70] Yeselson and Gaglione have questioned whether the UN Emergency Force (UNEF) efforts in the Middle East have had the same negative effect by providing an inferior substitute for a viable resolution in the region.[71]

Patrick Garrity has recently argued that UN peacekeeping efforts have allowed U.S. policymakers to postpone crucial security decisions that eventually must be made.[72] In this regard, we must question the effects of the UN in general and its solutions in particular on the relations between the superpowers. In the UN General Assembly, majorities have always favored one superpower over the other, offering more support to the United States in the early decades and more to the Soviet Union in later decades. Historically, the UN has provided a rational incentive for one of the superpowers to try to marshall collective support for a UN resolution against the other and thereby extract some desired action or policy through collective confrontation rather than through direct negotiations that would involve some form of concessions or quid pro quos. In short, given the tendency of UN members to automatically side with the appropriate superpower, collective confrontation via the UN has provided the superpowers with a relatively costless substitute for more costly direct bargaining. As Yeselson and Gaglione have observed, "Victories at the [UN] were cheap. They involved no

69. Pérez de Cuéllar, *Report of the Secretary-General on the Work of the Organization*, p. 3.

70. James Stegenga, *The United Nations Force in Cyprus* (Columbus: Ohio State University Press, 1968), p. 186.

71. See Yeselson and Gaglione, *A Dangerous Place*.

72. See Patrick Garrity, "The United Nations and Peacekeeping," in Pines, *A World Without a U.N.*, p. 155. See also Ruggie's response to Garrity, "The United States and the United Nations," p. 348.

cost in blood and very little in treasure, and they lent an aura of righteousness to . . . foreign policy."[73]

For the same or similar reasons, the diversion of important issues or controversies into IOs that are mainly ceremonial forums (which many are) is often counterproductive. Nations may perceive negotiations in international forums either as viable substitutes for more fruitful negotiations at the bilateral or multilateral level or as viable substitutes for real cooperation.[74] The result, as Robert Rothstein pointed out in his study of the UN Conference on Trade and Development (UNCTAD) is that "the situation may get worse simply because living with an increasingly ceremonial process is much easier than trying to reform it. . . . And, of course, the most obvious consequences ought to be reemphasized: problems get worse, time is lost, and resources are expended."[75]

Critics of IO-orchestrated development schemes argue that the public funds of IOs are inferior substitutes for private investments in the Third World and tend to generate negative externalities. IO funds are often tied to government planning that is antithetical to market processes. Because regulated economies are less attractive to international investors, this has the effect of driving out private investment, which is especially bad given the link between economic development and the growth of the private sector in underdeveloped nations.[76] Roger Brooks makes a related point with respect to agricultural development in Africa.[77]

Food aid, as commonly practiced before the 1970s, has encouraged LDCs to substitute food transfers for domestic agricultural production. This has served to reduce agricultural self-sufficiency in the long run through disincentive effects on local food production, thus compounding the problems of hunger and food dependence in underdeveloped nations. Moreover, food

---

73. Yeselson and Gaglione. *A Dangerous Place*, p. 178.

74. The literature on collective action suggests that sometimes it is to the benefit of a community as a whole for people not to have private substitutes for poor public services. The fact that they have such substitutes encourages them to exit (vote with their feet) rather than use their voice to contribute to the improvement of those services. For example, communities will be less likely to have poor public schools if private schools do not exist. This will encourage the wealthiest and most educated to contribute to collective action schemes designed to improve the school system. Collective action is enhanced to the extent that private substitutes for public goods are unavailable. One could make an interesting argument about the destabilizing nature of the "star wars" program on these grounds. The program's technology would increase the risk of war among the superpowers because if developed (even by both) it would represent a substitute for further cooperation. For a discussion about the adverse effects of private substitutes, see Russell Hardin. *Collective Action* (Baltimore, Md.: Johns Hopkins University Press, 1982), p. 73.

75. Robert Rothstein, *Global Bargaining: UNCTAD and the Quest for a New International Economic Order* (Princeton, N.J.: Princeton University Press, 1979), p. 20.

76. Data show that development is positively correlated with the growth of the private sector. See Edward Erickson and Daniel Sumner. "The U.N. and Economic Development," in Pines, *A World Without a U.N.*, pp. 1–22. See also Pilon, "The Center on Transnational Corporations."

77. See Brooks, "Africa Is Starving and the United Nations Shares the Blame."

transfers have disrupted local systems of food production and distribution, generated extremely expensive subsidy programs, created administrative nightmares, and encouraged corruption.[78]

It is interesting, Inis Claude notes, that some of the fiercest enemies of IO have been strong proponents of world government (federalists).[79] This animosity is not surprising, however, according to the federalist logic. As an unsatisfactory substitute for more comprehensive managerial arrangements, IO serves as a "palliative" that reduces the fervor for real world government. In this sense, IO is more antithetical to international government than anarchy is. Agreeing with this assessment, Claude has argued that world government requires an existing community. IO can delay or prevent that community from arising because it reduces the sense of urgency for real and substantive community building.[80] Consistent with this same line of argument, Adam Roberts and Benedict Kingsbury have argued that the UN has actually worked against international security in its function as a perceived potential substitute for arms control. "By presenting a mythological alternative to armaments," they argue, "it may distract attention from other possibly more fruitful approaches to the urgent problem of controlling and limiting military force."[81]

IO sometimes functions as another kind of substitute: a substitute for responsible domestic policies. In this function, IO can be destabilizing in the long run not only at the national level but also at the international level if domestic disorder spills over into international relations. In the case of the Plaza Accord, for example, the United States was given a way of escaping necessary and costly adjustments in government spending: bringing down the dollar through intervention was preferred to bringing down the dollar by cutting the budget, which would have brought interest rates down.[82] Defenders of the conditionality policies of multilateral lending institutions have used the substitution logic to justify their argument that unconditional lending would only make loans a substitute for responsible macroeconomic and foreign economic policy management.[83] In the case of the Bretton Woods

---

78. Hopkins identifies these problems as central targets for multilateral food aid reform in the 1970s and 1980s. See Hopkins, "Reform in the International Food Aid Regime."

79. See Claude, *Swords into Plowshares*, pp. 417–19.

80. Ibid.

81. Adam Roberts and Benedict Kingsbury, "The UN's Roles in a Divided World," in Adam Roberts and Benedict Kingsbury, eds., *United Nations, Divided World* (Oxford: Oxford University Press, 1988), p. 11. The problem is not a matter of nations believing that the UN is a real and significant instrument of world peace and that they therefore avoid other means of addressing global security issues. Rather, the problem is that any positive perceptions of the security-enhancing potential of the UN may alter their incentives to apply their full resources to other strategies. This suggests an element of moral hazard, a subject discussed in a later section of my article.

82. See Funabashi, *Managing the Dollar*, p. 41.

83. It is impossible to definitively state that in the absence of IO, nations would act more responsibly or make the necessary hard choices required for long-run stability in their econ-

system, liquidity became a substitute for adjustment. External adjustment was constrained by means of fixed exchange rates and rules governing trade policy, while internal adjustment was no longer accepted as a viable means of eradicating external payment imbalances.[84] In another context of adverse substitution, Vaubel argues that as a forum for collusion, IO can make it easier for governments to pursue unstable economic policies. Monetary collaboration, for example, can shield policymakers from criticism over high inflation by bringing inflation rates into conformity.[85]

Jan Tumlir and others have argued that it should be a principal goal of IO to limit this substitution and enhance responsible policies at home. According to Tumlir, IO should "help national governments . . . discharge those basic domestic functions on which the economic stability of their societies depends in the long run."[86] If nations would all follow responsible policies at home, then IO would be less necessary. Certainly this argument is common in the context of international economic relations. As a recent article in the *Economist* noted, economic ministers could "think of cooperation as a boring means to an end, not as a glorious goal in its own right. Because if they all stayed home and adopted sensible domestic policies there would be precious little need for cooperation on trade or exchange rates."[87] A similar view was offered by Max Corden: "It can be argued that if countries make adequate use of the policy instruments available to them, there is no need for coordination of policies. . . . One can thus imagine countries reacting quickly and atomistically to the events from outside them, including the consequences of other countries' stabilization policies. And if their policies are

---

omies. Certainly, nations might seek other ways to avoid making hard choices. However, to the extent that IO provides additional "outs" or, alternatively, fails to close off less responsible avenues, it augments or maintains the possibilities for destabilizing policy choices in the long run.

84. Some might argue that this tendency toward substitution was not as apparent to the founders of the Bretton Woods system, since their principal goal was to provide nations with liquidity as a way to avoid market intervention (prompted by balance-of-payments disequilibria) in the short run and thus give them the opportunity to develop more incremental adjustment policies in the long run. Furthermore, the fixed exchange rates and the circumscription of internal adjustment were a reaction to the problems that prevailed during the interwar period. The point to be made here is that the opportunities for adverse substitution which IO provides can as likely be unintended as intended. For a discussion of the early objectives of the Bretton Woods system, see Richard Gardner, *Sterling-Dollar Diplomacy: Anglo–American Collaboration in the Reconstruction of Multilateral Trade* (Oxford: Clarendon Press, 1956), chap. 5.

85. In "A Public Choice Approach to International Organization," pp. 47–49, Vaubel cites evidence that inflation tends to be higher among nations that exhibit more convergent inflation rates.

86. See Jan Tumlir, *Protectionism: Trade Policy in Democratic Societies* (Washington, D.C.: American Enterprise Institute, 1985), p. 12. On a related note, critics of super-301 and strategic American trade policy argue that these initiatives represent a destabilizing substitute for a long-term resolution to the trade deficit, which would require the elimination of the underlying microeconomic and macroeconomic causes. See "The Snit List," *Economist*, 3 June 1989, pp. 30–31.

87. *Economist*, 26 September 1987, p. 56.

intelligent and speedy, they will achieve whatever stabilization they wish to achieve."[88]

The argument for responsible domestic policies reflects the belief that domestic problems have a tendency to spill over and become international problems. In the economic realm, excessive internal deficits and inflation alter exchange rates, and this in turn influences external positions. Differential rates of inflation in a fixed exchange rate system redistribute trade surpluses to nations with low inflation. While these effects are unintentional (externalities), there are also intentional actions (policies) that are instituted to redistribute external surpluses—for example, tariff barriers and exchange controls keep imports down and capital in. Both externalities and policies can therefore be quite destabilizing internationally.[89] Similarly, in the political realm, domestic problems can become international problems. For example, oppressive authoritarian regimes may find foreign adventurism a necessary remedy to quell domestic unrest.

Dispute intensification

IO can be a destabilizing force when it intensifies disputes. Because IO can lend moral force to the foreign policy positions of nations, it has the tendency to be used by them as a means of statecraft to further their global interests. To the extent that these interests create confrontational behavior, IO generates utility not only as a forum in which accusations are made and brinkmanship is practiced in front of the community of states but also as a vehicle through which collusion and alliance building are effected.

In general, scholars have tended to underplay these and other negative uses of IO that interfere with negotiations and make agreements difficult to achieve. Rather than serving as vehicles to resolve conflict, IOs are often used to promote or magnify conflict. As Claude has noted, they frequently function as arenas "for the conduct of international political warfare."[90] The UN, for example, has historically served as a forum to embarrass nations. In 1956, Western nations brought up the Hungarian issue for the purpose of embarrassing the Soviet Union. The Soviets vindicated themselves in 1965 when they brought up the Dominican Republic issue to embarrass the United States. As Yeselson and Gaglione have pointed out, "Real negotiations

---

88. See W. Max Corden, "The Coordination of Stabilization Policies Among Countries," in Albert Ando, Richard Herring, and Richard Marston, eds., *International Aspects of Stabilization Policies* (Boston: Federal Reserve Bank of Boston, 1977), pp. 139–40.

89. See Giulio M. Gallarotti, "Toward a Business-Cycle Model of Tariffs," *International Organization* 39 (Winter 1985), pp. 155–87. The success of GATT in lowering tariffs may be counterproductive, given the fact that nations often substitute nontariff barriers. These barriers are more protectionist and more distorting of trade flows, since producers cannot compensate for them by managing prices and costs. This illustrates the fact that IO can channel policy into less stabilizing instruments.

90. Claude, *Swords into Plowshares*, p. 446.

require that the parties define differences as narrowly as possible, avoid recrimination, and exclude extremists from discussions. At the UN, issues are widened, insults are common, and the most violent spokesmen frequently dominate the debate. The effects of such deliberately provocative discussions is to contaminate efforts to achieve peaceful settlements."[91]

The "safety valve" rationale for IO, which reflects the famous Churchill quote "better to jaw, jaw than war, war,"[92] is based on the erroneous assumption that battle among diplomats is a perfect substitute for battle in the fields. In fact, however, "war jaw" in the UN merely compounds conflicts, as Maurice Tugwell has pointed out.[93] For example, the verbal aggression traditionally marshaled toward the United States by the Soviet Union and involving the use of terminology such as "racist," "imperialist," "antipeace," and "neocolonial" served to compound confrontations outside of the UN both directly and indirectly, since it prompted as well as justified the arms buildups and supported the extremist views of Cold Warriors in domestic debates over foreign policy. In this respect, Jeane Kirkpatrick, former U.S. Ambassador to the UN, was probably justified in saying that she has "never believed that the release of aggression is healthy or therapeutic" and that "it is a sorry state of affairs when the United Nations, which was conceived as an instrument for the building of peace, is now justified as an instrument for the release of aggression."[94] She was also at least partially correct in calling the UN a "dangerous place."[95]

The UN was historically used as an instrument of Cold War competition, with each superpower marshaling voting alliances against the other. Claude underscored the point that the superpowers competed for control of the organization and viewed it as the ultimate ally in the Cold War, while Ruggie added that the Soviets considered it "a vehicle to delegitimize the postwar international order constructed by the capitalist nations."[96] Yeselson and Gaglione have noted that what many have seen as UN failures in cooperation are in fact successful instances of the organization's use as a weapon to embarrass nations.[97] According to them, much can be understood about the UN if it is seen as a tool of statecraft in the Cold War. To say that this use has substituted for more direct confrontation assumes that the marshaling of alliances which occurred earlier outside the UN was subsequently re-

91. Yeselson and Gaglione, "The Use of the United Nations in World Politics," p. 396.

92. See Maurice Tugwell, "The UN as the World's Safety Valve," in Pines, *A World Without a U.N.*, pp. 157–74. The Churchill quote is from his speech on 26 June 1954 in Washington, D.C.

93. Tugwell, "The UN as the World's Safety Valve," p. 157.

94. Jeane Kirkpatrick, speech before the Anti-Defamation League on 11 February 1982 in Palm Beach, Fla., pp. 11–12.

95. Kirkpatrick, quoted by the Associated Press, 29 October 1982.

96. See Claude, *Swords into Plowshares*, pp. 89–94; and Ruggie, "The United States and the United Nations," p. 354.

97. Yeselson and Gaglione, *A Dangerous Place*, pp. 31–43.

placed by the formation of voting blocs within the UN forum. This is not the case, however, since confrontations within the UN were merely added to confrontations outside it. In this sense, according to Tugwell, instead of acting as a "safety valve," the UN became "a threat to peace."[98] This is also evident in the fact that the organization has actively taken part in conflicts and either escalated them, as in the Korean War, or intervened to suppress them, as in the siding with Kasavubu in the Katangan revolt led by Tsombe. In the latter case, Belgian Prime Minister Paul Henry Spaak cited the intervention in the Congo affairs as a "UN war operation."[99]

In addition to these direct effects, IO has had indirect international and domestic effects that run counter to the ideals of multilateral cooperation. The constant attacks of the UN on Israel, South Africa, and Rhodesia, for example, have had the unfortunate effects of strengthening the political position of "hawks" in Israel and of providing racial extremists in the African nations with a weapon to use against moderates.[100] For this reason, nations have become reluctant to bring disputes or problems to IOs that have historically been mobilized against them. Israel, a victim of Egyptian and Syrian attack in 1973, chose not to bring the problem to the UN Security Council because of the anti-Israeli sentiment there. The Soviets bypassed the UN often during the earlier period in which the Western coalition dominated the organization, and the United States has done so following the organization's shift to Soviet and Third World domination. Claude underscored this point with respect to the earlier period: "To the degree that the United States succeeded in using the [UN] as a pro-Western device, it reduced the utility of the organization as an agency of conciliation and stabilization in the Cold War."[101]

98. Tugwell, "The U.N. as the World's Safety Valve," p. 158.

99. The ultimate outcome in this intervention was markedly different from the original intention "not to take any action which would make [the UN] a party to internal conflicts in the country." See UN Security Council, *Official Records*, meeting no. 872, 7 July 1960, p. 5.

100. See Yeselson and Gaglione, *A Dangerous Place*, p. 203. With respect to the indirect effects of IOs on African politics, Jackson and Roseberg see a quite different deleterious effect. By accepting African nations as members regardless of their political regimes, IOs serve to legitimize oppressive political systems. See Robert Jackson and Carl Roseberg, "Why Africa's Weak States Persist: The Empirical and Juridical in Statehood," *World Politics* 35 (October 1982), pp. 1–24.

101. See Claude, *Swords into Plowshares*, p. 130. Some analysts might interpret the 1990 involvement of the UN in the Iraq–Kuwait crisis as a breakdown in the deleterious Cold War use of the organization and argue that with superpower agreement the UN can be a positive force in abating and preventing crises in global security. There are several problems with this interpretation. The first and most obvious is that it is premature to draw conclusions, given that the crisis is still in progress at the time of the writing of this article. The second is that we have to question whether the UN initiated or followed the U.S. lead in attempting to resolve the crisis. The United States, defending its geopolitical and resource-security interests in the Middle East, played the major role with regard to constructing a unified response to the invasion of Kuwait. Insofar as the 1990 UN resolutions called for actions that the United States and its allies had already committed themselves to, the organization merely served as a stamp of approval or vehicle for legitimating the actions. The European Community has, in fact, at the

In resolving smaller controversies or contentious issues, IO has often created roadblocks to the resolution of more important issues. For example, the 1948 Security Council resolution endorsing self-determination in Kashmir drove a major wedge into Indian–Pakistani relations, while resolutions favoring South Korea fueled bad North–South Korean sentiment. The result was that substantive relation improvements were impeded. In the greater scheme of international relations, it may have been better for the resolutions not to have been made, regardless of their short-run successes in addressing injustices.[102]

Furthermore, as a facilitator of issue linkage, IO has often had negative rather than positive effects. Scholars have argued that linkage leads to greater possibilities for exchange and bargaining and thus enhances the potential for substantive agreements. "Clustering of issues," according to Keohane, "facilitates side-payments among these issues: more potential *quids* are available for the *quo*."[103] Although linkage can be stabilizing if it encourages cooperation, it can have destabilizing effects if it instead fuels conflict. In 1974, the Arab states traded votes with the Black African nations in the UN: the former pledged their vote to silence the South African delegation in exchange for the latter's vote in support of the Palestine Liberation Organization (PLO). This not only intensified old disputes but also brought new participants into the disputes. In IOs, voting alliances whose purposes revolve principally around confrontation are quite the rule rather than the exception.[104]

Along this line of logic, it is not the case that IO always enhances the conditions favorable to cooperation or dispute resolution. In the case of dispute mediation, IO may restrict, rather than expand, the number of mediators. The restriction occurs as a result of nations being identified as biased either because they took a particular position on an issue in IO debates or because they failed to take sides. For example, India's abstention on a UN

---

time of the writing of this article made a collective request to the Security Council to pursue air blockade in addition to naval and ground coverage. Critics of the confrontational style within the UN forum might argue that since nations are committed to a confrontational response to the invasion outside this forum, it would behoove the UN to expend its energies toward engineering a diplomatic resolution. This would reduce the possibilities of pan-Arab antagonism (especially from Iraq, Iran, Yemen, and Jordan) toward the UN and would place the organization in a better position to fulfill its role with respect to resolving other disputes in the Middle East. Given the fact that Hussein has threatened war in response to the UN resolutions, we have to question whether confrontational resolutions are counterproductive and whether the UN has served as a positive force.

102. See Yeselson and Gaglione, "The Use of the United Nations in World Politics," p. 396.

103. Keohane, *After Hegemony*, p. 91. See also Robert Keohane, "The Demand for International Regimes," *International Organization* 36 (Spring 1982), pp. 325–56; and Robert Tollison and Thomas Willett, "An Economic Theory of Mutually Advantageous Linkages in International Negotiations," *International Organization* 33 (Autumn 1979), pp. 425–50.

104. See Yeselson and Gaglione, "The Use of the United Nations in World Politics," p. 397.

208   International Organization

vote regarding Soviet intervention in Hungary discredited India as a Cold War mediator in the eyes of the United States. The potential for such outcomes is high, given that IO normally puts nations in a position of appearing to choose sides on divisive issues whether they elect to vote or not. This destabilizing transitivity can manifest itself also in terms of the effects of inner-IO confrontations on outer-IO negotiations. In 1973, for example, Americans were quite apprehensive about Chinese–South Korean interaction in the UN, given its potential effects on Chinese–U.S. rapprochement.

This tendency of "leaning" international support to one side or another is not peculiar to IO but is a characteristic of such social functions in general. When IO takes sides, however, it can have adverse effects on both the longevity and the intensity of a dispute. As Yeselson and Gaglione have observed, "Victorious states are emboldened by the vindication of their policies, and losers are embittered by injustice."[105] Taking sides without regard to consequences—even in the form of condemning what is considered an illegitimate use of force, as in the cases of the Israeli occupation of Arab territories in 1967, the Falklands invasion of 1982, and Soviet intervention in Afghanistan in 1979—encourages the use of counterforce.[106] Critics have often lamented the overt UN support of groups such as the PLO, the Southwest African People's Organization (SWAPO), the African National Congress (ANC), and the Pan-African Congress (PAC) and have argued that these groups use UN support as a legitimization of violent methods.[107] The following statement by PLO spokesman Massur on the murder of two Israelis by a PLO terrorist group in 1975 is revealing: "We sponsored the operation because it is our right to fight for our rights, and the whole world sponsored it . . . because the [UN] General Assembly has approved the right of the Palestinians to pursue their struggle *with all means* to gain usurped rights."[108] In the Falklands case, it is difficult to separate the aggressive Argentine foreign policy of the late 1960s and the 1970s from the fact that the Falklands problem had been linked to decolonization by the UN after 1965. Great Britain asserted its sovereignty over the islands throughout the century, but

105. Ibid., p. 395.
106. See Roberts and Kingsbury, "The UN's Roles in a Divided World," p. 19.
107. See Gulick, "How the U.N. Aids Marxist Guerrilla Groups." It appears that this support has been uneven in a most destabilizing way, given the recent UN decision to allow South Africa to break Resolution 435 and confront SWAPO rebels in Namibia.
108. Massur, quoted in ibid., p. 4. The argument that IO is supposed to promote change and that the PLO and ANC are therefore justified in their use of the UN to promote conflict in the Middle East and Africa presents some problems. First, it assumes that people think it worth the costs of conflict intensification, including death and destruction, to promote change. Many would not think so. Second, it assumes that any parties advocating changes to some status quo are justified in using IOs to promote conflict. In fact, nations have historically been encouraged to bring their disputes to IOs as a way of avoiding conflict. Finally, there are both peaceful and conflictual avenues to change. Some think it a bad precedent for IOs to expend resources in anything but peaceful solutions. Certainly the traditional spirit of IO suggests diplomatic approaches to resolving conflicts of interests.

it was not until after 1965 that Argentine terrorism and militarism became pronounced.[109] The problem was probably compounded when the General Assembly passed a resolution in December 1976 praising the Argentine government for "facilitat[ing] the process of decolonization" and thus legitimized its confrontational methods of using verbal and military aggression in resolving the problem.[110]

Finally, and most obviously, IO can be destabilizing by stimulating cooperation in the negative form of predatory collusion. When nations collude for the purpose of exploitation, redistribution, or aggression, collective action is bad, just as it is bad for economic efficiency when firms with market power collude to restrict output. Nations perceive confrontational alliances as bad, just as consumer nations perceive international commodity cartels as bad. Depending on the goals of cooperation, it is sometimes in the interest of peaceful international relations for collective action and prisoners' dilemma problems to exist.

Moral hazard

Situations involving moral hazard are those in which a nation is relieved of the obligation of incurring the full costs of its social, economic, or political actions because some protective scheme allows it to impose those costs onto other nations through risk sharing. The problem of generating moral hazard has been most extensively discussed in the context of the social inefficiencies of insurance. An inherent problem of insurance is that it encourages individuals to be more reckless in the management of their possessions and consequently raises the risk of losses, which in turn imposes greater costs on society. Similarly, an inherent problem of IO is that by helping to ward off catastrophes or by insuring nations against them, it discourages individually responsible behavior on their part.

There are numerous examples in which IOs have functioned as providers of insurance. The International Energy Agency (IEA) has traditionally insured against energy shortages through resource-sharing schemes. The es-

---

109. Operation Condor in 1966 and the immediate reception of this terrorist operation on the part of the Argentine masses suggest a sharp turning point in Argentine policy toward the Falklands in the mid-1960s. See W. Michael Reisman and Andrew Willard, eds., *International Incidents* (Princeton, N.J.: Princeton University Press, 1988), pp. 121–22.

110. In 1974, the newspaper *Cronica* began a campaign for the invasion of the Falklands. In January 1976, the Argentine foreign minister predicted a head-on collision with Great Britain. Just one month later, an Argentine destroyer fired on the British research ship *Shakleton*. See ibid., pp. 122–27. UN involvement may have contributed to the Falklands episode by exacerbating the domestic antagonism toward Great Britain and driving policy toward a more militant response. While this is somewhat speculative, one thing is certain: in its resolutions and other involvement in this matter, the UN provided sources of legitimacy that could be used by Argentina as justification for confrontational approaches to the problem. This in itself violated the traditional spirit of the UN objective to encourage peaceful diplomatic resolution of international disputes.

cape clauses of the General Agreement on Tariffs and Trade (GATT) have provided partial insurance to domestic industries in distress and alleviated balance-of-payments difficulties. The Financial Support Fund, agreed to by members of the Organization for Economic Cooperation and Development (OECD) but never instituted, was meant to serve as a lender of last resort that would spread the risk of loans given to nations in economic difficulty. The compensatory and contingency finance facilities of the International Monetary Fund (IMF) were instituted specifically as insurance against sudden economic disruptions that negatively affect the balance of payments. And the Lomé Convention's Compensatory Finance Scheme for Exports (STABEX) was instituted as insurance against a sudden decline in the key exports of the African, Caribbean, and Pacific nations.

In their various protective or safeguard functions, these and other IOs have frequently generated adverse effects in encouraging nations to be reckless in the management of their domestic economies. As Charles Kindleberger has argued with respect to the debt problem, last-resort and crisis lenders reduce the incentives of nations to make the internal economic adjustments necessary for long-term domestic stability. The fact that trade deficits can be financed through external funds allows nations to overinflate without worrying about the adverse effects of high prices on their trade balances. The guarantee of external sources of liquidity also allows nations to increase government spending, to prolong or expand their budget deficits, to smooth over exchange rate mismanagement, and, worst of all, to compound their foreign debt.[111] These domestic problems, spread over many nations, have the capacity to spill over and become international problems. For optimal stability in the international economic system, Kindleberger thus prescribes a lender whose commitment is uncertain: "Because of moral hazard, there should be some ambiguity about whether there will or will not be a lender of last resort."[112] Shrinking the safety net would encourage nations to manage their external accounts and macroeconomies in a manner that makes them more self-sufficient in the long run and is conducive to both domestic and international stability.

The logic of moral hazard suggests that managerial schemes can create conditions that cut against the spirit of their original purposes. In the case of the Plaza Accord, for example, cooperation provided a multilateral substitute for addressing U.S. economic problems. Instead of encouraging U.S. policymakers to bring interest rates down by instituting domestic measures to reduce their budget deficit, the G-7 stepped in to manage the dollar. In the short run, this redistributed some of the costs of the large U.S. deficit

111. Historical limitations in the demands and enforcement of conditionality have given nations more leeway than is good for their own long-run economic stability.

112. See Kindleberger, *The International Economic Order*, p. 39. See also Charles Kindleberger, "The International Monetary System," in *International Money: A Collection of Essays* (London: Allen & Unwin, 1981), pp. 297–300.

to the community of industrialized nations. But because it also reduced the incentives for the U.S. government to manage its deficit more cautiously, the deficit worsened and has become a significant potential source of international economic instability.

A better approach: limited international organization

Managerial prescriptions for IO and proscriptions against deregulating relations have led to a predilection for big supranational government. However, as Keohane and Nye have pointed out, supranational institutions "are not desirable for their own sake."[113] Nor does a high level or large scope of international management ensure optimal results. More limited forms of IO are in fact preferable in many cases, particularly those in which IO is prone to managerial failures of the types noted above and those in which the interactive patterns among nations are less conflictual and thus more representative of coordination games than of stag hunt or prisoners' dilemma. Contributors to the revisionist literature on IO and the literature on cooperation have recognized the negative effects and conditionality of management and have provided a partial solution to these problems by recommending more limited managerial functions for IOs.

In determining the proper level and scope of IO, we should begin by questioning to what extent stable international relations in the past have been the result of extensive management. Contrary to common assumptions, history shows that extensive management of international relations in both orderly and disorderly periods has been more the exception than the rule. IOs have rarely been constructed to manage any issue-area extensively or even effectively. The constitutions of IOs, like most other constitutions, have commonly been so vague as to tolerate a wide range of behavior on the part of actors both close to and far from implicit principles. Rule breaking has been tolerated, escape mechanisms have always been pervasive, and the problems of compliance have been compounded by the lack or general underdevelopment of enforcement instruments.[114]

The calls for an escape from the present "nonsystem" (nonmanagement) of monetary relations and an adoption of a new Bretton Woods system on the part of managerialists such as Irving Friedman are rather curious considering that some have questioned whether management under the old Bret-

113. Keohane and Nye, *Power and Interdependence*, p. 274.
114. Interestingly, Puchala has argued that during the first half of the European Community's existence, much of its success was actually attributable to weaknesses in getting nations to follow rules. The Community has, however, shown itself to be much stronger in the second half of its existence in both generating legislation and encouraging adherence. See Donald Puchala, "Domestic Politics and Regional Harmonization in the European Communities," *World Politics* 27 (July 1975), pp. 496–520.

ton Woods plan was extensive or strong.[115] Robert Solomon has observed that under the old Bretton Woods system

> there were no accepted rules to govern changes in par values, yet such changes were necessary as economic policies and conditions diverged among nations. Furthermore, there was no systematic means for increasing countries' reserves in a growing world economy. The growth of reserves was the haphazard result of the outcome of the U.S. balance of payments, which then, as now, depended on developments in other countries as well as in the United States. For these two reasons alone, it may be concluded that the nostalgic desire to get away from the present "nonsystem" is a product of emotion rather than careful analysis.[116]

Furthermore, those who unequivocally profess the evils of decentralization and the superiority of extensive regulation ("bigger government is better") are sometimes guilty of overestimating the destabilizing elements in international relations and their effects on international politics, underestimating those forces which naturally inhibit nations from behaving predatorially in anarchic environments, and overestimating the capacity of IO to solve problems. Common rationales for extensive supranational management have centered around the conviction that international relations are permeated by prisoners' dilemmas, stag hunts, security dilemmas, and public goods problems. Under such conditions, even the least expansionist and aggressive nations would be rationally driven to participate in destabilizing behavior such as arms races, trade wars, and competitive depreciation. The result of the "pursuit of self-interest by each," Keohane and Nye have argued, would thus be a "disaster for all."[117] But as the growing literature on cooperation suggests, the incidence and the adverse effects of predatory games have been overstated. The games that nations play are much more varied than the traditional literature on international relations has suggested, and the effects of conflictual games can vary in their level of adversity. Moreover, even under conditions that are potentially destabilizing, such as relative gains maximization, cooperative outcomes are still possible. Interactional patterns, according to this literature, are not so inherently unstable that they cannot often converge toward orderly equilibria under more limited international management. As Keohane and Nye note, "Issues lacking conflicts of interests may need very little institutional structure."[118]

115. In "Fiscal Policies, Current Accounts and Real Exchange Rates," p. 426, Corden sees the post–Bretton Woods period as a period of decentralized monetary relations, "an international laissez faire system."

116. Robert Solomon, "Issues at the IMF Meeting," *Journal of Commerce*, October 1979, p. 4.

117. Keohane and Nye, *Power and Interdependence*, p. 274.

118. Ibid., p. 273. For other contributions to this literature, see John Conybeare, "Public Goods, Prisoners' Dilemmas and the International Political Economy," *International Studies*

The fears of less centralized management, which are frequently founded on the misconception that prisoners' dilemmas and stag hunts are ubiquitous in international relations, systematically discount the costs of predation. Imposing suckers' payoffs onto other nations incurs significant costs that are independent of those costs incurred as a result of retaliation. This is not to say that exploitation does not pay; rather, the point is that it does not pay as much as many believe and that, moreover, managerialists tend to mistake other games for prisoners' dilemma and stag hunt. With tariffs, for instance, there are obvious deadweight losses with respect to social welfare. Tariffs are conducive to inflation, which bears high economic and political costs. They raise the cost of domestic production as well as reduce the efficiency of a nation's capital stock in the long run by shielding domestic industries from competition and making it difficult to import foreign capital and inputs. Declining capital efficiency will also have adverse effects on wages in the long run. Finally, tariffs can adversely affect a nation's capital balance if investors perceive them as a sign of external difficulties or mercantilistic policy styles.[119] Competitive depreciation causes not only inflation but capital flight. Depreciation can also adversely affect current balances if a nation's demand for imports and others' demand for its exports are inelastic.[120] Brinkmanship and wars can incur preponderant political as well as economic costs, as the Cuban crisis, the Vietnam War, and the Falklands War have demonstrated. The more prolonged and unsuccessful the adventurism, the greater are the costs.

The fears of decentralization are also fueled by a propensity to see disorder where it may not exist. For example, external imbalances are not in themselves a sign of economic disorder, any more than traders exchanging resources are a sign of market disorder. Much depends on the structure of the imbalances. In the present external imbalance between the United States and Japan, the former is running a current deficit against the latter, and the latter is running a capital deficit against the former. There are some important

Quarterly 28 (March 1984), pp. 5–22; Conybeare, "International Organization and the Theory of Property Rights"; Arthur Stein, "Coordination and Collaboration: Regimes in an Anarchic World," *International Organization* 36 (Spring 1982), pp. 299–324; Duncan Snidal, "Coordination Versus Prisoners' Dilemma: Implications for International Cooperation and Regimes," *American Political Science Review* 79 (December 1985), pp. 923–42; Duncan Snidal, "Relative Gains Don't Prevent International Cooperation," paper presented at the annual meeting of the American Political Science Association, Atlanta, Ga., 31 August 1989; Timothy McKeown, "Hegemonic Stability Theory and 19th Century Tariff Levels in Europe," *International Organization* 37 (Winter 1983), pp. 73–92; R. Harrison Wagner, "The Theory of Games and the Problem of International Cooperation," *American Political Science Review* 77 (June 1983), pp. 330–46; and Robert Axelrod, *The Evolution of Cooperation* (New York: Basic Books, 1984).

119. The conventional argument about the advantages of optimal tariffs assumes that other nations will not retaliate.

120. In "The Logic of the International Monetary Non-System," p. 65, Corden implies that these predatory costs increase on the margin, thus suggesting that the restraints against predation will rise as predation increases.

gains from trade in this reciprocal imbalance: Japan is helping finance the
U.S. budget deficit in exchange for the exportation of goods.[121]

Various forms of limited IO have been suggested in the recent literature
on cooperation and the critical literature on IO as a partial solution to the
problems of managerial failure and the conditionality of international management.[122] The transaction costs approach to IO, for example, has modest
aspirations for the functions of institutions. Keohane and Nye specifically
cite them as facilitators "of bargaining among member states that leads to
mutually beneficial cooperation."[123] In this sense, order is institutionally
assisted rather than managed. Institutions, they argue, can "set the international agenda and act as catalysts for coalition formation and as arenas
for political initiatives and linkage by weak states."[124] The principal function
of IOs in this case would be the reduction of organization costs, such as
those deriving from asymmetric information, deception, irresponsibility, uncertainty, risk, and unstable expectations, all of which are potential im-
pediments to stable relations and exchange patterns. Cost reduction can be
effected through limited functions relevant to the roles of gathering and
disseminating data and information about the preferences of nations, facilitating side-payments and communication, and reducing the costs of decision
making. In general, in cases in which the construction of extensive managerial schemes (what Keohane refers to as "control" schemes) is fraught
with problems or is unnecessary, less ambitious schemes become desirable.[125]

The literature on regimes has also suggested substitutes for control schemes.
According to this literature, preexisting norms and principles can reduce the
need for extensive management in several ways.[126] First, they can render
strategic interactional patterns less conflictual by altering payoffs. For example, they can make defection more costly. Second, they can facilitate
intertemporal cooperation by generating expectations of reciprocity or, in
more static games, by enhancing expectations of "nice" moves. And, third,
in specific issue-areas where coordination games predominate, as described
by Arthur Stein, or where spontaneous regimes exist, as described by Oran
Young, the preexisting norms and principles either obviate the need for

121. See Corden, "Fiscal Policies, Current Accounts and Real Exchange Rates," p. 436.
This is not to say that the imbalance cannot be politically destabilizing.

122. Even those contributors to the literature on cooperation who are quite sympathetic to
the role of IO in world politics note that limited forms of multilateral management can be
desirable and effective given the proper underlying conditions in relations among nations. See
especially Keohane and Nye, *Power and Interdependence*, pp. 274–76; and Ruggie, "Collective
Goods and Future International Collaboration," p. 888.

123. Keohane and Nye, *Power and Interdependence*, p. 274.

124. Ibid., p. 35.

125. Ibid., pp. 35 and 274. See also Keohane, *After Hegemony*; and Keohane, "The Demand
for International Regimes."

126. See the special issue of *International Organization*, vol. 36, Spring 1982.

extensive regulation or eliminate the need for formal institution building.[127] The stable patterns of interaction in specific issue-areas, Duncan Snidal has argued, can be maintained through more modest functions concerned with "codification and elaboration of an existing or latent convention" and with "providing information and communication to facilitate the smooth operation of the convention."[128] In other words, by performing limited functions with regard to preexisting focal points, management can facilitate the convergence of expectations about international behavior.[129]

Ruggie has noted that epistemic communities can be viable substitutes for extensive control schemes.[130] They are capable, for instance, of generating stable structures of expectations that are conducive to nonconflictual relations. Some of the limited management functions in the case of communities concerned with technology, for example, relate to facilitating efficient exchange through consensus about how and under which conditions transactions can be effected.

As Keohane and Nye have pointed out and as the public choice literature on IO has demonstrated, in cases in which nations can agree upon reasonable entitlement rules, an institutionally assisted market solution is superior to an extensive managerial scheme.[131] The conventional minimum-support functions in these cases are the definition, adjudication, and enforcement of property rights; the dissemination of information about preferences; and other functions related to the elimination of market distortions such as externalities. Conybeare has noted that in international environmental law, for example, there has been an impressive evolution that "illustrates the ability of states operating in a market exchange environment to develop a system of property rights and liability rules consistent with global welfare, in the absence of any overarching supranational IO directly intervening to force

127. See Stein, "Coordination and Collaboration"; and Oran Young, "Regime Dynamics: The Rise and Fall of International Regimes," *International Organization* 36 (Spring 1982), pp. 277–98. See also Wagner, "The Theory of Games and the Problem of International Cooperation"; and Snidal, "Coordination Versus Prisoners' Dilemma."

128. Snidal, "Coordination Versus Prisoners' Dilemma," p. 932. Even with more conflictual payoff structures, such as that of prisoners' dilemma, notes Wagner, functions relating to the dissemination of information about preferences and potential choices can play an essential role in bringing about cooperative outcomes. Furthermore, in cases in which conflictual games generate horizontal proliferation (interissue linkage in games), modest managerial assistance is required to arrive at mutually beneficial equilibria. Snidal argues that to the extent that horizontal properties emerge, the game "becomes embedded in a broader social context, and cooperation is increasingly possible with less centralized enforcement." See Snidal, ibid., p. 939; and Wagner, "The Theory of Games and the Problem of International Cooperation."

129. For a discussion of the role of focal points in generating mutually beneficial outcomes in games, see Thomas Schelling, *The Strategy of Conflict* (Cambridge, Mass.: Harvard University Press, 1980).

130. Ruggie, "International Responses to Technology."

131. See Keohane and Nye, *Power and Interdependence*, p. 274; Conybeare, "International Organization and the Theory of Property Rights"; Vaubel, "A Public Choice Approach to International Organization"; and Wijkman, "Managing the Global Commons."

states to internalize the effects of externalities.''[132] Wijkman, who notes that environmental problems have historically been dealt with through the market approach of subdividing internationally shared resources into "national inheritances," has argued that this approach would be viable with regard to the deep seabed and the continental margin (which are less costly to subdivide than other environments) and possibly with regard to the orbital spectrum as well.[133]

Even the traditional literature on IO, which has a strong managerial orientation, exhibits strands of logic that attest to the utility of limited IO. The functionalist concept of "technical self-determination" suggests that the nature of technological problems will dictate the scope and level of supranational regulation. Although the mainstream vision of functional interdependence foresees a growing need for the integration and management of technical issues, there is nothing in the logic to suggest that decentralized solutions in which each nation addresses a problem independently of other nations cannot sometimes be viable. If autarkic solutions to technical and welfare problems do not suffice, IO can serve minor functions in facilitating stable relations. Moreover, limited technical integration need not spill over into greater political integration.[134] Neofunctionalists acknowledge that IO is sometimes ineffective in achieving specified goals.[135] If this is because the goals are set too high, as in the case of grand collaborative schemes, it may be preferable to moderate the targeted level of cooperation, since failure may serve to delegitimize cooperation not only in the short run but also in the long run.[136] Edward Morse has argued that in some ways modernization breeds conditions that abate conflict and tension in international politics, thereby reducing the need for international management. In bringing low politics to the fore (for example, making issues relating to welfare and technology as important as those relating to power and status), the content of foreign policies becomes less threatening because conflicts are diverted into the positive-sum contexts of economics and technology.[137]

The literature on collective action suggests another reason that limited IO can be viable. Russell Hardin, for example, has argued that it is easier to eradicate public "bads" than to procure or create public goods, since the goal of collective action in the former is more focused and since nations are likely to experience more "disutility" from bads than utility from goods.[138] In cases in which the elimination of bads is the primary goal, limited IO can

132. Conybeare, "International Organization and the Theory of Property Rights," p. 314.
133. Wijkman, "Managing the Global Commons," p. 527.
134. See Mitrany, *A Working Peace System*, pp. 28 and 73.
135. See, for example, Haas, *Beyond the Nation-State*, p. 126.
136. In *Power and Interdependence*, p. 276, Keohane and Nye make a similar point with respect to viable moderated management of crisis versus nonviable control management.
137. See Morse, *Modernization and the Transformation of International Relations*, p. 85.
138. See Hardin, *Collective Action*, pp. 62–65.

be effective. Moreover, the classic Olsonian treatment of collective action suggests that IOs with limited membership are more effective than large IOs in both eliminating bads and procuring goods.[139] Historically, however, the target of IO has tended to be the management of goods with little publicness. As Ruggie has pointed out, it has been "the production of [private] goods and services which accounts for most of the activities of international organization."[140] This essentially means that IO has historically been redundant in its managerial functions and has expended more managerial capital than is necessary, since relations involving private goods require the least supranational regulation.[141]

That limited IO can be effective, however, does not mean that it will be. For IO to be a viable means of contributing to order in international relations, the environment in which it functions must be conducive to the effectiveness of supranational management in general. It appears from the logic in this article that IO will be more effective in the management of relatively simple constellations of intra- or inter-issue relations than in the management of complex chaotic systems in which relations between relevant variables are difficult to understand and forecast. With respect to the complexity of the two major issue-areas of international economic and security relations, it is interesting to note that management will most likely be effective where it is least likely to emerge. The processes involved in economic cooperation are much more complex according to Perrow's definition than those involved in security cooperation, but cooperation in security relations has historically been much less visible than that in economic relations.[142]

Moreover, IO will be more effective when it facilitates or encourages substantive and long-term solutions to problems than when it offers short-run and ad hoc approaches to them. UN peacekeeping functions, for example, have historically specialized in the latter approaches to abating conflict.[143] As valuable as these may be in insulating and desensitizing conflict, they need to be bolstered by viable schemes that raise and maintain the incentives for nations to continue pursuing substantive and lasting settle-

139. See Mancur Olson, *The Logic of Collective Action* (Cambridge, Mass.: Harvard University Press, 1965).

140. Ruggie, "Collective Goods and Future International Collaboration," p. 888.

141. See ibid.; Conybeare, "International Organization and the Theory of Property Rights"; and Wijkman, "Managing the Global Commons."

142. Jervis argues that cooperation is more likely to occur in economic relations than in security relations because the underlying strategic structure of the former is positive-sum, while that of the latter is closer to zero-sum. See Robert Jervis, "Security Regimes," *International Organization* 36 (Spring 1982), pp. 357–78. Of course, a disaggregation of economic relations would show a significant variation in the complexity of the various forms, ranging from commodity agreements, which are relatively simple, to macroeconomic coordination, which is highly complex.

143. See Brian Urquhart, "International Peace and Security," *Foreign Affairs* 60 (Fall 1981), pp. 1–16.

ments to their foreign relations problems.[144] Economic cooperation among the G-7 has also had a history of ineffectiveness because it has remained open to and often encouraged domestic and foreign policies that are inconsistent with the intentions and spirit of substantive economic policy coordination. Economic summitry has exhibited a tendency to be a legitimator of national economic policies as well as an instrument of domestic politics, rather than serving exclusively as a forum for substantive negotiations.[145] While the United States was able to use macroeconomic coordination in the 1980s as a means of escaping tough but necessary adjustments in spending,[146] future effectiveness in coordination will depend on the resolve of nations to limit such domestic policy responses. Similarly, with regard to the debt problem, strengthening conditionality will make international monetary management more effective in the long run. Greater conditionality can be even more effective if accompanied by some uncertainties regarding the provision of crisis liquidity in the international system, as suggested by Kindleberger. Absolute guarantees not only generate excessive moral hazard in the management of debt but also make conditionality more difficult to maintain.

Finally, IO is more likely to be effective when it does not put itself in a position to be a vehicle of international competition. In managing international conflicts and disputes, the UN has had mixed results. Notwithstanding its value as a forum for positive interactions, it has (even when siding with a position that seems morally correct) added fuel to international fires by intentionally or unintentionally producing instruments of confrontation and competition. By discouraging confrontational rhetoric and debate and making other adjustments in style or function, the UN might be more effective in reducing international tensions. The argument that a world with an imperfect UN is preferred to a world without a UN does not sufficiently justify the continuation of a style of dispute settlement that exhibits destabilizing characteristics.

Conclusions

Contributors to the IO literature have traditionally been overly optimistic about the ability of multilateral management to stabilize international relations and have generally ignored the fact that IO can be a source of, rather

144. These schemes require neither extensive scope nor extensive level. Their effect depends on their ability to address the right issues in the right ways. Depending on underlying strategic structures in specific relational contexts, institutions that assist cooperation may be more substantive means of generating positive outcomes than institutions that manage cooperation. Often, as has been suggested in this article, big and broad functions make it more difficult to substantively address issues.

145. See Putnam and Bayne, *Hanging Together.*

146. Critics of super-301 would identify a similar motive behind the U.S. trade policy toward Asia.

than a remedy for, disorder in and across issue-areas. Although recent revisionist scholars have recognized the destabilizing effects of IO, they have
taken a somewhat restrictive view of organizational failure. In addressing
the general issue of the ways in which IO can fail and outlining the conditions
under which more limited and less centralized modes of regulation are preferable, this article has sought to develop a set of guidelines that are pertinent
to decision making and serve as a rationale for eliminating the excesses of
IO. The findings of the article have implications not only for policymaking
but also for theory and research in the field of international relations.

According to conventional theories of cooperation and conflict, the sources
of international disorder are the underlying strategic structures of relations
between nations. However, the findings presented here suggest that disorder
springs from more heterogeneous sources. Important sources of disorder—
sources that are seemingly unlikely and have thus tended to be overlooked—
are the solutions proffered by IOs. While these solutions are intended to
moderate or eliminate the disorder created by strategic structures, they often
have the opposite effect of exacerbating existing problems or creating new
ones. Theories thus need to endogenize these origins of disorder. They also
need to expand their menu of dependent variables, which has traditionally
been limited to the roles, goals, and functions of IOs. Far more attention
needs to be paid to the effects (impact) of management in shaping international outcomes. The finding emphasized here with regard to impact is that
IO has the potential for negative as well as positive results, a finding that
supports the view that conflict and cooperation coexist in close proximity
and even overlap in international relations.[147]

Recent research has tended to blur the distinction between international
relations on the one hand and the schemes and institutions that are created
to manage these relations on the other hand. In other words, it has failed
to distinguish the forest from the trees. By focusing on the processes of IO,
this article has attempted to avoid this pitfall. More work in this direction
is needed, however, particularly with regard to better differentiating the
impact as well as the roles, goals, and functions of IO.[148] Which specific IOs
are more likely to generate moral hazard?[149] Which are more likely to generate inferior substitutes? Questions such as these only partially reflect the
theoretical and empirical issues that need to be addressed.

Finally, international bureaucrats and national policymakers, like schol-

---

147. Nowhere is this more evident than in alliance relations. See Paul Diesing and Glenn
Snyder, *Conflict Among Nations* (Princeton, N.J.: Princeton University Press, 1977), chap. 6.
148. Jervis, for one, has differentiated between security and international economic regimes
in terms of viability and stability. See Jervis, "Security Regimes."
149. Discussions of moral hazard in international politics have generally focused on monetary
relations, but the possibilities for moral hazard appear to be more far-reaching. Jervis and Nye,
for example, make interesting albeit brief allusions to possibilities for moral hazard in security
relations. See Jervis, "Security Regimes," p. 368; and Joseph Nye, "Nuclear Learning,"
International Organization 41 (Summer 1987), p. 390.

ars, need to be more sensitized to the complexity of the effects of IO when considering optimal responses to international problems. The problems themselves should not comprise the sole criteria according to which managerial schemes are constructed but must instead be carefully considered in conjunction with the likely effects generated by these schemes. In other words, the specific roles, functions, and goals of IO should be dictated both by the nature or underlying strategic structures of the international problems and by the potential positive and negative effects of possible managed solutions. Such a "conditional orientation" toward organizational design seems best adapted to the realities of IO failure and the underlying relations among nations.

Part II
UN Financing

[9]

Futures, Vol. 27. No. 2. pp. 161–170, 1995
Copyright © 1995 Elsevier Science Ltd
Printed in Great Britain. All rights reserved
0016-3287/95 $10.00 + 0.00

0016-3287(94)00021–2

FINANCING THE UNITED NATIONS

Some possible solutions

Erskine Childers

This article suggests four basic propositions. First, financing is *not* an issue of UN policies or of UN management. Every member-state accepts an outright treaty obligation to pay its share of the organization's costs. The Charter gives no licence whatever to pay or not to pay one's dues according to whether one likes or dislikes some facet of UN work. Second, discussion of the financing of the UN should proceed from the Charter's principles of democratic revenue raising and governance, which plainly need reinforcement. Third, we should certainly explore additional sources, beyond the present triplicate framework of continuous dues assessment for regular budgets, *ad hoc* assessments for peacekeeping, and voluntary funding of development and humanitarian activities. But they should *be* additional sources—not devices to compensate for any state not paying its assessments. Fourth, UN financing is extremely vulnerable to disinformation and lack of information.

A picture has been painted for many years in some Northern countries of a UN budget that has massively increased. In 1946 the UN's regular budget—then raised from 51 states—was $21.5 million. In 1992 the budget was $1.2 billion. That looks like a 55-fold increase. But the budget has always been raised, and spent, in US dollars, and the dollar has lost about 85% of its value since 1946. In real terms the budget today is only eight times larger than it was 48 years ago for an organization

Erskine Childers (Ireland) retired in 1989 as Senior Adviser to the UN Director-General for Development and International Economic Cooperation. He may be contacted at 531 Main Street #1105, Roosevelt Island, New York, NY 10044, USA (Tel: +1 212 355 3174; fax: +1 212 980 0546). This article is an edited version of a paper presented to the Conference on Financing the United Nations, organized by the Society for International Development, New York, 30 March 1994.

starting virtually from scratch.

If we add the costs of peacekeeping and humanitarian relief, the UN's proper worldwide 1992 expenditures totalled a little over $5 billion. US citizens alone spend more than that on cut flowers and pot plants every year.[1]

The regular budgets of the specialized agencies are also financed by assessed membership dues, and they have also been the targets of demagogues. In 1992 the total worldwide expenditure of the whole UN system—the UN itself, all its development and humanitarian funds, and all its agencies except the World Bank and the International Monetary Fund, whose funds are raised in totally different ways—was $10.5 billion.[2] That, for example, would only sustain the alcoholic intake of UK citizens who so indulge for about 15 weeks.[3]

Table 1 shows all the expenditures including entirely voluntary contributions (for example to UNDP, UNFPA and UNICEF). Since the first pledging by governments of $20 million in 1950 this method has mobilized large additional sums for development and humanitarian assistance now aggregating to about $2.5 billion a year. But when high compound inflation over 40 years is factored in, that is nothing like the increase that is routinely claimed for this method.

Against record spending of about $*150* per human being alive in the world on military establishments and weapons every year, in 1992 governments spent through the UN system, in all fields, about $*1.90* per human being. Much of the budget goes on what we are constantly informed is 'a vast, sprawling, bloated bureaucracy'—a neat sound-bite and editorial phrase, powerfully conjuring up a picture of a huge and constantly multiplying staff, fecklessly frittering away the treasuries of the industrial countries.

First, as to the United Nations itself, its entire core, regular staff—general-service and professionals, worldwide, in New York, Geneva, Vienna, Addis Ababa,

TABLE 1. OVERALL WORLDWIDE EXPENDITURES OF THE UN SYSTEM IN 1992

Programme	UN and agencies (US$10⁶)	Emergencies (US$10⁶)	Per capita (US$)
Policy making	177.9		0.03
Political affairs	385.3		0.07
Peacekeeping operations		1400	0.25
Development	774.5		0.14
General statistics	145.9		0.03
Natural resources	403.5		0.07
Energy	81.5		0.01
Agriculture, forestry, fisheries	817.2		0.15
Industry	275.5		0.05
Transport	241.2		0.04
Communications	298.9		0.05
Trade and development	291.9		0.05
Population	268.8		0.05
Human settlements	127.9		0.02
Health	402.9		0.07
Education	418.5		0.07
Employment	284.4		0.05
Humanitarian assistance		2699.8	0.49
Social development	375.2		0.07
Culture	48.9		0.01
Science and technology	294.6		0.05
Environment	269.3		0.05
Totals	**$6383.8**	**$4099.8**	**$1.90**

Baghdad, Bangkok, Santiago and other offices—is now about 9000 (see *Table 2*).[4] That is less than the civil service of the City of Winnipeg in Canada.[5] It is some 14% less than the staff of the international advertising firm of Saatchi and Saatchi.[6]

The total regular and non-permanent staff of the whole UN *system*—the 9000 of the UN plus the staff of the agencies and the voluntarily financed development and relief funds, but not the Bank or IMF or, of course, contributed peacekeepers—is about 51 500. That is less than the total governmental staff in the state of Wyoming; it is less than the civil service of the city of Stockholm; it is less than the district health staff of the principality of Wales in the UK.[7]

We are not here discussing the inevitable improvements needed in the structure or the management of these civil services after 50 years. But let us be clear that we are talking about the financing of a world institution which has been kept perilously *small* and *under*-resourced because of all this disinformation.

When the UN was founded, only one method of financing it was envisaged. This was stated in Article 17 of the Charter: that 'the expenses of the Organization shall be borne by the Members as apportioned by the General Assembly'. This made payment of assessed dues obligatory in international treaty law. The method of apportioning these assessments is reviewed by the Assembly every three years. It allocates to each member a percentage of the total budget, calculated through a formula (currently) involving a 10-year average of its gross domestic product, with

TABLE 2. STAFF OF THE UNITED NATIONS SYSTEM[a]

Organization	Financed from regular budgets			Extra-budgetary (voluntary funds)			Total	
	Prof	GS	Total	Prof	GS	Total	Prof	GS
United Nations	3 265	5 829	9 094	1 604	3 198	4 802	4 869	9 027
UNHCR	106	179	285	643	1 198	1 841	749	1 377
UNITAR		1		10	8	18	10	9
UNRWA	51	2	53	67	7	74	118	9
ITC	1		1	181	192	373	182	192
ICSC	18	22	40				18	22
ICJ	19	28	47				19	28
UNU				36	65	101	36	65
UNDP				1 571	5 033	6 604	1 571	5 033
UNICEF				1 179	2 623	3 802	1 179	2 623
ILO	678	1 012	1 690	695	692	1 387	1 373	1 704
FAO	1 051	2 062	3 113	1 608	1 649	3 257	2 659	3 711
UNESCO	808	1 406	2 214	248	341	589	1 056	1 747
WHO	1 269	2 350	3 619	564	1 208	1 772	1 833	3 558
ICAO	248	350	598	231	223	454	479	573
UPU	62	84	146	25	1	26	87	85
ITU	240	395	635	135	99	234	375	494
WMO	104	124	228	78	72	150	182	196
IMO	88	146	234	34	47	81	122	193
WIPO	114	237	351	4	18	22	118	255
UNIDO	355	665	1 020	305	458	763	660	1 123
IAEA	684	958	1 642	15	108	123	699	1 066
Totals	9 161	15 850	25 011	9 233	17 240	26 473	18 394	33 090
Grand total UN system								**51 484**

[a] As of the end of 1990. There have been no major changes since then. Data derived from ACC document on 'The Budgetary and Financial situation of organizations of the UN system'. UN Doc A/47/593, 3 November 1992, and ACC/1991/Per/R 28, 5 July 1991.

downward adjustments for low per capita income and high foreign debt.

At the beginning, the US share of the regular budget was just on 50% and, of course, there were very few extremely poor members. Since then, in an agreed framework of special parameters, the US share has been adjusted downwards, and the contributions of the poorest countries cannot fall below 0.01% of the budget. To give a quick sketch of how the formula works, the USA is legally obliged to contribute 25% of the budget, currently $310 million; Japan half of that, 12.45%; Germany 8.93%; Russia 6.71%; France 6% and the UK 5%; Italy 4.29% and Canada 3.11% or $31 million; Brazil is assessed 1.59% of the budget; China 0.77%; India 0.36% which is $3.6 million, Nigeria 0.20% and Indonesia 0.16%; and so on down to 0.01%, or $102 000 for 87 member-countries at the bottom of the income scale.[8]

Late payment of these dues has been a chronic problem for decades, and there is to date no penalty interest charge. Late payments have steadily depleted the UN's Working Capital Fund (see *Figure 1*), and increased the running deficit, so that in October 1993, with 75% of the 1993 budget already spent, the equivalent of 72% of it had not yet been paid.[9] Governments have so far refused to allow the Secretary-General to borrow even for a week.

Every member-state has to pay its assessment in actual US dollars (we should actively campaign to establish a United Nations currency, a special drawing right (SDR) calculated on a representative basket of currencies). Protectionism in the North, and its refusal to discuss a fair trade strategy for the Charter's goal of the 'advancement of all peoples', have steadily reduced 75% of humankind to only having 18% of world trade, which drastically limits the ability of developing country members to earn hard currency. They have also suffered from unilaterally raised Northern interest on their loans. UNDP calculates that these North–South structural inequities are depriving developing countries of at least $500 billion a year in income that they could be earning.[10] Their indebtedness has multiplied 14-fold since 1970. Inevitably many have fallen behind in their payments, and we cannot hope for much improvement from that part of the assessment spectrum until industrial countries agree to discuss truly global all-win macroeconomic policies at the UN.

But the single most devastating impact on the assessments system came in 1985 when the US Congress decided to cut its legally obligated contribution by one-fifth

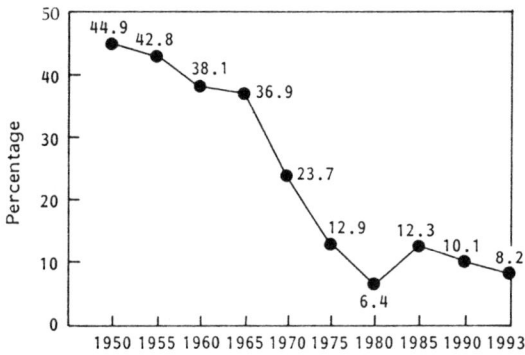

Figure 1.   Level of Working Capital Fund as % of regular budget appropriations.

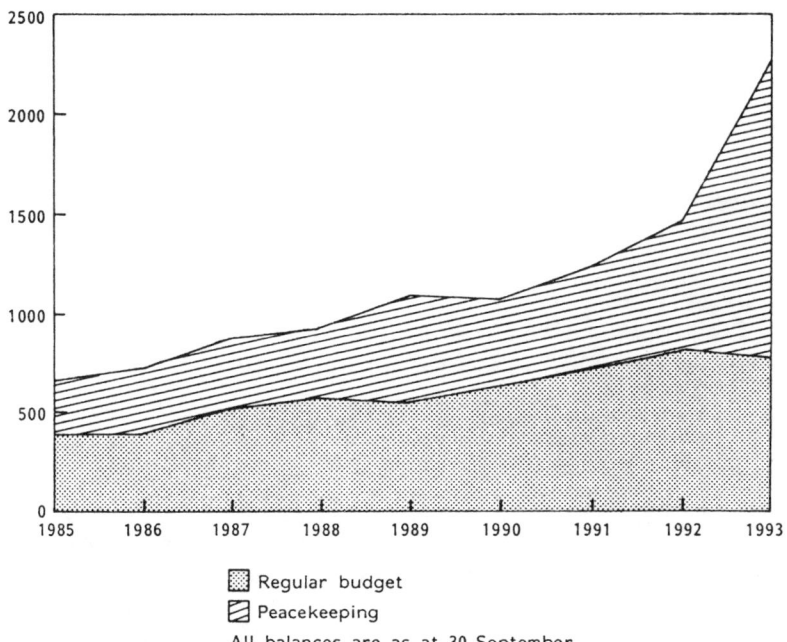

Figure 2.   Unpaid assessed contributions—regular budget and peacekeeping activities combined
(all balances at 30 September).

unless weighted voting was introduced in the UN, and then in 1986 when it applied
an additional across-the-board reduction in US government spending.[11] *Figure 2*
shows the impact.[12] Ever since the mid-1980s sheer cash-flow has been so uncertain
that there have been times when the staff have not known if they would be paid the
next month.

Peacekeeping costs are also assessed, but since 1973 the General Assembly has
applied a slightly different scheme for these. Each of the five Permanent Members of
the Security Council is supposed to pay 22% more than what its share would be
under the regular budget formula; a second group of affluent countries pays the same
percentages; a third group of the less well off pay one-fifth of their regular
apportionment; and a fourth pay one-tenth. A major problem is that the
Secretary-General only has a $150 million revolving fund, and each time the
Security Council approves a peacekeeping operation he has to get a projected
budget through the General Assembly before he can even send out a letter to
members with their assessments for that new operation. That in itself results in delay
in payments.[13]

The upper belt of unpaid assessments in the graph shows the consequences of
this seriously inadequate method of raising peacekeeping funds. Here, the largest
single delinquent is now Russia. Already crippled by Cold War armaments, its
economy is now nearly wrecked by the hectoring priests of the new fundamentalist
religion of the magic of the market. In October 1993 Russia owed nearly half the
current $1 billion in peacekeeping arrears.

Finally, these arrears have a circular effect. Reimbursements to troop-contributing countries—more than half of which are developing countries—are delayed.[14] This in turn affects not only their ability to contribute more troops to more operations, but even their ability to pay their regular-budget assessments.

The history of official, intergovernmental efforts to reform the assessment system is pretty dismal.[15] Working Groups and intergovernmental Committees of Experts have been repeatedly convened over the UN's financing—in 1961, 1964, 1965, 1970, 1975, 1980, 1983 and 1986. But they have only tried to deal with its financial crises, and even then not to correct their causes but to reduce or freeze the budget, or UN salaries—or to liquidate arrears in peacekeeping costs when various members had refused to pay their assessed share.

By my reckoning, all these exercises have produced only five concrete actions:

- one issue of UN bonds—but only to liquidate already incurred costs of peace-keeping in the Sinai and the Congo;
- one increase in the level of the Working Capital Fund (now $100 million);
- under massive Northern pressure exploiting the US withholding of dues, the 1986 'Group of 18' exercise pressured the majority of members to accept that budgets are approved by consensus. This did *not* then improve the assessment process; indeed, even after this major concession by the South the USA did not resume full payment of its dues;
- a fourth action was to give the Secretary-General an inadequate $150 million fund for peacekeeping;
- and the fifth concrete action was the creation in 1991 of a $50 million revolving fund for start-up costs of humanitarian relief operations, which the regular budget could never have funded.

During the Reagan assault on the UN, however, there was one extremely important proposal. In 1985 the Prime Minister of Sweden, the late Olof Palme, proposed in the General Assembly that a ceiling of 10% should be put on the assessed contribution of any member-state, with redistribution of the difference among capable members. India endorsed this idea. It got only silence from Washington, but it was no secret that the US administration did not wish to have its share—and therefore its leverage—reduced at all. Other industrial countries might have supported Mr Palme's proposal but they refused to risk having such a reduction seem to reward the USA for defaulting on its legal obligations.

Mr Palme had diplomatically but sharply enough suggested that, 'a more even distribution of the assessed contributions would better reflect the fact that this Organization is the instrument of *all* nations'.[16] Once upon a time that was indeed the idea. If nothing else were to be done with regard to the financing of the UN for another decade, relieving the organization from its perpetual threat of either political dictation or bankrupting by one member-state—*any* one state—would be a marvellous achievement. In autumn 1993 President Clinton told the General Assembly that the USA does now want a reduction in its assessment share of peacekeeping costs. It is time to get the Palme proposal adopted first, for the regular budget apportionment.

In 1993 a 'first-ever' was, however, achieved in this rather gloomy history, when a blue-riband group of the world's financiers, co-chaired by Shijuro Ogata of Japan and Paul Volcker of the USA, met under the auspices and facilitation of the Ford Foundation, and sent their report to the Secretary-General.[17] The group's recommendations essentially addressed flaws in the present assessment system. The main recommendations were that:

- Dues should be paid in four quarterly amounts, with interest charged on late payments; and countries whose appropriations calendar is late in the year should re-phase it for UN dues.
- The Working Capital Fund should be doubled, to $200 million.
- The assessment formula should work from three- rather than ten-year averages of GDP.
- Governments should consider financing peacekeeping from their national defence budgets, and the revolving reserve for peacekeeping should be increased to $400 million.
- And along the lines of recent Nordic proposals the group also recommended that the administrative costs of the voluntary funds should be met by assessment.

We are now waiting to see what the action will be on these perfectly sound proposals. Governments should be nagged.

In the *Agenda for Peace* report Dr Boutros-Ghali had already suggested that alternative, additional means of financing should be considered, including a Peace Endowment Fund to which private sources could contribute. The Ogata-Volcker group, however, said that 'current proposals for additional, non-governmental sources of financing the UN are neither practical nor desirable, and that the present triplicate system is the most logical and appropriate means of financing the UN as 'it permits governments to maintain proper control over the UN's budget and its agenda'.

Financing possibilities

I briefly sketch here some possibilities for such additional and alternative financing, and then suggest some guiding principles.

Various sources have proposed a range of schemes in 'international taxation'.[18] This has a certain logic and equity to it: it would be automatic, fairly universal, with higher yields from those profiting more. Member-states could agree to levy a United Nations surcharge on any one or several of the following:

- all arms sales in the recently established UN Register (I do not much like that but I would acclaim an immediate and serious tax on every single land-mine produced from this day forward); or
- a tiny, fractional levy on all transnational movement of currencies (if governments came out of their current state of trance in market religion long enough to agree)—it has been estimated that a levy of 0.003% on the $900 billion being traded daily would produce some $8 billion[19]—or even on all international trade; or on the production of such specific (and polluting) materials as petroleum and hydrocarbons, or on all mineral raw commodities.
- There is, of course, the revenue from the Seabed Authority when that finally gets moving.
- One more often proposed is a United Nations levy on all international air and sea travel, on the grounds that the UN must maintain a peaceful environment for international travellers.

Common to all these propositions except the Seabed Authority is that each member-government would have to agree to levy the tax, collect it, and transfer it to agreed parts of the UN system. I mention this simply for us to be quite clear that international taxation revenue would essentially be raised through and stay under the control of governments. To what extent, also, would citizens of the United Nations—'We, the Peoples'—feel more involved as a result of such taxation, and how much importance would we attach to that as one purpose and product of additional financing?

That thought leads to another range of possibilities—still needing the initial assent of member-governments, but thereafter far more visible and tangible to citizens. For example, if someone has not already done so, the Universal Postal Union should be asked to calculate what revenues could accrue if the national post offices of every member-country agreed to contribute the proceeds of sales of stamps for one, publicly well announced, day in each year. To make it a real event for information about the UN system, a tiny surcharge might be arranged through the International Telecommunications Union on all telephone calls that day, with a free dialling number for a recorded explanation.

Of course, here again the revenues would still move through each government, to the UN. One possibility for income moving more directly to the UN—but still with initial governmental licensing and auditing legislation in each country—would be an annual United Nations lottery, administered by a special authority under the Secretary-General. This might be sensitive in one or more cultures, but it would be a form of very visible and citizen-involved 'voluntary automaticity'. Lotteries painlessly raise lovely pots of money.

Finally, we come to the various forms of endowment funds to which citizens, foundations or corporations could contribute. Here, however, I would suggest considerable caution, lest before we knew it some ebullient corporation CEO arrived with several billion very attractive-looking dollars, but perhaps with all sorts of conditionalities attached in extremely small print. Through voluntary financing the UN system is already in danger of drowning under waves of donor conditionalities that are flatly against the Charter.

I have only touched on some possibilities in three broad categories, but let me now offer some guiding principles.

First, any additional, alternative financing of the UN and its system should be *supplementary to* a properly worked, more healthily apportioned, and fully *honoured* assessment system.

Second, we should be clear what we mean in terms of who would *govern* any such additional contributions to the UN and the system.

Third, and closely connected, such additional financing, in one way or another a tax or donations from citizens, must be transparently accountable to citizens. Here I simply enter a plea for all-out support for a United Nations Parliamentary Assembly, one of whose functions could indeed be to watch over such supplements.

In conclusion, I make a plea for another 'first-ever' on this subject. The entire question of putting financing on a more stable and even modestly expanding basis has been plagued for many years by pressures and even outright demands from those who claim they are 'contributing the most'.

The assessment system is squarely founded on the principle of *relative capacity to pay*. It is a fundamental principle of democratic revenue raising and governance that it is as difficult for the poorer citizen to find his or her lower money amount of tax as it is for the wealthier citizen or corporation to find higher money amounts. Accordingly, the wealthier should have no special voice or voting strength in government; and they do *not* have it in any of the established democracies.

In the United Nations system, it is at least as difficult for Jamaica, Ireland, Tanzania, Australia or Nepal to find their smaller money amount of assessment dues as it is for Germany or Japan or the USA to find their larger money amount of dues. Yet it is from countries claiming to be models of democratic governance that there has for several decades come this insidious, totally *anti*-democratic talk of who 'pays most' for the UN's budgets, and of demands for special influence. If anyone tried now to revert their *own* system of governance to what they are demanding in the UN—the wealthier citizens and corporations to have special voting strength in their parliaments and hold key cabinet posts and civil-service jobs—there would be another round of the bitter and bloody revolutions it took to establish this principle in those same democracies.

It is often claimed that those contributing the larger money amounts are justified in demanding a special voice and voting strength, because the UN secretariats do not handle funds well. I find this difficult to accept from countries that are currently reeling from the exposure of massive corruption and ineptitude in their political and administrative systems. Citizens of one country whose officials constantly lecture the UN recently lost the equivalent in savings of 250 years of UN budgets through mismanagement and corruption in public organizations. The UN's management needs improvement, of course; but let us *improve* it, not surrender it to pre-democratic and semi-feudal control.

An all-time record would be set if no one again uttered those totally undemocratic words, 'who pays most'. The fundamental principle in our United Nations Charter, at the very roots of our one universal public-service institution, is that for all we want it to achieve, *everyone* 'pays most'.

Notes and references

1. *Surveys of Current Business* (Washington, DC, US Dept of Commerce).
2. UN Document A/48/1, Table 4 and paragraph 108.
3. *Social Trends* (London, Her Majesty's Stationery Office, 1991).
4. This and further staff statistics are assembled from UN Docs A/47/593 and ACC/1991/Per/R 28. Data are as of 1991; there have been no significant changes since then.
5. The City of Winnipeg was employing 9917 staff in mid-1993 (data from its Personnel Office).
6. *Financial Times*, 14 February 1994.
7. Comparative data respectively from *Public Employment 1991*, Table 6, Doc GE/91-1 (US Department of Commerce); *Kommunal Personal 1991* (Svenska Kommunforbundet); *Public Bodies 1991* (London, HMSO).
8. UN Doc A/48/503/Add 1, 11 November 1993.
9. UN Doc A/48/503, paragraph 31.
10. Data and graph from *UNDP Human Development Report 1992* (New York, Oxford University Press, 1992).
11. For useful summary accounts of this and other periods of UN financial crisis see Joachim W Muller, *The Reform of the United Nations* (New York, Oceana, 1992).
12. Graph on unpaid assessed contributions is from UN Doc A/48/503, in paragraph 14.
13. For much useful data on financing of peacekeeping, see, *inter alia*, Anthony McDermott, *United Nations Financing Problems and the New Generation of Peacekeeping and Peace Enforcement* (Providence, RI, Watson Institute/Brown University, 1994), Occasional Paper No 16.
14. See UN Doc A/48/503, paragraph 37.
15. For useful background to the whole history of the assessment system and its bargaining dynamics see, *inter alia*, John G Stoessinger, 'Financing of the United Nations', in *International Conciliation* (New York, Carnegie Endowment, 1961); Robert F Meagher, 'United States financing of the United Nations', in Trister Gati (editor), *The US, the UN, and the Management of Global Change* (New York, New York University Press, 1983).
16. Statement in the General Assembly, 21 October 1985.

17. *Financing an Effective United Nations: Report of the Independent Advisory Group on UN Financing* (New York, Ford Foundation, 1993).
18. For useful background see, *inter alia*, Eleanor B Steinberg and Joseph A Yager with G M Brannon, *New Means of Financing International Needs* (Washington, DC, Brookings, 1978); Paper on Automaticity in Electronic Transfers for the InterAction Council; United Nations Bibliography Series, Dag Hammarskjold Library. At the Conference at which the present paper was presented the author learned of a valuable paper, 'Financing mechanisms and their implementation' by the NGO UNCED Task Force, contact Dr Lisinka Ulatowska, World Citizens (Tel: 1-718-658-5872).
19. See, *inter alia*, Martin Walker, 'Global taxation', *World Policy Journal*, 1993.

[10]

THE UN FINANCE CRISIS:
A HISTORY AND ANALYSIS

*Simon Duke**

It is a source of profound concern to me that the same membership which sees it appropriate to entrust the United Nations Secretariat with unprecedented new responsibilities has not taken the necessary action to insure that the minimum financial resources required to carry out those responsibilities are provided on a reliable and predictable basis.[1]

Javier Pérez de Cuéllar

Introduction

The United Nations is faced with a paradox; never before has it had the potential to do so much yet, at the same time, it has never been in such dire financial straits. The end of the Cold War has opened the way for the United Nations to play a critical role in the international system and the recent requests for its intervention in Yugoslavia, El Salvador, Cambodia and Iraq, with the likelihood of others seeking its help soon, could indicate a new lease of life for the organization, making it an essential component of the new world order founded on concepts of the 'rule of law and the principle of collective security'.[2] Until recently, the United Nations had effectively been blocked from playing a major role in the international system since, whatever the hopes and aspirations of the delegates at the San Francisco Conference, it still remained an organization subject to the whims of the great powers. While this is clearly less true in the contemporary international system, it is nevertheless worth noting that the high political profile which the organization is currently enjoying exists because the major actors so wish it. This consensus could vanish as quickly as it appeared.

The end of the Cold War has also opened the way to increased awareness of international issues beyond the confines of issues of peace and security. These are not necessarily new issues, but ones which had hitherto been subsumed under the general problems of the Cold War. For example, environmental problems have moved to the forefront of many developed countries' political agendas. The 'greening' of politics has led to increased awareness that the United Nations has an essential coordinating role as well as ensuring that the international community is aware of the magnitude of the issues. The environment is but one issue; others could be mentioned such as human

---

* The author would like to acknowledge the help given by Tae Kang in gathering documentation for this article. In addition the comments and criticisms given by Brian Anderson, Roberta Haar, Joo Seung-Ho and Richard Tucker were much appreciated.

[1] Quoted in *The New York Times*, 'UN asks Billion for Peacekeeper Fund', 25 November 1991, p. A3.

[2] See Bruce Russett and James S. Sutterlin, 'The UN in a New World Order', *Foreign Affairs*, Spring 1991, pp. 69–83.

rights, women's rights, refugee problems, recognition of new states and so forth. These are all pressing problems which need attention but which assume second place to the more general problems of peace and security.[3] For this reason, the main focus of this article is on the financial woes of the regular and peacekeeping budgets and not upon the budgets of the specialized agencies such as UNEP, UNESCO and UNICEF.

The post-Cold War international order has yet to establish itself in a completely coherent fashion. What is discernible is the gradual emergence of a system which is different from the bipolar system which prevailed until recently. The emergent system is one characterized by multiple players and with many new states emerging, with the result that the potential for instability may be high. Here again the United Nations is of the utmost importance since there is no obvious, existing security network to answer the security problems which will confront the international system in the years ahead. Many of the problems are beyond the purview of the existing alliance systems and are more appropriately dealt with at the international level. The salutary example of the civil war in Yugoslavia illustrates how inadequate traditional alliance systems or interest groups are at halting such internecine conflict. The call by the UN Secretary-General, Boutros Boutros Ghali, for UN intervention in Yugoslavia, which could involve over 10,000 troops, also brings us back to the fundamental point: who pays? Yugoslavia is but one example of the many which could be chosen; the UN force in Cambodia will be some 22,000 strong.

Never before has the international community looked to and entrusted the United Nations with such responsibility yet never before has the organization been so financially ill-equipped to deal with those responsibilities. Even if one confines the examination to the central role of the United Nations – the maintenance of international peace and security – the case for the UN's growing prestige is clear. In the first forty years of its existence, the organization took on thirteen peacekeeping jobs, ranging from full-fledged intervention in the Congo to observation tasks in the Middle East. Since 1988 the United Nations has adopted seven new peacekeeping jobs, excluding the Gulf War and Cambodia. In the light of its growing importance and prestige, why is there a lack of will to give the United Nations commensurate funding?

The finance issue at its most basic is this: the United Nations faces 'imminent bankruptcy'[4] because some UN members continue not to pay their dues fully,[5] the United States accounting for most of the shortfall, at the very time when the demands on peacekeeping operations as well as other areas of UN activity are soaring. In spite of the American underfunding of the organisa-

---

[3] This trend was emphasized at the Security Council meeting in New York on 1 February 1992, where peace and security were put forward as the prime issues of concern to the Council, with the attendant problems of nuclear proliferation, chemical weapons and ethnic strife all being features. Issues such as the environment received little or no attention, in spite of the forthcoming 'Earth Summit' to be held by the UN in Rio de Janeiro in June 1992.

[4] This phrase was used by Javier Pérez de Cuéllar to describe the financial plight of the UN. See General Assembly, *Current Financial Crisis of the United Nations, Report of the Secretary-General*, 45th session, 6 December 1990, (UN doc. A/45/830).

[5] At the end of November 1991 only 67 of the 159 countries assessed for 1991 contributions had paid.

tion, the United States has been among those calling for the expansion of the UN's agenda into areas such as international drugs control, the environment and international peacekeeping.[6]

To understand the nature of the current UN finance crisis it should be put into a historical context. The finance problem is not new; it has bedevilled the United Nations for at least three decades, imposing severe restrictions upon the organization's ability to assume a full role in the international system. Although its financial woes have long been understood by those directly connected with the organization, they were less well-known to the public. The preoccupations of the Cold War era had the effect of detracting from the relevance of the United Nations, and thus diminishing interest in the UN's funding, since it was generally seen as an organization which was largely at the mercy of the superpowers.

The finance question in a historical context

There are four types of budget in the United Nations: the regular budget, the peacekeeping budget, specialized agencies' budgets and voluntary programmes – the first two being the largest and of most interest. Contributions to the regular budget are assessed on a complicated ability-to-pay basis.[7] The United States, which accounted for around 40 per cent of global GNP in 1945, could have paid up to half of the organization's regular budget. Its initial assessment was 39.98 per cent. As the relative strength of the American economy declined, the assessment was reduced to one-third and eventually one-quarter. A minimum assessment of 0.04 per cent of the budget was set for those states with least assets. In 1973 this figure was reduced to 0.02 per cent and eventually, in 1978, to 0.01 per cent. As about 79 members pay the minimum assessment and another nine pay 0.02 per cent, it is possible for a majority of the General Assembly to represent less than 1 per cent of the UN regular budget. The scale of assessements, as it stands, imposes on 14 member states the burden of funding 84 per cent of the regular budget.[8]

The problems which have been caused in the regular budget through the assessment method exist also in the peacekeeping budget. This relies upon

[6] US Congress, Hearing before the Subcommittee on Human Rights and International Organizations, and on International Operations, of the Committee on Foreign Relations, House of Representatives, *Recent Developments in the United Nations System*, 101st Congress, second session (Washington DC: GPO, 1990), p. 95.

[7] Assessed contributions are calculated according to the type of economy involved. For market economies the starting point is the national factor income from the world (in other words GDP, expressed in US$), minus the consumption of fixed capital, which equals the national income. National income is then used as the basis of assessed contribution. There are however maximum and minimum assessment levels, being 25 per cent and 0.01 per cent respectively. If there were no limits the US contribution would be nearer 28 per cent. (See General Assembly, *Report of the Committee on Contributions*, Annex 1A, 1989, pp. 20–27 (Supplement no. 11;A/44/11)).

The assessment system has been criticised by many who point out that the national income of countries can be subject to manipulation by the use of unrealistic exchange rates or inflation, and more elaborate methods have been urged, such as the use of purchasing power parities and price-adjusted rates of exchange.

[8] General Assembly, 42nd session, Fifth Committee, 59th meeting, 10 December 1987. Agenda Item 117, *Financial Emergency of the United Nations*, p. 7.

a similar system with 78 countries being assessed at 0.02 percent or less, the United States at 30.7 per cent, Japan at 12.5 per cent and Germany at 8.9 per cent. Under UN financial regulations the member states are required to pay their assessed contributions within thirty days of receipt of notification of the amount; the majority fail to do so. The peacekeeping budget has been the most controversial of the various UN budgets because of the highly politicized nature of peacekeeping ventures, particularly during the Cold War years. There are also separate budgets for the specialized agencies which are arrived at independently, although they are formally subject to approval by the General Assembly. Lastly, the voluntary programmes include financial support, economic and technical assistance for several of the major UN programmes, such as the UN Development Programme (UNDP), the UN Fund For Population Activities (UNFPA), the UN Environmental Programme (UNEP) and the UN Children's Fund (UNICEF).

The derivations of the financial crisis are to be found in the early 1960s with the Congo crisis. The Congo crisis, which saw the United Nations commit around 20,000 personnel from 29 nations over a four-year period at a cost of $400 million, was the beginning of the serious financial problems for the organization. At that time the cost of the Congo forces exceeded the UN budget; a problem which was exacerbated because some members, like the Soviet Union and France,[9] refused to pay their share of the operations due to political objections. The Soviet Union rested its case against payment of its assessed costs for the Congo operations upon a constitutional argument; the Soviet representative argued that only the Security Council had the power under the Charter to raise and dispatch UN armed forces and to decide how they should be paid for. The Soviets and the French were joined by India, some of the Afro-Asian countries and Mexico. Mexico led a Latin American revolt against the US insistence on the applicability of article 17 and the penalties for non-payment contained in article 19. Mexico argued that the records of the San Francisco Conference of 1945 showed that the stipulations contained in articles 17 and 19 were not intended to apply to expenditures related to the use of armed forces. This position was rejected as a misinterpretation by Dag Hammarskjöld, on the grounds that the Congo operation was not related to article 43 of the Charter.[10] In a statement on 21 November 1960 to the UN's Fifth Commitee, which deals with finance questions, Hammerskjöld emphasized the gravity of the UN's financial situation when he observed that 'the present outlook is that the organization will begin the 1961 financial year with a virtually empty Treasury; with arrears of assessed contributions totalling approximately $31 million ($8.5 million on the regular budget and $22.5 million on the UNEF budget)'.[11]

The UN's financial problems can be understood by comparing assess-

[9] De Gaulle disliked the UN intervention in the Congo and the French government joined the Soviet bloc in refusing to pay its assessed share of the Congo operations and also refused to recognize that its obligations under article 17(2) (stating that the 'expenses of the Organization shall be borne by the members as apportioned by the General Assembly') of the Charter applied.

[10] A.J. Cordier and W. Foote, *Public Papers of the Secretaries-General of the United Nations: Dag Hammerskjold* 1960-61, vol. 5 (New York: Columbia University Press, 1975), pp. 438–43.

[11] *Ibid*. p. 232.

ments, decided by the General Assembly, with the estimates for the cost of an operation. For example, in the period between 1 July and 31 December 1963, the General Assembly assessed the expenses for the Congo operation for the 104 UN members according to their ability-to-pay criteria. The assessments amounted to some $30,034,744 while the total authorized expenditure amounted to $33,000,000. The United Nations was therefore dependent upon the international community for some $2,965,256 of 'voluntary contributions'.[12] The United States was assessed at just over 32 per cent of the expenses at this period. Two points are significant in this context; first, the United Nations was even then reliant upon members for 'voluntary contributions' to fill the gap between aspirations and ability, and secondly, the United States was the UN's financial bulwark. For the same period the USSR was assessed at 14.97 per cent of the expenses.

What accounts for the US willingness to shoulder such a disproportionate amount of the burden? The answer would appear to be twofold. On the one hand the United States was in the relative position of being able to afford it and, on the other, the contributions must be set in the context of superpower competition for influence in Africa in those years – a situation abetted by the emergence of a plethora of Marxist regimes.

The Congo crisis is also of interest because it illustrates a fundamental aspect of the UN financial crisis, namely that the UN's financial concerns arise in large part not just from the ability to pay but, more importantly, from whether UN actions are in accordance with the various national policies of the members. In other words, it is a question primarily of will and, to some extent, of legal interpretation.

The funding of the Congo crisis also raised other types of questions, amongst them being the question of the legality of deliberately withholding funds. This applies primarily to article 17 of the UN Charter, which states that the General Assembly shall consider and approve the budget of the organization and that the 'expenses of the Organization' shall be borne by members as apportioned by the General Assembly. The phrase, 'expenses of the organization,' has served as the basis for many budgetary wrangles, most notably when it comes to peacekeeping operations.

The General Assembly unambiguously has the right to decide on budgetary contributions, but it is the Security Council that can authorize a peacekeeping action. The Soviet Union and France both refused to pay their share of the costs involved in ONUC (*Opération des Nations Unies au Congo*) and UNEF (the United Nations Emergency Force established in 1956 in response to the Middle East Crisis) because the General Assembly had acted beyond its mandate. as laid out in the Charter, by authorizing a peacekeeping action and apportioning funding. The legal dispute was only solved in 1961 when the General Assembly sought an advisory opinion from the International Court of Justice (ICJ). The ICJ decided that peacekeeping expenses did indeed amount to 'expenses of the organization,' as defined in article 17 of the Charter. In spite of the ICJ's deliberations, their opinion was insufficient to levy the required funds for peacekeeping operations. In 1964 the financial crisis threatened the very survival of the United Nations and led to some highly unusual

---

[12] Figures are from UN doc. ST/ADM/SER.B/183 (10 January 1964).

improvisations designed to save the organization. Article 19 of the UN Charter states:

A Member of the United Nations which is in arrears in the payment of its financial contributions to the Organization shall have no vote in the General Assembly if the amount of its arrears equals or exceeds the amount of the contributions due from it for the preceding two full years.

The Soviet Union reached that point in 1964, and France came perilously close, with the result that the United States threatened to apply article 19. The Soviet Union promptly threatened to leave. What then happened must be considered extraordinary: the United Nations proceeded to hold a session (1964) of the General Assembly with no formal votes being taken and decisions being decided by consultation with the delegates and the President of the Assembly. As a result of the failure to enforce article 19, the United States reserved the right to reject compulsory assessments in the future if it deemed such funding to be contrary to the national interest. The *ad hoc* measures adopted were clearly designed to protect the United Nations; had the Soviet Union, and perhaps France, left, the organization would have been well on the way to unravelling completely. Nevertheless, the failure to implement article 19 for fear of key members resigning, has also demonstrated a lack of resolve and willingness to enforce the spirit and letter of the Charter. Members can fail to meet their assessments with little fear of the consequences.

The financial crisis continued into the 1965 session and a Committee of Thirty-Three was established to deal with the financial crisis. The solution proposed by the Committee was to solicit voluntary contributions which, in effect, left the Soviet Union and France open to decide on the terms of their contributions. The Soviet Union then insisted that any voluntary contributions must be matched by those from the United States. The Soviet Union ultimately withheld funds from peacekeeping operations as well as some additional funds from the regular budget.

Attempts to come to terms with the UN's financial shortcomings since the early 1960s have led to a variety of *ad hoc* solutions. One practice which was informally adopted in 1964 with the formation of the UN Force in Cyprus (UNFICYP) was the reliance on the disputing parties for contributions, as well as voluntary contributions, to meet the costs of peacekeeping operations. The funding for this operation came from three sources: the governments involved, the government of Cyprus and additional voluntary contributions. While not ideal, it kept the United Nations working and maintained its profile in the international system.

In part, the financial difficulties of the United Nations can be accounted for by superpower rivalry, but they also owe a certain amount to the internal political concerns within the organization. For example, the authorization by the Security Council of the creation of a 7,000-man peacekeeping force in the Middle East in October 1973 received no objections and the operation was funded on a scale related to members' contributions to the regular budget. The reason this was passed and funded where other earlier initiatives had not been is related to the source of the initiative. In the Congo case the General Assembly was felt by many, and particularly by the Soviet Union, to be an improper source for peacekeeping initiatives – a concern no doubt prompted

by the 1950 Uniting for Peace Resolution which was intended to by-pass the
Security Council when they were paralysed by a veto or similar obstructive
action. Generally, if demands for peacekeeping emanate from the Security
Council they are more likely to receive financial backing than demands from
the General Assembly, provided they are not blocked by a veto by one of the
five permanent members. There are exceptions to this observation, such as
the peacekeeping initiative in the Lebanon in 1978 which emanated from the
Security Council; on this occasion the Soviet Union and, initially, China
refused funding.

Such was the manner in which the United Nations struggled through the
1960s to the mid-1980s. In 1985 a new and potentially devastating problem
reared its head – the Kassebaum-Solomon amendment. This required that
the United States reduce its contributions to the regular budget from 25 per
cent to 20 per cent, which involved holding back around $42 million for
1987.[13] The reasons for the amendment were twofold; first, concerns over
reducing the US budget deficit prompted close scrutiny of expenditure to international bodies as well as more general overseas expenditure, and secondly,
the United States was concerned about voting procedure in the United Nations
which it felt was under the sway of bloc politics (most notably the Third
World). The Kassebaum-Solomon amendment demanded a weighted system
of voting on budgetary matters so that voting rights would be proportional to
budget contributions. In large part this was a result of mainly US exaspera-
tion at the fact that seven members contribute just over 70 per cent of the
budget, while the 150 small contributors provide just under 30 per cent. Yet
the seven main contributors had only nine votes (the Soviet Union had three
votes since Russia, Byelorussia and the Ukraine all voted)[14] while the small
contributors had 150 votes on budgetary matters.[15]

As a result of the Kassebaum-Solomon amendment, cuts were made in the
top administrative posts and, in December 1986, a twenty-one member Committee for Program and Coordination (CPC) was established. The United
Nations agreed that the spending limits established by the CPC would not be
overridden by the General Assembly. Decisions in the CPC are made by consensus which gives each of the committee members a veto on the size of the UN
biennial budget. In spite of the UN's attempts to meet the objections posed
by the Kassebaum-Solomon amendment, the United States has continued to

[13] Figure from R.E. Riggs and J.C. Plano, *The United Nations: International Organization and
World Politics* (California: Brooks/Cole Publishing Company, 1988), p. 52.

[14] Since the dissolution of the Soviet Union and the formation of the Commonwealth of
Independent States, Russia now occupies the permanent seat on the Security Council and has
assumed responsibility for the Soviet Union's arrears and debts to the United Nations.

[15] Prior to the breakup of the Soviet Union, the seven large contributors, with percentage of
regular budget contributions noted in parentheses, were France (6.26), Germany (8.31), Italy
(3.45), Japan (9.58), USSR (12.95), UK (4.46) and USA (25). Since the breakup of the Soviet
Union, Russia assumes approximately 9.5 per cent of the regular budget and 11.44 per cent
of the peacekeeping budget. The former republics make individual contributions to the UN
budgets and all the former Soviet republics are assessed on the market economy system (see note
7 above). Prior to the dissolution of the Soviet Union and the demise of the communist regimes
in Eastern Europe there was a separate assessment method used for non-market (centrally-
planned) economies which is still applied to the few remaining economies using this method, such
as the People's Republic of China and Cuba.

contribute less than its allotted contributions to both the regular budget and peacekeeping operations.

Several features are worth noting at this juncture. First, the Kassebaum-Solomon amendment is a violation of the UN Charter which could lead to a loss of voting rights in the General Assembly.[16] The introduction of a weighted voting system on budgetary questions, as called for in the amendment would violate not only article 18(1), which provides for one vote for each GA member, but also article 2(1) on the sovereign equality of all members. In spite of the illegal nature of the amendment in terms of the UN Charter there was little fear of article 19 being enforced since any attempt to do so would potentially lead to the loss of the remaining funding and, in all likelihood, the demise of the United Nations. Secondly, the position of the United States differs from that of the other six main contributors. The Soviet Union promised to pay its full share of all peacekeeping operations since 1956 (but was unable to meet this promise), China paid $4.3 million owed for the support of the UN Congo operations, and even India and Brazil have managed to pay some of their long overdue debts. Although it would be unjust to lay the UN's financial crisis solely at America's doorstep, the United States remains the largest withholder of funds and to a large extent the future of the United Nations rests in its hands. Why, in spite of the creation of the CPC, has the United States persisted in withholding funds from the UN budget?

The simple answer is that the CPC has not worked as it was supposed to. Initially, the CPC had twenty-one seats distributed between three categories according to financial liability. Thus, in 1986 the picture looked like this:

Composition of CPC in 1986

CPC Members by Assessment Percentages	Number of Members	Assessed Percentage	% of Seats Held
Major contributors (= 1% +)	8	68.67	38
Middle contributors (= 0.4–0.99%)	7	2.46	33
Small contributors (= 0.01–0.03%)	6	0.9	28

In this form the CPC answered some of the issues raised by the Kassebaum-Solomon amendment since it appeared to restore some of the budgetary control to those who paid the most. However, with the enlargement of the CPC from twenty-one to thirty-four members the principle of the broadest possible geographical representation was observed. By 1988 the CPC looked radically different:

---

[16] The American Bar Association's House of Delegates adopted a resolution both condemning the Congress's action and urging cooperation between the executive and legislative branches of government to restore payment in full.

Composition of CPC in 1988

CPC Members by Assessment Percentage	Number of Members	Assessed Percentage	% of Seats Held
Major contributors	9	71.24	26
Middle contributors	14	5.21	41
Small contributors	11	0.16	32

The growth in the number of middle contributors, mainly African states, shifted control decisively away from the major contributors whose burden, in financial terms, had actually increased. As a bureaucratic attempt at solving some of the budgetary control concerns, the CPC was a failure.

With the failure of the CPC to satisfy US concerns regarding financial liability and voting rights, the United States was obliged to enforce the Kassebaum-Solomon amendment terms, which meant a reduction of the US contribution from its assessed 25 per cent contribution, to 20 per cent. In financial terms the effects are clear:

Assessed Contributions outstanding to the UN Regular Budget at 31 December 1990 (in US$ millions)

Year	Owed by US	Total Outstanding	US % of Total
1981	24.2	145.6	16.6
1982	3.4	147.9	2.3
1983	27.4	170.5	16.1
1984	11.5	166.2	6.9
1985	85.5	242.4	35.3
1986	147.0	257.8	57.0
1987	252.8	353.4	71.5
1988	307.7	394.9	77.9
1989	365.1	461.2	79.2
1990	296.2	403.0	73.5

Source: Status of Contributions. UN Secretariat ST/ADM/SER B/1990

The enforcement of the Kassebaum-Solomon amendment in 1985 caused an obvious worsening of the financial position of the United Nations and while the United States is not the only country in arrears, the figures clearly illustrate that America controls the fate of the UN through its financial health. It should also be pointed out that at the same time as the United States began to withhold funds, the UN's regular budget increased from around $811 million in the period 1978–9, to $1.2 billion in 1980–1, and $1.5 billion by 1984–5.

The Kassebaum-Solomon amendment was only the tip of more widespread Congressional concern about the United Nations. The first complaint, which has already been touched upon, related to the need for a consensual decision-making mechanism for the budgetary process. Complaints in the US Congress were rife about exploitation of the budgetary process by Third World members. One of the catalysts for the Kassebaum-Solomon amendment had been the expenditure in 1984 of some $74 million on a conference centre for the Economic Commission for Africa in Addis Ababa. This was condemned by Senator Nancy Kassebaum as an example of the 'tyranny of the Third World majority'.[17]

The second complaint was that the principles laid out by Sir Eric Drummond, the first Secretary-General of the League of Nations, were being violated by the process of secondment. Drummond had advocated the creation of an international civil servant whose primary loyalty was to the organization and not to his or her country of origin and this was later enshrined in article 100 of the UN Charter.[18] There was concern in the United States, as voiced by the Senate's Select Committee on Intelligence and by other official bodies, that certain countries were violating this principle, in particular the Soviet Union whose 'civil servants' were obliged to respond to KGB calls for assistance. In its report of May 1985,[19] the Committee observed that approximately 25 per cent of all Soviets in the UN Secretariat were intelligence officers and that 'many more' were co-opted by the Soviet intelligence agencies. Other intelligence agencies estimated that 'as many as one-half of the Soviet and Soviet bloc nationals in the UN Secretariat are officers of the KGB or the GRU'.[20] As of September 1985, it was estimated that 442 of 446 Soviet nationals employed throughout the UN system were 'seconded'.[21] The charge, from the US perspective, was that the Soviet Union had effectively used the UN Secretariat in the conduct of its foreign relations. US ire was further stirred when the Secretary-General announced a hiring freeze in April 1986 which was designed to reduce UN personnel by 15 per cent over a three-year period. On 5 May 1987, however, the Secretary-General reported that he was considering granting 156 exceptions to the hiring freeze, of which 104 would be Soviet or Soviet-bloc nationals. The State Department alleged that this constituted a 'gross violation' of articles 100 and 101.[22]

These two overriding complaints led to the restructuring of the US contributions to the United Nations. The Foreign Relations Act, FY 1988–89, section 143, entitled *Reform in Budget Decision-Making Procedures of the United Nations and its Specialized Agencies*, demanded the adoption and implementation

---

[17] Senator N. Kassebaum, Statement on Amendment no. 293 to S1003, Foreign Relations Authorization Act, Fiscal Years 1986–7. Congressional Record, 7 June 1985, S7793.

[18] Article 100 of the UN Charter reads: 'In the performance of their duties the Secretary-General and the staff shall not seek or receive instructions from any government or from any other authority external to the Organization. They shall refrain from any action which might reflect on their position as international officials responsible only to the Organization.'

[19] US Senate Print 99–52, May 1985.

[20] Quoted in US Public Law 100–204, December 1987, p. 101 STAT 1384.

[21] *Ibid.*

[22] Article 100 is explained above in footnote 18. Article 101 stipulates, amongst other things, that 'appropriate staffs shall be permanently assigned to the Economic and Social Council, the Trusteeship Council, and, as required, to other organs of the United Nations.' It also specified that paramount consideration shall be given to 'securing the highest standards of efficiency, competence, and integrity'.

of decision-making procedures on budgetary matters. The Act stipulates[23] that the United States should pay 40 per cent of its assessment on 1 October. An additional 40 per cent should be provided on the condition that the President report to Congress that a consensus-based decision-making procedure is being created regarding the budgetary process. The President must also be satisfied that significant reductions are being made in the Secretariat staff (up to the designated 15 per cent level). The remaining monies can be paid to the United Nations within thirty days after Congress receives the Presidential assent, unless it is blocked by a joint resolution of the Congress. The President has yet to report to Congress that he is satisfied with the progress towards the required changes in the organization. More significantly, section 143 stipulates that US-assessed contributions to any UN specialized agency may not exceed 20 per cent in any calendar year unless the President overrides this stipulation. Although section 143 officially terminated on 30 September 1989, it effectively still exists in the form of an amended version of the Kassebaum-Solomon amendment (1990).

What have the results of the Kassebaum-Solomon amendment been? For the United States, the amendment was seen as a way of inducing some fundamental reforms and, for many in the US Congress, it was seen as the necessary catalyst to spur the United Nations to serious reforms. While the United Nations did respond to the amendment, as described below, it is by no means clear that the amendment produced the desired results. It has, for example, posed a logical conundrum for the United Nations. How are these reforms meant to be conceived of and implemented when there have been administrative cut-backs which have resulted in difficulties in financial forecasting, future planning and restructuring designs? How is the United Nations meant to plan for major restructuring and modifications when its financial plight is so uncertain and all that it can rely upon from its major financial backer is 40 per cent of its assessment, maybe more, if the organization is lucky? As Javier Pérez de Cuéllar commented before the General Assembly:

Planning a budget to match a programme was largely meaningless when neither the amount nor the timing of contributions could be predicted. Uncertainty would soon destroy the Organization's ability to enter into commitments.

The Secretary-General also commented on the 'atmosphere of perpetual crisis and the need for constant expedients to honour its mandate and the related expenses'.[24] If anything, the amendment has forced the United Nations to divert funds away from emergency uses, such as peacekeeping, and to use it to cover shortfalls in the day-to-day costs of the organization. Futhermore, by demonstrating its willingness to put national interests above those of the United Nations, the United States has damaged its credibility and trustworthiness as a leading member of the United Nations, and has cast doubt upon its adherence to the ideals and principles of the organization.

---

[23] Public Law 100–204, 22 December 1987.
[24] General Assembly, Fifth Committee, 12th meeting, 16 October 1987, *Address by the Secretary-General*. Doc. A/C.5/42/SR.12, p. 10.

The US message was heard and acted upon when the UN Secretary-General proposed in April 1988 that the Secretariat be reduced by around 13 per cent. In practice these reductions have been slow and exacerbated by the accession, and potential accession, of new members to the organization. In spite of US protestations, the General Assembly reconfirmed the views of the Fifth (Finance) Committee when they stated that 'the capacity to pay of member states is the fundamental criterion for determining the scale of assessments'.[25] Even when the Committee on Contributions delivered their report on assessment methodology which had been prepared at the request of the General Assembly, the hope of any internal UN relief for the United States was not forthcoming.[26]

An additional irritant to UN financing has been the discrepancies in the fiscal years of the United States and the organization. The UN fiscal year is the same as the calendar year, while the US fiscal year runs from 1 October to 30 September. This means that US payments to the organization will be on assessments made by the United Nations the previous year. In practical terms this means that the United States only completed its payments to the 1989 UN budget in August 1990.[27] The fact that US funds are not available to the United Nations during their fiscal year obviously makes the financing of UN activites difficult, quite apart from funding shortcomings. The US budget allocations for the United Nations are made as part of the overall budget for international organizations, as agreed by the House and Senate Appropriations Committee. Even when this is announced the organization is not guaranteed a specific allocation since the appropriated funds are then split between the various international organizations of which the US is a member. Since the late 1980s the United Nations has borne a higher proportion of the shortfall than have the UN specialized agencies. There are two reasons for this. First, there is a feeling in Congress that the specialized agencies represent US interests in a manner which reflects financial contributions more accurately than the United Nations. Moreover, the activities of the specialized agencies are seen as having a more direct impact upon the United States than those of the United Nations. Secondly, the UN specialized agencies have more highly developed lobbying groups in Washington DC than does the United Nations. Underfunding of the International Civil Aviation Organization (ICAO), the World Health Organization (WHO), or the International Atomic Energy Agency (IAEA), to name but a few, would be detrimental to US interests, damaging air traffic safety, research into AIDS or nuclear safeguards. Other specialized agencies such as the Food and Agricultural Organization (FAO) have not been so lucky. In spite of the FAO's work, which is 'vitally important and of substantial benefit to the United States and to world trade in agricultural commodities,'[28] the United States is in

---

[25] General Assembly resolution 43/223 A,B,C, December 1986.

[26] General Assembly, *Report of the Committee on Contributions*, Annex A, supplement no. 11; A/44/11.

[27] See Vita Bite, CRS Report for Congress, *US Withholding and Arrearages to the United Nations Regular Budget: Issues for Congress*, 19 June 1991, pp. 12 and 30.

[28] US Congress, Hearing before the Subcommittee on Human Rights and International Organizations, and on International Operations, of the Committee on Foreign Affairs, House of Representatives, *Recent Developments in the United Nations System*, 101st Congress, 2nd session, 25 April 1990 (Washington DC: GPO, 1990), pp. 112-3.

arrears to the agency, largely because it ignored the concerns of the United States and other major contributors and approved an 'excessive budget.'[29] Underfunding the United Nations, by contrast, has effects that are as not as immediately obvious or injurious to US interests. The effects for the UN are quite the opposite. The United Nations is virtually bankrupt at a time when, as one US official observed, 'the US is placing ever increasing demands on the UN to do more in key areas such as international drug control, the environment and international peacekeeping'.[30] Nor is the problem confined to the United Nations itself, similar problems haunt the UN Industrial Development Organization (UNIDO) and the International Labour Organization (ILO), where the United States is also responsible for 25 per cent of the assessed budget.

The current problem

The financial woes of the United Nations are not new but they have now become acute. What accounts for this? The simple answer is that the organization has, until now, muddled through in an unsatisfactory manner that provided stop-gap solutions but no long-term answers. The stop-gaps were akin to the strategy of robbing Peter to pay Paul. Two mechanisms have traditionally been used: the Working Capital Fund, which was raised in 1981 to $100 million from $40 million, and the UN Special Account, established in the mid-1960s with the objective of overcoming financial difficulties. The Special Account was overhauled in 1972 with the hope that it could address the UN's financial difficulties and to resolve the short-term deficit. By the end of 1990, however, Pérez de Cuéllar reported that both these funds were exhausted,[31] largely due to the feeling that the voluntary contributions were effectively subsidizing the American under-contribution. Both the funds were of modest proportion and certainly inadequate to solve the scale of the UN's financial problems that have existed since the mid-1970s. As a result of the failure of the Working Capital Fund and the Special Account, the Secretary General was forced to 'borrow' from the peacekeeping budget to cover short-term deficits in the regular budget. However, this has merely transferred problems from one place to another with the result that, for example, the UN Interim Force in Lebanon (UNIFIL) is now in arrears (the United States owes around $130 million to UNIFIL).[32] By the end of 1990 it had become painfully obvious that the Working Capital Fund had become woefully inadequate for the purpose that it was supposed to serve, with the result that Perez de Cuellar appealed for extra funding for the fund, to around $200 million.[33]

The new Secretary-General, Egyptian diplomat Boutros Boutros Ghali,

---

[29] *Ibid.*, p. 116.
[30] *Ibid.*, p. 95.
[31] *Current Financial Crisis of the United Nations*, *op. cit.* note 4 above.
[32] *Ibid.*
[33] *Ibid.*, p. 3. Pérez de Cuéllar also suggested that the Working Capital Fund should ideally be increased beyond the $200 million level to approximately 25 per cent of the regular budget. He described this measure as the 'only realistic buffer between the Organization and bankruptcy'.

140   Simon Duke

must put the finance question at the top of his agenda since, without a resolution of this question, the United Nations will be increasingly incapacitated
at a time when it has major commitments in Cambodia and Yugoslavia, and
may be called upon to undertake similar work in El Salvador and Somalia. The
gravity of the problem which faces Boutros Ghali should not be underestimated; on 31 December 1991, members who had not paid their dues owed the
regular budget and the already assessed costs of peacekeeping operations a
combined amount of $1 billion. The regular budget is owed around $439.3
million (the United States being responsible for $266.4 million of that) and
$463.5 million is owed to the peacekeeping budget (the US share being
$140.9). The United States alone owes the two budgets around $407.3
million,[34] but is not the only debtor. Russia owes around $172 million to the
regular and peacekeeping budgets, Brazil $18 million, Canada $11 million,
France $10.4 million and Britain $4 million. Washington went some of the
way towards amending the situation in October 1991 by paying $180 million
towards its assessed 1991 contributions of $272 million. The Bush adminis-
tration will withhold the balance to ensure that the General Assembly holds
expenditure level in the biennial budget it is drawing up. Both UN budgets,
the regular budget and the separate peacekeeping budget, are in dire straits.
At the end of November 1991, only 67 of the 159 countries assessed for 1991
contributions, had paid up.[35] By the end of 1991 the five largest debtors owed
the two UN budgets $678.4 million, the United States having the largest share
of the debts:

Debt at the UN, 31 December 1991 (US$ million)
Amount owed by the Five Largest Debtors

Country	Amount owed: Regular	Peacekeeping	Total
United States	266.4	140.9	407.3
Russian Federation	46.0	126.7	172.7
S.Africa	45.0	16.5	61.5
Brazil	17.8	1.0	18.8
Ukraine	5.7	12.4	18.1
TOTAL	380.9	297.5	678.4

Source: *New York Times*, 27 Jan. 1992. p. A8.

The gravity of the financial situation is either ignored or seen as somebody
else's responsibility; at a meeting between the fifteen Security Council members (the five permanent members and the ten rotating members) on 24
January 1992, the Security Council members called on the United Nations to
play a 'growing role' in preserving peace in trouble spots around the world.[36]

---

[34] *The New York Times*, 'UN Fund Crisis Worsens as Role in Security Rises', pp. A1 and A8.
The New York Times, 'UN Asks Billion for Peacekeeper Fund', 25 November 1991, p. A3, and *The
Economist*, 30 November 1991, p. 17 quoted a higher figure for the combined US debt, amounting
to $483.5 million.
[35] *The New York Times*, 'UN Asks Billion for Peacekeeper Fund', 25 November 1991, p. A1.
[36] *The New York Times*, 'UN's Fund Crisis Worsens as Role in Security Rises', 27 January
1992, p. A1.

At least three of the members who called upon the organization to assume this expanded role are major debtors to the regular and peacekeeping funds. The apparent ability to continue building wish-lists while ignoring how this can be done is worrying. At a rough estimate the 'wish-list' compared to the actual funds available looks like this:

Estimate of UN Peacekeeping Expenses for 1992* (US$ million)

A *Projected UN Involvement*	B *Current Involvement*	C *Task Completion*
Cambodia 750–1 billion Yugoslavia 350–450	Lebanon, Kuwait, Golan Heights, West Sahara, Angola, Central America, El Salvador	Cent/America (April 1992) Angola, (Oct. 1992)
TOTAL: + 1.1 – 1.45 billion	+ 500	– 150–175

* In addition three other peacekeeping operations are funded through non-peacekeeping fund routes. Around $30 million per annum is spent on peace-keeping operations in Cyprus, funded by voluntary contributions, and another $35 million is spent on truce observation in Jerusalem and the India-Pakistan border, paid for through the regular budget.

The figures above are rough estimates and give a somewhat distorted pic-ture. The figures in A represent extraordinary expenditure since start-up costs are always higher and thus do not necessarily represent normal peacekeeping costs. Nevertheless, if A is added to B, peacekeeping costs could amount to around $1.6–1.95 billion and if the savings from C are subtracted the total is still around the billion dollar range. Although the figures are extremely rough they do serve to illustrate that such activities are financially beyond the UN's peacekeeping budget which at the end of 1991 was $377 million in arrears, out of a projected budget of around $1 billion. Even if the UN's involvement in peacekeeping operations were cut, it is unclear how the organization is going to fund its involvement in Cambodia or Yugoslavia, let alone both. In financial terms, the call for the United Nations to play a growing role in preserving peace in trouble spots around the world is nonsense. The funds do not exist to finance even half of the desired peacekeeping projects. This, it should be remembered, is in addition to the $439 million that is owed to the regular UN budget. Even the old tactic of borrowing from the regular budget to pay for peacekeeping, or even vice versa, is no longer a viable notion.

Within the United Nations the gravity of the situation is well recognized. Various *ad hoc* and increasingly desperate remedies have been attempted. For example, in an attempt to save the organization from insolvency Secretary-General Pérez de Cuéllar proposed that those who owed money to the two budgets should pay interest and those who paid promptly and in full, like Australia and most of the West European countries, should pay their 1992 dues early so that December 1991 costs could be met. The latter proposal was unacceptable; nor would it have solved the problem, but merely have passed the buck to the new Secretary-General Boutros Boutros Ghali. The idea of charging interest to encourage settlement of overdue obligations is one that is potentially dangerous. While it is clearly designed with the United States in mind, it risks cultivating an antagonistic attitude in the United States towards the organization and it also risks exacerbating the already critical economic state of the Russian Federation. Such proposals do however illustrate the gravity of the UN's financial situation. So, what are the possible solutions to the problems facing Dr Boutros Ghali?

Six suggestions

1. The first suggestion is to persuade other rich industrial countries to assume more of the financial burden which has accrued to the United States or to adjust the assessments so that the United States assumes a lower portion. Such persuasion could be accompanied by inducements such as permanent seats on the Security Council or penalties for those who do not pay in a timely manner. This solution, though, seems unlikely to succeed as the two powers who are (or were) in a position to pay more, Germany and Japan, have preoccupations of their own. In the German case the preoccupation is obviously with the after-effects of unification and changes in the former Soviet Union. Chancellor Kohl has called on the industrialized nations to give support to the United Nations, while at the same time warning the international community, that '[We Germans] have reached the limit of our capabilities'. Kohl observed that Germany was shouldering 56 per cent of all Western aid to the former Soviet Union along with 32 percent of the aid to Central and Eastern European nations.[37] It is unlikely that Germany will be persuaded to pay more than its current assessment mainly because of its own preoccupations but also because of the feeling that the funding crisis in the United Nations is primarily of US construct. It should be noted that Germany has shown no willingness to restore its $17 million of unpaid assessments owed to the peace-keeping budget, presumably because it feels it is already shouldering more than its fair share of the burden in helping the struggling Commonwealth of Independent States as well as having made a considerable financial contribution to the Gulf War effort.

In Japan's case Prime Minister Kiichi Miyazawa suffered a setback when the motion to let Japan participate in UN peacekeeping operations was turned down by its parliament, the Diet. Miyazawa's position was also compromised by Japan's worsening economic situation. If Japan were to assume a major

[37] *The Week in Germany*, 6 September 1991, p. 1 (New York: German Information Centre). It should also be pointed out that the high proportion of aid that Germany gives to the Commonwealth of Independent States results largely from an arrangement to help the ex-Warsaw Pact forces move out of what was formerly East Germany. The former German Foreign Minister, Hans-Dietrich Genscher, called for a greater international role for the UN in disputes such as that in Yugoslavia, when he said that 'We expect the Security Council to adopt a clear unequivocal position so that the fighting can be stopped'. He also called for an 'International Court of Justice where crimes against humanity, crimes against peace, genocide, war crimes and environmental criminality can be prosecuted and punished'. *The Week In Germany*, 27 September 1991.

financial responsibility in the United Nations it is likely that this enhanced role would have a political price, in the form of a permament seat on the Security Council. It is not clear that this would be wholly welcome given the wave of anti-Japanese sentiment sweeping across the United States in early 1992.

The European Community may, eventually, be able to pick up some of the financial slack, but since Germany would be the main EC contributor the same objections outlined above would apply.[38] If, for the sake of argument, Germany, Japan or the European Community did pick up some of the arrears, there would be a political price to pay in the form of political concessions. A seat on the Security Council by any one of these parties, or a combination thereof, would have the effect of undermining US leadership and influence in the United Nations. Symbolically, too, it might be damaging to US prestige and lead to suspicions that the United States is a superpower in decline, with knock-on effects for other areas of US diplomatic activity.

The possibility of introducing penalties for late payment or incentives for early contributions is one that has some superficial attraction but may be problematic in practice. Penalty systems do exist elsewhere – in the International Telecommunications Union and the Universal Postal Union – but attempts to apply this to the United Nations as a whole are open to objection. The introduction of penalties would have to be voted upon and could be subject to veto by the main offenders. Penalties could also be seen as unjust unless they differentiated between those powers who for perfectly legitimate reasons could not meet their assessments and those who withhold funds for political reasons. Finally, there is a risk that the introduction of penalties could be interpreted as an anti-American move and achieve quite the opposite effect to that intended; instead of putting pressure on the United States to pay it could have the effect of confirming suspicions held by some in Congress of an anti-American bias in the United Nations and might exacerbate the UN's funding crisis.

Incentive schemes, designed to encourage early payment of funds, have been implemented by the ICAO, UNESCO, the International Maritime Organization (IMO) and the World Meteorological Organization (WMO). ICAO introduced incentives in January 1987 and the others followed a year later. All of these agencies engaged in intensive follow-up activities but it is difficult to attribute the results to the respective incentive schemes. It would be difficult, but not impossible, to apply such a scheme to the United Nations. It is open to the objection that any incentives offered would probably be too small to be of great interest to the United States and other members in arrears.

The adjustment of assessments has been suggested as one way of alleviating the US burden. If the minimum assessment of 0.01 per cent, paid by around eighty UN members, were adjusted upwards, the US share could be lowered proportionately. Although the minimum assessment seems low, in monetary terms it represents around $90,000 per annum (less than the cost of maintaining a diplomat in New York for one year), any increase could impose severe strains on the least developed countries who may rely upon the organization

---

[38] The twelve EC countries contribute around 30 per cent of the UN's regular budget.

144   *Simon Duke*

for their contact with the international community and the developed states. If the minimum assessment were doubled for half of the least developed states, the increase in revenue would be in the order of $3.7 million per annum. Attempts to increase contributions from developing states (who contribute between 0.4–0.99 per cent) would meet political resistance and, even if successful, would be insufficient to solve the UN's funding crisis.

2. The second suggestion concerns alternative fee sources, essentially the levying of taxes on 'international' goods and services. There are many possibilities: a fee could be charged for UN services; a surcharge could be applied to international communications or mail; a fee could be charged for the use of international water or airspace;[39] exploitation of the resources of the seabed through a UN agency could result in the surrender of a percentage of the profits to that agency; or a percentage of each member's national taxes might be devoted to the United Nations. There are, doubtless, many other such ideas. All, however, have significant drawbacks. The suggested sources of additional revenue outlined above would mean that the organization would be less dependent on national support but such a scheme could hit the poorest members and, if the contributions were graded according to the ability to pay or use of resources, the original assessment problem still exists with all of its attendant problems. The larger contributors might also view the increasing financial independence of the United Nations as a threat, but the unwillingness of those same states to fund the organization adequately could ultimately push it in this direction for funding.

3. Thirdly, Pérez de Cuéllar made a direct plea to governments and private corporations to contribute funds, with the objective of establishing a $1 billion Peace Endowment Fund, to help pay for future UN peacekeeping operations. This, together with interest charges on late contributions, would only amount to a stop-gap measure and would not constitute a long-term solution to the UN's finance problems. The Peace Endowment Fund, should it be established, also runs the danger of merely becoming another method of subsidizing the regular budget of the United Nations, as peacekeeping funds have done in the past. Indeed, with the potential for a rapid growth in the demand for UN peacekeeping and conflict resolution activities, the problem may only become worse as pressure on both budgets mounts. If direct pleas for voluntary contributions are made and the United Nations as a whole becomes more reliant upon voluntary contributions, this might solve the immediate budgetary crisis but could lead to others in the future. There are currently around twenty-five UN programmes which receive their funding from voluntary contributions and their experience provides a hint of what could happen. The key difficulty is that voluntary contributions are not consistent, making long-term planning extremely difficult and subject to national political whim. For example, the 1984 World Population Conference, held appropriately in Mexico City, was threatened with disaster when the United States threatened to suspend its contributions to the UN Fund for Population Activities (UNFPA) in protest against the support that the UNFPA gives to non-governmental organizations

---

[39] A precedent already exists for such a course of action. Under resolution 1212 (XII), adopted by the General Assembly on 14 December 1957, a surcharge of 3 per cent on Suez Canal traffic was imposed in order to repay the advances made by certain countries to the UN to meet the costs of clearing the Canal.

who perform or otherwise support abortion. Increasing reliance upon voluntary funding could lead to instability in the United Nations, with the organization subject to the political stratagems of the key players and dependent upon the whims of the key financiers. Whatever the flaws of the assessment system, it does at least have the potential for long-term planning. If the United Nations were to resort to commercial borrowing, as has been suggested, this would merely serve to burden the organization with more debt.

4. Fourthly, there is the 'muddle through' approach which applies in particular to peacekeeping operations. The obvious model for this is the funding of the Gulf War in 1991. This was an *ad hoc* response to the twelve Security Council resolutions. The Gulf War was not a UN operation as such but one conducted by UN member states in a coalition force, mandated by the resolutions. The funding for the operation cannot serve as a model since the Gulf War effort was the result of a particular set of circumstances at a specific point in time and, furthermore, it was only nominally a UN-related activity. The United Nations responded to the Iraqi invasion of Kuwait largely because of US objections to the invasion – unlike the invasions of Cyprus, Panama, Lebanon or Western Sahara.[40] The 'muddle through' approach is open to objections on the grounds that the financial crisis in the United Nations is acute and, barring the restoration of full funding, the organization cannot survive unchanged. To use the United Nations as the basis for international peacekeeping action is certainly better than the complete demise of the organization, but such a model does open up the possibility of the more powerful and affluent UN members being selective about what they choose to get involved in.

5. The fifth option is to make do with a far smaller United Nations or one that is radically restructured. At a minimum the Secretariat could be shrunk by 15 per cent, the Trusteeship Council abolished (there remains only one trust territory), the International Court of Justice could be given additional powers to levy substantial fines from UN member states which would then be surrendered to the organization, and there is clearly a need for a thorough review of the budgetary process. However, such suggestions for 'streamlining' hide the fact that far from being an over-bloated bureaucracy, the United Nations is suffering from a chronic staff shortage. In 1986 the Secretary-General implemented a recruitment freeze in an effort to cut-back, resulting in a vacancy rate of 10.8 per cent, a deferment of cost-of-living allowance increases in the General Service category and, in one regional commission, a professional vacancy rate of 25.5 per cent. The result of the recruitment freeze has been 'grave discrepancies between available skills and programme needs'.[41]

[40] For an extension of this argument see Noam Chomsky, 'The Use (and Abuse) of the United Nations' in C. Cerf and M.L. Sifry (eds), *The Gulf War Reader* (New York: Times Books/Random House, 1991), pp. 307–10. The United States has frequently frustrated UN peacekeeping efforts, including US vetoes of its invasion of Panama, a veto of a resolution condemning Israeli human rights abuses, another veto exercized against a resolution condemning US support for the Contras and another condemning its economic policies against Nicaragua. Other blockades within the United Nations are of longer standing, such as the twenty-year US opposition to a political settlement of the Arab-Israeli conflict.

[41] General Assembly, 42nd session, Fifth Committee, 12th meeting, 16 October 1987, *Address by the Secretary-General*. Doc. A/C.5/SR.12, p. 11.

146   *Simon Duke*

The image of UN officials being overpaid is also erroneous; the conditions of service have deteriorated and many staff members face financial hardship while serving the organization. Certain governments have even taken to offering financial inducements for their nationals to accept positions with the international civil service. Such adjustments have been of questionable benefit to the regular budget and any savings have been made at the expense of efficiency. The freeze, aimed at reducing the Secretariat by 15 per cent, does not answer the economic problems of the peacekeeping budget.

With the demise of many of the regional security organizations and the questionable utility of some of the remaining ones, most of which were built with Cold War exigencies in mind, a case could be made for the surrender of some of the funds used for these organizations to the United Nations to further international peace and stability instead of regional schemes. The chances of this happening are not encouraging; many figures about the US 'peace dividend' have been circulated but amongst the many ideas about what to do with the dividend (ranging from deficit financing to investment in civil and social programmes) there has been no mention of an increase of funding to the United Nations.

In terms of structural reform there are several options, some of which have been touched on already. One alternative is to reach a compromise between the seemingly intractable problem of funding versus voting in the budgetary process. Weighted voting could be introduced in the budgetary process, reflecting the actual contributions made by members. This might encourage Germany and Japan to contribute more. At the same time a move could be made to abolish the anachronistic permanent members' seats on the Security Council, i.e. those reflecting post-war conceptions of power in terms of military might which are less relevant to contemporary definitions of power which emphasize economic performance. This might have the benefit of enhancing the UN's potential to maintain international peace and stability. It might also alleviate the richer countries' needs for prestige and influence while at the same time reducing the likelihood of the Security Council being rendered helpless by paralysis due to the exercise of the veto.[42] Whatever the intrinsic benefits or demerits of such a scheme, it is clear that such a proposal, necessitating amendments to the UN Charter, would face objections from those with a vested interest in maintaining the status quo and would lead to protracted debate which would not answer the need for an urgent answer to the funding crisis.

6. The final option is for the United States to restore funding to the United Nations. Before this is done a persuasive case has to be made to Congress and the Bush administration by the US delegation to the United Nations. This should include the reminder that countries who do not pay their assessments are in violation of international law. There are signs that Bush is sympathetic to this line of reasoning, in part for personal reasons since he was US representative to the organization in 1973–4. The Bush administration, unlike that of Reagan, is sympathetic to the United Nations but the real problems still rest with Congress and the link made between the US budget deficit and

---

[42] An expansion of the Security Council's membership to include Germany and Japan might solve some of the funding concerns but might well lead to the institutionalization of existing disputes, such that between Russia and Japan over the Kurile Islands.

contributions to organizations such as the United Nations. The doubts about
the role and utility of the United Nations that existed in the early and mid-
1980s have lessened, largely in response to the end of the Cold War. The
problem of the general state of the US economy is one that is still seen as a real
obstacle to restoring full funding to the organization.

Bush has personally pledged to restore US arrears to the organization. In
a speech to the United Nations on 1 October 1990 he affirmed his administration's support for the organization and promised to pay 'what we are
obliged to pay by the Charter'. In part the Bush administration was responding to the more general changes in the international security environment
and the gradual change in attitude within Congress in some influential circles,
such as the Senate Foreign Relations Commitee.[43] As part of the Bush
administration's support for the organization a plan was announced to restore
the arrears over a five-year term, starting in 1991. While this is undoubtedly
good news for the United Nations the grounds for optimism have been
tempered by the decline in the dollar relative to other currencies, with the
result that the anticipated payment of arrears has actually been smaller than
expected.[44] Exchange rate fluctuations have caused problems for the United
States since the UN assessments, combined with the decline in the value of
the dollar, has led to underestimations of budget requests by the office of
Management and Budget. In the 1992 financial year, the anticipated contributions, alongside statutory and policy withholdings,[45] led to a US shortfall of
$34.7 million.[46]

Even with Bush's apparent goodwill towards the United Nations, which is
stressed in policy terms by the UN's central role in his 'New World Order',
there are still problems to be overcome in Congress before the US can restore
most of the funding. The problems range from the legal to the political. The
Kassebaum-Solomon amendment poses the most formidable legal obstacle to
the restoration of funds. The amendment still requires the withholding of up
to 60 per cent of the US assessment until the President can assure Congress
that the requisite amendments have been made. Upon Presidential assurance
that the changes have been made, it is then up to Congress to decide whether
or not to pay the remaining 20 per cent within a thirty-day period after the
Presidential report. The sticking point still remains the question of whether
the organization is willing to introduce budgetary reforms in return for the
restoration of the remaining 40–60 per cent of the US contribution. The political concerns revolve around the question of whether the UN represents 'good
value' for money at a time of financial stringency and whether the organization
is fully aligned with US interests. On the political front the potential for a

[43] See US Congress, Senate. Committee on Foreign Relations. Supplement to Foreign Relations Authorization Act, 1990. 101st Congress, 2nd session, Senate. Report 101–334 (Washington
DC: GPO, 1990).
[44] In the 1991 financial year some of the funds appropriated for payment of arrears were
reclaimed to make up for exchange rate losses in the funding of international organizations. The
amount that was thus deducted was held over to the following year. The same pattern was
replicated in 1992 and may well be so again until a final adjustment is made in fiscal year 1995.
[45] US statutory withholdings include those programmes associated with the PLO, SWAPO
and cost of living increases for UN employees in New York. Policy withholdings include support
for the Preparatory Commission for the Law of the Sea Treaty and the Tax Equalization Fund.
[46] Figure in Vita Bite, *op. cit.* note 27 above, p. 11.

restoration of partial funding looks brighter as the general attitude to the organization seems more munificent. Restoration of full funding is likely, however, to remain problematic. Full payment of arrears would require the removal of statutory prohibitions and there appears to be little desire to do this. Payment of the arrears does not appear to guarantee that funding to the individual organizational recipients would be guaranteed since the funds, if appropriated, would be 'directed toward activities mutually acceptable to both the United States and the respective international organizations'.[47]

The question for Congress is not whether the United States can afford to restore funding to the United Nations, it is ultimately a question of political will. Statements emanating from Congress insist that the United States is unable to meet all of its budgetary obligations to international organizations, but there is also a recognition that the allocation of funds is a political judgement made in the light of how a given organization is deemed to serve US interests. A typical example would be the following statement made in a 1990 Congressional hearing in reference to the US arrears to the Food and Agricultural Organization:

In recent years we have not had sufficient budgetary resources to pay our full assessments to the UN system organizations. We have had to make judgements in allocating the funds which have been made available. Those judgements have reflected the responsiveness of individual organizations to US desires for improvements in their program and budget process to enhance value for money spent.[48]

Arguments that the United States cannot afford to restore funding and pay its assessments look unconvincing in the light of the billions that the country spent on the Gulf War (where vital US interests were seen as being at stake) and when compared to its funding of other major international organizations. For example, the United States has no arrears with the Organization for Economic Cooperation and Development (OECD) nor with the North Atlantic Treaty Organization (NATO). The comparison with NATO is particlarly interesting since for the last four decades there has been a burden-sharing debate within NATO about whether the United States is assuming an unfair share of the burden. This has been accompanied, at times, by suspicions of incipient anti-American feelings within the organization. In spite of these problems the United States has continued to assume its portion of NATO's defence burden. The question of UN funding is ultimately a question of priorities and political will, not one primarily of resources.

Conclusions

Of the six options outlined above the last is the most desirable, at least in the short-term. Some may well challenge the logic of the argument but the case for the restoration of US arrears in the first place and, in the second, its assumption of responsibility for its assessments for the regular budget and

---

[47] US Congress, *Recent Developments in the United Nations System, op. cit.* note 6 above, p. 114.
[48] *Ibid.*, p. 116.

peacekeeping operations are strong. The main benefits for the United States in following this course of action are that it would restore international confidence in the United Nations as well as the sincerity of the Bush administration's proclaimed support of the organization as a cornerstone of the new world order.

The consistent US underfunding of the United Nations is largely a by-product of a Cold War mentality whereby it is politic to be seen as an admirer and supporter of the organization but, at the same time, words are not matched with deeds (or cash). The potential for the organization to play a valuable role in the international system and not to be hampered by alliance systems or superpower whims is new and should be encouraged. To strangle this potential at this historic point in time would be irresponsible when no other international or regional organization, or single country, could replicate the spirit and role of the United Nations. For most of the developed countries the cost of UN activities represents less that one per cent of their military budgets. The United States has embarked upon defence cut-backs which could amount to annual savings of $50 billion over the next five years. While much of the funding is already spoken for directly or indirectly, it seems that the restoration of funding to the United Nations would incur economic costs that are dwarfed by the political significance of the gesture.

Other countries, such as Britain and Germany, are carrying out similar military cut-backs, and they too could be encouraged to contribute more to the United Nations, with the example of the United States as a spur. While there are undoubtedly many pressing demands on any 'peace dividends', it seems that the wisest expenditure of some of these funds would be to wipe out UN debts on the regular and peacekeeping budgets and to match political design with financial responsibility. The worst-case scenario is that the essentially bureaucratic objections to the budgetary process and other woes (such as the over-emphasized mis-allocation of resources in UNESCO and other stories of Third World diplomats' high-living) will block any resolution of the funding crisis. We will then be faced with a world without the United Nations. This need not be a catastrophe if there were an alternative body or organization better suited to maintain international peace and security, or better suited to develop friendly relations among nations or to achieve international cooperation in solving international problems of an economic, social, cultural or humanitarian character or to be a centre for harmonizing the actions of nations in the attainment of these ends. Before the United Nations goes broke, the alternatives should be considered.

The objections to the other five suggestions as short-term solutions rest upon the time factor; the UN funding crisis is urgent, as are the demands being made upon the organization. The other possible solutions may serve for consideration for the long-term but do not answer the short-term problem, which is the ability of the United Nations to continue to play an indispensable role in the international community. Clearly, beyond the need for the restoration of funding to a level where the organization can play its required role, there is a need for a fundamental structural reform of the United Nations as an institution. Its present structure reflects the immediate post-war world, giving rise to questions about its current utility. As a long-term suggestion it might be worth considering the introduction of a weighted voting system on budgetary matters while, as a *quid pro quo*, abolishing the permanent seats on the Security Council. While this might not stop any one power from obstructing the work of the organization, it would encourage both Germany and Japan to assume a greater role in the long-term, while also answering some of Congress's objections to the full restoration of funding.

[11]

FINANCING THE UNITED NATIONS

Muchkund Dubey

Like all other international institutions, the United Nations depends upon adequate and timely flow of resources to its coffers for its survival. No discussion on the reform of the United Nations will be meaningful, unless it is possible to mobilise adequate resources for the functions of the reformed United Nations. Financing is therefore at the very core of the struggle for the future of the United Nations. Providing adequate financing to the United Nations is the litmus test of the loyalty of member states towards the United Nations and of the sincerity of their intentions to make it really effective. The kind of the United Nations we are going to have at the turn of the century will very much depend upon what magnitude and quality of resources we will be able to mobilise for the Organisation.

The present financial position of the United Nations is precarious. For the past several years, the Organisation has been on the edge of bankruptcy. The bankruptcy has become so chronic and the Secretary-General's appeals for financial rescue of the Organisation so frequent, that it has long ceased to be a news; sadly, it is no longer considered as a matter of great concern among the majority of the member states. It seems that these member states have got reconciled to what is taken to be the *fait accompli* and they have come to believe that the Organisation will somehow or the other limp along. This is a very poor reflection on these states' commitment to the United Nations, if not a sinister design to keep the United Nations ever weak and ineffective.

The United Nations finds itself in the present financial straitjacket partly because of the accumulation of huge arrears of payment, and also because of late payments by most of the Member States, and the insistence of the major contributors on zero-growth budget for all the organizations of the United Nations system. Another important reason is the increasing reliance, over the years, on voluntary contributions which are volatile, uncertain and unpredictable. A sudden decline in voluntary contributions to UN organizations results in a large scale retrenchment of their personnel and activities. And this trauma is administered at regular intervals. This leaves the Organisations truncated, demoralised and uncertain about its future.

As of 31 January 1995, total arrears of payment of contributions to the assessed budget of the United Nations were $3.6 bn. of which $1.4 bn. was against the regular budget and $2.2 bn. against the peace-keeping budget. The most disturbing part of the arrears picture was that out of the total arrears of $3.6 billion, as much as 2.5 bn. or 70 per cent were due from 5 top debtors (the largest amount being by the United States).

The arrears are of two types; the first from a large number of very poor member countries which are unable to pay, because of their precarious ways and means and whose cumulative defaults of payment constitute a very small part of the total arrears; and the second, from a handful of top contributors which are capable of making payment but are withholding their contributions as a standing blackmail against the United Nations. And among the top contributors, the United States is the biggest defaulter and also the most persistent blackmailer. These top contributors deliberately hold back their dues to compel the United Nations to reduce their sizes, to adjust their agenda and alter the thrusts of their activities in order to receive payment of their dues. And since a part of the dues is permanently held back, the pressure on the UN organizations to restructure their agenda and activities has become the permanent feature of the life of the UN system.

To buttress their position in favour of downsizing the United Nations, the major contributors - their governments, their intellectuals and their media - carry out a concerted campaign against and perpetrate all kinds of myths and distortions about the United Nations. One of such distortions is the so-called "high and excessive" cost of the Organisations "draining billions of dollars from the tax payers of the developed countries". In this connection, there are frequent references to the "bloated budget" of the United Nations. The reality, however, is different, which is brought out by the following facts and figures.

(a) The estimated total worldwide cost of the UN system (excluding the IMF, World Bank and IFAD average $ 10.5 bn. per annum during the biennium 1992/93. This included not only operating costs but also all development assistance funds and programmes, all peace-keeping and all the humanitarian emergency relief for the whole world.

(b) $10.5 billion represents under $2 per capita for the whole of mankind, at a time when the world's governments spend about $150 per capita on military expenditure. $10.5 bn. was only 0.0005 per cent of the world GNP in 1992.

(c) The regular assessed UN budget was only $1.06 bn. in 1994. The total UN budget (including contributions to peace-keeping and voluntary contribution for humanitarian assistance) is currently $4.5 bn. This budget is less than the combined annual cost of the Police and Fire Department of the New York City. It is a strange irony that the same level of resources should be made available for global fire-fighting and policing as for the Police and Fire Department of a single city in the United States!

The regular budget of the United Nations and those of the UN Specialised Agencies are financed on the basis of assessments related to a set of criteria laid sown by the legislative bodies of these organizations. As regards the UN budget,

Article 17.2 of the Charter provides: "The expenses of the Organisation shall be borne by the members as appropriated by the General Assembly".

Under this provision of the Charter, the General Assembly assesses for each member state the proportion of the expenses of the United Nations to be paid by it. The assessment is derived from the capacity to pay which is determined on the basis of usual economic indicators, including population, national income etc. The assessments are expressed in percentage terms which add up to the total UN budget. A ceiling of 25 per cent limits what any state pays - at present only the United States reaches that limit - and a minimum percentage of 0.01 of the total budget is fixed for payment uniformly by a category of lowest income members identified for this purpose.

The highest ceiling for the United States has been periodically coming down. It was a little under 50 per cent when the United Nations was established. It came down to 33 per cent in 1952, 30 per cent in 1955, 25 per cent in 1972 which is continuing till today. According to the criteria applied uniformly for determining the capacity to pay, the United States should be paying 31 per cent of the budget, instead of 25 per cent.

Article 17.2 ensures that every member state would have participated in the discussion of the budget, including its own share, and that once the budget was approved by the Assembly, each member state becomes party to this decision, and is, therefore, automatically obliged to pay the assessment established for it. This is apart from the treaty obligation of every member state to pay its dues without any conditionality.

Looked at in this perspective, no country pays more and no country pays "less". Each country pays according to its 'ability to pay' calculated by applying on a uniform non-discriminatory basis, a set of universally agreed criteria. The relative burden of the member states is equal which is the essence of the application of the democratic principle for determining shares for the payment of the total budget. The country which pays 0.01 per cent of the budget sacrifices as much as the one which pays 25 per cent of the share. The latter country has, therefore, no right by virtue of the payment of its share, unilaterally to lay down any conditionalities for payment. The country paying 0.01 per cent the lowest percentage, is entitled to equal participation in the governance of the United Nations.

There is no basis in the law of the Charter for any member state to withhold its dues on grounds that it dislikes any policy or administrative practice that has been adopted by a duly constituted organ of the United Nations. This is based on the same principle as that which enjoins that no citizen tax-payer can decline to pay his or her income tax, which was duly legislated, simply because he or she dislikes some policy of the government; if that were so, the revenues of a country (or of the United Nations) would be in perpetual uncertainty, indeed chaos. Article 19 of the UN Charter provides:

A Member (which) is in arrears in the payment of its financial contributions to the Organisation shall have no vote in the General Assembly if the amount of its arrears equals or exceeds the amount of the contributions due from it for the preceding two full years. The General Assembly may, nevertheless, permit such a Member to vote, if it is satisfied that the failure to pay is due to conditions beyond the control of the Member.

The United States is clearly in default under Article 19, as the amount of its arrears far exceeds the amount of its contributions for the preceding two years. The United States also cannot get a reprieve under the last sentence of this Article, because its failure to pay is not (by any criteria due to conditions beyond its control. Such conditions arise only in the situation of acute economic difficulties. The United States has never been in such a condition, as it has never claimed that the non-payment of its dues is due to the prevalence of such a condition.

Therefore, there is every justification for the General Assembly to suspend the voting rights of the United States. But this has never been done, on account of pragmatic political considerations. Given the overwhelming military and economic clout of the United States, it is very unlikely that any international organization will be able to function effectively without its full participation. Thus the United Nations is in a real dilemma on account of the US delinquency. There can be no effective or orderly international system if its most powerful member decides to default systematically on its financial obligations.

The UN peace-keeping budget is also based on assessment, though the formula applied for making the assessment of the contributions of member states is slightly different from that applied to the assessments for the regular budget. According to the formula approved by the General Assembly in 1973, each of the five permanent members of the Security Council pay 22 per cent more than their share under the regular budget assessment criteria; a second group of countries pays the same as in the regular budget formula; a third group of countries pays one-fifth of its regular assessment; and a fourth group pays one-tenth.

According to this formula, the United States is to pay 31.7 per cent of the peace-keeping budget. The major contributors have defaulted on the payment of their contributions to the peace-keeping budget also. They are also reluctant, among others, on financial grounds to permit the United Nations to take on too many peace-keeping operations. Of course, there are political reasons too, the most important of them being the desire of the major military powers to act on their own without involving the United Nations or just getting the stamp of United Nations, approval for their acting on their own in situations of threat to or breach of peace. As a combined result of both these economic and political factors, the United Nations is now reduced to a mere residual role in peace-keeping.

And the peace-keeping operations the United Nations is permitted to carry out, face uncertainty of resources and frequently run into problems. Owing to the arrears of the payment of the assessed shares, countries contributing troops have experienced up to 5 years of delay in the reimbursement of their costs. As of September 1994, the United Nations owned $1 bn. to some 70 member states contributing troops and equipment.

Another problem with the regular budget is its excessive dependence on a handful of countries for sustaining the UN budget. Out of the total 1994 regular budget amounting to $1,061.8 million, one state, i.e., the USA, paid 25 per cent and 24 states paid 64.6 per cent. This concentration holds the United Nations hostage to the whims of a few nations and enables these nations to exercise undue influence over the affairs of the UN system.

Yet another problem with the UN budget is that it has to be paid in dollars. Many smaller and less developed Third World countries suffer from serious dollar shortage and are therefore obliged to default in the payment of their dues.

According to Article 18.2 of the Charter, any decision of the General Assembly on substantive issues, which include all financial matters, is taken by a two-thirds majority of the members present and voting. This principle was scrupulously adhered to until the early 1980s when the major contributors started unfolding their designs on the budget. They wanted arbitrarily to freeze the budgets of the UN system or even to reduce them in real terms. They, therefore, sought to acquire a veto on the decision on the budgets. They achieved this purpose in 1986 when the President of the General Assembly made a consensus statement to the effect that the Fifth Committee to the Assembly make "all possible efforts with a view to establishing the broadcast possible agreement" on the budget. The United States and other developed countries took it to mean the approval of the budget by consensus. Since then the UN budget and those of the Specialized Agencies have been approved by consensus, that is, (in effect) under the veto power of the developed countries. As a consequence, all regular budgets of the UN system have remained more or less frozen for the last 11 years.

One of the most unfortunate developments in UN financing has been the steady growth of voluntary contributions. The founders of the United Nations envisaged only one method of raising resources for the financing of the United Nations, and that was through assessed contributions. This was the only method consistent with the obligations of the member states under the Charter (treaty) establishing the United Nations. The Charter, therefore, makes no provision for voluntary contributions.

When the practice of voluntary contributions was introduced, it was meant only to finance technical assistance activities. But by the late 1960s, this limitation was transgressed and voluntary financing was resorted to for financing other activities also. The situation has come to a pass where regular UN reports, seminars and inter-governmental meetings are also being financed through voluntary contributions. This has given the major contributors firm grip over the activities of the UN system. Today, by and large, the UN Organisations do what the governments of the countries making major voluntary contributions want them to do.

Till the early 1970s, there was only one principal source to which voluntary contributions for carryout out development assistance activities were made, and that was the UNDP and its predecessors in various forms. There were, of course, a few significant exceptions. UNICEF was funded on a voluntary basis from its very inception. Refugee assistance and relief activities carried out by the United Nations were also, right from the very beginning, financed through voluntary contributions.

Inspite of these important exceptions, the fact remained that voluntary contributions for development assistance activities *per se* of the United Nations were channelled mainly through the UNDP. UNDP was regarded as the central body of the UN system to provide resources for technical assistance. All Specialized Agencies, with the exception of WHO which started with resources of its own earmarked for financing technical assistance activities, looked up to the UNDP for finding resources for their technical assistance programmes.

In the country programming consensus of 1971, UNDP's central role in providing resources for technical assistance activities of the entire UN system and co-ordinating such activities, was reiterated. It was also provided that at the country level, the resources of all UN agencies and programmes will be pooled for preparing a single country programme for each of the recipient countries.

This system was inaugurated with due fanfare with the adoption of the first in the series of country programmes, in 1972. However, very soon, the fashion and predilections in major donor countries changed and the process of the dilution of the notion of central funding and joint programming began. Today UNDP has ceased to be a central funding body and the practice of pooling all the resources available at the country level, has been diluted beyond recognition. The first step in the direction of the proliferation of funds and the fragmentation of programmes was the establishment by most of the Specialized Agencies of funds of their own for carrying out their technical assistance activities. And then came the "multi-bi" in the UN system.

The trend in this direction coincided with the increasing trend of attaching conditionalities to resources provided by the major donors for development assistance. They were no longer content with the activities undertaken by the Organisations of the UN system, based on the decisions of the respective governing bodies of the programmes and the development objectives and priorities indicated by the governments of the recipient countries. They now wanted the United Nations Organisations to undertake activities of their choice in the countries of their choice. For this, they started making special-purpose resources available to UN Organisations which came to be known as "multi-bi", that is resources for bilateral assistance channelled through multilateral organisations. In several cases, trust funds have been created for these programmes. The extent of the proliferation of these trust funds is indicated by the fact that by 1991, against UNDP's total receipts of $1.34 bn. "multi-bi" direct funding to executing agencies was $0.67 bn. "Multi-bi" has become so much a part of the reality of raising resources for technical assistance that UNDP itself is no longer able to resist the temptation to avail itself of "multi-bi" resources.

The extraordinary expansion of the budgets of the UN systems based on voluntary contributions and the proliferation of funds financed by each contributors, has had very adverse consequences for the UN system. Firstly, it distorts the development priorities of the recipient governments, and even those laid down by inter-governmental bodies. It has also led to frequent shifts in priorities depending upon the priorities prevalent in donor countries and the ideas emanating from the think-tanks in these countries. We have thus seen during the last two decades the so-called global priorities shifting from poverty alleviation to human development, and so on. Added to these priorities have been such other objectives as growth in GNP, meeting basic needs, involvement of the people in the process of development, reducing unemployment, population management and removal of gender bias. Thus, today UN Organisations have a vast menu of global priorities to choose from which can justify any activity they intend to take up.

Secondly, the voluntary basis of financing UN activities has introduced uncertainty and unpredictability in UN development assistance programmes. It has also made it very difficult to plan for the future on any assured basis. The effectiveness of the programmes has been adversely affected and countries' confidence in the United Nations has been undermined.

Thirdly, voluntary funding has given tremendous fillip to conditionalities. Conditionalities are imposed not only for determining priorities, but also for getting the maximum out of the voluntary contributions made, in terms of export of personnel and equipment. In a "give and take table" which was informally circulating in the UNDP in the early 1970s, for every dollar paid as voluntary contribution, UK and France were getting back close to a dollar and half and the USA about 95 cents. Channelling UN assistance in the priority areas of their choice has also helped major donor countries to prepare the ground for larger scale export of goods and services to the recipient countries and for the penetration of their multinationals into these countries.

Fourthly, voluntary funding has undermined the democratic process of decision-making in the United Nations. The major donor countries, by virtue of their larger contributions, exercise dominant influence over this process.

Fifthly, voluntary funding has been an important factor introducing donor-recipient relationship in the United Nations. In the regular budget, there is no donor and no recipient. Every member country pays according to its capacity to pay, based on a formula uniformly applicable to all. But in voluntary funding, some contribute more and some contribute less. Some countries ostensibly do not get back anything out of their contributions, while other countries pay very little, but receive most of the funds as recipients of UN technical assistance. This donor-recipient syndrome has resulted in the dilution of the basic UN principle of "the sovereign equality of all its members". It has also lowered the very quality of relations among nations.

The most unfortunate part is that this donor-recipient syndrome engendered by the voluntary funding of UN activities has been transported to the regular budgets of the UN system where a group of countries are claiming that they have the right unilaterally to determine the priorities of the activities of the UN system by virtue of their being the "larger" contributors to the UN regular budget.

Sixthly, the rapid increase in the component of the UN budget financed through voluntary contributions has been a major factor preventing the desired growth in the regular budgets of the UN Organizations. This phenomenon has had the effect of diluting the concept of financing the United Nations as a matter of treaty obligation.

Finally, when the United Nations resorted to voluntary contributions for financing its activities, the expectation was that this will help in mobilizing additional resources for the United Nations. But things have not worked out that way. It is a matter of speculation whether in the absence of voluntary contributions, the United Nations would have been able to raise the present level of its budgetary resources from assessments from member states. However, the fact remains that even with voluntary contributions, the overall availability of resources has remained meager in relation to the expanding needs of the international community for such resources, that there have been prolonged and frequent periods of stagnation in the levels of resources mobilized through voluntary Security Council contributions and that the contributions has fluctuated very widely.

In view of the chronic nature of the resources constraint of the United Nations and the uncertainty surrounding the availability of resources, suggestions have been made from time to time to tap autonomous and predictable sources of financing. The person who carried out a veritable campaign for several years for raising such resources for the United Nations was Professor Jan Timbergen, the first Nobel Laureate in Economics and the Chairman of the UN Committee for Development Planning for the best part of the late sixties and early seventies. His favourite scheme was international taxation on the consumption of luxury goods. He got a recommendation to this effect included in successive reports of the Committee on Developing Planning. In 1980, in a conference in Bubrovnik, he presented a paper giving the economic rationale for instituting a system of international taxation to raise resources for multilateral organizations. His basic reasoning was the same as has been given in justification of national taxation, that is, the welfare argument and the inevitability of carrying out activities on behalf of the community (in the present context the community of nations) as a whole.

The proposals advanced for raising new resources for the United Nations on a stable and assured basis are either in the form of international taxation or incomes derived from the global commons like the sea, space, biosphere etc. Some of the proposals, if implemented, would, apart from raising incomes for UN organizations, have other important positive effects - like putting a measure of restraint on the exploitation of natural resources, moderating large scale currency speculations as in the case of the Tobin Tax, discouraging arms transfer etc. The following is a brief listing of some of the major proposals:

(a) Tobin tax - Explaining his proposal for a tax on currency speculation, Prof. Tobin has stated (see the 1994 Human Development Report, UNDP) that the capital flows needed to achieve an efficient allocation of world savings are today a minuscule fraction of the world-wide transactions in currency markets (1 trillion per day). The bulk of these transactions are speculations and arbitrates, seeking to make quick money on exchange rate fluctuations. They contribute little to rational long term investment allocations. An irrevocably unique world currency which can escape such a turbulence is decades away. So the second best solution is to tax speculations based on fluctuations in currency exchange rates. The revenue potential is $ 1.5 trillion per year for a 0.5 per cent tax. The proceeds should be devoted to international purpose and be placed at the disposal of international institutions. A 0.5 per cent tax is equivalent to a 4 per cent difference in annual interest rates on three-month annual interest rates on three-month bills, a considerable deterrence to persons contemplating a quick round trip to another currency. It will, however, be too small to deter commodity trade or serious international movements.

(b) A tax on the international sale of designated weapons.

(c) Pollution tax - A global carbon tax or tax on sales of fossil fuels. It is estimated that a $ 5 per barrel tax on oil would yield $ 100 bn. per year.

(d) Travel tax - Agreement on such a tax could be reached in the International

Civil Aviation Organization (ICAO). This could take the form of a flat tax on all air travellers in selected sectors. The justification would be that air travel depends on international regulations, as well as peace and stability, which the UN is supposed to ensure. It has been estimated that a flat charge of $ 5 per passenger covering 300 million travellers every year will fetch $ 1.5 bn. annually.

(e) Making available a part of the proceeds derived from the mining of the sea-bed.

(f) A tax on international trade.

(g) A tax for parking geo-stationary satellites.

(h) A tax for using the electromagnetic spectrum.

(i) Charges on marine ocean transport.

(j) Charges for fishing rights in the high seas.

(k) Charges on maritime dumping of wastes.

(l) Making available to the United Nations the proceeds from one day's sale of stamps by the world's post offices every year.

(m) A tax on the day's telecommunications every year.

Many of these proposals are viable and workable. What is lacking is the political will of the member states to reach agreement on one or more of these proposals and implement them. Until now, the governments of the major developed countries are not prepared to accept any of these proposals, because the main burden of payment will fall on them, and also because they do not want the United Nations to be an autonomous and stable source of financing its activities. In their bid to continue to exercise control over the Organisation, they want it to go on living from hand to mouth. Developing countries on their part have no unified position on any of these proposals. In any case, they do not want to confront the major powers on this issue.

On the occasion of the 50th anniversary of the United Nations, a number of studies on the finances of the United Nations were undertaken and suggestions made for improving the financial position of the United Nations. Some of the studies and reports were officially sponsored by the UN Secretary General and duly submitted to the General Assembly. However, even the modest proposals made in these reports have not, until now, been given due consideration, let alone being accepted. Therefore, prospects for improving the financial position of the United Nations in the near future do not appear to be promising. Neverthless, the following suggestions are made for overcoming the present financial crisis of the United Nations:

(a) **The problem of late payments and arrears**

(i) Interest should be charged on late payments by member states, except the low income countries facing genuine difficulties in making payments.

(ii) Arrears due from this group of countries should be liquidated by one-time proportional increase in the assessments of the other Member states.

(iii) The problem of deliberate defaulting cannot be ignored. The World Court should be moved to pronounce on the illegality or otherwise, in terms of

Article 19 of the Charter, of deliberate non-payment of dues and on the sanctions that can be applied against the defaulting state under the Charter.

(b) Concentration of assessed contribution

The present excessively high ceiling (25 per cent) of contribution by any single member state should be reduced to not more than 10 to 12.5 per cent. Other member states, particularly the middle economic powers which will include several developing countries, should be prepared to increase their own contributions to compensate for the loss of revenues on account of the lowering of the ceiling.

(c) Assessed Contributions

(i) The primacy of the regular budgets of the organizations of the UN system should be reaffirmed. These organizations should rely mainly on their regular budgets for financing their activities. All the operational and administrative costs of the organizations should be financed from their regular budgets.

(ii) All peace-keeping operations should continue to be financed on the basis of special assessments.

(d) Voluntary Contributions

(i) Urgent and decisive steps should be taken towards reversing the growing dependence of the United Nations on extra-budgetary sources of financing. The system of voluntary funding should be phased-out within a time-bound framework.

(ii) As an interim measure, all administrative and management costs of operating UN's development assistance programmes should be moved to financing by assessment.

(iii) As a part of phasing-out, a minimum of 25 per cent of the total budget for operational activities should be moved to the assessed portion of the over-all budget.

(e) New autonomous sources of financing

An expert group should examine the various proposals for providing to the United Nations access to autonomous sources of financing and recommend the most equitable, feasible and desirable proposals in order of *inter se* preference. The group should also work out in detail the modalities of implementing the recommended proposals. Negotiations should commence on reaching an agreement on one or more of these proposals, immediately after the completion of the work of the expert group.

(f) Resources for Peace-keeping

(i) Arrears on peace-keeping assessments should be cleared on an urgent basis.

(ii) Decisions should be taken urgently on the various proposals made by the Secretary General in his report *Agenda for Peace* for resolving the present difficulties in financing the peace-keeping operations of the United Nations.

(iii) In particular, his proposal to establish a reserve fund for pre-assessment start-up of peace-keeping operations should be accepted and urgently acted upon.

g) **Currency of payment of financial contributions to the United Nations**

All transactions of the UN System, either from the assessed or voluntary contributions, should be carried out, not in dollars as at present, but in Special Drawing Rights or any other unit of account based on a basket of currencies.

Part III
The UN, States, and
Non-Governmental Actors

[12]

Appraising the U.N. at 50:
The Looming Challenge

Richard Falk

IS THE U.N. FAILING?

In the spring of 1994, *The Economist* had on its cover a ghastly scene: a landscape of utter desolation, the sky and earth blood red, corpses littering the ground with a flagpole in their midst, its U.N. flag flying at half-mast and a large caption entitling the cover story, "SHAMED ARE THE PEACEKEEPERS."[1] Such an iconography of failure is sadly expressive of public disappointment with the United Nations' role in world affairs in light of its inability to avert tragedy in Somalia, Bosnia and Rwanda.

Such an assessment does not provide a promising background for this year's observance of the 50th anniversary of the U.N.'s founding, which, if nothing else, is certain to generate a multitude of discussions on the past, present and future of the Organization. My aim in this article will be to account for this current attitude of disappointment and to interpret expectations of the United Nations within the larger setting of global restructuring, especially the displacement and realignment of the sovereign state.

It should be noted by way of introduction that it is the peace and security agenda that serves as the prism through which the U.N. is judged by the media and the public. This is understandable, yet misleading. It is misleading because, even considered mechanically as an aggregate of its multifold distinct activities, actors and arenas, the U.N. consists of such diverse main organs as the Security Council, the General Assembly, the International Court of Justice, the Economic and Social Council, the Trusteeship Council and the Secretariat, as well as a long list of specialized agencies, among the most important of which are the United Nations

---

[1]   "Shamed are the Peacekeepers," *The Economist*, 331, no. 7861 (30 April - 6 May 1994); see also along the same line two featured articles in *Foreign Affairs* by Saadia Touval and Giandomenico Picco under the title "Why the U.N. Fails," *Foreign Affairs*, 73, no. 5 (September/October 1994) pp. 14-18, 44-57.

Journal of International Affairs, Winter 1995, 48, no. 2. © The Trustees of Columbia University in the City of New York.

Journal of International Affairs

Educational, Scientific and Cultural Organization (UNESCO), the Food and Agriculture Organization (FAO), the World Health Organization (WHO), the United Nations Children's Fund (UNICEF), the Office of the United Nations High Commissioner for Refugees (UNHCR) and the United Nations Development Programme (UNDP). Also formally part of the U.N. family, although fully autonomous in operation, are the international financial institutions, which include the International Monetary Fund (IMF) and the World Bank.[2] The U.N.'s range of activities thus encompasses virtually the whole gamut of human concerns. Its many constructive achievements over the years must be balanced against a plethora of shortcomings, making it complicated to evaluate any particular aspect of U.N. work.

At the same time, the tendency to conflate the U.N. in such a way that only the peace and security agenda is sharply profiled is understandable. The main goals of the Organization have always been related to the avoidance of war and the protection of weak states against aggression. That is why the U.N. response to the Iraqi conquest of Kuwait in 1990 seemed such a decisive test of the capacity of the Organization to act in the post-Cold War world, giving then-President George Bush's mobilizing call for "a new world order" much credibility, at least for the duration of the crisis. Two distinct conclusions emerge: First of all, the U.N. is a complex actor with multiple roles that have growing importance in many domains of international life; secondly, despite this diversity, the overriding test of U.N. success or failure focuses on its handling of peace and security challenges.

Overall, this emphasis on peace and security tends to give an undue prominence to the Security Council, and an unwarranted back burner status to other organizational facets of the U.N. Occasionally, the World Court will receive attention through rendering a controversial decision, as it did in 1986 when it held that the efforts of the U.S. government to overthrow the Sandinista government in Nicaragua violated international law; or the Secretary-General will make headlines by taking a strong, independent stand on a peace and security issue, such as fashioning a response to genocide in Rwanda. Normally, however, it is the Security Council that takes the heat and gets the credit. This has been especially true since 1989. No longer does the threat of a Soviet veto loom to produce either gridlock

---

[2]   For a convenient overview see figure in Robert E. Riggs and Jack C. Plano, *The United Nations: International Organization and World Politics*, 2nd ed. (Belmont, CA: 1994) p. 24.

Richard Falk

or an ineffectual compromise.[3] If the Organization fosters peaceful resolution of warfare or carries out its Charter mandate to protect member states that are victims of aggression, then its achievements are noted and celebrated. In this regard, the U.N. reached its peak of popularity, especially in the United States, after the Gulf War in 1991 by providing the auspices for successfully challenging Iraq's conquest and annexation of Kuwait.[4] This aura of achievement was reinforced by a series of seemingly successful mediation efforts from 1988 to 1990 related to long-festering regional conflicts: Iran-Iraq, Afghanistan, Cambodia, Namibia and El Salvador.[5] This string of successes, especially given the ending of the Cold War, lent some temporary credibility to expectations of a "new world order," guided by international law and institutionally upheld by a robust United Nations that would be strengthened gradually as public confidence in its effectiveness increased.

---

[3] Such consensus is evaporating rapidly. Russia used its veto to block a Security Council resolution calling on the U.N. to stop shipments of fuel to Serb-held areas of Bosnia. See "Russian Veto Protects Serbs," *New York Times*, 3 December 1994, p. 6. The events in Chechnya in early 1995 also disclose the extent to which current Russian security policy diverges from international legal and moral standards, as well as from the prevailing political consensus governing uses of force.

[4] This popularity was always somewhat contested, especially by those who perceived the war as "premature" or "unnecessary," implying that Kuwaiti sovereignty could have been reestablished by a combination of sanctions and diplomacy. Other critics complained that the United States had appropriated the Security Council as a vehicle of its foreign policy, ignored the requirements of the Charter to seek, if at all possible, a peaceful solution and resorted to war mainly to destroy Iraq's capability to molest others in the region, especially Israel, and to prevent the acquisition of nuclear weapons by a state perceived as both hostile and reckless. Even among those who were positively impressed by the U.N.'s effectiveness in reversing aggression, degrees of disillusion followed as a result of several factors: the plight of Kurds and Shiites living in marsh regions of the south, the failure to dislodge Saddam Hussein from power and the extent of suffering inflicted on Iraqi civilians.

[5] Some of these successes were not sustained, as in Afghanistan and Cambodia, where renewed conflicts overcame U.N. mediation efforts that earlier had achieved positive results. The outcome in Cambodia, as of late 1994, is not entirely clear, but the resumption of warfare is discouraging; the brutal execution of Western tourists by the Khmer Rouge, as well as its warning to foreigners to stay away, seems ominous. During 1994 two Australians, three Britons and a Frenchman were taken hostage and executed by Khmer Rouge forces operating in the southern jungles of Cambodia, and threats to expand such executions were made by representatives of the Khmer Rouge. See Teresa Oi, "Aussie embassy on higher alert against urban terror campaign," *The Straits Times (Singapore)*, 4 January 1995, p. 14. Reportedly, the Khmer Rouge has initiated this terroristic campaign against foreigners "to try to scare away investment and destabilize the shaky coalition government in Phnom Penh." Philip Sherwell, "Khmer Rouge bandits massacre Thai hostages," *The Daily Telegraph*, 26 November 1994, p. 15.

Journal of International Affairs

What, then, went wrong? Can it be corrected? At bottom, this pattern of popular attitudes, shifting back and forth between hopes raised and hopes dashed, reflects a failure to realize what the U.N. is currently capable of accomplishing and what it is not. This, in turn, relates to the precise type of Organization that the U.N. has become. Can such a family of entrenched bureaucracies, in some way answerable both to world public opinion and to the geopolitical will of its leading member states, be changed to any appreciable extent in the foreseeable future?

From the very outset of the U.N.'s history, it was recognized that the Organization could operate effectively only if its dominant members, the five permanent members of the Security Council, could act in concert. Constitutionally, this precondition was acknowledged in the form of both the veto and permanent membership, given to these five states and only to them. The optimists, such as Franklin Roosevelt, felt that the U.N. at its inception had a good chance of succeeding because these same countries had cooperated to defeat fascism, and thus would be able to suppress their differences well enough to keep their alliance together for the purpose of safeguarding the peace achieved in 1945 after their valiant and exhausting efforts during the Second World War.[6] The pessimists, such as George Kennan and Dean Acheson, anticipated the Soviet challenge, partly as an expected enactment of the Marxist-Leninist orientation and partly as a reflection of the inevitable tendency of leading states to engage in rivalry in the absence of a common enemy. They expected the U.N. to be quickly marginalized, thereby resting their hopes for future peace on a posture of containment and deterrence.[7] As we now know, the pessimists carried the day through the entire Cold War.[8]

---

[6]   See Willard Range, *Franklin D. Roosevelt's World Order* (Athens, GA: University of Georgia, 1959) especially pp. 175-9.

[7]   See for example Dean Acheson, *Present at the Creation: My Years at the State Department* (New York: Norton, 1969) pp. 160-1; and George F. Kennan, *Memoirs 1925-1950* (Boston: Atlantic Monthly, 1967) pp. 219-20.

[8]   The U.N. was not entirely marginalized, although it fell far short of the hopes of the optimists. It did validate a response to the North Korean attack on South Korea in 1950, but mainly to endorse the U.S.-led response, and then only because the Soviet Union was boycotting the Security Council to protest the U.N.'s failure to have China represented by the People's Republic of China leadership. Also, the U.N. did line up in opposition to the British/French/Israeli Suez Operation in 1956, but primarily because both superpowers opposed the invasion of Egyptian territory, and thus, for the only time, the U.S. government opposed an important initiative of its major European allies.

Richard Falk

Since 1989, the pattern of activities in response to peace and security challenges has reflected the changing character of the global setting — above all, the disappearance of the East-West axis of conflict and the emergence of a far more integrated pattern of economic activity on a global and regional basis. In a sense, the signature of this new era is the positing of a new arrangement of geopolitical priorities, subordinating most peace and security concerns to the issues of economic stability and the expansion of trade. The next section explores this rearrangement of priorities, especially in relation to the changing role of the state and the impact of this process upon the activities of the U.N. Security Council.

THE UNITED NATIONS AND THE CHANGING ROLE OF THE STATE

Although simple dualisms are not descriptive of complex reality, it is useful, as a first approximation, to appreciate that the U.N. is an extension of the states system rather than an alternative to it. States are, of course, the only entities eligible for membership, and, in terms of peace and security, completely dominate patterns of access and participation.[9] Furthermore, it is not only states as such, but rather the hierarchy of states that has given structure to international political life as the states system has unfolded over time.

Both points are critical. From a juridical perspective, rules of membership and participation, including procedures for financing, are exclusively premised on states' status as political actors; in the General Assembly, with its role confined to recommendatory authority, all states regardless of size are entitled to equal rights of participation — Liechtenstein's vote counts as much as the People's Republic of China's (PRC's) or that of the United States. In contrast, from a geopolitical perspective (one sensitive to the hierarchy of states that exert influence in the world) and in relation to the operational code of the U.N., the most powerful and influential states as of 1945 have privileged formal status,

---

[9]   In other domains of U.N. activity — in relation to human rights or environmental protection, or on such social issues as population policy or development — the interface between statism and transnational democracy is increasingly evident within U.N. arenas. For instance, at the U.N. "consciousness-raising" conferences, such as the 1994 International Conference on Population and Development, held in Cairo, social movements associated with women, indigenous peoples and environmentalists have had influential roles in reshaping the agendas planned by governments. However, with respect to security policy, the most traditional domain of geopolitics, civil initiatives have had almost no access or impact.

Journal of International Affairs

especially through their capacity to control the decision-making procedures of the U.N., either by mandating coercive action (as in the Gulf War) or by blocking action through the exercise of their veto power (as throughout the Cold War).[10]

But it is not only by way of its formal structures that the U.N. experiences this geopolitical imprint of inequality among states. It pervades the operations of the Organization, the role and selection of the Secretary-General, financing (especially of special budgets needed for peacekeeping), the selectivity practiced with respect to threats to the peace or severe abuses of human rights and the implementation (or lack thereof) of decisions taken by the Security Council. In this respect, the U.N. is often perceived, especially in Africa and Asia, as a virtual instrument of the foreign policy of its most powerful member, the United States, which is believed to exert an influence that extends far beyond its authority as a permanent member of the Security Council. While both the PRC and the United States are permanent members, their relative operational influence on the behavior of the U.N. is hardly comparable. Of course, neither is their share of the financial burden. Another aspect of U.S. influence undoubtedly arises from the location of the main U.N. organs in New York City.

In this respect, the U.N., especially in peace and security, essentially embodies the geopolitical priorities of the permanent members of the Security Council, and especially those of the United States. In this regard, the ascendant states have shared a continuing reluctance to endow the U.N. with autonomous capabilities either in relation to financing or to enforcement, although such endowments would not place any significant

---

10 One acknowledged weakness of the U.N. is its inability to adapt its embodiment of hierarchy in light of changes in the global setting over the past half century. As matters now stand, the Security Council is anachronistic in two dimensions: the failure to reconstitute permanent membership in light of changes in relative power and/or wealth (including Japan and Germany, while excluding either France or the United Kingdom, or possibly both); and the lack of addition of important countries from the South, which would acknowledge the globalization of the world power structure. This weakness of the Organization arises from its formal inability to displace entrenched interests in the original, now outmoded, structure, given a Charter amendment process that is itself subject to the veto, making it impossible to displace France or the United Kingdom without their acquiescence. See Charter of the United Nations, Article 108. But note that the Charter under Article 109 would permit a "General Conference ... for the purpose of reviewing the present Charter," (Article 109[1]), "if so decided by a majority vote of the members of the General Assembly and by a vote of any seven members of the Security Council." (Article 109[3]).

Richard Falk

strain on the resources of members.[11] It is a matter of political will, of leading governments not wanting to relinquish control over peacekeeping responsibilities, especially with respect to concerns that might collide with vital national interests and even challenge prerogatives associated with territorial sovereignty.[12] This position is currently unchallenged by weaker states or public opinion. The U.S. government recently has reaffirmed its opposition to either creating an independent U.N. peace force or substantially lengthening the short financing leash that restricts U.N. undertakings.[13] In this regard, the U.N.'s role in peacekeeping mirrors the priorities of leading states, and their capacity to form an operative consensus in critical situations.

As in the Cold War, to the extent that the U.N. is paralyzed formally such states will tend to revive more unilateral patterns of diplomacy, especially reliance on spheres of influence or regional frameworks. These patterns have been increasingly evident in the last several years: Witness France's role during 1994 in containing genocide in Rwanda; Russia's continuing role in overcoming ethnic strife in the Commonwealth of Independent States and claim of a sphere of influence within its "near abroad"; and the United States' revived reliance on a Monroe Doctrine

---

[11] Arguably, an autonomous U.N. might cut the overall costs of global security, which currently rest upon high levels of military readiness at the state level in peacetime, as well as wartime.

[12] It is conceivable that the U.N. would seek to authorize some undertaking that related to "the near abroad" of Russia, to ethnic conflict in Russia itself, or to the human rights and self-determination claims of Tibet if the Organization possessed its own peacekeeping capability. Even if the veto was exercised, the U.N. might exert pressure to take action, especially in extreme circumstances, by way of the General Assembly or even through an initiative of the Secretary-General. Such scenarios seem quite implausible, but a more realistic concern of the United States, and to a lesser extent the United Kingdom and France, is that a volunteer U.N. peace force would be far less amenable to geopolitical control than present ad hoc arrangements, especially with respect to the implementation of Security Council mandates. For instance, in the Gulf War, Somalia and Haiti, the Security Council essentially delegated full operational discretion to the U.S. government.

[13] See revised U.S. guidelines on U.N. peacekeeping set forth in Presidential Decision Directive 25 ("PDD 25"). See U.S. Department of State, "The Clinton Administration's Policy on Reforming Multilateral Peace Operations," *International Legal Materials* 33, no. 3 (May 1994) pp. 798-813.

Journal of International Affairs

rationale and practice with respect to its diplomacy in Central America and the Caribbean.[14]

The U.S. approach to Haiti in recent years discloses the terms of debate about whether the Monroe Doctrine is alive and well or, as Gaddis Smith contends, is fading away. Haiti is now governed by Father Jean-Bertrand Aristide, restored to power by a threatened U.S. military intervention that was formally premised upon a U.N. mandate to use force as necessary.[15] If the essence of the Monroe Doctrine is intervention to protect a country in the Caribbean or Central America from an extra-hemispheric threat, then the coercive diplomacy employed in Haiti cannot validly invoke the doctrine for support, as it was motivated by other factors. However, if the Monroe Doctrine, by virtue of its various extensions since 1933, refers to U.S. unilateralism in relation to its Latin neighbors, then the doctrine has not at all been discarded. One aspect of this latter view would be the marginalization of the influence of the United Nations, accentuating the unilateral nature of the basic interventionary claim.[16]

There is an unfortunate tendency in popular discourse, and even in much academic writing, to reify the state. The state acts through its governmental leaders, responsive to a range of social and political forces expressive of a specific power and ideological configuration and subject to change through time. Depicting these forces in relation to a given government at a particular time is bound to be controversial and inconclusive, yet indispensable. In the United States, with a governing process shaped by elections and constrained by a written constitution, there is a strong presumption that public policy is responsive to the wishes of the citizenry, or else it will be held accountable by way of electoral outcomes. Yet such a generalization is so incomplete as to be misleading. For one thing, foreign policy issues are quite often of little concern to the electorate, as compared to such domestic issues as taxes, jobs and inflation. In foreign policy, leadership is crucial and capable of shifting public opinion, and, more broadly, special interests and pressure groups in and out of

---

[14]   For authoritative interpretation of the controversy surrounding the invocation of the Monroe Doctrine rationale to validate recent U.S. interventionary diplomacy, see Gaddis Smith, *The Last Years of the Monroe Doctrine, 1945-1993* (New York: Hill and Wang, 1994).

[15]   Security Council Resolution 940 (31 July 1994).

[16]   See Smith, *The Last Years of the Monroe Doctrine*, especially pp. 211-30.

Richard Falk

government make public policy far less responsive and accountable than general attitudes toward democracy would have us believe.[17] In this regard, given the U.N. presence in the United States and considering the U.S. prominence within the Organization, it is hardly surprising that the U.N. has been made into a scapegoat or political football, depending on the circumstances. Also, the extent of reliance on the U.N. is taken as a litmus test in the persisting debate between liberal internationalists, who regard the U.N. as an important instrument for promoting U.S. interests and for improving the quality of world order, and arch-realists who view the U.N. as generally useless, or worse, as either a rubber stamp or a deforming obstacle to the clear pursuit of strategic interests in the world.[18]

Part of my contention is that states, including powerful ones, are losing their political room for maneuver in relation to a broad range of issues as a consequence of pressures from without and, to a lesser degree, from within. That is, the state is losing its autonomy as a global actor, and is changing its role in the process.[19] If this is a correct general assessment, then the U.N.'s peace and security activities will reflect both this reduction of autonomy and this changing role.[20] The relevance of the state's changing

---

[17]   Domestic pressure groups can impose boundaries on the discretion of leaders in relation to foreign policy. For instance, it would be difficult for any U.S. president to normalize relations with Castro's Cuba or to reduce significantly foreign economic assistance to Israel because of the leverage on policy exerted by well-organized constituencies with strong ethnic identifications with the subject matter. In general, see James N. Rosenau, ed., *Domestic Sources of Foreign Policy* (New York: Free Press, 1967).

[18]   More pragmatic realists will assess the instrumental value of recourse to the U.N. in each situation, as was done by George Bush (emphasizing U.N. legitimation in the Gulf Crisis, while avoiding the U.N. altogether in carrying out the 1989 intervention against Noriega's Panama). Also, conservatives traditionally have been skeptical about all efforts to internationalize foreign policy (believing that such moves imperil sovereignty), whereas liberals have tended to favor such moves (believing that strengthening international procedures contributes to a more peaceful and equitable world order).

[19]   For a significant exploration of this theme, see Joseph A. Camilleri, *The End of Sovereignty? The Politics of a Shrinking and Fragmenting World* (Hants, UK: Edward Elgar, 1992); also Phyllis Bennis and Michel Moushabeck, eds., *Altered States: A Reader in the New World Order* (New York: Olive Branch Press, 1993).

[20]   Note that part of the argument is that states are losing their freedom of action on the global stage; they are being shaped, although not deterministically or necessarily forever, by forces beyond their control. This loss can be phrased as an erosion of sovereignty as a result of a more integrated world economy. The identity and priority of these forces, exerting influence through changes in the nature of strategic interests, are defining the scope of effectiveness for the United

Journal of International Affairs

role with regard to the U.N. in relation to peace and security will be discussed in the next section, but it is important to emphasize that the overall impact could either weaken or strengthen the capacity of the U.N. to fulfill the security needs of the world community. For instance, should global market forces emphasize the importance of an overall climate of stability or the link between human rights and economic growth, pressure might mount for an expansion of U.N. roles and capabilities, including the establishment of a more autonomous U.N. to the extent that states were immobilized. Yet it is also possible that market forces will simply "write off" areas of turmoil and warfare, thus reinforcing the currently weak disposition of the U.N. to respond effectively to such challenges as, for instance, those being mounted in sub-Saharan Africa or the former Soviet Union.

GLOBALIZATION, THE STATE AND THE U.N.

The deepening of globalization, a long-term trend linked to technological innovation, business practices and moves toward the freer flow of trade and money, is significantly responsible for the new, outward orientation of the state, as well as its diminished autonomy. In such circumstances, enhanced competitiveness as a shared goal of national economic policy pushes down wages, and increased capital mobility weakens the capacity of organized labor to protect the interests of workers.[21] Such conditions are reinforced by the discrediting of socialism, the collapse of an anti-capitalist pole in international society and the shift in economic emphasis from manufacturing to service-oriented activities. These developments could occur quite independently of globalization, but their occurrence at the present time pushes globalization into the embrace of an unconditional market-driven ideology. For instance, the expansion of capital in the context of a growing transnational labor movement, or accompanied by an increasingly popular socialist challenge to a market orientation, would have led the state to play a more mediating role rather

---

Nations at this stage of international history, thereby helping us grasp why the U.N. was so effective in its initial defense of Kuwaiti sovereign rights and so ineffectual on behalf of Bosnian sovereign rights and in opposition to Serbian "ethnic cleansing."

[21] But see skeptical account by Paul Krugman, *Peddling Prosperity: Economic Sense and Nonsense in the Age of Diminished Expectations* (New York: Norton, 1994).

Richard Falk

than generally acting as an agent for global capital interests. As matters now stand, the state is put in the position of either adapting to globalization or experiencing economic decline, if not collapse. A partial explanation of the Soviet collapse lies in the inability of its command economy to adapt to the play of global markets. Even the far more efficient Scandinavian countries are finding their state-run welfare systems under pressure, as entrepreneurs deploy capital where taxes are lower, regulation less onerous and workers less secure.

The struggles over the ratification of treaties that push forward the consolidation of capital and markets at regional and global levels, such as Maastricht, the North American Free Trade Agreement (NAFTA) and the Uruguay Round of the General Agreement on Tariffs and Trade (GATT), illustrate the strength of global economic forces in overcoming the determined opposition of the most rooted, territorially-oriented elements in domestic society.[22] The political magnetism of globalization is reorienting the state and limiting the effective space open for domestic political rivalry, thereby rendering mainstream political parties incapable of providing choice and helping to give leaders an image that combines hypocrisy with ineptitude. These effects are registered most clearly, of course, in the constitutional democracies of the North, but are of systemic dimensions. The pattern is particularly manifest in the policies being pursued by socialist or left-liberal leaders and parties: President François Mitterrand in France abandoning socialism in favor of the discipline of the market; the Social Democrats in Sweden being instrumental in leading their country into the market-driven European Union; President Bill Clinton in the United States struggling to implement Republican priorities in relation to NAFTA, and thus overriding the opposition of the constituencies that elected him; the new leadership in the British Labour Party signaling similar intentions if returned to power; or a Socialist leadership in Japan renouncing its own ideology in order to achieve enough credibility to assume an unexpected role in running the government. There are additional examples, but the trend is unmistakable.

---

22   For useful discussions of this exceedingly complex phenomenon see Richard J. Barnet and John Cavanagh, *Global Dreams: Imperial Corporations and the New World Order* (New York: Simon & Schuster, 1994); and the essays in Ralph Nader et al., eds., *The Case Against "Free Trade": GATT, NAFTA and the Globalization of Corporate Power* (San Francisco: Earth Island Press, 1993).

Journal of International Affairs

The obvious question, even accepting this line of interpretation, is, "What has this got to do with the U.N.?" My response is, "It helps explain a lot." The state, as argued earlier, reflects the play of forces upon it; when this play shifts, its role in the world is adjusted correspondingly. The globalized state is increasingly responsive to global economic priorities, tending to push aside opposing societal claims on policy. Of course, these results cannot be reduced to one set of factors. Many cross-cutting developments are shaping globalization and its impact on states that are variously exposed to such pressures.

At the base of this integrative trend is technological innovation, its extension of administrative capacity and its transcendence of territoriality. The drift of this technological innovation is to associate efficiency in economic behavior, and hence growth, with the mobility of capital and the weakening of normative inhibitions relating to poverty, unemployment, environmental decline and health hazards. The interaction of globalizing pressure and responsive domestic conditions is distinctive for each state, although the general pattern of an overall pull toward conformity and subordination gives content to the assertion that the state is subject to pulls on behalf of global market forces that can no longer easily be balanced by pulls on behalf of territorial forces.

This pattern is confirmed by the major mobilization of effort in defense of privileged access to oil and regional stability during the early 1990s, which contrasts with the low level of concern about either the spread of civil strife and acute turmoil in sub-Saharan Africa or the restoration of order in the event of a breakdown of authority structures in economically inconsequential countries. During the Cold War, despite the parallel emergence of globalizing trends and the growing influence of market forces, statist priorities were quite different, as there was political space available for the adoption of socialist and social democratic programs. Global market forces were thus kept at bay to a greater extent. The perceived strategic interests of both superpowers were such as to reinforce prevailing structures of governance within their respective blocs, by intervention if necessary, sustaining the repression of ethnic and nationalist challenges and limiting ideological deviation from bloc affiliation. In the age of globalization, such a rivalry does not conform to the logic of market efficiency.

In effect, U.N. empowerment, beyond the level of shallow commitments, must therefore engage the globalized state in fashioning

Richard Falk

significant action in the peacekeeping domain. Such action is most likely to reflect a combination of pure economic considerations with more traditional efforts to restrain challenges to the established political and economic order in the world, as in the Gulf War but not elsewhere. The preoccupation of leading states with the proliferation of nuclear weapons is illustrative. It can be understood as a reaction against those political forces that challenge globalization, the so-called "backlash" states, but it can also be interpreted as a more traditional effort by the strongest states to prevent serious challenges by potential rival states. The globalizing of media activity, the so-called "CNN factor," may generate public pressures on states, and indirectly on the U.N., to act in the face of disaster and atrocity, but it does not create the leadership or rationale necessary for producing serious commitments of life and resources. The tendency, then, is to do something about these humanitarian challenges, but not enough, thus rendering the pattern of response exceedingly vulnerable to any serious effort to disrupt it. This has been the U.N.'s experience since the Gulf War. In contrast, during the Cold War, the opposite set of attitudes often prevailed, with almost every territorial struggle being perceived in global strategic terms, thus inviting interventions that were put forth as tests of strength and will and incurring costs often disproportionate to the material interests at stake.

In the absence of strategic rivalry, the outcomes of internal conflicts are of far less perceived consequence, with the major states' interest being the containment of a conflict and its ramifications, especially potential refugee flows. Again, the contrast is striking. During the Cold War, the westward flow of refugees was welcomed, generally encouraged and construed as evidence of the repressive nature of the communist regimes, offering valuable hostile propaganda that was deemed worth the costs incurred in resettlement. However, resistance to refugees and economic immigrants has been accentuated recently by higher levels of unemployment in the more affluent countries, making it far harder to incorporate additional potential workers. The U.N. is now encouraged to do its best to keep displaced persons from crossing borders, or remaining outside, while little effort is made to overcome the underlying cause of distress that accounted for the movement of large numbers of people in the first place.

Thus, the U.N., especially the Security Council, with its instrumental relationship to the largest and richest states, is limited to serving mainly those interests perceived as globalized: That is, it pushes forward the agenda of economic consolidation by protecting strategic resources and inhibits challenges to the established order by so-called backlash states (such as Iran, North Korea, Libya and Iraq). At the same time, the peacekeeping mandate is otherwise confined to containing the wider impacts of genocide and anarchy, as in Bosnia, Somalia and Haiti. However, the U.N. is still often seen as responsible for the persistence of violence and brutality, having been assigned a role in providing relief. Thus, the U.N. is held up to ridicule for its ineffectiveness, while not given the capabilities needed for success.[23]

A final aspect of this pattern is the restructuring of the U.N. with respect to its economic activity: The international financial institutions ("the Bretton Woods institutions" of the IMF and World Bank) have been strengthened and exalted, while development activities associated with the priorities of the South have been stripped down. The most notable expression of this trend was the elimination in the late 1980s of the U.N. Centre on Transnational Corporations, mainly an information-gathering unit but seen as potentially threatening to market-driven globalization. A further expression has been resistance to the treatment of economic and social rights as deserving of inclusion within the category of human rights by those seeking to confine U.N. human rights activities to the protection of the individual's civil and political rights.[24] Western opposition to "the right of development" reflects the same spirit of resisting any potential claims for redistributive justice in relation to the allocation of resources.

Globalization, then, because of the ideological and domestic setting, is accentuating a capital-driven image of the role of the state, and this is reflected in the priorities pursued within the various arenas of the U.N. A people-driven role for the state, a contrasting paradigm, would emphasize

---

[23] In fact, U.N. relief efforts in both Somalia and Bosnia have mitigated the suffering for hundreds of thousands of civilians. This is *a* success, but it is almost totally obliterated in public perception, because of *the* failure to stop the atrocities or reliance on military capabilities to reach forbidden goals. In fact, Senator Robert Dole has called for the removal of the U.N. Protection Force (UNPROFOR) from Bosnia so as to encourage an expanded NATO military role, allegedly inhibited by fear of Serb retaliation against U.N. forces. See for example Richard W. Stevenson, "Britain and France Criticize U.S. on Bosnia Positions," *New York Times*, 29 November 1994, p. A16.

[24] Textually, the two broad categories of rights are intertwined in the Universal Declaration of Human Rights and separated, yet equally delineated and acknowledged, in the Covenants of 1966. For convenient texts see Burns H. Weston et al., eds., *Basic Documents in International Law and World Order*, 2nd ed. (St. Paul, MN: West Publishing, 1990) pp. 298-301, 371-87.

Richard Falk

instead territorial human effects more directly, and this could be expressed by way of U.N. activities relating to human rights, market regulation and such matters as social development, with its stress on relieving poverty and reducing unemployment.[25] This latter emphasis would accord priority to the concrete and rooted concerns of citizens, even if this meant some setbacks with respect to market efficiency and capital opportunities, negotiating compromises rather than, as now, acknowledging the basic dominion of globalization.

PATHOLOGICAL ANARCHISM, STRATEGIC INTERESTS AND THE MARGINALIZATION OF THE UNITED NATIONS

The end of the Cold War, followed by the breakup of the Soviet Union, accentuated some powerful pre-existing trends in international society: an expanding claim of the right of self-determination and a growing preoccupation with the politics of identity, relating to ethnic and national consciousness. During the decades following the Second World War, the emergent norm of self-determination was mainly confined in practice to the struggle against the colonial order. In the background, however, were various other suppressed peoples that sought to assert their political autonomy and escape from structures and memories of oppression.[26]

---

[25] The World Summit on Social Development, to be held by the U.N. in Copenhagen in March 1995, represents an ideological attempt to moderate the human consequences of global market forces. Such a summit presupposes the support of leading governments. Such support can be obtained only by acquiescing in the basic standpoint of the capital-driven conception of economic development, thereby suppressing the tension arising from positing the claims of the people-driven perspective. The preliminary conference documents for Copenhagen pretend that it is possible to reconcile globalization with the realization of the goals of social development. To some extent, one can appreciate the "realism" of such a purported reconciliation, but at the cost of "false consciousness." It will be up to the NGO participants at Copenhagen to expose the tension between the two images of economic development. It is doubtful that this exposure will have much immediate impact. The relative influence of global market forces is too great. States and the mainstream media are aligned; there is not yet sufficient countervailing power and influence. At this stage, the social development theme offers a safety valve to those being victimized, but over time, depending on other developments, it could become an alternative that might mount a challenge to market-driven globalization.

[26] For a range of these claims as present in the early 1990s see Hurst Hannum, *Autonomy, Sovereignty, and Self-Determination: The Accommodation of Conflicting Rights* (Philadelphia: University of Pennsylvania Press, 1990); see also Morton Halperin and David Scheffer, *Self-Determination in the New World Order* (Washington, DC: Brookings, 1992); for a constructive perspective on how to address these claims with minimum disruption see Gidon Gottlieb, *Nation Against State* (New York: Council on Foreign Relations, 1993).

Journal of International Affairs

Throughout the Cold War there was a consensus that transcended the East-West divide to the effect that claims of self-determination had to be satisfied within existing state boundaries, even those that were artificial and had been contrived by colonial rulers. This conception of the limits of self-determination was endorsed by the United Nations and its full membership.[27] But with the breakup of the Soviet Union and Yugoslavia, a new form of state-shattering self-determination came into being. The claims of the Baltic states to statehood had a strong and distinctive pre-existing legal foundation, considering their coerced annexation by the Soviet Union in the setting of the Second World War, and, aside from tensions associated with Russians who had been deliberately settled to alter the demographic balance, these reassertions of independent statehood have been relatively unproblematic.[28] The more severe tensions were reserved for the former Yugoslavia and some of the Asian republics of the former Soviet Union, where overlapping ethnic identities, anguished historical memories of abuse and passionate expressions of ethnically exclusive nationalism induced claimants of self-determination, most notably the Bosnian Serbs, to embark on "ethnic cleansing" to ensure that whatever political entity was constituted would, to the extent possible, embody their aspirations of identity and security. It is at this point that the "politics of identity" has, to varying degrees, become genocidal, and hence pathological with respect to the values and presuppositions of a world order resting upon the major premise of the territorially (not ethnically) defined sovereign state. The United Nations, although not empowered to intervene in matters essentially within domestic jurisdiction unless a threat to international peace is posed (Article 2[7]), has asserted a limited competence to protect the basic normative idea of ethnic pluralism and to resist several of the most severe denials of human rights of the sort that

---

[27]   See, for example, the authoritative formulation of this understanding incorporated into the Declaration on Principles of International Law Concerning Friendly Relations and Co-operation Among States, United Nations General Assembly Resolution 2625(XXV), reprinted in Weston et al., pp. 108-14, adopted by consensus without recorded vote, 24 October 1970.

[28]   See Halperin and Scheffer, *Self-Determination in the New World Order*, pp. 27-29, 148-56.

Richard Falk

accompany such ethnic-nationalist crusades as occurred in northern Iraq, Bosnia and Rwanda.[29]

Examples abound. A tiny privileged elite exploits and brutalizes its own citizenry to such an extent as to depend on the continuing commission of crimes against humanity (in the Nuremberg sense) to remain in power.[30] South Africa in the era of apartheid was a strong instance of such criminalization of state power. The situation in Haiti after the 1991 coup d'état that displaced the democratically elected leader, Jean-Bertrand Aristide, raised another form of pathological anarchism to global consciousness, namely, the repudiation of an overwhelming electoral mandate, combined with reliance upon paramilitary forces to terrorize the citizenry — a process that combines severe violations of the most fundamental human rights with crimes against humanity (in the Nuremberg sense). Finally, the interplay of extreme poverty, ethnic strife, tribal or clan rivalry and religious extremism in several African countries illustrates yet another variant of pathological anarchy that challenges the conscience and capabilities of the United Nations, especially to the extent that the media spotlight generates strong grassroots demands for response.

Without entering into the details of specific cases, it is possible to generalize that the failure of responses associated with U.N. initiatives to restore normalcy or to protect the victims of atrocity has contributed, to some extent unfairly, to the declining reputation of the United Nations. In essence, the Organization, when pressured to act (as in Somalia), failed to mount an operation of sufficient magnitude to eliminate the pathological elements accounting for the worst human abuses. By mandate and capability, the U.N. role has been confined to the substantial mitigation of civilian suffering through the provision of food, medicine and other forms of relief, especially to those displaced from their homes. Such a role for

---

[29] This sovereignty-eroding practice is well-analyzed in an unpublished paper by Michael Doyle, "U.N. Intervention and National Sovereignty," dated September 1994. (Security Council Res. 688 [5 April 1991] with reference to Kurds; Security Council Res. 794 [3 December 1992] with reference to hunger in Somalia, Security Council Res. 841 [16 June 1993] with reference to the military coup d'état and violations of human rights in Haiti). A similar argument about the limits of acceptable diversity in the choice of public order systems is discussed in a powerful essay by John Rawls. See Rawls, "The Law of Peoples," in *On Human Rights: The Oxford Amnesty Lectures 1993*, ed. Stephen Shute and Susan Hurley (New York: Basic Books, 1994) pp. 41-82.

[30] For exposition of the evolution of international law to address such criminality see Richard Falk, Gabriel Kolko and Robert Jay Lifton, eds., *Crimes of War* (New York: Random House, 1971) pp. 73-176.

Journal of International Affairs

U.N. efforts may reduce the impact of barbarism to a significant degree, but not in a manner that generally engages the media, which emphasizes the persisting violence and unresolved political setting. The perception and assessment of U.N. effectiveness varies from case to case, but a current of disillusionment has been building since Somalia, focusing on Bosnia, and has created an overall impression of U.N. impotence in the face of the multiple challenges of pathological anarchism.

It is in these kinds of scenarios that the instrumental relationship between dominant states and the U.N. has again been crucial. Leading states in the post-Cold War setting have not treated pathological breakdowns of internal order in states marginal to the dynamics of the world economy as engaging their strategic interests sufficiently to justify the sort of open-ended, and possibly costly, commitments that would be needed to challenge successfully the agents of the pathology.[31] In contrast, during the Cold War, almost no country was perceived as marginal in relation to the East-West rivalry. The outcome of internal strife almost anywhere was perceived as weakening one side at the expense of the other, thus inducing strong pressures to preserve the status quo (however oppressive it might be), provided that an existing ideological alignment was maintained.[32] Under these new conditions, the call for response requires some sort of action, a politics of gesture, yet the main states remain unwilling to accept the requisite burdens or responsibilities. The result is a tendency by states to dump the situation on the Security Council, thereby

---

[31] Note that, as Hedley Bull so systematically depicted, anarchism is the structural condition of a world system constituted by distinct sovereign states. See Hedley Bull, *The Anarchic Society* (New York: Columbia University Press, 1976). Pathology emerges when the diversity of arrangements within boundaries crosses minimum normative thresholds of human security for the most vulnerable elements of society: the poor, minorities, or on occasion, as in Rwanda (although complicated by threats directed at minority Tutsi prior to the flight of the Hutu), and earlier in South Africa, majorities. In this terminology of international law and morality, such behavior constitutes genocide and crimes against humanity, as well as gross violations of human rights.

[32] Cuba's transfer of allegiance from one bloc to another was an exception, contributing, no doubt, to the inability of Washington in recent years to alter its Cold War posture despite the drastically altered global situation. Whatever else, Cuba no longer poses a threat to U.S. hemispheric interests, whether directly as a source of revolutionary politics, or indirectly as a base for Soviet penetration and influence. As a result, U.S. policy towards Cuba makes no geopolitical sense, and strikes the membership of the U.N. as vindictive and punitive. Its persistence, aside from the pressure mounted by the Cuban exile community, derives, I believe, from Castro's ability to flout the rules of the game associated with Cold War geopolitics, and the degree to which this has left an unhealed wound in the hegemonic sensibilities of U.S. government policy makers.

Richard Falk

shifting the focus of blame, yet at the same time eroding confidence in the peacemaking capabilities of the U.N. The argument being made here is admittedly convoluted. The allegation of "dumping" refers to the refusal to endow the U.N. with the capabilities and support needed for an effective response, and not to the appropriateness of U.N. action in such settings. It is dumping because states that call on the U.N. to act also control its purse strings and mandate. By withholding the means needed to be effective, leading states both shift some responsibility for inaction away from themselves and foster an impression of the U.N. as inept and ineffective.

Yet, given the instrumental relationship of leading states to the Security Council, the true locus of responsibility lies elsewhere, in a realist tradition of statecraft that is conditioned to disregard humanitarian claims unless intertwined with great power rivalry or threatening to wider patterns of political and economic stability. The maintenance of the multi-ethnic, secular state as the legitimate foundation of territorial sovereignty enlists widespread rhetorical support, but it is not seen as integral to either economic growth or global security. As long as the ascendent states (and their publics) are not threatened by pathological anarchism, the level of response is almost certain to remain minimal.[33] In light of this, it is implausible to expect the U.N. to perform miracles. Yet the scapegoating of the U.N. continues, thereby disguising the irresponsibility of the leading states and overlooking the achievements of the U.N. in mounting crucial relief operations in situations of acute danger and on the basis of constrained budgets.[34]

---

[33] To the extent action is taken, it is often to end the outflow of unwanted refugees, which in sufficient numbers do threaten the interests of powerful states, especially if producing racial tensions and adding to welfare and unemployment rolls.

[34] Such a generalization does not imply that valid criticisms of the U.N. cannot also be made for inefficiency or partisanship. The contention of the text is that U.N. failings of this sort are not the primary explanation of failure. It is also true that in the United States, and elsewhere, there is a generalized and influential hostility toward the U.N. as a political actor arising from ultra-conservative, highly nationalistic orientations. Here again, however, such ideological opposition does not explain public disappointment about the recent U.N. role, which is associated with the Organization doing too little, not too much. At the core of this disappointment is the dumping phenomenon, which creates expectations that exceed capabilities.

Journal of International Affairs

RESTORING CONFIDENCE IN THE UNITED NATIONS: SEIZING THE MOMENT

It may be helpful to reiterate the central thesis of this article: the U.N. engages in a range of useful activities (with greater or lesser success) that far exceeds its central peace and security mandate, but the *overall* reputation of the U.N. depends almost exclusively, especially in the media and with the citizenry, on how well or badly it does when called upon to act in relation to the global security agenda. To restore confidence in the U.N., then, depends on establishing a coherent and successful relationship with this agenda. Such an emphasis also underscores the relevance of leading states, especially in its orientation toward what is important enough to justify the risking of lives or the commitment of substantial resources. In the early post-Cold War period, the U.S. governmental orientation has been crucial to both the success and failure of the U.N. in the peace and security field.

The argument that has been presented is essentially structural and normative: The U.N. as an instrument of uneven state power is being shaped, primarily in relation to peace and security activities, by the priorities of an increasingly globalized world economy. Until this preponderant pattern of influence is offset by a resurgent labor movement or the further growth of transnational democracy, the role of the U.N., especially on matters of global security, is bound to be limited in contexts where G-7 leaders do not perceive strategic interests at stake.

Intriguingly, where the state is less engaged or supportive, that is, removed from the war-peace agenda, the U.N. can achieve some impressive results. For instance, the 1994 International Conference on Population and Environment, held in Cairo, was a great step forward for transnational efforts to address the issues at stake, especially the conditions of affliction confronting women in many societies around the world. Reversing a long-held demographic consensus that stressed reducing fertility rates as the best means to halt population growth, the Conference emphasized instead the improvement of the education and circumstances of women as the critical focus for population policy on a global level.

The U.N. can also contribute impressively, even to peace and security, in those settings where capabilities and mission are more or less congruent. Such has been the case in the settling of several long-standing conflicts in which either the contending parties struck a compromise (as in El Salvador)

Richard Falk

or one side surrendered (as in Namibia and Afghanistan).[35] In these situations, modest capabilities can suffice if the political will of the parties is sustained, but if consent is withdrawn, these efforts can end up inconclusively or in failure.

In peacekeeping, the eye of the storm, the challenge is more formidable, and its extent is often quite unpredictable. Such activity engages the use of force, the special domain of the state. What seems crucial at this stage is that the U.N. not intervene in situations it cannot reasonably expect to resolve in a satisfactory fashion. In this regard, the U.N. should be exceedingly wary about becoming committed to any undertaking that involves radical political restructuring, displacing by force patterns of governance in a state that are responsible for generating pathology. Under these circumstances, it should instead restrict its role to relief work (as in the early stages of its Somalia involvement or in relation to Bosnia), and make this restriction on its mission as clear as possible. One of the strengths of the International Committee of the Red Cross over the years has been its ability to delimit its role in manageable terms that do not generate disappointment. Unlike the U.N., the Red Cross does not generate unrealistic expectations.[36]

Where the rival territorial factions or parties have reached a point of exhaustion, the U.N. can often go further, by seeking a negotiated return to normalcy, as in such countries as Cambodia and El Salvador. The U.N. can usefully provide auspices for this process, resting its role on the consent of the parties. As recent events in Cambodia have demonstrated, consent can be withdrawn, making the U.N. role again precarious. As discussed earlier, this prospect of augmenting first-generation U.N. peacekeeping, in the spirit of Hammarskjold's original emphases, should remain a source of guidance, counseling action and restraint as appropriate.

---

[35] The U.N. "success" in Afghanistan involved the removal of the Soviet Union from the country, a step that has unfortunately produced neither normalcy nor peace for the country.

[36] Limiting expectations will be difficult, given the degree to which the Security Council is subject to the control of its leading members. As argued, it is often useful for these governments to use the U.N. as a shield behind which to obscure their own low levels of commitment. The U.N. is so used, and abused. To change this process is, in the first instance, an educational task, convincing both governments that it is more important to uphold the reputation of the Organization and public opinion that the U.N. needs capabilities commensurate with its responsibilities if it is to be held accountable.

Journal of International Affairs

A more ambitious approach would emphasize the need for a more autonomous U.N., an Organization more capable of responding without soliciting the heavy involvement of its leading members on an ad hoc basis. Essentially, this would require a more secure, independent financial base. Hovering at the edge of bankruptcy is not good enough for an effective U.N. More U.N. independence would also mean, over time, an independent, specially trained U.N. peace force that would seek to intrude itself in pathological conflict situations and exert leverage on behalf of a variety of humanitarian missions, including multi-ethnic tolerance as the basis of legitimate governance.[37]

With the 50th Anniversary Year of the U.N. upon us, it seems time to take stock of how to make the Organization better serve the needs of the peoples of the world, given changes in the patterns of conflict and considering the extent to which ascendent states are acting as agents of global market forces. Without establishing this wider structural framework, efforts to build wider public support for the U.N. are bound to fall short, particularly in the face of a continuing pathological anarchism assuming a variety of distressing new forms.

Perhaps, over time, the accumulation of human tragedy will build a consensus in the public, among leaders and within the boardrooms of transnational banks and corporations that an effective, autonomous U.N. is worth the investment. At present, the mood of disillusionment prevails, but it may turn out to be as transitory as the atmosphere of euphoria that emerged in the weeks after the cease-fire in the Gulf War. In any event, the public perception of an effective U.N. will remain tied, for the foreseeable future, to how well the Organization does in relation to peace and security. However, this should not blind more sophisticated observers from appreciating the many contributions being made by the U.N. with respect to its extraordinary range of activities.

---

[37] The scope of the U.N. role would have to evolve on a case-by-case basis, keeping in sharp relief the importance of conforming missions to available capabilities. Mistakes might still be made, but they would be seen more clearly for what they are, misjudgments as to means, not ambivalence as to ends. See suggestions along these lines in Sir Brian Urquhart, "For a U.N. Volunteer Military Force," *New York Review of Books*, 10 June 1993.

[13]

Review of International Studies (1995), *21*, 435 462 *Printed in Great Britain*

The influence of states and groups of states on and in the Security Council and General Assembly, 1980–94

SALLY MORPHET

Introduction

The aim of this paper[1] is to consider the way the main political groups of states, as well as important individual states, promote their interests in the Security Council and, where relevant, the General Assembly. It examines the composition, cohesion, interests and voting behaviour of these states and groups of states (and the way they have changed) between 1980 and 1994. It also discusses how they have used their political assets to increase their power overall within the whole system and how this has affected the development of both the Security Council and the General Assembly as well as their interrelationship.

The paper suggests that states on the Security Council over the period 1980 5 normally promoted their interests (as they did outside the UN) through their membership of three, familiar, political groups: the West (normally comprising the three Western permanent members, the United States, France and the United Kingdom, plus two non-permanent members from the Western European and other states group—see table 5); the Soviet Union and Eastern Europe (comprising one permanent member, the Soviet Union, and one from the Eastern European group); and the non-aligned[2] (comprising up to three African, two Asian and two Latin American states as well as, occasionally, one of the European members such as Malta or Yugoslavia). China, the fifth permanent member, remained separate, often not participating in votes. Each permanent member could use its veto to block any draft resolution which it considered inimical to its interests, and if members of a group wished to pass a resolution, they had to get nine or more members of the Security Council to vote for it. This meant that they normally had to ensure that the resolution was acceptable to some or all members of one or both the other groups. The paper does not discuss the behaviour of what is sometimes called the non-non-aligned group since they do not normally work together on the Security Council.

---

[1] The opinions expressed are the author's own and should not be taken as an expression of official government policy.
[2] A short account of the development of the non-aligned is given in my article on 'The Non-Aligned Movement and the Foreign Ministers' Meeting at Nicosia', *International Relations*, 9, No. 5, May 1989, pp. 393 6. The subject is well covered in Richard L. Jackson, *The Non-Aligned, the UN and the Superpowers* (Praeger Special Studies, New York, 1983). A useful account of the development of the Group of 77 is given in Robert L. Rothstein, *The Third World and US Foreign Policy* (Westview Press, Boulder, CO, 1981).

436 *Sally Morphet*

Member states of the General Assembly also promoted their interests through political groupings such as the European Union (formerly the European Community). One of the larger active groups consisted of the non-aligned whose ninety-seven-strong membership in 1980 included ninety-four members of the UN[3] (out of a total membership of 154). If they vote together the non-aligned can normally command over half the votes in the Assembly. This enables them to pass resolutions unless the question on which they are voting (relating to international peace and security or the budget or certain elections) is regarded as of particular importance (Article 18 of the UN Charter). The resolution then has to pass by a two-thirds majority. This paper examines the way the non-aligned in the General Assembly have tried to ensure the Security Council responds more appropriately to their concerns, and have (from within both bodies) prevented attempts to expand certain of its powers.

The paper suggests that by the mid-1980s (i.e. before the ending of the Cold War) the distinctive contribution of the Soviet Union and Eastern Europe on the Security Council began to disappear. Instead a new group was formed consisting of the permanent members of the Security Council (France, the Soviet Union, the United Kingdom, the United States and even China). They began to work closely together, fairly often but certainly not always, with the other main group remaining on the Security Council—the non-aligned.

These groups were not always cohesive. Each of the permanent members could defend its interests through the use of its veto power which did not depend on group cohesion. The non-aligned, without any veto power, needed to stick together (and promote their point of view) to maintain influence. This paper tries to show how they continued to do this (e.g. in 1989 when they made sure that the range of subjects the Council had authority to discuss was not increased).

The interests of the two groups continued to coincide more than they differed in the post-Cold War era, judging from the number of unanimous resolutions passed in the Security Council between August 1990 and 1994 (263 out of 310). Nevertheless the groups dissented in their voting on certain Security Council resolutions on such subjects as Libya, Iraq/Kuwait, former Yugoslavia and Rwanda. Dissent was also manifested in their attempts from 1991, from differing perspectives, to bring about Security Council reform. The paper looks at this and concomitant non-aligned attempts to change a number of the ways in which the Council related to the General Assembly. This battle has been affected by the expansion of UN membership from 159 in 1989 (only five more than at the end of 1980) to 185 (the non-aligned had 111 members, 109 with votes in the General Assembly,[4] and the Group of 77[5] had 131 members by the end of 1994).

The paper argues that the pattern of dissent within each group began to change in the 1990s though each group remained pretty cohesive, the permanent members

---

[3] The non-members of the UN were the PLO and SWAPO, both UN observers, and North Korea which was not then a UN member.

[4] The two without votes were Palestine which remains an observer in the UN system, and the Federal Republic of Yugoslavia (Serbia and Montenegro) which cannot participate in the work of the General Assembly since it cannot automatically continue the membership of the former Socialist Federal Republic of Yugoslavia. SCR 777, 19 September 1992.

[5] The Group of 77, formed in 1963, meets periodically to discuss economic issues. It consists primarily of members of the African, Asian and Latin American regional groups at the UN. See also n. 2 above.

voting together on 282 out of 310 resolutions and the non-aligned on 278. China, for the first time since 1981, began to vote differently from the other permanent members on certain constitutionally important resolutions beginning with SCR 678 (November 1990) which authorized UN members to take peace-enforcement measures against Iraq. It also began to work more closely with the non-aligned, becoming an observer in the movement in 1992.[6] Russia (which took over the responsibilities of the Soviet Union at the beginning of January 1992) began to dissent occasionally in 1993. It was joined by the United States in 1994. Members of the non-aligned did not always vote the same way on Security Council resolutions as they had between 1986 and July 1990.

The paper suggests that members of both major groups on the Security Council have, since August 1990, been prepared to accept the increased use of mandatory Chapter VII resolutions, mainly authorizing certain peace-enforcement operations and certain sanctions. They have also been prepared to accept certain instances of humanitarian intervention. All questions of this sort are considered on a case-by-case basis. They have agreed more easily to set up peace-keeping bodies, though this agreement is now in jeopardy since the United States has challenged the way they are financed. The non-aligned group have, so far, ensured (despite the fact they do not have veto powers) that the Council should not authorize any election monitoring (or human rights verification) not associated with peace-keeping. They have also succeeded in ensuring that the definition of 'security' has not been extended to cover narcotics or environment issues, besides pointing out firmly that the General Assembly, not the Security Council, deals with finance, even the financing of war crimes tribunals. The non-aligned have also won concessions from the Security Council in the context of its relationship with the General Assembly. The debate on the expansion and reform of the Council is not complete. It will be interesting to see how changes in this area affect the balance of forces on the Council and within the UN system as a whole.

Five tables (see annex) are relevant. Tables 1–4 consider Security Council resolutions and vetoes between 1980 and 1994[7] in terms, respectively, of:

(1) the number that were unanimous, the number voted for by all the permanent members and the number that were the subject of splits in voting between the permanent members;
(2) the number that were unanimous, the number voted for by all the non-aligned members on the Security Council and the number that were the subject of splits in voting between the non-aligned;
(3) the subjects on which the permanent members disagreed and on which the non-aligned members disagreed;
(4) voting patterns of the permanent members and the non-aligned on Chapter VII resolutions.

Table 5 gives an outline of the development of electoral, regional groups in the UN.

---

[6] Observers in the movement are states which are eligible to join the movement but have decided not to do so. They can participate in most, but not all, non-aligned activities.
[7] The details are taken from two FCO Research and Analysis Department Memoranda produced in January 1994: Summary of United Nations Security Council Resolutions 1946–1993 and Table of Vetoed Resolutions in the United Nations Security Council 1946–1993.

438   *Sally Morphet*

Three political groups, 1980–5

The primary responsibility of the Security Council is the maintenance of international peace and security in accordance with the purposes and principles of the
UN Charter. During the early 1980s the three major political groups on the Security
Council (the West, the East and the non-aligned plus an unsure China that often did
not participate in votes) continued to maintain their distinctive contributions (see
tables 1 and 2). This did not mean that the groups never voted together. They did.
At least half of the resolutions passed every year between 1981 and 1985 were
unanimous (this was not true of 1980).[8] Nor does it mean that countries within each
group always voted together. They did not. Nevertheless the continuing, distinctive
East–West non-aligned interchange over this period can be traced by looking at
some of the disagreements between the groups during this period.

The non-aligned on the Security Council had agreed to formalize their relationship under the guidance of Kuwait in January 1979 when the six non-aligned
members (Bangladesh, Gabon, Jamaica, Kuwait, Nigeria and Zambia) and one
non-aligned observer (Bolivia) on the Council agreed to form a G7 with a rotating
monthly chairmanship. This gave the group 'a new sense of non-aligned identity',
coherence and discipline which enhanced its subsequent performance besides contributing to its initiatives on southern Africa and the Middle East.[9]

Security Council reform 1979–80

Since the non-aligned succeeded in expanding the numbers on the Security Council
from eleven to fifteen in 1963 (the expanded Council came into operation at the
beginning of 1966), those occupying the ten non-permanent seats have come, as
agreed by General Assembly Resolution (GAR) 1991A (1963), from the following
regional electoral groups: five from Africa and Asia in a ratio of 3:2; two from Latin
America; two from Western Europe and other states (this includes Australia,
Canada and New Zealand); and one from Eastern Europe (see table 5). By 1980 this
meant that the non-aligned could gain up to nine seats on the Security Council if
non-aligned members filled all the available seats for Africa, Asia and Latin America
and if Malta (which belonged to the Western European electoral group and was also
a member of the non-aligned) and Yugoslavia (which belonged to the Eastern
European electoral group and was also a member of the non-aligned) were also
elected. The numbers of non-aligned on the Council between 1980 and 1994 have
varied between eight (1983–4) and four (1981 and 1986) (see table 2).

In 1979 a number of non-aligned countries including Algeria, Argentina (then a
non-aligned member) and India (supported interestingly by Japan) submitted a draft

---

[8] Over the forty-nine years the Security Council has been in operation (up to the end of 1994) the
number of unanimous resolutions passed has been equal to half or more of the resolutions passed in
thirty-two of these years. The last year in which non-unanimous exceeded unanimous resolutions
was 1980. The longest sequence of years in which non-unanimous exceeded unanimous resolutions
was 1947–53 inclusive.
[9] Jackson, *Non-Aligned*, pp. 116–19.

resolution to the General Assembly (Charter reforms are considered in the General Assembly not the Security Council) proposing an increase in the non-permanent membership of the Security Council from ten to fourteen; UN membership had increased from 135 in 1963 to 152 in 1979. Consideration of this matter was postponed. The sponsors put forward a revised resolution in 1980 suggesting an increase of six non-permanent seats: once again this was postponed. The subject remained on the agenda of the General Assembly and burst into life in 1991.

The United States, the non-aligned and UN finances

In the General Assembly the permanent members do not have the privileges they have on the Security Council since resolutions are passed by a simple majority unless they deal with important questions such as recommendations on international peace and security and finance (Article 18 of the UN Charter); the draft resolution has then to be passed by a two-thirds majority. Between 1980 and 1985 the non-aligned could, if they agreed, have commanded over half the votes in the Assembly if not quite two-thirds. They could also supplement their voting power through bringing pressure to bear on the few members of the Group of 77 that did not belong to their movement and thus reach a two-thirds vote. This gave them potential control over the General Assembly agenda including the very important control over votes on the UN budget (Article 17 of the UN Charter states that the General Assembly shall consider and approve the budget and apportion the expenses of the Organization).

However, the permanent members, particularly the United States which in the early 1980s was liable to pay 25 per cent of the budget (apart from the peace-keeping budget), also had a weapon to hand which was in effect the temporary non-payment of some or all of its dues (continuing non-payment raises problems since states lose their vote in the General Assembly under Article 19 if they are more than two years in arrears). The differences between the United States and the non-aligned were expressed most clearly in a battle about UN financing of the budget. The US Administration under President Reagan, reflecting the views of influential lobbying groups such as the Heritage Foundation,

complained with increasing vehemence that they were not prepared to pay excessive sums, providing a fixed percentage of a budget which they were unable to control. Too frequently, it was asserted, the Secretariats of international organizations consulted the major donors so late in the biennial budget cycle that the budget was then difficult to unravel. And too often states which contributed very little out-voted major donors in the plenary meetings approving such budgets.[10]

This attack on a major prerogative of the General Assembly was eventually dealt with by a compromise in December 1986 when the non-aligned agreed that financial decisions should be agreed by consensus. This gave the United States (and other

---

[10] Paul Taylor, 'The United Nations system under stress: financial pressures and their consequences', *Review of International Studies*, 17 (1991), p. 369. This study also shows that this assessment was somewhat simplistic.

440   *Sally Morphet*

permanent members) much more power in financial decision-making in the General
Assembly. This underlying conflict has continued to contribute to non-aligned/US
dissension.

Three vetoes, 1980

The three-sided interaction in the Security Council can be neatly demonstrated by
looking at the three vetoes cast in 1980. In January the Soviet Union (with East
Germany also voting against) vetoed a resolution voted for by all the Western and
non-aligned countries on the Council calling for the immediate and unconditional
withdrawal of foreign (Soviet) troops from Afghanistan. This was followed two days
later by a procedural resolution which could not be vetoed (voted against by the
Soviet Union and East Germany, with one non-aligned abstention, Zambia) calling
for an emergency special session of the UN General Assembly 'due to the lack of
unanimity among the permanent members of the Security Council'.

The Soviet Union subsequently vetoed a resolution calling for sanctions against
Iran because of the American hostages (China took the line of non-participation).
This split the non-aligned vote by one. Five voted for it as did all the Western
countries. One, Bangladesh, abstained. China once again did not participate in the
vote.

The third resolution, reaffirming that Israel should withdraw from all the occupied
territories including Jerusalem and affirming the Palestinians' right to self-
determination, was vetoed by the United States; four Western countries abstained,
France, Norway, Portugal and the United Kingdom. On issues concerning the
Arab/Israeli dispute and Palestine here, as in the past, the non-aligned and the
Soviet Union and the Eastern Europeans usually agreed. The fact that the Western
group did not vote together is worth noting. The United States and the rest of the
West have never been completely aligned on the question of Israel and Palestine.
The United States vetoed four more resolutions on this subject between 1982 and
1985. On three of these, Western countries voted for the draft resolution in question;
on the other they abstained.

The influence of peace-keeping finance on the roles of China and the Soviet Union

The Soviet Union had announced at the end of 1976 that it would pay only half of
its assessed expenses for UNEF II and UNDOF. It subsequently, at Arab request,[11]
only abstained on (rather than vetoing) the 1978 SCR setting up UNIFIL (the UN
Interim Force in Lebanon). It then refused to pay its assessed expenses for the
operation. China, which had taken the decision not to participate in voting on a
number of subjects, including peace-keeping, also pursued a policy of not paying its

---

[11] See p. 207 of the chapter on 'UN Peacekeeping and Election Monitoring' in Adam Roberts and
Benedict Kingsbury (eds.), *United Nations, Divided World*, 2nd edn (Clarendon Press, 1993).

peace-keeping dues. However, in the early 1980s the Chinese had to reappraise this policy since they were about to lose their vote in the General Assembly under Article 19. After detailed negotiation the General Assembly passed GAR 36/116A in December 1981. This was voted for by most countries with the exception of the Soviet Union and the Eastern Europeans. The resolution asked the Secretary-General to put past dues owed for peace-keeping by China into a special account; decided that the applicability of Article 19 in respect of these should not be raised; and welcomed China's decision to contribute its assessed expenses to UNDOF and UNIFIL from January 1982. This, in effect meant that China had been forced to become more committed to the UN. It was, perhaps, therefore more ready to become more creatively involved in using the UN to its best advantage. China also gave up its policy of non-cooperation in votes on peace-keeping. Its last move of that kind had come in November 1981 when it did not participate in a vote on the renewal of the mandate of UNDOF.

It was clear that the Soviet Union realised that its policy of non-payment of peace-keeping dues would need to be rethought once it, too, came close to losing its General Assembly vote. This turnaround was to come in 1986. This was, no doubt, one reason for its change in policy towards the UN system.

The Argentine invasion of the Falkland Islands, 1982

The differences between the permanent members, however, continued on certain major issues. A straightforward example is the Argentine invasion of the Falkland Islands. In early April 1982 all the non-aligned on the Security Council except Panama, plus France, the United Kingdom and the United States, voted for a Security Council resolution determining that there was a breach of peace in the Falklands, demanding a cessation of hostilities and the withdrawal of all Argentine forces, and calling on the UK and Argentina to seek a diplomatic solution to their differences. Both China and the Soviet Union abstained. The United Kingdom and the United States both vetoed a subsequent draft resolution in June 1982 requesting an immediate cease-fire and implementation of two previous resolutions. This was voted for by China and the Soviet Union; France abstained as did three of the non-aligned, Togo, Guyana and Jordan, who had particular ties with the United Kingdom.[12] This resolution was a Chapter VII resolution.

The Israeli invasion of the Lebanon, 1982

The Israeli invasion of the Lebanon in 1982 provoked a more complex response from the permanent members, who were able both to agree and to differ with the United States on aspects of the issue. In early June the permanent members (and the others on the Security Council) voted unanimously for two resolutions calling for an end to military activities within Lebanon and across the Israeli–Lebanese border and demanding the withdrawal of Israeli forces to the internationally recognized borders

---

[12] Jackson, *Non-Aligned*, p. 118.

442   *Sally Morphet*

of Lebanon. The United States vetoed two draft resolutions the same month condemning Israel for non-compliance and demanding the immediate cessation of hostilities. These were voted for by all other members of the Security Council. However, all the permanent members were able to vote for a resolution in August 1982 authorizing observers from UNTSO (the UN Truce Supervisory Organization) to monitor the situation in and around Beirut, though the United States vetoed another, to withhold military aid to Israel, with abstentions from the United Kingdom and two non-aligned.

Old Soviet attitudes, 1983–5

The continuation of old-style policies can be seen in the Soviet Union's voting pattern between 1983 and 1985. In September 1983 it vetoed (with Poland also voting against) a draft resolution deeply deploring the destruction of the South Korean civil airliner shot down by a Soviet plane. China and certain non-aligned members of the Council abstained. Western countries and certain non-aligned voted for. The Soviet Union's last veto (in February 1984, with a Ukrainian vote against) stopped the setting up of a UN force in Beirut supported by all other members of the Council. This force was to be selected, if appropriate, from UNIFIL, and the Soviet Union's veto reflected its continuing questioning of the role of UNIFIL. Between 1983 and 1985 it abstained on all resolutions extending UNIFIL's mandate besides continuing not to contribute to it.

Southern Africa

One major subject of dissension between Western countries, the Soviet Union and the non-aligned remained the question of South Africa. Western countries (the United States in all cases with the addition of the United Kingdom and France in certain cases) vetoed seven draft resolutions initiated by the non-aligned on Namibia and South Africa over this period, mainly because most called for Chapter VII imposition of sanctions. Meanwhile twenty-eight resolutions were passed: the United States abstained on eight. The United Kingdom joined in abstaining four times and France once. As Jackson noted in 1983 'the non-aligned have been successful in keeping Namibia and Palestine before the public through recourse to the Council and General Assembly. Without illusions that UN resolutions could lead to a breakthrough in either case, they have viewed the process as a long-term form of pressure on the West to intervene with South Africa and Israel.'[13]

Analysis of the tables 1980–5

Between 1980 and 1985 the tables show that the permanent members voted together on 75 out of 119 Security Council resolutions, as opposed to 68 out of the 79

[13] Ibid., pp. 128 9.

resolutions passed between 1986 and July 1990. They differed on such subjects as Afghanistan, Arab/Israeli issues, Cyprus, the Falklands, the Gulf, Iran/Iraq, Lebanon, Namibia, Palestine, South Africa, Syria, and the Israeli attack on PLO targets in Tunisia (see table 3). Vetoes were cast by four different permanent members (China cast no vetoes during this period, France cast four, the Soviet Union four, the United Kingdom seven and the United States twenty-five) on subjects including, besides many of the subjects noted above, US intervention in Grenada, Iran and Nicaragua.

In contrast the non-aligned on the Security Council voted together on 113 of the 119 resolutions passed between 1980 and 1985. This reflected the efficacy of the formalizing of the relationship of the non-aligned on the Security Council under Kuwait in January 1979 and compares well with their voting together on 79 out of 79 resolutions passed in the period 1986–July 1990. The non-aligned tend to split in their votes on resolutions when there is conflict between a regional and a non-aligned view and/or when pressure is applied by a superpower, which is particularly effective on weak countries. The former explains the Panamanian vote on the Falklands on Security Council Resolution (SCR) 502 of 3 April 1982. The latter explains, perhaps, the votes by Zaire on Arab/Israel vetoes by the United States at the end of 1982 and the beginning of 1983, and the votes by Zaire and Togo on a resolution on US intervention in Grenada in October 1983. A further example is probably the Egyptian abstention on a draft resolution vetoed by the United States in May 1985 regretting the imposition of economic sanctions against Nicaragua, the only non-aligned split that year.

The permanent members and the non-aligned, 1986–July 1990

This section looks at the British initiative at the end of 1986 which paved the way for the beginning of continuous permanent member cooperation as disagreements between the West and the non-aligned over UN finances were at least temporarily resolved. It goes on to look at the permanent member/non-aligned cooperation which developed in 1988 and 1989 over the setting up of peace-keeping bodies to help resolve regional disputes.[14] Their main disagreement centred on the question of whether the Security Council or the General Assembly should authorize election monitoring when peace-keeping bodies were not involved

UN finances, the Soviet Union and the non-aligned, 1986–7

The Soviet Union's changing attitude to the United Nations was demonstrated in April 1986 when it announced that it would pay its peace-keeping dues. This was no doubt partly due to the fact that its arrears were nearly two years behind so that it

---

[14] Members of the Security Council, with others, particularly regional groups, continued to attempt to find ways of settling long-standing regional disputes from the early 1980s onwards in the context of Chapter VIII of the UN Charter. These attempts included the peacemaking activities of the Contadora Group in Central America, whose actions were endorsed by the Security Council in 1983; of ASEAN in Asia; and of the United States in southern Africa. These were combined with renewed pressure by the UN Secretary-General to bring about an end to the conflict in Cambodia.

was coming near to losing its vote in the General Assembly. The same month the Soviet Union was given a demonstration of the usefulness of the UN system when the IAEA came to its aid over the nuclear reactor disaster at Chernobyl.

The permanent members particularly the United States also reached a *modus vivendi* with the non-aligned over finance, through a compromise in 1986, expressed through GAR 41/213 of December 1986, when major donors agreed that they would be consulted in the first year of the two-year budgetary cycle, about programmes and finance. Decisions about the budget would be taken on the basis of a consensus in the Committee for Programme and Co-ordination, on which major donors were represented, before being discussed first in the Fifth Committee of the General Assembly and second in plenary. The consensus has held though it almost broke in 1990 on the question of full funding by the United States. The quid pro quo underlying this agreement was that the United States would stop withholding and go back to full funding of the United Nations.

The permanent members begin to work more closely together

In late 1986 the British permanent representative at the UN invited all other permanent member representatives to meet to see if they could do more to stop the long-running regional conflict between Iran and Iraq. The permanent five were subsequently able to agree and to gain unanimous support in July 1987 for a resolution, SCR 598, containing a Chapter VII determination laying down a number of elements which, taken together, had to be fulfilled to bring about the ending of the war. This, the first Chapter VII resolution since that on the Falklands in 1982, can in retrospect be seen as the precursor of the greatly increased use of Chapter VII Security Council resolutions from 1990 onwards (see table 4).

It also, it can be argued, marked a change in the composition of the groups that operate the Security Council. The former West–East–non-aligned division still noticeable between 1980 and 1985 was replaced by more cohesion between the permanent members and the non-aligned. In both 1986 and 1987 the non-aligned and permanent members voted together on ten out of the thirteen resolutions passed each year. The United States abstained on resolutions relating to Israel/Palestine (two), Israel/Lebanon (one), South Africa (two; on one of these the UK also abstained) and Nauru and the International Court of Justice (one). The United States also vetoed ten draft resolutions, four on southern Africa, all of which were also vetoed by the UK, three on Israeli actions, two on the question of the ICJ judgment on actions against Nicaragua, and one accompanied by the UK and France on the US raid on Libya. Meanwhile the non-aligned on the Security Council voted together on all twenty-six Security Council resolutions passed (and all those vetoed) in 1986–7.

The expansion of peace-keeping bodies

The changed Soviet attitude was made explicit through the simultaneous publication of an article by Gorbachev in *Pravda* and *Izvestia* in September 1987. This noted that the world was becoming increasingly interrelated and interdependent. There was therefore a need for a mechanism which was capable of discussing common problems. The permanent members could become guarantors of regional security. More use should be made of UN peace-keeping bodies. This latter concern was subsequently given more credence by the Soviet government's announcement in early 1988 that it would pay arrears on its assessed contributions for peace-keeping operations.

In this climate it became increasingly possible for the permanent members and the non-aligned to vote to set up UN peace-keeping bodies to help resolve previously intractable regional disputes.[15] The Security Council was thus able, unanimously, to set up the UN Iran–Iraq Military Observer Group (UNIIMOG) which had been foreshadowed in SCR 598 in 1988, as well as approving the UN Good Offices Mission in Afghanistan and Pakistan (UNGOMAP) and deciding to authorize a UN Angola Verification Mission (UNAVEM 1) following the Angolan peace accords, to monitor the withdrawal of Cuban troops from Angola. In 1989 the Security Council went on to give a green light to the UN Transition Assistance Group (UNTAG; this had been authorized in 1978) to take charge in Namibia while pre-independence elections were held. In November, it set up a UN Observer Group in Central America (ONUCA) to monitor the Central American peace accords.

The non-aligned work against the expansion of the Security Council's powers

The ability of groups on the Security Council to do more to help resolve disputes in the late 1980s was due not only to the changing relationships among the permanent members, but also to a renewed determination by the non-aligned to adapt to changing political circumstances as shown by the concern for reform demonstrated at both the non-aligned foreign ministers' meeting at Nicosia in August/September 1988 and the Belgrade Summit in August/September 1989.[16] A further example of non-aligned adaptation to change could be seen in the unequivocal acceptance of the existence of Israel by the PLO, and the declaration of the state of Palestine in November 1988.

The dispute over ONUVEN. The non-aligned and those close to the non-aligned were happy to work with the permanent members to set up a variety of peace-keeping operations. They remained, however, concerned about any attempt by permanent members to enlarge the scope of the Security Council. The first major dispute in 1989 concerned the decision to deploy a UN electoral observer mission in Nicaragua (ONUVEN), the first such UN mission to an *independent* country.[17] The non-aligned were careful to ensure that the unanimous Security Council resolution

---

[15] See *The Singapore Symposium: The Changing Role of the United Nations in Conflict Resolution and Peacekeeping 13–15 March 1991* (UN DPI, New York, 1991).

[16] For discussion of this period see my article on 'The Non-Aligned in "The New World Order". The Jakarta Summit, September 1982', *International Relations,* 11 No. 4, April 1993, pp. 371–3.

[17] See *The Singapore Symposium,* pp. 42–6.

446   *Sally Morphet*

(SCR 637) of July 1989, *inter alia* commending the Esquipulas Agreement of 1987, only noted with appreciation (*not authorized*) the UN Secretary-General's agreement with Nicaragua to deploy a UN electoral observer mission. ONUVEN was subsequently *endorsed* in a General Assembly resolution. Non-aligned members of the General Assembly were prepared to accept that election monitoring in independent countries could be authorized by the Security Council *if* this was part of a peace-keeping operation. They had accepted in the mid-1960s that the Security Council alone, and not the General Assembly (the last peace-keeping operation authorized by the General Assembly was in 1962), could set up peace-keeping operations. They were not, however, prepared to accept that the election monitoring on its own was a matter of international peace and security, and thus within the ambit of the Security Council.

Narcotics and the Security Council. This contretemps was followed by an attempt by a permanent member, the United Kingdom, to enlarge the meaning of 'security' in the mandate of the Security Council in the context of a series of murders in August 1989 by drugs traffickers in Colombia. The United Kingdom began to seek support for a draft Security Council resolution on the subject. This initiative was pre-empted by the non-aligned on the Security Council and President Barco of Colombia who called in his plenary speech at the General Assembly for a special General Assembly session on narcotics. The draft resolution was withdrawn in early October.[18] The special session of the General Assembly was subsequently held in 1990.

The General Assembly/Security Council relationship. The concerns of the non-aligned members over attempts to increase the powers of the Security Council had not yet, however, reached their subsequent levels. In December members of the General Assembly normally consider a report from the Security Council to the Assembly (running in this case from June 1988 to June 1989). In December 1989 the President of the General Assembly asked, as usual, that the General Assembly should take note of this report, and this was so decided without any dissent.[19] This report was to become a focus of attention from 1990 onwards.

Election monitoring in Haiti. Non-aligned concern shown about any inappropriate precedent relating to the constitutional standing of ONUVEN did not diminish. In June 1990 the provisional government of Haiti requested assistance from the UN Secretary-General to observe and verify the forthcoming elections in December. No mention was made of peace-keeping. In August 1990, however, in a further letter, the provisional government specifically noted, 'the Haitian Government does not wish for, and is not requesting, the dispatch of "Blue Helmets" or of any peace-keeping force to ensure the security of the country, a task for which the Haitian Armed Forces are basically responsible'.[20] This specific distinction seems to have been pushed for by the Latin American and Caribbean Group of the UN, most of whom are either members or observers of the non-aligned group.

---

[18]   *The Times*, 13 October 1990.
[19]   A/44/PV.79 of 21 December 1989 for 11 December 1989. The question had been previously brought up in the early 1970s.
[20]   The texts of these letters are given in A44/965 and A44/973.

Latin Americans, who have a strong legalistic sense, obviously realized that the original request (in the context of only the second election to be monitored in an independent country by the UN) could have ensured that the Security Council, rather than the General Assembly, would, from now on, take on the task of authorizing the supply of election monitors to independent countries. Since the Latin Americans considered that election monitoring was not, *per se*, a question relating to the maintenance of international peace and security (i.e. a Security Council task), they were determined to ensure that this would not provide an opportunity for Security Council aggrandizement. These concerns were strongly argued by both Colombia and Cuba, the two (non-aligned) Latin American members of the Security Council in 1990. They succeeded in ensuring the other non-aligned members of the Council were brought round to their view. The matter was finally settled through a General Assembly resolution, adopted by consensus in October 1990, which *authorized* the sending of election monitors to Haiti.

The use of 'authorized' is worth commenting on here. This deliberately goes further than the resolution setting on ONUVEN. The General Assembly 'endorsed' ONUVEN in 1989: in mid-1990 it 'authorized' ONUVEN.

Analysis of the tables 1986–90

The new cooperation among permanent members of the Security Council and non-aligned attempts to adapt to a changing world, which developed in the mid-1980s, came about before the breaking down of the Berlin Wall in November 1989. Both the permanent members and the non-aligned were able to cooperate more between 1986 and mid-1990 (before the invasion and annexation of Kuwait by Iraq) than they had between 1980 and 1985. One indicator is the number of unanimous resolutions on the Security Council: there were 72 unanimous resolutions out of 119 between 1980 and 1985, and sixty-eight out of seventy-nine between 1986 and mid-1990. Between 1986 and mid-1990 the permanent members voted together on sixty-eight and the non-aligned voted together on all seventy-nine.

In retrospect 1986 to the end of July 1990 can perhaps be seen as a transition period between a world that included acceptance of certain fixed certainties relating to the continuing Cold War and the difficulties produced *inter alia* by its demise. The main continuing thread remained the need for the world community to find appropriate ways of settling regional conflict. A new era was highlighted in August 1990 by the unique challenge posed by the Iraqi invasion and annexation of Kuwait.

The permanent members and the non-aligned, August 1990–1994

The Security Council moved into the post-Cold War world with the Iraqi invasion and annexation of Kuwait. By the end of 1990 it had passed at least nine Chapter VII resolutions (table 4) followed by thirteen in 1991, ten in 1992, twenty-five in 1993 and twenty-three in 1994 in contrast to two in the 1980s. The prospect of a

448   *Sally Morphet*

Security Council that could use the provisions of Chapter VII more often and make collective security more of a reality made some of the non-aligned (and probably China) apprehensive and, in the case of the non-aligned (see below), more determined both to make the Security Council more responsive to the General Assembly and to reform and expand it. This section discusses the way both the permanent members and the non-aligned responded to the problems of the post-Cold War world, in particular concerning Iraq and former Yugoslavia.

The Security Council and the Iraqi invasion and annexation of Kuwait

The Iraqi invasion of Kuwait proved to be a watershed in the development of the Security Council in the post-Cold War period. It led to an unprecedented exploration of the powers of the Council under Chapter VII of the Charter. The most important resolution on Iraq/Kuwait in 1990 was SCR 678 of November 1990 and it was the only one on which China abstained, its vote differentiating it from all the other permanent members for the first time since 1981. SCR 678 authorized member states cooperating with the government of Kuwait to use all necessary means to uphold and implement SCR 660 demanding the withdrawal of Iraq from Kuwait, unless Iraq withdrew before 15 January 1991. This gave the green light for peace-enforcement by the UN for the first time (with the possible exception of the Congo) since Korea in 1950. The Chinese Foreign Minister, in his explanation of his country's vote, stated China was against the use of military action. China held that

relations between States should be based on the Five Principles of mutual respect for each other's sovereignty and territorial integrity, mutual non-aggression, non-interference in each other's internal affairs, equality and mutual benefit, and peaceful coexistence; and that international disputes should be settled through dialogue and consultations.[21]

The second major, unprecedented, resolution (not a Chapter VII resolution) concerned the obligation to allow *humanitarian* aid. SCR 688 of April 1991 insisted that Iraq allow immediate access by international humanitarian organizations to all those in need of assistance in all parts of Iraq and make available all necessary facilities for their operations, and requested the Secretary-General to pursue his humanitarian efforts in Iraq. A number of states, including China, considered that this sort of resolution could be used to undermine the territorial integrity of states.

Non-aligned attempts to make the Security Council more responsive to the General Assembly

The UN Charter in Article 24 lays down the pattern of the relationship between the Security Council and the General Assembly by stipulating that, in carrying out its

---

[21] S/PV.2693, 29 November 1990, pp. 61–2.

duties, the Security Council shall act on behalf of the members of the UN.[22] Both bodies, of course, have to act in accordance with the purposes and principles of the Charter. The Security Council has the primary responsibility for the maintenance of international peace and security; the General Assembly is specifically barred by Article 12 from being involved in such disputes when the Security Council is able to exercise its responsibilities.

Report of the Security Council to the General Assembly. Cuba, Colombia and Malaysia (all non-aligned members) were not slow in expressing their concern over developments in the Security Council, in the General Assembly debate in December 1990 on the report (June 1989–June 1990) of the Security Council to the General Assembly.[23] Colombia called for prompt action, otherwise

we shall ourselves be permitting the advent of a new era in which the dictatorship of the permanent members will prevail to the detriment of all countries including those industrialized countries that are not permanent members of the Council and the developing world.

These countries also drew attention to the need to address the veto question; raised fears about the exclusivity of decision-making on the Council; discussed the need for transparency, accountability and explanation of its decision-making in the Council's report to the Assembly; and also noted that SCR 678 had not provided for a clear system of reporting to the Council.

The following December (1991) Malaysia noted that agreement between the permanent members facilitated the settlement of political and security disputes.[24] The Security Council could, however, be undone if one power or a group of powers took control of decision-making. It agreed with the Secretary-General that the UN must seriously consider how the general membership could ensure that the Council remained accountable to it. Cuba drew attention to the informal consultations of the Council and the fact that these were not reflected in the report to the General Assembly. Brazil (a non-aligned observer) spoke of 'the need to listen to the wider membership of the UN in order adequately to ascertain and reflect the sense of the majority, if not the consensus, of the international community', as well as drawing attention to the financial burdens imposed through peace-keeping.

The next debate[25] on the report of the Security Council (of June 1991–June 1992) took place on 22 June 1993 (eighteen months after the discussion of the previous report). The eleven speakers (nine of them members or observers of the non-aligned) made much of the need for greater openness and transparency in the deliberations of the Security Council, particularly the closed informal consultations.[26] Colombia and Egypt drew attention to the need for the Security Council to respect the rule of law. Colombia also expressed concern over the excessive use of Chapter VII of the Charter. Algeria noted *inter alia* the non-aligned proposal to create an ad hoc working group of the General Assembly to study the

[22] See Sydney D. Bailey, *The Procedure of the UN Security Council*, 2nd edn (Oxford 1988), pp. 254–70.
[23] See A/45/PV.63 of 28 December 1990 for 10 December 1990.
[24] See A/46/PV.70 of 30 December 1991 for 12 December 1991.
[25] A/47/PV.106, 12 July 1993.
[26] Cuba noted (pp. 39–40) for instance that the consultations held in July 1991 on the need for transparency in the work of the Council did not even rate a mention in the report before them.

450   *Sally Morphet*

submission of reports to it from the other principal organs of the UN including the Security Council.

The campaign produced results. Eight days later, on 30 June, the President of the Security Council issued a note[27] on the issue of the format of the Security Council's annual report to the General Assembly. All Council members agreed to submit the report (mid-June to mid-June as before) before the end of September. They also agreed that Presidential statements should be published and that the report should be adopted at a public meeting of the Council. The Council also set up an informal working group to consider the question. Subsequently all members of the Council agreed to a tentative forecast of the Security Council's programme of work for the next month being circulated to all member states for information.[28] In October the President of the Security Council, Brazil, addressed the General Assembly about the next report of the Security Council (June 1992–June 1993).[29] He also referred to the new practice of regular consultations by the President of the Security Council with the President of the General Assembly and separately with the Chairmen of the five regional electoral groups (see table 5).

Colombia welcomed these innovations in the subsequent debate while drawing attention to 'the Council's tendency to broaden, arbitrarily, the definition of what constitutes a threat to international peace and security', in particular, coverage of human rights, humanitarian assistance, the restoration of democracy and certain legal controversies. Indonesia, the non-aligned Chairman, stated firmly that 'there should be greater accountability of the Council to the Assembly on decisions and actions affecting the interests of the entire international community'.

The momentum of the campaign continues. In December 1994 the Security Council President declared the Council's intention of ensuring 'increased recourse to open meetings, in particular at an early stage in its consideration of a subject'.[30]

Renewed disputes over finance. The preservation of the General Assembly's pre-rogative to make financial decisions was challenged when the Security Council unanimously passed SCR 827, a Chapter VII resolution, in May 1993 establishing a war crimes tribunal for Yugoslavia. Paragraph 5 urged states, inter-governmental and non-governmental organizations to contribute funds to the tribunal. Members of the General Assembly regarded this as an attack on their prerogative, noting in GAR 47/235 of 21 October the General Assembly's role in financing under Article 17 of the UN Charter as well as expressing concern 'that advice given to the Security Council by the Secretariat on the nature of the financing of the International Tribunal did not respect the role of the General Assembly as set out in Article 17 of the Charter'. The non-aligned and the permanent members have not yet been able to agree on the way the tribunal should be funded in the long term.

The Security Council and human rights. In 1994 the UN Secretary-General exposed

---

[27] S/26015, 30 June 1993.
[28] S/26176, 27 July 1993.
[29] See GAOR 41st and 42nd plenary meetings of 28 October 1993: A/48/PV.41, 17 November 1993 and A/48/PV.42, 19 November 1993.
[30] S/PRST/1994/81, 16 December 1994; see also S/1995/234, 29 March 1995.

a further clash of interests in his report on the establishment of a human rights verification mission in Guatemala.[31] As he said (para. 38):

> In view of the fact that the agreements that the United Nations will in due course be called upon to verify will include agreements on military matters, it had been my intention to address to the Security Council a recommendation that it take decisions now to establish a multidisciplinary United Nations mission in Guatemala and to deploy the human rights division of that mission immediately, in advance of its other components. This would have followed established United Nations practice in similar circumstances and would thus ensure that verification of the Agreement on Human Rights would begin as expeditiously as possible. However, I have received strong representations from some of the Member States who constitute the friends of the Guatemalan peace process to the effect that, as international verification will, in its initial phase, be concerned only with human rights, its establishment is a matter for the General Assembly rather than the Security Council. I have also been informed by the Government of Guatemala that, although it wishes the mission to be approved rapidly, it cannot for that reason favour a matter related to a specific mechanism for human rights being submitted to the Security Council.
>
> In these circumstances, I recommend that the General Assembly authorize now the establishment for an initial period of six months of a United Nations Human Rights Verification Mission in Guatemala.

The non-aligned, the permanent members and Security Council reform

The non-aligned agreed at their foreign ministers' meeting at Accra in September 1991 that the membership of the Security Council needed to be reviewed. In the subsequent General Assembly debate, India noted that after the increase in membership in 1963, the ratio of non-permanent Security Council membership to total UN membership (then 113) had been 11:3 compared with 6:6 in 1946. This figure now stood at 11:1 (total membership was 166). Was the Council 'representative enough to discharge its onerous responsibility in the expected transparent and democratic manner?' Algeria noted that the Council should be expanded to ensure more equitable geographical representation for the countries of Africa, Asia and Latin America. The question was then deferred to the next session of the General Assembly.[32]

The September 1992 non-aligned Jakarta Summit called for a review of the membership of the Security Council to promote a more balanced and equitable representation. In the subsequent General Assembly debate, once again dominated by the non-aligned, India pointed out that the ratio of United Nations membership to non-permanent membership in the Council was now 17:4 (total membership was now 179). The Security Council would lose the trust and faith of the overall membership unless it achieved a more balanced representation. Malaysia stated that the ratio of the number of countries in a region represented by one non-permanent seat was 22:1 for Asia, 17:1 for Africa and Latin America, 12:1 for Western Europe and others, and 10:1 for Eastern Europe. It went on to propose that three new seats

[31] A/48/985, 18 August 1994.
[32] A/46/PV.68, 23 December 1991 for 11 December 1991.

452   *Sally Morphet*

should be allocated to Asia, three to Africa and two to Latin America.[33] In December India introduced a draft resolution (sponsored *inter alia* by Algeria, Colombia, Egypt, Indonesia, Malaysia, Nigeria, Pakistan, Senegal and Zimbabwe besides two non-aligned observers and Japan) which was passed by consensus as GAR 47/62. This requested the Secretary-General to obtain member states' comments on a possible review of the membership of the Council by 30 June 1993 and to submit a report to the next General Assembly. The United States, the only country to speak after the adoption of the resolution, stated that it attached 'great importance to the work of the Security Council and would oppose revisions to the United Nations Charter that would undermine the Council's efficacy or efficiency'.[34]

In early October 1993 the Foreign Minister of non-aligned Singapore devoted his plenary speech to the General Assembly to the question of Security Council reform. He suggested the removal of the enemy states clauses from the Charter and that permanent members should pay at least 9 per cent of the UN's operating expenses as well as 11 per cent of the UN's peace-keeping expenses. He considered that Article 43 of the Charter should be reactivated and that member states should place their military forces at the disposal of the UN. In the subsequent debate in November.[35] the Indonesian representative endorsed the expansion of permanent and non-permanent seats 'in order to achieve equitable geographic representation and an acceptable balance between the developed and developing countries' besides calling for a review of the veto system. An open-ended working group was set up by consensus in December 1993 by GAR 48/26 to discuss the problem. This (in April 1995) is still in operation.

Agreement between the permanent members and the non-aligned

Despite the fact that the underlying divisions between the non-aligned and the permanent members, with the exception of China, widened over this period, it needs to be remembered that the non-aligned and permanent members were able to reach unanimity on 263 out of the 310 Security Council resolutions passed between August 1990 and the end of 1994. There continued to be much unanimity about setting up peace-keeping operations though less about setting up peace-keeping operations that might become (or were already) peace-enforcement operations. Nevertheless, the non-aligned and permanent members agreed unanimously to set up UNAVEM II in Angola; MINURSO in Western Sahara; UNAMIC in Cambodia; ONUSAL in El Salvador; and UNIKOM (on the border between Kuwait and Iraq) in 1991. These were followed by UNOSOM 1 in Somalia; UNTAC in Cambodia; UNPROFOR in former Yugoslavia; and ONUMOZ in Mozambique (and even the peace-enforcement force UNITAF for Somalia) in 1992. In 1993 it was possible to agree unanimously on the establishment of UNOMUR in Rwanda,

[33] A/47/PV.69, 10 December 1992 for 23 November 1992.
[34] A/47/PV.84, 8 January 1993 for 11 December 1992.
[35] GAOR 61st, 62nd and 64th plenary meetings on 23 and 24 November 1993: A/48/PV.61, 3 December 1993; A/48/PV.62, 3 December 1993; A/48/PV.64, 7 December 1993.

UNOMIG in Georgia, UNOMIL in Liberia and UNMIH in Haiti and, in 1994, on UNMOT in Tajikistan.

All members of the Security Council were also able to agree to set a peace-enforcement force for Somalia in December 1992 (UNITAF) as well as its successor UNOSOM II in March 1993. The problems that subsequently arose in Somalia led to second thoughts on peace-enforcement. Both the permanent members and the non-aligned split on a resolution setting up a similar operation (Operation Turquoise; SCR 929, June 1994) for Rwanda. This was passed by ten with five abstentions (China and two non-aligned Nigeria and Pakistan abstained as well as Brazil, a non-aligned observer, and New Zealand).

There were also more agreements than disagreements between the permanent members and the non-aligned on Chapter VII resolutions passed between August 1990 and December 1994 (see table 4). They agreed on fifty-four out of eighty Chapter VII resolutions passed during this period including all those on Angola, Liberia, Somalia, and South Africa (twelve resolutions in all, nine of them on Somalia). They also agreed on thirteen out of twenty-five resolutions relating to the Iraqi invasion of Kuwait and subsequent developments; twenty-one out of twenty-nine on former Yugoslavia; five out of seven on Haiti; two out of four on Libya; and one out of three on Rwanda.

Permanent member dissension

China's abstention on SCR 678 of 29 November 1990 authorizing member states to take all necessary measures (i.e. use force) against Iraq unless it withdrew from Kuwait on or before 15 January 1991, has already been discussed. This was the first time China had voted separately from all other permanent members since 1981. It announced the same month that it would be joining the non-aligned as an observer—the non-aligned accepted its application in May 1992. Since then it has voted separately from the other permanent members on a further nineteen occasions as well as twice with Russia (on former Yugoslavia in 1993). China's main aim in its separate voting during this period (through abstaining and not, so far, vetoing) seems to have been to continue to register three concerns. Its first, over the use of force by the Council (under Chapter VII), can be seen in its voting on the extension of the ban established on aircraft in Bosnian airspace and, at the same time, authorizing member states to take all necessary measures to ensure compliance under SCR 816; and on the setting up of the peace-enforcement operation for Rwanda under SCR 929. Its second, concerning certain authorizations of sanctions (under Chapter VII), can be noted in its voting on the sanctions imposed against Libya under SCR 748; against the Federal Republic of Yugoslavia under SCR 787; and those called for, but not mandated under Chapter VII, against Cambodia under SCR 792. Its third relates to its voting on humanitarian intervention (and for the territorial integrity of states) evident in its voting on SCR 688 on humanitarian intervention in Iraq; and on SCR 770 calling on states to take measures to deliver humanitarian assistance to Bosnia.

Russia was the only permanent member to use its veto between August 1990 and

454   *Sally Morphet*

May 1995,[36] once over the question of whether peace-keeping finance should become mandatory in the context of Cyprus, and once over the question of the imposition of more sanctions on the Federal Republic of Yugoslavia in December 1994. It also abstained, with China, on two resolutions in 1993: one imposing further sanctions against the Bosnian Serbs, and one deciding that the FRY could not participate in the work of ECOSOC. In 1994 it abstained unilaterally on two resolutions on Haiti. Its votes on former Yugoslavia are perhaps the most significant. Russia is the permanent member most involved in Slav concerns.

The controversies engendered by the war in former Yugoslavia were well shown by a vote on a draft resolution lifting the arms embargo in Bosnia in June 1993. US sympathies with certain non-aligned concerns were shown when it voted for this resolution with all the non-aligned on the Council and separately from the other permanent members. The resolution did not pass, as no other member of the Security Council voted for it. In March 1994 the United States registered its differences with all other permanent members (and all other states on the Council) on a question relating to Israel, for the first time since its last veto in May 1990. It abstained on separate votes on certain preambular paragraphs (one of which mentioned occupied Jerusalem) of a Security Council resolution condemning the Jewish massacre of Palestinians in Hebron and its aftermath. The resolution was adopted without an overall vote.

These developments have to be seen against a background of unanimity among the permanent members on 284 out of 310 resolutions passed between August 1990 and the end of 1994. But they could indicate a trend if the divergence of voting between China, Russia and the United States increases and if more vetoes are cast.

Non-aligned dissension

The non-aligned on the Security Council as has already been noted voted together on 113 out of 119 Security Council resolutions passed between 1980 and 1985 and 79 out of 79 passed between 1986 and July 1990. They voted together on 278 out of the 310 resolutions passed between August 1990 and the end of 1994 (see table 2). Their main disagreements were on Iraq/Kuwait and, subsequently, on former Yugoslavia. Cuba voted against nine (and abstained on two) Chapter VII resolutions on Iraq/Kuwait in 1990-1 besides abstaining on two others, including SCR 688 on humanitarian intervention in Iraq. India, which joined the Council in 1991, abstained on the call for a final cease-fire (and implementation of all resolutions on the annexation) as well as SCR 688, as did another new member, Zimbabwe. All these three non-aligned countries feared that humanitarian intervention could be used as an excuse to invade less powerful countries and to weaken the important principle of the territorial integrity of states. Both Cuba and India were also concerned about the use of Chapter VII. Yemen, the other major non-aligned dissenter, split, for regional reasons, on twelve resolutions dealing with Iraq/Kuwait.

---

[36] The United States vetoed a draft resolution in May 1995 on the invalidity of Israel, as occupying power, expropriating land in East Jerusalem.

The non-aligned internal rift between those supporting the territorial integrity of former Yugoslavia and Islamic states seeking to support Bosnia helps explain some of the non-aligned dissension shown on certain resolutions concerning former Yugoslavia.[37] Zimbabwe was among those more sympathetic to former Yugoslavia so it is not surprising to find that it (joined by India on three) abstained on five (three Chapter VII) resolutions on the FRY in 1992. Islamic Pakistan, by contrast, with Venezuela, showed its concern about SCR 836 authorizing the use of force by UNPROFOR to protect the safe areas of Bosnia in 1993 after both India and Zimbabwe had left the Council. In 1994 Djibouti and Pakistan showed their Islamic credentials by voting against SCR 943 partially lifting sanctions against the FRY, while Nigeria and Rwanda abstained and Oman (Islamic yet close to the West) voted for.

The most contentious resolution (SCR 748) in 1992 concerned the imposition of certain sanctions against Libya until it demonstrated its renunciation of terrorism.[38] Cape Verde, India, Morocco and Zimbabwe all abstained while Ecuador and Venezuela joined those voting for the resolution. Djibouti, Morocco and Pakistan voted for SCR 883 imposing further sanctions in 1993 while Cape Verde and Venezuela abstained. The other important resolution on which the non-aligned differed in 1994 was SCR 929, setting up a peace-enforcement force for Rwanda. Both Pakistan and Nigeria showed their disapproval by abstaining. Rwanda chose not to participate in four votes at the end of July 1994 for reasons relating to a change of government in the country.

The non-aligned and China

The growing interrelationship of China and the non-aligned (it became an observer in the movement in 1992) could also become significant particularly if it leads to China using its veto to promote its own and non-aligned interests. China distanced itself from the majority of the other permanent members on twenty-two occasions between August 1990 and 1994. On thirteen of these it was joined by one or more non-aligned. On Iraq/Kuwait these included SCR 678 (Cuba and Zimbabwe voted against) and SCR 688 (Cuba, Yemen and Zimbabwe voted against while India abstained).

On former Yugoslavia, Zimbabwe joined with China on all the resolutions on which it abstained in 1992 except for SCR 781; India joined in on three (SCRs 770, 776 and 777). Four out of six of the non-aligned joined China on the controversial resolution, SCR 748, on Libya, terrorism and sanctions. In 1993 China and Pakistan joined forces and abstained on the resolution on North Korea and the NPT, and, with Djibouti and Morocco, on the resolution imposing further sanctions on Libya.

Analysis of the tables August 1990–1994

The significance of the continuing, but so far limited, dissension within the groups

---

[37] See also my 'Non-Aligned in the "New World Order" '.
[38] This also made history as it was taken by Libya to the ICJ.

456   *Sally Morphet*

of permanent members and the non-aligned is, as yet, difficult to judge. It will be easier to do so in five years' time. Both groups were able to reach unanimity on 263 (including fifty-four out of eighty Chapter VII resolutions) of the 310 Security Council resolutions passed during this period. The permanent members voted together on 284 (including sixty-five out of eighty Chapter VII resolutions) while the non-aligned reached unanimity on 278 (including sixty-two out of eighty Chapter VII resolutions).

Conclusion

This paper has looked at the main political groupings in the Security Council and, where relevant, the General Assembly, and tried to explore how they exerted influence on these bodies (and the relationship between them) and, beyond that, on world politics. It has suggested that the familiar West, East and non-aligned pattern of political groups on the Security Council in the 1980s was replaced by a permanent member/non-aligned group pattern from the mid-1980s onwards. Although these two groups sometimes differed, they were (judging from their voting records between 1986 and mid-1990) able to work more closely on certain regional conflicts (often through a process which included setting up peace-keeping bodies) which had become easier to resolve as the Cold War came to an end.

Their major disagreement continued to be shown up through US vetoes. The continuing pressure by the non-aligned on southern African and Israel/Palestine issues can be seen by the fact that the United States cast twelve of its fifteen vetoes during this period on these issues (nine on Israel/Palestine and three on southern Africa). The non-aligned also exercised vigilance over attempts to enlarge the powers of the Security Council to the detriment of the General Assembly, where the group commanded a majority of votes, and on such subjects as the authorization of election monitoring and the expansion of the definition of security to include subjects like narcotics.

The non-aligned and permanent members' first major challenge in the post-Cold War era was to decide how they should deal with the Iraqi invasion and occupation of Kuwait in August 1990. They were able to handle the question through a series of Security Council resolutions (including an unprecedented series of twenty Chapter VII resolutions in 1990 1 table 4). The cohesion of each group was affected however: China voted differently on three resolutions from the rest of the permanent members, and the non-aligned split on twelve. The most contentious resolution was SCR 688 (not a Chapter VII resolution) which demanded that Iraq should allow international humanitarian organizations into its territory. Four out of five of the non-aligned and China dissented on this resolution (Cuba, Yemen, and Zimbabwe voted against and India abstained) since it could be regarded as a direct attack on the important international principle of the territorial integrity of states. China was, however, not prepared to use its veto on the question.

Both the non-aligned and the permanent members have continued to work together on a number of questions that have since confronted the Security Council. They have continued to set up a number of peace-keeping bodies despite financial problems, and they have agreed on all Chapter VII resolutions dealing with Angola, Liberia, Somalia and South Africa. They have also agreed on twenty-one out of twenty-nine Chapter VII resolutions on former Yugoslavia; five out of seven on Haiti; two out of four on Libya; and one out of three on Rwanda.

However, each group has continued to express a certain amount of internal disagreement through their votes on certain Security Council resolutions.[39] China, has differentiated itself more than the others. However both Russia and the United States have occasionally voted differently from the other permanent members. China has been concerned with issues such as the authorization of the use of force, the application of some sanctions and humanitarian issues. The United States has differed on the question of lifting the arms embargo against Bosnia and on Israel/Palestine. And Russia has supported the FRY (Serbia and Montenegro) besides being concerned about paying more for peace-keeping.

The non-aligned group has found it difficult to agree on the question of former Yugoslavia; its Islamic members have taken a more proactive line on Bosnia than countries such as India and Zimbabwe. But they have also differed on the imposition of sanctions against Libya as well as the setting up of a peace-enforcement force in Rwanda.

Non-aligned cohesion has been demonstrated in a successful campaign, begun in the General Assembly in December 1990, to make the Security Council more responsive to the General Assembly. The non-aligned are keen proponents (since 1991) of Security Council reform (Charter reform must be debated and voted on in the General Assembly), though they, like the permanent members, have found it difficult to agree on all aspects of what they want to achieve.

The Security Council itself has, of course, been affected by the way members of both major groups on the Security Council have responded to major political crises. Both have, since August 1990, been prepared to accept the increased use of mandatory Chapter VII resolutions mainly authorizing certain peace-enforcement operations and certain sanctions. They have also been prepared to accept certain instances of humanitarian intervention. Each question of this sort is considered on a case-by-case basis. They have agreed more easily to set up peace-keeping bodies, an agreement that is now in jeopardy since the United States has challenged the way they are currently financed. The non-aligned group has, so far, despite its lack of a veto, ensured that the Council should not authorize any election monitoring (or human rights verification) not associated with peace-keeping. They also have succeeded in ensuring that the definition of security has not been extended to cover narcotics or environmental issues, besides pointing out firmly that the General Assembly, not the Security Council, deals with finance, even the financing of war crimes tribunals.

The debate on the expansion and reform of the Council is not complete. It will be interesting to see how changes in this area affect the balance of forces between these groups on the Council and within the UN system as a whole.

---

[39] Translated into percentages the permanent members voted together on 63% of resolutions passed in 1980–5, 86% between 1986 and July 1990, and 92% between August 1990 and December 1994. The equivalent figures for the non-aligned are 95%, 100% and 90%.

458   *Sally Morphet*

Table 1. *Security Council resolutions and vetoes, 1980–94: unanimity and splits between permanent members. ToP, total passed; V, vetoed; U, unanimous; PMU, permanent members unanimous; VC, vetoes cast.*

Year (Agg. voting)	No. of resolutions				Splits on SC (No. of vetoes)						
	ToP	V	U	PMU	Tot	By Chi	By Fra	By SU/Ru	By UK	By US	VC
1980 (462–84)	23	3	8	8	15	7	1	4(2)	2	7(1)	3
1981 (485–99)	15	5	10	10	5	4	(4)	2	(4)	(5)	13
1982 (500–28)	29	8	21	21	8	1	—	5	1(1)	3(8)	9
1983 (529–45)	17	3	10	12	5			3(1)		2(2)	3
1984 (546–59)	14	3	7	8	6	—	—	2(1)	2	4(2)	3
1985 (560–80)	21	7	16	16	5	—	—	2	2(2)	3(7)	9
1986 (581–93)	13	8	10	10	3	—	(1)	—	1(3)	3(8)	12
1987 (594–606)	13	2	10	10	3	—	—	—	(2)	3(2)	4
1988 (607–26)	20	6	17	17	3	—	—	—	1(1)	3(6)	7
1989 (627–46)	20	5	18	18	2	—	(2)	—	(2)	2(5)	9
1990 (647–83)	37	2	29	36	1	1	—	—	—	(2)	2
Jan–Jul	13	2	13	13	—	—	—	—	—	(2)	2
Aug–Dec	24	0	16	23	1	1	—	—	—	—	—
1991 (684–725)	42	0	36	40	2	2	—	—	—	—	—
1992 (726–99)	74	0	64	65	9	9	—	—	—	—	—
1993 (800–92)	93	1	85	87	6	6	—	2(1)	—	—	1
1994 (893–969)	77	1	62	67	10	5	—	3(1)	—	2	1

Table 2. *Security Council resolutions and vetoes, 1980–94: unanimity and splits between non-aligned. ToP, total passed; V, vetoed resolutions; U, unanimous; VC, vetoes cast; NV, non-vetoed resolutions*

No. on SC*	Year (Agg. voting)	No. of resolutions				Non-aligned voting		
						U	Splits	
		ToP	V	U	VC		NV	V
6	1980 (462–84)	23	3	8	3	22	1:Zam	1:B
4	1981 (485–99)	15	5	10	13	15	0	0
6	1982 (500–28)	29	8	21	9	28	1:Pan	5:G,J,Pan, T,Zai
8	1983 (529–45)	17	3	10	3	15	2:J,Ma, Nic,Pk2	3:G,Nic,T, Zai2,Zim
8	1984 (546–59)	14	3	7	3	12	2:Nic,Pk, Zim	0
6	1985 (560–80)	21	7	16	9	21	0	1:Eg
4	1986 (581–93)	13	8	10	12	13	0	0
5	1987 (594–606)	13	2	10	4	13	0	0
6	1988 (607–26)	20	6	17	7	20	0	0
7	1989 (627–46)	20	5	18	9	20	0	0
7	1990 (647–83)	37	2	29	2	29	8:Cu7,Y6	0
	Jan–Jul	13	2	13	2	13	0	0
	Aug–Dec	24	0	16	0	16	8:Cu7,Y6	0
7	1991 (684–725)	42	0	36	0	36	6:Cu6,Ec, In2,Y5	0
6	1992 (726–99)	74	0	64	0	67	7:CV,Ec, In4,Mo, Zim6	0
5	1993 (800–92)	93	1	85	1	89	4:Dj,Mo, Pk4,V1	0
5	1994 (893–969)	77	1	62	1	70	7:Dj, Nig2,Pk2, R6	0

*Details of the non-aligned on the Security Council between 1961 and 1989 are given in Table 3 of my article. 'Resolutions and vetoes in the UN Security Council: their relevance and significance', *Review of International Studies*, 16 (1990). Those on the Council in 1990 were Colombia, Côte d'Ivoire, Cuba, Ethiopia, Malaysia, Yemen, Zaire; in 1991 Côte d'Ivoire, Cuba, Ecuador, India, Yemen, Zaire, Zimbabwe; and in 1992 Cape Verde, Ecuador, India, Morocco, Venezuela, Zimbabwe. The five non-aligned in 1993 were Cape Verde, Djibouti, Morocco, Pakistan and Venezuela, and in 1994 Djibouti, Nigeria, Oman, Pakistan, Rwanda.

Key: B, Bangladesh; Cu, Cuba; CV, Cape Verde; Dj, Djibouti; Ec, Ecuador; Eg, Egypt; G, Guyana; In, India; J, Jordan; Ma, Malta; Mo, Morocco; Nic, Nicaragua; Nig, Nigeria; Pan, Panama; Pk, Pakistan; R, Rwanda; T, Togo; V, Venezuela; Y, Yemen; Zai, Zaire; Zam, Zambia; Zim, Zimbabwe.

460   *Sally Morphet*

Table 3. *Security Council resolutions and vetoes, 1980–94: subjects of split between permanent members and between non-aligned. ToP, total passed; V, vetoed resolutions; U, unanimous; VC, vetoes cast; NV, non-vetoed resolutions*

Year (Agg. voting)	No. of resolutions				Issues splitting perm. mem.		Issues splitting non-aligned	
	ToP	V	U	VC	NV	V	NV	V
1980 (462–84)	23	3	8	3	Af,A/I,Cy, Le,Rh,SA, Sy	Af,Ir, Pl	Af	Ir
1981 (485–99)	15	5	10	13	A/I,Cy,Le, Sy	Nb,SA	----	----
1982 (500–28)	29	8	21	9	A/I,F,Le	A/I,F, Ni	F	A/I,F,Ni
1983 (529–45)	17	3	10	3	Le,Nb,SA	A/I,G, SU/Ko	Cy,IIW	A/I,G, SU/Ko
1984 (546–59)	14	3	7	3	Cy,Le,SA	Le,Ni	Gulf	----
1985 (560–80)	21	7	16	9	Tu,Le,Nb, SA	A/I, I/L,Le, Nb,Ni,SA	Ni	Ni
1986 (581–93)	13	8	10	12	A/I,Le,SA	A/I,I/L, Le,Ni,SA	----	A/I,Ly,Ni
1987 (594–606)	13	2	10	4	A/I,Nb	Nb,SA	----	----
1988 (607–26)	20	6	17	7	A/I,ICJ,Tu SA	Le,Pl,SA	----	----
1989 (627–46)	20	5	18	9	A/I	Ly,Pl, Pan	----	----
1990 (647–83)	37	2	29	2	Ku	Ni,Pan	Ku,Pu	----
1991 (684–725)	42	0	36	0	Ku	----	Ku	----
1992 (726–99)	74	0	64	0	Cb,Y,Ku,Ly	----	Y,Ku,Ly	----
1993 (800–92)	93	1	85	1	Y,Ko,Ly,	Cy	Cy,Y,Ly	----
1994 (893–969)	77	1	62	1	A/I,Y,H, Rw,So	Y	Y,Rw	----

Key: Af, Afghanistan; A/I, Arab/Israeli issues; Cb, Cuba; Cy, Cyprus; F, Falkland Islands; G, Grenada; H, Haiti; ICJ, International Court of Justice; IIW, Iran/Iraq War; I/L, Israeli/Libyan incident; Ir, Iran; Ko, Korea; Ku, Kuwait; Le, Lebanon; Ly, Libya; Nb, Namibia; Ni, Nicaragua; Pan, Panama; Pl, Palestine; Pu, Palau; Rh, Rhodesia; Rw, Rwanda; SA, South Africa; So, Somalia; SU/Ko, Soviet/South Korean incident; Sy, Syria; Tu, Israeli/Tunisian incident; Y, former Yugoslavia.

Table 4. *Security Council resolutions and vetoes, 1980–94: Chapter VII resolutions.* *
ToP, total passed; U, unanimous

Year (Agg. voting)	Chapter VII resolutions**				
	ToP	Subjects	U	perm. mem. splits	non-aligned splits
1982 (500–28)	1	F	0	1:Ch,SU	1:Pan
1987 (594–606)	1	IIW	1	0	0
1990 (647–83)	9	Iq/Ku9	3	1:Ch	6:Y5,Cu5
1991 (684–725)	13	Iq/Ku11	6	1:Ch	5:Cu5,Y4,I,Ec
		Y2	2	0	0
1992 (726–99)	10	Y5	2	3:Ch3	3:Zim3,I
		So2	2	0	0
		Iq/Ku	0	1:Ch	0
		Lr	1	0	0
		Ly	0	1:Ch	1:CV,I,M,Zim
1993 (800–92)	25	Y13	10	2:Ch2,Ru	1:Pk,V
		H4	4	0	0
		So4	4	0	0
		Iq/Ku2	2	0	0
		An1	1	0	0
		Ly1	0	1:Ch	1:Dj,M,Pk
1994 (893–969)	23	Y9	7	1:Ch	1:Dj,Pk,Nig,R
		H3	1	2:Ch,Ru	1:R
		R3	1	2:Ch2	2:Nig,Pk,R
		So3	3	0	0
		Iq/Ku2	2	0	0
		Ly2	2	0	0
		SA1	1	0	0

*Explicit Chapter VII resolutions are easy to identify; there is often some amount of disagreement about others. Many would suggest that SCR 743 setting up UNPROFOR is a Chapter VII resolution; it is not included here.
**These are SCRs 502, 598, 660, 661, 664, 666, 667, 670, 674, 677, 678, 686, 687, 689, 692, 699, 700, 705, 706, 707, 712, 713, 715, 724, 733, 748, 757, 760, 770, 771, 778, 787, 788, 794, 806, 807, 814, 815, 816, 819, 820, 824, 827, 833, 836, 837, 841, 844, 859, 861, 864, 869, 870, 871, 873, 875, 878, 883, 886, 897, 899, 900, 908, 910, 913, 914, 915, 917, 918, 919, 923, 929, 940, 942, 943, 944, 947, 949, 954, 955, 958, 967.

Key: An, Angola; Cu, Cuba; CV, Cape Verde; Dj, Djibouti; Ec, Ecuador; F, Falkland Islands; H, Haiti; I, India; IIW, Iran/Iraq War; Iq, Iraq; Ku, Kuwait; Lr, Liberia; Ly, Libya; M, Morocco; Nig, Nigeria; Pan, Panama; Pk, Pakistan; R, Rwanda; SA, South Africa; So, Somalia; V, Venezuela; Y, former Yugoslavia; Zim, Zimbabwe.

462   *Sally Morphet*

Table 5. *Regional electoral groups at the UN, 1946–94*

Year		Africa		Asia	E. Europe	Latin America	Middle East	W. Europe & others	Perm. mem.	Common-wealth
1946	SC				1	2	1	1	5	1
1963	SC	3	+	2	1	2		2	5	
	GA	34		23	9	22		19		
1978	SC	6		5	1	3		2	5	
	GA	50		37	10	28		20		
1994*	SC	3		2	1	2		2	5	
	GA	53		47	20	33		27		
1993**	SC	7		5	1	3		2	5	
	GA	52		47	20	33		27		

* Of the 185 members of the UN in December 1994, four were not in regional groups.
** Proposal: did not get through in the context of the revitalisation of the work of the UN. The material relating to the General Assembly refers to the way the Vice-Presidencies are distributed.

[14]

Third World Quarterly, Vol 16, No 3, 1995

Pluralising global governance: analytical approaches and dimensions

LEON GORDENKER & THOMAS G WEISS

Nongovernmental organisations (NGOs) have in increasing numbers injected unexpected voices into international discourse about numerous problems of global scope. Especially during the last 20 years, human rights advocates, gender activists, developmentalists, groups of indigenous peoples and representatives of other defined interests have become active in political work once reserved for representatives of states. Their numbers have enlarged the venerable, but hardly numerous, ranks of transnational organisations built around churches, labour unions and humanitarian aims.

The United Nations (UN) system provides a convenient, accessible vantage point to observe some of the most active, persuasive NGOs in the world. During the last 50 years, various UN organisations have felt the direct and indirect impact of NGOs. According to the Union of International Associations, the NGO universe includes well over 15 000 recognisable NGOs that operate in three or more countries and draw their finances from sources in more than one country; this number is growing all the time.[1] In their own ways, NGOs and intergovernmental organisations (IGOs) grope, sometimes cooperatively, sometimes competitively, sometimes in parallel towards a modicum of 'global governance'. We define global governance as efforts to bring more orderly and reliable responses to social and political issues that go beyond capacities of states to address individually. Like the NGO universe, global governance implies an absence of central authority, and the need for collaboration or cooperation among governments and others who seek to encourage common practices and goals in addressing global issues. The means to achieve global governance also include activities of the United Nations and other intergovernmental organisations and standing cooperative arrangements among states.

This introductory essay generally discusses the NGO phenomenon. It proposes a definition of NGOs to serve for the purpose of this issue, although much controversy remains about the concept and individual authors may offer refinements. It also provides a general backdrop of historical, legal and political factors for the study. It offers some analytical detail needed for deeper understanding of the phenomenon, and outlines a set of fundamental factors for studying NGOs. It does not assume that NGOs always or even usually succeed in reaching their goals or, if they do, that the result is beneficial for peace, social or personal welfare, or human rights.

The studies that follow all employ the United Nations as a central and reasonably transparent point of observation that has legal and historical underpinnings, and branching activities that reach to the social grass roots. Moreover, NGOs are omnipresent in many aspects of international relations, and they may

0143-6597/95/030357-31 © 1995 Third World Quarterly

LEON GORDENKER & THOMAS G WEISS

have become crucial to the UN's future. It is significant that in its essay, 'Reforming the United Nations', the Commission on Global Governance—whose members are virtually all former governmental officials or international civil servants—examined NGOs and observed that 'in their wide variety they bring expertise, commitment, and grassroots perceptions that should be mobilized in the interests of better governance'.[2] NGOs assume centre stage for activities that once 'were irrelevant to the overall plot'.[3] The case studies, each written by an author who has directly observed or experienced NGO activities, examine NGO work on human rights, complex humanitarian emergencies, the United Nations relationship, the global environment, AIDS, the international women's movement, scaling up and scaling down, operational coalitions and state relations. The final essay draws on the specific studies to reach conclusions about the nature, function and prospects for NGOs in relation to the UN system.

The phenomenon

In spite of the growth of the NGO phenomenon, confusion or ignorance persists as to the definition of the participants and the nature of their relationships to the UN system and to one another. Theoretical explorations have tended to be few in number and specific to a particular sector of activity, especially aspects of economic and social development and of the environment. A considerable body of writing has a primarily legal character, which overlooks or understates the richness of NGO activity and politics. Definitional clarity connects closely with concepts of structure, organisation and institutionalisation.

The very site of NGO activity under examination here suggests paradoxes. IGOs join with governments in common undertakings. By definition, NGOs have no formal standing in this realm. Yet they have become exponentially more visible precisely in connection with governments. IGOs were intended to serve governments and to assist in cooperatively reaching goals on which both generally agree. Yet NGOs have now become an integral part of the process of setting agendas for cooperation and in carrying the results not only to governments but to other NGOs and individuals. This study seeks to analyse this process, which requires examining both broad and deep interorganisational relationships.

The term 'nongovernmental organisation' itself is challenged by a host of alternative usages. These include officials, independent sector, volunteer sector, civic society, grassroots organisations, private voluntary organisations, transnational social movement organisations, grassroots social change organisations and non-state actors. Some of these refer to highly specialised varieties and many are synonyms for each other. There seems no quarrel, however, with the notion that these organisations consist of durable, bounded, voluntary relationships among individuals to produce a particular product, using specific techniques. Like-minded organisations may analogously develop lasting relationships to one another and thus form meta-organisations.

Although the term 'non-state actors' may more closely resemble our inclusion of several varieties of meta-organisations that are engaged in transnational relationships, we maintain the term 'nongovernmental organisations' because of its common currency and because this is the term that appears in article 71 of the UN Charter. At the same time, 'non-state actors', according to a Lexis-Nexis search, connotes a host of transnational entities that we deliberately exclude from our inquiry. These include profit-making corporations and banks, criminal elements (both organised crime and terrorists), insurgents, churches in their strictly religious function, transnational political parties and the mass communication media.

A metaphor suggested by Marc Nerfin provides a starting point for locating NGOs in the political realm: the prince represents governmental power and the maintenance of public order; the merchant symbolises economic power and the production of goods and services; and the citizen stands for people's power.[4] As such, the growth of NGOs arises from demands by citizens for accountability from the prince and the merchant. In this perspective, NGOs compete and cooperate with the prince and the merchant for guidance in aspects of social life. They function to 'serve undeserved or neglected populations, to expand the freedom of or to empower people, to engage in advocacy for social change, and to provide services'.[5]

Such an approach contains much that is subjective. Citizens may believe themselves under-served by, or deprived of, rightful power, or they may seek more freedom and advocate change. Doing so implies reform or drastic changes in existing societies. Yet it is equally conceivable that citizens could demand preservation of the status quo as part of the accountability of merchants and princes. The objective point of such approaches, however, lies in the identification of organisation and activity beyond the conventional categories of state and business.

Questions can be raised about the accuracy of this metaphor. Although recognising the legitimacy of each sector of society, it tends to glorify NGOs at the expense of states and markets. NGO 'citizens' are portrayed as vanguards of the just society, as 'princes' and 'merchants' strive to dominate or to make profits. In a study of environmental NGOs in world politics, two authors concluded that the crucial function of NGOs was to create transnational links between state and non-state. NGOs, in this model, politicise the previously unpoliticised and connect the local and the global.[6]

Some NGOs do, in fact, politicise issues otherwise regarded by some as part of the nonpolitical realm, AIDS being a recent case in point. They also bring local experience to bear on international decision making. This may be the most important contribution NGOs have made to global governance. Once again, however, generalisation is dangerous because some NGOs continue to lead a more marginal existence, without links to international bodies. Most NGOs have not managed to break out of the local setting and become engaged in transnational activities.

If NGOs exist and operate above and beneath the level of government, they parallel the pattern of IGOs, particularly those of the UN system. These entities, too, are intended to operate to some degree beyond the states that form them. IGOs do not govern; they attempt to cope with and help manage complex interrelationships and global political, economic and social changes by arranging cooperation of other actors, especially governments. In doing so, they have also

LEON GORDENKER & THOMAS G WEISS

extended their operations below the classical boundaries of governmental autonomy.

Distinctions between IGOs and NGOs rest on legal grounds and tend to
exaggerate the boundary between the two categories. In reality, there are great
variations within, and unclear borderlines between, the two categories. The sheer
number of different types of NGOs, ranging from community-based self-help
groups to international NGOs with staff and budgets surpassing those of many
IGOs, calls for conceptual differentiation and clarification.

Students of international relations have proposed alternative terminologies to
conceptualise transnational relations. James Rosenau, for instance, distinguishes
between sovereignty-bound and sovereignty-free actors.[7] While sociological
rather than legal, this dichotomy can also be misleading insofar as organisations
composed of governments are automatically assumed to be sovereignty-bound
and other actors sovereignty-free. Perhaps it would make more sense to speak of
sovereignty-bound and sovereignty-free behaviour.[8] Regardless of their legal
status, organisations may engage in behaviour that is guided by, or pays heed to,
state sovereignty to varying degrees. Loyalties do not always follow state
borders, and secretariats of IGOs are not necessarily more dominated than
secretariats of big NGOs.

This essay and this journal issue retain the traditional IGO–NGO distinction for
lack of better alternatives, while remaining attentive to sovereignty-bound and
sovereignty-free behaviour by IGOs and NGOs alike. The important puzzle is what
specific roles NGOs may play in transnational networks as intermediary organisations that provide links between state and market, between local and global
levels.

The challenges to sovereignty, according to a recent analytical study, include
four categories of interdependence—trade and finance, security, technology and
ecological problems—and 'the emergence of new social movements with both
local and transnational consciousness'.[9] Both NGOs and IGOs, then, busy themselves with the paradox of global economic and technological integration with
local fragmentation of identities.

Apart from the function of representing people acting of their own volition,
rather than by some institutional *fiat*, NGOs have other defining characteristics.
They are formal organisations that are intended to continue in existence; they are
thus not *ad hoc* entities. They are or aspire to be self-governing on the basis of
their own constitutional arrangements. They are private in that they are separate
from governments and have no ability to direct societies or to require support
from them. They are not in the business of making or distributing profits. The
NGOs of interest here have transnational goals, operations or connections, and
have active contacts with the UN system.

Not every organisation that claims to be an NGO exactly fits this definition of
a private citizens' organisation, separate from government but active on social
issues, not profit making, and with transnational scope. At least three significant
deviations from these specifications can be identified. The first of these is a
GONGO—government-organised nongovernmental organisation. They achieved
notoriety during the Cold War because many so-called NGOs owed their very
existence and entire financial support to communist governments in the Soviet

bloc or authoritarian ones in the Third World. There were also a few such 'NGOs' in the West, particularly in the USA, where they were often a front for administration activities. Although the Western species may have been more nongovernmental than their Soviet or Third World counterparts, they were not created for the classic purposes of NGOs. Thus, GONGOs can be treated as only tangential to our examination.

The second special type of NGO is QUANGOs (quasi-nongovernmental organisations). For example, many Nordic and Canadian NGOs, a handful of US ones, and the International Committee of the Red Cross (ICRC) receive the bulk of their resources from public coffers. The staffs of such organisations usually assert that as long as their financial support is without strings attached and their own priorities rather than those of donor governments dominate, there is no genuine problem. This is clearly a subjective judgment, but most of these NGOs are relevant for our discussion. Their services aim at internationally-endorsed objectives and their operations are distinct from those of governments, even if their funding is public.

We are at an early stage in understanding how NGOs adapt to changing external and internal environments. In examining recent trends at the domestic level in the USA and Britain, one analyst has gone so far as to call into question voluntary agencies as a 'shadow state'.[10] With more governmental and intergovernmental resources being channelled through international NGOs, the issue of independence—or a willingness to bite the hand that feeds in order to make autonomous programmatic decisions in spite of donor pressures—assumes greater salience. 'One of the real issues for NGOs is how much money can they take from the government while still carrying out advocacy activities that may involve criticizing the source of those funds'.[11]

The third mutant type—the donor-organised NGO (DONGO)—is also distinguished by its source of funds. 'As donors become more interested in NGOs, they also find themselves tempted to create NGOs suited to their perceived needs'.[12] Both governments and the UN system have 'their' NGOs for particular operations and purposes. The United Nations Development Program (UNDP) has been involved in fostering their growth for a decade. The UN itself created local NGOs that contributed to mobilising the population for elections in Cambodia[13] and to de-mining in Afghanistan.[14]

QUANGOs and DONGOs fit well enough in the general definition to warrant inclusion in this study. They aim at internationally-endorsed purposes and have a private status, even if their funding is public. They offer services that clearly fall within the usual range of NGO operations.

Relationship to the UN

A conventional, legally-based way of describing NGOs and their relationship to the United Nations begins with the formal structure that derives from UN Charter article 71.[15] It empowers the Economic and Social Council (ESOSOC) to 'make suitable arrangements for consultation with non-governmental organizations which are concerned with matters within its competence'. It is the only mention of NGOs in the Charter, largely an afterthought stimulated by the Soviet

Union's attempt to put a GONGO on a par with the International Labour Organisation (ILO), another IGO dating to the formation of the League of Nations that constitutionally included representation of labour and management in its governing structure.[16] Early attempts to give meaning to article 71 were heavily coloured by cold-war manoeuvers, but a growing list of organisations with consultative status developed around fairly restricted practices laid down by ESOSOC.[17] Historically speaking, the UN Charter formalises the relationship between NGOs and the world organisation in a significantly different way from the previous experience with international organisation. For example, NGOs were completely excluded from the Hague Conferences in 1899 and 1907. At the League of Nations, NGOs achieved only an informal consultative arrangement that had some effect, however, on proceedings there.[18]

The present legal framework dates from 1968 in the form of the elaborate ESOSOC Resolution 1296 (XLIV). It is now undergoing reexamination in a stately process whose diplomatic tone is heavily coloured by NGO participation. Resolution 1296 retains but refines the earlier UN principle that any international organisation not established by intergovernmental agreement falls into the NGO category. In 11 paragraphs of principles, the text emphasises that NGOs that seek consultative status must have goals within the UN economic and social ambit. These NGOs must also have a representative and international character, and authorisation to speak for members who are supposed to participate in a democratic fashion. The text requires submission of data from organisations on their budgets and the sources of their financing. It also promotes a vague hierarchy by encouraging the formation of umbrella organisations composed of organisations with similar purposes that pool their advice to the council and transmit results of consultations from national organisations. The process of admission to consultative status is supervised by the Committee on Non-Governmental Organizations, elected each year by ESOSOC from among its member governments, 19 of which provide the actual personnel.

Consultations remain largely under ESOSOC control, in contrast to the fuller rights of participation available to IGOs in the UN system. NGOs can be granted status in one of three categories, designated as 'I', 'II', and 'the roster'. Those in category I are supposed to have broad economic and social interests and geographical scope; those in category II have more specialised interests. The remainder of accepted applicants are listed in a roster for organisations that may make occasional contributions. Category I organisations have the broadest access to the council. They may propose ESOSOC agenda items to the Committee on Non-Governmental Organizations, which in turn can ask the secretary-general to include their suggestions on the provisional list. This is far from a right to submit agenda items. Like category II NGOs, category I organisations may send observers to all meetings and may submit brief written statements on their subject matter. The council has the right to ask for written statements from any of the consultative NGOs, and it may invite category I and II organisations to hearings, which, in fact, are rare. Other rules set out limitations on NGOs in dealing with ESOSOC subsidiaries and international conferences summoned by it.

The UN Department of Public Information simultaneously developed a

PLURALIZING GLOBAL GOVERNANCE

parallel set of relationships with NGOs under its own legislative authority.[19] This emphasises the information-disseminating function of NGOs, rather than any input in policy formation. It includes briefings, mailings, access to documentation and an NGO Resources Center in New York.[20]

Both of these consultative arrangements gave birth to meta-organisations representing NGOs. Some of those in contact with ESOSOC soon formed a Conference of Non-Governmental Organizations in Consultative Status, which adopted the acronym CONGO. It takes no substantive positions, but concentrates on procedural matters and the promotion of better understanding of the ESOSOC agenda. For the organisations in the public information orbit, an NGO/Department of Public Information (DPI) Executive Committee serves as liaison.[21]

These consultative arrangements signal the presence of two trends. One of them indicates the almost unprecedented establishment of 'formal relations between "interest" groups and an intergovernmental body'.[22] Even though this relationship was conditioned by the Cold War, both in the formation of the list of accredited organisations and the attention given them by the largely diplomatic ESOSOC, it offered some access to the UN system by NGOs. The fact that this access was seen as worthwhile by NGOs may be inferred from the growth in category I listings from seven in 1948 to 41 in 1991, and in category II organisations from 32 to 354 during the same period, while an even faster expansion took place on the roster.[23]

The other trend looks towards the vast broadening of scope and reach of the programmes reviewed in ESOSOC. Although this organ by itself has never achieved the influence implied by its place in the UN Charter,[24] reports submitted from elsewhere in the system make it a central source of documentation and information. Senior officers of other IGOs also appear as authors, and those related to ESOSOC in the UN system make statements. The subject matter covers not only old-style international cooperation, but also takes in new subjects such as the environment, an enlarged operation to succour refugees and disaster victims, and a variegated web of economic and social development projects.[25]

Furthermore, the ESOSOC machinery and the international secretariats that serve it are intimately involved in the organisation of large-scale international conferences on special themes, such as population, the status of women and the environment. Such gatherings, in which governments are represented by senior officials, attract heavy NGO interest. The UN Conference on the Environment and Development in Rio de Janeiro in 1992, for example, registered 1 400 NGO representatives who formally participated in a Global Forum and informally did their best as lobbyists. Only a minority of these NGOs had official consultative status with ESOSOC.

Consequently, over the years ever more officials and members of NGOs have come into contact with UN affairs or see some reason to seek such connections. In addition, the formation of NGO alliances and coalitions among them—the UN has picked up social science jargon and calls them 'networks'—has become a routine response to activities in the UN system.[26]

LEON GORDENKER & THOMAS G WEISS

A salient phenomenon

Evidence of an NGO presence around the IGOs of the UN system alone hardly demonstrates what the Club of Rome has called 'the barefoot revolution' and the Worldwatch Institute has called 'people power'.[27] Instead, both external and internal factors can be cited in what has become a salient phenomenon in international policy making and execution.

End of the Cold War

The first and perhaps most important explanation of NGO expansion is the end of the Cold War. With the breakdown of ideological and social orthodoxy, the reluctance of many, perhaps most, diplomats and UN practitioners to interact with nongovernmental staff evaporated. This has opened new possibilities of communication and cooperation within decision-making processes. With the waning of East–West tensions, the United Nations has become a better forum for the reconciliation of views among governments on the old geopolitical compass of North-South-East-West. The UN also has become an obvious forum for discussions between governments and NGOs. 'Before it was not possible to have any contact with nongovernmental organizations in the Soviet Union, for example, because this would be seen as neo-imperialist intervention', said UN Secretary-General Boutros Boutros-Ghali. 'On the other side, it was called communist intervention'.[28]

The explanation goes beyond procedures. Issues recognised in the revealing light of the post-Cold War world as extending beyond and below state borders also needed and demanded the strengths of NGOs. As part of a major reappraisal of the role of the state and of alternative ways to solve problems, NGOs are emerging as a special set of organisations that are private in their form but public in their purpose.[29] The environment, grassroots development, more equitable trade relations, human rights and women's issues had been on NGO agendas throughout the last two or three decades. But now they have assumed new vitality. Additional pressures for NGO involvement grew around such new issues as investment needs of the erstwhile socialist bloc and ethnonationalism, with its accompanying flood of refugees and internally displaced persons. These issues simply could not be addressed solely through intergovernmental operations and recommendations characteristic of the United Nations.[30]

Moreover, when high politics and security, particularly over nuclear issues, dominated the international agenda, NGOs were at a comparative disadvantage. They obviously had no weapons and only limited access to people wielding decision-making power. As low politics rose on the international agenda, NGOs that had promoted relevant policies and actions energetically exploited or expanded direct access to policymakers. For example, NGOs not only have a capacity for direct action but they may also bring advanced knowledge to bear on such issues as gender, the environment, AIDS, relief assistance, human rights and community development.

Technological developments

Technological developments represent a second explanation for the increasing salience of NGOs in UN activity. '[New] technologies increasingly render information barriers either ineffective or economically infeasible'.[31] Governments that are hostile to NGOs fail in their sometimes zealous efforts to prevent information flows, interaction and networking through the Internet and fax communications. Electronic means have literally made it possible to ignore borders and to create the kinds of communities based on common values and objectives that were once almost the exclusive prerogative of nationalism.[32]

Modern communications technology is independent of territory. 'By providing institutional homes in the same way that states have accommodated nationalism', one observer suggests, 'NGOs are the inevitable beneficiaries of the emergence of the new global communities'.[33] Consequently, global social change organisations (GSCOs), another study claims, 'may represent a unique social invention of the postmodern, postindustrial, ie information-rich and service-focused, globally-linked world system'.[34]

Growing resources

A third explanatory factor can be found in the growing resources and professionalism of NGOs. Both indigenous and transnational NGOs have recently attracted additional resources from individual donors, governments and the UN system. In 1994 over 10% of public development aid ($8 billion) was channelled through NGOs, surpassing the volume of the combined UN system ($6 billion) without the Washington-based financial institutions. About 25% of US assistance is channelled through NGOs; at the Social Summit in Copenhagen, Vice-President Al Gore committed Washington to increasing this figure to 50% by the turn of the century.[35] Western governments have increasingly turned towards NGO projects on the basis of a reputation for cost-effectiveness.

This trend fits well with the progressively declining funds for foreign assistance and generally with domestic pressures in donor countries to cut back on overseas commitments. In fact, two prominent analysts have recently written: 'The increase of donor-funded NGO relief operations and Western disengagement from poor countries are two sides of the same coin'.[36]

Interorganisational relations in the NGO realm

Networking is perhaps a cliché in the lexicon of transnational organisation, but it aptly points to a key function of many NGOs: the process of creating bonds, sometimes formal but primarily informal, among like-minded individuals and groups across state boundaries. New communications technologies are helping to foster the kinds of interaction and relationships that were once unthinkable except through expensive air travel. Scaling up certain kinds of transnational efforts from neighbourhoods and regions to the global level and scaling down to involve grassroots organisations are no longer logistic impossibilities, but may be treated as institutional imperatives.

Claims about NGOs' eclipsing the role of the state are exaggerated, but significant change is nonetheless taking place regarding their weight in world politics. NGOs may 'create conditions that facilitate the formation of international institutions' and 'reinforce the norms promoted by these institutions through public education as well as through organized attempts to hold states accountable to these, and enhance institutional effectiveness by reducing the implementation costs associated with international institutions'. Moreover, the potential for enhanced networking increases the 'capacity to monitor states' compliance with international agreements, promote institutional adaptation and innovation, and challenge failed institutions'.[37]

NGOs that have relations with IGOs go far beyond the officially-sanctioned diplomatic networks and the narrowly-defined contacts implied by a legalistic approach. NGOs are based upon interpersonal ties and relationships among people with similar convictions, goals and interests. The result is a web of personal connections that do not fit within a formal, legal framework.

NGOs employ a variety of devices to increase the persuasiveness and efficiency of their work in conjunction with IGOs. Some of these have formal structures, while others rely primarily on interpersonal relationships. Some are constructed for service with only one UN organisation, while others have a more general scope across the UN system. Four types of interorganisational devices that involve NGOs—formal bridging groups, federations, UN coordinating bureaus and connections to governments—can be identified. Aside from these fairly defined structures, many NGOs coordinate their activities with others for a specific issue or within a particular geographical area. These occurrences may be formal but are probably usually informal and may last only briefly. There is a variety of mechanisms for NGOs to relate collectively to the UN system. Probably the best known coordination mechanisms are represented by the World Bank within its own investment or aid projects, or by the United Nations Development Program within a country-wide framework. Many NGOs coordinate their own activities for a specific issue or within a particular geographical area through formal coalitions and these, too, should be considered in understanding NGOs and the United Nations.

Some NGOs have a long institutional history or are part of federations of the organisations that they represent. Others get together only for particular issues for short periods. In either form, NGO coalitions seek to represent the views of their constituent members and to pursue shared goals. Examples would be the International Council of Voluntary Agencies (ICVA) in Geneva, originally for European NGOs but now composed primarily of Third World ones; Inter-Action in Washington, DC for US-based NGOs; or a gathering of the various Oxfams or country chapters of Médecins Sans Frontières (MSF). Within a recipient country where UN organisations operate, there sometimes exist umbrella groups for indigenous NGOs—for example, Coordinación in Guatemala facilitates contacts between external donors and local groups working with uprooted populations. Within a region there can also exist a similar pooling of efforts—for example, Concertación links development NGOs in five Central American countries.

PLURALIZING GLOBAL GOVERNANCE

Formal coalitions of NGOS

A main function of formal coalitions of NGOs is to develop as far as possible or to harmonise common positions for issues. Some examples are the lobbying efforts within the United States for the extension of Public Law 480, the source of foodstuffs for relief and development; or the search for a common stance by women's groups for international conferences on human rights in Vienna and on population in Cairo. Concrete examples include an invitation to ICVA to address the Executive Committee of the UN High Commissioner for Refugees (UNHCR), and a request to EarthAction (one of the largest global NGO networks with over 700 member associations in about 125 countries) to put forward views to the Commission on Global Governance.

These formal coalitions may attempt headquarters-level coordination of activities within a certain region or in relationship to a specific crisis, as for example, Somalia and Rwanda. Member NGOs of formal groups are not, however, bound by organisational decisions, and dissenters are free to follow their own counsel or take individual positions on policies of IGOs.

'Bridging organisations', created for service in developing countries, seek on one hand to create both horizontal links across economic and social sectors and vertical links between grassroots organisations and governments. On the other hand, they try to form similar links to external donors, whether governmental, intergovernmental or nongovernmental.

Constituent NGOs working in different sectors can interact in these bridging organisations that furnish what otherwise would be absent—a forum for discussion and cooperation. As a consequence, grassroots groups get a voice and attempt to influence policy-making. Bridging organisations function as a conduit for ideas and innovations, a source of information, a broker of resources, a negotiator of deals, a conceptualiser of strategies and a mediator of conflicts. Such organisation, it is argued, helps lead to sustainable development.[38] Examples of such bridging organisations include the Asian NGO Coalition for Agrarian Reform and Rural Development (ANGOC Asia), the Society for Participatory Research in Asia (PRIA), Savings Development Movement (SDM, Zimbabwe), and the Urban Popular Movement and the Coalition of Earthquake Victims (MUP and CUD, Mexico City).

Relief operations, and to a lesser extent development efforts, have drawn together in-country consortia of local and international NGOs with the support of donors. These groupings are often shaped to accommodate a division of labour for a geographical region or for a function like transport.[39] The Khartoum-based Emergency Relief Desk, for example, was backed by a number of European religious NGOs and then reorganised and adapted to help crossborder operations into Eritrea and Tigray.[40] In the southern Sudan, the combined Agency Relief Team was established in the mid-1980s as a relief transport consortium.[41]

Transnational federations of NGOS

Save the Children, Oxfam, Amnesty International, MSF, the International Federation of Red Cross and Red Crescent Societies (IFRC) and CARE are examples of large NGOs with a global scope and autonomous chapters in individual countries. Organisational members of a federation share an overall image and ideology. For example, Oxfam's ideology sets out a grassroots development orientation that all its national affiliates employ. But the national groups are responsible for their own fundraising and projects. Although members of such federations meet periodically at both the management and working levels to discuss common problems, each national member maintains autonomy.

Federations of NGOs try to, and frequently do, present a united front on the policies that they advocate in IGOs and in their field operations. Yet this is not always possible because of differences in view and leadership styles, and the needs in respective country branch offices and headquarters. Federations differ in how much control they can exert over their branches and how much branch activity can be coordinated with worldwide partners as well as how they finance administrative costs for common activities.

For example, Save the Children US has limited coordination with its European partners, and there is little consensus about how to address this rift. Save the Children UK does not necessarily wish to increase coordination, but the US headquarters seeks to increase interaction to improve cost-effectiveness. Also, some Save the Children branches and projects have different emphases and agendas. For example, Save the Children Sweden acts as a sort of amnesty international for children, focusing on child abuse and child advocacy to a greater extent than other chapters do.

Large federations with headquarters and many branches face the tension of accountability versus autonomy and independent action by their many satellites. Friction rises when branch offices stray from a supposedly common vision of a federation or engage in controversial or unprofessional activities. These could have negative repercussions for other chapters. At the same time, imposing constraints on branch offices may be impossible and may risk sacrificing independent and innovative thinking and acting.

UN coordination of NGOs

In contrast to the conventional Roman wisdom of divide and conquer, UN officials concerned about the proliferation of nongovernmental entities have responded with the attitude: 'If you can't beat 'em, organize 'em'. The efforts by the World Bank, UNHCR and the UNDP to structure project relationships are probably the best known.[42] UN organisations vary not only in how they coordinate their activities with NGOs but also in the extent to which they work with NGOs in the first place. When no formal structures for coordination exist, cooperation often proceeds on a case-by-case basis. Even with the existence of formal mechanisms, coordination is often *ad hoc*, based on individual relationships. Especially in crises, coordination may occur spontaneously. Nevertheless, NGOs are notorious for their independence; coordinating NGOs is 'like herding cats', according to one UN official.

Cooperation is not cost-free for NGOs. From a logical management perspective, for example, the current systems for development cooperation or humanitarian action have too many moving parts.[43] Greater collaboration among the various agencies would appear at first glance to be helpful in limiting random activity, overlap and duplication. Yet, assuming it could be arranged, even improved coordination may involve significant opportunity costs for NGOs in terms of use of personnel, resources or even diminished credibility because of their association with the United Nations. There is no guarantee of greater effectiveness or savings. As James Ingram, the former executive director of the World Food Programme (WFP), has written: 'The appearance of improved coordination at the center is not necessarily a factor in more effective and timely interventions in the field'.[44] Hence, formal UN-led efforts at coordination, comprehensive or not, are not viewed by NGO leaders as always desirable.

Such coordinating bodies in fact have a mixed record for viability and effectiveness. They have often struggled to find funding, a task that is more than a mere forum for endless NGO meetings.[45] If the main concern is effectiveness, then both formal and informal coordinating should be able to increase contact and collaboration among NGOs (exchange ideas and information); provide genuine services to members; improve liaison with governments and the UN system; and increase resources available for NGOs.

An intriguing question arises as to why certain operational IGOs—observers point to UNICEF and UNHCR—cooperate easily with NGOs while others experience considerably more difficulty. The structures, charters and goals of these UN organisations play a part, but more intangible elements such as organisational culture are among the plausible explanations.

A significant number of staff in both UNICEF and UNHCR have themselves worked in NGOs and appreciate their strengths and weaknesses. The rough-and-ready, roll-up-the-sleeves approach to disasters also makes cooperation seem more necessary and sensible than in other contexts, where the lack of an emergency permits more time and leisure for turf battles.

On a more political level, one possible explanation for easy cooperation is complementary tasks. For example, in election monitoring within UN-orchestrated operations in El Salvador and Cambodia, NGOs could more easily make public pronouncements about irregularities than could the civilian or military staff of the UN Observer Mission in El Salvador (ONUSAL) and the UN Transition Authority in Cambodia (UNTAC). In such circumstances, rather than rivalry, a sensible division of labour appeared between NGOs and IGOs. For some of the same reasons, discernible complementarity has developed between Amnesty International or Human Rights Watch and the United Nations. Because NGOs can push harder and more openly for more drastic changes, which can then be codified over time by the UN, a 'symbiotic' relationship has developed in the context of establishing new human rights standards and implementing existing ones.[46]

Some participants view the coordination effort launched in the early 1990s by UNHCR and ICVA as promising. It is titled PAR in AC (Partners in Action) and is intended to 'enhance dialogue and understanding between UNHCR; to facilitate closer collaboration and increase the combined capacity to respond to the global refugee problem and ... the problem of internal displacement'. PAR in AC aims to 'enhance and improve future NGO/UNHCR collaboration', and is motivated by UNHCR's belief that NGOs have a 'community-based approach [that] is an asset in bridging the gap between relief and development'.[47] Behind the official language lies the intense field experience of Bosnia and elsewhere in the former Yugoslavia and northern Iraq as well as the belief among some leading participants that earlier contact mechanisms delivered less than was hoped.

NGOs and governments

The relationships between governments and NGOs take several forms. Some of these are adversarial, as certain NGOs criticise and hope to change governmental policies. Other relationships are cooperative and businesslike. Host governments regulate activities by NGOs through domestic legislation and activities of international NGOs by administrative procedures (for example, visas and foreign exchange procedures). Donor governments hire NGOs to implement projects and sign contracts subject to national legislation. NGOs may lobby governments for altruistic reasons, such as new international agreements and policies, and for more self-serving reasons, such as increased budgetary allocations for their own work. In the process, they must abide by national regulations governing such activity. In some extraordinary situations, NGOs have provided services to citizens that are normally expected from governments. For example, the primary education system in the north of Sri Lanka was coordinated largely by NGOs after the government system collapsed following the onset of civil war in 1987; and the Bangladesh Rural Action Committee (BRAC) is responsible for 35 000 schools.

In general, throughout much of the Third and former Second World, the decline of oppressive regimes and the rise of democracy mainly since the end of the Cold War has tempered the former automatic hostility by governments toward the activities of local and international NGOs. Previously, NGO–government relationships were often ones of benign neglect at best, or of suspicion and outright hostility at worst.

A significant experiment

One noteworthy international experiment in combining intergovernmental and nongovernmental action in a coordinated policy and resource mobilisation for refugees and internally displaced populations took place in the early 1990s when the International Conference on Refugees in Central America (CIREFCA) brought together UN organisations and the NGO community.[48] With UNHCR in the lead, such organisations as UNDP and WFP were brought into greater contact with external and local NGOs.

Actual and potential beneficiaries were involved from the outset in project design, implementation, and monitoring. The process induced governmental, intergovernmental and nongovernmental organisations to forge new relationships with one another as well as with dissident and insurgent groups outside internationally recognised governments. This wider orchestration also took into consideration the activities of the various UN peacekeeping and peacemaking operations.

Finances, size and independence

The relationship between governments and NGOs includes many complexities and rapid changes that sometimes run parallel to the pluralism permitted by governments. Most governments that decide to do so have little difficulty in crippling NGO activities or favouring those that increase governmental capacity either to do harm or to provide popular benefits. Foreign-based NGOs may be particularly vulnerable to host government pressure since they need permission to bring in personnel and goods, such as automobiles and communications equipment. Relief NGOs that must import large quantities of supplies, as was repeatedly demonstrated in the Horn of Africa during the two decades beginning in the 1970s, can encounter direct limitations emanating from political authorities, either in the host government or in insurgent territory.

At the same time, some NGOs operating outside of their base countries have reached formidable proportions. Agencies such as CARE or Oxfam have enough prestige not to be easily or silently dismissed with the wave of an authoritative hand. Some have programmes that, once begun, burrow deep into the social fabric. To liquidate such activities can cost a government popularity and even stimulate resistance. Moreover, development NGOs may have close working relationships and direct support from IGOs, thereby raising the potential that a local incident of interference can become a matter of unpleasant discussion in an international forum. In addition, other NGOs have impressive bases of popular support. Repressive governments, for instance, intensely dislike the activities of human rights monitoring groups and try to inhibit them. Yet such interference is also restrained by the sure knowledge that these groups have developed the ability to persuade powerful governments in Western countries. Thus, a government or an insurgent group that acts in an unrestrained manner against human rights monitors may soon be faced with formal protests and action through bilateral or intergovernmental channels.

The vigour of NGO activities may ultimately be determined by the levels and sources of their finances. Some of the largest NGOs, such as the International Committee of the Red Cross and CARE, rely on contributions from governments of rich countries for most of their operating funds. As much as 90% of financing emanates from governments. The World Bank has entered into numerous partnerships with DONGOs that execute projects financed by the International Bank for Reconstruction and Development (IBRD). In 1993, for example, 30% of Bank projects had provisions for NGO participation.[49] The UNDP has changed policy over the last decade so that local NGOs are receiving allocations in the Indicative Planning Figures (IPFS) that used to be exclusively reserved for governments. The depth of such relationships, however, may vary from formal to close collaboration in phases from planning to execution.

Many organisations of the UN system routinely rely upon both international and indigenous NGOs for the delivery of relief and development assistance. For instance, in northern Iraq since the April 1991 Kurdish crisis, NGOs (including the Red Cross) have been responsible for 40% of refugees, whereas the UN system has been responsible for about 30%.[50]

Putting an exact dollar value on these resources is not easy. It would be hard to prove the contention that '[i]n net terms, NGOs now collectively transfer more resources to the South than the World Bank'.[51] Over time, however, shifts of a significant magnitude have taken place. During the last two decades, private grants from the 21 Western countries of the Development Assistance Committee (DAC) to DAC-country NGOs for use in developing countries have grown dramatically. NGO activities represent well over 10% (perhaps even 13%) of official development assistance (ODA) in comparison with only 0.2% in 1970.[52] Particularly over the last decade, when ODA has stagnated, NGOs have positioned themselves for a greater proportional share of total resources. Moreover, the visibility and credibility of such efforts have increased dramatically.

From another direction, private foundations have increasingly stimulated the growth of NGOs and added to the knowledge base for their work.[53] Favourable tax laws and a tradition of voluntarism have made this influence particularly important in the USA, where the family names of Ford, Rockefeller, MacArthur and Pew are familiar philanthropic entities. In fact, 5500 independent foundations, not including those from corporations, have assets in excess of $2 million or give grants of at least $200 000 per year.[54] Such institutions as the Volkswagen Foundation attest to the significance of this type of source in other parts of the Western world as well. Although the exact numbers are difficult to gauge, many directly finance operational activities, institution-building and research by NGOs at home and in connection with partners in other countries.

All NGOs and foundation donors operate under some governmental, donor-imposed or doctrinal restrictions. Especially in the USA, foundations owe their prosperity to provisions of tax laws that could be changed. They are also forbidden to act in electoral and other political spheres, and may not lobby in the way that special interest groups do. As for NGOs receiving outside governmental or IGO financing, these set out in programme proposals their plans for using funds. Proposals for programmes that ran counter to donor policies would hardly be likely to succeed.

Conversely, NGOs dispose of some persuasiveness in relations with donors, whether official or private. No donor would wish to invest in a programme that was foredoomed to failure. NGOs can thus signal their estimate of the practicality of policies. Moreover, once embarked on the execution of an agreed project, the NGO is in a good position to suggest policy and methodological changes, if only because the donors prefer their funds to be used in ways that can be defended against criticism.

Theories of international cooperation

Despite the rapidly rising curve of NGO numbers and activity in the context of the UN system, a firm consensus about their nature and function remains elusive. Consequently, some generalising about NGOs that operate in the international environment is necessary for a better understanding of NGO roles, but it is larded with uncertainty. The rest of this essay takes up some of the theoretical approaches that pertain to NGOs and sets out a set of dimensions that may be useful in drawing conclusions.

In general, theoretical approaches to explain international cooperation provide little specific insight into the nature and function of NGOs. Most are based on the state as the only noteworthy entity in international cooperation, and provide no category for considering the possibility that NGOs are significant actors in their own right.

States as actors

The dominant approaches employed by governmental representatives, international officials and academic scholars to transnational cooperation emphasise states as the basic units of analysis.[55] Officials usually leave this assumption in implicit form, although international civil servants constantly underline the role of member states in their organisations. Academic scholars of this persuasion quite explicitly use the state as the basic counter, although biodiversity is increasingly obvious for a category that cannot be captured by narrow nations.[56]

Since the state stands by definition, not to speak of ideology, as an autonomous organisation in a universe where only consensual limits to action are accepted as binding, an explanation is needed as to why they sometimes cooperate. Two main possibilities, both based on promotion of national interest, emerge.

The first is that cooperation among states is actually induced by the use of persuasion or coercion by one state over another.[57] This line of argument accords with analyses that set out mainly military power as the final arbiter of international relations. No state finds it in its interest to be expunged or defeated militarily, and therefore it eventually bows to superior force, whether it is latent or applied. Thus, a hierarchy based on military calculation in fact reigns among nominally equal states. This approach, incidentally, accords with much of the rhetoric of diplomats and foreign policy specialists.

The second explanation relies implicitly or explicitly on a market rather than a military calculation.[58] States cooperate in the search for material advantages. Thus, they reckon whether there is more to gain from cooperation than from withdrawal or conflict. If they do not cooperate, in all but a few instances coercion to do so is absent.

This line of reasoning is the basis for the extensive academic theorising about international regimes.[59] These institutions for international governance, based on the voluntary acceptance of rules of state conduct in regard to specific issues, do not require explicit international organisations or even formal international accords, but they continue over extended periods of time as the actual guides to state policy. Thus, international regimes do not necessarily always have much relationship to the organisations of the UN system, even though their concerns may overlap.

Paralleling these approaches is the conventional legal approach to NGOs.[60] This depends on the exercise of authority by states, on the consent of states as the basis of application of rules, and on the notion of some type of self-interest as the underlying reason for acceding to cooperative arrangements. International organisations are treated ultimately as creatures of national self-interest, however and by whomever that is defined. NGOs fit into this scheme of thinking as entities whose activities have to be regulated to conform to the broader undertakings of states.

Even if it is accepted that the state is the primary unit of international relations, the political and legal explanations based on self-interest leave little room for autonomous NGO activity. If such theoretical approaches are made more sophisticated by incorporating considerations of domestic political processes as the determinant of national interest, a focus on transnational NGO activity in shaping decisions is usually left distant or obscured. Moreover, the national self-interest approaches imply a crisp consensus within governments as to the degree of international cooperation and its desired outcome. Whether this can be demonstrated empirically is subject to doubt. Finally, the implicit emphasis of rational decision making on the basis of national interest draws attention away from the social bases of the state. The state is an abstraction. Governments, not states, actually make decisions to cooperate or not. Governments consist of people, a point that NGOs obviously do not neglect.

Social approach

A different and less widely accepted approach to international cooperation emphasises the social bases of politics.[61] It begins with the proposition that governments are social organs made up of people who have complex relationships with other parts of their own and other societies. It is presumed that these relationships may have a bearing on the decisions taken by governments as the vital representation of states to involve themselves in international cooperation.

Among such approaches, organisation theory has general application but has been infrequently used as the basis for research on international cooperation.[62] This theory abandons the traditional view of organisations as formal and self-contained units. It is concerned with relations between formally autonomous organisations with diffuse accountability and division of responsibility, whether in the national or international arenas. Such relations typically involve interorganisational bargaining where informal organisation is of the essence.

Organisation theory posits that organisations are made up of people who work together to produce a particular product by means of a relevant technique. From this base, propositions can be developed to analyse at least subgovernmental units, if not governments as a whole, as well as international agencies and NGOs. It asks what people are involved, what joint work they perform, what methods they use, and what emerges from their work. Such analyses can also trace changes taking place in organisations and their products.

Organisations, moreover, can be bound together to form new organisations, or what could be termed meta-organisations. International organisations such as the UN system, for instance, can be viewed as such meta-organisations, as can federations of NGOs. This notion necessarily involves interorganisational relationships that have great importance at the international level and in particular in connection with NGOs. But these relationships are carried on by people, rather than by abstractions, just as is the case within organisations made up only of individuals.

A commonplace of organisational analysis holds that informal links among organisational participants congeal alongside formal structures. This is a phenomenon that every diplomat and political leader acknowledges by seeking personal contacts with people who have ability to persuade within their own circles. Informal links often prove to be essential to organisational work, adaptation to changing conditions and continued existence. In transnational organisational relationships, which include those formed by NGOs, it is natural that a web of informal links develops to confront issues defined in the formal structures.

This points in the direction of network analysis, which focuses on the links between interdependent actors. Formal organisations—private and public, national and international—form the foundation of transnational networks. However, participants in networks are not organisations in their entirety but certain individuals in the constituent organisations. The interface between organisations consists primarily of boundary-role occupants. As 'activist brokers' between their organisation and its environment, boundary-role occupants must represent the organisation to its environment, and also represent the environment to their constituents.[63]

Students of networks have pointed to the centrality of so-called linking-pin organisations, which occupy central positions in terms of being reachable from and being able to reach most other organisations in the network. Serving as brokers and communication channels between organisations in the networks, linking-pin organisations are the 'nodes through which a network is loosely joined'.[64] One research question is to what extent NGOs have been able to assume linking-pin positions in transnational networks.

The sophisticated conceptual device of the social network has found little use in research on international cooperation. What exactly are the durable sets of relationships among individuals who are in a position to exchange information, resources and prestige? Individuals in this position in interorganisational relationships can usually be described as occupying boundary roles. In that role, they can easily be engaged in the activities characterised as a social network, which affect their own organisations as well. Thus, a transnational social network would depend on persons from different countries and organisations who engage in their relationships over a considerable period. The network, then, is defined by what it does, not by an organisational form, defined structure or material appurtenances.

In brief, networks represent flat or horizontal organisational forms in contrast to vertical ones based on hierarchical authority. Networks, in other words, rest on the coexistence of autonomy and interdependence. Whereas hierarchy is the natural organising principle of states, and markets are the natural organising principle of business organisations, networks are readily associated with NGOs.[65] By positioning themselves centrally in informal networks, NGOs can exert an influence above and beyond their weak formal status. In the international arena, these possibilities are enhanced because effective cooperation among states operating in an anarchic environment often implies precisely the kind of informality and network-building that work well for NGOs. Although network analysis requires the assembly of detailed data and sometimes lengthy observation, it would seem a most promising technique for analysing the function of transnational NGOS.

Another socially-oriented analytical concept that has been applied to international cooperation is that of the epistemic community.[66] This notion seeks to explain changes in the programs and doctrines of international organisations through the operation of transnational sets of experts. Their common vision on the proper outlook on a set of issues—protection of the environment has featured most prominently—underlies their efforts to capture existing organisations and redirect their work. Their persuasiveness derives from consensual knowledge growing from advanced technological competence. It eventually convinces other leaders and organisational managers. This concept, too, would appear to be relevant to a better understanding of NGOS, although its emphasis on technological expertness may limit its appropriateness to a narrow range of issues.

An even less formally organized type of participant in international policy and administrative processes is composed of prominent persons who, by dint of expertise, experience, office or other distinguishing characteristic, earn deference. They may be asked to serve on honorific official commissions and as highly expert technical consultants on defined issues. Many have high visibility and credibility from their previous tenure in senior positions in governments and parliaments, or from their reputations as insightful intellectuals. Some work on their own accounts, others for governments, corporations, universities and specialist firms. Some of the assignments are ongoing, some are for a fixed period. Their tasks are sometimes performed for immediate consumption by UN organisations but also with an eye on other consumers in a broader public. Examples are the members of the UN Advisory Committee on the Peaceful Uses of Atomic Energy (appointed by Dag Hammarskjöld) or Max van der Stoel, former foreign minister of the Netherlands, who was appointed by the Commission on Human Rights as Rapporteur on Human Rights in Iraq. Such 'influentials', with or without official appointments, are often consulted informally by opinion leaders and national and international officials.

An increasingly common practice has been to ask such prominent individuals to serve as members of high-visibility *ad hoc* commissions—those headed by Willy Brandt, Olaf Palme, Gro Harlem-Brundtland, Sadruddin Aga Khan, Julius Nyerere and, most recently, by Ingmar Carlsson and Sonny Ramphal are perhaps the best known.[67] They constitute visible groups that come together for short-term specialised advisory assignments. Their work has much in common with the efforts of educational NGOS. Other groups of less prominent professionals—not just Médecins Sans Frontières but also, for instance, architects and physicists without borders—attempt to make their collective views known in international policy circles and among broader publics. Parliamentarians for Global Action (PGA) is one such pooling of politicians who have a primary interest in global problem-solving and in the United Nations.

Broad roles for NGOS

These theoretical approaches to international cooperation could aid in analysing NGO activity and in reaching conclusions, but none of them appears fully apt for an investigation that emphasises concrete activities and observation born of participation. Rather, it might be better to base such an examination on a close scrutiny of goals. relationships among various organisations and operating methods. This may eventually lead to more general conclusions about the weight and scope of NGO participation in international cooperation. An initial sorting, suggested to the authors of the case studies that follow in this issue, sets out two general roles that reflect both goals and operating methods. Few if any NGOs are likely at all times to set out goals and use methods that are confined exclusively to these discrete categories, but this broad typology can help point out their main thrust.

Operational roles

At least part of the activities of most NGOs falls into the category of operations. Operational NGOs are the most numerous and have the easiest fundraising task. They are more and more central to international responses in the post-cold war world. Most NGOs provide some services, if only to their members, while others concentrate on providing them to other organisations and individuals. The delivery of services is the mainstay of most NGO budgets and the basis for enthusiastic support from a wide range of donors. Such services include intangible technical advice as well as more tangible resources for relief, development and other purposes. Many NGOs operate development programmes; they have become increasingly active in migration and disaster relief, which may now be their most important operational or advisory activities in total financial terms.

Bilateral and multilateral government organisations are relying upon NGOs more and more as project subcontractors. Some of these contractors, known as DONGOs, could be dedicated organisations and even disappear after the conclusion of a project. Others have long histories as contractors. NGOs recover their staff costs and overheads in addition to the direct costs of the products that they deliver but, unlike private contractors, they do not make a profit to redistribute since there are no shareholders. Some NGO managers are delighted with this trend since it expands the scope of their activities with increased resources. Others, however, are troubled about being exploited by governments or intergovernmental organisations rather than remaining institutions with their own unique purposes and independent wherewithal.

Such contractual relationships on the one hand offer opportunities to NGOs to persuade donors to adopt their approaches; but on the other hand they include powerful incentives in the form of financial support to accede to the views of donor organisations. The key to operational integrity is being a partner and not simply a contractor. The former term connotes authentic collaboration and mutual respect, and it accepts the autonomy and pluralism of NGOs. Such relationships are rare, more an aspiration than a reality.[68] It is difficult to imagine NGOs enjoying authentic collaboration and genuine partnership with large and powerful agencies. However, in certain circumstances and as mentioned earlier, there seems to be a greater possibility with more sympathetic funders like UNICEF and UNHCR.[69]

Educational and advocacy roles

The targets of operational NGOs are beneficiaries (or victims in emergencies), whereas those for educational and advocacy NGOs are their own contributors, the public and decision makers. Educational NGOs seek primarily to influence citizens, whose voices are then registered through public opinion and bear fruit in the form of additional resources for their activities as well as new policies, better decisions and enhanced international regimes. They often play a leading role in promoting the various dedication of 'days', 'years', and 'decades' that the UN system regularly proclaims. NGOs can help to reinforce various norms promoted by intergovernmental organisations through public education campaigns. This heightened awareness among public audiences can then help hold states accountable for their international commitments.[70]

Western operational NGOs are under growing pressure from their Third World partners to educate contributors and Western publics about the root causes of poverty and violence. This logic is driving some organisations to adapt to such harsh criticism as the following: 'Conventional NGO project activities are manifestly "finger-in-the-dike" responses to problems that require nothing short of worldwide and whole-hearted governmental commitment to combat'.[71] Hand-in-hand with operational activities is the need to educate populations and mobilise public opinion about the requirements for fundamental alterations in the global order.

Educational NGOs direct activities towards a broad public or towards specifically differentiated publics in order to persuade them to voice opinions on governmental policies in international organisations. The primary tool of the educational and advocacy NGO is collecting and disseminating information, which sometimes incorporates a high degree of expertness and sometimes consists of mainly emotional appeals.

Educational as well as other varieties of NGOs can be distinguished from social movements,[72] even if the aims and methods are sometimes similar. The former are organisations with visible structures, are generally tolerated as parts of the polity and can make sure that their interests are represented in decision processes. Social movements, in contrast, have loose or skimpy structures to give effect to a rather spontaneous coming together of people who seek to achieve a social goal that may include changing or preserving aspects of society. One or more NGOs may be associated with social movements but do not define or direct them.

Linked to education are the related concerns of NGOs working primarily in the corridors of governments and intergovernmental organisations. Using a distinctive venue for advocacy, these organisations aim at contributing to international agenda-setting, the design of programmes and overall supervision of international organisation activities. They do so by seeking discussions with national delegates and staff members of international secretariats. Under some circumstances they can make formal statements before UN deliberative organs, and they frequently submit documentation for use by government representatives. In the corridors of UN organisations, they offer expertise, research, drafting and even mediation to governmental representatives and organisational staff. In

PLURALIZING GLOBAL GOVERNANCE

doing so, the NGO representatives hope to promote acceptance of their positions, which involve adjustment or change of policies.

These advocates pursue discussions with national delegates and staff members of international secretariats in order to influence international public policy. Calling this activity 'lobbying' is perhaps an accurate image but an inaccurate description according to dictionary definitions. In seeking to alter the policies of governments as well as of governmental, intergovernmental and nongovernmental agencies, these NGOs seek to influence all policy makers, not only legislators.

Rather than aiming at beneficiaries or the general public, as is the case for the operational and educational types, advocacy NGOs target key decision makers in parliaments as well as in governments and intergovernmental secretariats. Because they have a direct impact on international responses, advocacy NGOs have the most difficulty raising funds.

NGO advocacy may be generally described as unofficial participation by internal and external modes.[73] Internal modes can be observed in capitals and domestic arenas. They include such things as pressure on a government to participate in a treaty-making effort; formation of domestic coalitions and the mobilisation of public opinion to influence the positions a state takes during treaty negotiations; public pressure on a government to sign a treaty; and using the strengths and weaknesses of a country's domestic system to challenge governments, companies and others to comply.

External modes consist of urging the United Nations or one of its associated agencies to add an issue to the agenda; gathering data to help frame or define a problem or a threat in ways that influence the work of official UN-sanctioned conferences; and contributing to the implementation of treaties by assisting countries without expertise to meet their obligations. Through formal statements in UN forums and through informal negotiations with international civil servants and members of national delegations, advocacy NGOs seek to ensure that their positions, and those of their constituencies, find their way into international texts and decisions. They sometimes offer their research and drafting skills, and they provide scientific or polling data to support their positions.[74] Also, first-hand reports and testimony from field staff can be powerful tools before parliamentary committees.

External functions generally require mobilisation across state boundaries. Independent researchers and scholars, usually as part of transnational networks, contribute theoretical arguments or empirical evidence in favour of a particular response. This information is used by NGOs and helps build coalitions of individuals and groups that otherwise would not join forces.

A great deal of past NGO advocacy has been directed against government and UN policy. An important evolution is that a growing number of NGOs are eager to institutionalise a 'full-fledged partnership with the governmental members of the United Nations'.[75] Historically NGOs have had some responsibility for treaty implementation, but they may aspire to a more direct involvement in treaty-making. Some NGOs have contributed substantially to international agenda-setting, as at the San Francisco Conference in April 1945, where NGOs played a pivotal role in securing the inclusion of human rights language in the final draft of the UN

Charter. In fact, they have spurred action since the middle of the 19th century at each stage in the evolution of international protection for human rights.[76]

As with the venerable debate over the impact of the media on foreign policy, there is disagreement about NGO influence on governmental responses. However, NGOs that seek government policy change can be crucial for the timing and nature of international responses, even in such controversial arenas as civil wars. NGOs in the USA, for example, failed to get the Clinton Administration to acknowledge genocide and to take action in Rwanda in April and May 1994, but eventually they were more successful in getting the Pentagon to help in Zaire and Tanzania. For three years, many US NGOs encouraged a robust enough military invasion to restore the elected government of the Rev Jean-Bertrand Aristide in Haiti. In France, NGOs have been successful in launching and sustaining an activist humanitarian policy, *le droit d'ingérence*, which became the official policy of the Mitterrand government and its visible Minister Bernard Kouchner, and which survives both of their departures.[77]

NGOs that focus exclusively on education or advocacy in their own countries without overseas activities are not numerous, but they exist. For example, the Refugee Policy Group, Refugees International, and the US Committee for Refugees all focus on research with a view towards informing the public and altering public policy on people displaced by war. However, many of the most effective educators and advocates are those with the credibility, knowledge and convictions resulting from substantial operational activities.

Many NGOs that started their work at a project level mitigating the symptoms of problems have moved into attacking the structural roots of those problems. As such, they draw away from an exclusive concern with projects and move towards preventing the need for the assistance in the first place. Projects alone cannot promote structural change and prevention. The logic of the shift towards educating the public about the necessity for systemic change moves away from a preoccupation with relief, and is summed up by two observers: 'Many of the causes of underdevelopment lie in the political and economic structures of an unequal world ... and in the misguided policies of governments and the multilateral institutions (such as the World Bank and IMF) which they control. It is extremely difficult, if not impossible, to address these issues in the context of the traditional NGO project.'[78] In these efforts to target officials within governmental and intergovernmental institutions, NGOs can be loud and theatrical, like Médecins Sans Frontières and Greenpeace, or discreet and more subtle, like the International Committee of the Red Cross.

Advocacy is an essential and growing activity. As such, the debate about possible modifications of consultative status in UN forums is important at least for some NGOs. Consultative status provides additional access to and enhanced authority in the eyes of many governments and UN officials.

Political levels and constraints

A complementary or alternative approach to NGO roles depends on identifying relationships among them and their governmental levels of activity.[79] Primary associations are those serving members at the community level; these may be called people's organisations. As their base, scope of operations and methods are circumscribed, they can be excluded from the group of transnational NGOs with direct relevance to the UN system. Secondary organisations include public-serving groups that operate at the community level as well as federations of member-serving primary associations. Tertiary organisations are those that do not operate at the community level and also comprise federations of secondary organisations. Thus, only public-serving organisations and meta-organisations that they form may be considered as NGOs with transnational significance.

Further distinctions can be drawn between organisations that work at the community level and those that do not. National NGOs that work only within the boundaries of one developing country can be distinguished from international NGOs that are based in developed countries. Refining classificatory factors include constituency, primary functions and activities, ideology/philosophy, scale and coverage or organisational structure.

NGO interactions may be constrained or facilitated according to the consensus surrounding the issues that they address. Environmental NGOs, for instance, work within an overall and seemingly expanding agreement about protecting the biosphere. Development NGOs, in contrast, are partly sustained by a consensus about the necessity for growth, even though they often encounter significant discord when they begin to threaten elites. Human rights NGOs, however, pursue agendas in which governments, intergovernmental organisations and NGOs disagree profoundly about goals, ideas, the nature of violations and appropriate forms of redress. Therefore, NGOs working on the front lines where ethnic cleansing takes place, lobbying for human rights changes, or doing education and advocacy work face different constraints from NGOs struggling to save rain forests or to advance development.

Separate microsystems of issues have their own attributes and exigencies that condition the existence of NGOs. Within each microsystem, the potential for collaboration or conflict by NGOs and the UN is distinct.[80] Moreover, the varied aims and methods of NGOs range from constructive dialogue, that is incrementalism or reform from within, to shouting from the sidelines for revolution, rejection and nihilism.

Dimensions for analysing NGOs

A search for identities within the explorations in the specific case studies in this volume offer data on which further research could be based and would provide tests of the appropriateness of typologies and theoretical approaches. Accordingly, four sets of dimensions—organisation, governance, strategies and output—were suggested to the authors of subsequent essays. These dimensions are displayed in Table 1 and discussed in the succeeding paragraphs; they also provide a structure for the concluding essay.

The dimensions are divided into four categories. The first two, organisation and governance, have special relevance to locating the site of activities within governing structures and understanding the structures and aims of NGOs. The second two, strategic and output, have to with the techniques and products of NGOs.

TABLE 1
NGO dimensions

Organisational dimensions	Governance dimensions	Strategic dimensions	Output dimensions
Geographic range	*Governmental contact*	*Goal definition*	Information
Community	Intergovernmental	Single issue	Expert advice
Subnational	International conferences	Multisectoral	Financing
National	Regional	Broad social	Material goods and services
Regional	National	Church related	Support for policies
Transnational	Subnational	Social ideology	Mobilisation of opinion
	Community	Revolutionary/rejectionist	(leaders and followers)
Support base	Informal transnational		Maintenance of
Personal memberships		*Tactical modes*	interorganisational relations
Other organisations	*Range of concern*	Monitoring	Political feedback among
Quasi-governmental	Norm setting	Advocacy/lobbying	governmental units
Mixture of above	Policy setting	Mass propaganda	Encouragement of networks
	Policy execution	Mass demonstration	Education of specific publics
Personnel	Contractor		
Managerial	Mediation between levels		
Basic research			
Expert and professional (applied)			
Undifferentiated			
(popular, voluntary)			
Financing			
Membership dues			
Contributions			
Endowment income			
Compensation			
Legal relationships			
General rules			
Regulations			
Ad hoc guidelines			

PLURALIZING GLOBAL GOVERNANCE

Organisational dimensions

These dimensions are intended to make clear two aspects of NGO existence and operation. The first is where they fit in an organisational framework that extends from the village to the globe, and who supports them. The second aspect concerns their internal arrangements and participation, their resource bases, and their legal status. Membership and financial information make possible comparisons relating to the size of NGOs. Since the legal dimensions of NGOs have had a great deal of attention, they are touched on only briefly in the case studies.

Governance dimensions

These dimensions comprise information about the instruments of governmental policy and programme administration with which NGOs come into contact. The subcategory, 'Range of Concern', helps distinguish among the characters of the arrangements for governance in which NGOs may participate. For example, a substantial difference in governance may be presumed between a situation in which an NGO simply works as a contractor for a regional intergovernmental agency from one that is involved in the discussion of a new global law-making treaty.

Strategic dimensions

These dimensions set out what NGOs hope to achieve within the organisational and governance dimensions. The emphasis here is on relationships directed inwards, ie, how NGOs choose to relate to IGOs and governments on policy issues and design of projects. They include both the normative basis for action and, under tactical modes, the methods employed for reaching the goals. A wide range of data can be expected by searching out the effects of these dimensions. Along their lines, NGOs differentiate themselves from each other and reinforce their support bases. The tactical modes, however, have primary significance in the relation to the UN system.

Output dimensions

These dimensions are framed to make evident the results of NGO activity within the framework of the UN system. They are highly significant in determining whether NGOs can reach their goals. They include a set of products of organisational work that bear on how the UN system reacts and also on how NGOs maintain relationships with one other in reaching their goals. The outputs relate to services delivered to organisational membership as well as to external persons and organisations.

Conclusion

NGOS are omnipresent in the policy and administrative process of UN organisations; the extent of their participation has progressively deepened. The turbulent

LEON GORDENKER & THOMAS G WEISS

pluralism of the NGO realm has clearly brought new and unanticipated groups into the process. Without attributing either a positive or negative value to NGO activity, it can nevertheless be recognised as a factor in global governance. Yet this phenomenon, contrary to the conventional assumptions about the virtually exclusive role of governments in international politics, has not been fully described nor adequately encompassed in theoretical approaches.

Defining categories of NGO tasks, their transnational relationships and the impact of their efforts marks an initial step towards understanding the variety of nongovernmental interactions with the UN system. They form part of a larger set of analytical challenges as the international community gropes and copes with changing world politics and trends towards the decentralisation and democratisation of global governance. These include a vast variety of cooperative structures and practices that have emerged in and around the United Nations and its associated organisations.

There is an obvious hypothesis: NGOs have been essential in this evolution. Because NGOs, both local and international, increasingly affect world politics, theoretical and practical understandings of NGO activities are intrinsically important. Moreover, they are crucial for comprehending the problems and prospects of the UN system more generally. It is to an examination of cases of NGOs in action that this volume now turns.

Notes

The authors acknowledge the assistance of Carrie Murphy and Minh Vo in the preparation of this article.

1   *Yearbook of International Associations*, Brussels: Union of International Associations, 1993/94. The actual figure is 16 142 but it is increasing constantly. In fact, the figure more than doubled from 1991. The OECD *Directory of NGOs* (Paris: Organisation for Economic Cooperation and Development, 1991) estimates some 2500 INGOs in OECD countries in 1990, up from 1600 a decade earlier. They also estimate some 20 000 local NGOs in developing countries, although the UNDP's *Human Development Report 1994* (New York: Oxford University Press, 1994) estimates that the number is considerably higher, at about 50 000.

2   Commission on Global Governance, *Our Global Neighbourhood*, Oxford: Oxford University Press, 1995, p 254.

3   John Clark, *Democratizing Development: The Role of Voluntary Organizations*, Hartford, CT: Kumarian Press, 1991, p 3.

4   Marc Nerfin, 'Neither prince nor merchant: citizen—an introduction to the third system', *IFDA Dossier*, 56, November/December 1986, pp 3–29. See also David C Korten, *Getting to the 21st Century: Voluntary Action and The Global Agenda*, Hartford, CT: Kumarian Press, 1990, pp 95–112.

5   Kathleen D McCarthy, Virginia Hodgkinson, Russy Sumariwalla *et al.*, *The Nonprofit Sector in the United States*, San Francisco, CA: Jossey-Bass, 1992, p 3.

6   Thomas Princen & Matthias Finger, *Environmental NGOs in World Politics*, London: Routledge, 1994.

7   James N Rosenau, *Turbulence in World Politics: A Theory of Continuity and Change*, Princeton, NJ: Princeton University Press, 1990 and *The United Nations in a Turbulent World*, Boulder, CO: Lynne Rienner, 1992.

8   The authors are grateful to Christer Jönsson and Peter Söderholm for their formulations.

9   Joseph A Camilleri & Jim Falk, *The End of Sovereignty? The Politics of a Shrinking and Fragmenting World*, Aldershot, UK: Edward Elgar, 1992, p 3.

10   Jennifer Wolch, *The Shadow State: Government and Voluntary Sector in Transition*, New York: The Foundation Center, 1990.

11   Brad Smith, President of the Inter-American Foundation, quoted by Mary Morgan, 'Stretching the development dollar: the potential for scaling-up', *Grassroots Development*, 14 (1), 1990, p 7.

12   David L Brown & David Korten, *Understanding Voluntary Organizations: Guidelines for Donors*, Working Papers No 258 (Washington, DC: Country Economics Department, World Bank, September 1989), p 22.

13   *UNIFEM Annual Report 1993*, New York: United Nations Development Fund for Women, 1993, p 9. See also

PLURALIZING GLOBAL GOVERNANCE

Stephen P Marks, 'Forgetting "the policies and practices of the past": impunity in Cambodia', *The Fletcher Forum of World Affairs*, 18 (2), 1994, pp 17–43; and Jarat Chopra, *United Nations Authority in Cambodia*, *Occasional Paper #15*, Providence, RI: Watson Institute, 1994.

[14] Antonio Donini, 'Missions impossibles', *Le monde des débats*, July-August 1994, p 4.

[15] For a useful discussion of the literature about NGOs in the context of teaching international relations, international law and international organisation, see Lawrence T Woods, 'Nongovernmental organizations and the United Nations system: reflecting upon the Earth Summit experience', *Research Note*, 18 (1), 1993, pp 9–15.

[16] Leland M Goodrich, Edvard Hambro & Anne Patricia Simons, *Charter of the United Nations*, New York: Columbia University Press, 1969, pp 443–446.

[17] See United Nations, Economic and Social Council Resolutions 3 (II) (1946) and 288 B (X) (1950).

[18] Chiang Pei-Heng, *Non-Governmental Organizations at the United Nations: Identity, Role and Function*, New York: Praeger, 1981, pp 19–57. For historical discussions, see also J Joseph Lador-Lederer, *International Non-governmental Organizations and Economic Entities: A Study in Autonomous Organization and Ius Gentium*, Leiden: Sythoff, 1963; Borko Stosic, *Les Organisations non Gouvernementales et les Nations Unies*, Geneva: Librarie Droz, 1964; and Lyman C White, *International Non-Governmental Organizations: Their Purposes, Methods, and Accomplishments*, New Brunswick, NJ: Rutgers University Press, 1951.

[19] UN, General Assembly Resolution 13 (1), Annex I (1946); and ECOSOC Resolution 1297 (XLIV).

[20] UN, Economic and Social Council, Open-Ended Group on the Review of Arrangements for Consultations with Non-Governmental Organizations, 'General review of arrangements for consultations with non-governmental organizations', UN Doc. E/AC.70/1994/5 (26 May 1994), p 18. Hereafter cited by document number. The ILO tri-partite structure was an earlier precedent.

[21] Ibid, pp 17–18.

[22] Ibid, p 11.

[23] Ibid, p 17.

[24] Johan Kaufmann & Nico Schrijver, *Changing Global Needs: Expanding Roles of the United Nations System*, Hanover, NH: Academic Council on the United Nations System, 1990, pp 40–45.

[25] See Francesco Mezzalama & Siegfried Schumm, *Working with NGOs: Operational Activities of the United Nations System with Non-governmental Organizations and Governments at the Grassroots and National Levels*, Geneva: Joint Inspection Unit, 1993, document Jiu/REP/93/1.

[26] UN Doc. E/AC.70/1994/5, p 8.

[27] Bertrand Schneider, *The Barefoot Revolution*, London: IT Publishers, 1988; and Alan Durning, 'People power and development', *Foreign Policy*, 76, Fall 1989, pp 66–82.

[28] Barbara Crossette, 'UN Leader to Call for Changes in Peacekeeping', *New York Times*, 3 January 1995, A3.

[29] For a theoretical and empirical investigation, see Lester M Salamon & Helmut K Anheier, *The Emerging Sector: An Overview*, Baltimore, MD: Johns Hopkins University Institute for Policy Studies, 1994.

[30] See Jackie Smith, Ron Pagnucco & Winnie Romeril, 'Transnational social movement organizations in the global political arena', *Voluntas*, 5 (2), 1994, pp 121–154.

[31] Maria Garner, 'Transnational alignment of nongovernmental organizations for global environmental action', *Vanderbilt Journal of Transnational Law*, 23 (5), 1991, p 1077.

[32] See Benedict Anderson, *Imagined Communities: Reflections on the Origins and Spread of Nationalism*, London: Verso, 1991.

[33] Peter Spiro, 'New global communities: nongovernmental organizations in international decision making institutions', *Washington Quarterly*, 18 (1) 1995, p 48.

[34] David Cooperrider & William Pasmore, 'The organization dimension of global change', *Human Relations*, 44, (8), 1991, p 764.

[35] 'NGOs and conflict: three views', *Humanitarian Monitor*, 2, February 1995, pp 32–33.

[36] Rakiya Omaar & Alex de Waal, *Humanitarianism Unbound?* Discussion Paper No 5, London: African Rights, November 1994, p 6.

[37] Janie Leatherman, Ron Pagnucco & Jackie Smith, *International Institutions and Transnational Social Movement Organizations: Challenging the State in a Three-level Game of Global Transformation*, Working Paper Series, South Bend, IN.: Kroc Institute, October 1993, p 4.

[38] L David Brown, 'Bridging organizations and sustainable development', *Human Relations*, 44 (8), 1991, pp 807–831. Brown argues that 'development sustainability depends in part on institutional factors—effective local organizations, horizontal linkages that enable intersectoral cooperation, and vertical linkages that enable grassroots influence on policy-making—that can be influenced by bridging organizations'. Ibid, p 825.

[39] See Mark Duffield, 'Sudan at the cross roads: from emergency preparedness to social security', *IDS Discussion Paper #275*, Brighton: Institute for Development Studies, 1990.

[40] Barbara Hendrie, 'Cross border operations in Eritrea and Tigray', *Disasters*, 13 (4), 1990, pp 351–360.

[41] R Graham & J Borton, *A Preliminary Review of the Combined Agencies Relief Team (CART), Juba 1986–1991*, London: Overseas Development Institute, 1992.

[42] UN Doc. E/AC.70/1994/5, pp 67–71.

[43] For a discussion in relationship to the UN, see Erskine Childers with Brian Urquhart, *Renewing the United Nations System*, Uppsala: Dag Hammarskjöld Foundation, 1994.

[44] James O Ingram, 'The future architecture for international humanitarian assistance', in Thomas G Weiss & Larry Minear (eds), *Humanitarianism Across Borders: Sustaining Civilians in Times of War*, Boulder, CO: Lynne Rienner, 1993, p 181.

[45] Carolyn Strenlau, 'NGO coordinating bodies in Africa, Asia and Latin America', *World Development*, 15, Supplement, 1987, pp 213–225.

[46] Ramesh Thakur, 'Human rights: Amnesty International and the United Nations', *Journal of Peace Research*, 31 (2), 1994, pp 143–160.

[47] Sadako Ogata, UNHCR High Commissioner, 'Opening statement to the 44th Session of the Executive Committee of the High Commissioner's Programme', PARinAC Information Note and Update No 1, Geneva: UNHCR and ICVA, 1993, p 1.

[48] See Adolpho Aguilar Zinzer, *CIREFCA: The Promises and Reality of the International Conference on Central American Refugees*, Washington, DC: CIPRA, 1991; and Cristina Eguizábal, David Lewis, Larry Minear, Peter Sollis & Thomas G Weiss, *Humanitarian Challenges in Central America: Learning the Lessons of Recent Armed Conflicts*, Occasional Paper #14, Providence, RI: Watson Institute, 1993.

[49] World Bank, *Cooperation Between the World Bank and NGOs: 1993 Progress Report*, Washington, World Bank, 1993, p 7. Some NGOs would contest that 'participation' is not as meaningful as these statistics might imply.

[50] Judith Randel, 'Aid, the military and humanitarian assistance: an attempt to identify recent trends', *Journal of International Development*, 6 (3), 1994, p 336.

[51] Mark Duffield, 'NGOs, disaster relief and asset transfer in the Horn: political survival in a permanent emergency', *Development and Change*, 24, 1993, p 140.

[52] UN Doc. E/AC.70/1994/5, Annexes IV and V.

[53] See James G McGann, *The Competition for Dollars, Scholars and Influence in the Public Policy Research Industry*, Lantham MD: University Press of America, 1995.

[54] Margaret M Feczko (ed), *The Foundation Directory*, New York: The Foundation Center, 1984, p vii.

[55] See, for example, Hans J Morgenthau, *Politics Among Nations*, New York: Knopf, 1973; and Kenneth N Waltz, *Theory of International Politics*, Reading, MA: Addison-Wesley, 1979. See also Robert O Keohane, *Neorealism and Its Critics*, New York: Columbia University Press, 1986.

[56] See Stephen J Del Rosso, Jr, 'The insecure state: reflections on "the state" and "security" in a changing world', *Daedalus*, 124 (2), 1995, pp 175–204.

[57] Robert Gilpin, *The Political Economy of International Relations*, Princeton, NJ: Princeton University Press, 1987.

[58] See for example, Joseph S Nye, Jr, *Bound To Lead: The Changing Nature of American Power*, New York: Basic Books, 1990, which makes a case for the validity of 'soft power'. See also Hedley Bull, *The Anarchical Society*, New York: Oxford University Press, 1977.

[59] See, for example, Stephen D Krasner (ed), *International Regimes*, Ithaca, NY: Cornell University Press, 1983; and Robert O Keohane, *After Hegemony: Cooperation and Discord in the World Political Economy*, Princeton, NJ: Princeton University Press, 1984.

[60] See Henry G Schermers, *International Institutional Law*, Alphen aan den Rijn, Netherlands: Sijthoff & Noordhoff, 1980, pp 15–18, 164–75. Much legal commentary relates to specific subject matter, eg the UN Conventions on Human Rights, the UN Convention on the Status of Refugees and a host of other legal documents in force or in the developmental stage.

[61] An overview of this approach is found in Leon Gordenker, Christer Jönsson, Roger A Coate & Peter Söderholm, *International Responses to AIDS*, London: Pinter, forthcoming 1995.

[62] Gail D Ness & Steven B Brachin, 'Bridging the gap: international organizations as organizations', *International Organization*, 42 (2), 1988, pp 245–274.

[63] Dennis W Organ, 'Linking pins between organizations and environment', *Business Horizons*, 14, 1971, pp 73–80.

[64] Howard Aldrich and David A Whetten, 'Organization-sets, action-sets, and networks: making the most of simplicity', in Paul C Nystrom & William H Starbuck (eds), *Handbook of Organizational Design*, Vol 1, New York: Oxford University Press, 1981.

[65] Grahame Thompson, Jennifer Frances, Rosalind Levacic & Jeremy Mitchell (eds), *Markets, Hierarchies and Networks: The Coordination of Social Life*, London: Sage, 1991.

[66] Ernst B Haas, *When Knowledge Is Power: Three Models of Change in International Organizations*, Berkeley, CA: University of California Press, 1990; and Peter M Haas, 'Introduction: epistemic communities and international policy coordination', *International Organization*, 46 (1), 1992, pp 1–35, and 'Do regimes matter? Epistemic communities and Mediterranean pollution control', *International Organization*, 43 (3), 1989, pp 377–403.

[67] Independent Commission on International Development Issues, *North–South: A Programme for Survival*,

PLURALIZING GLOBAL GOVERNANCE

London: Pan, 1980; Independent Commission on Disarmament and Security Issues, *Common Security: A Blueprint for Survival*, New York: Touchstone, 1982; World Commission on Environment and Development, *Our Common Future*, New York: Oxford University Press, 1987; Independent Commission on International Humanitarian Issues, *Winning the Human Race?*, London: Zed, 1988; South Commission, *The Challenge to the South*, Oxford: Oxford University Press, 1990; and Commission on Global Governance, *Our Global Neighbourhood*.

[68] See International Council of Voluntary Agencies, NGO Working Group on the World Bank, 'Brief history of the NGO Working Group on the World Bank', informal document dated December 1993.

[69] Part of the explanation may be that many UN staff members in these institutions have actually worked in NGOS or are at least very sympathetic towards goals and styles of operation. For example, see the UNHCR's special issue of *Refugees*, 97, March 1994, entitled 'Focus: NGOS & UNHCR'.

[70] See Leatherman *et al.*, *International Institutions*.

[71] John Clark 'Policy influence, lobbying and advocacy', in Michael Edwards & David Hulme (eds), *Making a Difference: NGOS and Development in a Changing World*, London: Earthscan, 1992, p 199.

[72] Dennis R Young, 'The structural imperatives of international advocacy association', *Human Relations*, 44 (9), 1991, p 925. See also M N Zald & J D McCarthy (eds), *Social Movements in an Organizational Society*, New Brunswick, NJ: Transaction Books, 1987.

[73] Lawrence Susskind, *Environmental Diplomacy: Negotiating More Effective Global Agreements*, New York: Oxford University Press, 1994, p 50.

[74] For discussions, see Cynthia Price Cohen, 'The role of nongovernmental organizations in the drafting of the convention on the rights of the child', *Human Rights Quarterly*, 12 (1), 1990, pp 137–147; Thakur, 'Human rights'; and Princen & Finger *Environmental NGOS in World Politics*.

[75] Susskind, *Environmental Diplomacy*, p 51.

[76] See David P Forsythe, *Human Rights and World Politics*, Lincoln, NB: University of Nebraska Press, 1989, pp 83–101, 127–59.

[77] See Bernard Kouchner & Mario Bettati, *Le devoir d'ingérence*, Paris: Denoël, 1987; Bernard Kouchner, *Le malheur des autres*, Paris: Odile Jacob, 1991; and Mario Bettati, 'Intervention, ingérence ou assistance?', *Revue Trimestrielle des Droits de l'Homme*, 19 July 1994, pp 308–358.

[78] Edwards & Hulme (eds), *Making a Difference*, p 20.

[79] The authors are grateful to Marty Chen for suggesting these categories.

[80] The authors are grateful to Charles MacCormack for having helped develop ideas along these lines during the July 1994 summer workshop organised by the Academic Council on the United Nations System.

[15]

Nongovernmental Organizations in the United Nations System: The Emerging Role of International Civil Society

Dianne Otto

INTRODUCTION

In February 1993, the United Nations' Economic and Social Council (ECOSOC) established an open-ended working group (OEWG) to update, if necessary, its arrangements for consultation with nongovernment organizations (NGOs) and to introduce coherent rules to regulate the participation of NGOs in international conferences organized by the United Nations (UN).[1] The review provides an important opportunity to clarify the roles and functions of NGOs in the international community, issues which have always been controversial. The review also has the potential to contribute to

---

1. E.S.C. Res. 1993/80, U.N. ESCOR established the OEWG to conduct the review outlined by E.S.C. Res. 1993/214, U.N. ESCOR.

Human Rights Quarterly 18 (1996) 107–141 © 1996 by The Johns Hopkins University Press

108   **HUMAN RIGHTS QUARTERLY**   **Vol. 18**

current debates about the growing importance of civil society[2] in international norm-setting, although this possibility seems, as yet, remote.[3]

My aim is to foster connections between the related projects of the ECOSOC review and post–cold war reconceptualizations of international civil society and governance. Without linking with theoretical debates about the future shape of the international community, it is likely that the review will be narrow in its scope and reach myopic and pragmatic, rather than visionary, conclusions. Alternatively, as I will argue, the review could help to foster new forms of relationships between NGOs and states in the context of new understandings of international democracy.

My discussion is divided into two sections. Part I examines the history and context of the ECOSOC review and its likely outcomes, focussing on what principles should guide UN-NGO consultative relations. This examination reveals the tenacity of many of the issues which have precipitated the review and the likelihood that, like its forerunners, this review will leave these issues unresolved, resulting instead in piecemeal readjustments to the *status quo*. I argue that this would be a regressive outcome, muffling the innovative contributions of the more recently formed NGOs and ensuring a chaotic, rather than orderly, movement of civil society from the fringes to the center stage of the UN system.

Part II canvasses some of the theoretical debates about the growing importance of international civil society. The dominant realist view of international relations is contrasted with alternative liberal and postliberal paradigms which place importance on individuals and social movements as international actors. These perspectives present a challenge to the statist supremacy assumed by current international arrangements and provide an important context for the ECOSOC review by recognizing the crucial role of international civil society. I conclude that the potential for the ECOSOC review to fail to come to grips with the fundamental tensions of the historical relationship between states and NGOs could be reduced by situating its deliberations within the broader context of the future of international governance. If such a contextualization were achieved, the review could assist in the urgent task of reconceptualizing relations between

---

2.   "Civil society" can be understood in many different ways. I am using the term to refer to the networks, movements, and organizations of nonprofit interest groups which form to assert interests, identities, or causes outside state-based and controlled political institutions.

3.   Only a small number of contributions to the review appear to recognize this potential. They include *General Review of Arrangements for Consultations with Non-Governmental Organizations: Report of the Secretary-General*, U.N. ESCOR, Open-Ended Working Group on the Review of Arrangements for Consultations with Non-Governmental Organizations, 1st Sess., Prov. Agenda Item 3, U.N. Doc. E/AC.70/1994/5 (1994) [hereinafter *Report of the Secretary-General*].

states and nonstate entities and extending the discourse of international law beyond the interests of states to hear the many voices currently excluded.

I. THE ECOSOC REVIEW

The UN Charter makes one reference to NGOs, in Article 71, which allows that ECOSOC "may make suitable arrangements for consultation with nongovernmental organizations which are concerned with matters within its competence."[4] The effect of this provision was unprecedented in that it formalized the extensive consultative relationships which had existed during the years of the League of Nations.[5] But Article 71 also limited the earlier practices by confining mandated consultation to the areas covered by ECOSOC[6] and by limiting involvement to "consultation" in contrast, for example, to the ability of representatives of UN specialized agencies and member states to "participate without vote" in ECOSOC deliberations.[7] The present arrangements for consultation with NGOs, the subject of the review, are set out in ECOSOC Resolution 1296(XLIV) of 27 May 1968 (hereinafter Resolution 1296).[8] By 1993, nearly 1000 NGOs had been granted formal consultative status with ECOSOC by way of these arrangements.[9] There is no doubt that the extent of NGO involvement in UN activities has vastly exceeded the expectations of those who drafted the Charter and dramatically outstripped the scope of these legal provisions.

In this part of my article the primary focus is the principles which should guide UN-NGO relationships. I turn first to issues associated with defining international NGOs. Second, I briefly map a background to the current state of UN-NGO consultative arrangements. Third, I examine the issues which have precipitated the OEWG review. Finally, I consider the

---

4.   Article 71 continues, "Such arrangements may be made with international organizations and, where appropriate, with national organizations after consultation with the Member of the United Nations concerned." U.N. CHARTER art. 71.

5.   CHIANG PEI-HENG, NON-GOVERNMENTAL ORGANIZATIONS AT THE UNITED NATIONS 34–39 (1981).

6.   The areas that fall within the competence of ECOSOC are "international economic, social, cultural, educational, health, scientific, technological and related matters and to questions of human rights." E.S.C. Res. 1296 (XLIV) B, U.N. ESCOR, art.1 [hereinafter Resolution 1296].

7.   U.N. CHARTER arts. 69 & 70.

8.   This resolution superseded earlier arrangements set out by E.S.C. Res. 3 (II), U.N. ESCOR (1946) and E.S.C. Res. 288B (X), U.N. ESCOR (1950).

9.   *Report of the Secretary-General, supra* note 3, at 17. In 1993 there were 978 NGOs in consultative status over the three categories of status recognized by Resolution 1296: forty-two in category I (NGOs with general competence in ECOSOC activities), 376 in category II (NGOs with special competence in particular ECOSOC activities), and 560 on the roster (NGOs who can make occasional useful contributions to ECOSOC activities). *Id.*

responses the review has elicited and, in light of these, its possible out-comes. I conclude that there is a chance that the result will be an erosion of the current levels of NGO participation in the UN system.

1. Defining International NGOs

The negative language of the UN Charter, which simply defines NGOs as *not* governmental organizations, gives little guidance to the question of what constitutes an NGO. But it does reveal the defensive position of states towards NGOs and their insistence that the status of an NGO is peripheral to that of a state. An early example of the strength of states' resolve on this issue was the decision of ECOSOC that its subsidiary commissions be entirely composed of states representatives, despite the Dumbarton Oaks proposal that they be made up of experts.[10] This guarded state-centric approach reflects a continuing and pervasive tension in UN arrangements for cooperation between states and NGOs.

The restrictive system envisaged by the Charter was further narrowed by Resolution 1296, which was shaped by cold war paranoia about the political allegiances that some NGOs, particularly those with a human rights orientation, were perceived to have with states on either side of the East-West divide. New provisions enabling the suspension or withdrawal of consultative status were added to the previous arrangements,[11] and strict financial procedures were set out, requiring NGOs to declare the sources of their funds and fully account for any financial or other support received from governments.[12]

Resolution 1296 has certain other requirements of NGO candidates for consultative status which influence definition. The organization must not have been established by intergovernmental agreement;[13] its aims and purposes must be consistent with the principles and spirit of the UN Charter;[14] its work must support and promote the work of the UN;[15] it must be broadly representative of its field of competence, have recognized international standing, and cover, where possible, a significant number of countries in different regions of the world;[16] it must have an established headquarters and a democratically adopted constitution which provides for

---

10.   Declan O'Donovan, *The Economic and Social Council, in* THE UNITED NATIONS AND HUMAN
        RIGHTS 107, 110 (Philip Alston ed., 1992).
11.   Resolution 1296, *supra* note 6, pt. VIII.
12.   *Id.* art. 8.
13.   *Id.* art. 7.
14.   *Id.* art. 2.
15.   *Id.* art. 3.
16.   *Id.* art. 4.

determination of policy by the membership;[17] and a national organization would only qualify under exceptional circumstances and then not without the agreement of the state concerned.[18] These criteria have been narrowly interpreted[19] and have shaped the form and operation of international NGOs. Controversies associated with these requirements include concern about their Western bias, the restrictiveness of the stipulations of cross-regional membership, "international standing," and "established headquarters," and the virtual exclusion of national NGOs. These issues will be discussed in the following sections.

Other factors, besides ECOSOC guidelines, influence the shape and purposes of NGOs in the international community. Of primary importance are developments that occur over time, as local, regional, and international communities become more interdependent and as the dominant discourse of international relations changes. Angus Archer, for example, notes a shift in the "nonpolitical" orientation of NGOs during the 1960s as many questioned the effectiveness of their benevolent humanitarian focus and, as a result, broadened their mandates to ensure that the root causes of poverty, hunger, social, and economic injustices were included on their agendas.[20] More recent changes in types of NGOs and their modes of operation are due in part to the globalization of information and communication technology, as observed by the Secretary-General in his report.[21]

It is clear that NGOs are not satisfactorily defined by a unitary category and that this is an important issue for the OEWG.[22] There are many possible typological approaches to classification of NGOs, including their function, size, resource base, geographical spread, membership, area of interest,

---

17. *Id.* art. 5.
18. *Id.* art. 9.
19. Adama Dieng, *NGO Access to United Nations Human Rights Procedures: How Can It Be Improved without Affecting the Rights Already Acquired by NGOs in Consultative Status with ECOSOC?* at 1 (on file with author). Dieng is the Secretary-General of the International Commission of Jurists and prepared this discussion paper for the World Conference on Human Rights, Vienna, 1993.
20. Angus Archer, *Methods of Multilateral Management: The Interrelationship of International Organizations and NGOs, in* THE US, THE UN, AND THE MANAGEMENT OF GLOBAL CHANGE 303, 309 (Toby Trister Gati ed., 1983).
21. *Report of the Secretary-General, supra* note 3, ¶¶ 4, 5, 7, and 43. The report mentions, as examples, the growth of informal international, regional, and national coalitions and networks, and national and regional organizations that are not affiliated with any international NGO.
22. *Id.* ¶¶ 9–10. The Secretary-General suggests some general characteristics:

> An NGO is a non-profit entity whose members are citizens or associations of citizens of one or more countries and whose activities are determined by the collective will of its members in response to the needs of the members or of one or more communities with which the NGO cooperates.

Id. ¶ 9.

degree of institutionalization, and philosophical orientation. However, these typologies are, at best, partial. At a minimum, the elusiveness of a satisfactory definition should encourage flexibility and open-endedness.[23] Even better would be to reject the quest for certitude altogether on the basis that closed categories tend to control rather than encourage participation and creativity. An alternative would be to use inclusive definitional tools based on the principle that NGOs are essential to participatory democracy in the international community. This would prioritize definitional concepts that ensure a diversity of viewpoints, legitimate a heterogeneity of NGO forms, and encourage an open and dynamic exchange of ideas and experience.

For the purposes of my analysis, which seeks to link the ECOSOC review with developments associated with international governance and civil society, it is instructive to use as my reference point those NGOs that have their foundations in the "new social movements." By this I mean organizations that aim to represent values and aspirations associated with peoples rather than with states,[24] including the promotion of human rights, gender and race equality, environmental protection, sustainable development, indigenous rights, nonviolent conflict resolution, participatory democracy, social diversity, and social and economic justice.[25] The aptness of focussing this discussion on the consultative status of peoples-based NGOs is three-fold. First, the issues of international democratization link squarely with the concerns of these movements which aim to promote links between the global and local participation of individuals and communities.[26] Second,

---

23. *Working with Non-Governmental Organizations: Operational Activities for Development of the United Nations System with Nongovernmental Organizations and Governments at the Grass-Roots and National Levels: Note by the Secretary-General*, ¶ 15, U.N. GAOR, 49th Sess., Preliminary List Item 12, U.N. ESCOR, Substantive Sess. 1994, Prov. Agenda Item 10, U.N. Doc. A/49/122-E/1994/44 (1994) (Joint Inspection Unit Working with Nongovernmental Organizations) suggests that UN agencies and other organizations working with NGOs must determine for themselves the types and categories of NGOs that they wish to work with, rather than trying to formulate a single common definition.

24. Lorraine Elliott, *International Conference on Diplomacy and the Changing Role of NGOs, in* Australian and New Zealand Society of International Law: Proceedings of the Second Annual Meeting 223, 225 (1994), refers to them as NGOs that "speak not for themselves, but in the interests of broader social values." In this context, "peoples" has a much broader meaning than groupings who identify on the basis of race, culture, or ethnicity.

25. Richard Falk, *The Global Promise of Social Movements: Explorations at the Edge of Time*, 12 Alternatives 173 (1987); Marc Nerfin, *Neither Prince nor Merchant: Citizen— An Introduction to the Third System, in* World Economy in Transition 47 (Krishna Ahooja-Patel et al. eds., 1986). States may also share some of these aspirational goals, but my interest is in those nonstate entities that are speaking for groups and individuals who do not believe that states are adequately representing their interests.

26. Dianne Otto, *Challenging the "New World Order": International Law, Global Democracy and the Possibilities for Women*, 3 Transnat'l L.& Contemp. Probs. 371, 399 (1993).

the focus of many long-standing NGOs has also shifted to include the participation of local communities.[27] And third, the recent upsurge of NGOs wishing to participate in UN policy development comes largely from this grouping, as will be discussed in the next section.

2. Background to Current UN-NGO Relationships

The relationship between the UN and NGOs has always been one of controversy and fluctuation. In the early years of the UN, there was strong cooperation between ECOSOC and those NGOs with social and humanitarian concerns.[28] However, Communist and Third World states adopted a general policy of opposition to NGOs, for different reasons,[29] and the attitude of Western states was often characterized by prevarication and opportunism.[30] In the early 1950s, consultative status was withdrawn from four NGOs as the result of efforts of the United Kingdom (UK) and the United States (US), who were unhappy with the NGOs' criticisms of the US and the UN's role in Korea.[31] In this situation, the Soviet Union (USSR) defended the NGOs involved. The expulsions were achieved despite there being no provision for this in ECOSOC Resolution 288B(X), which governed consultative arrangements at the time.[32] Since then, there has been only one expulsion—that of the International Lesbian and Gay Association (ILGA) in 1994—which I will discuss later in this section.[33]

As the cold war intensified and its effects devastated ECOSOC, the UN-NGO relationship deteriorated further. The perception that ECOSOC was Western-dominated led to many of its functions being usurped by the Third World dominated General Assembly, and UN specialized agencies established good working relationships with NGOs, regardless of their consultative status. Most damaging was ECOSOC's inability to assume its important

---

27. *Report of the Secretary-General, supra* note 3, ¶ 19 notes that development NGOs have moved from an initial focus on "relief and welfare to community development to [,currently,] sustainable systems development" which emphasizes the link between local and global issues.
28. Archer, *supra* note 20, at 306.
29. Pei-Heng, *supra* note 5, at 185.
30. *Id.* at 201.
31. *Id.* In 1950 the International Association of Democratic Lawyers (based in Brussels) and the International Organization of Journalists (based in Prague) were expelled, and the World Federation of Democratic Youth (based in Budapest) was demoted to the Register. E.S.C. Res. 334A (XI), U.N. ESCOR (1950). In 1954 the Women's International Democratic Federation (based in Berlin, GDR) was also expelled. E.S.C. Res. 529B (XVII), U.N. ESCOR (1954).
32. Provisions for suspension and withdrawal of consultative status were included in Resolution 1296, *supra* note 5, pt. VIII.
33. Melbourne Star Observer, 12 Oct. 1994. The International Gay and Lesbian Association (ILGA) was expelled in September 1994.

economic role, which, instead, became spread throughout the UN system.[34] In Archer's view, the consultative status relationship plunged to its lowest ebb in the late 1960s.[35] This crisis, most evident in the political sensitivities that surrounded the role of NGOs, led to the first major review of consultative arrangements in 1968–1969. Four issues dominated this review: concerns about the Western domination of NGOs in consultative status;[36] the extent of government influence on NGO activities;[37] the expanding numbers of NGOs;[38] and the criticisms of governments by human rights NGOs.[39]

Resolution 1296 was the formal outcome of this review. It introduced new mechanisms of control which enabled periodic reviews and the suspension or withdrawal of consultative status in certain circumstances, including where there was evidence of secret financial influence by governments[40] or where an NGO had "systematically engag[ed] in unsubstantiated or politically motivated acts against [s]tates."[41] It should be noted that the latter provision, in combination with the UN Charter's protection of states' domestic autonomy,[42] could conceivably be used to gag the contributions of human rights NGOs and others critical of states' domestic activities.

Although the review highlighted fundamental divisions between states and further politicized UN-NGO relationships,[43] paradoxically, there were also some positive outcomes. In spite of the blistering attacks made on many NGOs in the course of the review, ultimately the consultative status of most NGOs remained the same, and no organization was suspended or expelled.[44] Also, the review revealed a shift over the years in the attitudes of Communist and Third World states which was leading to the establishment of more NGOs based in the East and a revaluing of NGOs by the South, particularly those involved with development.[45]

---

34. Archer, *supra* note 20, at 306.
35. *Id.* at 307.
36. Pᴇɪ-ʜᴇɴɢ, *supra* note 5, at 175. More than 90% of the NGOs reviewed had their headquarters in the West.
37. I have already referred to the paranoia of the cold war, which led to the adoption of strict procedures to police financial accountability.
38. Pᴇɪ-ʜᴇɴɢ, *supra* note 5, at 176. At various stages both the US and the USSR proposed grouping similar NGOs in order to reduce their number. The proposed groupings unashamedly reflected the interests of the super powers. For example, the USSR review proposal was that all Jewish, Catholic, and social welfare NGOs be grouped so that they were represented by three overarching NGOs.
39. *Id.* at 178.
40. Resolution 1296, *supra* note 6, art. 36(a).
41. *Id.* art. 36(b).
42. U.N. Cʜᴀʀᴛᴇʀ art. 2(7).
43. Pᴇɪ-ʜᴇɴɢ, *supra* note 5, at 185.
44. *Id.* at 182–83.
45. *Id.* at 186.

The shift towards wider state support for NGO participation in the UN was clearly apparent by the second review in 1978. It was initiated almost single-handedly by Argentina, and the sole motivation was to condemn activities of human rights NGOs.[46] The review underlined the fundamental nature of the continuing antipathy of states towards these NGOs. As Chiang Pei-heng observes, "NGO criticism of human-rights violations seems to be one of the few issues which cause many governments of both the right and left to close ranks, ignoring ideological differences."[47] However, many states confined their criticisms to a few NGOs and took the opportunity to praise the work of others, pointing to the fact that the UN is almost totally dependent on NGOs to provide expertise in many areas.[48] Some states went further suggesting that NGOs play an important role in representing aspects of global public opinion and aspirations of peoples of the world,[49] although there were ominous signs that proponents of the opposing view remained undeterred.[50]

The implementation of Resolution 1296 has been discussed by the Committee on NGOs over a number of years.[51] Recurring problems have included the lack of uniform rules and procedures for NGO participation throughout the UN system, including UN conferences; the lack of resources available for implementation of Resolution 1296; the need for a special fund to encourage greater participation by Third World NGOs; and the need to rationalize the workload of the Committee, perhaps by reducing the numbers of NGOs seeking consultative status.[52] These issues remain unresolved.

The Committee on NGOs has itself been consistently controversial. Early discord about the Committee's Western bias was resolved in 1966 when ECOSOC decided that membership be based on equitable geographical

---

46.   *Id.* at 187.
47.   *Id.* at 193.
48.   *Id.* at 192, 194. Examples given are the areas of human rights, women, development, apartheid, and refugees.
49.   *Id.* at 191. For example, in the view of the UK government, NGOs "represent large segments of public opinion throughout the world," and the government of the Federal Republic of Germany commented that NGOs "can be regarded as a kind of spokesman [sic] for those who, due to political situations, cannot raise their voice in the UN."
50.   *Id.* at 193. The view of the Syrian Arab Republic described many NGOs as "blatantly violating . . . the principles and provisions" of the UN Charter by acting according to "political or local regional motives."
51.   The Committee on NGOs (a committee of states) was established by E.S.C. Res.3(II), *supra* note 8. Its current role and functions are set out by Resolution 1296, *supra* note 6, pt. IX. They include dealing with applications for consultative status, quadrennial reports from NGOs in categories I and II, and other aspects of the implementation and monitoring of Resolution 1296.
52.   *Report of the Secretary-General, supra* note 3, at 18–24.

distribution.[53] Its current membership comprises nineteen states. Arguably, the most contentious aspect of the Committee's practice has been its informal adoption of consensus decisionmaking. During the cold war this meant that member states were able to veto applications from the opposing side of the East-West dichotomy.[54] This practice has proved effective in preventing or deferring the granting of consultative status to controversial NGOs.[55]

Unfortunately, decisions of the Committee on NGOs have not been any less "political"[56] since the end of the cold war.[57] States who have been criticized by human rights NGOs continue to attempt to block accreditation.[58] This forced the Committee to a vote for the first time in March 1993, and, as a result, majority decisions were made to recommend to ECOSOC that both Human Rights Watch and ILGA be accredited.[59] ECOSOC accepted these recommendations in July 1993 with significant support coming from Western, East European, and Latin American states and strong opposition from Asian and African states.[60] Following this, antihomosexual groups in the US began questioning the US's support for ILGA, claiming that its accreditation gave pedophile groups access to the UN. This campaign

53. The Committee had an original membership of five. E.S.C. Res. 288B (X), *supra* note 8, increased this to seven. E.S.C. Res. 1099 (XL), U.N. ESCOR (1966) introduced equitable geographical distribution of membership and raised the number of members to thirteen. E.S.C. Res. 1981/50, U.N. ESCOR raised this again to nineteen. Membership comprises five from African states, four from Asian states, two from Eastern Europe, four from Latin American and Caribbean states, and four from Western Europe and other states.

54. Laurie Wiseberg, *NGO Self-Examination is the Missing Link in ECOSOC Review*, Hum. Rts. Trib., Apr. 1994, at 11, 12. Wiseberg points out that during the cold war, this practice led to NGO accreditation only after "backroom deals."

55. O'Donovan, *supra* note 10, at 111.

56. I do not confine the meaning of "political" to its narrow liberal conceptualization as an autonomous sphere of social activity defined by the formal political processes of states. Rather, I define politics as involving all aspects of interpersonal and intercommunity social arrangements, including, in the international sphere, the "private" or domestic activities of peoples and states. For further discussion, see Hilary Charlesworth, *The Public/Private Distinction and the Right to Development in International Law*, 12 Austl. Y.B. Int'l L. 190 (1992); Lester Edwin J. Ruiz, *After National Democracy: Radical Democratic Politics at the Edge of Modernity*, 16 Alternatives 161 (1991).

57. O'Donovan, *supra* note 10, at 111. In 1991 applications by Human Rights Watch and the International Movement Against All Forms of Discrimination and Racism were deferred.

58. Wiseberg, *supra* note 54.

59. ILGA, *Out at the U.N.: UN Accredits the International Lesbian and Gay Association* 2 (31 Aug. 1993) (media release). Nine states voted in favor of ILGA's application, four voted against, three abstained, and three were not present. The most vocal opponent was Sudan.

60. *Id.* Twenty-two states voted to accept ILGA's application out of a total of fifty-four. Only four states voted against its acceptance: Togo, Swaziland, Malaysia, and Syria, who claimed to speak on behalf of the Third World alliance Group of 77.

gathered momentum, and, in January 1994, the US Senate voted unanimously to withhold $129 million from the UN if it continued to support ILGA.[61] Meanwhile, ILGA was recommending to its members that they vote at its annual conference in June 1994 to expel any member organizations supporting pedophilia. This occurred, but it did not avert the decision by ECOSOC, under intense pressure from the US, to expel ILGA in September 1994.[62] These events raise serious questions of principle about UN/US policing of "unacceptable" international NGOs and reveal the strength of the continuing animosity that many powerful Third World states feel towards human rights NGOs.[63]

A factor that simultaneously compounds and diminishes the difficulties associated with ECOSOC granting of consultative status is the plethora of UN-NGO relationships that operate outside the Resolution 1296 arrangements. These relationships are governed by a broad range of formal and informal procedures. I have already alluded to the relationships that developed between NGOs and UN specialized agencies. International NGOs have also collaborated with UN funds and programs,[64] cooperated with states in UN campaigns,[65] played key roles in devising new human rights standards,[66] provided invaluable assistance to human rights treaty bodies[67] and special rapporteurs,[68] and become increasingly visible in the

---

61. ILGA, UN Newsletter, Mar. 1994.
62. Melbourne Star Observer, *supra* note 33.
63. *See generally* Michael H. Posner, *The Establishment of the Right of Nongovernmental Human Rights Groups to Operate, in* Human Rights: An Agenda for the Next Century 405 (Louis Henkin & John L. Hargrove eds., 1994).
64. *Report of the Secretary-General, supra* note 3, Annex II *(Relations between Non-Governmental Organizations to the Funds Programmes of the United Nations)* summarizes relationships between UN funds and programs and NGOs.
65. Archer, *supra* note 20, refers to campaigns about hunger, environment, and women's issues.
66. Several collaborations are notable: Amnesty International's role in the adoption of the Convention against Torture, see Peter R. Baehr & Leon Gordenker, The United Nations in the 1990s 116 (1992); NGOs' participation in the drafting of the Convention on the Rights of the Child and in its implementation, see Cynthia Price Cohen, *The Role of Nongovernmental Organizations in the Drafting of the Convention on the Rights of the Child,* 12 Hum. Rts. Q. 137 (1990); and the role of indigenous groups in formulating the Declaration on the Rights of Indigenous Peoples, see Catherine J. Iorns, *Indigenous Peoples and Self Determination: Challenging State Sovereignty,* 24 Case W. Res. J. Int'l L. 199 (1992).
67. The Committee on Economic, Social and Cultural Rights is currently the only treaty-monitoring body that encourages NGOs to formally submit written submissions, but all treaty bodies are heavily dependent on NGO input. Posner, *supra* note 63, at 416–17. *See* Howard B. Tolley Jr., The International Commission of Jurists: Global Advocates for Human Rights (1994).
68. Bacre Waly Ndiaye, UN Special Rapporteur on Summary or Arbitrary Executions, said, when he visited Australia in 1993, that he relies on Amnesty International for over 65% of the information he uses. 11(10) Amnesty International Australian Newsletter 10 (1993).

work of many General Assembly committees.[69] In addition, many NGOs are "listed" with the UN's Department of Public Information (DPI), which ensures that they receive regular information on UN activities.[70] Of unique significance in the array of UN-NGO relationships is the tripartite system of the International Labour Organization (ILO), where workers' and employers' NGOs participate, as full members, alongside states.[71]

Arguably the most far-reaching of the UN-NGO relationships that exist outside the purview of Resolution 1296 is the role that NGOs have assumed in relation to UN intergovernmental conferences.[72] The participation of NGOs, as members of states' delegations[73] and in activities run parallel to the governmental conferences, has snowballed over the last twenty years. As NGOs gradually develop cooperative strategies and adopt collectively determined positions, their impact is becoming increasingly influential. These developments peaked with the open accreditation processes of the 1992 UN Conference on Environment and Development (UNCED), which formally recognized the participation of some 1500 NGOs.[74] The resulting Rio Declaration and plan for sustainable development, Agenda 21, spell out a continuing critical role for regional, national, local, and specialized NGOs.[75] To this end, the Commission on Sustainable Development (CSD) has liberalized access to its ongoing consultative processes in order to

---

69. Archer, *supra* note 20, at 310, identifies the promotion of the New International Economic Order by the Third World as playing a significant role in forging these relationships. *See also Report of the Secretary-General, supra* note 3, at 42. *See generally* THE NEW INTERNATIONAL ECONOMIC ORDER (Karl P. Sauvant & Hajo Hasenpflug eds., 1977).

70. Archer, *supra* note 20, at 307–08. About 1500 NGOs were listed in 1992. These arrangements were set up in 1946 and, in Archer's view, have tended to reinforce the idea that NGOs are relatively passive conduits of information in the UN system. G.A. Res. 13 (I), U.N. GAOR, Annex I provides the mandate for DPI work with NGOs.

71. Virginia A. Leary, *Lessons from the Experience of the International Labour Organisation,* in THE UNITED NATIONS AND HUMAN RIGHTS, *supra* note 10, at 580, 584.

72. In this respect, Archer emphasizes the significance of the World Food Congresses organized by the Food and Agricultural Organization (FAO) in 1963 and 1970. Archer, *supra,* note 20, at 311–14.

73. Joann Schmider, *International Conference Diplomacy and the Changing Role of NGOs in International Law,* in AUSTRALIAN AND NEW ZEALAND SOCIETY OF INTERNATIONAL LAW: PROCEEDINGS OF THE SECOND ANNUAL MEETING 235 (1994) [hereinafter PROCEEDINGS].

74. G.A. Res. 44/228, U.N. GAOR, 44th Sess., Agenda Item 82(f), U.N. Doc. A/Res/44/228 (1990); G.A. Res. 45/211, U.N. GAOR, 45th Sess., Agenda Item 80, U.N. Doc. A/Res/45/211 (1991); G.A. Res. 46/168, U.N. GAOR, 46th Sess., Agenda Item 78, U.N. Doc. A/Res/46/168 (1992); PrepCom Decision 2/1.

75. *Report of the United Nations Conference on Environment and Development,* U.N. Conference on Environment and Development, U.N.Doc.A/CONF.151/26 (Vol.III) § III (1992) (*The Rio Declaration on Environment and Development*), recognizes "major groups" as important segments and constituencies of civil society which are indispensable to the success of Agenda 21.

include the UNCED NGOs.[76] In addition, these NGOs have been granted ECOSOC Roster status if they comply with criteria that are much broader than those set out by Resolution 1296.[77] This has created a second track to accreditation under Resolution 1296 that operates according to less rigid criteria.[78] Many states and NGOs already in consultative status are concerned that this will lead to a flood of management problems and an erosion of the rights currently enjoyed by accredited NGOs.[79]

In marked contrast to UNCED, the 1993 World Conference on Human Rights (WCHR) largely excluded NGOs from the official process because of the efforts of many Arab and Asian states who argued for restricted NGO access at every opportunity.[80] As a result, the Vienna Declaration implicitly established restrictions on NGO activity.[81] The UN Secretariat unfortunately added legitimacy to the antagonistic positions of some states in attempting to exclude references to specific states in the parallel NGO Forum's program and in excluding the Dalai Lama from speaking at it.[82] Despite this, large numbers of NGOs attended the parallel conference activities which nevertheless impacted on the official deliberations. Since then, UN world conferences on population and development, social development, and women have continued the practice of adopting liberal criteria for NGO participation.[83] As a result, these conferences were fundamentally influenced by the nongovernmental sector, and this is reflected in their outcomes. The Platform of Action of the 1994 International Conference on Population and Development (ICPD) devotes an entire chapter to strengthening the partnership between governments and NGOs, which is described as "essential . . . to assist in the formulation, implementation, monitoring and evaluation of population and development objectives and activities."[84] In a similar vein, the Programme of Action adopted by the 1995 World Summit for Social Development (WSSD) also stresses that the involvement of civil society is required for its effective implementation and that particular support must be directed towards the development of community

---

76. *Report of the Secretary-General, supra* note 3, ¶ 101.
77. E.S.C. Res. 1993/215, U.N. ESCOR. About 550 NGOs were added to the roster as a result. *Report of the Secretary-General, supra* note 3, ¶ 131.
78. *Report of the Secretary-General, supra* note 3, ¶ 132.
79. Dieng, *supra* note 19, at 7–8.
80. *Id.* at 8.
81. Thomas Hammarberg, *A Question of Principle, in* Human Rights—The New Consensus 23 (Richard Reoch ed., 1994).
82. Schmider, *supra* note 73, at 239.
83. G.A. Res. 48/108, U.N. GAOR, 48th Sess., Agenda Item 111, U.N. Doc. A/Res/48/108 (1994) (*Implementation of the Nairobi Forward-Looking Strategies for the Advancement of Women*); PrepCom, organizational session (World Summit for Social Development).
84. *Report of the United Nations Conference on Population and Development,* U.N. Doc. A/CONF.171/13, ch. XV, ¶ 15(1) (1994).

organizations and NGOs among disadvantaged and vulnerable people.[85] Most recently, the 1995 Fourth World Conference on Women (FWCW) proved to be the largest UN conference ever held.[86] In addition to 400 participating NGOs with ECOSOC accreditation, there were almost 2500 other NGOs accredited to the conference.[87] Echoing the earlier conferences, the Declaration and Platform for Action identify the participation of women's groups and networks and other NGOs as critical to follow-up and the implementation of conference commitments.[88]

Richard Falk refers to the NGO activities run parallel to intergovernmental conferences as "counter-conferences" whose outlook is "instinctively based on human solidarity."[89] This is consistent with my view that the growing force of NGOs in the international community is due primarily to the emergence of new social movements consciously concerned with issues of peoples rather than states. The growth of international civil society is both reflected and bolstered by the groundswell of NGO participation in international conferences. It has introduced a new dynamic of embryonic participatory democracy to the global community and to the shaping of international law.[90] This development has also played a major part in precipitating the current ECOSOC review.

3. Issues Precipitating the Review

The burgeoning number of NGOs seeking to participate in UN conferences, and other processes which enable them to have an ongoing involvement in UN legal and political decisionmaking, is a primary impetus for the ECOSOC review. The uncoordinated array of arrangements operating outside the Resolution 1296 mechanisms are of concern to many players. Related to this issue is the constraint, set in place by the UN Charter, which limits official consultative relationships to activities of ECOSOC. Yet the competence of NGOs covers the entire breadth of UN activities. This includes the work of the General Assembly (GA), as evidenced by the existing strength of many GA-NGO relationships, and that of the Security

---

85. *Report of the World Summit on Social Development*, ch. V, ¶ 85.
86. AMNESTY INTERNATIONAL, REPORT ON THE FOURTH WORLD CONFERENCE ON WOMEN 22 (1995).
87. *Id.* at 17.
88. *Fourth World Conference on Women: Action for Equality, Development and Peace, Beijing Declaration and Platform for Action* ¶ 20 (advance unedited draft). NGOs are identified throughout the Platform for Action as playing a role in achieving the strategic objectives identified. *See, e.g.*, ¶ 62.
89. Falk, *supra* note 25, at 187.
90. Elliott, *supra* note 24, at 232.

Council, which currently dominates the work of the UN, yet is the least democratic UN structure.[91]

A second stimulus for the ECOSOC review is the growing recognition of the indispensability of NGOs to many aspects of the UN's work, particularly in the area of economic and social development. The UNCED process left this beyond doubt. Sustainable development simply is not possible without the empowerment of communities to participate in decisions that affect their lives.[92] Since UNCED, recognition of the necessity of NGO participation in global, as well as national, affairs has been consistently reaffirmed by successive UN world conferences. The restrictive criteria of Resolution 1296 militate against these developments, especially with the requirements that NGOs have "international standing" and "established headquarters." In combination with the exclusion of most national NGOs by the guidelines and the ability of states to veto applications from NGOs within their territory, the vast majority of the new peoples-centered NGOs are precluded by the current arrangements. Resolution 1296 is simply inconsistent with movement towards recognizing a diversity of NGOs and broadening and deepening their role in the international community.

A third concern, related to the second, is that Resolution 1296 favors Western-dominated NGOs which are more likely to have the resources to develop "international standing" and less likely to be thwarted by legal and other intimidatory restrictions set in train by the state at the domestic level. This raises the important question of the responsibility of the international community to ensure that all states allow NGOs to operate freely within and across their borders.[93] Despite these obstacles, the number of NGOs in Third World countries has increased dramatically in the last ten years, but most of them are small.[94] The exclusion of national organizations from ECOSOC accreditation operates to specifically disadvantage Third World NGOs.

A fourth catalyst for the review is the equivocal (if not hostile) attitude of many states towards NGOs, particularly those NGOs involved with challenging human rights violations by states. This factor offsets the desire of some states to see an enhanced role for NGOs in UN activities and

---

91. International peace and disarmament have been primary issues for international NGOs, many of whom predate the formation of the UN and even the League of Nations.
92. *Agenda 21, Report of the United Nations Conference on Environment and Development,* U.N. Conference on Environment and Development, U.N. Doc. A/CONF.151/26 (Vol.I), Annex I, at 8–13 (1992). The preamble refers to "a new and equitable global partnership" between "states, key sectors of societies and peoples," and Article 27 refers to "states and people" cooperating "in good faith and in a spirit of partnership" in achieving sustainable development.
93. Posner, *supra* note 63, at 409–11.
94. *Report of the Secretary-General, supra* note 3, ¶ 17.

threatens to limit the review's scope to the defense, rather than the promotion, of international NGO participation.

Finally, the review has many financial, administrative, and operational issues to address. The limited resources of the UN, seriously eroded by the US decision not to honor hundreds of millions of dollars in UN debts and by the late payment of dues by most member states,[95] place the review in an environment of economic restraint. In addition, the cumbersome bureaucratic processes involved with the current arrangements need urgent attention. A detailed examination of these issues is beyond the scope of this essay, but they potentially place powerful limitations on the review's scope.[96]

The issues precipitating the current review are strikingly similar to those which have plagued the operation of Article 71 since its initial draft. They go to the core conundrum of the unresolved relationship between states and NGOs in the international community. The efforts by states to control the activities of international NGOs by regulation and powers of veto are opened, by the review, for questioning. But there is the real possibility that the combined effects of states' paranoia about human rights NGOs, states' fears about loss of domestic power, financial pressures, and lack of vision about future arrangements able to cope with large numbers of heterogeneous NGOs will result in a reaffirmation of the need for tight and restrictive consultative arrangements.

4. Responses to the Review and Possible Outcomes

The response to the review from NGOs who currently enjoy consultative status has been varied.[97] An examination of fourteen NGO statements submitted to the OEWG at its first substantive session in June 1994 reveals one conditional area of agreement—there is support for expanding UN-NGO relationships *provided* that this does not reduce any of the rights currently attached to Resolution 1296 status.[98] Although the self-interest in

---

95. Richard W. Nelson, *International Law and US Withholding of Payments to International Organizations*, 80 Am. J. Int'l L. 973 (1986); William Pace, *Guest Editorial*, 43 Go-Between (UN Nongovernmental Liaison Service) 20 (1993).

96. See Joint Inspection Unit Report, JIU/REP/93/1 which was presented to ECOSOC as a Note by the Secretary-General. A/49/122-E/1994/44, *supra* note 23. The Secretary-General's report also deals with many operational issues. *Report of the Secretary-General, supra* note 3, ¶¶ 102–07.

97. Wiseberg, *supra* note 54, observes a split between those veteran NGOs who are worried about being squeezed out by the newer grass roots organizations and those who want the guidelines broadened.

98. *General Review of Arrangements for Consultations with Non-Governmental Organizations*, U.N. ESCOR, Open-Ended Working Group on the Review of Arrangements for

many of these statements is palpable, this concern is well-founded. Adama Dieng catalogues an emerging pattern of reduced participation rights accompanying expanded NGO access to UN bodies like the CSD and the Committee on the Rights of the Child.[99] There is no doubt that trading off increased access with reduced quality of participation is not an acceptable solution.

A majority of the NGO statements take the conservative position of support for Resolution 1296 as a valuable framework for future consultative arrangements and suggest that it is necessary to safeguard the procedures and categories outlined in it. Suggestions for minor reform include expansion of its range to include all UN bodies[100] and some ability for national NGOs to be accredited.[101] Unfortunately, most NGOs revealed a defensiveness about the proposition that Western NGOs currently dominate. Many responded to this charge by stressing that their membership comprised a majority of Third World affiliates.[102] This response avoids the issue of the Western form of most international NGOs which *is* an issue of major concern. Most NGOs also defended the importance of maintaining a distinction between global NGOs and those which they perceive to be more limited in focus and base.[103] It was suggested that alternative methods be explored for creating opportunities for nonglobal NGOs to participate meaningfully in UN activities.[104] The majority also argued for consistency and transparency in rules regulating participation in UN conferences.

A minority of NGOs took a broader approach, arguing that Resolution 1296's exclusion of local, national, and regional organizations with global concerns was inappropriately restrictive in a context of diverse forms and roles of NGOs.[105] Concern was expressed about the hierarchical structure of

---

Consultations with Non-Governmental Organizations, 1st Sess., Prov. Agenda Item 3, U.N. Doc. E/AC.70/1994/NGO/1–11; and statements from the Australian Conservation Foundation (ACF), Women's Environment and Development Organization (WEDO), and Amnesty International (AI).

99.   Dieng, *supra* note 19, at 7–10. Dieng refers to abolition of the right to have NGO written statements circulated as official UN documents, reduced speaking rights in official sessions, and removal of the rights to participate in negotiating working instruments.

100. E/AC.70/1994/NGO/6, *supra* note 98, ¶ 10 (Conference of NGOs (CONGO)).

101. E/AC.70/1994/NGO/1, *supra* note 98 (World Federation of UN Associations (WFUNA)); E/AC.70/1994/NGO/2, *supra* note 98 (International Confederation of Free Trade Unions (ICFTU)).

102. For example, E/AC.70/1994/NGO/2, *supra* note 98, ¶¶ 2–3 (ICFTU); and E/AC.70/1994/NGO/4, *supra* note 98, ¶ 7 (International Chamber of Commerce (ICC)).

103. E/AC.70/1994/NGO/4, *supra* note 98, ¶ 6 (ICC).

104. E/AC.70/1994/NGO/1, *supra* note 98, ¶ 3 (WFUNA); E/AC.70/1994/NGO/6, *supra* note 98, ¶ 3 (CONGO); Statement on behalf of AI, *supra* note 98; and statement on behalf of the International Federation of Human Rights.

105. E/AC.70/1994/NGO/7, *supra* note 98, ¶ 8 (ActionAid); ACF, *supra* note 98; WEDO, *supra* note 98.

the existing system of classification of NGOs,[106] and it was suggested that it be altered to reflect NGO function or area of expertise.[107] The Women's Environment and Development Organization (WEDO), ActionAid, and the Australian Conservation Foundation (ACF) were the only three NGOs in this sample who explicitly made the important link between the review and issues of the democratization of international governance.

States are likewise divided in their responses to the review. The report of the first substantive session of the OEWG, attended by about sixty states, allows only limited insight into differences in states' views, especially because states' comments are not attributed.[108] Some states argued that Resolution 1296 needed updating to allow expanded NGO participation, while others stressed the importance of retaining the ability to exclude NGOs whose objectives were incompatible with those of the UN and recommended enforcing a strict code of NGO conduct.[109] A number of states argued for mechanisms that would ensure greater participation by Third World NGOs, including adoption of the principle of equitable geographical representation and the establishment of a fund to facilitate this.[110] States' views on the present system of NGO categorization ranged from supporting maintenance of the *status quo* to suggesting a total revamp.[111] Many states supported extension of consultative arrangements to encompass other bodies of the UN, but differed about how far this should spread.[112]

According to some commentators, the strongest views expressed at the OEWG were those of states who are antagonistic to NGOs, including Cuba, India, Indonesia, China, and African and Middle Eastern countries.[113] Regrettably, Western delegations were generally reticent about expressing their views which, it could be surmised, may have been due to a fear that opening the scope of the review could result in a downward revision of the existing consultative arrangements.

In contrast to the prevarications of NGOs and states, the Secretary-General's approach to the review is emphatic about the importance of placing it in the broad context of the developing relationship between the

---

106. WEDO, *supra* note 98, at 3.
107. ACF, *supra* note 98.
108. *Report of the Open-Ended Working Group on the Review of Arrangements for Consultation with Non-governmental Organizations*, U.N. GAOR, 49th Sess., Preliminary List Item 12, U.N. ESCOR, Substantive Sess. 1994, Agenda Item 10, U.N. Doc A/49/215-E/1994/99 (1994).
109. *Id.* ¶¶ 55–57.
110. *Id.* ¶¶ 66–73.
111. *Id.* ¶¶ 79–82.
112. *Id.* ¶ 84.
113. These comments have been made to me in confidence. I would hope that acknowledgement of the sources may be possible in due course.

UN system and civil society.[114] The Secretary-General's report to the OEWG is unreservedly positive about the pioneering role that NGOs have played, in national as well as international developments, and categorical about the indispensability of NGO participation in the international community.[115] In this view,

> [Agenda 21] marks a new point of departure for cooperation between institutions of civil society, Governments and the United Nations since it defines a relationship in which the broad non-governmental sector is no longer seen as an instrumentality of governmental and intergovernmental action but as a wide range of institutions that should be involved at all levels . . . and that need to be strengthened in their capacities.[116]

The Secretary-General suggests that the primary objective of the review be to ensure an environment that encourages a strengthened relationship between the UN and institutions of civil society and promotes principles that support civil contributions to global governance.[117]

In summary, there appear to be three potential outcomes from this multifaceted situation. First, there is the possibility that the review will result in a reduced role for NGOs in the UN. If the conservative alliances of states, apparent at the WCHR and other recent world conferences, were able to gain the upper hand, NGO influence would be diminished on the grounds that they are tools of Western governments with little relevance to the heterogeneous international community. Second, the *status quo* of the current arrangements could be reaffirmed, leaving NGOs to continue to play both formal and informal roles that are supportive of and ancillary to states. This outcome would leave most of the issues precipitating the review unresolved. Third, if the Secretary-General's contribution is able to set the framework for the review, it could result in a reconceptualization of the relationship between states and NGOs in the international community. This result would make an important contribution to the democratization of international governance by formally empowering the peoples of civil society to represent their aspirations and values in the global context. This possibility will be explored further in Part II.

II. INTERNATIONAL CIVIL SOCIETY

In tandem with heightened concern about the scope and function of ECOSOC consultative arrangements with NGOs, the end of the cold war

---

114. *See Report of the Secretary-General, supra* note 3.
115. *Id.* ¶ 14.
116. *Id.* ¶ 47.
117. *Id.* ¶ 111(a)(i).

has precipitated a reevaluation of the appropriateness of a UN shaped by post–WWII practicalities and sensibilities. As commentators portend the ascendancy of liberal democracy as a global phenomenon,[118] it is hardly surprising that the dearth of democratic mechanisms in the structure of the UN is under the spotlight. Until now, the lack of democracy in the UN has been justified by the dominant realist discourse of international relations which accepts that realities of global power arrangements, rather than shared values or interests, form the foundational principle of international cooperation.[119] This discourse is now facing serious challenge from both liberal and postliberal camps, which are disputing the statist supremacy assumed by the current arrangements and asserting the importance of international civil society.

A fundamental claim of those promoting change is that the interests of states and peoples are not necessarily coterminous. They are asserting that the multidimensional identities of the world's peoples are not adequately represented by the unidimensional idea of nationality. Liberals argue that this is particularly so in the case of undemocratic states,[120] while proponents of a postliberal future reject the individualism and free market orientation of liberalism and seek, instead, to transform the liberal paradigm.[121] Both liberal and postliberal perspectives have played a part in informing the expanded UN-NGO relationships that have developed in recent years. While some lament that the end of the cold war has left us with a world devoid of alternatives,[122] others argue that the new social movements and their companion NGOs are leading the way towards a more egalitarian and socially just international community.[123]

In this part of my article, I look at discussions of the future shape of the international community and, in particular, at the roles envisaged for international civil society. I commence by examining what is meant by international civil society and what part international NGOs play within it, focussing again on the new social movements as in Part I. Second, I canvass the different alternatives posed by liberal and postliberal perspectives. Finally, I relate these theoretical perspectives to the ECOSOC review and its

---

118. Thomas M. Franck, *The Emerging Right to Democratic Governance*, 86 Am. J. Int'l L. 46 (1992).
119. Gerry Simpson, *Some Recent Theoretical Orientations in International Law*, in Proceedings, *supra* note 73, at 142, 146.
120. Fernando R. Tesón, *The Kantian Theory of International Law*, 92 Colum. L. Rev. 53 (1992).
121. *See* Leslie P. Thiele, *Making Democracy Safe for the World: Social Movements and Global Politics*, 18 Alternatives 273 (1993).
122. *See* Rajni Kothari, *The Yawning Vacuum: A World Without Alternatives*, 18 Alternatives 119 (1993).
123. *See* Falk, *supra* note 25; Thiele, *supra* note 121.

potential to contribute to a new vision of international relations which gives prominence to the institutions and other formations of civil society and the multilayered identities that are thereby expressed and represented.

1. The Emergence of International Civil Society

The UN Charter is a statement of "we, the peoples of the United Nations."[124] Yet the system it set in place is a system of states rather than of peoples. A growing number of commentators are drawing attention to the many undemocratic features of the UN that circumvent the capacity of peoples, as individuals or nonstate groupings, to participate in international legal processes.[125] This structure institutionalizes the longstanding antipathy of states towards the idea of NGOs and individuals assuming an autonomous role in international affairs.

Despite the Charter's vision of an ancillary role for nongovernmental entities, confined to ECOSOC responsibilities, there is no doubt that nongovernmental players have had a major effect on global affairs. International organizations and movements have been very influential in shaping the discourse within which international decisionmaking and action occurs. Concern for the environment, for women's equality, and for disarmament would not have achieved international expression without the backdrop of social and political understandings promoted by NGOs. This civil activity has supported a "quiet revolution" in the UN system.[126] As mentioned earlier, it has enabled nongovernmental input to enrich the soft law processes of the General Assembly, to contribute informally to areas within the responsibility of the Security Council, and to influence international legislative processes, particularly in the area of human rights. Gus Speth goes so far as to claim that "[a]ll really basic and fundamental changes have been people-led, bottom-up movements" and sees the UNCED process as the most recent confirmation of this view.[127]

The tenacious activity of NGOs in the international sphere, despite rigid institutional barriers, reflects the power that people have as citizens. This

---

124. U.N. CHARTER pmbl.
125. James Crawford, Democracy in International Law, Inaugural Lecture, Cambridge University 8–10 (5 Mar. 1993). His examples include the assumptions that the executive has plenary power to assume and apply international legal obligations, that an individual has no autonomous right to make a claim at international law, and that the principle of self-determination prevents modification of states' territorial boundaries.
126. See Toshiki Mogami, The United Nations System as an Unfinished Revolution, 15 ALTERNATIVES 177 (1990).
127. Gus Speth, Guest Editorial, 42 GO-BETWEEN (UN Nongovernmental Liaison Service) 20, 20 (1993).

power expresses an identification or viewpoint, autonomous from governments and markets, which can operate as a "third system" either within
institutional arrangements or as an alternative to them.[128] Marc Nerfin
describes this third system as functioning benignly, helping the people to
assert their own power and making efforts to listen to those who are never
or rarely heard, rather than seeking governmental or economic power.[129]
But this is a little short-sighted. It is inevitable that the power of the
nongovernmental sector will at least mitigate the exercise of economic and
formal political power, and it may eventually provide an alternative that
entirely transforms the current arrangements.[130] This is, of course, what
many states fear.

There is no single narrative that describes the significance of this third
voice in international relations. Broadly, it is based on identification as
transnational citizens.[131] In the postliberal view, this identity is multilayered,
multinational, and highly participatory. It manifests the force of a common
interest that is something more than the aggregate of separate national
interests and vastly more fluid and empowering than the homogenizing
hegemonic liberal idea of the universal citizen.[132]

The strength of the emergent transnational social movements indicates
that it may be possible to build a socially just global society on diverse and
multinational identities. The new social movements are seen by many as
heralding an extensive reorganization of international life that simultaneously affirms both local and transnational emancipatory identities.[133] Yet
others point out that transnational social movements are limited by their
failure to become a coordinated force and are continually fending off
cooption by the established structures of power.[134]

There is no doubt that increasing activity in international civil society
has catapulted the issue of democracy in the global polity squarely onto the
international agenda. The question is whether the UN, with its state-centric
world view, can rise to the challenge of reorienting its focus to be inclusive
of peoples as well as states. Further, if the UN achieves this first step, the

---

128. Nerfin, *supra* note 25, at 54–57; RICHARD FALK, REVITALIZING INTERNATIONAL LAW 208–13
     (1989), points to the civil initiatives of the MacBride Commission and the Permanent
     Peoples Tribunal as challenges to statist international law.
129. Nerfin, *supra* note 25, at 54.
130. FALK, *supra* note 128, at 3.
131. Thiele, *supra* note 121, at 281–82. "To hazard a summary statement: social movements
     are political organizations that attempt to restructure attitudes, values, and behavior;
     they are composed of and oriented to a relatively nonexclusive population; and they
     function primarily through communicative rather than coercive means." *Id.*
132. *Id.* at 287.
133. Elliott, *supra* note 24, at 24.
134. Kothari, *supra* note 122, at 133–34.

next question is whether this will lead towards a withering away of the system of states. The answer is not clear, but fear of it should not thwart open discussion and debate. States may be an important defense against the emergence of a monotonic, vertical, and hierarchical international government or, alternatively, they may act to impede the development of a more horizontal participatory democratic structure.

As a global community, we need to explore what international democracy might mean. Elements of the third system of international civil society are becoming increasingly insistent that the quiet revolution of their emergence as international actors is as yet unfinished.[135] In the following sections, I outline how liberal and postliberal perspectives imagine transnational cosmopolitan democracy before going on to link this discussion to the ECOSOC review.

2. Liberal Alternatives

Classical liberalism, supplemented by realism, characterizes the current Westphalian model of international relations.[136] The liberal ideas of consent, liberty, and equality are applied to states and operate alongside the realist imperative that ultimately there will be acquiescence to *de facto* power differences between states. The UN Charter reflects all of these components: the consent of states determines the content of international law; the liberty of states is protected by the principle of nonintervention in domestic jurisdictions;[137] sovereign equality is recognized by membership of the UN and GA;[138] and the balance of world power is acknowledged by the membership, powers and voting rules of the UN's most powerful body, the Security Council.[139]

The UN Charter's failure to outline a significant international role for the NGO community is a consequence of its liberal-realist pact. This scheme constructs the primary identification of individuals as associated with their membership in a national polity. It operates to minimize the

---

135. *See* Mogami, *supra* note 126.
136. David Held, *Democracy: Past, Present, and Possible Futures*, 18 ALTERNATIVES 259, 266 (1993).
137. U.N. CHARTER art. 2(7).
138. *Id.* arts. 2(1) & 9.
139. *Id.* arts. 23, 24, & 27. The power arrangements recognized by these rules are now outdated. There is a lively international debate about whether the permanent membership of the Security Council should be expanded to include, at least, Germany and Japan, if not also a member from the regions of the world currently unrepresented. These debates are not questioning the underlying realist principle of deference to power realities.

opportunity for identification across territorial boundaries which, in turn, creates the optimum civil environment for the pursuit of power politics in relations between states.[140] In this view, human rights violations are matters for the state concerned except where states have agreed to international supervision by way of a treaty or convention or where norms of *jus cogens* are violated.

In the post–cold war environment, realism still provides a powerful explanation of the relations between states as the US incontrovertibly dominates world affairs, and classical liberalism continues to justify the interstatal structure of the UN, while it also legitimates supremacy of the global marketplace. However, the difference between the rhetoric and realities of the post-Communist "new world order" has given proponents of a second strand of liberal thought, democratic liberalism, renewed scope to challenge the dominance of realism and classicism in the international sphere, despite fundamental questioning of liberalism itself by critical legal scholars.[141]

The most forthright proponent of democratic liberalism in international law today is Fernando Tesón.[142] He draws on the Kantian tradition of republican liberalism[143] to argue that the individual should be the normative unit in international law and that the international legitimacy and sovereignty of states is merely derivative of the confidence of their citizens. This confidence is the outcome of a state's full respect for universal human rights and its republican democratic processes which ensure just representation of its people.[144] The dual paradigm of the realist world view, which justifies different principles of justice for the domestic and international spheres, is thoroughly rejected. The ultimate goal of Kantian liberalism is a just civic society, resulting from founding all political arrangements on individual freedom and autonomy and respect for individual preferences.[145]

Kant's republican liberalism imagines the state as an entity created by a social contract with its civil society, rather than as an entity defined

---

140. Thiele, *supra* note 121, at 276.
141. *See* Anthony Carty, *Critical International Law: Recent Trends in the Theory of International Law*, 2 Eur. J. Int'l L. 66 (1991); Hilary Charlesworth, *Subversive Trends in the Jurisprudence of International Law, in* ASIL Proceedings 125 (1992); Nigel Purvis, *Critical Legal Studies in Public International Law*, 32 Harv. Int'l L. J. 81 (1991); Brian Fitzgerald, Theorizing About International Law through the Liberal Paradigm (unpublished paper).
142. *See* Tesón, *supra* note 120.
143. Immanuel Kant, Perpetual Peace: A Philosophical Sketch (1795). This was his most important work on international relations.
144. Tesón, *supra* note 120, at 61, describes this type of democracy as "republican democracy," as a system where the "participatory political process [is] constrained by respect for rights."
145. *Id.* at 54–55.

primarily by its territorial control.[146] In this view, the international society of states should be a federation of only those states that are liberal democracies that, by definition, favor a global free market and share a commitment to the "categorical imperative," Kant's foundational moral principle. Tesón describes the categorical imperative as "a universal law that all rational beings can make and act upon for themselves as free, self-determining agents whose actions are morally good . . . [i]t enjoins us to 'act autonomously and respect the right and obligation of everyone else to do the same.'"[147] The distinctly modern characteristics of this formulation's confidence in rationality, individualism, and universality combine to provide emphatic support for a masculinist and Eurocentric conception of universal human rights. In Tesón's view, respect for human autonomy is the result of achieving an "equilibrium" of rights which, in the post–cold war environment, would include socioeconomic rights.[148]

Republican liberalism does not portend an end to the system of states in the international community. Quite the reverse. The liberal democratic state is identified as providing important protection against the possible emergence of a global "super-state" which would pose a great threat to individual liberty and cultural diversity based on individual autonomy.[149] The sovereignty of the state is, however, limited by the universal system of human rights and the democratically determined priorities of its citizens.

Republican liberalism's emphasis on the normative unit of the individual leads to a conception of international civil society as populated by individual actors. Group autonomy, whether in the form of the state, family, or cultural community, is rejected by Tesón as an "illiberal" notion.[150] In his conceptual framework, the primary identification of people arises from their individual cosmopolitan citizenship and not from national, cultural, class, gender, racial, or other associations. In the Kantian paradigm, mechanisms for the expression of that citizenship lie chiefly at the state level, and democratic states remain the subjects of international law.

This leads to a limited role for international NGOs, understood as voluntary associations of individuals with self interest and risk averse preferences.[151] Logically, in this view, the primary interest of NGOs, whether national or international, would lie in restricting state autonomy and

---

146. *Id.* at 71.
147. *Id.* at 63 (quoting Roger J. Sullivan, Immanuel Kant's Moral Theory (1989)).
148. *Id.* at 65.
149. *Id.* at 87–88.
150. Fernando R. Tesón, *Feminism and International Law: A Reply*, 33 Va J. Int'l L. 647, 658 (1993).
151. *See* Andrew Moravcsik, Liberalism and International Relations Theory 6–9 (The Center for International Affairs, Harvard University Working Paper No. 92-6, 1993).

keeping a check on states' political power in order to maximize individual autonomy. Internationally, this would include making claims against states that violate human rights and promoting cosmopolitan education about the universality of human rights.[152] However, Kantians emphasize that expression of public opinion through freedom of the press is the key device operating to restrain the encroachment of states on civic freedom.[153] This is a more diffuse and individualized understanding of the importance of civil society than that traditionally associated with the idea of NGOs and more recently assumed by the new social movements.

A third strand of liberal approaches to global governance, distinct from both the classical and republican traditions, can be described as the Grotian school, which bases its vision of the ideal world order on the principle of respect for the dignity of human beings.[154] This vision relies on the ethical foundation of collective human solidarity, in contrast to Kantian individualism.[155] The Grotian school is critical of both state-centered classicism and individualistic republicanism. Grotians argue that group-based identities provide a third important normative category that must be acknowledged internationally, alongside national and individual identities. Grotians are skeptical of many other aspects of republicanism including its uncritical embrace of representative democracy; its simplistic assertion of the possibility of a free press; its unqualified confidence in the global free market; and its failure to acknowledge its own potential to result in the enforcement of Western-style global homogeneity.

A Grotian-inspired world order includes states, individuals, and nonstate entities as primary international actors.[156] Advocates would envisage an expanded and central role for international NGOs as representatives of diverse interests within the global community. For example, Marc Nerfin's suggestion of a "citizen's parliament" within the UN, operating in tripartite relationship with the GA and the Security Council, is consistent with this approach.[157]

The Grotian strand of liberalism has contributed to the growth of transnational social movements and to the development of both liberal and postliberal proposals for change. In fact, in this area of liberal thought, the

---

152. Tesón, *supra* note 120, at 75–76. Kant had a well-developed theory of cosmopolitan education.

153. Simpson, *supra* note 119, at 153.

154. Gerry Simpson, *False Harmonies and Tragic Ironies: Human Rights in the New World Order*, Int'l Legal Sec. J. 5, 6 (1991).

155. Falk, *supra* note 128, at 8.

156. Myres McDougal et al., Human Rights and World Public Order: The Basic Policies of an International Law of Human Dignity (1980).

157. Nerfin, *supra* note 25, at 55.

boundaries with postliberalism often blur. Rather than treating them separately, I will discuss Grotian-based options in more detail under the next heading of postliberal alternatives.

3. Postliberal Alternatives

Many transnational social movements define their goals as transformative of the present international order.[158] These visions are based on critiques that question the ability of liberalism to actualize its rhetoric of equality, neutrality, openness, freedom, and rights. They are also concerned with the rigidity of liberal rationality and the privileging of certain perspectives over others by the dualisms implicit in liberal thought.[159]

A significant contribution of postliberal paradigms is their insistence that human identities are multidimensional and fluid. While the importance of national and autonomous individual identities is emphasized in liberal thought, the new social movements stress that identity is considerably more complex. The importance of relational allegiances and commonalities are obvious additional factors. This has been argued for many years by Third World theorists and is implicit in the idea of transnational human solidarity associated with the new social movements.[160] Contributing to these new perspectives are feminists, who highlight the importance of the ethic of care that comes with the recognition of relational connections,[161] and environmentalists, who expand the relational polity to include the rights of future generations.[162]

The multiplicitous foci of the new social movements are in themselves indicative of the enormous potential for human identification—indigeneity, race, culture, spirituality, class, gender, sexuality, and ideology, to name a few. This suggests that identity can be simultaneously local and transnational. While identity is clearly situational, located in a person's specific history

---

158. Thiele, *supra* note 121, at 279.
159. *See, e.g.*, Dianne Otto, *Violence Against Women—Something Other than a Violation of Human Rights?*, 1 AUSTRALIAN FEMINIST L. J. 159 (1993); Joan Scott, *Deconstructing Equality-Versus-Difference: Or, the Uses of Poststructuralist Theory for Feminism*, 14 FEMINIST STUD. 33 (1988).
160. FALK, *supra* note 128, at 8, describes human solidarity as "a shared responsibility to seek equality and dignity for every person on the planet without regard to matters of national identity, territorial boundary, or ideological affiliation."
161. Hilary Charlesworth et al., *Feminist Approaches to International Law*, 85 AM. J. INT'L L. 613 (1991).
162. WORLD COMMISSION ON THE ENVIRONMENT AND DEVELOPMENT, OUR COMMON FUTURE (1987) (The Bruntland Report) first coined the term "sustainable development" to refer to development which does not compromise the needs of future generations. The term has since been embraced by the Rio Declaration.

and social context, a postliberal view proposes that this can enrich, rather than thwart, a transnational identification that makes experience of the local an important aspect of the global paradigm.

Allied to the idea of multilayered identity is the postliberal emphasis on participatory democracy, in contradistinction to the reliance of republican liberalism on electoral formality and the highly artificial notion of consent through the ballot box.[163] The new social movements are keen to "scramble" the distinction between national and international polities that characterizes liberal thought.[164] Clearly, national governmental decisionmaking can have effects that extend beyond territorial boundaries, and it is apt to ask who constitutes the relevant community to whom they should be accountable.

A postliberal conception of cosmopolitan democracy draws on an emancipatory democratic tradition that Chantal Mouffe describes as "composite, heterogeneous, open, and ultimately indeterminate."[165] In David Held's view, this would go well beyond the steps of, first, living up to the UN Charter and, second, extending it to include, for example, compulsory jurisdiction to resolve international disputes, including human rights violations, and enabling the GA to generate international law.[166] Held's central concern is that mechanisms be established which can hold states and other international actors directly accountable to the peoples of civil society. In his view, this would include the formation of regional and international democratic assemblies and crossnational referenda, complemented by the deepening and strengthening of local participatory democratic processes.[167] The core emphasis is on open debate and promoting egalitarian values that embrace participation and diversity.

The postliberal perspective, which decenters states and stresses the importance of local participation in the international community, is allied with a postmodern understanding of power. Power is conceptualized as dispersed throughout the global polity rather than, as constructed by liberal theory, centralized in the state and the economy. In the postmodern understanding, the relations of domination and subordination at the micro, local levels of society make possible the global systems of inequalities in power.[168] Consequently, changes in the distribution of power locally will impact upon the macro level of power relations.

---

163. Otto, *supra* note 26, at 383.
164. Thiele, *supra* note 121, at 278.
165. Chantal Mouffe, *Radical Democracy: Modern or Postmodern? in* Universal Abandon? The Politics of Postmodernism 31, 41 (Andrew Ross ed., 1988).
166. Held, *supra* note 136, at 267–68.
167. *Id.* at 268–69.
168. Jana Sawicki, *Feminism and the Power of Foucauldian Discourse, in* After Foucault: Humanistic Knowledge, Postmodern Challenges 161, 164 (Jonathan Arac ed., 1988).

The emergence of the new social movements can itself be understood as "resistance," which in the postmodern view is one of the products of power. Michele Foucault describes how the micromechanisms of power at the local level produce local criticisms which, if organized politically, develop into strategies to resist the mechanisms of power.[169] Such an understanding of power leads to a distrust of entities which seek to concentrate power, like the state and perhaps the UN. Alternatively, political formations which promote decentralization, decisionmaking at the local level, and redistributive justice are supported.

In the postliberal view, international civil society consists of a diversity of individuals, institutions, and informal peoples' networks and coalitions. It is a vast, shifting web of interconnections and alliances involving multidimensional human identities. People, rather than governments, are seen as the progressive agents of social history.

The question of the role of NGOs in the international community raises a critical tension within postliberal thought which is perhaps one way of distinguishing between liberal and postliberal Grotians. On the one hand, liberal protagonists are keen to devise alternative institutional arrangements that will change the current system. Leslie Thiele's proposal for international and regional democratic assemblies is one example. On the other hand, postliberals share a basic distrust of institutional structures because of their tendency to homogenize, control, and conservatize participants. Richard Falk's suggestion that the new social movements might be best advised to carve out less compromising spaces at the margins of institutional systems is informed by this latter view.[170] Another approach is Marc Nerfin's suggestion that networking, which operates horizontally and cooperatively, may be an alternative to hierarchical institutional structures.[171]

For present purposes, liberal and postliberal Grotians would generally promote an expansive and emancipatory role for NGOs in the UN. Emphasis would be placed on mechanisms which are inclusive of a diversity of formal and informal NGO formations, which encourage the building of global perspectives from local participation, and which foster open debate and criticism. The assessment of an NGO's "international standing" would be related to the transnational nature of its concerns and alliances rather than its geographical spread. A high priority would be given to the development of global civil information systems and networks by ensuring that information technology is widely accessible.[172] The implications

---

169. Michele Foucault, The History of Sexuality: An Introduction 95–96 (1978).
170. Falk, *supra* note 25, at 194.
171. Nerfin, *supra* note 25, at 56–57.
172. *Id.* at 58.

of these liberal and postliberal perspectives for the ECOSOC review will be explored in the next section.

4. The Potential of the ECOSOC Review

The state-centric liberal realism of the UN Charter, overlaid by the influence of the cold war environment, continues to guide the operation of formal UN-NGO consultative arrangements. The emphasis is on tight control and limited access to UN decisionmaking. Concurrently, a multitude of informal UN-NGO relationships has developed, guided by democratic liberal ideas and, more recently, by postliberal alternative paradigms. These arrangements are characteristically more open and flexible than those set out by Resolution 1296.

Recently, UNCED and the FWCW attracted the largest gatherings of international civil society ever. Much of the energy and vision that made this possible emanated from the new transnational social movements. At UNCED, this resulted in a radical rewriting of the relationship between states and NGOs involved with sustainable development processes. The effects of the new partnership have been reverberating throughout the UN ever since and helped to instigate the ECOSOC review of consultative arrangements. At the FWCW, despite the logistical difficulties of geographical separation of the NGO Forum from the government conference, women's groups and feminist movements were acknowledged as indispensable to women's empowerment. This puts further pressure on the review to transform the current consultative arrangement.

The initial responses to the review can be grouped into three main clusters which correspond to the theoretical frameworks outlined above. First, the realist defenders of states' autonomy and supremacy in the international sphere would like to see the review result in a diminished role for NGOs. Second, the proponents of democratic liberalism support the current arrangements with varying degrees of reform. They would be likely to endorse proposals which strengthen the domestic operation of NGOs but leave the international system much as it is. Third, those included in the diverse range of views that I have grouped together as "Grotian" would seek a reconceptualization of the UN-NGO relationship resulting in the empowerment of international civil society to participate in a more democratic international system.

The optimum review outcome lies somewhere between the second and third positions, but it will not be easily achieved. The states who have pitted themselves against NGO participation have drawn into their service a number of powerful arguments which associate NGOs with the hegemonic reach of the West. They have commandeered the platform of the nonaligned movement to question the universality of human rights norms promoted by NGOs and to characterize the idea of international civil society as a form of neoimperialism. While there is no doubt that the potential for Western expansionism must be resisted, the strengthening of the civil infrastructure provides an important means for such resistance.

One way to avert a regressive outcome would be to restrict the scope of the review and confine its potential to make change. But this approach concedes too much power to the anti-NGO camp and misunderstands the historical backdrop to the review. The quiet revolution of progressive NGO influence at many levels of the UN will not be so easily halted. In addition, the strengthening of transnational identities and the growing self-consciousness of international civil society as a player in world affairs are developments that are virtually impossible to stop. Also, the enormous untapped potential of a partnership between the UN and institutions of civil society is too promising to derail, especially in the crucial areas of sustainable development, women's equality, and the emerging global social agendas.

While it is utopian to expect that the OEWG will adopt a postliberal approach to future arrangements for NGO participation, it is not unrealistic to expect that its deliberations might result in a strengthening of international civil society and a liberalization of mechanisms which enable NGO access to UN decisionmaking forums. It could open the way for new relationships to emerge in the future.

Such a strategy, aimed at achieving an outcome consistent with the quiet revolution and the post–cold war developments in international civil society, would be associated with the Grotian spectrum of theoretical perspectives. It would support the Secretary-General's suggestion that the review promote principles that assist and nurture civil contributions to global governance.[173] Before concluding, I will outline several principles which might guide such a strategy.

The first principle necessary to ensure an environment of strengthened relations between the UN and international civil society is a commitment to the development of international participatory democracy. On the basis of this principle NGOs assume an essential, independent status in international affairs that is not confined to "consultation." The international order is understood as dependent on local empowerment, similar to the sustainable development paradigm, and NGOs are recognized as forming a vital link between the local and the global. The interests of peoples are acknowledged as having a different foundation than the interests of states, although

---

173.   *Report of the Secretary-General, supra* note 3, ¶ 111(a)(i).

they are not necessarily mutually exclusive. In ECOSOC review terms, this would mean arguing for measures that attach more participatory rights to NGOs who have consultative status and extending such arrangements to all UN organs, including the Security Council.

The principle of participatory democracy should also underlie the accountability of NGOs to their constituencies in civil society. This is a responsibility of NGOs, not something which states should impose, as the autonomy of NGOs is critical. In order to develop participatory models and norms, international NGOs need to evolve an infrastructure which would assist with such projects. Two key aims of NGO participatory strategies might be to build in protections against Western domination and to promote the strengthening of transnational identities. Global and regional NGO infrastructures would also encourage cooperation, coordination, and coalition activities which, in turn, would help to resolve some of the current difficulties with unmanageable numbers of NGOs seeking to participate. The review could assist the development of transnational NGO systems and networks by making this a priority area for resourcing and assistance.

A second principle, related to participatory democracy, is to encourage UN-NGO relations rather than control them. Compliance with the formal requirements of official status should be secondary to seeking ideas and input. The view shared by many states that they should retain a general right to veto or expel NGOs from consultative status, as shamefully exercised in relation to ILGA, should not be condoned. In terms of the review, this could mean formally introducing a voting system to replace the consensus model, suggesting that a body constituted by NGOs should replace the Committee on NGOs, and reorienting formal requirements to prioritize NGO input that results from participatory processes. In addition, concerns raised by Michael Posner about the domestic restrictions placed on NGOs by many states[174] need to be addressed by the international community, and the review could consider methods of ensuring the protection of civil initiatives in hostile states.

A third principle which would improve the quality of UN-NGO relationships is that of recognizing and encouraging diversity in the form and orientation of NGOs. The present arrangements exclude many NGOs that have transnational concerns, particularly those associated with the new social movements and those based in the Third World. It was suggested earlier that inclusive definitional tools should be adopted by the OEWG. In addition, institutional requirements should be minimized in order to open access to more fluid transnational formations like networks and coalitions as well as to regional, national, and local NGOs that have transnational

---

174.   Posner, *supra* note 63.

interests. The requirement of "international standing" should be revised to refer to an organization's area of concern rather than placing so much emphasis on geographical spread and "expertise" in a narrow sense.

A fourth principle is the desirability of promoting the dispersal of power and information rather than relying on centralized mechanisms. The global extension of information technologies to link individuals and groups within civil society is essential. Also, regionalization of many of the functions of the UN should be considered because it would make NGO access easier. Holding the meetings of treaty-monitoring bodies, commissions, specialized agencies, and intergovernmental organizations in places other than New York or Geneva would help to forge stronger connections between UN policy and lawmaking forums on the one hand and international civil society on the other.

The most immediate practical barrier to achieving a forward-looking outcome from the review that is consistent with developments in international civil society is its time lines, although progress has fallen behind. The aim was to finalize the review in 1995 to correspond with the fiftieth anniversary of the formation of the UN. To this end, an informal intercessional meeting was held in 1994, and only one further substantive session of the OEWG was arranged for early 1995. It was intended that a draft agreement on the future of consultative arrangements be negotiated at the substantive session.[175] However, these time lines were extended by ECOSOC, in mid 1995, into 1996.[176]

Many participants in the OEWG's first substantive session in July 1994 stressed the importance of facilitating widespread discussion of the review within the NGO community, including in developing countries. To this end, it was agreed that the report of the OEWG be given the broadest dissemination. However, the report has still to materialize. Without extensive discussion and input, the OEWG misses an important opportunity to broaden the scope of its deliberations and enhance the likelihood that the fundamental issues will be tackled.

The second major barrier to the adoption of progressive principles by the review is the hostility of many states to an outcome which bolsters the power of the NGO community. The wisdom and practicability of this hostility needs to be challenged. There are increasing numbers of NGOs in the South, and there is much to be gained by states who work cooperatively with NGOs in the processes of development. There is also evidence that the

---

175. *A/49/215-E/1994/99, supra* note 108, ¶ 52.
176. *Report of the Open-Ended Working Group on the Review of Arrangements for Consultation with Non-Governmental Organizations on Its Second Session, E/1995/83,* U.N. ESCOR (1995).

historical tensions between states and NGOs have been slowly dissipating over time and that the world conference processes, particularly associated with UNCED and the FWCW, have ameliorated many states' fears.

Unfortunately, the activities of human rights NGOs remain a critical point of contention because they pinpoint the feature of a global community that states fear most—that states should be accountable to international civil society. It is clearly preferable, and consistent with the spirit of the UN Charter, that accountability mechanisms are cooperatively developed and jointly implemented. To force the issue off the agenda is to invite ongoing chaos and subdue the dynamism and vision of international civil society.

CONCLUSION

The quiet revolution spawning the emergence of international civil society has burst onto the international agenda with the end of the cold war and the recent UN world conferences. The democratic credentials of the UN are in question and the dominant realist discourse of international relations is under challenge. The ECOSOC review of consultative arrangements with NGOs provides an opportunity to support a move towards democratic reform of the UN by carving out a more substantial role for NGOs as a voicepiece for multilayered transnational identities that are barely audible in the current state-dominated system.

States, and NGOs themselves, are divided about the desirability of such an outcome. Many states are opposed to the power that democratic change would concede to NGOs, particularly those concerned with human rights. Many international NGOs who are accredited under the current arrangements for consultative status are fearful of having their power diluted. In contrast, the Secretary-General and other states and NGOs have strongly advocated that the review mark a point of departure with past UN-NGO relationships which position NGOs as supportive adjuncts to states. By acknowledging the transformed international political climate, it is suggested that the review could contribute towards states and civil society developing more collegiate, responsive, and flexible relations.

The advocates for fundamental reform share a vision of the future of international society that draws on the Grotian tradition and extends into postliberal paradigms. This vision is of an international polity where the interdependence of the local and the global is realized through the operation of multilayered processes of participatory democracy and celebration of the diversity of human identifications.

Although the articulation and realization of this vision is the work of many generations, there is potential for the review to contribute to its evolution. The hostility of many states may be more a relic of the past than congruent with current realities of partnership with NGOs. If the review adopts visionary principles associated with participatory democracy, NGO representativeness and autonomy, global diversity, and decentralization of power and information, NGOs would be a step nearer to being recognized as independent actors in the international community. This would bring the unfinished revolution of emergent international civil society a little closer to fruition.

[16]

Breaking the Realists' Cabal: citizens' rights in the UN

ERSKINE B. CHILDERS

"Everything will be all right when people stop seeing the United Nations as a weird Picasso drawing, and see it as a drawing they made themselves."

(*Dag Hammarskjöld*)

Introduction

If, thirty-five years ago, Secretary-General Hammarskjöld felt that people found it difficult to see the UN clearly, and to see themselves involved in it, what would he say today? This year the drawing is festooned with jubilee decorations, but under these ephemera it is, if anything, more bizarre, daubed in even heavier contradictions.

The basic contradiction, of course, concerns the numerous, first-ever strides the UN has in fact made 'despite' the attacks on it. Some quick examples:

'The General Assembly has been scorned by northern democrats (of all people) as a "useless talking shop" ever since it achieved virtually universal membership; but its "irresponsible majority" has by now created humanity's first-ever *magna carta*, comprising some seventy legal instruments of human rights.' (United Nations, 1995)

The UN's founders did not predict decolonization even within this century: they directed the architects of the new seat at New York to allow for a possible maximum of some seventy member-states. The buildings with these essentially north-centred space assumptions were hardly opened when the UN's own charter and first human rights declarations motivated a grassfire sweep of liberation movements that have by now ended — at least legally — the age of northern empires.

• With virtually universal access to humankind for the first time, a breathtaking succession of UN World Conferences began in the 1970s, preceded by well-organized national research, regional analyses, and

Erskine B. Childers exposes the inner workings of the UN in a plea for citizens to assert their rights in 'their' UN.

then global assessments. For the first time in its history, humankind took inventory of itself, and of its planetary environment. (For the first time, too, governments lost the last excuse for inertia, that of ignorance.)

• Those conference processes themselves required and generated hitherto unimagined exercises in co-operation between governments. An illustration of what can be achieved in such co-operation through the UN System — and down to the smallest health clinic in every country on the planet, day in day out, year after year for one specific goal — was the total eradication of smallpox, from 1967 with some fifteen million known cases, to only 1980 when the World Health Organisation could announce the whole planet free of that ancient scourge.

• As one illustration of the progressive products of UN human rights legislation combined with the results of UN mega-conferences, in only a quarter of a century the UN Population Fund has implemented everywhere the concept of social responsibility for human fertility rates, and of the right of every woman to control her fertility.

• From the first (Stockholm) Conference on the Environment in 1972, a relentless mobilization of public concern and a progressive development of public policy culminated at the UN Rio conference in 'Agenda 21', to chart our way back from the brink of destroying this planet.

• After three hundred years and four conferences between 1958 and 1982, the UN inter-governmental community has made the conduct of nations on and under the seas and oceans far more responsible with the giant Law of the Sea.

A full listing of all the solid achievements of our universal public-service institution in only half a century would consume many pages of this journal.

And yet . . . what people 'see' from day to day is so very contradictory, so filled with evidence of indifference to the Charter and UN goals, as to raise in question whether the same governments could possibly be

15

responsible. Consider the following Picasso-like slashes of nonsensical, regressive and undemocratic behaviour on our UN canvas in 1995:

• The UN is kept on the brink by the refusal of its 'Host Government' to pay its full membership dues unless all other members accept its multi-lateral policy and managerial demands. The Host Country is withholding some $1.2 billion, but is still allowed to profit from the UN about $1.2 billion of UN procurement awards and income from the headquarters being in New York.[1] European governments not only accept the situation but subsidize the delinquency, and many developing countries, providing about half the UN's peace-keeping forces, are nor reimbursed for their costs.

• Fifty years after they were already archaisms, the power of veto and the claim to permanent, un-elected seats in the Security Council are still insisted upon by five out of one hundred and eighty-five member-countries. In the so-called Age of Democracy, another two industrial states are demanding to join this unseemly club, and try to secure this, efforts are being made to seduce several large southern countries into it, and thus to prolong these flaws in the Charter;[2]

• Running their special cabal within the Five, the three western 'Permanent Members' have brilliantly demonstrated their superior diplomatic wisdom and military power in former Yugoslavia. In a brutal conflict on its own continent that Europe not only failed to avert but has by unilateral diplomacy actually exacerbated, the Three have involved the UN in a miasma of ambiguous mandates with a protection force which the Secretary-General warned would be utterly inadequate — while their spokespeople have seized every possible opportunity to call the resultant tragic shambles and destruction of a people's human rights and homeland 'a UN fiasco'.[3]

• Throughout their Cold War, the nuclear powers insisted to all who demanded that they eliminate such weapons that their contest required such 'mutual deterrence'. Their Cold War has evaporated, but they have now forced through the General Assembly an indefinite extension of the Nuclear Non-Proliferation Treaty (NPT) which is to allow them to keep their weapons as long as they wish. The methods they used in the Assembly to secure this decision constitute one of the most disgraceful displays of brute power in the UN's annals.

When asked about this pressure and intimidation, however, Indonesia's Foreign Minister responded 'So what else is new? It happens every day'. (Menon, July 1995) In the Security Council routinely, and in the General Assembly whenever they deem it also important, the major powers, they have national laws even making the extortion of votes a criminal felony, use precisely such methods at the UN against any recalcitrant weak member-country. Their

Ambassadors are quite likely the next day to pontificate on the virtues of their democratic systems.[4] The practice is so consistent that at least one poorer country withdrew its candidacy for a Security Council seat rather than face the special intimidation to its economy that membership in the Council entails. The head of one Latin American delegation to the NPT Conference resigned rather than implement his government's instructions after it had been successfully coerced into accepting the nuclear power's demands.

• Through the UN's development funds and agencies as well as by bilateral aid, northern 'donor' governments have for decades assisted developing countries in building their health and education services. The same 'donor' governments have, however, authorized the International Monetary Fund (IMF) and the World Bank to require the same developing countries to dismantle up to 35 percent of the health and educational services thus built. Meanwhile, numerous northern authorities complain that the UN Economic and Social Council has 'failed to co-ordinate'.

• The Charter commits all member-governments to work for 'the economic and social advancement of all peoples'. But as the UN turned fifty, the richest one-fifth of humankind was earning over sixty times what the poorest one-fifth could earn — twice as wide a gap as in 1960. Yet amid donor complaints of 'aid fatigue', northern trade barriers and other northern-imposed structural inequities are depriving the South of over $500 billion a year that it could be earning . . . about ten times all the 'aid' the donor North says it is fatigued about providing. (Human Development Report 1992 *et seq.*, UNDP, New York)

The UN is virtually powerless to remedy such behaviour because the industrial powers refuse to discuss global macroeconomic policy in any UN forum, claiming that the Bretton Woods institutions are so mandated. This claim is false, and in any case the Bretton Woods institutions do not discuss, leave alone formulate any kind of macroeconomic policy for the full world of 5.7 billion people.[5] Nor do the G-7 'industrial powers' club; their 'global economy' in their summit *communiqués* is only the Japan–North America–Europe economy (less than a quarter of humankind). With the UN denied its Charter mandates to exert global economic leadership, humankind is thus totally bereft of strategic policy to bring it through the increasing dangers of a North–South convulsion.

• This gigantic problem is well-illustrated in world trade. Where the South did at least have 28 percent of world trade in the early 1970s, today the majority of humankind have only 19 percent of world trade (Mahbub ul Haq, 1994), a prescription for global conflict. Yet major industrial powers are determined to prevent the new World Trade Organization from being made a specialized agency in the UN system lest the majority might be able to exert some serious influence over this increasingly dangerous trade gap. The WTO is bidden by its northern controllers instead to work closely with the IMF and World Bank, whose track record on behalf of the poor is well-known. Meanwhile, efforts are being exerted finally to close down UNCTAD, such as stratagems even penetrating into the supposedly 'representative' report of the Global Governance Commission. (Commission on Global Governance, 1995, pp. 280–1)

Riddles on the canvas

How can such behaviour ranging from the inefficient to the brutal, come from within the same inter-governmental community responsible for so many genuinely global and history-making UN achievements? The question is not rhetorical; it strikes to the heart of the UN's problems at fifty.

There is not one answer but several, and they may guide us to needed action. They concern the intimidation of the weak countries by the strong which have led to the 'hardball diplomacy' and 'realism', burying the powers the majority possess in the Charter and a fragility of national government when extended into multilateral structures. This combined with the lack of public knowledge of international law has resulted in a continued inertia of 'We the Peoples of the United Nations'.

Programmed subservience of the mind

The first and most important key to these riddles is intimidation. The international community as a whole is still partly caught in the traps of imperialism and colonialism which was built largely on bluff about 'power', punctuated by periodic massacres. The difference between then and now ought to be that the world was then a far less open and transparent place, where today it ought to be very easy to call the bluff. Why it has so seldom been called needs exploration.

The two words 'great powers' still have a kind of automatic reflex impact. Northern journalists as a whole still worships this kind of power, does not question its premisses or the realities of its claims, and constantly regenerates an unhealthy respect for these powers by its choice of topics and its language. From officialdom through decision-influencers to citizens, most people do not stop to question the proposition in the phrases; do not stop to ask, who said they are 'great powers'; 'in what are they so powerful'?

The moment such questions are asked the bluff is useless. Even the 'single superpower' does not withstand serious examination. Like any other country, the United States of America has many good qualities. But its physical infrastructure is stated by its own authorities to be in advanced decay; its surface economic superiority can be destroyed overnight by decisions in Berlin and Tokyo; the

majority of its citizens have steadily lost real income in the last two decades; homelessness, urban violence, and even child malnutrition have increased, the USA has over two hundred million guns in private hands, and the highest rate of imprisonment in the world; and in its last major foreign military adventure in the Gulf War it had to go hat in hand among its allies and other clients to finance the operation.

An intelligent visitor from another planet would be extremely puzzled about all this worshipful respect and semi-fear of a handful of countries, and would check through their credentials to ascertain what lay behind this. They would almost certainly report back that the only serious claim they had to such 'power' was that they have indeed abused science to refine weapons expressly designed to incinerate, irradiate, flay alive, and otherwise hideously maim and disfigure the largest number of human beings in the shortest possible time.

But this kind of examination seldom happens among the terrestrial beings who are imbued with all this intimidation.

'Hardball diplomacy'

Sustaining the myths has been made easier by another form of intimidation, and never more so than at the United Nations. The practice of extortion and surrender of votes and voices in United Nations organs is a reality which would be more difficult to overcome. For, just as the individual victim of blackmail is required to stay silent and not seek support in the community, so the individual member-government of the United Nations, ordered to vote a certain way by Washington and/or London and/or Paris, feels helpless.

The Ambassador at the UN who receives cabled instructions from their home capital to do the bidding of 'the powers' over some coming vote in the Security Council or the General Assembly cannot call in the Press Corps and announce this to the world as the blatant violation of the Charter and international law that it is.[6]

Nor can they count on the Press somehow independently finding out what is being threatened and forthrightly reporting it; the most that happens is that a news item about the results of the resolution may say, 'after particularly intensive diplomatic pressure, the western powers succeeded. . .'.

The nearest a media report may come to the truth is the occasional use of a colloquialism which, itself, is part of the intimidation — 'hardball diplomacy'. It sounds tough, masculine, above all effective . . . a short distance from 'just the way things are done' . . . only a short move to 'the way things always are and always will be'.

The Ambassador receiving the cabled instruction to suborn their Charter-protected vote for their country to the wishes of one of the three northern regimes knows that the threat delivered to their government may be real indeed. These realities often just below the surface of UN deliberative processes, are real threats, because they have actually

17

been carried out against weak developing countries. For example, for opposing the force-authorizing Security Council resolution in the Gulf Crisis, Yemen's 'aid' was immediately halted and eight hundred thousand of its remittance workers expelled overnight from Saudi Arabia.

These are threats to the lives, health, education, and all other elements of even only sustained life, for tens of thousands even millions of human beings, depending on the size of the targeted country. They are a form of state terrorism, carried out by the same governments that have invoked that charge most often and loudly against others.

The extortion technique invariably involves the 'targeting' of a number of developing countries carefully selected for maximum psychological effect among all other southern governments. By this device southern solidarity at the UN is already half-broken before anyone may begin to gather the courage to suggest a united stand. Everyone of up to a hundred or so governments knows that 'we may be next'.

The two kinds of intimidation — the inheritance of colonialism and the real threat — play enormous roles inside the United Nations, both among delegations and in the calculations of any Secretary-General lacking the straightforward courage to defend the Charter and dare the 'powers' to have him removed. Simply because it is repeated often enough in the corridors and coffee-breaks, UN processes are often enough virtually timetabled by the syndrome of 'waiting for the Permanent Members' to indicate of what they approve or disapprove, how they will react to a draft resolution.[7] There are times when the ambience of an institution whose Charter proclaims 'the equal rights of nations large and small' is more like that of a mediaeval Court where everyone waited breathlessly upon the next pronouncement from the Inner Chamber before daring to speak.

Thus, the weaknesses of the United Nations are by no means only those recognizable controversies of the size and quality of its staff, the relevance or not of all agenda items, the usefulness or not of one or another organ. Few citizens of the United Nations can ever know that it is an organization under constant cynical domination by the elites of a mere handful of countries — whose own citizens do not know this because it is quite as thoroughly concealed from them, usually in the din of demagogic disinformation purveyed to them about the UN by their own elected representatives.

The role of 'realism'

The profound disjunctures between the noble goals and the actual achievements of the UN on the one hand, and the kinds of behaviour sketched earlier, are strengthened by another influence of our times, the school of 'realism' in international affairs. This, too, is profoundly anti-democratic but it, too, is strongest within precisely those

countries whose leaders continually pontificate that they are the exemplars of democracy in the world.

The 'realists' have it that economic and military power are now and always will be the over-riding forces governing the conduct of world affairs, the condition of the international community, and of course the continuation or decline of the United Nations. The 'realist' is an academic intellectual, an editor, a politician, an international lawyer, or a diplomat who stands comfortably behind this nostrum. A tiny fraction are women who have advanced by imitating men; the overwhelming majority of 'realists' are men, and it is a very *macho* perspective on our world and its public-service institutions.

The 'realist' tells anyone who invokes something called ethics, or ideals, that these are almost entirely irrelevant unless they are espoused by the mighty for-some specific and probably short-term *real politik*. The real reforms needed in the UN have always been nonchalantly dismissed by the adherents of this cynical school as 'starry-eyed' and 'utopianist' — code-language for, not acceptable to the powers, and therefore silly.

Above all in this anniversary year when many more minds than usual turn to strengthening our United Nations, the realists are ever-present to advise with that all-knowing smile that the only reforms that will ever be adopted are those that will suit the powerful. Such an attitude has influenced on some of the specially commissioned reform studies, but so subtly that it required a re-reading to detect it.

The key to these hidden roles of 'realism' in such reform papers is to see where the reason for the alleged 'failure' of a part of the UN that is to be turned over to the tender mercies of the minority is not given. It is simply fudged in a sudden turn of grammar — like, 'For reasons of realism attention has switched (from the UN) to the Bretton Woods institutions.' (Commission on Global Governance, 1995, p. 155) Concealed in this single innocent-looking sentence are such important facts as that the Bretton Woods institutions were deliberately built up by the industrial powers, while the economic staff of the UN were deliberately cut down.[8] Like an Act of the gods, the 'switching of attention' is described as having no known source, no deliberate provenance; it just happened. And so, once having happened, 'realism' would argue that it must continue to be so . . .

A majority not using the powers it has

If 'hardball diplomacy' and 'realism' have wrought havoc within the citizen's dream for the United Nations, they have also helped to disable the majority of the world's nations of the powers it does possess. This may seem almost a contradiction in terms at first sight, but not when the influences of intimidation and 'realism' are taken into consideration.

The sheer psychological effect of the presence of the power of veto in the hands of five 'Permanent Members' has had the effect of putting out of sight and out of mind numerous defensive and assertive powers and authorities which the majority could readily invoke in the present Charter. There has been down the years the constant, drumming effect of the dictum that 'the Security Council takes binding decisions, the General Assembly only passes recommendations'. Intimidation and 'realism' have nearly defeated all the strenuous efforts made by the smaller countries fifty years ago to write into the Charter untouchable powers for the General Assembly. Three quick examples must suffice:

• In the Gulf Crisis the General Assembly was virtually inert because Article 12.1 states that if the Security Council is already seized of a dispute, the Assembly cannot make a recommendation on it unless the Council so requests. Yet this does not bar the Assembly from debating such a crisis — which would have enabled the great majority of the world's governments to make clear their profound disagreement with what was being contrived, towards war, in the Security Council.
• Through the elections of all six Secretaries-General to date, there has been the same pernicious waiting upon the Permanent Members to see which candidates might survive their veto powers over the post. The result has been that the General Assembly which, in the Charter, alone has the actual power of appointment of the Secretary-General, has played little more than a rubber-stamping role. Yet because it has the sole power to appoint, nothing and no one could stop the General Assembly majority from rejecting any recommendation from the Council, and indeed rejecting its candidate as often as necessary. If the General Assembly were to make this clear to the Council at the very onset of the selection process — better still, to send the Council instructions as to how the Assembly expected the recommendation stage to be conducted by the Council — the Permanent Members might take their self-arrogated role more seriously as long as they are allowed to retain it.
• The Security Council is presumed to have sole authority to mount a UN peace-keeping operation, and to have this decision binding on all members. But the Security Council cannot appropriate a single dollar of UN funds; under the Charter, only the General Assembly has budgetary powers. The General Assembly must approve the actual funds that alone give effect to a 'binding' Council deployment decision. Nothing except intimidation could bar the Assembly from using this power to nullify a Security Council decision which the majority of members could not support.

Many other examples of the written yet, in effect, buried powers of the majority of the members in the United Nations could be cited. It is very human, it is all too understandable, but is no longer tolerable, that intimidation prevents greater democracy in the UN.

Governments disuniting themselves at the UN

Another contribution to the bizarre drawing has been the fragility of national government when extending itself into the UN System. An example was cited earlier, of the same 'donor' governments helping to build health services with one hand while having IMF order them torn down with the other.

When the UN was being founded, professional and technical 'sectorialism' and 'functionalism' were strong.[9] Several of today's Specialized Agencies were already in gestation as entirely separate international organizations before the UN founder even assembled at San Francisco. Yet it was well appreciated at San Francisco that the new UN was to address the causes of conflict, and to succeed in promoting 'the economic and social advancement of all peoples', the emergent very loose 'system' of UN and Agencies must be held together and be well co-ordinated by the UN.

The founders adopted many carefully debated and constructed measures to achieve this — including adopting the principle, never implemented to this day, that the Headquarters of all specialized agencies should be located at the Seat of the United Nations. (Childers and Urquhart, 1994) They also wrote into the charter what they intended to be the powerful Article 58, mandating 'the General Assembly to co-ordinate the policies' of all such agencies (including the policies of the IMF, World Bank and the later US-blocked International Trade Organization); and Article 17.3 under which the General Assembly should have been reviewing the budgets of the Agencies, the ultimate hope of the founders being a single consolidated budget of the whole UN System.

However, so apprehensive were the founders about the ultimate Achilles Heel of this entire architecture to bring the UN and agencies together, that they ended their recommendations to the first, 1946 General Assembly on implementing the new Charter with a warning. They warned that if individual member-governments did not co-ordinate their own policies — in their own capitals where their delegations to each separate entity would be instructed — then the whole design might falter.

Their warning was all too prophetic; for among the greatest single causes of the weakness of the UN System — and of the bewilderment of people before Hammarskjöld's drawing — is the kind of failure to co-ordinate national policies within the UN System. Equally, this has afforded one of the special advantages the northern minority has had in ensuring that it retains control of the UN. The full strength of developing-country governments is dissipated in their separate delegation at the tragically scattered headquarters of the System in nine cities in seven countries on two continents and across one ocean.

The Cinderella of International Law

Running through all the causes of the numerous contradictions, there is also lack of public knowledge of international law.

The UN has in fact an astonishing body of achievement in this field in its half-century record: more international law has been developed under the auspices of the General Assembly in the last fifty years than in all previous history. But not only is this breath-taking accomplishment of well over twenty thousand legal instruments deposited at the UN hardly known; the international law of the Charter itself is very little known.

At first sight this again may seem as bizarre a proposition as perceptions of 'the UN' itself: how can the citizen of the United Nations possibly relate to, leave alone invoke, so abstruse and complex a thing as International Law? The first answer is that this is precisely part of the problem — the perception of international law as impossibly remote. The 'realists' constantly tell us that international law is of very little 'operational relevance'.

Only one part of a more full answer can be outlined here. The citizen of any member-country of the UN has, at international law, the right to benefit from the 'useful effects' of the treaty obligations which their government has ratified in accepting the Charter.

In a generally cautious and conservative profession, the concept of 'useful effect' in a treaty is not yet granted enthusiastic endorsement by every international lawyer, but it exists, and support for it is growing, and it is being used in actual litigation. (Russbach, 1994, *passim*)

In essence, it is possible for any one of 'We, the Peoples of the United Nations' to demand, at law that their government properly account for its efforts to secure the fullest implementation of the promises in the United Nations Charter.

And it is possible for any one of us to organize to sue one or more governments for violating our UN Charter. A strikingly successful illustration of this has already been the World Court Project. An increasingly powerful number of professionals' and citizens' organizations around the world have managed to provide sufficient support for a majority of governments, first in the World Health Assembly and last December in the UN General Assembly, to have the threat of use of nuclear weapons referred to the World Court under the Charter for an advisory Opinion whether such threat violates international laws.

'We, the Peoples' coming out of our long sleep

In this and in a thousand far more well-known and more dramatically reported ways, the single most encouraging phenomenon as the United Nations enters its second half-century is the awakening of its citizens to its vital roles. In ever growing numbers, they are perceiving how the UN is indispensable, even in their 'issues', which they once held wary distance. In turn, they are becoming more and more concerned about their governments' inadequate discharge of their duties in the UN.

The NGO movement is in turns exhilarating and scaring the UN diplomatic and civil-service community. The spectacle of 'inter-governmental' UN World Conference being transformed into world citizens' meetings of thousands is acknowledged by more and more officials to be at least a help and an energy-charging phenomenon, even if by other officials it is a blasted nuisance. The former need more of it; the latter need to be even more bothered by it.

Mahatma Gandhi proved that people power — unarmed impoverished people power — was the one certain means of bursting the giant bubble of bluff that imperial 'power' really was.

The entire ground upon which the 'realists' feel safe to tread and purvey their projections of our children's future is the hallowed ground of 'power' that has not been challenged by people power. The 'other' power that can expose 'realism' is the power of an alert, impatient, and when necessary, very angry citizenry.

Citizens in countries whose governments — as in Europe — acquiesce in the incompetent and undemocratic grip of the 'powers' over the UN can now effectively demand that those governments have nothing to lose but their shame. For no government in Europe needs to fear economic retaliation as the price of insisting on its right to bribe-free and non-intimidated voting in United Nations organs.

The directly affected citizens in weak developing countries can do more to support their governments in principled stands against such state intimidation, but as the potential further victims and so often already destitute, they need and deserve the help of their northern sisters and brothers. It is time for the NGO movement to establish a 'Blackmail Watch' at the United Nations.

All NGOs that have by now discovered how vital the United Nations is to the issues they work on need to form effective consortia to watch over the behaviour of their governments in the forthcoming UN-reform processes. Plenty of compromises are being hatched — like extending the archaic privileges of the 'Permanent Members' by luring a few more from both North and South into their antiquated clique.

Citizens in the countries still calling themselves 'Permanent Members' must realize that they never in fifty years had the courage to stand for election to the Security

Council like all others. The International NGO movement needs to generate a strong and continual demand that the entire veto system be abolished. A simple start can be made by mobilizing a campaign publicly to invite even one Permanent Member to show that it does wish to enter the modern world by simply relinquishing its veto power over the next appointment of our universally responsible chief public servant, the Secretary-General.

It should also be a watchword of invigilating NGOs that they will not allow their governments to be rushed into any reforms of any part of the UN, if the result is either an incompetent change or a disguised protraction of the *status quo*.

The agenda for genuinely improving reform of the United Nations is considerable. Amid the many solid achievements of our governments through it, their obeisance to 'the

powers' combined with their recurring fragility in their own home structures has left our world organization very weak at the very moment when neglect of the causes of conflict is coming home to roost. We have no time to lose in organizing — to support government when it is doing well by us, to challenge and demand that it do better when it is failing us at the UN.

For the United Nations is ours, not theirs. 'We, the Peoples' must resolve in this anniversary year never again to leave our United Nations to governments; for it is a far too important a matter to be safely entrusted to them alone.

Erskine B. Childers *is an internationally known writer and lecturer on development issues and senior advisor to the UN.*

Notes

[1] The United States was the largest debtor to the UN for $1.2 billion as of 12 July 1995, UN Press Statement of that date. The next largest debtor was the Russian Federation, owing $559 million; but only the United States was a deliberate debtor, withholding dues to the regular and peace-keeping budgets for stated political reasons. UN public documents for 1994 record that the US earned $377.5 million from procurement awards; the City of New York's UN Commission's last estimate, now undoubtedly lower than current benefits, recorded over $800 million in income flowing into greater-New York area from the presence of the UN.

[2] By any definition, provisions in a constitution whereby an unelected small minority has permanent seats on a key decision-making body; can veto all police actions and all peaceful settlement actions in the community; can veto any candidacy for the community's elected chief public servant; and can veto any amendment to the constitution entrenching these privileges, are severe flaws in even an otherwise beautiful document.

[3] For a complete recounting of the ambiguous mandates, see the *Report of the Secretary-General Pursuant to Security Council Resolutions 982 (1995) and 987 (1995)*, 30 May 1995, New York.

[4] The extortion of votes is carried out by the ambassador(s) of one or more of the powers informing the developing country government(s) that there will be less or no aid, less or no debt relief, less or no credit rating by the IMF, less or no capital financing from the World Bank, unless the government instructs its delegation at the UN to vote the way the power(s) wish. Alternatively, outright bribery with debt relief or financial transfers or most-favoured nation trade treatment may be used. The victim government, as with the individual victim of extortion, blackmail, dare not publicly expose this coercion. The semblance of 'unanimity' in the Security Council during the Gulf Crisis, over its cease-fire resolution, and over sanctions against Libya was obtained by these methods. In addition to the NPT decision delegations in the General Assembly have been similarly coerced over votes on Palestine, referral of the threat of nuclear weapons to World Court, and many other critical issues.

[5] The actual stature and operational power of the Bretton Woods institutions has been grossly inflated as part of the G-7 strategy. The IMF is not allowed by its controllers to have responsibility for more than about 10 percent of total world liquidity. The World Bank has so little command over surplus financial resources that in 1990, when there was a global surplus of $180 billion, the Bank was only able to recycle $1.7 billion to developing countries. (Data from SID Roundtable Papers by Dr. Hahbub ul Haq, 1994)

[6] It is not worth using the term 'he or she' about Ambassadors to the UN, because out of one hundred and eighty-five there are only some seven who are women; but that is yet another story about the world organization at fifty . . .

[7] Of the five Permanent Members, of course, China makes all possible efforts to stay detached from this cabal, and now accepts designation with the Group of 77 of the developing countries under the formula, 'the G-77 and China'. The Russian Federation, its already Cold-War bankrupted economy further wrecked by the hectoring incompetence of western 'market magic' experts, is a sometime partner in what is really a bluff of three — the 'PermThree', Britain, France and the United States.

[8] The staff of the World Bank, for example, was 'doubled' between the late 1970s and 1990, while in one single exertion of pressure in 1986, the industrial powers had the entire UN Secretariat staff slashed by 13 percent. (World Bank Annual.Reports) The powers have repeatedly claimed that UN salaries are too high (while many northern governments subsidized their nationals in UN posts because the salaries were too 'low' for them); there have seldom even been murmurs out of the same governments about 35 percent higher Bretton Woods salaries, leave alone such Bretton Woods prerequisites as First Class air travel.

[9] 'Functionalism', a term usually attributed to David Nitrany, held that international collaboration in technical fields like agronomy and public health, education and telecommunications merited their own institutions, and in any case must not be put at risk in an integrated United Nations — lest some co-operation be destroyed if the politicians failed again as they had in the League of Nations.

References

Childers, E. B. and Urquhart, B., *Renewing the United Nations System*, Uppsala, Dag Hammarskjöld Foundation, (1994).
Global Governance Commission, *Our Global Neighbourhood*, Oxford, Oxford University Press, (1995).
Human Rights — A Compilation of International Documents, United Nations, (1995).
Menon, B. K., *International Documents Review*, Vol. 6, No. 27, New Jersey, (17–21 July 1995).
Report of the Secretary-General Pursuant to Security Council Resolutions 982 (1995) and 987 (1995), New York, (30 May 1995).
Russbach, O., *ONU contre ONU*, Paris, Editions La Découverte, (1994).
UNDP, *Human Development Report 1992*, UNDP, New York, (1992).

Part IV
The UN Secretariat
and Secretary-General

[17]

RESILIENCE AND REFORM:

SOME THOUGHTS ON THE PROCESSES OF CHANGE IN THE UNITED NATIONS*

Antonio Donini

There is a fundamental ambiguity surrounding reform attempts in the United Nations. For some insiders and many outsiders – at least those on the outskirts of the UN system – the associations that come to mind when the United Nations is mentioned are: crisis, mismanagement, paper factory, useless palaver, wasted resources, politicization, and so on. The situation is viewed as *negative* and, depending on the vantage point, 'the time has come' for more or less radical reform, reorientation, restructuring (if not for withdrawal as advocated by the most virulent critics). There is also something *positive*, however, since the deepening of the crisis at last brings 'opportunities' or opens 'windows' for corrective action. The concept of reform assumes that there is a crisis and that change for the better is required; at the same time it hints that it is necessary to reform, i.e. re-create something that has been lost or which has deviated from its original purpose.

At a second glance, however, things may not be so simple. The first manifestation of a crisis – and the so-called crisis of multilateralism is a case in point – is perhaps a dramatic increase in static. As this increases, communication becomes more difficult and messages are either distorted or not received at all. In the case of the United Nations it might seem that static has reached such high levels that it is attracting all the attention while concealing the real nature of the problem. Critics of the present state of the United Nations tend to assume that there is a broad consensus on the 'ills' of the Organization, even if there is less general accord on the prescriptions for reform (and even less on the root causes of the malady). The accent is therefore put on the managerial, administrative and structural measures aimed at static-reduction, or, to use another analogy, at oiling the machine and getting the train to run according to schedule.

There is another view, however: while not discarding altogether the oiling of the machine, the authority of the station-master in deciding where the train should go is being questioned. True, the railway line was built by the company for the benefit of all users (and of the shareholders), but now the number of users has grown somewhat unexpectedly; they have formed a user-committee and have started complaining that they had no say in the drafting of the company rules, that fares are too high, service is poor, and that there is no reason why some should be entitled to first or second class, while the majority is crammed in third or on the roof.

Reform is an elusive concept: it means different things to different groups. For some, mainly in the North, UN organizations need to be streamlined,

* This paper was presented to the Conference on 'Teaching about International Organizations from a Legal and Policy Perspective' organized by the Fletcher School of Law and Diplomacy, Boston, October 28–30, 1987. An abridged version appeared in *Geneva International Yearbook*. (The Hague: Martinus Nijhoff, 1989). The views expressed are the responsibility of the author alone.
© International Relations, 1988

restructured, reactivated, made more accountable. The issue is basically one of control. For others, mainly in the South, issues of management and structure are secondary. The 'crisis' is seen in political terms as a Northern response to the South's challenge to the existing world order. For others still, what has to be reactivated is not so much the organizations themselves but the 'sense of purpose' of member states *vis-à-vis* the international system which otherwise runs the risk of marginalization and total loss of responsiveness to the challenges of the coming decades.

In the following pages, after briefly summarizing the main clusters of reformist activity in recent UN history, we shall try to provide some markers which may be helpful for the understanding and interpretation of the current reform proposals. Given the vastness of the subject, and the fact that change and reform, whether administrative, structural or substantive, have been permanent features of the UN agenda since 1945, no attempt is made to record systematically all reforms projected or actual. A selective and somewhat subjective approach had to be followed in deciding which reforms or reform attempts to include and which to exclude.

This article deals mainly with the process of reform in the United Nations (i.e. the United Nations itself and its affiliates UNDP, UNICEF etc.) since this is where efforts have been concentrated. When the 'UN system' is mentioned, unless otherwise specified, this is not meant to include the Bretton Woods organizations. The latter have attracted little reformist attention in the past, a fact which is perhaps explained by the West's firm grip on the management and operations of these organizations and which increases their 'separateness' from the UN system. This separateness is, however, not without implications for UN reform since the Bretton Woods organizations are perceived as being the places 'where the real action is' – for better or for worse – while the United Nations, in the economic sphere at least, is left with the management of residual functions.

What follows deals both with reforms which have been implemented and with constructive proposals for reform which have come from 'within' or 'around' the UN system. 'Destructive' proposals, such as those of the Heritage Foundation, have not been considered.[1] Practically all attempts are aimed at improving efficiency, effectiveness, impact, co-ordination and usually provide a blueprint for the ideal structure. Few address higher level considerations of the nature of the activities to be undertaken, of 'whither?' or 'what for?', or present an articulated vision of 'how' the world problems of the 21st century might be solved. Reformatory zeal therefore appears to be of a pragmatic and technocratic nature, and its key concepts are variations on the themes of simplification, concentration, integration, co-ordination and, overtly or covertly, centralization and control.

A short digression on the nature of change in the international system is in order here. Much water has flowed down the East River since 1945 and the founding fathers of the United Nations would hardly recognize the organization that they painfully patched together at the drawing-board. The world outside changed rapidly and utopia soon had to come to grips with *Realpolitik*. But the Organization did not wither away; on the contrary it adapted. This capacity

---

[1] See *A World Without A UN: What would happen if the UN shut down*, edited by B.Y. Pines, (Washington DC, 1984). Interestingly, similar points are made at the opposite end of the political spectrum: see C. Krauthammer, 'Let it Sink' in *The New Republic*, 24 August 1987.

The Processes of Change in the United Nations 291

to adapt, or resilience, is perhaps the major characteristic that has marked the life of the Organization at least during its first thirty years. Depending on the point of view, value judgements on *how* it has adapted will vary, but the sheer quantity of change cannot be denied. In the main, it has grown in an aggregative fashion, with new committees, processes and entities cropping up as new problems appeared on the international scene – just to mention a few: assistance to Palestinian refugees, operational activities for development, the North-South economic *problématique* which led to the creation of UNCTAD, the environment, the Law of the Sea . . . The UN system has not developed according to an abstract plan, it has developed in an incremental, pluralistic, decentralized manner. Change has been substantial and the nature of the change has been quite different from mere 'tinkering with organizational charts'.[2]

The result is that although the structure of the system looks 'messy, untidy and confusing, it does in a very real sense reflect the world which could be characterized in like terms.'[3] It has been argued that sectoral pluralism and decentralization constitute the hidden strengths of the system[4] and that the structuralist reform proposals which focus on these 'original sins' are in fact reductionist and conservative since the reinforcement of central controls in the name of 'coherence' is bound to stifle the system's vitality, innovativeness and capacity to adapt to new challenges.[5] From this point of view the issue of reform becomes one of 'Whose interests are being curbed or controlled in the name of efficiency and structural coherence?' This is a highly political point, to which we shall return later.

For the time being, it is sufficient to note that the UN system is (among other things) a political space in which reform proposals, and the reactions they spark off, depending on the interests they represent or purport to defend, are in a dialectical, antagonistic relationship each having conquered various beachheads and positions. The current for efficiency + effectiveness + control is one of the forces in presence. The other main force sees the problem in more political-ideological terms. The geography of attitudes towards UN reform could be plotted around the four cardinal points below:

political-ideological

control and   **adaptation and**
centralization   **decentralization**

structural-technocratic

[2] Mahdi Elmandjra, 'UN Organizations: Ways to their Reactivation', paper submitted to the Tokyo International Roundtable on 'Future of International Co-operation', September 1986, p. 5.

[3] John P. Renninger, *Survey and Analysis of Evaluations of the United Nations Intergovernmental Structure and Functions in the Economic and Social Fields* (New York: UNITAR, July 1987), p. 37.

[4] Renninger, *Survey and Analysis*, op.cit, pp. 36-7 and Philippe de Seynes, 'Plaisirs et périls de la réforme. L'utopie de l'organigramme', in *The Adaptation of Structures and Methods at the United Nations*, report of a workshop in The Hague, 4-6 November 1986 (Martinus Nijhoff, 1986), pp. 67-80.

[5] See de Seynes, *Plaisirs et périls* op.cit, p. 68; Renninger, *Survey and Analysis* op.cit, p. 36.

292   *Antonio Donini*

In practice, however, things are more complex and distinctions between these two main orientations are often blurred: efficiency-minded technocrats, obsessed as they may be with the joys of organizational charting, are not insensitive to political-ideological arguments (nor, of course, are they immune from ulterior political motives) just as the ideological militants for a new order are not deaf to structural and managerial considerations. Whatever the arguments for pluralism and decentralization, the system does have the potential of becoming totally unmanageable. Extreme fragmentation, overlap, inefficiency, poor administrative practices, and lack of accountability are very real problems, as has so often been pointed out. There is probably a point of no return where resilience loses all meaning and bureaucratic decay becomes a circular and cumulative process. But collapse has been predicted so often in the past that any speculation as to how close we are to that point becomes essentially a value judgement. The present financial crisis and the general feeling of moroseness surrounding the Organization and the international system make the outlook seem bleak; on the other hand, the extraordinary flourishing of reform proposals which, as we shall see, have marked and followed the United Nations' fortieth anniversary, are an indication that a new historical compromise is being seriously debated even if it may not yet be within reach.

Reform proposals and attempts have had different foci. Leaving aside the purely political plane of peace and security which up to now has been largely intractable to reform, proposals and actual changes affecting the United Nations fall into the following categories:

Institutional growth and development. As mentioned earlier the UN system has grown in an *ad hoc* manner, with new organs, bodies and institutions being established on the basis of newly perceived needs. This can be exemplified by the setting up of totally new entities whether global (UNEP, UNCTAD, HABITAT etc.), regional (the regional economic commissions) or with special functions (various research and training institutions) and by the occasional merger of existing entities (e.g. the merger of TAB and EPTA to form UNDP);

Structural changes within existing bodies, both at the intergovernmental and secretariat levels, which have clustered mainly in the economic and social sectors of the UN (e.g. the 1977 'restructuring exercise');

Reforms of organizational policies and procedures aimed generally at improving effectiveness and accountability (e.g. the introduction of programme-budgeting and medium-term planning, evaluation, personnel policy reforms, various attempts at administrative and substantive co-ordination, etc.).

It should be recognized however that many of the reforms do not fall neatly into one category. In particular, the distinction between the two latter categories – on which the analysis in the following pages concentrates – is often blurred.

The early years

Reform has been on the United Nations' agenda almost since its inception. The first General Assembly resolutions on co-ordination and concentration of resources date back to 1948. Resolution 413(V) of 1950 entitled 'Concentration of efforts and resources' states: '. . . The successful carrying out of the economic and social work of the United Nations and the specialized agencies may be jeopardized by undertaking so many projects as to exceed the available technical, administrative and financial resources.' This was the beginning of a never-ending series of similar texts.

The quest for efficiency and effectiveness in United Nations activities can likewise be traced back at least to 1953 when the Secretary-General was requested to undertake a comprehensive review of the work and structure of the Secretariat. Subsequent reform actions sought to concentrate efforts and resources on those priority programmes which the United Nations could 'perform efficiently and effectively', avoid a 'dangerous' dispersion of these resources on a 'miscellany of projects' and launch a 'continuing self-criticism of the way in which various tasks are carried out'[6] – a familiar language which has recurred persistently in documents and resolutions for some thirty-five years.

In 1958 in response to 'repeated calls' for concentration of effort and budgetary stringency, an attempt was made to reform the then annual budgetary format to make it more transparent. In a 1961 report, a Committee of Experts noted member states' discontent with the high rate of increases in expenditures and demands for services. It called for budgetary stabilization and more effective processes to establish and enforce programme priorities. It also urged actions to achieve closer scrutiny of the total budget by governing bodies, and greater administrative control and analysis of the budget by the Secretariat. In the following year, the General Assembly elaborated on these themes with a call for an integrated programme and budget policy.[7]

Confronted in 1965 with a financial crisis caused by disputed peacekeeping operations, the General Assembly established another group of experts (known as the 'Committee of 14') to examine the financial situation and procedures for preparing, approving, and overseeing the implementation of budgets. In a pivotal report which has guided efforts ever since, in 1966 the Committee called for 'early steps' to develop integrated systems for planning, programming, budgeting and evaluation in each organization of the United Nations system. The Committee stressed the need for programme planning and budgeting to provide a clear picture of objectives and strategies for using the organizations' limited resources. It also urged a corresponding effort to strengthen evaluation processes and internal reviews of operations, with timely reporting every year to governing bodies and member states on progress made and results obtained.[8]

These early steps in the art of streamlining led to the establishment of a host of new bodies: in 1962, the Committee on Programme and Co-ordination (CPC), the main subsidiary body of ECOSOC and the General Assembly for planning, programming, evaluation and co-ordination; in 1964, the Committee for Development Planning (CDP), a group of independent experts

[6] The quotations are from UN documents A/2554 (1953) and A/2663 (1954). A forthcoming JIU report on programme performance and evaluation in the UN describes these early efforts and the subsequent ones in greater detail.

[7] Report of the Committee of experts: document A/4776 and GA resolution 1797 (XVII) of 11 December 1962.

[8] 'Second Report of the Ad Hoc committee of Experts to examine the Finances of the United Nations and the Specialized Agencies' document A/6343.

appointed 'to consider and evaluate the programmes and activities of the organs of the United Nations and of the specialized agencies' relating to economic matters; in 1968, the Joint Inspection Unit (JIU), whose members have 'the broadest powers of investigation in all matters having a bearing on the efficiency of services and the proper use of funds' and who have also been given the task 'of achieving greater co-ordination' between the organizations of the UN system.

By the end of the 1960s, CPC and JIU had embarked on a painstaking and more or less concerted effort aimed at injecting more sense into the planning, programming and budgetary methods of UN organizations. In 1966, the General Assembly had requested CPC to make a full review of UN system economic and social activities to ensure *inter alia* the maximum concentration of resources, the development of an integrated system of programme planning, and the institution of systematic evaluation procedures.[9] The CPC reported in 1969 that the rapid proliferation of UN system programmes would encounter increasing criticism from member governments and increasing public disillusionment, unless greater efforts were made through effective review and evaluation to ensure that these programmes met the needs of member states and provided concrete benefits. The Committee also stressed the need for more systematic review and evaluation on behalf of intergovernmental programme bodies,[10] a responsibility which the General Assembly subsequently assigned in part to CPC itself.

In 1969, the JIU – thanks to the pioneering work of Maurice Bertrand – issued its first report on programming and budgeting questions[11] to be followed by many others – on medium-term planning, cost-accounting, the introduction of systematic evaluation techniques as part of the planning, programming and evaluation cycle, more precise and transparent rules and regulations concerning this cycle, programme performance reporting, etc.[12] – all aimed at increasing the general accountability and transparency of the Organization's activities.

The reforms urged by CPC and JIU as well as by other groups – the Advisory Committee on Administrative and Budgetary Questions (ACABQ), the 'Capacity Study' (see below) – had produced tangible results by the mid-Seventies. The first UN biennial programme budget was approved for 1974–75, along with the first medium-term plan (a four-year rolling plan, revised every two years) for 1974–7. Both documents have continued to evolve in this format up to the present, with the exception that the medium-term plan became a fixed-term four-year plan for 1980–3, and then a fixed-term six-year

---

[9] GA resolution 2188 (XXI) of 13 December 1966.

[10] 'Enlarged Committee for Programme and Co-ordination: Final Report', doc. E/4748 of 2 October 1969.

[11] 'Report on Programming and Budgets in the United Nations Family of Organizations', JIU/REP/69/7.

[12] See in particular: 'Report on the Introduction of Cost-Accounting in the Organization of the UN Family', JIU/REP/72/10; 'Report on Medium-Term Planning in the UN system', JIU/REP/74/1; 'Report on Evaluation in the UN system', JIU/REP/77/1; 'Report on Programming and Evaluation in the United Nations', JIU/REP/78/1; 'Medium-Term Planning in the United Nations', JIU/REP/79/5; 'The Setting of Priorities and Identification of Obsolete Activities in the United Nations', JIU/REP/81/7; Reports 82/10 and 83/6 on the establishment of rules and regulations concerning the planning cycle in the UN; 'Status of Internal Evaluation in Organization of the UN system', JIU/REP/85/10; 'Third Report on Evaluation in the UN system: Integration and Use', JIU/REP/85/11.

plan for 1984–9 and beyond. Progress on monitoring, evaluation and performance reporting has, however, been much slower.

Meanwhile, the JIU – again at the initiative of M. Bertrand – had started pursuing another ambitious objective: the reform of UN personnel policy. In a report[13] issued in 1971, flagrant shortcomings were identified: lack of objective recruitment methods, poor personnel management practices, non-existent career development, inadequate and antiquated training, but above all, the inadequate level of the average qualifications of professional staff members – the main cause of the poor quality of so many of the outputs – was singled out. A detailed blueprint for reform was provided, but although it was formally approved by the General Assembly in 1974 and despite numerous follow-up JIU reports [14] and GA resolutions, resistance to change has been particularly persistent. The International Civil Service Commission (ICSC), established in 1975 did not, unfortunately, contribute significantly to the reform process.[15]

The great expectations and failures of personnel policy reforms cannot be described in detail here.[16] After fifteen years of efforts in this field, M. Bertrand concluded that the situation was 'extremely bad and far removed from the principles laid down in the Charter', and that

. . . there is nothing to indicate today that systematic efforts are being made either to require a high level of qualifications or to train professional staff for the specific tasks they will be called upon to perform. On the contrary, the laxness that prevails in this matter would seem to put a premium on mediocrity. In the United Nations, some efforts have been made to begin shaping a recruitment policy (competitive examinations in the junior professional grades) and to establish a career development policy (definition of occupational groups). But these measures, which have not been adopted by the other agencies, have so far remained half-hearted and have not even been properly applied; and nothing has been done either to extend objective recruitment methods to all grades or to guarantee a climate of responsible work, or to institute a system of training, or to develop within this environment where cross-cultural communication is difficult an esprit de corps and a dedication in keeping with the letter and the spirit of the Charter.[17]

Or, as another critic has remarked, 'There is no valid reason why international secretariats should not be of the highest quality. The present situation is impossible to justify.'[18]

[13] 'Report on Personnel Problems in the United Nations', JIU/REP/71/7.

[14] See the first, second and third reports on the implementation of the personnel policy reforms approved by the General Assembly: JIU/REP/76/8, JIU/REP/78/4 and JIU/REP/80/9, also 'Competitive Examinations in the United Nations', JIU/REP/84/11.

[15] On the failings of ICSC, see John P. Renninger, *Can the Common System be Maintained? The Role of the International Civil Service Commission* (New York: UNITAR, 1986).

[16] The main UN personnel policy issues, including the differences in the JIU and ICSC approaches are detailed in 'Personnel Policy Options', JIU/REP/81/11 and in 'Second Report on the Career Concept', JIU/REP/82/3, both by M. Bertrand. See also Renninger, *Can the Common System be Maintained?:, op. cit*, pp. 33–4 and Douglas Williams, *The Specialized Agencies and the United Nations: The System in Crisis* (London: Hurst, 1986).

[17] M. Bertrand '*Some Reflections on Reform of the United Nations*', JIU/REP/85/9 (GA document A/40/988), paras 37–40.

[18] Renninger, *Survey and Analysis*, op. cit, p. 44.

The Capacity Study

The first major attempt to reform the overall UN system structure in the economic and social fields was issued in 1969.[19] This was the work of a team of experts, led by Sir Robert Jackson, who were requested by the Governing Council of UNDP to make a study of the capacity of the UN development system to handle the resources made available through the UNDP – which it was thought at the time would continue to increase steadily.

The report did more than this; it presented a severe indictment of the short-comings of the system – much of which is, unfortunately, still valid today. The UN development system was described as 'a non-system' lacking a 'central brain'. Extreme decentralization and lack of co-ordination both at the head-quarters and at the regional and field levels made it an 'administrative jungle'. Because of the polycentric nature of the UN system, the specialized agencies tended to behave like independent 'principalities'. Jackson's oft quoted con-clusion reads as follows:

The question must be asked 'Who controls this "Machine"?.' So far, the evidence suggests that governments do not, and also that the machine is incapable of intelligently controlling itself. This is not because it lacks intelligent and capable officials, but because it is so organized that managerial direction is impossible. In other words, the machine as a whole has become unmanageable in the strictest sense of the word. As a result, it is becoming slower and more unwieldy, like some prehistoric monster.

The Capacity Study put forward a package of recommendations forming a coherent plan to rationalize UN system development activities and some addi-tional ones which were wider in scope (on programme budgeting, staff training, the setting-up of a unified UN Development Service). Implementation, how-ever, has been piecemeal. In 1970, the new system of 'country programmes' for technical co-operation activities financed through UNDP started to be set in motion. This was the centrepiece of the reform and was predicated on the assumption that UNDP would continue to be the central financing mechanism for the technical co-operation activities of the whole UN system. Many other administrative, managerial and operational measures related to the execution of these activities were also implemented. But change was mostly limited to UNDP itself. Since a reduction of the independence of the 'principalities' was not considered to be politically acceptable, UNDP's role as 'hub' of the system's development activities was dependent on the goodwill of the specialized agencies and on its 'power of the purse' as a funding agency. With the benefit of hindsight, both assumptions proved to be incorrect. Centrifugal forces increased and with the growth of the agencies' regular budget and funds-in-trust technical co-operation programmes, neither of which are subjected to the country programming exercise, UNDP's role as a central funding and co-ordinating mechanism suffered a progressive deterioration.

As for the suggestions for long term reform included in the study – the strengthening of ECOSOC which was to become a 'one-world parliament', the consolidation of certain governing bodies and secretariat units, the harmonization of developmental policies, etc. – these have largely remained on paper. A post of Director-General for operational activities in the United Nations was however instituted several years later (see below).

---

[19] *A Study of the Capacity of the United Nations Development System*, UNDP document DP/5, 1969.

The issues of rationalization and co-ordination continued to be on the agenda throughout the 1970s. Several JIU reports – on the introduction of cost-measurement techniques, on harmonization of medium-term planning in the UN system, the first reports advocating more and better evaluation – deserve at least to be mentioned here.[20] Another source of research and analysis was UNITAR: in 1974, Martin Hill, a former Assistant Secretary-General for Inter-Agency Affairs, produced a study for UNITAR entitled 'Towards Greater Order, Coherence and Co-ordination in the United Nations system', later to be revised and published as a book. The study describes the history of co-ordination efforts in the system and argues for a simplification of structures and a greater concentration of authority at the intergovernmental level but does not advocate any reform of the present pluralistic, decentralized structure of the United Nations system.[21]

Restructuring

The dynamic for change was once again put in motion in 1974, by a Group of twenty-five independent experts appointed by the Secretary-General to prepare a study containing proposals aimed at re-shaping the economic and social sectors of the UN system. The experts issued their reports, containing numerous recommendations, in 1975.[22] This was followed by more than two years of deliberation by an *Ad Hoc* Committee and by the adoption in 1977 by the General Assembly of resolution 32/197 known as the 'restructuring resolution'.

The 'restructuring exercise' resulted from the conjunction of two different but converging forces: on the one hand, the continuing dissatisfaction of many Third World countries with the lack of progress towards the lofty goals proclaimed in the Development Decades and the Programme of Action on the Establishment of a New International Economic Order (NIEO); on the other, increasing concern, especially among the industrialized countries, with the apparent intractability of the issues of proliferation, fragmentation, absence of co-ordination and inadequate planning, programming, budgeting and evaluation systems which had been highlighted during previous reform attempts.

Although the recommendations of the Group of Experts were significantly diluted when they were tested against the political wisdom of the Ad Hoc Committee and the General Assembly, the restructuring resolution did represent an attempt to bring about limited but important structural change. The most important changes actually implemented were the following:

– an Office of Director-General for Development and International Economic Co-operation was created to provide 'effective leadership to the system in development' and 'to exercise overall co-ordination within the system in order to ensure a multidisciplinary approach to development on a system-wide basis';
– co-ordination of operational activities at the country level was to be enhanced through the appointment of 'Resident Co-ordinators' (normally the local UNDP Resident Representative) and the use of the UNDP country programme

---

[20] See note 12 above.
[21] Martin Hill, *The United Nations System: Coordinating its Economic and Social Work* (Cambridge University Press for UNITAR, 1978).
[22] UN document E/AC.62/9.

298   *Antonio Donini*

as 'a frame of reference' for all UN system operational activities for development in each country;
– an Office for Programme Planning and Co-ordination was set up to examine
system-wide co-ordination problems and to undertake cross-organization programme analyses;
– the Administrative Committee on Co-ordination's (ACC) subsidiary bodies
were re-organized and a Consultative Committee on Substantive Questions
was set up to enable UN system organizations to co-ordinate the preparation of
their programmes and even to make 'joint planning in the medium-term at
system level'.

All this looked promising, but the actual results in no way met the expectations. Once the excitement of resolution 32/197 had faded away, the
momentum for change dropped and business continued more or less as usual.
Potent and entrenched forces were opposed to change and resorted to resistance. There is little evidence to suggest that the ACC machinery is more
effective now than it was ten years ago, or that the Director-General for Development is actually providing 'effective leadership' to the system's baronies and
principalities, or that Resident Co-ordinators have improved co-ordination at
the field level.[23]
As has been pointed out:

The cumulative impact of the changes that have been made is not overwhelming.
Despite literally hundreds of documents and resolutions and untold hours of Governments and secretariat time and energy, what has restructuring accomplished? Are the
activities of the United Nations and the United Nations system better co-ordinated
today than ten years ago? Is a coherent and consistent multidisciplinary approach to
development now being followed by the organizations of the United Nations system?
Perhaps the best that could be said is that things might have been worse if restructuring
had not taken place. But is such a level of benefits commensurate with the costs?[24]

Renninger rightly concludes that:

any review of the 1977 restructuring exercise should consider if the structural changes
proposed were too timid and if many of the supposed agreements concerning changes
were cast at such a level of generality that their implementation was rather easily
sabotaged by forces resistant to change. The implication is that more far-reaching
changes with more attention to implementation could succeed.[25]

The Bertrand connection

The fortieth anniversary of the United Nations provided a timely opportunity
for stock-taking and advocacy for reform. The most wide-ranging and coher-
ently structured proposals are contained in Maurice Bertrand's 'Some
Reflections on Reform of the United Nations'.[26] After seventeen years of experience

___

[23] There is actually evidence to the contrary, see the JIU report on 'Field Representation of
Organizations of the United Nations system: Structure and Co-ordination', JIU/REP/86/1
(GA doc. A/41/424).
[24] Renninger, *Survey and Analysis*, op.cit, p. 42. The failure of the 'restructuring exercise' is also
analyzed in Williams, *The Specialized Agencies*, op.cit, pp. 51–3.
[25] Ibid., p. 43.
[26] The ideas contained in the report (see note 17 above) are expanded in *Refaire l'ONU! Un
programme pour la paix* (Geneva: Zoé, 1986). The Bertrand report was reviewed by A.F. Ewing in
'Reform of the United Nations', *Journal of World Trade Law*, vol. 20, no. 2, March-April 1986. A
detailed analysis also appears in Williams, *The Specialized Agencies* op.cit, pp. 181–95.

as a member of the Joint Inspection Unit, and having personally witnessed the difficulties in getting reforms approved and seen the resistance to their implementation, he provides what has been termed a 'savage indictment' of the Organization's illnesses.[27] Commenting on the reform attempts of the 1960s and '70s he writes:

This extraordinary perseverance produced no results. This mass of efforts, changes in structure, work on methodology and recommendations, precise though they were and formulated in an imperative way by the General Assembly, have in no way improved co-ordination. 'Joint planning' has remained wishful thinking; development strategies applied by each organization have continued to diverge; and 'country programming' and 'field co-ordination' have never been anything more than meaningless terms. (paragraph 29)

This 'useless effort at co-ordination' has in fact over the last 15 years gone hand in hand with a parallel effort towards planning, programming, monitoring of the implementation of programmes and evaluation. Progress has been made 'on paper' in these fields: 'There have been better descriptions of the existing activities, but there has been no improvement in either their design or their implementation.' (paragraph 31)

Improvements in method have thus not succeeded in correcting the structural shortcomings. The extreme decentralization of the system, deliberate at the outset and then aggravated by the establishment of dozens of new organs, has not been able to be made up by 'co-ordination' imposed on agents who did not want to be co-ordinated. (paragraph 32)

If it is true that 'the way in which the mill operates becomes much more important than the quality of the flour it produces' (paragraph 22), does this mean that if problems of management and functioning of the system could be remedied the Organization would be able to carry out its mandate more effectively? Bertrand confronts this issue squarely: it is the structures that need changing, but most of all the very concept of the World Organization needs to be redefined.

For the reader's convenience we reproduce below a summary of the main points put forward in the report:[28]

1. A reform of the United Nations and its system is urgent, and in spite of deep-seated prejudice existing on the subject, it is feasible to envisage this seriously.
2. The time has come to begin to reflect in a serious and ambitious way on the definition of a third-generation World Organization. The introduction of reforms will be a lengthy process and will call for difficult searchings and negotiations.
3. The structures of the present system rest on three fallacious notions, false from the outset or gradually distorted – to the effect that the 'maintenance of peace' can be achieved through an institution, that the development of the poor countries can be achieved through a sectoral approach, and that negotiations among 159 States are possible without a prior definition of agreed negotiation structures.
4. In the present political context it is unrealistic to believe that sovereign States can deal in common with activities outside the limited sphere where a broad consensus exists. The basic role of a World Organization can only be the

---

[27] Williams, *The Specialized Agencies*, op.cit, p. 184.
[28] Bertrand, *Some Reflections*, op.cit., pp. 67–9.

determined search for a better or a different type of consensus which will lead towards the far-off ideals set forth in the Charter.

5. In the present political context, reform cannot be focused on modifying the structures for the maintenance of peace or more generally the structures of a political United Nations. The successes achieved using an instrument ill-suited for the purpose already constitute a paradox. We must continue, as the Secretary-General did in a recent report, to encourage the member states to make the most of it. But it is impossible today to propose other structurs which would be an improvement on the Security Council.

6. On the contrary, the reform should focus on the transformation of the structures that support development and on the institution of a genuine world economic forum. The aim would be to build up an 'economic United Nations' side by side with the political United Nations.

7. On one front, the reform should be a total recasting at system level of all structures concerned with development in order to constitute regional or sub-regional development agencies or enterprises. It might be hoped that the drive resulting from so radical a transformation of this part of the system would lead to a re-examination of the other regional or sub-regional intergovernmental structures. It would obviously be desirable for the World Bank to consider the possibility of taking a hand in the thinking and in the reform, and for joint efforts to be developed in this connection between the other aid systems, multi-lateral or bilateral.

8. On the other front, the reform should be to set up a genuine world forum to deal essentially with economic problems. The developing countries should not continue to be left out of the discussion at the negotiation tables where economic and financial problems are concretely discussed. This situation does harm to the international community as a whole. Hence we must give some thought to the replacement of the present dual forum: Economic and Social Council and UNCTAD, by a more restricted Council of the type envisaged in the original Charter, which set at 18 the membership of the Economic and Social Council. Calculations indicate that if this 'Economic Security Council' had twenty-three members, the main major States and the main regions of the world could be represented on it. It should be possible for the secretariats of the United Nations and the major agencies to be reorganized under the authority of one or more 'Commissions' made up of independent persons of distinction.

The purpose of the thesis propounded in the Bertrand report is to try to make a contribution to a body of reflections inspired by the fortieth anniversary of the United Nations. In doing this, the author has been led to formulate critical judgements 'whose severity may at times be calculated to surprise or even to shock'. The light thus thrown on the scene should on the contrary help towards a better understanding of the real situation of the UN and to provoke a debate on the possibilities of a reform.

This raises the question of the responsibility of those who have the wherewithal to achieve wholesale reform. Bertrand does not believe the theory, widely held today, that Machiavellian designs on the part of states – and in particular the great Powers – are what keep the United Nations in a state of helplessness and impotence. He feels rather that there is a great deal of misunderstanding concerning the possible role of a World Organization and that the confusion in people's minds on this subject is itself a political phenomenon whose harmful effects could be mitigated by reflection and clarification.

The seriousness and the urgency of the problems justify focusing the search in directions little explored up to now. A proposal to devise and install entirely new structures at least in the development area and in that of the system of negotiation at world level 'may strike some people as rash or utopian and others as mealy-mouthed'. The author has confined himself to the universal UN system, without including the Bretton Woods organizations. In his opinion it is obvious, however, that the construction of an economic United Nations is not conceivable without them, and it is desirable that the thinking on the subject should be broadened to include them.

As can be seen, the radical structural and institutional reforms advocated by Bertrand go much further than any of the reform proposals reviewed so far. It is now becoming increasingly clear that the Bertrand report represents a kind of demarcation line: the small world of UN system reform attempts will not be the same again. The emphasis has shifted from a predominantly managerial and administrative perspective to one focusing on structural and systemic change. Whether the approach recommended in Bertrand's seminal contribution is ultimately successful or not, the international community is now confronted with the challenge of a 'third generation World Organization'. The 'Council-Commission' idea, largely inspired by the relatively successful experience of the European Community, will be attractive to some but may not be acceptable, for geopolitical reasons, to Third World or Eastern European representatives. However, the current financial crisis – triggered by the Gramm-Rudman-Kassebaum syndrome – is another potent, though contradictory, impetus for reform. As we shall see, a convergence of the powers of reflection and the powers of the purse in re-shaping the United Nations is not altogether to be excluded.

The Bertrand report attracted considerable attention among unofficial circles within and outside the UN system. It became a best-seller with academics, NGOs and various UN staff groupings on both sides of the Atlantic.[29] Interestingly, though, the official response was at best lukewarm.

The question of the soundness of the existing institutional machinery, not to mention any suggestion of tampering with the Charter, is something of a taboo among delegates and officials. As Renninger points out:[30]

Any serious discussions of reform would presumably begin with this question. The fact that it is infrequently raised, let alone discussed, in intergovernmental forums is not surprising. The very question seems to make Governments uncomfortable. Their reluctance to entertain questions which might lead to unpalatable conclusions is surpassed only by that of executive heads of agencies.

Within days of the publication of the report 'a senior UN official in New York' is reported to have stated that the author 'was out of touch with the political realities of the institution'.[31] The Secretary-General's initial comment was that the report 'merits careful and thoughtful examination',[32] but the ACC's knee-jerk reaction was to bury it. The ACC is required to issue inter-agency comments on any JIU report having system-wide implications.

[29] It was much debated in *UN Special* and *Secretariat News*, the Geneva and New York UN internal staff journals, also at a UN symposium on '*Is Universality in Jeopardy?*' held in Geneva in December 1985.

[30] Renninger, *Survey and Analysis*, op.cit, p. 38

[31] Quoted in *The Guardian*, 10 October 1985.

[32] Document A/40/988, add. 1 of 6 December 1985.

302   *Antonio Donini*

However, the supreme body for administrative co-ordination argued that the
report presented 'a personalized view of the United Nations system' and considered it 'inappropriate to comment on the report'.[33]

The Group of 18

Bertrand's reflections on reform were provisionally overtaken by events when
it became apparent towards the end of 1985 – just as the United Nations was
preparing to celebrate its fortieth anniversary – that an unprecendented financial crisis had hit the Organization. Financial emergencies have been more or
less permanent features of the UN system,[34] but this time the situation was
more serious. The crisis was precipitated by the adoption of the Kassebaum-
Solomon amendment which was intended to cut the US contribution to the UN
from 25 to 20 per cent, unless a weighted voting system was introduced for
financial decision-making. This was compounded by further cuts resulting
from the Gramm-Rudman-Hollings Act aimed at reducing the US federal
deficits. Despite the fact that withholdings of contributions represented an
arbitrary violation of article 17 of the Charter and that both texts were clearly
undefendable from the point of view of internationl law, such parliamentary
action was widely supported by US public opinion. Inside the UN and outside
the US and especially in the Third World this was mostly perceived as a wanton
attempt to blackmail the Organization in order to make it 'behave'.

At the end of 1985 the Secretary-General was faced with a short-term deficit
of $390 million and had to resort to unexpected budgetary cuts. Meanwhile at
the General Assembly the crisis was forcing member states to take corrective
action and the familiar issues of the functioning and effectiveness of the
Organization were once again put on the agenda. During the general debate,
Japan proposed the setting-up of a group of 'eminent persons', to study the
problem. This met with the resistance of many Third World delegations who
questioned both the idea of an 'independent' group and the proposed
mandate – which they feared might lead to a discussion on the possible introduction of a weighted voting system while down-playing the 'political' origins
of the crisis. Finally agreement was reached on the setting up of a Group of
High-Level Intergovernmental Experts with a more technical mandate, i.e. to
review the efficiency of the administrative and financial functioning of the
United Nations (resolution 40/237).[35]

The report of the Group of 18, containing 71 recommendations, was issued
in August 1986.[36] The report did not contain proposals to solve the immediate
financial problems of the UN; this was not its mandate. In the meantime
(end-April 1986), the Secretary-General had had to reconvene the General
Assembly to discuss an urgent set of measures – deferment of expenditures,

[33] Document A/41/639 of July 1986.
[34] A very similar crisis had arisen in 1972 when the United States obtained a reduction of its
share of the budget from 31.52 to 25 per cent. During the 1960s the Soviet Union and France had
also precipitated a crisis – which led to the establishment of the Committee of 14 – by refusing to
pay their share of the Congo operations. The US withdrawals from ILO (1977–8) and UNESCO
(1985) also caused financial crises and led to streamlining efforts.
[35] For a detailed discussion of the establishment, mandate and recommendations of the Group
of 18, see V.Y. Ghebali, *La crise du système des Nations Unies* (Paris: La documentation française,
1988).
[36] Document A/41/49.

reductions in meetings, curtailment of various programmes – designed to keep the Organization financially afloat.

The report of the Group of 18 contains a familiar assessment of the State of the Organization: 'overlapping agendas and duplication of work', 'overly complex structure which generally lacks of cohesion', 'the volume of documentation' has 'surpassed the limit of what can be studied' by member states, 'management capacity' has lagged behind the growth of the organization, 'the quality of work needs to be improved', 'qualifications of staff, in particular in the higher categories are inadequate', etc. The corresponding recommendations are in many cases simply repetitions of past proposals concerning the functioning of intergovernmental organs, co-ordination, planning, programming and evaluation, personnel policy etc. Nevertheless, as pointed out by M. Bertrand (who was one of the 'intergovernmental experts'):

A relatively *new tone* was identifiable in the consensus report of the Group of 18. Several abusive practices and problems of mismanagement affecting the Secretariat were confronted directly for the first time, including the harmful proliferation of the posts of Under-Secretary-General and Assistant Secretary-General, the inadequacy of qualifications of staff, particularly in these top posts, and the complex, fragmented, and topheavy structure of the Secretariat. The report represented a sincere effort to reverse past tendencies.[37]

It recommended reducing the number of Under-Secretary-General and Assistant Secretary-General posts by 25 per cent over a period of three years, and pursuing in-depth studies of the structure of the intergovernmental machinery, a subject until now shielded from critical investigation.

The Group of 18 devoted particular attention to a possible reform of the intergovernmental mechanisms regarding the preparation of the budget. Although, as had been often proposed in the past, several experts advocated the establishment of a Committee on Programme and Budget with a limited membership, a composition which would give 'major contributors' a stronger voice and consensus decision-making, the report was inconclusive on this point. In the final analysis, it seems quite clear that the Group of 18 tried to steer clear of the most controversial political issues – i.e. the root causes of the crisis (lack of consensus amongst member states on the role of the Organization) and its immediate manifestations (the question of 'weighted voting'). It concentrated on technical issues – perhaps with the half-hearted hope that this would contribute to the solving of the political ones – and on this terrain its work was far from negligible.[38]

By its resolution 41/213 of 19 December 1986, the General Assembly finally approved, with a number of reservations, the recommendations of the Group of 18 concerning the structure of the Secretariat, reduction of staff, personnel policy, inspection, co-ordination, etc. On the budgetary process, the General Assembly decided to request the Secretary-General to prepare an outline of the programme budget one year in advance, and to give the existing Committee for Programme and Co-ordination the mandate to consider this outline. The

---

[37] M. Bertrand, '*Can the United Nations be reformed*', in Roberts and Kingsley (eds), *United Nations, Divided World*, (Oxford: Oxford University Press, 1987).

[38] From the inside, the Group of 18 will however be remembered for its recommendations to cut staff by 15 per cent, to reduce annual leave to four weeks and to abolish education grants for post-secondary education. This was seen as an attempt by member states to solve the crisis on the back of the Secretariat.

CPC will 'continue its existing practice of reaching decisions by consensus', and will transmit its conclusions and recommendations to the General Assembly. The General Assembly will continue to decide on the programme-budget in conformity with Articles 17 and 18 of the Charter.

In response to what it perceived as a major success, the US Administration indicated that it would recommend to Congress that it be more positive in its financial support of the United Nations. While it is true that a number of housekeeping measures have been taken by the Secretary-General (reductions in staff, including high-level posts, streamlining of the Secretariat structure, consolidation of various units etc.),[39] the changes in the budgetary review process are more symbolic than real and will only function if all sides are prepared to play the same game. It is therefore still difficult to judge whether GA resolution 41/213 represents real long-term progress toward a better mutual understanding of the role of the UN, or even whether it will contribute to the solving of the financial crisis.

Other proposals

Three studies which were issued while the Group of 18 was preparing its report and which were aimed at influencing its deliberation should also be mentioned here:

The first was issued under the auspices of the Heritage Foundation and is mentioned only *pour mémoire*.[40] It contains 59 recommendations in response to General Assembly resolution 40/237 which established the Group of 18;

The second[41] was initiated by an informal Commission under the auspices of two UN 'old hands' – Sadruddin Aga Khan and Maurice Strong – who commissioned former Under-Secretary-General for Administration and Finance George Davidson to study possible cost savings and budgetary cuts both from a short-term and longer-term point of view. The draft report was discussed at an informal consultation held in August 1986 at which three members of the Group of 18 participated. The final report may therefore have had some influence on the deliberations of the latter group. The study focuses specifically on an analysis of the UN regular budget and points to areas where changes could produce reductions in staff and the overall level of the budget while retaining the effectiveness of the Organization. While the vast majority of the measures recommended are essentially of a stop-gap nature – ranging from a salary reduction of 'not less than 3%', to the discontinuance of some 200 'lower priority' programme elements, and to the merger of a number of Secretariat units – it also proposes some major strutural changes such as the abolition of the Economic Commission for Europe, UNDRO, and the Department of Technical Co-operation for Development (whose functions wuld be transferred to other UN system executing agencies). The report also touches upon the issue of the scale of contributions – proposing various alternative assessment formulae where the maximum contribution allowed would be reduced to 10, 15

---

[39] See the Secretary-General's progress report on 'reform and renewal' in the UN, document A/42/234 of 23 April 1987.

[40] *The United Nations: its Problems and What to do About them*, (Washington, DC: Heritage Foundation, 1986).

[41] *United Nations Financial Emergency: Crisis and Opportunity*, New York, August 1986.

or 20 per cent – an area which was cautiously avoided by the Group of 18.

The third proposal came from the UN staff in Geneva.[42] An *ad hoc* independent group of staff members – 'The Study Group for the 40th Anniversay' – took the initiative of sending a questionnaire to all Geneva-based UN staff to give them an opportunity to express their views on how they perceived their Organization and their role in it and to make suggestions to improve not only their daily environment but more generally the functioning of the Organization. On the basis of the numerous replies to the questionnaire (about one-third of the staff responded) and other suggestions received – which provide an interesting x-ray of the staff's motivations and aspirations – and after a round table debate in which one of the members of the Group of 18 participated, the Study Group elaborated '13 Proposals for the Future' which were submitted to the Secretary-General as a contribution to the process of reflection on the crisis of the Organization. The Group's main proposal was the establishment of a Governing Body for the United Nations, composed of a small number of Government representatives, and resulting from the merger of ACABQ, CPC and some of the functions of the subsidiary bodies of ECOSOC. Its principal role would be to define the Organization's priorities and work programme and to ensure continuity in supervision and management between General Assembly sessions. Other proposals dealt with the reinforcement of the Secretary-General's management responsibilities; the establishment of a single autonomous inter-agency body responsible for inspection, audit and evaluation; a more dynamic approach to information and better relationships with NGOs; the introduction of more selective and objective recruitment methods; a reduction in the number of high level posts; the definition of performance evaluation and career development criteria, etc.

Three passports for Utopia

The sub-heading is not meant to be derogatory. The studies reviewed below are on another plane and are perhaps for another century. Although they have a common point of departure with the preceding ones – the occasion of the fortieth anniversary – they go further in their questioning of conventional wisdom. It is therefore easy to dismiss them for not being 'realistic' and not advancing recipes for immediate application. But given the dismally slow pace of change which has resulted from the 'realistic' proposals hitherto reviewed, more far-reaching ideas may become the realistic programme of tomorrow.

A three-chamber UN? Marc Nerfin,[43] President of the International Foundation for Development Alternatives (IFDA), considers that the crisis of multilateralism is also an identity crisis: any serious discussion should start by clarifying what the United Nations really is, and what it can or cannot do. It is necessary to understand better the distance between the UN as an aspiration and the UN as a reflection of realities and explore the margin of liberty that

---

[42] *Study Group for the 40th Anniversary of the United Nations*, 'Results of the Questionnaire', February 1986 and '13 Proposals for the Future', June 1986. These documents can be obtained from the present writer.

[43] Marc Nerfin, 'The Future of the United Nations system: Some questions on the Occasion of an Anniversary', *Development Dialogue*, 1 (1985).

such a distance may offer. Being *le fait du Prince*, the UN is fundamentally an instrument of governments, and this is not only its 'original sin' but also its 'major shortcoming'. It can function properly only when there is agreement among governments. Still the 'UN entity' enjoys a margin of authority, extremely limited in the political sphere, but somewhat larger in the development co-operation sphere. This 'entity' is something more than the mere sum of the governments composing it. But there are other social actors: the economic powers, transnationals, the international banking system, and people in their diversity and movements – religious, peace, consumer and ethnic movements, trade unions etc. Can the UN system accommodate these actors?

'In the global sphere where the UN evolves, the Prince (or governmental power) and the Merchant (or economic power), which control most decisions, have proven unable to offer effective approaches to peace and development. The voices of the third power, that of the people and of the peoples – in whose name the UN Charter was promulgated – remain largely unheard. Could not the people and their associations, which we call the third system – or the Citizen – have a say in the Organization?

Utopian as it may appear today – as did so many ideas, now part of the conventional wisdom, before someone took the first step towards implementing them – couldn't we sketch out a possible UN of 2025? Redeeming its original sin of having been conceived, brought into being and grown up as an organization of governments, the UN of our children and grandchildren will probably reflect better the societies of the world and the actors who make them alive.

This could for instance be achieved through a three-chamber General Assembly of the United Nations. The Prince Chamber would represent the governments of the states (not likely to wither away). The Merchant Chamber would represent the economic powers, be they transnational, multinational, national or local, belonging to the private, state or social sectors, since at the same time we need them and need to regulate their activities – which is better done with them. The Citizen Chamber, where there should be as many women as men, would, through some mechanism ensuring adequate representativity, speak for the people and their associations. At the very least, this would make it possible for citizens to hold Princes and Merchants accountable for the consequences of the exercise of their power.'

Johan Galtung's eight proposals.[44] This study starts with an assessment of the achievements of the United Nations: judged against our goals and aspirations the Organization has fallen far short of what we had hoped for. But 'looking backward in time, judged by what has happened during the last forty years it is a tremendous success': it has quasi-universal membership, it has played a very important role in the process of decolonization, a number of conflicts have been handled through dialogue, advances have been made in development and human rights. Galtung sees the UN's basic role as a forum where problems and conflicts can be articulated and made transparent and where ideas can be formulated about their solution – whether or not it is in a position to actually solve them (implementation resting principally with member-states). Member states should use the United Nations as training in 'world citizenship': if

[44] Johan Galtung, *The United Nations Today: problems and some proposals*, (Center of International Studies, Princeton University, November 1986)

The Processes of Change in the United Nations 307

conflicts cannot be resolved, member states should learn to 'put them aside, forget about them until something happens that makes it possible to solve them peacefully'. His eight concrete proposals are summarized hereunder:

1. Change the UN contribution structure: the US 25 per cent contribution gives it a *de facto* economic veto (in addition to the political veto it enjoys in the Security Council). The present situation is intolerable, because the whole organization is 'kept on its toes, anxiously counting signs of pleasure and displeasure from the major contributor'. The Soviet contribution stands at 12 per cent; it might be a good idea to reduce the US to an equivalent amount.
2. Cut UN salaries by 30 per cent. High salaries do not necessarily attract the best people; they attract 'the type of people who are interested in high salaries'. Cut them down, especially for high ranking postings, and people motivated by other things than money will be attracted.
3. Stop using the UN as a dumping ground for failed politicians in member states.
4. Dewaldheimization of the UN system! Until now Secretariats have been indoctrinated in the sacredness of governments in general and the United Nations as a trade union of governments in particular.
5. Reduce the significance of the executive heads of the UN agencies. More internal democracy and freedom of expression would contribute to higher staff morale.
6. Move the United Nations out of the United States, i.e. away from a hostile environment which has a detrimental influence on the Organizations. His preferred locations are Berlin, with the headquarters bridging the 'infamous wall', or Southeast Asia thus giving more prominence to this dynamic part of the world.
7. Abolish the Security Council.
8. Make the United Nations less a government monopoly: the other actors, such as transnational corporations and international peoples organizations, should be granted some kind of representation.

One Europe: One World: a first exploration of Europe's potential contribution to world order. This report[45] by Christopher Layton, a former high-ranking EEC official, starts by registering humanity's failure to develop the institutions and means of international action which are needed if the 'threats to the human condition' – ecological disaster, poverty, economic failure and war – are to be overcome.

Within Europe, the European Community despite its weaknesses is an island of relative peace and stability, a living example of practical co-operation between former enemies. Yet so far, the European nations, despite immense economic strength and political potential, have largely failed to apply their strength creatively to the reform of the world's economic and political institutions. It is time for the European Community to develop initiatives, and strategies to help build a more stable, just and harmonious world. Europe needs to work systematically to promote and encourage regional unity in other parts of the world, as a means towards peace and greater prosperity. The report sets out the following key proposals:

[45] Christopher Layton, 'One Europe: One World. A first exploration of Europe's Potential Contribution to World Order', Special Supplement no. 4, *Journal of World Trade Law*, 1986.

- The infant impulse towards regional unity in Latin America, Africa and the Pacific, the Middle East and elsewhere needs to be accelerated and encouraged from outside. It is one key element in resolving conflict and achieving sustainable development and joint protection of the environment. It can help build a more balanced, multipolar world.
- The debt problem must be tackled boldly, partly in a regional context, by writing off the debts of the poorest countries, and reducing others. In return key environmental assets, like major parts of the tropical forest, should be placed in a world environmental trust, regionally administered.
- At world level, the economic system desperately needs reform, in the short run by making exchange rates more stable and realistic, stabilising capital movements and developing greater harmony in macroeconomic policy. But in the medium term there will have to be a radical reconstruction of the world's financial and economic institutions.
- A world reserve currency is needed, issued and controlled, not by the most powerful country, but by a world institution in which power is better balanced between the major regions of the world. Overcoming world poverty requires the rich North to accept responsibility for a transfer of resources to the poorer South on a scale comparable to the transfers within a modern welfare state.
- New worldwide agreements, backed by actions in the regions, will be needed to legislate against pollution and preserve key resources, such as forests and coastal seas.
- The arms race cannot go on indefinitely. Either it will stop or we will. The process of disarmament, however, will require a sustained effort of confidence-building, and political detente. Within that essential framework the tide can first be stopped by a comprehensive test ban, a moratorium on new weapons, a freeze – and then systematically rolled back by cuts and mutual force reductions. All that, however, will require institutions, for inspection – such as a joint satellite-monitoring agency – and, in the end, a new system of collective security.

These practical steps, however, will not succeed unless they are inspired by a political commitment to build and support international institutions that work. Just as the European Community was inspired by a long-term political vision, so progress towards world order needs to combine functional steps to cope with economic, ecological and security challenges with a readiness to build 'a system of world governance that works'.

The report therefore concludes by exploring ways in which the United Nations might be made more effective: reform of the Security Council, reducing the use of veto, and the replacement of present national representatives by a representative from each of the major regions of the world; the gradual development of some kind of parliamentary forum, perhaps including delegates from regional parliaments; a more effective Secretary General with greater powers of initiative.

The UNA–USA's successor vision

The use of the European experience as a model or as an inspiration for reform of the United Nations seems to be gaining popularity. We have seen that the underlying theme of the Bertrand report was the establishment of a small

Economic Security Council – meeting at the ministerial level – and of a Commission of eminent and independent personalities each in charge of directing specific sectors of the UN system. Very similar ideas have now been put forward in the recent report of the United Nations Association of the USA.[46] This is not altogether surprising since M. Bertrand worked as consultant for the UNA-USA's 'UN Management and Decision-Making Project'. What is more surprising – and encouraging – is the fact that far-reaching ideas for reform of the United Nations were endorsed by an international panel chaired by former Attorney-General Elliot L. Richardson and comprising some twenty personalities from North and South (but none from the Eastern bloc) ranging from Mrs Kassebaum and Mrs Kirkpatrick to Mr Salim-Salim (Tanzania) and Olara Otunnu (Uganda).

The report's fundamental recommendation is the re-organization of the entire UN system – including to some extent the Bretton Woods Organizations – around a small 25-member Ministerial Board within ECOSOC and a UN Commission both largely inspired by the EEC model. The vision of the future United Nations proposed in the report is based on the idea that the UN lacks a small political centre for high level consultations on urgent matters of human security and welfare. This 'global watch' function would be the prerequisite for 'Consensus-building' by providing an appropriate framework for negotiations and for the third function, i.e. the 'conversion of agreements into action'. The report is bold enough to recognize that its recommendations go beyond tinkering with the structure of the Organization and require a modification of the Charter. That the panel was prepared to infringe this 'taboo' is particularly encouraging. Whether this package of coherent proposals, many of which are far-reaching – such as the recommendation to merge the executive boards of UNDP, UNICEF and the World Food Programme in order to increase the effectiveness of UN operational activities – will eventually pass the test of intergovernmental scrutiny remains to be seen. The strength of the report lies in that it attempts to provide the basis for the establishment at the global level of a credible institution with a reasonable and clearer mandate: i.e. analysis and joint action to confront the global problems that nation states are no longer in a position to cope with. This is indeed a *sine qua non* in any attempt to check the seemingly unabating marginalisation of the United Nations.

Elusive reform: Some questions and conclusions

At the end of our journey through the labyrinth of UN reform attempts, it may be worthwhile to pose some pertinent questions on the meaning of all these efforts. Can they be reduced to a common denominator? What convergent points emerge from the analysis? Where do they lead us?

The analyses/proposals/blueprints for reform reviewed above can be seen as forming three concentric circles, with the two outer circles adding on new features to those identified in the inner one:

1. The inner circle is the one of *managerial and administrative reform*. Everyone agrees on the identification of the ills and on the need for change. Structural change is seen as either unnecessary or impossible to bring about because of

---

[46] *A Successor Vision: The United Nations of Tomorrow*, Final panel report of the UNA-USA United Nations Management and Decision-Making Project, New York, September 1987.

'political realities' or, as the UN catch-phrase goes, because of 'lack of political will'. It is, however, possible and indeed necessary to introduce important changes by refining existing mechanisms and techniques for co-ordination, planning, programming, and evaluation. The goal is to shape a tidier and more effective organization through incremental measures and selective tinkering. This is what has been convincingly described by Renninger as 'the theory and practice of muddling through'.[47] It is how most of the changes which have taken place in the United Nations over the past forty-odd years – with the exception of the setting up of new institutions – have in fact occurred. It is the preferred approach of government delegates and Secretariat officials since it does not really call their respective roles into question. The fact that it has been an obvious failure – many of the reports or analyses written fifteen or twenty years ago could be re-issued today with the same validity – has not yet discouraged its advocates and it is certainly in this circle that formal consensus on issues for reform can most easily be reached.

2. The middle circle is the one for *structural change*. Here the existing constitutional and institutional foundations of the Organization are seen as sound, but the problems of the Organization are of such magnitude that mere tinkering with organization charts is not enough. The typical examples of advocacy for structural change are the Capacity Study and the Restructuring exercise: in both cases, a lot of time, effort and dedication went into the preparation of a well-thought out, coherent proposal. However, they were more or less diluted when they went through the meat-mincing exercise of intergovernmental scrutiny. Compromise texts were adopted, but implementation was further diluted if not defeated either by the 'sociological weights' built into the system (the principality syndrome) or by outright Secretariat resistance to change. As for the Group of 18 report, one hesitates even to include it in this circle. The fact that a financial crisis gives birth to a committee of experts is certainly not a new phenomenon and many of the Group's recommendations are simply repetitions of past proposals concerning the functioning of the intergovernmental machinery or the streamlining of the Secretariat. What is new perhaps is the aggressive tone and a sense of urgency which transpires from the Group's report and from the Secretary-General's reports on the implementation of the measures decided by the General Assembly.

3. The outer circle is the realm of not only structural but also *institutional change*. It contains the UNA/USA 'successor vision' straddled across the border with the middle circle, Bertrand's realistic diagnosis but partly visionary prognosis for a 'third generation international organization', and, on more distant clouds, the utopian proposals mentioned in the preceding section. The common characteristic of the inhabitants of this circle is their belief that it is necessary to put the purpose of international co-operation before the tinkering with modalities and instrumentalities.

Change is on the agenda. Managerial and administrative no doubt there will be. How much structural change will accompany it to prevent managerial and administrative advances from being swallowed by inertia and entropy is difficult to say. Will there be any institutional change? It must be recognized that this approach, tempting as it may be for outsiders, has very few proponents either among governments or in the higher strata of the Secretariat. At present, the political climate can hardly be considered favourable, but things may

[47] Renninger, *Survey and Analysis*, op.cit, p. 38.

evolve if the other approaches do not yield durable results. Some infinitesimal shifts indicating that the climate may be warming-up a little are, however, perceptible. Without being unduly optimistic, the following may be worth noting:

– The general mood in the UN is one of preoccupation and concern. On the one hand, there is recognition on the part of the US Administration that the congressional chain-reactions to its 'firmer' attitude towards the United Nations have gone awry. On the other, changes in attitude are also perceptible within the Group of 77. It has become less monolithic. Less Developed Countries, Newly Industrialized Countries and debt-burdened countries do not automatically pursue convergent tactics. The atmosphere in UNCTAD VII was less confrontational with an emphasis on problem-solving rather than on the quest for a new order (if confrontation there was, it was mainly between the United States and the rest of the world);
– The Soviet attitude towards the United Nations is changing. The recent signing of the Common Fund agreement, overtures in the direction of GATT, the World Bank and the IMF, and Mr Gorbachev's generally supportive tone vis à vis the UN – as shown by recent declarations[48] – are signs that the Soviet Union may revert to active rather than passive diplomacy in UN fora, while respecting the spirit of the game;
– There seems to be a discernible convergence to at least seriously consider the 'Council-Commission' idea. The UNA-USA report has given it quasi-official standing in Western circles. The Secretary-General's latest annual report on the state of the Organization,[49] hints positively at it and although a cautious conditional tense is used, this is perhaps a recognition that it is not such a 'personalized' idea any more.

The ways to reform are most certainly paved with good intentions, but before concluding this article it is necessary to underline the rather peculiar nature of UN reform proposals which reflects the peculiar nature of the complex world of the United Nations. This world is inhabited not by laymen but by specialists – diplomats, international civil servants, experts and other specialists of various kinds. The UN system is perhaps the most complex organizational entity in the world: nothing falls outside its all-encompassing mandate. As has been pointed out, because of the complexity of their universe, these specialists tend to 'limit their examination to the organization itself, and to forget the outside world'.[50] Analyses are made 'through the filter of collective interests' which is strengthened by the frequent professional mobility of the same individuals who alternatively hold positions as experts, professors, diplomats and international civil servants. This 'revolving doors' aspect of careers taking place within or around UN organizations has seldom been studied and its impact on the creation of a kind of 'UN collective unconscious' or 'UN vision of the world' is probably underestimated.

The reform proposals/attempts reviewed here have a slightly incestuous flavour. Practically all are by-products of the UN collective unconscious in the sense that their authors (and the official or *ad hoc* committees who reviewed

---

[48] Mikhail Gorbachev's article. 'The Reality and Guarantees of a Secure World', *TASS*, Moscow, 16 September 1987.
[49] 'Report of the Secretary-General on the Work of the Organization', A/42/1, September 1987.
[50] M. Bertrand, art.cit.

312 *Antonio Donini*

some of the studies) *all* come from within or around the UN system. With the exception of Layton, all the principal authors have been either staff members, 'officials' or experts of the United Nations.

Another constant that must be underlined is the convergence of all the studies reviewed on key concepts which are basically of a technocratic nature: simplification, concentration, integration, co-ordination, efficiency, effectiveness, accountability. Few attempt higher level considerations such as 'whither?' or 'what for the United Nations?'. Such persistence in managerial and technocratic recipes seems perfectly natural for the defenders of the logic of Western reason. It tends to conceal, however, the ideological foundations of the crisis and it is far from being universally accepted. Many Third World countries have no reason to go along with this vision of reform. They are suspicious, because they are afraid, not without reason, that technical and managerial solutions will result in a reduction of their political strength in the main UN organs.[51]

This leads us to another disturbing common characteristic: ethnocentrism. The initiative for reform – with the possible exception of the 'restructuring exercise' – has come exclusively from the West. The South has of course participated in the debate, but from a basically defensive position. As for the East, Krushchev's proposal of 1960 for a 'troika' of three Secretaries-General has not been followed by any significant ideas for reform. Does this mean that the United Nations as it is corresponds to the *needs* of the South (and the Eastern bloc), while it no longer corresponds to the *interests* of the North? What are the chances of reform if the South and East are either not interested or are merely reacting defensively to reform proposals?

The ethnocentricity of reform zealots is compounded by their relationship with the academic community, especially in the United States, where because of the geographical proximity with the UN headquarters, much interaction presumably takes place. The present writer is by no means a specialist in the subject but he was surprised – in fact, shocked – that so little attention is being paid by the US academic community to research efforts on UN questions being conducted outside the anglo-saxon world. A cursory look at the bibliographical entries in the main academic journals dealing with international organizations will provide ample proof of this monocultural pervasiveness – the overwhelming majority of the studies and scholars quoted are anglo-saxon, the remainder (say 10 per cent) are emigrés or . . . translations. Take as an example the otherwise stimulating analyses on international organizations as a field of study which have appeared in *International Organization*.[52] The impression is that it is taken for granted that the universe of UN studies belongs to anglo-saxon academics; nothing is said of what is being produced in continental Europe, not to mention the socialist countries or the Third World. This one-sidedness does not augur well for the interactions between the academic world and the United Nations. Or should one assume, *horresco referens*, that the US academic community is convinced that 'science is on its side', much in the same way that the US political community believed that the United Nations had been set up to further the propagation of US values and interests?

At the beginning of this article we noted that a lot of static stood in way of

---

[51] On this point see Pierre de Senarclens, *La dérive. Essai sur la crise des Nations Unies* (Paris: Presses Universitaires de France, 1988), chapter IX.

[52] *International Organization*, vol. 40, no. 4, Autumn 1986.

reform. Will reform come from outside the system? Judging from past attempts this is less than certain. But what is the place of the United Nations in the outside world? Many of the reformist studies reviewed have pointed to the increasing marginalization of the Organization. Can an inversion of this trend take place if the political and ideological dimensions of the crisis are not clearly put on the negotiating table? This is doubtful. A new historical compromise on the reactivation of the UN system will only come about if all the parties concerned become convinced that the game is worth the candle.

It has become a truism to predicate the future existence of the United Nations on the challenges of interdependence, on the recognition that the problems of the 21st century do not end at the borders of nation states. But is there sufficient evidence to prove that a 'universal membership' Organization is the best possible framework to come to grips with these problems? The experience of recent years would seem to show that there is a growing tendency to attempt to govern world problems elsewhere: through the Bretton Woods Organizations, through a 'Condominium of the Powerful' (the Western economic summits, the USA-USSR summits) and through increasing integration, whether on a regional or like-minded states basis (EEC, CMEA, ASEAN, OECD). Because of the marginalization of the United Nations, the Third World – and especially the smaller countries who cannot make their voice heard in any other forum – is effectively excluded from the picture.

How can this situation be redressed? Should one conclude that the reactivation of the UN system cannot be convincingly based on 'objective' facts and that the *problématique* of reform can only be seen in ideological or idealistic terms? Is an act of faith the prerequisite for reform?

For fundamental ethical reasons the only reasonable course of action might be to 'take a bet' that the global challenges of tomorrow – the debt, ozone layer depletion, AIDS, the drug problem, refugees, international migrations, etc. – can best be confronted in a 'universal membership' organization. If this is the case, i.e. if a number of sufficiently representative member states are prepared to accept this risk, then, the terms of the new compromise could be worked out. The support of outside public opinion would also have to be mustered: the 1985 famine in Africa has shown that this can be a potent force in spurring slow-moving superstructures to action. It is not inconceivable that the peace movements, the Greens and other environmental citizens' movements which mobilize on issues of human survival, might apply the proper pressures, nationally and internationally.

This is not the place to provide an outline for a possible compromise. Many issues, both conceptual and substantial, still need to be studied and clarified. However, in the view of the present writer, two important issues require priority attention if a meaningful institutional reform of the United Nations is to take place.

The first is the smokescreen surrounding the Charter. As has often been pointed out,[53] the UN Charter is an expression of Western – if not Anglo-Saxon – values, but forty years of post-war history are showing that the West's Law is no longer universal.[54] This is being made abundantly clear not only by

---

[53] De Senarclens, *La dérive*, op.cit; Williams, *The Speicalized Agencies*, op.cit. Preface; see also the stimulating points made by M. Elmandjra, *UN Organizations* op.cit.

[54] M. Bertrand, 'Universality', in *Is Universality in Jeopardy* (UN publication, 1987); see also de Senarclens, *La dérive*, op.cit., chapter X.

314   *Antonio Donini*

the spawning of fundamentalism but also by the fact that the values and lifestyles of the West are being increasingly challenged – not least by groups in the West itself. There has been a fragmentation of the dominant technocratic model. It is becoming increasingly difficult to export it without exporting its antibodies (ecology, 'another development', grass-roots initiatives, etc.). More important perhaps are the symbolic consequences of this fragmentation: the Charter was drawn up by roughly one-third of the present UN member- ship. More than 100 countries joined the club without having a say on what the rules really meant. Would the Charter be the same if they had had a chance to negotiate it? In these circumstances is it reasonable to expect that the Charter can be fully internalized by all the membership? Should not a compromise be based on give and take by all groups and on an agreement which every signa- tory can consider as 'his own'? Attempts to revise the Charter have until now encountered the entrenched opposition of the five Permanent Members of the Security Council to all but the most minor and non-controversial changes. As all revisions are subject to veto it does appear highly unlikely that any substantive changes could be introduced in the foreseeable future, but this is not a sufficient reason for avoiding the problem. If a climate for reform develops, ultimately the Charter will need to be revised.

The second important issue concerns UN system development activities. These were not really foreseen in the Charter and represent a deviation from the principle of international co-operation for the benefit of all members. These activities are operationally restricted to one part of the membership, and have acted as a conveyor-belt for Western rationality. They are based on the concept of 'assistance' – often a euphemism for charity and mendicity – rather than co-operation, and the pressure to spend and do good has often had counter- productive results. UN technical co-operation activities have often been criti- cized for their fragmentation, lack of impact, small size of the projects and of the overall amounts of money involved, but the fact that they divide the membership of the United Nations into two groups of unequal value – the 'haves' and 'have-nots' – thereby introducing a dangerous dichotomy between the normative and operational functions of the Organization, has seldom attracted serious attention.[55] Unless the 'invention' of technical assistance is a part of a Machiavellian ploy to reinforce the *status quo* in international relations, the time has come to question the validity of the approach. Some have argued for the pure and simple abolition of UN system technical co-operation activities – with the possible exception of emergency and humanitarian relief operations.[56] Should not this lop-sidedness in the relationships among mem- bers be replaced by co-operation for the benefit of all? Why should operational activities related to, say, rural development, unemployment or the homeless be restricted to the South? Are there no problems in the North, or is this not a convenient way of keeping the Organization from looking at problems and contradictions within the North? Should not co-operation be looked at globally taking into account not only the international dimensions of particular issues but also the intra-national dimensions in both North and South?

The reactivation of the UN will in the final analysis depend on the narrow- ing of the gap in perceptions as to what the United Nations is and what it can do

[55] This point was convincingly made in 1973 by M. Elmandjra, *The United Nations System: An Analysis* (London: Faber and Faber), p. 316.
[56] See Elmandjra, *Ways* etc., op.cit.

to improve the quality of international co-operation. At present the dominant perception in the North is that the United Nations is 'all give and no take'. The dominant perception in the South is probably that the North's attitude in international relations is 'not much give and all take'. As President Alfonsin put it – he was referring to the debt problem but the analogy is wider in scope – these relations are 'like an inverted Marshall plan where the South is helping the industrialized countries to get richer'.[57]

[57] Quoted in *Le Monde*, 8 October 1987.

[18]

PUBLIC ADMINISTRATION AND DEVELOPMENT, VOL. 16, 43–56 (1996)

Towards a management renewal of the United Nations—Part I

MICHAEL GURSTEIN

University College of Cape Breton, Canada

JOSEF KLEE

New York, NY, USA

SUMMARY

This article addresses the hitherto largely neglected subject of administrative reform of the United Nations—without which, the capacity of the Organization to carry out its increasingly critical global mandates effectively and efficiently, is severely constrained, with efforts in this direction being for the most part incremental, indecisive and ineffectual. The problems arise partly from the originating and continuing model for the UN's organization and culture, which predate the advent, for example, of modern automated systems of personnel and financial management. Other elements of the problem arise from the UN's system of governance—the oversight committees, senior staff nominations by Member States, allocation of funds or approvals for critical management and administrative reforms. As at the national level, impactful UN reform also requires internal management leadership, follow-up, the continuity and UN experience of top officials, capacity to design and implement measures, and budget flexibility to procure outside expertise.

In a second, concluding, part of the article, the authors will suggest a strategy for UN reform and a process for carrying forward a 'renewal exercise' to equip the Organization for its role beyond the year 2000.

UNITED NATIONS REFORM MATTERS

On its 50th birthday, the United Nations is in trouble. More and more countries are becoming concerned with entrusting their young men and women in arms, their diminishing public funds, and the awesome mandates attempting to stitch together an increasingly factious world to an organization whose decision-making, leadership, budgeting and financial administration are so evidently inadequate to the task.

An organization whose recruitment procedures can take up to 18 months and still end up with mediocre appointees, where procurement of even the most vital goods or services—airplanes to deliver peacekeeping troops to battlefields, for example—may require 6 months simply to process the paper when the requirement is to have the

Dr Gurstein is SSHRC/NSERC Associate Chair, Management of Technological Change, and Associate Professor, School of Business, University College of Cape Breton, Sydney, Nova Scotia. He was formerly Management Adviser, Audit and Management Consulting Division, Office of Internal Oversight Services, United Nations, New York and Dr. Klee was formerly Deputy Director of the same Division.

troops on the ground in 2 weeks; where at any one time (at least up to recent months) perhaps one-third of all staff members may be working (and being paid) without having a valid contract; where the phone book and organization charts are prepared by telephone round robins to individual units so that whole sections can be left out if someone happens to be on vacation, is not an organization that inspires confidence in even the least advanced of national administrations.

Still the United Nations is worth saving if only because if it did not exist it would need to be created anew, and who knows whether a 'new' United Nations would not have the same or even more debilitating problems than the current one.

The United Nations matters even if its failings and limitations sometimes prevent it from carrying out the expanded and extended mandates that a globalizing, contracting, economically stagnating, environmentally degrading, culturally eroding, institutionally disintegrating world is anxious to pass on. The global problems are beyond what any one country can or should address on its own. The world needs a body that looks after the whole, the commons, the planet, the well-being of all of us as 'we the people'.

There is widespread acknowledgement that not only does the United Nations need reform of its political and deliberative institutions (the Security Council, the General Assembly and the Economic and Social Council) but it also needs reform in its administrative structures and the processes that underlie and support all of the other activities and responsibilities. There is an emerging recognition that if these 'plumbing' i.e. administrative and managerial activities, are ineffectively executed or grossly inefficient, it is difficult to see how the Organization can successfully carry out its political or economic mandates.

United States President Clinton said in his General Assembly remarks on the occasion of the UN's 50th Anniversary, 'All who contribute to the UN's work and care about its future must also be committed to reform—to ending bureaucratic inefficiencies and outdated priorities. The UN must be able to show that the money it receives supports saving and enriching people's lives, not unneeded overhead. Reform requires breaking up bureaucratic fiefdoms, eliminating obsolete agencies, and doing more with less. The UN must reform to remain relevant and to play a still stronger role in the march of freedom, peace and prosperity.'

A renewal of the United Nations must have as its goal to shift the Organization from the patterns and culture of the 'old' United Nations, those of stalemate, compromise and the Cold War, to that of a 'new' modern United Nations, effectively organized and managed to execute the broadened and globally critical mandates that have been assigned to it.

Some observations might be of interest especially in the context of attempting to stimulate change within the Secretariat towards a modern, efficient and well-managed organization. Given the 'business' of the UN, and given the collapse in a significant element of the external political and values framework within which the UN has undertaken its business for the first 50 years of its existence, how best can it 're-invent itself' to appropriately meet the ever-mounting challenges it faces in the next 50 years.

United Nations renewal and management reform must be comprehensive and should address a number of new and different concerns and responsibilities:

- The end of the Cold War has changed the context for United Nations operations and management in general. Member States have higher expectations concerning the nature, quality and cost-effectiveness of the United Nations' activities and services. Thus, all management systems and practices must be re-thought and rebuilt not only to promote economy in the use of United Nations' resources, but also to encourage efficient, effective, timely and 'quality' results that are responsive to the wide variety of global needs the United Nations is now expected to address.

- The United Nations faces tremendous political and management challenges due to the evolution and growth of the United Nations's role in peace-keeping and its extension into peace-making and peace-building and related humanitarian missions; and also its efforts in elections monitoring and the rebuilding of government structures where these have corroded or collapsed. To operationalize these roles the United Nations must become action-oriented and develop competencies in a number of operational area as well as requiring the design and implementation of new systems for large-scale management.

- There are concerns that the United Nations has too narrow a base of representation and that the voices of the non-governmental organizations specifically, and more broadly the general public, are not being heard. Changes in these areas will require, and can be facilitated by, changes in management and administrative practices.

THE UNITED NATIONS IS NOT WORKING AS WELL AS IT SHOULD

In many respects the United Nations more closely resembles a *colonial (or post-colonial) administration of the 1950s* than a modern global and world-impacting organization. Its personnel practices, financial rules, and procurement procedures largely predate the existence of automated information management systems and global telecommunications networks. Its management practices reflect little awareness of developments in the last 40 years and the fact that management has become a 'professional' activity.

The result of the 'time warp' is that the United Nations' administrative systems are inefficient and ineffective in achieving its objectives and ill-equipped to deal with the additional demands that are being placed upon it. Cost savings of tens of millions of dollars would be available with relatively modest capital investment.

The United Nations is almost certainly one of the most tightly, if ineffectively, supervised and overseen organizations in the world. It is directly overseen by a number of legislative and oversight bodies such as the Advisory Committee on Administrative and Budgetary Questions, the Committee for Programme and Co-ordination, the Fifth Committee, the Board of External Auditors, the Joint Inspection Unit, the Office of Internal Oversight Services, the General Assembly of course, and for many matters, the Security Council. Budgetary scrutiny, including to the classification level of individual posts (United Nations-ese for positions), or the amount of money to be assigned by individual departments to travel or to consulting may be the subject of discussion and debate in the legislative bodies. Indeed, they frequently become part of the *political* deal making of the Organization.

The effect is an organization in which managers not only are not allowed to manage but may on a regular basis be subject to external interference from bodies who do not fully understand the UN's administrative requirements. In this context managers become passive and reluctant to exercise management initiatives or to accept full responsibility for their assigned activities and allocated financial and personnel resources.

With few exceptions (the recently created post of US Ambassador for United Nations Management and Reform being one), there is remarkably little sustained support for United Nations administrative reform. Perhaps reflecting their own inexperience with administrative and management matters, the contributions of delegates in these areas rarely go beyond exhortations to operate efficiently, to expand mandates 'within existing resources', or to find and punish the perpetrators of what is considered to be the 'widespread' instances of 'waste, fraud and abuse'. While at least some Member States are becoming perceptibly more critical of the administrative weaknesses of the Organization, this stance has not translated into an upgrading of the professional level of expertise in the various United Nations Management oversight committees (as, for example, through the use of national management experts as a source of delegates), or to the nomination of technically or managerially experienced staff to those senior level staff positions where such nominations are routinely solicited.

The lack of political attention for administrative reform has meant that efforts towards broader systematic reform do not gain the kind of political support that they require, including the legislative decisions regarding changes in financial and personnel rules that would facilitate such developments.

Perhaps inevitably there is also little or no recognition or support for such initiatives from senior managers within the Organization itself. Little active support from the Office of the Secretary-General is evident for significant reform initiatives and little public leadership is available in these areas. Occasionally there will be a public pronouncement *but no follow-up*.

The Secretary-General, no doubt correctly, seems to see his primary responsibility as being that of global statesman *rather than as the CEO of the United Nations Secretariat*. However, Article 97 of the United Nations Charter stipulates that the Secretary-General is 'the Chief Administrative Officer of the Organization'. From this it follows that all final decisions in administrative, as in other matters, rest with the Secretary-General and in practice no truly significant reform initiative could be undertaken without the active participation of the Secretary-General acting as CEO/CAO.

In the absence of concern or experience on his part or that of his immediate office in administrative matters, the cause of administrative reform is left as an orphan. Normally, the Under-Secretary-General for Administration and Management is expected to initiate and promote better management and higher productivity. However, in recent times this post has been occupied on a transient basis often with senior officials who themselves have had very limited management experience or experience in the UN and thus were compromised in their effectiveness. Moreover, this post itself lacks direct access to the range and depth of human and especially financial resources that would be required for truly effective reform initiatives. Close observers of the Organization are not particularly optimistic that current efforts at reform from this source will prove to be any more successful than *earlier efforts*.

Reflecting the lack of attention by the Secretary-General to administrative reform, it has not been possible to develop a *coordinated and integrated strategy* to deal with administrative renewal. The result has been a number of initiatives, isolated and incremental—'management accountability and responsibility' directives, the Integrated Management Information System (IMIS), procurement task forces, personnel strategies—announced with significant fanfare, pursued with ever-decreasing enthusiasm and in the end perhaps to be buried with the least publicity possible as have *so many previous efforts.*

Because so many of the problems in the United Nations are at the level of overall administrative systems, *dealing with problems incrementally* has meant that no resolution could be effectively achieved for many of them. Thus, for example, in the area of procurement, not only is there a need to reform the procurement procedures to make them more responsive, transparent and accountable but there is the even more basic need to modify the financial and personnel rules of the Organization to accommodate the procurement reforms that are widely acknowledged as being necessary.

The United Nations lacks professional managers and a *cohesive management culture.* Originally, the United Nations was designed, from a personnel perspective, on the model of the British or the French colonial services where if one chose appropriately educated entry level personnel there was no need for technical or professional staff except in supporting or highly specialized capacities. Managers were trained as they rose through the ranks. This approach worked remarkably well for both the British and the French until the need for a high degree of knowledge and professional managerial capacity to handle technology and increasingly complex administrative environments forced changes even in these administrations. In any case, these services were both large enough and operated well enough initially that potential high level managers were given sufficient breadth of experience and ongoing senior level support and mentoring.

The United Nations has virtually no capacity for launching and implementing profound management reforms and productivity improvements. The Organization lacks experts who could carry out this renewal work and has no budget flexibilities to allow it to procure external expertise for administrative planning or analysis. Senior staff are almost without exception, either generalists who have worked their way up through the system or specialists in one or another UN service area with no broad management experience or perspective on how things are done outside the UN. There is little capacity for acquiring the services of trained or experienced management outsiders for the Organization. Frequently, where outsiders are brought in, it is into positions where a deep knowledge of United Nations practice (and not incidentally personalities) would be beneficial. And perhaps not accidentally these outsiders are generally not provided with the means of readily familiarizing themselves with the Organization as, for example, through personally being able to select professional staff aides and assistants. A number of competent and experienced outsiders brought in (or pushed in by Member States) to significant administrative positions have found themselves isolated and bewildered by the gnostic world of United Nations administrative practice and, frustrated, they have left (or even been forced out) after relatively short and ineffective tenures.

The United Nations, as with any large organization, develops internal resistances to change or, looked at another way, commitments to maintaining the status quo. The United Nations, however, with the complexity of its rules and the heterogeneity of its staff, has perhaps a greater reluctance to change than many organizations.

Existing staff have a significant investment in the current rules since it is these that give them their influence and status in the Organization. The more esoteric the system, the more influence it gives to those few who understand it even if such knowledge is of little value outside the Organization.

PAST ATTEMPTS TO REFORM THE UNITED NATIONS' STRUCTURES AND MANAGEMENT

In the past, a number of initiatives have been launched to improve United Nations' management and to make the Organization more effective and efficient. Most of these reform efforts were limited to streamlining the organizational structure. The United Nations has never undergone a *comprehensive management renewal exercise based on an in-depth review of all management processes* with the objective of increasing productivity and administrative efficiency and reducing costs. The practical results of these *past reform attempts* have been minimal. It is, however, worthwhile to take a *brief look at some of these efforts* because many of the issues remain and *certain of the proposals for improving the United Nations are still valid.*[1]

The Group of 18

A comprehensive reform exercise was launched in 1985 in response to a General Assembly resolution requesting a 'review of the efficiency of the administrative and financial functioning of the United Nations'. The review group consisted of 18 representatives of Member States, most with very limited management experience. The Group of 18 conducted its review in accordance with normal United Nations meeting procedures and with the assistance of United Nations' staff members. The Group did not undertake or request any in-depth management studies or system analyses.

The Group of 18 held 67 meetings in 4 sessions. It produced a report summarizing the findings and made 71 recommendations covering 6 areas: inter-governmental machinery, the structure of the Secretariat, measures regarding personnel, monitoring, evaluation and inspection, planning and budget procedures, and implementation of the Group's recommendations (United Nations, 1986).

The quality of the findings and recommendations could be described as 'uneven'. Some issues were discussed in detail while others were put forward in a statement or recommendation. Two issues and recommendations have had a *lasting impact and deserve mentioning.* One was the recommendation for *substantial staff reduction* (Recommendation 15). The Group proposed a 15 per cent cut within 3 years in the overall number of regular budget posts and a 25 per cent cut in the number of posts at the level of Under-Secretary-General (USG) and Assistant Secretary-General (ASG). The second issue was reform of the *planning and budget mechanism.* The Group put forward alternatives for the preparation and processing of the medium-term plan and the programme budget. The final outcome, however, was the present

[1]See also Collins, 1987, p. 129.

cumbersome and lengthy process of submitting to and reviewing the United Nations' medium-term plan and budget by the various legislative bodies.[2]

Implementation of the recommendations was done in a half-hearted fashion without strong management commitment. The Secretary-General submitted to the General Assembly *two progress* reports on the implementation of the measures proposed and a final report in 1989 (Document A/44/22). A number of the recommendations were indeed implemented; certain personnel-related recommendations were submitted to the *International Civil Service Commission* for further study with, in some cases, the Secretary-General arguing that implementation would not be feasible or beneficial. As regards the recommendation on the 15 per cent post reduction, the Secretary-General established a task force to work out a reduction proposal. The task force, rather than conducting a strategic productivity or workload review, took the 'easy' approach by simply proposing in the main the abolition of those posts that were vacant at the time of the review.

The Boutros Ghali-restructuring/revitalizing exercises

Another recent major attempt at reforming the UN was undertaken when the present Secretary-General took office. At that time, there was a 'widespread feeling within the Membership that the Secretariat should be restructured in order to respond effectively to the challenges facing it' (United Nations, 1995, para 4). The Secretary-General began his restructuring efforts with considerable rhetorical force, his initial plan being 'to consolidate and streamline the Organization's activities into well-defined functional categories aimed at ensuring effective implementation of the objectives of the Charter . . .'.

Moreover, it was always understood that the restructuring of the Secretariat would be a *first* phase in a revitalization process (United Nations, 1992, para 5). This restructuring exercise consisted primarily of the merging of departments and other organizational units and, as a result, a considerable number of senior posts were eliminated. The original reorganization plan included merging the existing two departments concerned with economic and social development into one. However, only a few months after the announcement of the restructuring, the Secretary-General decided to subdivide the single consolidated department into three separate departments.[3]

The rationale given by the Secretary-General for creating the three new departments remains murky. To date there is no clear demarcation among the functions, responsibilities or missions assigned to the three departments. As Dick Thornburgh, at the time just completing his stay as Under-Secretary-General for Administration and Management predicted, this arrangement has led 'to turf battles, duplication and mal-coordination, as well as to additional post and costs' (United Nations, 1993).

---

[2]See also Collins, 1987, p. 122.

[3]*The rumour* has been that senior posts needed to be found for nationals of India, France and China and for protocol reasons these had to be at the Under-Secretary level. By UN rules, Under-Secretaries manage departments and thus departments needed to be created to justify the appointment of these Under-Secretaries, with of course the usual complement of Assistant Sercretaries, administrative officers, support staff and so on.

50   *M. Gurstein and J. Klee*

This exercise towards 'reform and revitalization' most evidently did not go beyond simply moving boxes on organization charts. There was none of the needed rationalizing of functions; work flow streamlining or re-engineering, or revising of job definitions, classifications and functions that would have resulted in improvements to operational efficiency and effectiveness in this key mandated area of UN responsibility. In addition, the whole reorganization process was poorly communicated to the managers and staff and there was very little planning and assistance in implementing the changes.

It has taken several years for new organizational charts for the affected departments to be prepared and the job descriptions adjusted. Since no other measures for updating management expertise were undertaken the overall results have been, if anything, counter-productive and the major outcome has been *confusion*. It is noteworthy, that Gustavus (Gus) *Speth*, Administrator of the UN Development Programme has recently been given the responsibility *to review once again* the UN's activities and structures in support of economic and social development (apparently in response to pressures from the largest of the donor states who are concerned with overall efficiency, duplication and operational effectiveness of the several UN agencies active in this area).

Dick Thornburgh's efforts

Another serious effort to reform UN management was initiated by Dick Thornburgh as the Under-Secretary-General responsible for the Department of Administration and Management, the senior administrative post in the Organization, and appointed by the current Secretary-General. In comparison to his predecessors, Thornburgh was a seasoned executive (a former Governor of Pennsylvania) and was committed to improving and upgrading United Nations management capabilities. He understood the politics of administration probably more than most. His tenure however, was short—barely a year—and his efforts were undone by not having a good understanding of the politics of the Organization nor having the ongoing political support of either his own Mission or delegations concerned with the functioning of the Organization.

Dick Thornburgh initiated a number of steps for streamlining the UN administrative systems. It was his decision to bring in a team from *McKinsey Consultants* to conduct a comprehensive strategic management review covering the key administrative areas such as procurement, personnel, cash management and peace-keeping operations. The McKinsey proposals for the improvement of management included both top-down and bottom-up approaches. McKinsey's project suffered from a *lack of sensitivity* to the peculiar political constraints and responsibilities of the Organization and from a failure to develop a constituency of supporters within the UN apart from Thornburgh and his office. With Thornburgh's departure, the 'McKinsey proposals', to which few had access, became the touchstone for rejecting any sort of management reform in the Organization, especially reforms proposed by outsiders or consultants or those with private sector experience or frames of reference. Whatever the proposal for reform being presented, the almost automatic response from many long-term officials would be that 'like those McKinsey consultants, the proposer just didn't understand the peculiar "culture" of the UN and its political masters the Member States', and the proposal could not be proceeded with as a consequence.

Unfortunately, Dick Thornburgh did not stay long enough to make a difference. Before leaving he prepared a paper, which outlines UN management deficiencies from his perspective and suggests recommendations for improvement. His findings are still valid and the United Nations would be well-advised to take a second look at the paper (United Nations, 1993).

In the introduction Thornburgh states that he accepted his appointment 'to assess and evaluate the operations of the Organization from an "outside" viewpoint, with particular emphasis on their integrity, efficiency and cost-effectiveness'. One of his key conclusions was that 'at a time when the United Nations is called upon to play an ever more active role throughout the world, many of the administrative and management practices of the past 45 years are wholly inadequate to meet the demands of the current era'.

His report addresses a large number of specific management issues regarding restructuring, redeployment, personnel, budget/finance, peace-keeping, economic and social development and 'fraud, waste and abuse'. He put forward a number of far-reaching reform proposals, some of which remain as directions for future changes: re-vamping personnel management by permitting managers to terminate incompetent staff, reducing the number of permanent contracts, redesigning the performance evaluation system, and providing intensive management training, overhauling the budget processes, modernizing cash management, putting into place sound management infrastructures and procedures for peace-keeping operations (with estimated cost savings of as much as $100 million), and *phasing out* the *Joint Inspection Unit (JIU) and establishing a strong Inspector General's office.*

Thornburgh was followed in his Under-Secretary position by a State Department insider with little administrative skill or experience, Ms. Melissa Wells, who quickly retired from the scene in favour of Joesph Connor, an accountant and former head of the audit and consulting firm Price Waterhouse International.[4]

CURRENT UNITED NATIONS ADMINISTRATIVE REFORM EFFORTS

Under-Secretary-General Joseph Connor

The present head of the Department of Administration and Management, Joseph Connor, is an experienced executive and seems committed to reforming United Nations management. So far, while not presenting a broad plan for comprehensive reform, he has launched or re-inforced certain specific reform initiatives.

It is notable that Mr. Connor, in effect, has few staff resources personally available to him to assist in assessing, planning or executing his initiatives. (His

[4]As with certain other senior UN positions the post of USG/DAM has become 'informally' designated as belonging to a particular Member State, in this case the United States. This method of selection would not necessarily be a problem except that those nominated for these positions by Member States are not always chosen for their administrative competence or experience.

'office' consists of a handful of staff chosen from the permanent roster of the Organization and whose selection and retention are the result of internal personnel processes). This lack of staff resources, whether deliberate on the part of forces in the Organization resisting reform or simply a product of an Organization that is tied up in its own knots, is a major impediment to his capacity to effect change. Furthermore, all of his actions and decisions must be formulated and put into effect by permanent staff whose own experiences with and future in the Organization are more directly linked to their capacity to maintain their relations with their long-term colleagues than to carrying out the wishes of an 'outsider' such as the already once retired, Mr Connor, whom no one expects to remain in his position for a lengthy period.

Mr Connor has identified three areas for primary attention in conjunction with management reform:

- Establishment of a transparent and effective system of accountability and responsibility.
- Implementation of a Human Resources Management Strategy, and
- Completion and full implementation of the Integrated Management Information System (IMIS).

Connor's success in any of these initiatives, after approximately 1 year on the job, remains to be seen and with these go the hope for a more or less 'bloodless' reform of the Organization.

System of accountability and responsibility

Mr Connor's first major initiative is the attempt to hold managers accountable for the achievement of results and for the effective management of personnel and financial resources. For this purpose Connor established, effective 1 January 1995, a 'transparent and effective system of accountability and responsibility', which is described in a General Assembly document (United Nations, 1994a). It is a very ambitious programme, which consists of a number of elements requiring considerable work for their design and implementation. Some of the key elements include: the elaboration of specific management plans, the establishment of performance indicators for each manager, a functioning performance evaluation system for managers, and a system of rewards and sanctions for managers.

The report to the General Assembly clearly acknowledges the enormous difficulties of establishing such a system. 'It would be unwise to downplay the magnitude and complexity of the problems and obstacles in the culture of the United Nations, which has been evolving over the course of almost half a century.'

After an initial flurry of activity and some indication of Secretary-General level support, it appears that the work on the system has become bogged down and little is currently heard of it.

The strategy for the management of human resources

As Dick Thornburgh noted, 'the present outmoded system of personnel management constitutes a major stumbling block to any reform within the Organization'. Mr

Connor must have come to the same conclusion and is vigorously pursuing the reform of personnel policies and practices. As one of his first personnel decisions, he brought in the former head of personnel for the United Nations Development Programme, *Denis Halliday*. Whatever his own feelings in the matter, Connor was almost certainly forced to find his head of personnel from within the United Nations system, since the United Nations' personnel rules and procedures are so complicated, specific to itself and in many cases counter-intuitive that no outsider could get mastery of these in sufficient time to be effective.

Halliday has taken an in-depth look at the United Nations' personnel practices and has produced a new 'Strategy for the management of the human resources of the Organization', which is summarized in a General Assembly report of that name. This is a very comprehensive and *ambitious* reform proposal, which addresses a broad spectrum of present ailments and issues in UN personnel management. 'The goal of the Secretary-General is to develop and implement a modern human resources management system for the United Nations Secretariat worldwide that meets the requirements of the Charter and the expanding and increasingly varied mandates and expectations of Member States' (United Nations, 1994b).

The proposal consists of some 27 projects and measures and provides specific performance indicators for the implementation of each individual improvement step. Some of the key areas of the proposed strategy aim at the establishment of a human resources planning function, the development and training of managers, the introduction of a performance appraisal system (PAS) based on work plans, decentralization and delegation of authority to empower managers, enhanced attrition at senior levels, improvement of recruitment including exploring the use of executive search agencies; and simplifications of functions and procedures consistent with Total Quality Management.

So far, little progress has been made in the implementation of this most ambitious effort, with one exception; *more than a dozen outside experts* have been engaged to execute the implementation of the PAS. However, despite all the efforts in training managers and staff in the procedures of the PAS there seems to be a lack of support for the new system. Staff reportedly are finding it overly complex and time consuming and in many areas inappropriate to those parts of the Organization providing 'secretariat' support services, which by their nature are *ill-adapted to output measurement*. In addition, the history of previously failed performance evaluation approaches, on-going staff–management suspicion, and an evident failure of the system to take into account the multi-cultural character and political complexity of the Organization, all appear to be impeding its effective implementation.

The Integrated Management Information System (IMIS)

Begun in 1988, the Integrated Management Information System project (IMIS) has grown in budget (while declining in scope) from an initial US$12 million to the current $70 million. The initial intention to develop an integrated administrative management system for the automated processing of all personnel, financial and related transactions was an appropriate and a far-seeing one. Unfortunately, the Organization was ill-equipped to plan, develop, manage or implement such an

54	*M. Gurstein and J. Klee*

ambitious project. The internal data processing unit (Electronic Services Divison), with virtually no technical competence of its own and evidently recognizing the pitfalls which such an ambitious project presented, has left it to a special team formed specifically for its development and execution.

After a number of false starts, with several consulting groups coming close to the United Nations' *administrative fire and backing away*, Price Waterhouse eventually was contracted to develop the system. In being so contracted, Price Waterhouse essentially took over the project, with on-going liaison being provided by a United Nations IMIS team, which lacked manpower, technical expertise or experience in developing or implementing such a complex project.

The initial, and in many respects the most visible, part of the system, the handling of personnel-related paperwork, moreover, was designed with a fatal flaw. Rather than—as would have been done in most organizations—redesigning or re-engineering the administrative policies, procedures and practices *before* writing the software and developing the automated system, IMIS was designed so as to reflect the *existing* procedures and practices that had been universally acknowledged as being overly complex, inefficient and terribly slow. What IMIS has done is to automate a personnel management system that should have been re-designed from the beginning. However, now it has been etched in very expensive software with associated computer networks and protocols designed around its peculiarities. The result is that while *individual* personnel-related activities are apparently being conducted more efficiently, the overall personnel *system* is, if anything, managing personnel matters in a *less* timely fashion since considerable time is being spent by staff in attempting to manage the computer's operations, in addition to their on-going personnel responsibilities. So much effort and money has now been expended on a system, which at its very core is misdirected, that there would appear for the foreseeable future to be no resources left to address the real problems in personnel, which are the out-moded but continuing system of policies, procedures and practices.

The project is now 3 years behind schedule and some *$60 million over budget* but the Organization is too far along with it, and its current administrative systems are in such disrepair that the UN has no choice but to carry on to completion at whatever cost.

While the technical system developed to date appears to have its flaws, its essential problem, and the source of the overruns in cost and time, is that the United Nations has been almost completely unable to organize itself effectively to support the development, implementations or use of IMIS. Key policy decisions, which go to the very core of the system's design, remained unresolved for *years* (at extraordinary cost to the Organization) until Mr Connor forced their resolution. With four heads in 3 years and an ongoing culture of paralysis and indecision, the primary 'client' for IMIS's Release 1, the Office of Human Resources Management, remains unable to this day to use the system effectively to process the complex procedures of recruitment, staff claims and benefits in anything like an acceptable time-span.

Mr Connor, to his credit, has given the implementation of IMIS much of his attention and put the weight of his office behind it. It is possible that the implementation may, in areas other than human resources, be more successful and not, as was widely feared, cause such administrative difficulties that the entire Organization would be brought to collapse through an inability to process any administrative actions whatsoever.

But considerable additional efforts and almost certainly money will be required before IMIS is fully operational, and whether it will have any positive effect on the administrative operations of the Organization still remains to be determined even after 7 *years* of planning efforts and development.

The Office of Internal Oversight Services

The recent establishment of the Office of Internal Oversight Services is a major attempt by the Member States to improve the effectiveness and efficiency of the Organization. Over the years United Nations operations have been the target of criticism as wasteful, fraud ridden and subject to insider abuse. While undoubtedly there is waste, fraud and abuse in the United Nations system, it is very likely, given the overwhelming weight of existing scrutiny and oversight, that there is less of these to be found in the UN than in the government systems of most, if not all, Member States.

Responding to Member States' concerns, the Secretary-General in 1993 established an Office of Inspections and Investigations by integrating four existing units—Internal Audit, Evaluation, Monitoring and the Management Advisory Service—which had been performing oversight or management assistance functions. Evidently, the Member States were not satisfied with this measure and in 1994, after considerable deliberation, the General Assembly decided to create an Office of Internal Oversight Services (OIOS) headed by an Under-Secretary-General. The head of the Office is appointed in accordance with special provisions of the General Assembly, for one fixed-term of 5 years without possibility of renewal, and can only be removed with the approval of the General Assembly. This means that the head of OIOS has a very considerable measure of independence. The Office has a broad mandate, which consists of five functions: monitoring of programme implementation, internal audit, inspection and evaluation, investigation, and support and advice to management. The first appointee to the new USG position was a German, Karl-Theodor Paschke, a former head of administration for the German Foreign Service.

The new office has yet to make its presence felt either as a 'watchdog' for performance or as a 'champion' of organizational change as was hoped for by its many proponents. The designated components have carried on with their pre-existing activities although perhaps with increased visibility and credibility. 'Investigations', the new function, has suffered from an absence of any trained investigators in the Organization—with the only major publicly acknowledged incident subject to investigative activity, the theft of more than $3 million from the United Nations mission in Somalia, being turned over to Scotland Yard for resolution.

The other new function, and perhaps the one most in need of execution—that of providing support and advice to management improvement—so far has been ignored except for the changing of the name of the Audit and Management *Controls* Division to Audit and Management *Consulting* Division. It is notable that the Organization, in the course of establishing the new Office, allowed the internal management consulting unit of the United Nations, the Management Advisory Service, to be absorbed into the Internal Audit Division with its management support functions essentially disappearing.

56   *M. Gurstein and J. Klee*

The office, moreover, suffers from its past, as having been constituted from existing units retaining into the new organizational structure their existing mandates, personnel and operating procedures. These units, as with other parts of the Organization, all carry forward approaches and methodologies that are out of step with contemporary requirements and practices—an emphasis on compliance auditing where most national audit agencies have shifted to performance of comprehensive auditing, a concern with the monitoring of narrowly defined service outputs rather than with dynamic and strategically integrated performance indicators, and individual unit level assignments rather than integrated approaches to broader problem areas with greater impact on the Organization's acitivities.

REFERENCES

Collins, P. D. (1987). 'Implementing Administrative Reforms in International Development Organisations', in Collins, P. (ed), *The Administrative Reform Process in International Development Organisations, Special Issue of Public Administration and Development*, 7(2) April–June 1987, Wiley, Chichester.

United Nations (1985). Document A/46/882, New York.

United Nations (1986). Report of the Group of High-level Intergovernmental Experts to review the efficiency of the administrative and financial functioning of the UN, Document A/41/49, New York.

United Nations (1992). Document A/46/L.67, New York.

United Nations (1993). Report to the Secretary-General of the United Nations by Dick Thornburgh, Under-Secretary-General for Administration and Management, 1 March, New York.

United Nations (1994a). Document A/C/5/49/1, New York.

United Nations (1994b). Report of the Secretary-General, Document A/C.5/49/5, New York.

PUBLIC ADMINISTRATION AND DEVELOPMENT, VOL. 16, 111–122 (1996)

Towards a management renewal of the United Nations—Part II

MICHAEL GURSTEIN

University College of Cape Breton, Canada

JOSEF KLEE

New York, NY, USA

SUMMARY

In the first part of this article, the authors examined the historical and structural factors constraining the effectiveness of the Organization's capacity to carry out increasingly critical global mandates. In a second, concluding part of the article, the authors will suggest a strategy for UN reform and a process for carrying forward a 'renewal exercise' to equip the Organization for its role beyond the year 2000.

Effective UN administrative reform, unlike so many previous attempts that were characterized by tinkering with its structure or taking isolated measures to improve performance, will require a comprehensive overhaul of, inter alia, the following: the professional management environment and culture, personnel, financial and supportive information management and technologies, the establishment of an effective oversight function and the development of operational management capabilities.

The proposed post-50th anniversary 'renewal exercise' brings together the governmental, senior management and staff levels of the Organization, along with outside experts, to develop a long-term strategy and an integrated and practically implementable action plan for facilitating UN administrative reform. The exercise would also be guided by global experience and look to its success in charting the future by involving both member states and UN staff. Only such an approach will ensure that accountability for results is effectively in-built.

KEY AREAS FOR MANAGEMENT RENEWAL

The United Nations cannot be made more effective and cost-efficient by *tinkering* with its structure or by taking isolated measures to improve performance. The UN needs a comprehensive overhaul based on sound professional management principles and starting at the top. Such a renewal programme should include the following areas.

Dr Gurstein is SSHRC/NSERC Associate Chair, Management of Technological Change, and Associate Professor, School of Business, University College of Cape Breton, Sydney, Nova Scotia. He was formerly Management Adviser, Audit and Management Consulting Division, Office of Internal Oversight Services, United Nations, New York and Dr Klee was formerly Deputy Director of the same Division.

CCC 0271–2075/96/020111–12

112   *M. Gurstein and J. Klee*

Professional management environment and culture

The notion of professional management is almost completely under-developed in the UN. The Organization is *administered* instead of *managed*. Senior UN officials often have a diplomatic background and very limited experience in managing complex activities or operations with large budgets and staff components. In addition, the UN has never created a cohesive management philosophy and does not hold managers accountable for their decisions or for achieving their mandated outputs.

The key element in a renewal exercise would be the development and implementation of a true professional management culture. To realize this would mean a revolution in the way in which the UN is managed and it has to be initiated by the Secretary-General as the Chief Administrative Officer of the Organization. In broad terms this crucial reform project should design and implement the following elements: mission statement, criteria for selection of candidates for management positions (solid managerial record would be essential), empowerment and training of managers, adequate management tools, regular management meetings, and guidelines for carrying out management tasks, etc. The Secretary-General's report on the 'Establishment of a transparent and effective system of accountability and responsibility' (United Nations, 1995) provided a good description of the tasks involved in the creation and promotion of a professionalized management and a management culture.

Overhaul of management tools

The UN has in place an elaborate reporting system with four key instruments: medium-term plan, programme budget, performance reports and evaluation. Both Member States and the UN managers agree that the current reporting system is extremely complex, uncoordinated, costly and cumbersome to operate and not effective for oversight and management purposes. Some have even suggested the discontinuance of the medium-term plan and the performance report because they are seen as paper exercises, unrealistic and having no impact.

In recent years there have been attempts to improve the reporting system. According to Joachim Mueller, a UN budget official, 'recent changes have been rather selective, focusing on specific aspects of the process and responding to specific needs'. Mueller observes that there is a 'need to draw *together the various reform efforts in order to advance the overall system in a rational manner*'.[1]

At this stage, the UN reporting system must undergo a comprehensive overhaul to achieve two objectives: (a) to streamline and simplify all aspects of the system, and (b) to give managers effective tools for day-to-day decision-making.

In its efforts to increase management effectiveness the UN should consider the introduction of 'modern' management approaches, tools such as Total Quality Management (TQM) or process re-engineering, which have been successfully implemented in both private and public organizations. The application of the

---

[1]Joachim Mueller's 1994 article, 'Planning, Budgeting and Performance Reporting in the United Nations', (Mueller, 1994) though widely circulated within the UN administration, remains unpublished.

principles of re-engineering, for example, to various of the UN service delivery elements such as printing, document distribution, translation and interpretation would allow for the smoothing out of workflows, reduction in the number of processes that individual documents must undergo as they move through the system, and potentially highly significant reductions in overall costs. In addition, attention to operational processes might lead to an increase in user/client satisfaction as the needs of service clients, both internal and external, begin to be taken into account in the formulation of plans and service strategies.

In addition, the UN could introduce benchmark comparisons to performers or providers of similar services in other public sector organizations as well as in private sector organizations in such areas as procurement, building management, publishing and so on. (By developing numerical performance indicators it will be possible to develop better approaches to staff performance assessment and thus to more closely and effectively manage the Organization's service output and performance.)

Complete overhaul of personnel management

The UN personnel management system has evolved over the years with reform attempts having been undertaken at various times. As a result, bits and pieces have been added to the overall structure without an overall reform of the conceptual framework. The UN personnel function could best be described as a 'patchwork'. It is extremely complex, cumbersome and costly to operate and does not appear able to attract and maintain the highly skilled and motivated work force necessary for the UN's evolving mandates.

Among the greatest deficiencies in UN personnel management has been the lack of appropriately trained and experienced human resource professionals among those occupying the top posts (D-2 and above). In addition the pattern has been that top officials in the Office of Human Resources Management serve only for relatively short periods of time (3 years or less). Staff have consistently lacked a pertinent academic background or proper personnel management training.

To add to the problem, UN managers, in general, have very limited management skills and expertise, particularly in personnel management. Managers are often unable to take initiatives or decisions to solve problems on their own. They feel the need to follow written instructions in carrying out their personnel management tasks. The result is a bureaucratic and rigid UN personnel management practice, which is unable to motivate staff and results in inefficiencies, long delays, and costly litigation when things go excessively off-track as they frequently appear to do. In addition flawed and outdated personnel policies and practices lead to deep frustration among UN managers and staff at large.

A complete overhaul of the UN personnel functions must have a top priority in the overall reform strategy of the UN. No further attempt should be made to do a partial 'fix' of existing personnel policies and instruments as has been done in the past. Reform should begin with a fundamental re-examination of the principles and practices that for too long have been taken for granted and have guided UN personnel practice.

As noted earlier, the Secretary-General has fully recognized that UN personnel management must be 'modernized and re-energized' and has put forward an ambitious state-of-the-art proposal 'to develop and implement a modern human resources management system'. In this context, the Secretary-General and his senior managers in the Department of Administration and Management should make the implementation of the key components of the strategy a major reform priority.

Development of operational management capabilities

There are two areas where the UN lacks operational management capability: (a) for peace-keeping missions, and (b) for facilities management. Today, the UN is responsible for some 16 peace-keeping missions of which several, such as UNPROFOR, have very large-scale operations. In terms of budget volume, this year the UN will spend approximately *US$3.5 billion*, with 'regular' activities making up approximately *$1 billion* (about the size of the budget of a medium-sized Canadian city), and some *$2.5 billion* allocated for peace-keeping. Overall the UN is unable to cope in an orderly and professional way with the management demands this scale of activities, and especially of peacekeeping, requires. That, in spite of all the constraints, the UN was able to launch and operate so many peace-keeping missions is a major accomplishment. However, to get the job done the UN has had to resort to *ad hoc* arrangements and a heavy reliance on experts on loan from Member States and short-term recruitment of managers and staff with special operational skills. It is obvious that *ad hoc* management cannot over the long term ensure either effective or cost-efficient operations.[2]

The management challenge for the setting-up of peace-keeping missions in a very short period of time and for operating these missions is tremendous. It requires capabilities in a variety of different professional fields in which the UN has no or very limited expertise. They include such areas as: large-scale procurement of transportation equipment and services, operation of warehouses and storage depots, inventory and asset management, shipping and transportation by road, sea and air, repair of trucks and cars, and construction engineering, among others.

The development of strong operational capabilities for peace-keeping missions is a gigantic task for senior management. It will take many years to accomplish and must be well-planned and closely monitored. Core elements of such an undertaking should include: recruitment and training of managers and staff in the above listed fields, the establishment of management structures and methods, the design and implementation of new systems and subsystems in each field administrative and operational area and, where necessary, the substitution of these for unreformed UN headquarters systems, and the introduction of the latest management information

---

[2]It should be noted that the challenge of '*getting the job done*' has led many of the best of UN staff to find ways of *short-circuiting or by-passing the paperwork straight-jacket* they inherited from the pre-peace-keeping era. Many dedicated UN staff have put their careers on the line to expedite critical matters in emergency environments, (La Munière, 1987). The consequence of this for a few has been disastrous as more senior managers perhaps interested in currying favour with certain Member States, an uncomprehending press, and unreformed oversight agencies have attempted to 'throw the (extremely overweighted) UN rule-book' at these staff members.

technologies. For this programme the UN could benefit from the advice and assistance of outside consultants and experts.[3]

The facilities management unit is responsible for large office and conference buildings in eight duty stations and numerous smaller offices. The costs for maintaining these facilities are very considerable. The UN has, as permanent employees, managers and staff to operate their facilities; however, the UN is not applying modern industrial engineering techniques to these activities. Based on the experience of other organizations, the UN could expect major productivity gains and cost savings through the introduction of modern methods such as preventive maintenance and the planning and monitoring of maintenance work assignments in the facilities management area.

Modernization of text and conference management

A service area where the UN is widely acknowledged as being among the world's leaders is in the management of conferences and meetings and in the production of the output of those conferences in the form of text. The UN has developed world class capabilities in conference planning and management, interpretation and translation, text production and document distribution.

These areas, however, have to a degree suffered from their success in that they have continually been passed over for renewal and investment so that in many respects, they are now out of step with the most advanced practices in the corporate and public sector worlds. These services would benefit significantly from a fundamental re-thinking of the nature and the objectives of conferences and meetings in the context of the development of very low cost telecommunications and information dissemination technologies. While face-to-face meetings still have a valuable role to play in the activities of the UN there would appear to be an opportunity for substantial cost savings and for achieving wider participation in the conference process through the use of such technologies as video and audio conferencing, the Internet (and the worldwide web), remote interpretation, decision support software and so on.

Text management and document production and distribution equally would benefit from a fundamental re-examination in the context of such technologies as 'print on demand', FTP (file transfer protocol) via the Internet, the World Wide Web and Gopher Internet facilities, and even such basic approaches as the networking of document producers with document editors with document formatters and printers. Thought should be given to reducing or even eliminating the printing step altogether by providing direct access to UN documents via Wide Area Networks or the Internet and thus putting the onus of accessing and 'printing' document on users rather than the UN. Truly dramatic savings in personnel and other resource costs are achievable with current technologies and with a root and branch re-engineering of the entire language management activity of the UN. Such innovation, however, is only possible

---

[3]In a number of areas including personnel management and electronic data processing, and in the absence of an updating of headquarters systems, certain of the larger missions have implemented their own more modern systems leading to the anomalous situation where the administrations in the field are more advanced than those at headquarters.

116   *M. Gurstein and J. Klee*

if the UN has access to resources for technology innovation and, most importantly, to the technical capability and managerial vision which such initiatives require (Gurstein, 1993).

Professional financial management

A further area in which the UN could and should take immediate action to upgrade current practices is in financial and especially cash management. Present systems and techniques are outmoded, based on manual processes and lacking even rudimentary information technology support such as would allow for more effective management of both cash on hand and payments. The effect of the current system where there are archaic procedures for cash management and where there is an overall lack of effective management of cash on hand, results in millions of dollars annually in lost revenues for the Organization.

Senior UN finance managers have not pursued modernization in this area as vigorously as would appear warranted. Several consultants and auditors have studied the UN treasury operations and have made concrete proposals, which call for conversion of imprest to zero-balance accounts, consolidation of funds in fewer bank accounts, introduction of value-dating of transactions, computerized verification of interest earnings, the transfer of funds through the SWIFT (Society for Worldwide Inter-bank Financial Telecommunications) network, obtaining better service from the Organization's banks through competitive bidding and generally tighter controls. According to Thornburgh, 'these changes are calculated to provide as much as US$12–15 million per year in cost savings and increased income' (United Nations, 1993).

Recently a first step towards improving the UN's cash management system has been taken. However, in light of the potential income earnings and savings, this modernization project should have a very high priority and needs the involvement of senior financial managers. In implementing the various proposals the UN could greatly benefit from the experience of the UN Development Programme, which has a very efficient treasury operation using up-to-date EDP systems and procedures.

Application of new technologies

Technology implementation can have a tremendously catalytic effect on an organization. It provides the opportunity for a re-examination of the Organization's functioning and a lever for a 're-engineering' of its work. By throwing into relief what the Organization is doing and how it is doing it, areas for further improvement are identified. This laying bare of the operational skeleton of the Organization allows for interventions and possible solutions based on an up-to-date understanding of expectations, resources and technology capabilities.

A global information-rich organization such as the UN can expect considerable benefits in terms of cost savings and better service from the application of new technologies in the areas of telecommunication and information processing. With some 16 peace-keeping missions, 2 regional headquarters, 5 regional commissions and numerous information centres, the UN's effectiveness is a direct function of the effectiveness of its communications system.

Similarly, in information areas, among the UN's primary activities is the servicing of the conference/meeting deliberations of its Member States. In this context having ready access to the most advanced means of storing and processing information would seem to be a basic requirement. It is surprising then, how limited in many respects is the capability of the UN in these areas. From its tardiness in the effective implementation of electronic mail and, more recently, access to the Internet, to lack of a clear strategy for managing or making more effective use or access to its information resources, to its inability to train staff or managers in the use of information technology systems or to obtain the services of staff with the requisite degree of technical competence, the UN is unable to use the most advanced available systems and must operate with outdated technologies and staff who are technically sub-par.

Partly the fault lies in the absence of any orientation towards the merits of technically trained staff in management positions, partly it is a consistent lack of authorization of new investment in technical areas, and partly it is the over-attention and investment given to a single system—IMIS—which itself, because of the technical limitations of the UN, has to date been poorly managed and even more inadequately implemented.

The Electronic Services Division, which is responsible both for information and communications technologies, is perhaps the most ill-served by current UN practices of any service unit in the Organization. Its lack of skilled and experienced professionals, its inability to command budgetary resources, its failure to make its voice heard in the higher reaches of UN management is a major burden, not only on the Organization but to those who may rely on the UN for any of its services or for the effective execution of any of its mandates. If any element of the UN is crucial for its long-term success, it is its managers of telecommunications and information technology. That the UN is still not effectively served by electronic mail; that its library resources are only accessible by UN insiders knowledgeable in an obsolete computer command language; that UN staff have no reliable links to the Internet and that the Internet world has no reliable access to UN documents; that the UN has to rely on costly and *ad hoc* arrangements to communicate with its peace-keeping missions and military contingents are all symptoms of a serious lack of leadership in the informatics and telecommunications area and of a failure by the most senior managers in the Organization to realize how transformative these technologies have become for all globe-spanning organizations.

Not only does the UN's technical management appear to be unable to cope with current demands and opportunities, more crucially they lack the vision to provide leadership to the Organization and to the world in these areas. Freely and ubiquitously available information; global observation of, and even participation in, the global agenda setting of conferences such as the Social Summit or the Conference on Environment and Development; the use of information and communications technologies as an active agent in peacemaking, peace-monitoring and peace-keeping; new methods of accessing and using information in support of economic and social development; all could be stimulated by a United Nations that was in tune with the opportunities that current technologies provide.

There is a need for a fundamental re-examination of the role of information and communications technologies in the Organization. This should include a review of the current structure of the units, their reporting relationships (their status should be upgraded), current and future requirements for expert staff and knowledgeable and experienced management, training of UN staff and especially managers in the use of existing systems, and the development of approaches to the use of these technologies in active support of the full range of UN activities.

Establishment of an effective oversight function

A strong independent oversight mechanism is an essential component in the UN renewal effort. It must fulfil a dual role: (a) performance of audits, inspections, evaluations and investigations to ensure compliance with regulations and rules, appraise the use of resources, prevent abuse and misconduct, etc. and (b) promotion of management improvement and cost-efficiency through advice and assistance to managers.

The new Office of Internal Oversight Services (OIOS) is still in an infancy stage with limited resources and professional capabilities. It can barely cope with its basic audit, evaluation and investigation mandates. At this juncture, the first priority for the Head of OIOS must be to build an effective management structure for the Office, to hire and/or train staff in the under-developed areas, such as investigation and inspection, to establish sound working procedures and to implement a tight compliance monitoring system for the implementation of OIOS recommendations.

The second role of OIOS, to promote and facilitate better management practices, cost reductions and productivity gains in the UN, is as critical as the first oversight responsibility. However, in this latter area, OIOS has almost no expertise. It lacks trained management analysts or consultants who can carry out productivity and cost reduction studies or provide advice and assistance to managers. To establish this management advisory role will be a major challenge of the Head of OIOS.

INITIATING MANAGEMENT REFORM AT THE UN

The circumstances that have taken decades to develop cannot be rectified in months. The 're-invention' of UN structures, management practices, systems and operations is a monumental task and will take many years, if similar exercises in the public and private sectors are taken as examples. The overall transformation process could take several biennia to reach the point where systems are self-correcting and self-sustaining, and where the Organization's culture consistently promotes high levels of performance.

What is needed is a comprehensive plan for organizational renewal that reflects the need for broad systemic renewal efforts, the requirement for participation by existing staff, and which is broken down into do-able but integrated components, small but significant first steps, as demonstrations of the usefulness and value of organizational renewal, combined with assessments of the need for broader change and the wide dissemination of the Organization's commitment to these initiatives.

In addition, past efforts at organizational reform have not incorporated the detailed knowledge of UN operations possessed by current UN managers and staff nor have they attempted to enlist the active cooperation and participation of staff in the development and execution of their recommendations.

It is proposed that a central component of the Organization's follow-up plans to the 50th Anniversary celebrations and re-dedications be a 'renewal exercise' and that:

- this 'renewal' effort have as its overall goal to create an organization whose operations, resources and results are commensurate with the mandates entrusted to it by the Member States;
- the exercise be undertaken to reinforce ongoing efforts to ensure the accountability and effectiveness of management and staff;
- included in the exercise is the introduction of measures to ensure continuing innovation and performance improvement in the operating environment; and
- the process of renewal and re-dedication of staff to the UN Charter include measures to promote permanent learning and adaptation to an evolving global environment.

In sum, the objective would be to develop, implement and implant the means for the continuing self-renewal of an innovative and results-oriented UN Secretariat.

The effort towards United Nations 'renewal' to be successful should draw on the knowledge and experience of UN staff currently living with the ineffective and wasteful systems and who should understand better than any others the reasons for inefficient and non-accountable organizational performance.

Global experience with public sector reform efforts would become the basis for UN renewal efforts. Outside experts would be invited to contribute their techniques and facilitation skills. The activities would focus on implementing change and achieving results, not just on producing reports. Top UN management and interested Member States would be entrusted with ensuring that accountability for results is built into the new systems. UN staff would be asked to participate in 'renewal laboratories' (Gurstein, *et al.*, 1994) to implement new practices and to learn lessons of renewal as they emerge, even as major UN systems are being re-designed. UN staff involvement, and their early implementation experience, would increase the credibility of the new systems and practices, and greatly improve the chances for successful large-scale implementation.

The exercise would be launched with a 'Big Bang' including presentations by the Secretary-General, and by the senior managers of a number of national efforts for public sector reform.

A 'Renewal Secretariat' under the direction of a 'Renewal Board' including Ambassadors to the United Nations, senior UN officials and eminent authorities in organizational reform, would develop long-term plans, and define project objectives, methods and workplans. The staff of the 'Renewal Secretariat' would be allowed to challenge and modify existing UN policies and procedures as required and involve UN staff in the execution of the projects.

A key element of this renewal activity would be the establishment of a *'UN 2000 Vision'* exercise. Interested Member States together with a mixed group of staff and management would begin thinking through future directions for the development of the UN administration. The intent would be the identification of a set of longer-term goals and requirements in the light of changing environmental conditions—demographic, technological and 'political'. This would lead into a 're-dedication' of the operating environment of the United Nations to the fundamental goals and objectives of the Organization as presented in the Charter.

As part of the renewal efforts a team would look at the proposals concerning the 'governance' of the multilateral system and develop recommendations for taking the system through *the next half century*, including re-examining the role of non-governmental organizations and popular participation in United Nations' deliberations and decision-making and the resources required to support these, as well as ways of incorporating the opportunities for increased participation provided by the new technologies.

Another team would be concerned with defining the structures needed to allow the system to more effectively execute its expanding responsibilities in peace-keeping and peacemaking, in development and industrial support, in matters concerning the environment and in creating a global rule of law.

All efforts would be linked to and reinforce ongoing reform initiatives i.e., the Integrated Management Information System (IMIS), the new 'System of Accountability and Responsibility' and the 'Strategy for Human Resources Management', creating a broad Organization-wide renewal effort.

CONCLUSION

Much of the current discussion about administrative reform of the United Nations has focused on the elimination of 'waste, fraud and abuse'. No doubt there is a measure of waste, fraud and abuse in the UN as there is in any large-scale public organization. Whether in the unlikely event that all such circumstances were to be eliminated, this would have any appreciable effect in 'reforming the UN' is at best questionable.

Much more important in fostering the effectiveness of the Organization would be the provision by the Member States of the resources and board level direction commensurate with the continuing and increased responsibilities of the UN. The lack of a stable financial environment is, at a deep level, one of the main reasons for the ongoing rigidity of the UN's systems and its inability to reform itself administratively.

There has been much talk of UN reform, of restructuring, of revitalization—but still the problems persist and ever newer efforts are proposed. Rather than another round of 'reforms', which deal with symptoms and not causes, 'restructuring', which does little but rearrange boxes on organization charts, or 'revitalizations', which contribute to little but pervasive cynicism among staff and delegates, what is required is a significant measure of management change and organizational 're-invention'. Just as the world has changed irrevocably and fundamentally in the 50 years since the UN began its odyssey, so must the UN re-invent itself to deal with this changed world.

The UN is administratively old, rigid and bureaucratic, and administratively and managerially perhaps the last of the organizational products of the 'Cold War'. It needs more than reform or the piecemeal, lip-service, restructuring or renewing that each generation of representatives feels compelled to inflict on it. There needs to be a vision of a 'new' post-Cold War twenty-first century UN.

Many States are currently re-assessing the efficiency, effectiveness and economy of their own public services, including major revamping of the internal operations of public sector activities—eliminating unnecessary 'paperwork', making management and staff more accountable for results, and streamlining procurement, personnel and budget functions.

It is our belief that a 're-invention' takes place *from the bottom up* as well as from the top down, and that before it is possible to re-conceive of a changed mandate for the UN it is necessary to bring the operations, administration and management of the Organization in line with the best practices and systems available in the world, and which, in turn, could provide a framework and a platform on which the aspirations of the world can be built and can flourish.

It is time to *draw on the experience and expertise to be found in many countries that* have *'renewed' or 're-invented' their public sectors* to begin the task of 'renewing' the operations of the United Nations especially as it enters its second half century. This 'renewal' must take place at several different levels but critically it must address the current operational limitations of the system through:

- the development and implantation of a professional management culture;
- the establishment of sound and cost-effective management and operational systems and practices in all parts of the Organization;
- the implementation of measures to ensure management accountability and effectiveness;
- the development of management and staff to ensure their responsiveness to the evolving requirements of the UN's mission;
- the integration of advanced technologies and information systems as constituent components of all aspects of UN operations;
- the reduction of needless constraints on operational performance and the 'paperwork burden'; and
- the development of results-oriented performance indicators for use in operations, planning, budgeting and personnel management.

In the meantime the UN Secretariat remains an organization of largely dedicated individuals with neither the resources nor the authority to execute their mandates effectively nor to revise them.

In the absence of other modalities, the UN has emerged as the forum of choice in the widest range of areas. The issue to be addressed is how best the UN can renew and 're-invent' itself to appropriately meet the ever-mounting challenges it faces in its next 50 years.

REFERENCES

Gurstein, M. (1993). *'A Vision for the Foreseeable Future: Text/Document Flow in the UN Secretariat'*, Management Advisory Services, United Nations, New York.

Gurstein, M., Klee, J. and Epstein, P. (1994) 'A Proposal for Re-inventing the United Nations', unpublished paper, New York.

La Munière, C.-H. (1987). 'Managing the UN's emergency operations in Africa: lessons for Organisational Development', in Collins, P. (ed), *The Administrative Reform Process in*

122   *M. Gurstein and J. Klee*

International Development Organisations, Special Issue of Public Administration and Development, 7(2) April–June 1987, Wiley, Chichester.

Mueller, J. (1994). 'Planning, Budgeting and Performance Reporting in the United Nations', mimeo, New York.

United Nations (1985). Document A/C/5/49/1, New York.

United Nations (1993). Report to the Secretary-General of the United Nations by Dick Thornburgh, Under-Secretary-General for Administration and Management, 1 March, New York.

[19]

The History, Role and Organization of the "Cabinet" of the United Nations Secretary-General

By B.G. Ramcharan[*]

I. Introduction

The belief that international organizations can play a role in promoting peace, justice, human welfare and freedom is one which has animated a long line of thinkers and peace strategists.[1] As international organizations began to develop in the second half of the 19th century, they started to develop secretariat services to help them in the performance of their functions. By the time the League of Nations was established, there were some embryonic international secretariats — although experience was still meagre in the organization and running of such an entity. The secretariats of the League of Nations and of the International Labor Organization thus charted new ground in international administration.

During the years of the League of Nations, the Secretary-General came to play an increasingly important political role although, as Sir Eric Drumond observed about his own position as Secretary-General of the League, "It had to be done behind the scenes, but I do not think it was any less effective because of this. To take sides publicly in a political dispute would certainly have lessened my political influence."[2]

Albert Thomas, the first Director of the International Labor Office, took the view that, to the Director 'fell of necessity the task of leadership, the task of initiative, the task of taking all those measures which might be necessary to defend the Organization'. Mr. Thomas, through his determination and his awareness of the need for exerting public as well as private leadership, lent credence to the view that a Secretary-General can be of great value in bringing political as well as administrative direction to an international organization composed of sovereign states with their multiplicity of interests and policies.[3]

By the time the United Nations was established in 1945, there were thus two clear patterns for the drafters of the Charter to choose from. One of the striking innovations of the Charter, as compared to the Covenant of The League of Nations, was that it gave an explicit political role to the Secretary-General of the United Nations, which is provided for in Article 99 of the Charter. That article reads: "The Secretary-General may bring to the attention of the Security Council any matter which in his opinion may threaten the maintenance of international peace and security."

Besides this explicit political role, the Secretary-General is, under Articles 97 and 98 of the Charter of the United Nations, the Chief administrative officer of the

[*]The views expressed are those of the author in his personal capacity

103

Organization and acts as Secretary-General in all meeting of the General Assembly, of the Security Council, of the Economic and Social Council and of the Trusteeship Council. He is the administrative head of the Secretariat. All functions of the Secretariat are carried out in his name or on his behalf. Among the Secretary-General's functions are to:

- Oversee the working of the major units of the Secretariat and provide guidance to them;
- Indicate priorities for the major units;
- Identify matters which in his opinion may threaten the maintenance of international peace and security;
- Exercise, at his discretion, the good offices of the Secretary-General;
- Conduct negotiations;
- Hold consultations with Heads of State or Government;
- Serve as the Chairman of the Administrative Committee on Co-ordination.

In a perceptive study of "Creative Leadership in International Organizations",[4] Professor Robert Cox suggested that there are three ways in which an executive head may seek to control his top staff so as to maintain his political initiative. These are:

1) *Complete domination and centralization of power in his own hands*. This would overcome "feudal" tendencies by making top officials dependent of the executive head.

2) *Presiding over a cabinet of top officials*. This can be a means of keeping top officials informed about important matters outside their own particular sphere and it may help the executive head to smoke out differences among his staff. Collective discussion, he argues, can be used as an instrument favoring a certain conformity of policy. "But it would be an unwise executive head who did not take his major decisions on policy *after* consultation rather than *in* consultation with his top officials. The cabinet technique is, at best, an instrument of communication and of limited control over the top-level officials. It has not proven to be an effective instrument of decision-making".

3) *The "reserved area" of policy*. In this approach the executive head reserves certain types of decisions to himself an equips himself with a personal staff so as to be able to act within this area of policy. Cox suggested that the executive head could thus reserve to himself:
   a) questions relating to the definition of the major goals and policy orientation (including programme priorities) and the development of organizational ideology; and
   b) matters of direct concern to the executives head's base of political support and his coalition policy for the construction of alliances to support his programme. This, Cox submitted, is the most usual method for executive heads to follow, using it in some combination with the cabinet system for communications and general supervision.

104

The "reserved area", Cox pointed out, implies that the executive head acquires his own staff distinct from the staff controlled by his senior officials. This personal staff can provide an executive head with several essential, effective components to his job:

a) a few people in whom he has virtually complete confidence, with whom he can talk frankly about all the issues arising within the organization. With his top officials, because of their political position, he is usually in a posture of negotiating;

b) channels of intelligence providing accurate assessment of the expectations and demands from the membership of the organization. His top officials provide a sounding board for sectional reactions but, in addition, the executive head needs his own research and intelligence network to assess the possibilities and limits presented by the world situation in terms of the policy objectives which he determines to pursue;

c) competent advisers to help him redefine as necessary the major aims which the organization is to pursue and to explain these in such a way as to gain the necessary political support. In other words, the staff would effectively command programme and policy development and avoid determination of the programme by specialists committed to sub-goals and subject to the special influence of particular outside pressure groups.

Cox' framework provides a good background to discuss the leadership role of the United Nations Secretary-General and the organization of his immediate staff — the Executive Office of the Secretary-General.

II. The Leadership Function of the Secretary-General

The following propositions about the role of the Secretariat and the Secretary-General would seem to be generally agreed upon. First, policy in the United Nations is set by the Member States, who also determine the priorities of the Organization. Second, when Member States are in dispute, they should be given an opportunity to resolve their difficulties before the Secretary-General "dives in". Third, the Secretary-General should be a facilitator, a positive agent, rathen than jumping into controversies and becoming a source of contention.

Having said this, however, the following propositions would also appear to be incontrovertible: First, the Secretariat, headed by the Secretary-General, is the only continuous focal point for thinking about, and planning, the activities of the Organization. Second, the Secretariat prepares draft programmes and strategies for the consideration of the membership. Third, the Secretary-General is expected, under Article 99 of the Charter, to act in such a manner as to head off potential threats to, or breaches of, the peace. Fourth, Member States often, themselves, turn to the Secretary-General for assistance. Fifth, the public usually looks to the Secretary-General for leadership in tackling international problems or for articulating the concerns or the sentiments of the international community.

Therefore, while, formally, the mandate of the Secretary-General is to serve and to implement the decisions of the policy-making organs, *de facto* the Secretary-

105

General has an important leadership responsibility in the international community. The late Dag Hammarskjold sought to establish:

> "a forward momentum by himself taking intiatives, instead of simply reacting to events. He believed that a reliable and just world order could only be built pragmatically by making precedents and by case law. He advocated a fearless adherence to the principles of the Charter which, he told the Security Council in 1956, "are, by far, greater than the Organization in which they are embodied, and the aims which they are to safeguard are holier than the policies of any single nation or people'".[5]

The current Secretary-General, Mr. Javier Perez de Cuellar, told the General Assembly in his acceptance statement, following his election to the post of Secretary-General:

> "I am convinced that the Organization must constantly reflect the world's conscience. In order to ensure that this shall be so, I will do everything in my power to ensure scrupulous respect for the purposes and principles of the Charter. I will tackle all the problems with an open mind and I will act according to my conscience on the basis of right and justice."[6]

Of course, to be able to do all of these things, a Secretary-General must have assistance. A Cabinet is one possibility and we shall turn to see how it has fared so far in the United Nations.

III. The Cabinet of the Secretary-General

On the basis of the recommendations of the Preparatory Commission, the General Assembly had agreed, initially, that the Secretariat should be organized in the following eight Departments, each under an Assistant Secretary-General:

1. The Department of Security Council Affairs

2. The Department of Economic Affairs

3. The Department of Social Affairs

4. The Department of Trusteeship and Information from Non-Self-Governing Territories

5. The Legal Department

6. The Department of Public Information

7. The Department of Administrative and Financial Services

8. The Department of Conference and General Services.

Even before the Secretariat began to function, the five permanent members of the Security Council had arrived at a gentlemen's agreement allocating to one of their nationals the Assistant Secretaryship-General of the five principal Departments. Sydney Bailey tells the story thus:

> "there was a good deal of improvisation in the early years. Lie was often preoccupied with major political quetions and left administrative matters to his colleagues. He normally held a weekly meeting with top officials. An agenda was circulated in advance and minutes were kept, but the matters discussed tended to be relatively trivial. Lines of authority became increasingly blurred, and it was not entirely clear whether the Assistant Secretaries-General were officers in charge of departments or a panel of top-level advisors to the Secretary-General — or both."[7]

Lie himself wrote in his memoirs:

> "The group of Assistant Secretaries-General was to be my official "cabinet", available for advice on all matters — not least on questions relating to their respective "home areas". They were also the responsible heads of their departments. I delegated to them broad administrative authority from the very beginning. As the work developed, it gradually fell to their deputies, the top-ranking directors, to assume many of the administrative duties; and then they too were called in for my regular meetings. This division of work was intended to permit an extensive political liaison activity to the Assistant Secretaries-General; but I soon found that many Member governments, and particularly their permanent delegates, insisted on bringing to the Secretary-General's personal attention not only all major political questions but even such infinitesimal administrative matters as the proposed appointment of a wife's nephew or a Minister's protégé to the Secretariat staff. In later years this practice went so far that one Ambassador insisted that it would be below his dignity to call on an Assistant Secretary-General! In other cases, not least in the Councils and Committees, very good contacts were established and maintained, as part of the liaison work; but as time went on, and the pressure for greater economy was added to my other considerations, I eventually concluded that the number of my "deputies" might be reduced to three (or four) provided they were of the highest caliber and could be selected freely by the Secretary-General according to his needs — and without having to please everyone. This conclusion in no way reflected upon the chief lieutenants assigned to me; in fact, several among them had personal qualifications that would have enabled them easily to fit into the proposed new pattern. But the change never went into effect, for my resignation intervened before I had finalized my proposal for consideration by the General Assembly."[8]

Sir Brian Urquhart, in his recently published memoirs, *A Life in Peace and War*, comments as follows on the performance of the Lie Cabinet:

> "The eight Assistant Secretaries-General constituted the nearest thing Lie had to a cabinet. They would meet each week with the Secretary-General, ostensibly to report progress and discuss serious problems. I was the secretary and minute taker of these meetings, and they were a disillusioning experience. Most of the time was taken up with trivial and peripheral matters such as the allotment of office space and cars. We even had an interminable discussion over the final salutation in official correspondence... There was little sign of the high-level interplay of statesmanlike ideas that I had anticipated. Lie seemed more flustered than ever in these meetings, and I think he found them as irritating as I did."[9]

Secretary-General Hammarskjold undertook a complete review of the organization of the Secretariat. He decided to change the previous pattern of eight Departments, headed by Assistant Secretaries-General, by adding to his own Executive Office: a Personnel Office, a Finance Office and a Legal Office, thus doing away with the Department of Administrative and Financial Services, as such. He also recommended that the Departments of Economic and Social Affairs should be made into one Department.

Originally, the eight Assistant Secretaries-General were intended to be politically representative of the spectrum of Member States and, under each of them, a principal Director was responsible for the day-to-day work of the Department. The Assistant Secretaries-General were supposed to provide a form of political liaison with their own governments or regions. This function, however, had more or less lapsed with the establishment of permanent national delegations at UN Headquarters. Hammarskjold, therefore, proposed that the main Departments should henceforth be headed by one echelon of officials instead of two. These officials, in principle, would be administrative and would undertake political responsibilities only

107

at the direction of the Secretary-General. Their title would be changed from Assistant Secretary-General to Under-Secretary.

Hammarskjold's changes gave rise to objections by the Soviet Union from the outset. During the General Assembly of 1958, the Advisory Committee on Administrative and Budgetary Questions expressed some misgivings about the workings of the Secretariat. Urquhart provides the following account:

> "The feeling persisted that Hammarskjold had gone too far in diminishing the authority of the Administrative and Financial Services and the Bureau of Personnel and had taken on his shoulders a burden that was too heavy and too time-consuming."[10]

In December 1959, the Assembly, therefore, called for an overall review of the organization of the Secretariat by a Committee of six outside experts to be appointed by the Secretary-General. Hammarskjold invited three former Presidents of the General Assembly to give him their views. The "three wise men" recommended increasing the Under-Secretaries for Special Political Affairs from two to five in order to constitute a group that the Secretary-General could consult on political and diplomatic questions. Their suggestions were eventually passed to the Committee of Eight and, in April 1967, in commenting on the Committee's provisional findings, Hammarskjold dealt with the problem of how the Executive Office of the Secretary-General of the United Nations should be organized. Urquhart relates his approach in the following manner:

> "*The Secretary-General, as the only elected official, inevitably carried the ultimate personal responsibility for running the Secretariat.* "This creation of a one-man office with very wide ultimate responsibilities and a position detached from all national links, dependent solely on an international staff that the man himself has recruited, has necessarily led to difficult and untried political and administrative problems." *He disagreed with the Committee's effort to solve the problem by the introduction of a Cabinet system, because it was based on an analogy with national governments for which the basis was lacking at the UN.* This was not only true during the current cold-war situation but also "so long as national interests are bound to clash and so long as an only limited number of international civil servants can be counted upon as wholly uninfluenced by national considerations". He also disagreed with the Committee's idea of reducing the responsibilities of the Secretary-General and strengthening the corporate nature of the Secretariat on the grounds that the ultimate personal responsiblity of the Secretary-General was based on the Charter. He denied again that too much authority was concentrated in the hands of the Secretary-General. "If publicity gives a false impression and tends to highlight the person of the Secretary-General, this I can tell you from rather bitter personal experience is very much against the efforts of the Secretary-General, and is the result of the present tendency, all over the world, to dramatize issues by personalizing them."

> "The creation of a new level of six to eight more senior officials as deputies would be expensive and inefficient, quite apart from making life more difficult for the Secretary-General. If the proposed deputies acted as a Cabinet and disagreed on controversial issues, they would embarrass the Secretary-General, who would then have to take one side or another; and if they were merely to act as an advisory committee they would not have enough to do. Hammarskjold conceded that the Committee had "very clearly seen the extremely difficult problem created by the form in which the executive aspect of the Secretariat has been handled in the Charter," but so far they did not seem to have found a workable solution to the problem."[11]

The Committee of Eight finally agreed to disagree on the organization of the top level of the Secretariat, three of its members favouring the establishment of three Deputy Secretaries General while four others favoured the designation of not more than eight major areas of responsibility to be run by the eight most senior Secretariat officials.

In his comments on the Report of the Committee of Eight, Hammarskjold put forward his own suggestions about the top level organization of the Secretariat. He thought that *there should be one top level, but its members would be grouped into two categories: Assistant Secretaries-General who would be "political" and Under-Secretaries who would be "administrative"*, although both would have the same rank. The former would serve for one term of three to five years, the latter might serve for up to two terms. Equitable geographical distribution would apply to both categories.

Hammarskjold died before these ideas could be considered by the General Assembly and the structure of the Secretariat would turn out to be a major issue at the time of the appointment of his successor. In his memoirs, *View from the United Nations*, U Thant relates the different views of the permanent members of the Security Council on the composition of the upper echelons of the Secretariat. In the end, it was left up to him to decide on the future pattern of organization of the Secretariat. In his acceptance statement, he informed the General Assembly as follows:

> "It is my intention to invite a limited number of persons who are at present undersecretaries, or to be appointed as undersecretaries, to act as my principal advisers on important questions pertaining to the performance of functions entrusted to the Secretary-General by the United Nations Charter."

> "In extending this invitation, I am fully conscious of the paramount consideration of securing the highest standards of efficiency, competence, and integrity, and with due regard to the importance of as wide a geographical basis as possible, as laid down in Article 101 of the Charter. I intend to include among these advisers Dr. Ralph J. Bunche and Mr. Georgi Petrovitch Arkadev."

> "It is also my intention to work together with these colleagues in close collaboration and consultation in a spirit of mutual understanding. I am sure that they will seek to work with me in the same manner."[12]

In a report on the organization of the top echelon of the United Nations Secretariat, which Secretary-General U Thant submitted to the General Assembly in 1967, the Secretary-General announced his intention to appoint a small team of experts to consider reorganization of the Secretariat and to make appropriate recommendations to him. The group, appointed by the Secretary-General, consisted of the following persons: Manuel Pérez Guerrero, Louis Ignacio-Pinto, Bernard de Menthon, Platon D. Morozov, C.V. Narasimhan, Andrew A. Stark and W.H. Ziehl.

The group submitted its report to the Secretary-General on 11 October 1968 and it was transmitted to the General Assembly at its 23rd session.

The Committee reviewed the grading of posts in the top echelon of the Secretariat. It noted that until 1955 the top echelon had consisted of 8 Assistant Secretaries-General and a number of top ranking Directors. As a result of a reorganization carried out that year, those two categories had been merged into one designated as Under-Secretary. The single level structure had remained in force until the end of 1967 when the Secretary-General had submitted to the General Assembly new proposals based on the re-establishment of two levels, Under Secretary-General and

Assistant Secretary-General. The Assembly had endorsed the Secretary-General's proposal and the new system took effect from the beginning of 1968.

The Committee made a number of recommendations which are relevant in the present context:

a. *Grading of Posts in the Top Echelon*
   The Committee more or less concurred with the two tier structure of the upper echelon. It discussed a suggestion that a new grade (D-3) be created between the level of D-2 and Assistant Secretary-General. It "had serious doubts concerning this suggestion."

b. *Interrelationship between Organizational Units*
   From a management standpoint, the Committee considered it advisable, as a general principle, that the Secretary-General should deal with the questions brought to his attention through established organizational units. It considered that, in those exceptional cases when the Secretary-General in his discretion finds it necessary to enlist the participation, in the implementation of any action, of persons who are not members of established organizational units, he may wish, to the greatest possible extent, to avail himself of the advice and assistance of all the senior officials who, by virtue of their functions or experience in the field of activity in question, could help him in the decision-making process. To that effect, as a general rule, these officials — and in particular the heads of the established organizational units concerned — should be kept currently informed of developments that have a bearing on these questions and also be given the opportunity to comment on them and to bring their suggestions to the attention of the Secretary-General.

c. *Periodic Meetings of Top Echelon Officials*
   The Committee noted that the Secretary-General had reinstituted the practice of having weekly meeting of his senior colleagues with a view to effecting coordination at the highest level. It felt that such meetings facilitate a broad exchange of information and views on all important problems arising in the Secretariat's various fields of activity and thus serve to keep the senior officials acquainted with developments outside their immediate fields of competence.
   The Committee believed that those meetings also served a useful purpose by involving the top officials more intimately in the process of formulating measures to be taken by the Secretary-General within the framework of decisions of the principal organs in various fields.
   While by their nature those meetings did not lend themselves to the circulation of a formal agenda in advance, the Committee was glad to note that participants were encouraged to inform the Secretary-General, through the Chef de Cabinet, of any matter they wished to raise at a particular meeting and to circulate in advance a note on the subject.
   It felt that thought might also be given to ensuring more effective participation in those meeting by Under-Secretaries-General and Assistant Secretaries-General stationed outside New York when they visited Headquarters. All Under-Secre-

110

taries-General and Assistant Secretaries-General stationed at Headquarters should, it advised, be informed in advance of such visits.

d. *Executive Office of the Secretary-General*

At the time that the Committee examined the Executive Office of the Secretary-General, it was responsible not only for the normal functions of such an office "which involved the implementation of the decisions of the Secretary-General and assisting him in the direction of the work of the Secretariat" but also for the work of the General Assembly. The Committee recommended that the Secretary-General consider the separation of the functions of Chef de Cabinet and Under-Secretary-General for General Assembly Affairs (which has since been implemented).

The Committee commented, in general terms, "that the organization of the Executive Office of the Secretary-General must remain responsive to his needs and therefore should be organized in a manner which serves him well".

The Committee also had various other observations, for example on responsibilities of a proposed Under-Secretary-General in charge of Administration and Management. The Secretary-General, in his comments on the Committee's report, made the following observations on the functions of the proposed Under-Secretary-General:

> "The intention is that the Under-Secretary-General would not be saddled with the day-to-day responsibilities (of the Offices of Controller and the Director of Personnel) but that he would devote his time to the larger questions of management and co-ordination which have become so important during recent years."

The Secretary-General further commented that:

> "The establishment of the new post of Under-Secretary-General for Administration and Management has, as the Committee recognized, given an opportunity for a fresh and comprehensive approach to some of the most stubborn problems in the area of administration, personnel and budget. The Committee suggested, in its report, that the new Under-Secretary-General "be kept relatively free from the routine work connected with either the Office of Personnel or the Office of the Controller. He needs to have both the time and the opportunity to study and chart new courses, which will lead to an increase in efficiency and economy through improved management for the United Nations as a whole"."

In his memoirs, *In the Eye of the Storm*, Secretary-General Waldheim made the following case for a Deputy Secretary-General:

> "*The situation today is a bureaucratic nightmare. Because of the lack of a proper hierarchical structure, no les than seventy Under-Secretaries-General, Assistant Secretaries-General, and other officials of comparable rank, in New York and around the world, reported directly to me. This is an impossible span of managerial control. Moreover, whenever I left New York, no matter how pressing my business, I was constantly pursued by telephone and cable to make decisions that no one else was empowered to handle.*"

> "The common objection to proposals for a Deputy Secretary-General is that his selection would pose an insuperable political problem. Presumably he would be chosen by the General Assembly. Given the political atmosphere in which that body works the Deputy would have to be drawn from a political group different form the Secretary-General's. In the bureaucratic interplay in the Secretariat, he would be used as a counter-balance to his chief. This arouses memories of Nikita Khrushchev's 1960 "troika" proposal for a group of three, from the West,

111

East and The Third World, to manage the Secretariat by consensus. The General Assembly has already decided to create the post of Director-General for Development and International Economic Co-operation, whose name appears directly under the Secretary-General's on the organization charts. But he is not a deputy, and his responsibilities are limited to his own sphere, i.e. economic and development matters."

"There is no denying the cogency of these objections. But I would point out that in the specialized agencies of the United Nations there are deputies, and they are selected by a political process. If no other satisfactory way can be found to choose a United Nations Deputy Secretary General, why should the choice not be left to the Secretary-General, in the same way as the candidates for President of the United States and Prime Minister of many other countries in effect choose their own deputies."[14]

It is interesting to compare Waldheim's approach with the views of Hammarskjold on this subject. Hammarskjold told the General Assembly in 1957:

"The head of each department and office is directed to carry on his operations and to make such decisions as are necessary within the limits of established policy. Where marginal policy questions or new questions of importance not covered by existing policy, arise, the daily contact maintained by the Secretary-General through the Executive Office provides a basis for his continuing direction of the Secretariat. It is only on those occasions when, due to unsatisfactory communications, the Secretary-General is both absent and unavailable, that some special measure would appear to be indicated. In these circumstances, it is my view that an arrangement should be made whereby a group or "panel", consisting of the Under-Secretary confronted with an urgent and important policy decision, not covered by existing policy lines, associated with two other Under-Secretaries selected on the basis of geographical distribution should make the decision."[15]

After the scheme introduced by U Thant, as related earlier, it was only in 1986 that the United Nations would look again at the upper echelons of the Secretariat. In 1985 the General Assembly established the Group of 18 to look at the administrative and financial functioning of the Secretariat of the United Nations. That group recommended that the number of Under and Assistant Secretaries-General be reduced by 25%. Following reforms instituted in the light of this and other recommendations of the Group, the number of senior officials has been reduced but the arrangements at the upper echelons of the Secretariat have not changed appreciably.

Secretary-General U Thant had announced, at the outset, his intention to invite Under Secretaries to serve as his "principal advisers". It seems that he and Secretary-General Waldheim did have regular meetings of senior officials. However, it is understood that, under the current Secretary-General, those meetings have lapsed.

It would thus seem that, up to now, the Cabinet system has had *mixed results* at the United Nations. Nevertheless, there continues to exist in the Secretariat a post of "Chef de Cabinet" who heads the "Executive Office of the Secretary-General". It is to that Office that we shall now turn.

IV. The Executive Office of the Secretary-General

Sir Brian Urquhart provides the following account of the early days of the Executive Office of the Secretary-General:

"Almost since our arrival in New York I had been appalled by the disorganization and slipshod medthods of the Secretary-General's office. In this I may have been over-zealous, applying military standards to the far wider and foggier area of international affairs and bureaucracy. But there was certainly much room for improvement, and early in 1948 David Owen and I hit upon a plan to do something about it. Owen and I persuaded Lie to take Commander Robert Jackson on in February 1948 as his *coordinating executive,* a job which Jacko, in his naval way, insisted on referring to, to the resentment of his colleagues, as Chief of Staff."

"Jacko's high-pressure ability and wide experience alienated his fellow ASGs, a stuffy and insecure lot to begin with. I soon began to see that we had installed a racing engine in a family automobile and could expect trouble. (He was fired by Lie shortly afterwards)."[16]

Goodspeed, writing in 1959, described the Executive Office of the Secretary-General, as it had evolved, as follows:

"This office is headed by an Executive Assistant to the Secretary-General (now Chef de Cabinet) who aids the Secretary-General in the *overall coordination of the work of the departments and offices* of the Secretariat...
Assistance is also provided with respect to *relations with the governments of members and non-members,* the *specialized agencies,* and the *various missions of the United Nations abroad.*"[17]

Since the establishment of the United Nations Secretariat, the following persons have held the position of Chef de Cabinet or Executive Assistant to the Secretary-General:

1. David Owen (UK)

2. Andrew Cordier (USA)

3. C.V. Narasimhan (India)

4. Esmat Kittani (Iraq)

5. Rafeeuddin Ahmed (Pakistan)

6. M'Hamed Essafi (Tunisia)

7. Virendra Dayal (India)

In 1989, the Executive Office of the Secretary-General had a complement of 29 professional and 42 general service staff. In practical terms it was organized around the following clusters of function:

1. The function of *the Office manager* — the Secretary-General's office manager (The Chef de Cabinet).

2. The Secretary-General's *political adviser and confidante* (The Executive Assistant to the Secretary-General).

3. *Peace-making functions* (Asia, Middle East, Central America, Africa).

4. *Representation functions* (Representation Unit).

5. *Editorial functions* (editing the Secretary-General's statements and reports).

6. *Note-taking, correspondence and secretarial functions.*

7. *Budgetary and administrative functions* (for the Secretary-General's office).

The Executive Office is complemented by some other "Offices of the Secretary-

General" — Research and the Collection of Information, Legal, Special Political Affairs, Political and General Assembly Affairs.

The current Chef de Cabinet has described his approach as follows:

> "There is really no "model" for a chief of staff. People are different, circumstances are different and the challenges are different. Every chief of staff needs to strike a balance for himself or herself. What you have to be is true to yourself.
> ...
>
> "I must try to ensure that the Secretary-General's menu for the day makes sense and that, faced with a multitude of serious matters, his time is used in the most creative and productive manner. I must help to keep the doors to the Secretary-General's office open, but not open to a stampede. I must never try to build a wall between the Secretary-General and others... but I must siphon away the in-essentials. Working in the Secretary-General's office one naturally develops an instinct for what the essentials or priorities are. But that's an advantage of where I am, not who I am..."
>
> "I would hope that my advice, on occasion, would be of help to the Secretary-General in his onerous responsibilities. However to be of help, that advice must always be straightforward. Anyone can give the good news, the Chef de Cabinet must be prepared to give the bad.", he said.
>
> "The staff of the office of the Secretary-General, Dayal said, had been kept deliberately small. "I do not think the Office of the Secretary-General should become a kind of mini-White House set up... I think there should be a healthy degree of decentralization"..."[18]

The main functions of the Executive Office of the Secretary-General are to:

- Assist the Secretary-General in the executive direction co-ordination and expedition of the work of the Secretariat and of the programmes and other elements of the Organization, as well as in the follow-up of the implementation, within the Secretariat departments and offices, of decisions taken by the Secretary-General;

- Assist the Secretary-General, in his capacity as Chairman of the Administrative Committee on Co-ordination, in his co-ordinating function in relation to the entire United Nations system of organizations;

- Supervise and co-ordinate the activities of certain political missions;

- Assist the Secretary-General in his contacts with Governments, delegations, the press and the public;

- Prepare drafts of speeches and statements by the Secretary-General and brief summary papers on subjects with which he is concerned;

- Deal with protocol, liaison and representation and with organizing official ceremonies and similar functions;

- Make arrangements for official receptions and other functions hosted by the Secretary-General, make travel arrangements for the Secretary-General and his party for official trips; maintain the personal security of the Secretary-General and his family;

The Chef de Cabinet, for his part:

- Regulates the flow of communications to and request for meeting with the Secretary-General in the light of priorities set by him and the inherent importance of the subject of communications or meetings for the Organization;

- Assigns tasks and issues instructions within the Executive Office and, on behalf of the Secretary-General, to the heads of departments and offices, and keeps the Secretary-General informed on important assignments and instructions;

- Clears important draft communications, instructions and reports to be issued on behalf of the Secretary-General and, whenever considered desirable, submits them for his approval;

- Assists the Secretary-General in remaining informed on the progress and effectiveness of work in the Secretariat by administering a progress reporting system and organizing periodic meetings of selected heads of departments/offices and relevant officials with the Secretary-General;

- Follows up on the implementation of instructions issued personally by the Secretary-General;

- Ensures the presence of officials required by the Secretary-General for consultation and the timely availability of all information desired by him;

- Supervises the work of the other officials and organizational elements in the Executive Office of the Secretary-General.
  The Executive Assistant, Special Assistants and other officers:

- Undertake studies, analysis, discussions, missions, preparation of notes and correspondence, and other tasks as assigned from time to time by the Secretary-General and/or the Chef de Cabinet.

Concluding Observations

The United Nations is being called upon to assume more and more responsibilities to help protect common interests, to promote human welfare, to help keep the peace and to uphold human rights and fundamental freedoms. Often, expectations of the United Nations are expectations of its Secretary-General. The lone occupant of the high office of Secretary-General must administer a large Secretariat, help solve international disputes, alert the Security Council to impending threats to international peace and security, engage in early-warning and peace-making, administer peacekeeping forces and provide leadership and direction in the diverse areas of activities of the United Nations: environmental, political, economic, social, cultural, humanitarian, legal and parliamentary. It does not take much imagination to realize that to be able to perform his numerous functions well, the Secretary-General needs around him talented aides, organized in such a manner as to enable the Secretary-General to provide the leadership and orientation that can come only from him. It is with this in mind that we have sought to present in this short essay, a description of the history, role and organization of the 'Cabinet' of the United Nations Secretary-General. More and more, "organizing for leadership" will be a major challenge for the Secretary-General.

115

Notes

1. See: F.H. Hinsley: Power and the Pursuit of Peace. (1963) See also: S.S. Goodspeed: The Nature and Function of International Organizations, 1959, Oxford University Press.
2. Goodspeed, *op.cit.*, p. 343.
3. *Ibid*, p. 344.
4. International Organization...
5. B. Urquhart: *Hammarskjold*, (1972), p. 353.
6. United Nations Press Release SG/SM/448, 16 December 1981.
7. Sydney Bailey, The Secretariat of the United Nations (1964), p. 66.
8. T. Lie: *In the Cause of Peace*, 1954, p. 44.
9. B. Urquhart, *A Life in Peace and War*, (1988), p. 103-104.
10. B. Urquhart: *Hammarskjold*, 1972, p. 523.
11. B. Urquhart: Hammarskjold, 1972, p. 526. See also Bailey, *op.cit.*, p. 56.
12. U Thant: *View form the UN*, (1977), p. 18.
13. (A/7359, 27 November 1968).
14. K. Waldheim: *In the Eye of the Storm*, (1985), p. 18.
15. S. Bailey, *op.cit.*, p. 69.
16. B. Urquhart: *A Life in Peace and War*, pp. 115-116. (Emphasis added).
17. Goodspeed, *op.cit.*, p. 350.
18. "Dayal, Powerful, Low Key as Secretary-General's Chef de Cabinet", Diplomatic World Bulletin, 31 August, 1987, p. 7.

THE OFFICE OF THE SECRETARY-GENERAL
AND THE MAINTENANCE OF INTERNATIONAL
PEACE AND SECURITY

By

Dr. Nabil Elaraby

Ambassador, Legal Adviser
Ministry of Foreign Affairs
Cairo

I. THE EXPANSION OF THE OFFICE OF THE SECRETARY-GENERAL

It must be admitted, at the outset, that the Charter vested the Secretary-General with explicit political powers but the role he eventually assumed surpasses the expectations of those who drafted the Charter provisions in 1945. The founding fathers did not anticipate the evolution of a trend to increase the reliance on the Office of the Secretary-General (1). The analysis of the factors that contributed to the emergence of an enhanced Office of the Secretary-General requires a brief examination of the constitutional framework defining his responsibilities under the relevant Charter provisions. Particular emphasis will be later focused on his authority under Articles 98 and 99.

Article 97 provides that the Secretary-General shall be the Chief Administrative Officer of the Organization. Thus he is to assume responsibility for all the administrative and operational tasks of the United Nations. This would include the servicing of the various consultative organs as well as being the focal point for the collection of information in the United Nations. The inclusion of this provision in the Charter makes it perfectly clear that the Administration

---

(1)   Sydney Bailery, The Secretary-General of the United Nations, The World Today, January 1961, p. 3.

of the United Nations shall be left to the Secretary-General. His discharge of this administrative responsibility was considered by the Preparatory Commission to involve the essential tasks of preparing the ground for the decisions of the organs and of «executing» them in cooperation with the Members (2). The entails that the Secretary-General should always be in close contact with the work of all the subsidiary organs. It follows that even without the development of the trend to delegate responsibilities directly to him he and his subordinates in the Secretariat were indirectly responsibile for the orderly functioning of these organs and for the successful discharge of their mandate.

Another point related to the Secretary-General's administrative duties which has a bearing on subsequent developments is the fact that to him all United Nations resolutions are mandatory and hence he should meticulously strive for their scrupulous implementation. It is worth noting that this legal obligation to carry out by all means the implementation of resolutions is different from the obligations of States under the Charter. In the political field only the decisions of the Security Council are obligatory on States. It is not therefore a theoretical proposition to consider that States sometimes refuse to assist in the discharge of a resolution they oppose. The annals of the United Nations abound with State refusal to abide by or assist in the implementation of resolutions. The Secretary-General's position, on the other hand, is prescribed by the Charter as an integral part of the implementation process. Cognizant of his complete dependability to strive for the discharge of their declared wishes, it seems logical that policy-making organs would reflect this fact by assigning more responsibilities on his shoulders.

Article 98 provides that the Secretary-General «shall perform such other functions as are entrusted to him.» This provision has substantial significance for it entitles the General Assembly and the Security Council to delegate political tasks to the Secretary-General, tasks which may bring him into the arena of possible political conflict with States (3).

---

(2) Article 7. The other five being the General Assembly, the three Councils and the International Court of Justcie.

(3) Hammarskjold, The International Civil Servant in Law and in Fact, Press Release SG/1035, p. 7.

Dr. Nabil Elaraby - The Office of the Secretary-General 3

It must be pointed out, moreover, that by increasing the delegation of political functions to the Secretary-General, the Assembly and the Security Council are not in conflict with the spirit of the Charter.

This emanates from the fact that the Charter confers on the Secretary-General in Article 99 an explicit political role which cohently refutes the interpretation of the phrase «Chief Administrative Officer» contained in Article 97 in a normative and limitative way as argued by some (4).

It is significant to mention also that the Charter stipulations setting forth the nature of the Secretary-General's activities should be considered in conjunction with the provisions of Article 100. This article is of fundamental importance for the status of an independent international civil service. Its provisions envisage and safeguard a position of full political independence for the Secretary-General and his staff from any influence flowing from national Governments. These provisions also place an obligation on States «to respect the exclusively international charter of the responsibilities of the Secretary-General and the staff».

The concept of an independent Secretary-General implies that when he is intrusted to seek the implementation of a resolution he has to be impartial and objective as well as closely adhere to the purposes and principles of the Charter.

In the course of implementing resolutions, the Secretary-General was, in many cases, confronted with a delicate problem of unclear and vague mandates. The character of some mandates has been such that it carrying out his functions the Secretary-General has found himself forced also to interpret the resolutions of the policy-making organs (5). Whenever the Secretary-General is confronted with a mandate requiring interpretation, he becomes «under obligation to seek guidance to all possible extent, from the main organs» (6). However, when such guidance is not forthcoming, as

---

(4) Ibid. Further discussion of the various implications of Article 98 and 99 will follow.

(5) Introduction to the Annual Report 1960-1961, A/4800/Add. 1, p 5.

(6) Ibid.

did happen in various cases, he assumed the role of interpretating
the resolution in the light of the Charter, the United Nations relevant precedents and the aims and intentions expressed by Members (7).

The move towards the Secretary-General orginated from the
accumulation of numerous elements. Perhaps the most mentioned,
though it is submitted not the only element, is that the Security
Council, because of the lack of unanimity between the Permanent
Members was not able, at the height of the Cold War between
1945 and 1950, to exercise its primary responsibility for the maintenance of peace and security (8). By 1950, particularly due to the
events of the Korean conflict, it was considered essential to sidetrack the Council when the unanimity principle is not forthcoming.
On 3 November 1950 the General Assembly adopted resolution 377
(V) called the «Uniting for Peace» resolution. This resoultion contained substantive and procedural provisions which was an attempt
to by-pass the veto in the Council by convoking an emergency session
of the General Assembly, This procedure has been invoked several
times to face highly explosive situations (9).

Thus the General Assembly was to have recourse to its residual
responsibility for the maintenance of world peace whenever the
Council is deadlocked and unable to take action. The General Assembly, however, due to its large membership could not handle
executive and operational tasks well and hence a vacuum was being
felt throughout the Organization. The vacuum was further brought
to the focus in subsequent years when the trend towards non-align-
ment among the Afro-Asian States made it a no easy task to mobilize the required votes for any resolution of substance in the General
Assembly (10). This situation had a favorable impact on the trend
to entrust responsibilities to the Secretary-General. If the Security
Council cannot act due to the lack of agreement between the «big
rive», and if no resolution of substance can secure the required votes
in the General Assembly, the only course available to United Na-

---

(7) Ibid. The problem of interpreting resolutions by the Secretary-General Will be elaborated upon in the following section.
(8   Ibid.
(9- In Suez, 1956; Hungary, 1956; Lebanon, 1958; the Congo, 1960;
and the Arab-Israeli Conflcit of 1967, update.
(10) Bailey, p. 3.

tions Members then would be to refer the problem to the Secretary-General (11).

The authors of the Charter had originally envisaged a wider range of executive actions to be undertaken under the aegis of the Security Council. For reasons already referred, to, the Security Council was rendered incapable of discharging its Charter responsibilities effectively and no specific machinery was established for directing these actions. Even the Military Staff Committee which the Charter established and defined its functions, became a still-born project.

The required executive functions and their form have been left largely to the practice and evolution in the United Nations (12). The forms used for executive actions by the Security Council and the General Assembly have varied, however some main types, such as Sub-Committees and peace-keeping and observation operations in general are, as previously pointed out, recurrent. As experience has revealed, these arrangements require centralized administrative measures which cannot be performed by the Council or the Assembly (13). The States Members of the United Nations came to realize that the best choice might be to request the Secretary-General to perform the necessary executive functions with a view to implementing their decisions. By having recourse to the Secretary-General with respect to field operations the Members avail themselves of the invaluable asset of the element of «continuity». Unlike Committees comprised of Member States, the Secretary-General enjoys relative permanency which enables him to acquire indispensable experience and insights in supervising operational tasks.

Dumping problems on the Secretary-General has been an accepted practice in the United Nations ever since 1954 when the General Assembly adopted resolution 906 (IX) which requested him to seek the release of members of the United States Armed Forces under the United Nations Command in Korea who were imprisoned in China. His effective and successful intervention on their behalf, which entailed personal representation in Peking, were

---

(11)   Ibid., p. 4.
(12)   Introduction to the Annual Report of the Secretary-General 16 June 1960 — 15 June 1961 (A/4800/Add. 1), p. 5.
(13)   Ibid.

undertaken by him as the Secretary-General of the United Nations and note merely as the agent of the General Assembly. The Chinese episode certainly could be considered as an extraordinary case since the Chinese Government was not then represented at the United Nations. However, there are many cases where it became apparent that one objective person would be more effective than a Committee.

Committees and Commissions composed of States may be inclined to reflect the line of policy of the majority of these States regardless of the merits of the case. To argue that a Committee's terms of reference when carefully delineated would constitute guidelines adequate to secure objectivity might not be substantiated by past events. Bodies comprised of Member States are subject to the influence, if not the direct instructions, of their respective Chancelleries. Each State usually has its own position and its preconceived ideas with respect to any problem and is inclined to interpret the mandate of the Committee in the light of its interests.

This, it is submitted, does not apply to the Office of the Secretary-General which should not be subject to special interests as Member States usually are. The Office of the Secretary-General has been, in fact, considered as «a servant of the principles of the Charter, and its aims must ultimately determine what for him is right and wrong.»

Article 98 provides that the Secretary-General «shall perform such other functions as are entrusted to him by these organs.» This provision has substantial significance for it entitles the aforementioned organs to entrust the Secretary-General with various tasks tn the implementation cf their resolutions including the execution of political decisions. Apart from delegated functions, Article 98 refers also to annual reports which the Secretary-General «shall make» to the General Assembly on the work of the Organization.

Through the performance of delegated functions and the submission of reports the Secretary-General strives for the implementation of the pronounced will of Member States as embodied in a. resolution. The requirement to submit an annual report by the Secretary-General has, moreover, created a unique opportunity for him to supplement the report with an introduction. This introduction has usually contained his personal assessment of the work of the

Organization during the previous year, the stages reached on the most important items, and his proposals, if any, to achieve better results.

The Secretary-General is also required, under Article 12 (2) of the Charter to «notify the General Assembly at each session of any matters pertaining to the maintenance of international peace and security which are being dealt with by the Security Council.» This latter responsibility might be considered relevant to the implementation of resolutions for the notification to the Assembly would usually include the stages reached in carrying out the provisions of resolutions

It is suggested to examine briefly the constitutional and legal limitations which have a direct bearing on the Secretary-General's functions. The purpose would be to ascertain the role the Secretary-General is able to perform within the framework prescribed by the Charter and then to examine his practice in interpreting the mandates entrusted to him and consequently to assess his influence in the process of achieving peaceful settlement of disputes.

It is to be noted that the framework laid down by the Charter within which the Secretary-General operates contains several basic concepts and norms which define the limits of his role. He cannot go beyond certain principles prescribed by the Charter as fundamental from which no derogation is permitted. Some of these basic principles relate to the structure of the United Nations system itself and the competence of the various organs within that system. Others directly pertain to powers of the Secretary-General.

Before any attempt is made to outline the limitations on the Secretary-General which affect the implementation process, it is proper to state two observations of a general nature.

The first observation pertains to the nature and philosophy of the United Nations Charter. As a constitutional instrument the Charter is subject to development and evolution according to the needs of the Membership and to the pressures of circumstances. It was this elementary fact which motivated the former Secretary-General to write that the United Nations is conceived by some as a dynamic instrument of Governments through which they should seek reconciliation and develop form of executive action aimed at forestalling conflicts and resolving them. (14)   This concept envisages the possibility of continued growth of effective forms of active international cooperation adopted to experience (15).   This approach to the United Nations points to the needs of the present and the requirements of the future.   It follows that the limitations contained in the Charter on the Secretary-General are not all sacrosanct and inviolable.   Some are subject to modifications in order to adapt to the ever-changing needs of the international system.   It is hoped that the following discussion of the limitations on the office of the Secretary-General will bear out the validity of this approach.

The second observation flows as a corollary from the previous concept and has its reflection on the Secretary-General's powers. To a large extent the possibility of expanding the Secretary-General's powers does exist notwithstanding the various limitations imposed by the Charter.   It might therefore appear that the authors of the Charter intended to put the Secretary-General on the same level with the other principal organs.

The study of the role assigned in the Charter to the Secretary-General, does not support the aforementioned view.   The Charter imposes certain constitutional limitations on the Secretary-General which differentiates between his role and that of the other principal organs.   These constitutional limitations define the relationship between the various organs and the Secretary-General. They also define his relationship with Member States.

The main limitation on the Secretary-General has its origin in the natures of the decision-making system in the United Nations. Decisions are to be reached by voting in the policy-making organs. The Secretary-General is not one, and the Secretariat, of which he is the head, was not originally conceived as a formal policy-maker. Only Member States have the right to vote and only the deliberative organs, whether principal or subsidiary, have the right to adopt. resolutions (16).   His role is thus to afford every assistance in facilitating the discharge of the adopted resolutions which are always bind-

---

(14)   Introduction to the Annual Report of the Secretary-General 1960-1961   (A/4800/Add. 1), p. 1.
(15)   Ibid.
(16)   The International Court of justice does not adopt resolutions but it passes judgements and decides on advisory opinions by voting.

ing upon him and the Secretariat Staff. When the adopted resolutions confer additional responsibilities on the Secretary-General, he is required to carry out these responsibilities (17) as effectively as possible.

The trend to increase the delegation of functions in the implementation process to the Secretary-General have entailed a significant increase in this responsibilities. However, his involvement in implementing resolutions was not accompanied by additional formal powers.

Some of these constitutional limitations however, are not rigidly imposed. In fact the flexibility of certain provisions allowed for the development of new practices to fill some gaps and inadequacies that appeared later on. It was therefore possible to pave the way for the evolution of the Secretary-General's role. As a relevant example, it might be pointed out that the Charter provides in Article 99 that the Secretary-General may bring to the attention of the Security Council any matter which in his opinion may threaten the maintenance of international peace. No similar provision exists with respect to the relationship between the Secretary-General and the Assembly (18) The rule of procedure of the Assembly, however, compensated for this gap by providing that the provisional agenda shall include all items which the Secretary-General deems necessary to put before the General Assembly (19).

It might also be pointed out that some changes in the constitutional structure as laid down in the Charter were undertaken through practice without any textual alteration. To demonstrate further this point, it might be recalled that the Charter conceives that the collective security system will be directed by a Military Staff Committee composed of representatives on the five permanent

---

(17) Article 98 obligates the Secretar-General to perform the functoins entrusted to him by the Assembly and the three Councils.

(18) Article 12 (2) provides that the notification of matters relative to the maintenance of peace and security shall be with the consent of the Security Council. Hence this provision does not confer upon him a right to act in accordance to his discretion as in Article 99.

(19) Rule 13 (G) for regular sessions and Rule 18 for special sessions.

10   Revue Egyptienne du Droit International, Vol, 42, 1986

members.   The Military Staff Committee was supposed to advise and assist the Security Council on all matters relating to the military requirements to maintain peace and security.   The Committee would also be responsible for the strategic direction of any armed forces placed at the disposal of the Counci l(20).   Due to the profound differences between the permanent Members on the composition direction stationing and size of the forces, the Article 43 agreements never materialized.   Consequently, no national contingents were put under the disposal of the Council.   In 1950 when the Security Council resolved to take military action against North Korea, it was deemed inevitable to avoid the Military Staff Committee and search for a new device for the command of the United Nations forces.   In the Korean episode the United States Government was required to appoint a Commander.   Six years later, however, when the Assembly established UNEF it was decided that the command of the Forces be assumed by a Commander under the direction of the Secretary-General.   The relevant provision in the resolution which established UNEF states that the Assembly «invites the Secretary-General do take such administrative measures as may be necessary for the prompt execution of the actions envisaged in the present resolution (21)».

Although the United Nations Charter prescribed a detailed system for the direction of United Nations forces, a practice, however, developed under the pressure of circumstances to assign the Secretary-General with the role of Supreme Commander.   True, UNEF and all the other peace-keeping operations, with the possible exception of the Congo operation, were not enforcement measures under Chapter VII.   Yet these operations were, nevertheless, military oriented, composed of uniformed forces with adequate authority to employ armed force under certain conditions (2).   The relevant point to be stressed is that, constitutionally, it was not provided that the Secretary-General would assume command of military forces, however, there

---

(20)   Article 47 (3).

(21)   General Assembly resolution 1000 (ES-1).

(22)   UNEF was not authorized to take the initiative in the use of armed force but is entitled to respond with force to an attack with arms including attempts to use force to move UNEF from its positions. The basic element is clearly the prohibition against the taking of initiative.   G.A.O.R., Thirteenth Session, Dec. A/3943, para. 179.

was no expressed prohibition to prevent him from performing such a role. It could be argued that the provisions of Charter VII pertaining to the establishment and composition of the Military Staff Committee amount to an implicit limitation on the Secretary-General to impinge on what some might construe as the competence of the Council. (23)   In the case of the Secretary-General assuming command of United Nations military forces the need did not arise for textual changes. No addition to or deletion from the rules of procedures of the Council and the Assembly was required. It was an evolution in the practice of the Council and the Assembly complemented by either the approval or the acquiescence of the majority which permitted the removal of what is inferred or implied to be a constitutional limitation.

Thus some of the Charter concepts which impose certain limitations on the Secretary-General in the discharge of the responsibilities delegated to him may incur changs and adjustments according to the needs and requirements of the Organization. This should be considered as a healthy sign in any constitutional instrument such as the Charter.

However, it must be emphasized that certain basic constitutional limitations could never be changed without the revision of the Charter itself. The most fundamental limitations on the Secretary-General with respect to the implementation of resolutions relate to the fact that he must carry them out. He is not a policy-making body. His role is to strive for the implementation of the decisions and recommendations of the deliberative organs as entrusted to him. He could not modify the resolutions by addition or delction. It follows that when embarking on the implementation of a given resolution the Secretary-General is bound by the text of that resolution.

The terms of the delegation of responsibility to the Secretary-General set the limit of his authority (24). If, however, there remains some doubts about the nature of the mandate delegated to

---

(23) The Soviet Union have always held the view that all U.N. military operations, whether enforcement actions or by consent, should be authorized by the Security Council, the competent organ for the maintenance of international peace and security.

(24) G.A.O.R., Thirteenth Session, Doc. A/3943, para. 175.

the Secretary-General, it has been the practice for him to request further clarification from the competent organ. It is to be noted that sometimes resolutions are passed in a most general form as a compromise and the Secretary-General might not receive adequate guidelines from the competent organ (25). In such cases, the Secretary-General would be forced to interpret the resolution himself. His interpretation however, is confined to the framework determined by the competent organ in the original resolution. As Hammarskjold once stated in the Security Council «it is not the Secretary-General who has determined the mandate, nor it is the Secretariat which has decided on what means they should use to fulfill it». (26)

Uis duty to implement could not be relinquished on the basis of the difficulties he may encounter. The Charter law on this point appears to have been correctly stated by Mr. Hammarskjold when he wrote in 1961 with respect to this responsibility of the Secretary-General

> «Is he (The Secretary-General) entitled to refuse to carryout the decision properly reached by the organs on the ground that the specific implementation would be oppoesd to positions some Member States might wish to take as indicated, perhaps, by an earlier minority vote ? Or course, the political organs may always entrust him to discontinue the implementation of a resolution, but when they do not so instruct him and the resolution remains in effect, is the Secretary-General legally and morally free to take no action, particularly in a matter considered to affect international peace and security ? Should he, for example, have abandoned the opesration in the Congo because almost any decision he made as to the composition of the force of its role would have been contrary to the attitudes of some Members as reflected in debates and maybe even invotes, although not to decisions.
>
> The answers seem clear enough in law ; the responsibilities of the Secretary-General under the Charter cannot

---

(25) The Congo operation is a relevant example and will be outlined later.

(26) S.C O.R., Sixteenth Year, 935th Meeting, 15 February 1961, p. 5.

be laid aside merely because the execution of decisions by him is likely to be politically controversial. The Secretary-General remains under the obligation to carry out the policies as adopted by the organs. The essential requirement is that he does this on the bais of his exclusively international responsibility and not in the interest of any particular State or group of States». (27)

To discharge his mandate effectively it is expected that the delegation of responsibility will be as clear and precise as possible.

Experience has, however, revealed that many resolutions have been passed in a most general form due to a manifold of reasons including the impossibility of reaching a more precise wording out of the divergent and firmly held views. Resolutions have been found to contain ambiguities, silences and pags which affect the implementation process and complicates the Secretary-General's task. It has been noted that even when the original resolution was adopted in a clear and precise form subsequent development may render the action called for in the resolution highly controversial, if not impossible to implement. The classical example for such a situation is the Congo episode which will be considered at a later stage. The wording may be agreed upon as a compromise to obscure or sidetrack some points with respect to which no agreement could be expected. The working of a resolution could also be the result of haste in drafting due to the need for urgent action or even as an escape from responsbiility. It is relevant to recall, in this connection, that some peace-keeping operations could not have been launched in time if the competent organs were to become bogged down in formulating a precise mandate and considering the various political implications involved. A prime example to be found in the resolutions of the first emergency session of the General which was convened after the failure of the Security Council to take any action. The General Assembly did not attempt to draft a blueprint for the establishment of the proposed United Nations Force. The international setting was threatening and fraught with danger and it was obvious that swift action was urgently needed. The Assembly passed a resolution, hastily drafted to request the Secretary-General

---

(27) Hammarskjold, The International Civil Servant in Law and in Fact, Press Release, SG/1035, 29 May 1961, p. 17.

as a matter of priority to submit within forty-eight hours a plan for the setting-up, with the consent of the nations concerned, of an emergency international United Nations Force. (28)　The Secretary-General was able to submit a report on a plan for the proposed Force within twenty-four hours.　The Assembly noted his report with satisfaction and established a United Nations Command for an emergency international Force to secure and supervise the cessation of hostilities (29).

When confronted with similar resolutions, the Secretary-General has, as a matter of record, tried to seek clarification from the competent organs.　The required clarification has not always been extended and the Secretary-General was forced in many cases to use his discretion in filling the pags and resolving the ambiguities in the resolutions.

Hammarskjeld expressed his views on this point by stating, on the occasion of his re-election in 1957, that he believed that it was «in keeping with the philosophy of the Charter that the Secretary-General should be expected to act also without such guidance, should this appear to him necessary in order to help in filling any vacuum that may appear in the systems which the Charter and traditional diplomacy provide for the safeguarding of peace and security ». (30)　This view disclosed his concept of the Office and his reading of the implications of the inherent powers with respect to his interpretative role in the implementation process.

It should be clear that an intensified burden would be placed on the Secretary-General whenever he is entrusted to carry out the provisions of such resolutions.　In situations where the delegation of responsibility is loosely drafted, the Secretary-General has found it desirable to benefit in carrying out his mandates from the day-to-day advice he could receive from representatives of Member States in order to be awlays fully aware of the wishes of the Membership. Hammarskjold considered that the idea of establishing advisory committees to consult with its members and hence be **au courrant**

---

(28)　Resolution 998 (ES-1).
(29)　Resolution 1000 1000 (ES-1).
(30)　G.A.O.R., Twelfth Session, A/PV. 690, 26 September 1967.

with the views of Member States might be a useful device (31). This device proved to be most helpful to ensure that, in implementing difficult and complex problems, the interpretation he gives to his mandate remains «on the rails» and as consistent as possible with the views of Member States (32).

It seems evident, on the basis of the record of the General Assembly and the Security Council resolutions, that the Secretary-General is sometimes faced with serious responsibilities in discharging mandates of a general character. If the Secretary-General can refer the matter back to the competent organ for more detailed guidelines then his task is greatly facilitated. However, this is not always the case. It has been correctly observed that Member States become perhaps with the exception of those directly concerned, less deeply engaged and less vigilant after the passage of the resolutions than before (33). Their interests in executing the mandate may wane and subsesquently the support the Secretary-General needs from Member States, which is imperative for any successful implementation, may not be forthcoming. The Secretary-General therefore would find that his actions do not represent the consensus of Member States.

In practice, his ability to execute his mandate depends, to a large extent, on his perception in following the consensus of the majority. The position of the super-powers is of significant importance in this respect. The need for their support would be more clearly manifested when the efforts to secure implementation are being resisted, or sometimes frustrated, by some States who happen to be friends or allies of the super-powers.

---

(31) Advisory Committee were established to assist the Secretary-General with respect to UNEF and the Congo operation.
(32) Cordier in The Role of the Secretary--General Annual Review of United Nations Affairs, 1961, p. 10.
(33) Ibid., p. 9.

16   Revue Egyptienne du Droit International, Vol, 42, 1986

II. ARTICLE 99 AND ITS SIGNIFICANCE : A NOTE ON THE INHERENT RIGHTS :

The Significance of Article 99

Article 99 has been rightly described by the late Secretary-General Dag Hammarskjold as «more than any other which was considered by the drafter of the Charter to have transformed the Secretary-General from a purely administrative official to one with an explicit political responsibility (34).

In point of fact, it is the only Article in the Charter which confers on the Secretary-General authority and responsibility comparable to Member States. Article 99 provides the Secretary-General with a license to undertake initiatives unlike his other functions under the Charter, which are mainly confined to strive for the execution of a mandate decide upon by another organ (35).

The interpretation of the significance of Article 99 is borne out by the Report of the Preparatory Commission of the United Nations which states in relation to the functions of the Secretary-General that «under Article 99 of the Charter, moreover, he has been given a quite special right which goes beying any power previously accorded to the head of an international organization, viz., to bring to the attention of the Security Council any matter which, in his opinion, may threaten the maintenance of international peace and security » (36). The Report further states that «it is impossible to foresee how this Article will be applied ; but the responsibility it confers upon the Secretary-General will require the exercise of the highest qualities of political judgement, tact and integrity». (37)

It was, therefore, to be expected that the performance of the five Secretaries-General has not, obviously, been uniform with respect to invoking Article 99 or its implications. The personality and character of the incumbent would be reflected in his conceptual

---

(34) Address by Mr. Hammarskjold at Oxford University, «The International Civil Servant in Law and in Fact», U.N. Press Release SG/1035, p. 7.
(35) Leon Gordenker, The UN Secretary-General and the Maintenance of Peace (Princeton University, 1964), p. 138.
(36) Report of the Preparatory Commission of the United Nations.
(37) Ibid.

reading of the Charter provisions, and his political judgement and style. Secretary-General perez de Cuellar recognized this fact and considered it important to recommend that «it may well be that the Secretary-General should play a more forthright role in bringing potentially dangerous situations to the attention of the Council within the general framework of Article 99 of the Charter. My predecessors have done this on a number of occasions, but I wonder if the time has not come for a more systematic approach. Most potential conflict areas are well known. The Secretary-General has traditionally, it informally, tried to keep watch for problems likely to result in conflict and to do what he can to pre-empt them by quiet diplomacy. The Secretary-General's diplomatic means are, however, in themselves quite limited. In order to carry out effectively the preventive role foreseen for the Secretary-General under Article 99. I intend to develop a wider and more systematic capacity for fact-finding in potential conflict areas » (38).

It was Hammaskjold more than any other Secretary-General who succeeded in developing a doctrinal expansion of his office based on the inherent powers which Article 99 bestows. He once said the right to bring matters to the attention of the Security Council «Carries with it, by necessary implication, a broad discretion to conduct inquiries and to engage in informal diplomatic activity in regard to matters which «may threaten the maintenance of international peace and security» (39)

Though Article 99 is generally considered as the most powerful weapon at the disposal of the Secretary-General, yet it has rarely been used. The first time a Secretary-General overtly brought a matter to the attention of the Security Council occurred in July 1960 in the Congo case. He was able to invoke this special right and it seems that this was a result of the steady stream of information reaching the United Nations from various sources, including reports from Under-Secretary Raiph Bunche, who was in the Congo as Special Representative at the Congolese Independence celebration. However, it is doubtful that the Secretary-General would have con-

---

(38)   Report of the Secretary-General on the Work of the Organization (Doc. A/37/1), p. 8.

(39)   Address by Mr. Hammarskjold, United Nations Press Release, SG/1035, p. 7.

voked the Council had he not received a written request for military aid from the Congolese Government. Though many believe that Hammarskjold was instrumental in writing the Congolese request for assistance.

In two earlier acute political crises, indirect reference to Article 99 was made. In June 1950, Secretary-General Lie indicated a willingness to invoke the Council ; however, it was the United States which called for the meeting of the Council after the North Korean invasion of South Korea. «Again, in October 1956, when Anglo-French-Israeli forces invaded Egypt, the United States grasped the initiative by asking for an urgent meeting for the Security Council. Nevertheless, Mr. Hammarskjold deemed it necessary to state in the 751st meeting that» ... yesterday morning on the basis of the information then available — I would have used my right to call for an immediate meeting of the Security Council, had not the United States Government in the course of the night taken the initiatvie » (40)

Secretary-General Waldheim invoked Article 99 twice. In 1974 to convene the Security Council to authorize the strengthening of the U.N. role in Cyprus. Again in 1979, Waldheim requested a Council meeting to deal with the U.S. Iranian hostage crisis. His request referred to the exercise of his responsibility under the Charter to seek a peaceful solution of the problem in conformity with the principles of justice and international law.

It is of significance to note Article 99 was not more frequently used. One obvious reason to explain the reluctance of the five Secretaries-General to use it more often in bringing matters to the attention of the Security Council is that the Secretary-General initiates the Council meeting under Article 99 but he could not determine the outcome of the Council's deliberations. (41) The Secretary-General's initiative could lead to prompt action by the Council or to inaction and deadlock. The incumbents of the Office realized the extent of their powers under Article 99 and appear to have preferred to invoke its collateral consequences rather than having to shoulder responsibility for confronting a Council determined or unable to take the requisite action.

---

(40) S.C O.R., S/PV 751st meeting, 31 October 1956, p. 1.
(41) Gordenker, op. cit., p. 138.

The provisions of Article 99 do not impose on the Secretary-General a duty to bring to the attention of the Security Council any matter which threatens international peace and security. At the San Francisco Conference, it was debated whether the invocation of Article 99 should be regarded as a right to be exercised at the discretion of the Secretary-General or an obligation which he is in duty bound to carry out (42). Supporters of the latter view proposed a motion to the effect that the Secretary-General «shall bring» instead of «may bring» (43). This view, however, did not enjoy the endorsement of the majority and the motion was withdrawn. (44) Most writers tend to regard that the provisions of Article 99 operate under the full discretion of the Secretary-General (45).

It is suggested to explore what has come to be considered as the two basic implications of Article 99 ; namely, the Secretary-General's implied authority to conduct inquiries and his authority to use his «good offices». Needless to add that the examination of these two points will be confined to the Secretary-General's practice when his actions are not authorized by a competent United Nations deliberative organ.

The Right to Conduct Inquiries

It is generally acknowledged that to admit that the Secretary-General has the right to use discretion on what «in his opinion may threaten» peace ought to entail accepting the preposition that the provisions of Article 99 confer upon his the competence to gather information and ascertain facts. How can the Secretary-General decide on what to bring to the attention of the Council without possessing acurate facts to determine whether a matter constitutes a threat to the maintenance of international peace and security. This determination necessarily requires a factual examination of the situation under consideration which in essence implies the power to in-

---

(42) Stephen Schwebel, The United Nations Secretary-General, (Harvard University Press, Cambridge, 1932), p. 19.

(43) Idem.

(44) U.N.C.I.O. Document, Vol. 7, Draft Rep. of Sub-Com. 1/2/D, p. 556.

(45) Kelsen, The Law of the United Nations, p. 303, writes that «the function determined in Article 99 is to be exercised at the discretion of the Secretary-General.

vestigate.   A brief historical examination appears to be appropriate.
At the San Francisco Conference, the debate on Article 99 did not
extend to a profound exploration of its scope and implications (46).

The records of the Security Council demonstrate that the Secretary-General asserted his investigatory powers as early as 1946
during the consideration of the Greek question.   In the course of
the Council's consideration of the Greek complaint in September
1946, a United States sponsored resolution asked that a commission
of three individuals be nominated by the Secretary-General to investigate the relevant facts.   Before the vote on the draft resolution
was taken, the Secretary-General intervened in the discussion and
stated : «... Just a few words to clear my own position as Secretary-
General and the rights of this Office under the Charter.   Should the
proposal of the United States not be carried, I hope that the Council
will understand that the Secretary-General may reserve **his right to
make such inquiries or investigation as he may think necessary,** in
order to determine whether or not he should consider bringing any
aspect of this matter to the attention of he Council under the provisions of the Charter ». (47)

This statement had far-reached implications for the future developments of the Secretary-General's functions.   By making this
statement, Mr.   Lie affirmed his right to conduct investigations
without authorization from the Security Council.   It was apparent
from the reference he made to bringing aspects of the matter to
the attention of the Council that he considered this investigatory
power to be a direct corollary of Article 99.

What is of particular importance in this connection is that the
Secreatyr-General's assertion went unchallenged. (48)   Ironically, it
was even endorsed bythe representative of the Soviet Union who

---

(46) Schwebel in The Secretary-General of the United Nations,
states, on page 19, that under Article 99, three issues Were considered :
whether the Article confers a right or a prescription of a duty; whether
its provisions extends to the General Assembly; and whether its provisions include violations of the Charter and not only threats to the peace.

(47) S/PV 70th Meeting of the Security Council, S.C.O.R. September 20, 1946.

(48)   Schwebel, op. cit., p. 89.

said : «... I think that Mr. Lie was right in raising the question of his rights. It seems to me that in this case, as in all other cases, the Secretary-General **must act.** I have no doubt that he will do so in accordance with the rights and powers of the Secretary-General as defined in the Charter of the United Nations ». (49)

It is thus possible to state that United Nations Members have accepted the right of the Secretary-General to carry out investigations without prior authorization from the Council. Before drawing any definite conclusions, however, one should be extremely cautious. For accepting that the Secretary-General has the right under the Charter to investigate in the abstract would not mean, by necessity, that he can apply this right and conduct investigations whenever he deems necessary and that States would have to acquiesce. In actual practice, it is submitted, the key factor is the willingness of the parties concerned to permit the Secretary-General to carry out his inquiry. It is evident, on the basis or past experience that the Secretary-General's success in executing a fact-finding mission, even when armed by a mandate from the Security Council, depends primarily on the willingness of the parties directly concerned to furnish him with the facilities necessary to accomplish his task. Once the parties are not willing to render their cooperation, then his task is gravely impaired if not doomed.

At this point, it appears that two factors which affect the Secretary-General's investigationary role merit mentioning. The first related to the scope and nature of fact-finding in international disputes, and the second, to the political and legal position of the Secretary-General as an impartial international civil servant.

First, it is noteworthy to bear in mind that international disputes are not a facsimile of domestic disputes. Each category has its separate characteristics and traits. Fact-finding in this context will assume the character of facilitating the process of resolving a conflict through the objective elucidation of the basic facts circumscribing a dispute or a situation. The purpose behind the inquiry by the Secretary-General is to determine whether to bring a specific issue before the Council, hence, it may be sufficient for him to undertake

---

(49) S.C.O.R., S/P. V. 70th Meeting, 20 September 1946.

22   Revue Egyptienne du Droit International, Vol, 42, 1986

activities limited the elucidation of the basic facts. Ultimate facts which have been described as a conclusion of law stated that if it were a conclusion of fact, (50) such as a finding that a State has exceeded its rights, transgressed or trespassed, are not likely to be undertaken by the Secretary-General.

It would, therefore, be reasonable to maintain a distinction between the nature and scope of fact-finding or inquiry under the United Nations practice from investigation under national laws in domestic disputes by national courts or boards of inquiry. The object of the latter, is usually, the discovery of new facts in order to establish responsibility. In the international arena, under the United Nations system, the emphasis is on fact disclosure by an impartial credible third party. The need to establish juridical responsibility is marginal in international disputes since the general orientation of the Charter is universally recognized to be political and not legal. The Security Council has consistently opted to tacke disputes in a political framework (51). Conflicts and disputes in the General Assembly also were seldom resolved in accordance with legalities. It is true that the parties concerned usually inject legal arguments to give support and countenance to their respective positions. The Council and the Assembly, however, do not, as a general rule, pronounce themselves, on the specific legalities involved. The practice has developed to patch up disputes and contain conflicts without strictly adhering to the requirements of applying legal norms.

The second factor to the consideration of the Secretary-General's investigatory role has its origin in the legal and political traits of the Secretary-General's position. As an international official, the Secretary-General has to be extremely careful when he decides to bring a matter to the attention of the Security Council. His position is not similar to that of States, who can afford to take initiatives in bring disputes to the attention of the Council without having to fully substantiate the existence of a threat to the peace. In fact, it should not escape the attention that sometimes states bring disputes

---

(50) Virginia Journal of International Law, United Nations Fact-Finding, Vol. 9, December 1968, p. 156.

(51) Despite the express provision in Article 36 (3) to take into consideration that legal dsiputes shoudl be, as a general rule, referred by the parties to the International Court of Justice.

before competent United Nations organs because it suits their strategy to display interest in upholding the Charter principles by being the first to put a given dispute before the United Nations. Another relevant factor which tends to explain the Secretary-General's reluctance in bringing matters to the attention of the Council is that he is more likely «to wear out his welcome» than a State (52). A determination by the Secretary-General that peace is threatened should not be announced publicly until he has ample evidence to substantiate the veracity of his assertion. This is one of the basic factors which significantly contributed to the rare, if indeed ever, resort to Article 99 (53).

As already pointed out, the Secretary-General's statement on the Greek question was supported by the Soviet Union and was not challenged by any other Member (54). This statement might in itself be considered as a precedent. The actual assertion by the Secretary-General, however, occurred in 1959 when he first put to test his right to carry out fact-finding responsibilities without specific authorization, with respect to the 1959 tension on the Laos borders. It was spelled out publicity in the form of a statement issued on 27 August 1959 concerning principles regarding political fact-finding or good offices missions (55). It might be appropriate to scrutinize the relevant aspects of this statement which proved to be of significance in the evolution of the Secretary-General's Office.

The statement pointed out to the hitherto established practice of basing such missions on decisions by the General Assembly or the Security Council, unless the Secretary-General goes on the mission personally after arranging the matter with the Government concerned and within the range of his competence (56). He has, in the case of a conflict between two Member countries, the statement con-

---

(52) Schwebel, Op. Cit., p. 86.
(53) Some writers doubt that Article 99 Was very expressly invoked. Even with respect to the Congo case, it is noteworthy that the Congolese letter to the Secretary-General (S/4382) Was the bassi for the convening of the Council. However, it is submitted that it was the Secretary-General who asked for the Council's meeting and not the Government of Congo.
(54) Schwebel, op. cit., p. 89.
(55) United Nations Press Release SG/849.
(56) Ibdi.

tinues, and without decisions by the General Assembly or the Security Council, sent a personal representative at the joint request of those countries. (57) Referring specifically to Laos, Mr. Hammarskjold stated that «the sending of a representative to Laos for fact-finding purposes, would be in line with the Secretary-General's attitude in similar cases, and would be arranged by him provided that the legal situation were to develop so as to make it constitutionally possible for him to act (58). However, Mr. Hammarskjold considered that «on the basis of a desire expressed by the Government of Laos, only with terms of reference limiting his task to developments proper to Laos itself which would not seem to serve the intended purpose». (59)

The essence of the Secretary-General's reasoning seems to be that he :

1) could send a representative for fact-finding purposes if the Governments concerned consented to a directive of the Assembly or the Council (60) and accepted the dispatch of his representative; or

2) could send a fact-finding mission to Laos without prior approval of a competent organ if the Government of Laos were to request him to do so.

Another statement to the same effect was repeated by the Secretary-General with respect to the consideration by the Security Council or the Tunisian complaint on 28 July 1961. On that date, Mr. Hammarskjold had this to say in connection withthe Tunisian President's invitation to the Secretary-General to visit his country :

«Quite apart from the fact that it is naturally the duty of the Secretary-General to put himself at the disposal of the Government of a Member State, if that Government considers a personal contact necessary, my acceptance of the invitation falls within the framework of the rights and obligations of the Secretary-General, as Article 99 of the Charter authorizes him to draw to the attention of the Security

---

(57)   Ibdi.
(58)   Ibdi
(59)   Ibdi.
(60)   Richard Miller, Dag Mammarskjold and Crisis Diplomacy.

> Council what, in his views, may represent a threat to international peace and security, and as it is obvious that the duties following from this Article cannot be fulfilled unless the Secretary-General, in case of need, is in a position to form a personal opinion about the relevant facts of the situation which may represent such a threat ». (61)

On other occasions, too, the Secretary-General reiterated his interpretation that by implication Article 99 confers upon him the right to conduct inquiries without authorization from any consultative organ. This occurred in an intervention in the deliberations of the Fifth Committee on budget estimates in 18 October 1960 stating in summary :

> «... If the Secretary-General was entitled to draw the attention of the Security Council to threats to peace and security, was he to rely on reports in the press or from particular Governments ? Certainly not. He had to find out for himself, and that could mean that he had to go himself, as he had gone to Laos in November 1959. To deny the Secretary-General the right to such personal fact-finding was, in fact, to erase Article 99 from the Charter » (62).

Hammarskjold's conception of Article 99 was unequivocably enunciated in his Oxford Address when he pointed out that Article 99 would authorize the Secretary-General» ... to start the whole United Nations machinery moving on the basis of his own judgement regarding what is a threat to peace and security ». (63) This, according to him, «implies a broad discretion to conduct inquiries and to engage in informal diplomatic activity in regard to matters which may threaten the maintenance of international peace and security». (46)

It might thus be adduced that the Secretary-General has consistently asserted to his Office the right to conduct fact-finding on his own authority pursuant to Article 99. In his 1982 report, Sec-

---

(61) S.C.O.R., S/PV 964, 28 July 1961, Para. 86.
(62) G.R.O.R., 15th Session. A/PV 769, 18 October 1960.
(63) Mr. Hammarskjold Oxford Address. «The International Civil Servant in Law and in Fact.» U.N. Press Release, SG/1035, p. 7.
(64) Ibid.

26   Revue Egyptienne du Droit International, Vol, 42, 1986

retary-General perez de Cuellar went further in endorsing the right
of the Secretary-General to ascertain fact. He wrote that «... I intend to develop a wider and more systematic capacity for fact-finding
in potential conflict areas ». (65) Member States have not challenged this interpretation of Article 99. Han Kelsen has written, however,
that «it might be doubted whether this interpretation corresponds
to the intention of the framers of the Charter » (66) He considers
that extending the Secretary-General's powers in this manner presupposes that not only the Security Council but also the other United
Nations organs would have a right to investigate if this were necessary to exercise the power conferred upon the organs with respect
to the matter (67). It is submitted that the Secretary-General's investigation in this respect has a direct bearing on the maintenance of
international peace and security and hence, should be compared
only to the right of the Security Council to investigate under Article
34.

Moreover, the intention of the founding fathers could not possibly be interpreted in a manner which denies the Secretary-General
the right to investigate. By vesting the Secretary-General with wide
discretionary powers in Article 99 they have, in practice, conferred
upon him a right to determine what may constitute a threat to international peace and security. The maintenance of the peace and
security is, in accordance with the United Nations Charter, the
primary responsibility of the Security Council. (68) The Secretary-
General, as a consequence, has to bring what he may deem a threat
of the peace to the Council in order to enable it to exercise its primary responsibility.

The Secretary-General's right in this respect could not be compared with the Council's right to investigate under Article 34 when
the Security Council resolves to investigate its decision might be
considered as mandatory since Article 34 investigations are undertaken to determine the competence of the council to deal with a given

(65) Report of the Secretary-General on the Work of the Organization (Dec. A. 37/1), p. 8.

(66) Kelsen. The Law of the Untied Nations, p. 304.

(67) Ibid,

(68) United Nations Charter, Article 24.

question. (69). The determination of competence of the Council is essential to the proper functioning of the Council and for the activation of the collective security system which could hinge on the outcome of the investigation. It is, therefore, suggested that the decision of the Council to dispatch a fact-finding to the territory of a State could be assumed as falling within the scope of Article 25 and hence mandatory.

In practice, however, the pattern of action in the Security Council does not support this view. States do not, as a general rule, consider calls for fact-finding as binding decisions. In point of fact, the Council has for all practical purposes binding decisions under its vast powers to restore and maintain peace and security. So, it may be stated that, from this aspect the Secretary-General's Article 99 powers to investigate are a significant importance to the functioning of the Council. Perhaps, it will not be an overstatement to point out that his inherent powers to investigate may, in certain instances, be more effective than investigatory activities pursuant to a formal resolution. Sometimes a formal fact-finding mission has been denied the necessary facilities to perform its functions while the Secretary-General was granted such facilities. A pertinent example is that the United Nations committees charged with investigating **Apart**heid practices in South Africa were unable to enter the Union while the Secretary-General was able to visit Pretoria in Januray 1961 at the request of the South African Government. (70)

In general, it is to be noted that the presence of a fact-finding mission initiated by the Secretary-General has been acceptable when its findings are going to be reported to United Nations competent organs at the discretion of the Secretary-General. It is possible also to foresee a situation where the Secretary-General will use his discretion and decide that the time to publish the findings is not ripe. The Secretary-General has, in fact, taken such a decision in 1958 in a mission undertaken by his representative pursuant to resolutions which would appear to apply **a tortiori** to those missions undertaken on the initiative of the Secretary-General. In 1958 the

---

(69) Kerley, Powers of Investigation of the United Nations Security Council A.J.I.L., Vol. 55, No. 4, October 1961, p. 897.

(70) Bowett in the Davies Memorial Institute Study on the Peaceful Settlement of Disputes, para. 55.

28　　　**Revue Egyptienne du Droit International, Vol, 42, 1986**

Secretary-General informed the General Assembly that «... The reports to the Secretary-General from the representative stationed in Amman would not be public documents unless the situation were found to call for their circulation as official documents of the United Nations ... Were the findings to be a serious nature, they may, under the present circumstances, be regarded as indicating a threat to peace and security in the sense of Article 99 of the Charter. This fact, and the possibilities for action which it opens for the Secretary-General, lends added weight to the planned arrangement as a means to help in upholding the purposes of the Charter in relation to Jordan » (71)

It should be also taken into account that while a State may be expected to refuse to comply with a politically-motivated decision of a policy-making organ to send a fact-finding mission into its territory, it would think twice before refusing to comply with the Secretary-General's request to send a representative to observe and report to him. The sheer presence of such a representative, who symbolizes the concern of the United Nations and its cognizance of potential dangers involved, and whose findings might not be automatically publicized, would probably be more palatable to recalcitrant states. Moreover, the presence of a Secretary-General's representative would contribute to creating conditions in which it would become difficult to assault the representative of the United Nations without at the same time assaulting its principles (72).

It would be appropriate to point out again here that the nature and characteristics of international disputes do not, usually require thorough in-depth investigatoin by the United Nations or any other third party. T he role of third party intervention in international disputes could be confined to providing information collected with the consent and cooperation of the concerned parties. Moreover, it is submitted that all third party interventions at the present phase of evolution in the international system, are, in the final analysis, subject to the consent of the parties. It should be noted, in this connection, that in international disputes, what is required more than anything else when a United Nations inquiry is to be conducted.

---

(71)　Doc. A/3934/Rev. 1, para. 38.
(72)　Bailey, The Troika and the Future of the United Nations Secretary-General, (Carnegie Endowment for International peace, 1962), p. 50.

is objectivity. Facts pertaining to international disputes are usually widely reported in the press and by the parties themselves. This fact tends to focus the role of the Secretary-General in fact-finding to that of the impartial observer whose sheer presence might be adequate to confer credibility on the reported facts. Sometimes the presence of the Secretary-General or his representative had a considerable effect in inducing the parties to reach a solution. In this latter case, the Secretary-General or his representative would be, in fact. a face-saving device which provides a leeway for the parties to decline their previously held positions. A relevant example is the Secretary-General's initiatives in the Bahrain findings in April 1970.

The Right to Use Good Offices

Dag Hammarskjold once stated that

> In recent years the secretary-General has increasingly been uesd for operations of a purely diplomatic type, either on behalf of the United Nations as such, or for one Government in relation to another on a good offices basis. He is in a position of trust **vis a vis** all the Member Governments. He speaks for no Government. It should go without saying that in the course of a negotiation or a mission of good offices, he must respect fully the laws of diplomatic discretion. He can never give away what must be considered the property of the Government with whom he is working. Nor could he pass public judgement upon their politics without working the use of his Office for the diplomatic purposes for which experience shows that it is much needed (73).

Then nature and scope of the Secretary-General's good offices could not be clearly defined (74). It appears, however, that in the Secretary-General's practice, extending his good offices would usual-

---

(73) Address at Ohio University, The Elements of Privacy in Peace-Making. U.K. Press Release, SG/665, 3 February 1958.

(74) U Thant wrote with respect to this point that "the nature of the Secretary-General's good offices, their limitations and the cond-itions in which he may hope to achieve results are perhaps less well understood.» Introduction to the 1969 Annual Report, A/7601/Add. 1, para. 178.

30   **Revue Egyptienne du Droit International, Vol, 42, 1986**

ly enatıl a host of activities to facilitate the settlement of disputes. Secretary-General Perez de Cuellar recently wrote that «it would be in the interests of the Organization as a whole if the Secretary-General's capacity to serve as an objective third party were to be further developed. There is much, of course, to be said for quiet diplomacy, but sometimes more is required. I am thinking in particular of a wider and earlier use of fact-finding and observation. I am also thinking of the need to survey more regularly and systematically the worldwide state of international peace and security a task in which the Security Council and the Secretary-General should be jointly involved » (75).

That considered these activities to cover «a considerable part of the workload of the Secretary-General.» (76)   His conception of the importance of the good offices was given in the 1969 Annual Report wheh he wrote that «it is natural that Governments, when faced with delicate problem which urgently deemed solution, should ask the Secretary-General for such help as he personally may be able to give through discreet approaches to the other party or parties concerned. The Secretary-General himself, in the very nature of his position and responsibilities, on occasion also takes initiatives in an attempt to promote a satisfactory solution to a difficult or dangerous problem which unless solved, might deteriorate to the point where peace and security would be threatened» (77).

In fact, the concept of good offices of the Secretary-General has come to the fore and has been employed in various instances for over thirty years now due to the necessity of devising new means to facilitate the resolution of international disputes. In 1959, Mr. Hammarskjold drew attention to this point when he wrote that the procedures and methods used by the United Nations «may be supplemented by others under the pressure of circumstances and in the light of experience if these additional procedures are not in conflict with what is prescribed …. such an evolution has in fact taken place, and it has thus been recognized that such new procedures may be developed when they prove productive in practice for efforts

---

(75)   1985 Report of the Secretary-General on the Work of the Organization (Doc. A/40/1), p. 5.
   (76)   G. A. O. R., 24th Session, Doc. A/7601/Add. 1, para. 178.
   (77)   Ibid., para. 177.

towards the objectives of the Charter. In this respect, the United Nations, as a living organism, has the necessary scope for a continuouns adaptation of its constitutional life to the neds ». (78)

The record of the Secretary-General's diplomatic achievements in the mid-fifties particularly with respect to the Suez and Lebanese crises, demonstrated the value of the «good offices» role which his Office is capable of performing. It moreover indicates the possibility of resort to an appropriate method to resolve international conflicts which, if properly explored and developed, may be instrumental in bridging the gaps which have come to the fore within the formal machinery of the United Nations. The significance of this new concept lies mainly in the fact that it provides a flexible means for smooth and fast action by the United Nations. The discreet off-the-record nature of the good offices endeavors by the Secretary-General have been regarded of «special value in situations in which prior public debate on a proposed course of action might increase the difficulties that such an action would encounter, or in which a vacuum might be feared because Members may prove hesitant, without fuller knowledge of the facts or for other reasons, to give explicit prior support in detail to an action, which, however, they approve in general terms or are willing should be tried without formal commitment (79).

Mr. Hammarskjold has drawn attention in his 1959 Introduction to the Annual Report of the Secretary-General to a new development which he considered as marking a new phase in the evolution of his Office. His reading of Article 99 convinced him that its provisions were meant for rare formal use. However, its implications were of considerable importance. In practice, he confirmed that the implications of Article 99 should by far exceed the formal resort to it (80). He wrote that the dispatch of special representatives of the Secretary-General

«May be regarded as a further development of actions of

---

(78) Introduction to the 1959 Annual Report of the Secretary-General (A/4132/Add. 1), p. 2.

(79) Smimonds K. R., Good Offices and the Secretary-General, Nordisk Tidsskift for International Ret. ,1959, p. 33.

(80) Introduction to the 1959 Annual Report (Doc. A/4132/Add. 1), p. 3.

32   Revue Egyptienne du Droit International, Vol, 42, 1986

a good offices nature, with which the Secretary-General said now frequently charged. The steps to which I refer here have been taken with the consent or at the invitation of Governments concerned, but without formal decisions of other organs of the United Nations. Such actions by the Secretary-General fall within the competence of his Office and are, in my view, in other respects, also in strict accordance with the Charter, when they serve its purpose. As a matter of course, the members of the appropriate organ of the United Nations have been informed about the action planned by the Secretary-General and were given an opportunity to express views on it.» (81)

The concept of good offices intervention by the Secretary-General without prior authoritzation from deliberative organs was thus enunciated. The Secretary-General, however, must have realized that any new development need time to penetrate the doubts usually created by novelty for in the same Introduction he underlined the fact that this concept will not affect «the basic character of the Office of the Secretary-General, or its place in the Organization in relation to the General Assembly, the Security Council or other main organs. They represent, from a constitutional viewpoint, an intensification and a broadening of the interplay these main organs and the Secretariat for purposes for which these organs maintain their primary responsibility ». (82)

The Secretary-General, moreover, appears to have wished to allay further the fears of those who follow the strict interpretation of the Charter. He therefore advanced two arguments in this direction. The first is that his good offices activities «should not be considered as setting precedent, especially as it always remains open to the appropriate organs to request that such an action, before being taken by the Secretary-General, be submtited to them for formal decision ». (83) The second point, on the toher hand, was motivated by his belief that it is necessary to emphasize to Member States that, in the final analysis, it is the policies they adopt that he executes. He, therefore, wrote in the same Introduction that «the wider

(81)   Ibid.

(82)   Ibid.

(83)   Ibid.

functions which in specific cases have been exercised by the Secretary-General fully maintain the charter of the United Nations as an organization whose activities are wholly dependent on decisions of Governments .. the development reflects an incipient growth of possibilities for the Organization to operate in specific cases within a latitude of independence in practice given to it by its Member Governments for such cases (84).

It would be useful to refer briefly to some cases where the Secretary General exercised his good offices without prior authorization from a policy-making organ. It should, however, be pointed out that the Office of the Secretary-General is consistently involved in diplomatic activities which fall under the general rubric good offices. Some of these activities were never publicized since they are conducted in such a manner that «there is no public knowledge at all of specific activities of this kind ». (85) U Thant expounded in his 1969 Introduction on the nature and limitations of the Secretary-General's freedom to use his good offices. He very aptly alluded to the insoluble difficulty of not affecting the prestige and public position of the Governments concerned. He further pinned down the essence of the problem of confidence in the Secretary-General, which is a prerequisite to his assuming mediatory functions, by saying that «if a way to be found, it must, therefore, be through mutual confidence, mutual respect and absolute discretion. Any hint that an action of the Secretary-General might serve to score political points for one party or another, or indeed, that credit might be claimed publicly on his behalf for this or that development will almost invariably and instantly render his efforts useless. Any public pressure on him would usually have the same result and any publicity at all for what he is doing is likely to have a severely adverse effect on his effort. (86)

Hammarskjold had considered that the provisions of Articles 98 and 99 endow the Secretary-General with a political role. He, moreover, considered that Article 99 was meant for rare formal use. However, its implications were of considerable importance. In practice, the implications exceeded by far the formal resort to Article 99.

---

(84)   Ibid.
(85)   A/7601/Add. 1, para. 176.
(86)   Ibid., para. 178.

34   Revue Egyptienne du Droit International, Vol, 42, 1986

He once stated that» ... it is in keeping with the philosophy of the Charter that the Secretary-General should be expected to act ... should this appear to him necessary in order to help fill any vacuum that may appear ». (87)

The views advanced in the 1969 Introduction to the Annual Report appear to represent U Thant's conception of the nature and scope of the Secretary-General's initiatives. It would seem rather clear that he has discarded his predecessor's attempts to «fill vacuums». He did inject, and one must admit successfully, United Nations presence in troubled areas. But this was never undertaken in the face or political obstruction by a group of States. U Thant s role has been limited, generally, to «good offices» procedures aimed at bringing the parties to a dispute together to negotiate a settlement or by the assumption of mediatory activities ». (88)

Examples of this type of diplomatic initiative abound. West Irian, Cuba, Yemen, Bahrain, Equatorial Guinea, Iran-Iraq and the Falklands are relevant illustrations. In the minute crisis relating to Equatorial Guinea, U Thant went further than his predecessor in asserting the authority inherent in his Office. He asserted in a letter to the President of the Security Council that «when I saw you earlier today, I told you, as a matter of information, of my intention to send a Representative to Equatorial Guinea. It was not a consultation in any sense, during my tenure as the Secretary-General of the United Nations, I have taken similar action several times in the past without prior consultation with the President or members of the Security Council ; I have only reported the action taken on my own initiative. It was not my purpose, on the present occasion, to establish any precedent of prior consultation ». (89)

CONCLUSION

As some already pointed out, the Office of the Secretary-General has become a focal point for conducting needed United Nations activities. The scope and the dimensions of his role have expanded and have included disputes and conflicts which are not

---

(87)   A/PV. 690, 26 September 1957.
(88)   Ibid.
(89)   S/9055 dated 7 March 1969.

under formal United Nations consideration. Secretary-General's initiatives have encompassed many highly sensitive international problems such as Vietnam, Berlin, and Biafra which were not under consideration by any United Nations organ. Many such initiatives have been devised as a pragmatic and flexible response to counterbalance the inability of the competent deliberative organs to cope with events. Inaction by the formal machinery could sometimes be substituted with quiet, behind the scenes interventions by the Secretary-General.

The Secretary-General's interventions could be even more useful and conceivably more influential when extended before the flare-up of a given crisis. Debates in United Nations organs tend to register the positions of the parties publicly and commit Governments to a line of policy which the cannot easily abandon without less of face and prestige. It is precisely in situations where disputes have not been the subject of public deliberations that the Secretary-General's initiatives and inquiries would be most effective.

The success of such initiatives would depend, **inter alia,** on the willingness of the parties to reach a peaceful settlement, as well as the support the Secretary-General receives from the Members; prerequisite for the success of this type of inquiry by the Secretary-General. The initiatives which flow from the need to extend assistance by the Security Council would vary depending on the characteristics of each case. It would, usually include, however, ascertaining basic facts

States might even agree to confer on him such a role as the United Arab Republic and Saudi Arabia did in 1963 with regard to the Yemen conflict. His presence might take the form of a Representative dispatched with the consent of the State concerned. Or the United Nations might be required to assume admniistrative functions as supervising a referendum or elections. This last form was used in West Irian, the Cameroons, Togo and Bahrain.

It is worth noting that all third party interventions, at the present stage in the international system, are, in the final analysis, subject to the consent of the parties. Even the Securiy Council has not been able to utilize its Charter powers of coercion and had to confine its actions within the provisions of Chapter VI. This, in turn, led to the increased importance and relevance of the pacific settlement procedures of the Charter. Thus, persuasion and not coercion has become the dominant feature of all United Nations actions.

The Secretary-General's role might be considered as providing alternative avenues to facilitate the pacific settlement. Such a role could be supported by all United Nations Members including those who follow a narrow interpretation of the Charter provisions. It is of relevance to recall, in this connection, that the Security Council's Committee of Experts, while examining the question of competence, decided that the Council could, with the consent of the Secretary-General, appoint the Secretary-General as rapporteur or mediator in any controversy within the Council. (90)

It is precisely the role of mediator or rapporteur, which was often used in the League of Nations, that should be considered now for the Secretary-General. Such a role is recommended for the Secretary-General to undertake at an early stage before public positions are declared.

The United Nations, as observed by a scholar, «has unique advantages as a form in which to exercise the techniques of behind-the-scenes persuasion ». (91) The impartiality, quasi-permanency, independent authority and prestige of the Secretary-General have made his Office the most suitable institution to carry out the techniques of persuasion. It is now an established practice in the United Nations that the Secretary-General undertakes extensive diplomatic contacts and initiatives in respect to international disputes and conflicts. These initiatives are taken with the full consent of the parties concerned. Often, the parties themselves take the initiative by resorting to the Secretary-General for assistance, whether as a middleman, supervisor or mediator, in resolving their disputes.

The resultant balane sheet of past activities by the Secretary-General in the field of fact-finding and good offices are indeed impressive and imaginative. A United Nations presence has been injected in varying situations in order to provide the United Nations with

---

(90)   Rule 23 of the Provisional Rule of Procedure of the Security Council.

(91)   Oran Young. The Intermediaries. p. 310.

accurate information on the true facts. This technique has been utilized with great success also as a buffer zone between combatants.

The prophylactic activities of the Secretary-General, with and sometimes without authorization from United Nations political bodies, have proved most useful in respect of actual and potential tension areas (92). The knowledge that the United Nations, through its executive head, is perturbed with the turn of events in any tension area and intends to initiate contacts with the parties could contribute towards simmering down potential conflagration.

The presence of the United Nations in a potentially troubled area would be useful in more than one way. It could provide the the parties with objective information, with a face-saving device or with assurances against future detrimental developments, all of which would contribute in resolving disputes and conflict peacefully. The United Nations presence would also provide the Secretary-General with information on the nature of the dispute which would enable him to use his discretion in accordance wit Article 99. In other words, good offices methods, both on the spot presence and exploratory consultations, might be essential to enable the Secretary-General to ascertain whether the given dispute is likely to endanger or endangers inctrnational peace and security. The United Natoins presence in Korea and in the Congo facilitated the task of the Secretary-General by securing and providing with the necessary information.

There is, however, some controversy with respect to the Secretary-General's role in peace-keeping. (93) Some States maintain that the Secretary-General's involvement in peace-keeping operations impinges on the jurisdiction of the Security Council in the peace and security area. (94) This argument, however, was not upheld by the International Court of Justice in its 1962 Advisory Opinion. It might be relevant to quote the following paragraphs from the Court's opinion :

> «The primary place ascribed to international peace and security is natural, since the fulfilment of the other purposes

---

(92) The prophylactic actions by the United Nations are lucidly described by Alan James in his valuable book, The Politics of Peace-Keeping, pp. 177-371.
(93) Particularly the Soviet Union and to a lesser extent France.

38   Revue Egyptienne du Droit International, Vol, 42, 1986

will be dependent on that basic condition. These purposes are broad indeed, but neither they nor the powers conferred to effectuate them are unlimited. Save as they have entrusted the Organization with the attainment of these common ends, the Member States retain their freedom of action. But when the Organization takes action which warrants the assertion that it was appropriate for the fulfilment of one of the stated purposes of the United Nations, the presumption is that such action is not **ultra vires** the Organization.

It is agreed that the action in question is within the scope of the functions of the Organization but it is alleged that it has been initiated or carried out in a manner not in conformity with the division of functions among the several organs which the Charter prescribes, one moves to the internal plane to the internal structure of the Organization. If the action was taken by the wrong organ, it was irregular as a matter of that internal structure, but this would not necessarily mean that the expense incurred was not an expenses of the organization. Both cases in which the body corporate or politic may be bound, as to third parties, by an **ultra vires** act of an agent. (95)

As a result of the controversy over the United Nations peace-keeping operations, including the role performed by the secretary-general, an acute financial and constitutional crisis was about to wreck the whole United Nations structure in 1964. The peace-keeping crisis did not, however, work to the detriment of the Secretary-General's utilization of his inherent political powers in dispute settlement. It seems that the objecions by certain States, France in particular, did not apply to actions not involving military operations. France, in fact, never raised any objectives to the Secretary-General's role in the settlement of disputes. The Soviet Union, on the other hand, has come out against them in a very mild tone. In the course of the Bahrain Question, the Soviet representative merely reserved his country's position with regard to the «procedure» employ by the

---

(84) Advisory Opinion on Certain Expenses of the U.N., I.C.J. Reports 1962.
(95) Ibid.

Dr. Nabil Elaraby - The Office of the Secretary-General 39

Secretary-General (96). Even during the peak of the peace-geeping crisis in 1963-1964, the Secretary-General did not hesitate to take certain initiatives without prior authorization from consultative organs. He relied, during this period, on the inherent political powers in his Office to initiate the Yemen Observation Operation in 1963 in order to facilitate the disengagement of the forces of the United Arab Republic and Saudi Arabia (97). He also dispatched, on his own authority, a Personal Representative to Cyprus. (89)

It might thus be stated that the practice in United Nations organs provides a set of precedents which serve as general guidelines for further initiatives by the Secretary-General. It must, however, be added that past precedent do not, by necessary, embrace sufficient guidelines for the future.

The rationale behind the resort to the Secretary-General is to benefit from, inter-alia, the flexibility and pragmatism innate in his Office. The main attraction of the Office of the Secretary-General is its proven ability to innovate discreetly. It might therefore be illuminating to bear in mind what Hammarskjold wrote in another context with respect to the lessons to be dranw from a previous innovation :

> In view of the impossibility of determining beforehand the specific form of a United Nations presence of the type considered in this report, which would be necessary to meet adequaately the requirements of a given situation, a broad decision by the General Assembyl should attempt to do no more than endorse certain basic principles and rules which would provide an adaptable framework for later operations that might be found necessary. In a practical sense, it is not feasible in advance of a known situation to do more than to provide similar forms of a United Nations presence ». (99)

Having outlined the framework, both legal and practical, which marks the scope and nature of the Secretary-General's role, it is

---

(96)   S/P.V. 1536.
(96)   S/5321.
(98)   S/5514.
(99)   G.A.O.R D.oc. A/3943,9 October 1958, para 154.

not called for to endeavor to put forward a short compendium of the
modalities used to facilitate the settlement of disputes. The main
reason lies in the fact that past precedents do not comprise an
adequate indication of the methods needed for the future. The
flexibility inherent in the Secretary-General's Office, which is one
of his main assets, calls for innovation on his part in accordance
with the circumstances of the dispute. As a prerequisite for any
attempt to decide on any particular method the Secretary-General
has to conduct adequate consultations with the parties concerned
and also with the Great Powers. It is to be noted that as a general
rule the Secretary-General is kept abreast of the major international
developments by the parties themselves. Every important development is, usually reported to him and his views normally carry considerable weight and influence on the parties. The establishment
of Permanent Missions accredited to the United Nations offered
the Secretary-General a year-round access to the view and thinking
of Governments. This enabled the Secretary-General to discuss
every topic of international interest whether on the agenda of
United Nations organs or not. On occasions he advises for or
against inscribing a dispute or situation on the agenda of a United
Nations organ. In 1967 the Secretary-General extended his good
offices in the dispute between Guinea and the Ivory Coast over
the detention of the Guinea delegation to the United Nations. Then
after resolving the dispute by the release of the Guinea delegation
he requested the inscription of an item entitled : «The Situation
Which Has Arisen Between Guinea and the Ivory Coast Involving
Section II of the Convention on Privileges and Immunities of the
United Nations.»

In the conduct of the informal consultations the Secretary-
Genreal may serve as a form to be used by the parties to harmonize
their views. In this respect, he may be symbolizing one of the basic
purposes of the Charter namely «to be a center for harmonizing the
actions of nations in the attainment of these common ends » (100
The objectivity, discretion and independence of the Secretary-General, which are considered inherent characteristics embedded in his
Office are prerequisites for affording him with the intimate informa-

(100)   Article 1, para 4.

Dr. Nabil Elaraby - The Office of the Secretary-General   41

tion needed for the performance of his role in the settlement process.

It should be pointed out that one cannot easily discern between some of the means which the Secretary-General employs as facilitative interventions. For example, most good offices activities are carried out through a special representative who, in a sense, also undertakes on-the-spot fact-finding functions and might be assisted by a United Nations presence.

The modalities which the Secretary-General employs are not easily defined even under general rubric. One, however, may refer to the various methods of United Nations «presence», the dispatch of special representatives, either to gather information or to mediate and use good offices, the supervision of the execuiton of agreements, the personal representation by the Secretary-General, the multitude of forms of diplomatic activity conducted by the Secretary-General as the main features of the methods usually used.

It is significant to note that in some of the burning international problems which are not on the United Nations agenda, the only effective means for the United Nations to exert pressure is through the Secretary-General. This might tabe the form of an appeal to Governments or just frank discussions with its Permanent Representatives or even a press conference. They have managed to make their views clearly felt through puhlic statements.

Another important area for the Secretary-General's diplomatic interventions is humanitarian assistance, where his attempts to alleviate the plight of the victims in certain conflicts through extending different forms of humanitarian help (101). This is, no doubt, one way, though a rather limited one, of positive contribution for eventual settlement.

It is submitted that all efforts aiming at bringing out settlement of disputes are, by their very nature, based on persuading the parties and not on forcing them. The dogma of enforcement was based on the asumption that international problems are, as in pre-League,

---

(101) In July 1979, Secretary-General waldheim convened, on his own initiative, a 65-nation conference in Geneva on Veitnamese refugees and displaced persons.

42   Revue Egyptienne du Droit International, Vol, 42, 1986

black and white and have not worldwide ideological implications.
Hence, the need to intensify dispute settlement methods through
quiet diplomacy and persuasion is acquiring greater importance and
urgency.

It is also significant to note in the context that, as already pointed out, the provisional rules of procedure for the Security Council
envisages a broad role for the Secretary-General's conciliatory and
mediatory role.   Rule 23 proivides.

> The Secretary-General may be appointed by the Security
> Council, in accordance with Rule 28, as rapporteur for
> a specified question.»

It is submitted that this rule might be taken as institutionaliz-
ing a useful practice. In the absence of radical changes in the Security Council structure, concepts and procedures which will render
it capable of enforcing its decisions, the Secretary-General, notwithstanding the constitutional and political limitations, imposed upon
his Office, will continue to be the most suitable institution to undertake these activities. As professor Thomas Franck has pertinently
observed «in one measures effectivesness in terms of impact on
the real world beyond the precincts of United Nations chambers, it
is the Office of the Secretary-General which has enjoyed modest
success ». (102)

---

(102) Unpublished study presented in November 1985 at The
Hague Academy for International LaW

[21]

Selecting the World's CEO

Remembering the Secretaries-General

Brian Urquhart

During periods of international disaster, a troubled world feels the need for an outstanding full-time supervisor. At first, with the horrors of World War I still fresh in their minds, the founders of the League of Nations considered calling the head of their organization "chancellor." When World War II was at its height, the title "moderator" was suggested for the head of the future United Nations. In both cases, the wartime mood passed, and the more bureaucratic title of "secretary-general" was chosen.

From the outset, the U.N. secretary-general has been an important part of the institution, not only as its chief executive, but as both symbol and guardian of the original vision of the organization. There, however, specific agreement has ended. The United Nations, like any important organization, needs strong and independent leadership, but it is an intergovernmental organization, and governments have no intention of giving up control of it. While the secretary-general can be extraordinarily useful in times of crisis, the office inevitably embodies something more than international cooperation—sometimes even an unwelcome hint of supranationalism. Thus, the attitude of governments toward the United Nations' chief and only elected official is and has been necessarily ambivalent.

THE ROLE

Fifty-one years ago at Dumbarton Oaks, when the Allied powers met to discuss some of the details of a future international organization, their ambivalence about the secretary-general's role was already evident. They strongly opposed a secretary-general directly elected by the General Assembly, and they defended the veto held by the Security Council's permanent members—Britain, China, France, the Soviet Union (now Russia), and the United States—over the selection process. In fact, the permanent members have always controlled the appointment of the secretary-general, a responsibility that they have often failed to live up to.

The founders of the United Nations were purposely ambiguous about the secretary-general's responsibilities. Despite President Roosevelt's vision of the job as a moderator, the primary function of the

---

BRIAN URQUHART is a Scholar in Residence at the Ford Foundation. His most recent book is *Ralph Bunche: An American Life.*

Brian Urquhart

secretary-general as outlined in the U.N. Charter is to act as the chief administrative officer of the organization. Secondarily, he is obligated to carry out the decisions of the main organs of the United Nations. Only Article 99 of the charter opens the door to independent political action, and then not very wide. Under Article 99, the secretary-general "may bring to the attention of the Security Council any matter which in his opinion may threaten the maintenance of international peace and security." If the secretary-general has any independent political role, this article provides the mandate for it.

When the time came to appoint the first secretary-general, governments were extraordinarily vague regarding the position's qualifications. In September 1945, for example, the U.S. representative on the preparatory commission, Adlai Stevenson, told Secretary of State Edward R. Stettinius, "We favor the choice of an outstandingly qualified individual, preferably a figure who has attained some international position and preferably a national of a small or middle power"—not exactly an overwhelming job description. (The idea of a female secretary-general was never even considered.)

After some eminent names—Dwight Eisenhower, Anthony Eden, Lester Pearson—had been bandied about and turned down by the Soviets, it became clear that the secretary-general's appointment would be a purely political decision, determined by what the United States and the Soviet Union could agree on—a lowest common denominator if ever there was one. Qualifications, stature, and leadership qualities would all be secondary considerations. This depressing reality

dawned on me in January 1946, when the General Assembly was considering nominations for the first secretary-general. At that time, among other duties, I ran the speakers' list in the General Assembly. Stettinius came up to my table and asked me to identify Trygve Lie, who was then foreign minister of Norway. I pointed out Lie's ample figure to Stettinius, who then proceeded to the rostrum to nominate Lie as "a statesman well known to all." Even then, a sincere search for the best possible candidate was obviously not in the cards.

The job descriptions given by its various incumbents also show some ambivalence, born, no doubt, of bitter experience. Lie referred to it as "the most impossible job on this earth." Dag Hammarskjöld said that the secretary-general was "a sort of secular pope, and, for much of the time, a pope without a church." U Thant, a courageous and modest man, said that the secretary-generalship was "the most varied, most interesting, and most challenging political job on earth." To Kurt Waldheim it was "at the same time one of the most fascinating and one of the most frustrating jobs in the world, encompassing as it does the height of human aspiration and the depth of human frailty."

The secretary-generalship, at least on paper, is indeed an impossible job. Quite apart from unrealistic public expectations, large responsibilities without significant power or resources, and the contrary attitudes of governments, the job comprises an unmanageable number of major functions. These include managing a worldwide secretariat and a global organization on a shoestring budget, a sizable part of which is usually overdue (the United Nations is not allowed to borrow); imple-

Selecting the World's CEO

menting the decisions of the Security Council and other organs of the United Nations; running peacekeeping and other highly sensitive field operations; being the world's mediator in an endless series of "good offices" missions involving quiet diplomacy all over the world; providing good offices in human rights and humanitarian situations; coordinating the so-called U.N. system of specialized agencies and major economic and social programs; representing the United Nations worldwide at conferences and regional meetings, and to the media and public; maintaining a watch on major developments of all kinds and alerting governments to them; generating ideas and strategies on global problems; and being the world's number one fig leaf and scapegoat.

The secretary-general is an international civil servant with 185 masters who is also periodically expected, especially when everyone else has failed, to be a leader. As U Thant put it, "The secretary-general's activity will usually seem to some governments too much, and to others too little. He must thread his way through the jungle of conflicting national policies with the U.N. Charter as his compass, and, if he is lucky, with a directive from one of the main deliberative organs as his guide." When crises arise, the secretary-general may be the world's last hope. He must be prepared to act without regard to political reputation.

THE ACTIVIST TRADITION

The main factors in the development of the office of the secretary-general have been the incumbents' personalities and the political climate in which they worked. The secretary-general is now

recognized as the world's foremost honest broker, but this was not originally the case. In 1946, governments were extremely reluctant to delegate political responsibilities to the secretary-general. When discussing the ideal secretary-general, the British reverently invoked the almost obsessive discretion of Sir Eric Drummond, the British secretary-general of the League of Nations, who never made a public statement or addressed a public meeting of the league in his entire time as secretary-general.

The sad history of the League of Nations indicated to the U.N. founders the potential importance of a strong chief executive for the new world organization, and the paralysis of the Cold War soon made a more active political role necessary. It was difficult, however, for the secretary-general to avoid confrontation with the Soviets or Americans when they disagreed on the appropriate course of action in an international crisis. Lie's break with the Soviets over the U.N. operation in Korea and Hammarskjöld's problems over the Congo attest to that. But the Cold War also made a nonpartisan third party indispensable to avoiding total paralysis in the Security Council during a crisis. Consequently, and with the genius of Hammarskjöld, the activist role of the secretary-general evolved.

After failing to agree on a score of other candidates, the Security Council in early 1953 appointed Hammarskjöld to succeed Lie under the delightful misapprehension that Hammarskjöld was a nonpolitical technocrat. Hammarskjöld soon showed his mettle. In his first triumph, during one of the Cold War's more dangerous moments, he secured the

Brian Urquhart

release from China of 17 U.S. airmen who were prisoners of the Korean War. He subsequently developed the secretary-general's negotiating role, as well as the concept of fielding U.N. peacekeeping forces, first deployed on a large scale in the Suez crisis in 1956. Thus Hammarskjöld pioneered a new role for the secretary-general as negotiator, crisis manager, and director of active peace operations.

Hammarskjöld paid a heavy price for his activism. He fell out of favor with the United States over Guatemala in 1954, and with the French and the British over the Suez operation in 1956. In the Congo, he infuriated both the Soviets and the French, alienating President Charles de Gaulle for good by his actions when the French clashed with newly independent Tunisia over Bizerte. Hammarskjöld believed that the independence, integrity, and activism of the secretary-general and the international secretariat were vital to the future of the United Nations. In fighting to preserve and develop those attributes, he suffered many setbacks in his final years in office.

Hammarskjöld was a practical visionary who regarded his task at the United Nations as "working on the edge of human society" to promote the "creative evolution" of human institutions. His aim was the gradual construction of a reliable and just world order through the establishment of international legal precedents and case law, especially in emergency situations. The United Nations would thus be gradually transformed from an institutional and diplomatic mechanism into a constitutional and operational system better equipped

to deal with the world's problems. In the daily frustrations of the post–Cold War world, it is worth reassessing our progress toward this ambitious goal.

AFTER HAMMARSKJÖLD

Hammarskjöld's death in Africa in September 1961 left the United Nations split on Cold War lines. His successor, U Thant, picked up the pieces and reunited the organization. Of all the secretaries-general, he has been the most unjustly judged. This is perhaps not too surprising. In U Thant's view, moral issues overrode political ones. He was a person of great honesty and courage, and he was not always appreciated in the cynical world of international politics. He brought the U.N. involvement in the Congo to an end. He played an important role in resolving the Cuban missile crisis. He was also instrumental in securing a cease-fire in the ominous war between India and Pakistan in 1965. On his own initiative, he made a prolonged and spirited effort to bring the Vietnam War to an end. But the collapse of the U.N. peacekeeping force in the Middle East in 1967 and the ensuing Six Day War overshadowed all the positive achievements of his stewardship. He served as a convenient scapegoat on that occasion, although he was the only world leader to go to Cairo to try to persuade Egyptian President Gamal Abdel Nasser to reconsider his fatal demand for the withdrawal of the U.N. peacekeepers. Despite a Security Council hopelessly divided along Cold War lines, he made valiant efforts to stave off catastrophe.

U Thant's successor, Kurt Waldheim, and his rival, Max Jakobsen of Finland,

Selecting the World's CEO

were the first candidates to campaign actively for the office, setting a disastrous precedent that has been followed ever since. Since that time, self-appointed candidates have lobbied for the post, confusing and monopolizing the already feeble efforts of the Security Council to recommend a suitable candidate to the General Assembly. Waldheim was neither an inspiring leader nor an original thinker, but he maintained stability throughout the tumultuous 1970s. He reestablished peacekeeping as an indispensable diplomatic tool of the United Nations after the 1973 Middle East war. After Waldheim left the United Nations it was discovered that he had misrepresented his war record, and he became the subject of universal opprobrium in the West. It would have been perfectly possible to verify Waldheim's war record *before* he was appointed secretary-general, but nobody bothered. Indeed, but for China's veto, Waldheim would have been elected to a third term with the active support of the United States, France, the United Kingdom, and the Soviet Union. The whole Waldheim episode speaks volumes about the quality and spirit of the appointment process—no open search procedure, no vetting of candidates, and a list virtually restricted to those who have declared themselves. In such circumstances, it is something of a miracle that the United Nations has been as well served as it has.

Waldheim's successor, Javier Pérez de Cuéllar, was a quiet and experienced diplomat who presided skillfully over the transition into the uncertainties of the post–Cold War era. He kept on good terms with all governments and was a well-liked but not striking international figure. His strongest suit was quiet diplomacy, which by definition does not gain public acclaim or recognition for its practitioners. After years of frustration, he enjoyed considerable success in the short-lived and illusory renaissance of the United Nations in the early 1990s.

The present secretary-general, Boutros Boutros-Ghali, has inherited the morning-after hangover from that false renaissance and the difficult problems of policing the tumult of the post-Cold War world. Like his predecessors, he is criticized for being both too activist and too passive. Compounding his difficulties, he has also been obliged to reorganize the secretariat when the organization is more heavily involved than ever in field operations. In a discouraging political climate, he is courageously fighting to keep the organization on course and enhance its effectiveness.

In the post–Cold War world, the secretary-general is perhaps less essential as a political intermediary than before. As the operational director of the United Nations, however, he (or in the future, let us hope, she) will undoubtedly have a huge and expanding task, with inadequate resources and often with inappropriate mandates. In an age when the media have a commanding position in international life, the secretary-general is also increasingly in demand as a spokesman for the United Nations and the emergent "international community."

In a period of resurgent nationalism and ethnic strife, growing distrust of international institutions, and diminishing support from governments, the secretary-general is busier—and perhaps lonelier—than ever. The original spirit of

Brian Urquhart

international solidarity embodied in the U.N. Charter has weakened in recent years. The essential institutions of an effective world community, based increasingly on law, are urgently needed. However, the inclination of U.N. members appears to be a continuation of ad hoc crisis management, which is often too late and sometimes inappropriate, ineffective, and expensive. A crisis of credibility has resulted. For this failure to adapt, the secretary-general will continue, unjustly, to be held accountable.

The United Nations now deals less with conflicts between states, for which it was established, than with civil and ethnic conflicts, for which it was not designed. Most of the critical situations in which the United Nations is now involved do not impinge on the national security concerns of the major powers. They concern, in the main, humanitarian issues. Altruism is a far weaker catalyst for international action than the threats to international peace and security that demanded U.N. action during the Cold War. This does not mean that the United Nations will not continue to be in demand when governments need a dumping ground for an urgent yet unwelcome problem, but it makes the secretary-general's capacity for effective action more uncertain.

GETTING THE BEST

It remains to be seen whether U.N. members have any interest in improving the selection process for the secretary-general. Miraculously, the process thus far has produced no outright disasters, but it would be rejected as a bad joke by any serious institution in the private sector. It

requires neither a search procedure nor an interview with the appointee. At a minimum, the Security Council and the General Assembly should define the essential qualifications necessary in determining the best person for the job. Ability, authority, and leadership capacity, rather than political convenience, must take priority if the United Nations is to shoulder its increasingly vital responsibilities and make the necessary transition to a very different world in the 21st century.

A few obvious changes would substantially improve the selection process. Besides initiating a more thorough search procedure, individual campaigning should be barred. The veto should not apply to the Security Council's recommendation of a candidate, and the ban on candidates from the five permanent members of the Security Council should be lifted. The temptation to run for a second five-year term can only disrupt the performance of an incumbent secretary-general. A single seven-year term would allow plenty of time to carry through serious policies without the pressure and distraction of a time-consuming reelection campaign. It should become the rule.

For all the burdens and difficulties of the position, the secretary-general, as the executive head of a world organization representing all governments, has a unique responsibility to foster the "creative evolution" of human institutions of which Dag Hammarskjöld spoke. The office and its incumbent will continue to be a central element in what is our only long-term hope, and probably our only alternative to a decline into chaos: the development of a global society based on the rule of law.⊛

Name Index